GOD'S RULE

GOD'S RULE

GOVERNMENT AND ISLAM

✦ ✦ ✦

PATRICIA CRONE

COLUMBIA UNIVERSITY PRESS
NEW YORK

Columbia University Press
Publishers Since 1893
New York

First published in the United Kingdom by
Edinburgh University Press Ltd 2004

Library of Congress Cataloging-in-Publication Data

Crone, Patricia, 1945–
God's rule : government and Islam / by Patricia Crone.
p. cm.
Includes bibliographical references and index.
ISBN 0–231–13290–5 (cloth : alk. paper)
1. Islam and state—Islamic Empire—History. 2. Islam and politics—Islamic Empire—History. 3. Islamic Empire—Politics and government. 4. Ummah (Islam) 5. Islamic Empire—History—622–661. 6. Islamic Empire—History—661–750. 7. Islamic Empire—History—750–1258. 8. Political science—Islamic Empire—History. I. Title.

DS38.2.C76 2003
320.5′5—dc22

2003062537

Columbia University Press books are printed on permanent and durable acid-free paper.
Printed and bound in Great Britain.

c 10 9 8 7 6 5 4 3 2 1

CONTENTS

III. COPING WITH A FRAGMENTED WORLD

IV. GOVERNMENT AND SOCIETY

CHARTS

PREFACE

Political thought may be broadly identified as thought about power formulated in a prescriptive rather than a descriptive vein: how should power be distributed, to what uses should it be put? Of power there are innumerable types, but political thought is primarily concerned with just one: that exercised by the governmental agency above the level of family, village, and tribe that we know as the state. It is however difficult to think about the state without attention to the social order on which it rests, and it is quite impossible to do so without considering its relationship with other organizations coordinating human activities above the domestic and local levels. Of such organizations there are many today, some nationwide and others international or global, but in a medieval context they were few and far between. Most associations in those days were local, and usually kin-based. Coordinating people's activities above the level of village or kin was difficult due to slow means of communication, poverty, local diversity, and lack of trust. It could be done by force: this was the typical manner in which the state established itself. But it could also be done, or assisted, by religion, which offered a common idiom, shared ideals and trust, and which was accordingly the main source of organization transcending locality and kin apart from the state. In the Islamic world it was originally the source of the state itself.

In part for this reason, the political thought of medieval Islam is difficult to understand for a modern Western reader. One might fondly have assumed political thought to be a subject open to discussion at a high level of generality, for what could be more universal than power and the problems it begets? But as everyone knows, it is in fact highly context-bound, and that of the Muslims seems to a novice to be based on a particularly odd set of premises. It also appears to come in a particularly heavy encrustation of strange-sounding names. The aim of this book is to make it intelligible to those who cannot get their minds around it, and to advance the understanding of those who already know what it is about. It is addressed to Western students of Islamic history, historians of adjacent periods and places (notably the classical world and medieval Europe), and, optimistically, the general public; and wherever possible, it asks questions of the type that preoccupy Western readers, in order to move from the familiar to the unfamiliar. It is devoted to political thought in the broad sense, not just theory, and tries to bring out the tacit assumptions and unspoken premises without which one cannot understand the edifice of explicit theory on top. Some very general knowledge of classical and European history is presumed (for example, I do not take it upon myself to explain who Alexander the Great or Louis XVI were), but no knowledge of Islamic history is required, though it would certainly be an advantage. All concepts have been glossed, and all persons, events, and historical developments have been identified or summarized (or so at least I hope) on first encounter and/or in the index, which doubles as a glossary. I do take the liberty of addressing specialists in the footnotes, but non-specialist readers are free to skip them. Though readers with some background knowledge will find the book much easier than those with none, it should be accessible to all.

Some conventions may be noted here. First, where double dates are given in the form 290/902f., the first figure refers to the Muslim calendar and the second to the Christian. Muslim years usually begin in one Christian year and continue into the next: continuation is indicated by 'f.', for example, 902f. stands for the relevant parts of 902 and 903. When only one date is given, it refers to the Christian calendar unless the contrary is specified. Secondly, I have opted for the term 'medieval', which some readers may dislike, because it can be used of both the Muslim world and the Latin West and because 'the formative period' does not yield an adjective. The centuries covered in this book were not of course in the middle of anything, but the same is true of their counterparts in the West: in both cases, the 'middle ages' are really the beginning. Thirdly, when I translate passages, referring the reader to both the original text and a translation, my own English version is not necessarily that of the translation, though it is often a modified version of it. I only follow other translators faithfully where no reference to the original text is given. Finally, though this is not a matter of conventions, I feel I must apologize for the inordinate number of references to publications of my own. Originally, the book was meant to be a short textbook codifying existing knowledge. There proved to be insufficient knowledge for that purpose, however, and as the book turned into a project of research, it inevitably came to build on earlier work of mine. I also wrote a fair number of articles on the way with the express purpose of being able to refer to them instead of cluttering the book with details. This may not mollify the reader, but all I can say is that I sympathize.

I should like to thank Maroun Aouad for much help and encouragement when I ventured into the alien field of *falsafa*, and also for making me look at the rhetorical works, more often than not supplying xeroxes along with the references and patiently answering questions of every kind. To Mohsen Ashtiany I am indebted for help with Persian matters (along with my share of his delectable wit). I am also grateful to him, Tamima Bayhom-Daou, Anthony Black, Bernard Haykel, Carole Hillenbrand, Stephen Menn, and Lennart Sundelin for comments on the book, or parts of it, in various stages of completion, to Firuza Abdullaeva for finding the illustration on the cover, and to Michael Cook for characteristically helpful and incisive comments on what was meant to be the final draft. I must also extend further thanks to Carole Hillenbrand, who put the idea of writing this book into my head and graciously waited the many years it took me to complete it.

Patricia Crone

I

THE BEGINNINGS

CHAPTER

1

THE ORIGINS OF GOVERNMENT

How did medieval Muslims think that humans had come to live under government? Differently put, how did they explain the origin of the state? The short answer is that they did not normally see government as having developed at all, but rather as having existed from the start. It is worth examining this answer in greater detail, however, for it brings out some of the most basic assumptions behind their political thought. It is to such fundamental concepts and ideas that this chapter is devoted.

Terminology

The word 'state' in modern parlance refers sometimes to a set of governmental institutions which constitute the supreme political authority within a given territory (as when we grumble about the state and wish that it would wither away) and sometimes to a society endowed with such institutions, that is a politically organized society or polity (as in the expression 'nation state'). In the question of how the state originated, the emphasis is on the agency, but the two meanings are closely related. Medieval Muslims had no word for states in either sense, however. They saw themselves as governed by persons rather than institutions and would speak of a ruler, such as a caliph (*khalīfa*) or king (*malik*), where we speak of the state in the first sense of the word; and they would identify the society of which the ruler was in charge as a nation (*umma*) or a religious community (*milla*), where we speak of states in the second sense of the word. (The term *khilāfa*, caliphate, only referred to the caliph's office, not to his polity, though modern scholars freely use the word in both senses.) The Muslims did pick up from their Greek forebears the habit of describing a politically organized society as a city (Greek *polis*). They did not know that Greek cities had once been states themselves and that this was how the habit had originated. They simply continued it by using the word *madīna* in the same way that their counterparts in Europe would use *civitas*, as a term for polities of any kind, in a close approximation to the modern word 'state' in the second sense. But *madīna* in the sense of polity was a fairly arcane usage in the Muslim world, confined to the philosophers and the few who read them. To everyone else, it just meant a city in the plain sense of the word.

The concept of the state as an impersonal institution emerged in Europe from the sixteenth century onwards and eventually passed to the Middle East. In the nineteenth century the Muslims gave it the Arabic name of *dawla* (Persian *dowlat*, Turkish *devlet*), and this is now the standard word in the Middle East for a state in both senses of the word. In pre-modern usage, however, *dawla* meant a turn of fortune (and of the stars in their spheres) and thus the era in which a particular dynasty held sway rather than the governmental institutions or the polity of which it was in charge.[1] But though the pre-modern Muslims lacked the concept of the state, they certainly had governmental institutions which conform roughly (if rarely precisely) to the modern definition of states in the first sense of the word and which held sway in units that we would identify as states in the second sense. How then did they explain their origin?

Adam and Eve

When medieval Muslims pondered the question why government exists, they formulated their answer in functional terms: rulers performed such and such roles for which there was a need thanks to the nature of human beings (see below ch. 17). They rarely addressed the historical question how rulers had developed or when they had first appeared, but it is clear from their creation myth that they did not share the medieval Western view of government as a secondary development of human history rooted in the Fall. They tacitly assumed government had existed even before the creation of mankind.

The relevant part of their creation myth may be summarized as follows. When God had created heaven, earth, the angels, and the *jinn* (i.e. spirits), He created Iblīs (the future devil), who was the first to receive power (*mulk*).[2] God made him ruler and governor of lower heaven and earth, as well as keeper of Paradise, or, according to another version, He made him judge among the *jinn*, who were the first inhabitants of earth and who had kings, prophets, religious

For abbreviations, see the bibliography.

1. Cf. Lewis, *Political Language*, chs 2–3.

2. Thus Tab., i, 78.10.

faith, long life, and blessings in abundance. The *jinn* grew wicked and caused corruption on earth, whereupon Iblīs sent an army against them and defeated them, which made him haughty; others say that Iblīs was a captive taken by an army of angels sent against them by God and that he became haughty because he grew up among the angels as a result of his capture; or, according to another version, Iblīs was so successful a judge among the *jinn* that he grew haughty and started fighting them. In any case, God knew that Iblīs was growing haughty and created Adam to bring out his true colours. Iblīs duly refused to bow down to Adam, whereupon he was cast into the lowest Hell. God then created Eve, but she was subverted by Iblīs in the form of a snake and both she and Adam ate of the forbidden fruit, whereupon they were expelled from Paradise. Eve was punished with menstruation, pregnancy, childbirth, and stupidity; Adam accidentally brushed his head against heaven when he fell to earth (they do not simply walk out of Paradise in the Muslim version), and so he became bald; both suffered the indignity of having to defecate: Adam wept when he smelt the stench. But above all, they lost their freedom from work: they and their descendants now had to do all the "irksome ploughing, planting, irrigating, reaping, threshing, milling, kneading, spinning, weaving and washing" which they had been spared in Paradise.[3] This was the crucial way in which the Fall affected the human condition. There was no forfeiture of immortality. Humans did not become more sinful than they had been from the start either, and human history did not turn into a story of Paradise lost and regained. In fact, many scholars denied that the Paradise from which Adam and Eve were expelled was identical with that in which God's righteous servants would eventually find themselves.[4]

Their fall notwithstanding, Adam and Eve continued to live a sub-Paradisical existence. Adam was God's deputy (*khalīfa*) on earth (cf. Q. 2:30), where he had been given power and authority (*mulk wa-sulṭān*). Both he and his son Seth were also prophets through whom God revealed His law. When Adam died, he passed the leadership (*riyāsa*) to Seth, and thereafter each leader passed his deathbed instructions (*waṣiyya*) to his successor along with "the political governance and management of the subjects under his control" (*siyāsat al-mulk wa-tadbīr man taḥta yadayhi min raʿiyyatihi*).[5] They lived a life of religious purity and piety, spending their time in worship of God without any impure thoughts or feelings of envy, hatred, or greed.[6]

3. *RIS*, ii, 229 = Goodman, *Case*, 73; Tab., i, 103, 129. For the antecedents of this idea, see below, note 10.

4. Cf. Māwardī, *Aʿlām al-nubuwwa*, 78f,; Ibn Bābawayh, *Iʿtiqād*, 130 = 81 (ch. 29).

5. Tab., i, 165.1.

6. Thus YT, i, 5 (closely following the account in the Syriac *Cave of Treasures*).

But when Cain killed Abel, he left the sub-Paradisical mountain on which Adam had settled to live somewhere else, where his descendants became 'despots and Pharaohs' (*jabābira wa-farāʿina*), that is, godless tyrants.[7] They invented musical instruments and took to entertaining themselves with music, wine-drinking, and sexual promiscuity. This caused an ever-growing number of Seth's descendants to leave the sacred mountain in order to join the fun. Enoch, *alias* Idris, and his son Methuselah both fought holy war against the Cainites and enslaved some of them, but to no avail: hardly any of Seth's descendants were left on the mountain by Noah's time, so God sent the Flood and wiped out the entire sinful lot. After the Flood, Noah's sons dispersed to become the ancestors of mankind as we know it.

The fundamental assumption behind these accounts is that all the power in the universe and all the physical and moral laws by which it is regulated reflect the same ultimate reality, God. God rules in the most literal sense of the word, appointing rulers, governors, judges, and deputies and ordering armies to be sent against insubordinate subjects. Divine government has always been and always will be, and it must necessarily manifest itself as government on earth. Adam represents the fullness of God's power on earth, and both the Sethians and the Cainites are envisaged as living in politically organized societies, as are the *jinn* who preceded them. Contrary to what medieval Christians said, coercive government did not develop among humans as a result of the Fall. All God's created beings were subject to His government, directly or through intermediaries, whether they sinned or not, and divine government was certainly coercive. Of course God would not need to use violence against His subjects if they would obey, but all have a tendency to rebel, for reasons which the myth leaves unexplained; there is nothing special about humans in this respect: God sent armies against unruly *jinn* long before humans had been created. Disobedience, *maʿṣiya*, is the Muslim word for what the Christians call sin, and the archetypal act of disobedience is Iblīs' refusal to bow down to Adam, not Adam and Eve's eating of the forbidden fruit, which only plays a limited role in the Muslim explanation of the human condition and none at all in the Muslim account of the origin of states.

Right and wrong government (imāma *and* mulk)

Government was an inescapable feature of the universe. But not all government was right, and sin certainly played a role in its corruption. The key event here is Cain's murder of Abel. Having killed his brother, Cain left Adam's

7. Tab., i, 167.14.

community to found one of his own, in which his descendants came to be ruled by godless tyrants. As we have seen, the creation myth calls them *jabābira wa-farāʿina*, despots and Pharaohs. Another word for such rulers was *mulūk* (sing. *malik*), kings. Either way, they were rulers who seized power for their own aggrandizement rather than the execution of God's will, turning God's slaves (that is, human beings) into slaves of their own and using their power for the satisfaction of private interests rather than the fulfilment of collective needs.

To call a man a king was not necessarily to denounce him. A *malik* was simply somebody who lorded it over others, especially one who did so sitting on a throne and wearing a crown. You could describe a ruler as a king in neutral or flattering terms, but in the first centuries of Islam you could only do so as long as you were speaking in a secular vein. As far as religious language was concerned, the only being to whom you could legitimately apply the awesome titles of king (*malik*) and despot (*jabbār*) was God. One could not question the overweening power of ultimate reality, but it was both presumptuous and rebellious for humans to claim such power for themselves, and those who did so merely branded themselves as kings in the sense of impious tyrants. Yet claim it often did: the despots of the Cainites were wiped out in the Flood, but they reappeared in Pharaonic Egypt, to be followed by Greek, Roman, Byzantine, Persian, Indian, and many other kings. The vast majority of humans had been, and continued to be, governed by wrongful rulers of this kind.

There was also another form of corruption, though it does not appear in the creation myth. After the Flood some people stopped having government altogether, as the Muslims knew from their own history: Islam had originated in a stateless society. The Muslims took no pride in this aspect of their past, at least not when they were religious scholars,[8] for in their view the absence of government in pre-Islamic Arabia reflected the failure of the pagan Arabs to acknowledge God. As pagans, the Arabs had lived in *jāhiliyya*, ignorance and barbarism, not in a state of aboriginal freedom and equality such as that which the Greeks and their Western epigones were apt to impute to tribal peoples. Without recognition of God's sole government there could be no proper relations among people, only tyranny or anarchy, with all the bloodshed, arbitrariness, and immorality that both implied.

Adam embodied the alternative to tyranny and anarchy alike. His leadership had been *imāma*, religious and political leadership in accordance with God's will. As *khalīfat allāh fī 'l-arḍ*, God's deputy on earth, he had dispensed God's law among his offspring as they multiplied. This was what government

8. For the attitude of specialists in tribal lore, see below, 268f.

should be and what it had remained among the Sethians down to the Flood. Thereafter right government had existed only sporadically, but it had been restored to the world by Muḥammad, the prophet who founded the Muslim polity, and it had been maintained (according to most Muslims) by his immediate successors, the first caliphs in Medina. It was their time which constituted the golden age. As always, proper government was coercive. Like Adam's successors, Muḥammad and the first caliphs had used institutionalized violence: they imposed penalties, suppressed revolts, and conducted campaigns against infidels. But they always did so in accordance with God's law; their coercive power was wielded only against evil-doers. This was the essence of good government, and it was such government, not a pre-political stage of alleged freedom and equality, that the most Muslims hankered for and hoped to restore.

The law (sharʿ, sharīʿa)

As the ruler of the universe, God issued laws. Adam had received a set of them; so had later prophets, most recently Muḥammad, whose version was final. Living in accordance with God's law was the essence of religion. In the early centuries it was practically all there was to religion. There soon came to be so much more to it that some would have liked to jettison the law altogether, much as the early Christians had done; but it remained the heart of Islam in all its forms.[9] The word *sharʿ* was often used to mean revealed religion in general.

What medieval Muslims regarded as law included much that modern students have trouble recognizing as such. A traditional handbook of Islamic law will start with the *ʿibādāt*, 'acts of service/worship',[10] that is to say the five daily prayers, the month of fasting, the annual alms tax, and the pilgrimage to Mecca once (or more) in a lifetime for those who were capable of making it. Dietary law (rules about permissible and prohibited food and drink) also formed part of the *ʿibādāt*, though its positioning in the lawbooks was unstable. None of this is law to a modern Westerner.

Next, the manuals moved on to the *muʿāmalāt*, 'mutual dealings', meaning people's relations with one another. Here they regulated marriage, divorce,

9. Cf. below, ch. 15.

10. In the ancient Near East it was by labour services that humans did the will of the gods, who had created them as their slaves in order to save themselves the trouble of procuring their own food and housing. (From the dawn of history in Mesopotamia, it was unremitting hard work that people saw as the distinguishing feature of human, or at least civilized, life.) This is the ultimate root of the Christian concept of worship as 'liturgy' (from *leitourgia*, public service or works) and the Muslims concept of it as *ʿibādāt*.

inheritance, slavery and manumission, commerce, torts, crimes, war, taxation, and more besides, all of which the modern Westerner instantly recognizes as law on the grounds that rules of this type are enforced by the authorities. But the *ʿibādāt* might also be enforced by the authorities (attending Friday prayer or fasting in Ramaḍān was not a matter of choice). Conversely numerous rules counted as law even though they lacked this feature, for the law extended into areas such as filial piety, the proprieties of clothing, behaviour at funerals, how to greet non-Muslims, and other matters that a modern Westerner would treat as purely moral, or as mere etiquette (and which in fact were not usually covered in the legal manuals, but rather in separate works). What distinguished a law from other rules was not that it could be enforced by the authorities, but rather than it defined the moral status of an act in the eyes of God. The key question to which the law provided answers was how far doing something would assist or impede the journey to salvation, not whether it was allowed or forbidden in the here and now. Assessing the moral status of human acts was the work of the jurists (*fuqahāʾ*). They classified human acts as either forbidden or permitted, and, within the latter category, as disapproved, indifferent, commendable or obligatory, trying to work out God's view of them on the basis of the Qurʾān and statements by the Prophet, plus some subsidiary sources. It was permitted to repudiate a wife, provided that the rules were followed, but it was not commendable; it was commendable to free a Muslim slave, but it was not obligatory; it was normally indifferent whether one wore this type of clothing or that, provided that the rules of modesty were satisfied and no silk was worn by men, and so on. The jurists did take an interest in how far the moral assessments should be backed by coercive power, but it was to God and His Prophet as represented in the here and now by the jurists that the law owed its authority, not to the rulers.

*Prophethood (*nubuwwa*)*

God revealed His laws to mankind by means of prophets. Adam, the first man on earth, was not just an imam but also a prophet, and the same was true of Muḥammad. Prophets play a key role in Islamic political thought.

A prophet (*nabī*) was a human being through whom God communicated with mankind, or more commonly with some subdivision of it (usually a people). He was not primarily someone who could predict the future, though he might be able to do that too; rather, he was a transmitter of God's wishes.[11]

11. Predictive abilities came to be regarded as one of the ways in which the line of transmission was authenticated.

Such mouthpieces were required because humans no longer knew God directly, as they had done in Paradise, and as the angels still did. Cut off from God, humans would corrupt His religion and government until nothing remained of either, but in His mercy God would respond by sending them a prophet to inform or remind them of the true way. Every time God selected a person for prophethood (*nubuwwa*), a window onto the unseen was opened up and a glimpse of ultimate reality was transmitted to the earth. After Muhammad's death the window was shut and so it would remain until the end of times, but it had been opened many times before him, maybe as many as 124,000 times.[12] Most of the 124,000 prophets before Muḥammad were merely sent to warn particular communities against their evil ways, but some brought a new version of God's law, and thus a new religion. The latter, numbering 315 at the most,[13] were prophets of the type called messengers (sing. *rasūl*). Messengers would found polities, for a law requires government for its realization. This is why they were of great political importance.

Some 1,400 years ago God in His mercy sent a messenger to the Arabs. He chose Muḥammad, a trader who was born in Mecca in c. 570 and who began to preach when he was about forty in response to periodic revelations brought by Gabriel. (Unlike Moses he did not speak to God directly, and he also differed from Moses in receiving his revelation in instalments rather than all in one.) Some people converted, but most Meccans reacted with sneers, ridicule, and eventually persecution of Muḥammad and his followers, many of whom were people in a weak position, such as slaves and freedmen who had no kinsmen to defend them. When things became intolerable in Mecca, Muhammad and his followers emigrated to Medina. His emigration (*hijra*) took place in 622, which later came to serve as the starting point of the Muslim calendar. When he arrived in his abode of emigration (*dār al-hijra*), he set about forming a community (*umma*) there with himself as leader, and took to consolidating his position with caravan-raiding, military expeditions, and battles with the Meccans, whose city he conquered in 630. He died in Medina in 632, whereupon his followers began the conquest of the Middle East. This, in a nutshell, is the story of how the Muslim community was founded.

Religion and politics

Westerners do not normally have any problems with the first part of this story, which follows a familiar model: Muḥammad was a prophet who preached to

12. Tab., i, 152; Ibn Bābawayh, *Iʿtiqād*, 137 = 92 (ch. 35); cf. Wensinck, 'Muhammed und die Propheten', 169ff.

13. Wensinck, 'Muhammed und die Propheten', 171.

the meek and who was persecuted for his faith. But they usually react with bewilderment to the second half, in which he goes off to found a polity in Medina instead of suffering martyrdom. Since modern Christians (and ex-Christians) typically think of religion as something transcending politics and other mundane pursuits, Muḥammad comes across to them as having abused religion to make a success of himself. This is why Western scholars have in all seriousness debated the absurd question whether he was sincere or not.[14]

Medieval Muslims did not generally see religion as above politics and other worldly affairs, but on the contrary as a prescription for their regulation. They granted that it could be abused, of course, and held numerous 'false prophets' to be guilty on that score. But they took the abuse to lie in the falsehood of the claims advanced by such prophets, not in the worldly use to which the claims were put, except in the sense that they resented the benefit that such prophets derived from them; for religion was actually meant to put things right for people in this world no less than the next, and it stood to reason that the bearer of the true religion had to acquire political power in order to bring this about. The more power you have, the more good you can do. Some prophets were assisted by worldly rulers, but others, such as Moses, David, Solomon, and Muḥammad, acquired worldly power themselves.[15] In Mecca, Muhammad had been constrained by the pagan power of Quraysh, but in Medina he had gained the power to execute God's law and to embark on warfare.[16] God had allowed Muḥammad to unite prophethood and kingship (in the flattering sense of great political power) so that he could accomplish his mission, see to the execution of the law, and overcome the infidels, as al-Thaʿālibī (d. 429/1038) put it.[17] It is not that Muḥammad was desirous of this world, the tenth-century Ismaili philosophers known as the Brethren of Sincerity explained, but God wanted Muḥammad's community to have religion and this world together; and when the Jews and Christians found this hard to understand, God sent down the story of David and Solomon, in whom kingship and prophethood had similarly been united without their prophethood being degraded thereby, so that the Muslims could argue their case with reference to them.[18]

14. The question was, however, put to them by their sources: it was Muslim freethinkers who first dismissed Muḥammad as a trickster who abused religion for worldly ends (cf. below, 172f.).

15. Juwaynī, *Ghiyāth*, §267.

16. Māwardī, *Aʿlām al-nubuwwa*, 316ff.

17. Thaʿālibī, *Ghurar*, 4 (where Adam, Joseph, David, Solomon, and Alexander are said similarly to have combined prophethood and kingship).

18. *RIS*, iii, 496. By the thirteenth century people wondered why Muḥammad had not been *more* of a king: "If kingship and sovereignty have so many advantages, and are means

All this is religious polemics, of course, here concerned with the moral status of power in the service of the truth. In terms of historical explanation – why and how things happen, whatever one's moral evaluation of them – the fact that Muḥammad was a political prophet is clearly related to the stateless environment in which he was active. The Buddha and Jesus had both lived in societies in which political authority already existed so that it was possible, prudent, or positively liberating to leave politics alone. Both preached messages which were largely about how to transcend politics along with everything else in this world: the Buddha is said to have been a prince who renounced his kingdom; Jesus was a carpenter who declared his kingdom to be not of this world. But Muḥammad was active among warring tribes and had to take political and military action if he was to accomplish his mission. The religion could not survive without communal embodiment, and the community could not survive without defence. Hence it had to have political organization.

To put this point at greater length, in tribal Arabia all free males protected themselves and their dependents in cooperation with their kinsmen by threatening to avenge any injury inflicted on them: there were no other ways of insuring oneself against murder, assault, robbery, theft, and the like. It is true that some Arabs had been incorporated in the Byzantine and Sasanid empires, in which there were armies and police, and that imperial subsidies had enabled others to develop petty kingdoms of their own, but most Arabs lived under conditions of self-help. Chiefs should not be envisaged as petty kings. Their role was to keep their tribes together by engaging in dispute settlement, helping the needy, and presiding over discussions of public issues in which all or most male adult tribesmen would participate and in which the chief would formulate the consensus as he saw it emerge. Chiefs might or might not be military leaders too, but they could neither coerce nor protect their fellow-tribesmen after the fashion of kings. Every tribesman defended himself and his dependents.

The sources say that when Muḥammad and his followers adopted their new religion, they severely tested the loyalty of their fellow-tribesmen and (in the case of slaves and freedmen) their masters and protectors, so that it was clear that the latter's cooperation would eventually be withdrawn. That would have left the Muslims in the position of outlaws, and as such they probably would not have survived for long. But Muḥammad hoped that another tribe could be persuaded to adopt them, and those of Yathrib (the later Medina) did eventually agree to afford them protection, apparently because statelessness in

---

for drawing near and gaining closeness to God, then why was the kingship of this world not given to the Prophet in the same perfection that it was given to Solomon?" (Dāya, *God's Bondsmen*, 406).

their case manifested itself in the form of endless feuds: they wanted peace and hoped that a man of God could provide it. They did not offer him protection as a host to a guest, but rather joined Muḥammad's followers to form a new community in Medina in which all members defended one another *as if* they were kinsmen. It could be said that Muḥammad created a new tribe, a super-tribe of believers; but it was led by a prophet with powers unknown to tribal chiefs. "Whenever you disagree about something, the matter should be referred to God and Muḥammad," as Muḥammad laid down in the document generally known as the Constitution of Medina.[19] Muhammad was the ultimate decision-maker. His community was a politically organized society, if only in a minimal sense. By claiming divine authority he had created an embryonic state.

Thanks to the environment in which it originated, Islam was thus embodied in a political organization almost from the start: the *umma* was a congregation and a state rolled together. Christians originated with dual membership. As believers they belonged to the church and were administered by the clergy; as citizens they belonged to the Roman empire and were ruled by Caesar. Islam originated without this bifurcation. As believers *and* as citizens they were members of the *umma* and ruled by the Prophet, thereafter by his successors.

Thanks to Muḥammad's career, Muslims came to think of prophets as the paradigmatic founders of states. Far from being assumed normally to transcend political organization, messengers of God were assumed normally to create it. The well-known fact that pagans also had polities was not normally perceived as a problem in this connection. The tenth-century Ismaili philosopher Abū Yaʿqūb al-Sijistānī observes that kingdoms are to be found all over the world whereas prophethood has only flourished in a small part of it, but he nonetheless insists that kingship arises by usurpation of leadership established by a prophet. This was indeed how kingship arose in the Islamic world, but it is hard to see how it could account for the kingdoms of the Indians, Chinese, Turks, Slavs, Africans and other peoples, to whom no prophets had been sent according to his own explicit statement.[20] It took the fourteenth-century Ibn Khaldūn to point out, in polemics against the philosophers, that in purely historical terms it was kings rather than prophets who were the paradigmatic founders of states: most of the world's inhabitants had rulers even though they had not received any prophets; and contrary to what the philosophers said,

19. Ibn Hishām, *Sīra*, i, 503.10; tr. Wensinck, *Muhammad and the Jews of Medina*, 56.
20. *Ithbāt*, 172, 174.

authority could be established without religious law, for people in power could and did devise injunctions of their own.[21] In short, the philosophers had been wrong to generalize on the basis of the Muslim experience. But Ibn Khaldūn's ability to see the formation of his own polity as an exception to the norm was highly unusual.

Restating the question

We are now in a position to restate the question with which we began. How did medieval Muslims imagine the state to have originated? Clearly, the question is misformulated. As medieval Muslims saw it, government was the inseparable companion of monotheism, and since humans had originated in a monotheist polity, the problem was not how they had come to live in states but rather why government had so often been corrupted thereafter, or disappeared altogether. The answer was that human disobedience repeatedly caused things to go wrong so that God had to send messengers to set things right again. But why had God implanted this propensity for disobedience in human beings, or indeed all his creatures? And why did He send messengers to some people and not to others? Such questions seem to have been regarded as beyond human understanding. The problematic fact that some people had government even though they had not received prophets was normally left as a loose end.

The unusual nature of the paradigm

But Ibn Khaldūn was right: most polities in history have indeed been founded by men who accumulated power from below rather than by prophets who received it from above. Consequently, most polities in history have also been characterized by a distinction between the political and religious spheres rather than by their fusion. There was no fusion of the religious and the political spheres in the complex societies of the Middle East that the Muslims were to conquer, nor had there been as far back as people could remember. It is true that Hellenistic kings and, following them, the Byzantine and the Persian emperors were credited with power over all things material and spiritual, but the fusion was limited to the ruler; it did not obtain in the society beneath him. Thus the subjects of Hellenistic kings were not expected to worship the same gods or to follow the same laws, except in the area pertaining to the shared government; and though both the Byzantines and the Persians did expect

21. *Muqaddima*, 48, 212 = i, 93, 390; cf. Nagel, *Staat und Glaubensgemeinschaft*, ii, 100; below, 268.

religious uniformity, they had to cope with an ecclesiastical organization distinct from their governmental agency beneath them. In Sasanid Iran, the two agencies were held to be twins; in the Byzantine case, they were unrelated partners. Either way, they were separate, despite the monarch's fullness of power. What is so striking about early Muslim society is precisely that it started out without such a separation. The monarch's fullness of power here reflected a complete fusion of the religious and the political all the way through: there was no religious community separate from the politically organized society, and no ecclesiastical hierarchy separate from the political agency. One has to go all the way back to the ancient Near East to find a situation comparable to that of early Islam. The Sumerians may have started their history with temple communities ruled by priests alone. But that was thousands of years ago by Muḥammad's time, nobody in the Middle East remembered it, and modern scholars usually deny it.[22]

The fusion (as opposed to blurring) of political and religious communities has not in fact been common in the history of complex societies at all, be it in the Middle East or elsewhere. Complex societies are usually much too differentiated in social, economic, intellectual, and cultural terms to tolerate the incorporation of all their interests in a single structure; and their rulers are usually much too coercive and rapacious for their subjects to have any desire to entrust them with the ultimate meaning of their lives. The Muslims were soon to find this out for themselves. The simplicity of Muḥammad's all-purpose community matched the undifferentiated nature of the tribal society in which he was active. Like everyone else in the Middle East, the Arabs were affected by the Hellenistic concept of kings as endowed with a fullness of power. ('Hellenistic' here is a shorthand for a mixture of ancient Near Eastern, Persian, and Greek ideas.) It shows in their conception of the caliph.[23] But there is only one real precedent for their all-purpose community in Middle Eastern history, and that is the federation of Israelites that Moses took out of Egypt for the conquest of Palestine (which he, like Muḥammad, did not live to see). Moses was a prophet and statesman like Muḥammad, and he is also the paradigmatic prophet in the Qurʾān.

Wittingly or unwittingly, Muḥammad was a new Moses. Like him, he united scattered tribes in the name of God and led them on to conquest (though for one reason or another the conquest continued far beyond Palestine this time round). Moses was an inspiration to many people, but his admirers were not usually able to imitate him in any literal way since they lived under

22. Cf. Crone, 'The Tribe and the State', 58ff.

23. Cf. below, 34, 40f.

such utterly different conditions. This was where Muḥammad differed. He could and did re-enact Moses' career. Thanks to the astonishing military success of the people he united, an antique model of prophetic state formation developed by a minor tribal people of the ancient Near East thus acquired paradigmatic status in the complex society of the medieval Middle East in which Islamic civilization took shape.

It is this starting point which gives Muslim political thought so different a character from that of its counterpart in the West. The Christians, as noted already, started with the conviction that truth (cognitive and moral) and political power belonged to separate spheres. Ultimately, of course, both originated with God, but they had appeared at different points in history, they regulated different aspects of life, and though they had to be coordinated for the common good, they could not be fully identified. The Muslims started with the opposite conviction: truth and power appeared at the same times in history and regulated the same aspects of life, more precisely all of them. It was a conviction that the post-conquest developments were soon to make untenable, but which was nonetheless difficult to give up. The result was an intense debate along utterly new lines dictated by the unusual starting point. In medieval Europe, where religious authority and political power were embodied in different institutions, the disagreement over their relationship took the form of a protracted controversy over the relationship between church and state. But in the medieval Middle East, religious authority and political power were embodied in a single multi-purpose institution, Muḥammad's *umma*. Here, then, the disagreement took the form of a protracted controversy over the nature and function of the leadership of the *umma*, that is the imamate.

CHAPTER

2

THE FIRST CIVIL WAR AND SECT FORMATION

The reader is warned that there are a lot of names, dates, and Arabic terms in this chapter. The first four caliphs, the first civil war, and its aftermath form part of the elementary vocabulary without which one cannot even begin to understand what medieval Muslims said about government. What follows is an attempt to serve the requisite knowledge in as short and simple a manner as possible.

The succession to the Prophet

We saw in the previous chapter that the leader of Muḥammad's community (*umma*) was called the imam. The dictionaries define an imam as somebody to be imitated, whether head of state or not. A simple prayer leader was an imam: you stood behind him and did as he did in performing the ritual prayer. Other righteous leaders were imams too: one modelled oneself on what they said and did. Great scholars, for example, came to be known by that title. But the head of state was the supreme imam. His imitators were not merely a small group of people at prayer or a major school founded by a great scholar, but rather the entire community of believers, the entire *umma*. At some point his leadership was dubbed 'the great imamate' (*al-imāma al-kubrā/ʿuẓmā*) to distinguish it from leadership of other types.[1] Unless otherwise specified, the imamate always means the great imamate in this book.

1. The earliest attestations known to me are Abū Yaʿlā, *Aḥkām*, 24.-10; Bāqillānī, *Tamhīd*, 183.-4; Naysābūrī, *Imāma*, 60.12, 61.2.

The first imam was the Prophet himself.[2] When he died in 632, the imamate passed to Abū Bakr (632–4), an early convert and emigrant from Mecca who was of the same tribe as the Prophet – the tribe known as Quraysh. We are told that he was elected at a public meeting at the initiative of another companion, ʿUmar; some sources describe his election as a kind of coup.[3] When Muḥammad died, we are told, his Medinese supporters, known as the Helpers (Anṣār), wanted to dissolve their union with Quraysh by electing a ruler of their own: "we'll have our leader and Quraysh can have theirs," they said. But ʿUmar got wind of their plans and foiled them by gatecrashing their meeting and pushing through the election of Abū Bakr as leader of the undivided community in a sequence of events which came to be known as 'the Day of the Portico' (*yawm al-saqīfa*). Whatever the truth of all this, Abū Bakr's position as leader of the community did not rest on prophethood, so he had to identify it in other ways and he is said to have adopted the title of *khalīfa* (caliph), meaning deputy or successor. One would assume this title to have stood for *khalīfat allāh*, 'deputy of God', the expression that God uses of Adam and David in the Qurʾān (2:20; 38:26) and which is attested for the caliphs from the 640s or 650s onwards.[4] But the religious scholars deny it. According to them, it stood for *khalīfat rasūl allāh*, 'successor of the messenger of God', a more modest title which no caliph is on record as having used until the early ʿAbbāsid period (750 onwards), except for Abū Bakr, who is said by the scholars to have adopted it in this version. The scholars, who emerged in the course of the century after Abū Bakr's death, disliked the grander title. They also denied that the caliph of their own time should be accepted as a guide in religious matters. Presumably, their insistence that the more modest form of the title was the original one reflects their attempt to cut the caliphs down to size (which will figure prominently in what follows). It has to be said, however, that modern scholars usually accept the scholars' claim at face value.[5]

Abū Bakr was succeeded by the above-mentioned ʿUmar (634–44), who was also an early convert of Quraysh. This time there was no crisis. Abū Bakr had designated ʿUmar as his successor, and/or ʿUmar's standing was such that his succession was a foregone conclusion. He called himself *amīr al-muʾminīn*, 'Commander of the Faithful', which became a standard title of the imam along with *khalīfa* (however completed). The sources also credit ʿUmar with the

2. Cf. Kumayt, *Hāšimijjāt*, 1:46; BF, 454.9; Ibn al-Muqaffaʿ in Kurd ʿAlī, *Rasāʾil*, 111.-5; Jāḥiẓ, 'Maqālat al-zaydiyya wa'l-rāfiḍa', *Rasāʾil*, iv, 321.

3. Cf. Madelung, *Succession*, ch. 1.

4. The first caliph known to have used it is ʿUthmān (644–56) cf. Crone and Hinds, *God's Caliph*, 6ff.

5. For all this, see Crone and Hinds, *God's Caliph*, ch. 2.

byname of al-Fārūq, a loanword from Aramaic meaning 'redeemer'. There is some additional evidence that ʿUmar was once cast in a messianic role, but tradition has forgotten about it and it plays no role in later political thought.[6] ʿUmar's byname is accordingly explained as an Arabic word meaning a person good at distinguishing right from wrong, and when the messiah reappears, he does so under the native Arabic label of *al-mahdī*.[7] It was under ʿUmar that the conquest of Syria, Egypt, Iraq and Iran was achieved. Much wealth and numerous captives were brought to Medina. Among them was an Iranian slave who developed a personal grievance against ʿUmar. In 644 ʿUmar was stabbed by this slave and died after having instructed the main contenders for the succession, of whom there are usually said to have been six, to choose a caliph from among themselves. This method of election, known as *shūrā* (consultation), was designed to prevent the contenders from fighting it out among themselves.[8]

Armed conflict was narrowly avoided when the members of the *shūrā* agreed on ʿUthmān (644–56), yet another Qurashī[9] and early convert. But it was under him that things began to go seriously wrong. Large numbers of Arab tribesmen had now settled in Syria, Egypt, and Iraq. The provinces had not so far played a role in high politics in Medina, but it was above all among the Arabs in the provinces that there was dissatisfaction with ʿUthmān, and in 656 delegates from Egypt and Iraq went to Medina to complain of his methods of government. They ended up by killing him. This act split the community down the middle, with reverberations that continue to this day.

The killing of ʿUthmān was a deed of the same order as the execution of Charles I in the English Civil War, or of Louis XVI in the French Revolution. Unlike the two European kings, ʿUthmān was not subjected to a formal trial, and his killers did not proceed to abolish the monarchy either: instead they elevated Muḥammad's cousin, ʿAlī, to the throne. But the fact that disgruntled subjects should have claimed the right to take the life of their monarch was as shocking to the early Muslims as it was to the later Europeans.[10] By what right had they acted? The answer took the form of an intense debate, not over the relative rights of rulers and subjects, but rather over the moral status of ʿUthmān himself: if ʿUthmān had been a rightly guided imam, the rebels had

6. Except perhaps in al-Mukhtār's revolt; cf. below, ch. 7.

7. Cf. Crone and Cook, *Hagarism*, 5; Bashear, 'The Title "Fārūq"'; *EI*², s.v. 'mahdī'; Donner, 'La question du messianisme'; below, ch. 7.

8. *EI*², s.v.; Crone, '*Shūrā* as an Elective Institution'.

9. This is the normal Arabic form, not 'Qurayshī', a medieval variant used by modern scholars on the assumption that the reader would find 'Qurashī' confusing.

10. For the Europeans, see Walzer, *Regicide and Revolution*.

been wrong to kill him; but if he had forfeited his imamate by his 'innovations' (*aḥdāth*), as his misdeeds were usually called, then the rebels had been entitled, or indeed obliged, to remove him by force, inasmuch as he had refused to abdicate. The vast majority of Muslims adopted what one might call a royalist position: ʿUthmān had remained a legitimate ruler till the end; it had been wrong to kill him; he should now be avenged and a new caliph elected by consultation (*shūrā*). Adherents of this position were known as ʿUthmānīs or *shīʿat ʿUthmān*, ʿUthmān's party. The rebels adopted the opposite position: ʿUthmān had violated the law in a manner incompatible with his status as imam and had been killed as a wrongdoer (*ẓāliman*), not as somebody wronged (*maẓlūman*); ʿAlī was now the legitimate imam and everyone ought to obey him. Adherents of this position were known as ʿAlawīs or *shīʿat ʿAlī*, ʿAlī's party.[11]

ʿAlī's caliphate is co-terminous with the first civil war (656–61). He began by leaving Medina for Iraq, where he established himself at Kufa and defeated a section of the ʿUthmānīs in the so-called Battle of the Camel in 657. The leaders of these ʿUthmānīs were two distinguished Companions of the Prophet, Ṭalḥa and al-Zubayr, both of whom fell in the battle, and Muḥammad's widow ʿĀʾisha, who was sent back to Medina. But ʿAlī could not defeat the other section of ʿUthmānīs, which was headed by Muʿāwiya b. Abī Sufyān, a Qurashī of the same Umayyad lineage as ʿUthmān. Muʿāwiya lacked the distinction of early conversion, but as a kinsman of ʿUthmān's he was well placed to demand vengeance for him; and having long been governor of Syria, he had a good power base. In 658 he met ʿAlī in the famous battle at Ṣiffīn in northern Mesopotamia, which the Syrians claimed to have won,[12] but which the Iraqis say they would have won if the Syrians had not cleverly called a halt to the fighting by hoisting Qurʾāns on their lances, signalling that the dispute should be submitted to arbitration. The Iraqi tradition further claims that the call for arbitration split ʿAlī's party into two: when he accepted the call for arbitration some remained loyal to him, but others left his camp, protesting that "judgement belongs to God alone" (*lā ḥukma illā li 'llāh*). These dissenters came to be known as Khārijites. Whatever the truth of all this, the Khārijites proved to be ʿAlī's downfall: he was assassinated by one of them in 661. His followers then paid allegiance to his son al-Ḥasan, but al-Ḥasan stepped down when Muʿāwiya claimed the caliphate, and in 661, the so-called 'year of unity' (*ʿām al-jamāʿa*), Muʿāwiya was generally recognized as caliph. He moved the capital to Syria and founded the Umayyad dynasty, which lasted down to 750.

Muslims are today divided into Khārijites (less than 1 percent), Shīʿites (c. 10 percent), and Sunnīs, an amalgamation of earlier groups (close to 90

11. For all this, see *EI*², s.v. 'ʿUthmāniyya'.

12. See the references in Crone and Hinds, *God's Caliph*, 69, note 67; add Tab., ii, 139f.

percent), and the key issue that divides them is the legitimate leadership of the Muslim community after the Prophet's death: who was entitled to the imamate? This was endlessly discussed with reference to the participants in the first civil war, and eventually the caliphs before it too, so that by the time the sources available to us began to be compiled (roughly a century after the events), the historical events had been through too many polemical mills to be retrievable today. (In fact, all narratives relating to pre-Umayyad history in this book are given without commitment to their historical truth unless the contrary is specified.) But why did the events get to be so disputed? How did the succession to Muḥammad come to generate *sects*? That is the question to which the rest of this chapter is devoted.

The imamate and salvation

A modern reader has trouble seeing how the civil war could generate sects, for it comes across as a purely political conflict: the protagonists were rivals for power; no disagreement over religious doctrine was involved, except perhaps in the opaque case of the Khārijites. For this reason it is commonly said that the parties, or at least ʿAlī's party, only acquired a religious dimension at a later stage.[13] But this is difficult to accept. More probably, we should correct our modern perspective. It is perfectly true that the civil war did not confront the participants with a choice between different articles of faith or concepts of spirituality, but this does not mean that it was purely political. On the contrary, it went to the heart of religion as understood by Muslims at the time in that it confronted them with a fatal uncertainty over the whereabouts of the path to salvation.

To understand this, it helps to envisage the community (*umma*) as a caravan. The early Muslims saw life as a journey through a perilous desert in which one could all too easily go astray and perish. To survive, one needed to band together under the leadership of a guide (*imām al-hudā*, *hādī*, *mahdī*) who knew the right paths, often called the paths of guidance (*manāhij* or *subul al-hudā/al-rushd/al-rashad*), that is the right things to do: the terms *sunna* (normative custom), *sīra* (exemplary behaviour), and *sharīʿa* (Islamic law) are all derived from roots to do with travelling and roads.

The imam performed two tasks indispensable for the achievement of salvation. First and most fundamentally, he gave legal existence to the *umma*. Without him there was no caravan, only scattered travellers; they became a community by their agreement to travel under him. Hence one could not be a

13. E.g. Sanhoury, *Califat*, 74n.; and, most recently, Halm, *Shīʿa Islam*, 6, 16 (at first the Shīʿites were "merely a party in the struggle for power"; there "was no religious aspect to Shīʿism prior to 680").

member of the Muslim community without declaring allegiance to its leader: in the Prophet's days one converted to Islam by paying allegiance to him (with a handclasp), be it in person or via tribal delegates; thereafter one remained a member of the *umma* by paying allegiance to his successor, in person or via his governors. The Prophet is credited with the statement that "he who dies without an imam dies a pagan death."[14] Nobody could achieve salvation without an imam (or at least agreement that there ought to be one), for there was no community without such a leader, or in other words there was no vehicle of salvation. Thus we are told that when the Prophet died, the Muslims hastened to elect a new imam because they did not want to spend a single day without being part of a community (*jamāʿa*).[15] For all that, both the Khārijites and the Shīʿites combined living without an imam with a strong sense of being the only saved, apparently by deeming agreement on the obligation to establish a true imamate, if and when it should prove possible, sufficient for the creation of a community, a saving vehicle.[16]

The second task of the imam was to lead the way. He did not simply cause the caravan to exist: he also guided it to its right destination. An imam was 'somebody to be imitated', as the dictionaries say: one went where he went and expected to prosper together with him in this world and the next. For a true imam was an *imām al-hudā*, an imam of guidance who could be trusted to show his followers the right paths. He was compared to way-marks, lodestars, the sun, and the moon for his ability to show the direction in which one should travel.[17] Without him one would not know where to go. He knew better than anyone else because he was the best person of his time: it was his superior merit that made people follow him. His guidance was seen as primarily legal, or in other words he declared what was right and wrong, for it was by living in accordance with God's law that people travelled to salvation. The coercion he might use to prevent people from straying from his caravan, or sowing dissension in it, was part of his guidance too, for anyone who strayed from the right path was lost and everyone would perish if the caravan broke up. His duty was to get people into the caravan and to make sure they stayed there without raising trouble or trying to go off on their own. This done, he could lead them along the right track until they reached their destination. Everyone who travelled with him would be saved, everyone else was lost.

14. E.g. Ibn Saʿd, v, 107 (B, 144) (cited by Ibn ʿUmar to make Ibn Muṭīʿ pay allegiance to Yazīd I); Ibn Abī Shayba, xv, no. 18997, cf. 19047; Ibn Ḥanbal, *Musnad*, iv, 96.

15. Tab., i, 1824.16.

16. Cf. further below, 287.

17. Cf. Crone and Hinds, *God's Caliph*, 34ff, (Umayyad), 82 (ʿAbbāsid; add Azdī, *Mawṣil* 427, on al-Muʿtaṣim: *aqāma 'l-imāmu manāra 'l-hudā*).

A true imam was the opposite of an *imām al-ḍalāl*, an imam of error, somebody who claimed to be a rightful leader, but who was actually illegitimate and who would thus take his caravan to Hell. If you paid allegiance to a false imam, you were doomed, for you would necessarily end up in the same place in the hereafter as the man whose caravan you had chosen to join. Anyone who joined the wrong caravan became an unbeliever (*kāfir*), for there was only one community of believers. It travelled under the one and only imam of guidance representing the one and only God. All this was generally agreed. But who was the imam of guidance when ʿUthmān was killed? How could one be sure that one was travelling to Paradise rather than to Hell? That was the problem raised by the first civil war.

Fitna

"The imam [ʿUthmān] Ibn ʿAffān has been killed and the Muslim cause has been lost. The paths of guidance have become dispersed," the poetess Laylā Akhyaliyya complained: not knowing where to go when ʿUthmān was killed, the believers had gone in different directions, inevitably meaning that some of them had gone astray.[18] Where *was* one to go? "Which party shall I deem infidel and which believing?," as a young man asked himself with reference to the followers of ʿAlī and Muʿāwiya.[19] If ʿUthmān had remained an imam of guidance till the end, he had been unlawfully killed and his position was in abeyance until he had been avenged and a new caliph elected; ʿAlī was in that case an imam of error leading a party of infidels who had condemned themselves to Hell by murdering a caliph and supporting a usurper.[20] But if ʿUthmān had fallen into error, he had forfeited the caliphate and been lawfully executed for his refusal to mend his ways or step down; ʿAlī was in that case the true imam and it was his opponents who were "calling to hellfire".[21] But maybe ʿAlī had forfeited the caliphate as irrevocably as had ʿUthmān, by accepting the call to arbitration at Ṣiffīn. This is what the Khārijites claimed: after all, it showed that he doubted his own entitlement to the office.[22] In that case, both ʿUthmān and ʿAlī had turned into unbelievers. In short, to choose one's leader was to choose one's vehicle of salvation. It was because the civil

18. Zubayr b. Bakkār, *Muwaffaqiyyāt*, 511, no. 326.

19. Ibn Saʿd, vii, 1, 82 (B, 114).

20. Cf. MM, v, 16f., (iii, §1774), where Muʿāwiya asks Ḥujr's followers to repent of their *kufr*.

21. Hence Ḥujr saw renunciation of allegiance to ʿAlī as leading to *dukhūl al-nār* (MM, v, 17 (iii, §1774)).

22. Thus the Najdiyya (cf. Crone, 'Statement by the Najdiyya Khārijites', 63).

war forced people to make up their minds about the whereabouts of this vehicle that it was known as *fitna*, test or trial: God was testing the believers to see how many of them would come out of it with their sense of guidance intact.

The first civil war (656–61) was soon followed by a second, in which the sons took over from their fathers. Muʿāwiya was succeeded by his son Yazīd I in 680. The latter's caliphate was contested by a son of al-Zubayr's, ʿAbdallāh, and also by a son of ʿAlī's, Ḥusayn (for some reason no son of Ṭalḥa's appeared).[23] ʿAbdallāh b. al-Zubayr, who ensconced himself in Mecca, refused to pay allegiance to Yazīd I and, when Yazīd died prematurely at the end of 683, claimed the caliphate for himself. ʿUthmān's party thus split into two. Just as 'ʿAlawī' had come to mean an adherent of ʿAlī – and later his kinsmen – to the exclusion of the Khārijites, so 'ʿUthmānī' now came to mean an adherent of ʿUthmān and his Umayyad relatives to the exclusion of those who supported the Zubayrids.[24] ʿAlī's son, al-Ḥusayn, set off for Kufa in 680 in the expectation of Kufan support against Yazīd I, to be cut down by Umayyad troops at Karbalāʾ. To Shīʿites, this became an event of almost the same importance (though not the same meaning) as the crucifixion of Jesus to Christians. When Yazīd I died in 683, the Kufans repented of having left al-Ḥusayn in the lurch. Some of them (known as the Tawwābūn, 'Penitents') marched off on a suicidal mission against the Syrians. Others stayed in Kufa, where they accepted the leadership of a rebel by the name of al-Mukhtār, who proclaimed another son of ʿAlī's by the name of Muḥammad b. al-Ḥanafiyya to be the messiah (*mahdī*).[25] Meanwhile the Khārijites were busy rebelling in Arabia and Iran under leaders of their own. Like the first civil war, the second was won by the Umayyads in Syria, now represented by ʿAbd al-Malik (685–705), whose troops defeated and killed Ibn al-Zubayr in Mecca in 692.

So once again the believers were afflicted with *fitna*. "Until now we have been brethren with the same religion and community . . . if the sword is used . . . we will be an *umma* and you will be an *umma*," a supporter of al-Ḥusayn told a supporter of the government.[26] "I am a friend (*walī*) of (ʿUthmān) Ibn ʿAffān in this world and the next, and a friend of his friends, an enemy of his

23. One of Ṭalḥa's sons, Mūsā, was held by some to be the messiah (*mahdī*); but instead of seeking a political role, he reacted to the *fitna* by withdrawing from human society (Ibn Saʿd, v, 120f. (B, 162); Nuʿaym b. Ḥammād, *Fitan*, 88 (S, §401)).

24. Cf. *EI*², s.v. 'ʿUthmāniyya'. Eventually, of course, ʿAlawī came to mean a descendant of ʿAlī's rather than an adherent of his, the latter being known as a Shīʿite; and in scholarly circles, ʿUthmānī came to mean an adherent of the three-caliphs thesis, not a devotee of the Umayyads.

25. Cf. below, 77f.

26. Tab., ii, 331.7.

enemies," Ibn al-Zubayr declared in the course of negotiations with Khārijites,[27] who had hoped for a different response. They told him that he should "treat as an enemy him who was the first to institute error and make innovations, and to depart from the judgement of the book (i.e. ʿUthmān); if you do that, you will satisfy your Lord and save yourself from painful chastisement"; he would forfeit his life in the next world if he did not, they said.[28] "What do you say of Muṣʿab (b. al-Zubayr)?," other Khārijites asked of Basran troops with reference to Ibn al-Zubayr's brother and governor of Iraq; "is he your friend (*walī*) in this world and the next . . . are you his friends (*awliyāʾ*) in life and death . . .? What do you say about ʿAbd al-Malik? . . . are you quit of him in this world and the next . . . are you his enemies in life and death?"[29] To the Khārijites, neither the Zubayrids nor the Umayyads were rightly guided. In the same vein the famous exegete, Ibn al-ʿAbbās, reputedly declared the Zubayrids and the Umayyads alike to "call to hellfire".[30] One's imam in this world was still one's imam in the next. Choosing him was still to choose one's vehicle of salvation.

Affiliation and dissociation

The first civil wars thus split the community into rival communities (*umma*s). Since each was seen by its members as a vehicle of salvation, each was a potential sect, and its members would certainly do their best to insulate themselves in social terms: having chosen their *umma* (or, as time passed, been born into it), they would publicly declare their loyalty to its imam and his adherents and dissociate from everyone else. Thus Ibn al-Zubayr would declare his loyalty for (*wālā*, *tawallā*, also translated 'affiliate to', 'associate with') ʿUthmān's party by declaring himself a friend (*walī*) of the latter, meaning that he accepted ʿUthmān as a true imam, supported his cause and had a relationship of loyalty and support (*walāya*) with everyone else who did so. The Khārijites by contrast would dissociate from (*tabarraʾa min*, also translated 'declare themselves quit of') ʿUthmān's party. The people with whom one had *walāya* were those with whom one would socialize. One would eat with them, sit with them in the mosque, intermarry with them, allow them to inherit from other members of one's community, accept inheritances from them, help and assist them, pray for forgiveness for them, and hope to see them again in Paradise: they formed one's community in this world and the next. But those from whom one did *barāʾa*

27. Ibid., ii, 517.2.
28. Ibid., ii, 515.10.
29. Ibid., ii, 821.13.
30. BA, v, 195f.

were not members of one's community, not believers, and not destined for Paradise, and one should not eat with them, sit with them in the mosque, intermarry with them, have relations of mutual inheritance with them, visit them, pray for forgiveness for them, greet them, or even smile at them.[31] One might well curse them. Muʿāwiya's governor of Kufa would curse ʿAlī and all the murderers of ʿUthmān, and pray for forgiveness for ʿUthmān and his party (*shīʿa*);[32] the adherents of ʿAlī would curse ʿUthmān or Muʿāwiya, dissociate from them, and stay away from the Friday service and other public prayers led by Muʿāwiya's governor.[33] People suspected of Khārijism would be asked to curse the Khārijites: a young man in Basra refused to do so, just as he refused to declare himself *ʿalā dīn Muʿāwiya*, 'a follower of Muʿāwiya's religion', or better, 'in a state of obedience to Muʿāwiya'.[34] When people declared themselves to be *ʿalā dīn fulān*, 'followers of the religion of so-and-so', they did not mean that they had opted for a particular set of religious doctrines associated with that person, though this is precisely what later Muslims took them to mean. To them, the usage came across as offensive: there was no separate 'religion of ʿAlī', all there was to ʿAlī's religion was Muḥammad's.[35] But when first-century Muslims declared themselves to be *ʿalā dīn fulān*, they simply meant that they accepted the person in question as the true imam and his party as the saving community. The declaration was synonymous with one of allegiance (*walāya*). "I, Ibn Shaddād, am in obedience to ʿAlī (*ʿalā dīn ʿAlī*) and not a friend (*walī*) of ʿUthmān b. Arwā," as an adherent of al-Mukhtār in Kufa declared, derisively identifying ʿUthmān with reference to his mother rather than his father.[36] When a Syrian chief prepared for action to save the Umayyad house, he made a speech saying, "I bear witness that if obedience to Yazīd b. Muʿāwiya (*dīn Yazīd b. Muʿāwiya*) was right when he was alive, then it is still right today and his party are in the right too; and if Ibn al-Zubayr and his party stood for falsehood at that time, then he and his party still do so today."[37] People would constantly declare their communal stance. Others would know where they stood and socialize accordingly. It was by mechanisms of this kind

31. For example Nasafī, *Radd*, 58f. Ibn Bābawayh, *ʿUyūn*, ii, 202.7; Nagel, *Rechtleitung und Kalifat*, 268, citing *TB*, viii, 144.

32. Tab., ii, 112.

33. Ibid., ii, 115, 147, 234.

34. Abī 'l-Aswad al-Du'alī, *Dīwān*, 92ff., no. 47.

35. Thus ʿAlī himself in Madelung, *Succession*, 178, citing Ibn Durayd. Of the young man in the previous note we are similarly told that he would only declare himself to be *ʿalā dīn Ibrāhīm*.

36. BA, v, 233.2.

37. Tab., ii, 469.13.

that sects in the sense of bounded communities identified by different views on religious questions began to emerge.

Needless to say, there must have been a good deal more to it than this schematized account suggests. The initial outcome of the debate over the caliphs seems to have been a confusing welter of small groups with slightly different views; amalgamation probably played as great a role in sect formation as splits. But whatever the details (which may prove beyond reconstruction), the reason why seemingly political disagreement led to the formation of sects is that the political leaders were religious guides and that their followers could not disagree about their identity without thereby assigning themselves to different vehicles of salvation.

Past caliphs

All Muslims needed to be sure that the community they travelled in was that founded by the Prophet himself: they would not otherwise be Muslims. They thus needed to know the genealogy of their community, in the sense of the legitimate succession of rightly guided leaders from the Prophet to their own time. In tracing this genealogy all focused their attention on the point at which the disagreement about the succession set in, or, as one might also put it, the point at which the genealogy branched out. (For what follows, see charts 1 and 2.)

The Prophet was succeeded by Abū Bakr, who was succeeded by ʿUmar, who was succeeded by ʿUthmān: there does not initially seem to have been any disagreement about the succession up to here; it was the civil war that started the disputes. The earliest sources to survive present the civil war and aftermath as a conflict between *shīʿat ʿUthmān* and *shīʿat ʿAlī*, no more and no less: the ʿUthmānīs said that ʿUthmān had remained a lawful caliph till the end, the Khārijites and Shīʿites said that he had not; the issue was whether one should attach oneself to the Prophet via ʿUthmān or ʿAlī; that the first two caliphs had been legitimate imams was taken for granted.[38] But the possible lines of descent soon multiplied. The Khārijites attached their community to the Prophet via Abū Bakr and ʿUmar without recognizing either ʿUthmān or ʿAlī as legitimate imams: though both had been rightly guided at the time of their accession, both had forfeited their imamate and indeed their status as believers by their sins. The Murjiʾites ('suspenders of judgement'), who appeared c. 700 AD, also accepted Abū Bakr and ʿUmar as legitimate caliphs, but without pronouncing on the status of the two disputed caliphs who followed: it was no

38. Noted by Ibn Taymiyya, *Minhāj al-sunna*, i, 7. See further below, 71ff.

Khāriytes - Abū Bakr + ʿUmar - hate others
Murji'ites - Abū Bakr + ʿUmar - no jude. on others
Shi'ites - Ali - hate others

longer possible to establish whether ʿUthmān or ʿAlī had been right, they said; one should not affiliate to or dissociate from either of them. About the same time some Shīʿites began to argue that the Prophet himself had designated ʿAlī as his successor: they thus traced their community to the Prophet directly via ʿAlī without going through Abū Bakr and ʿUmar, let alone ʿUthmān, rejecting all three as usurpers. In the early ʿAbbāsid period the so-called Rāwandiyya (named after a member of the ʿAbbāsid army) argued that the Prophet had designated his uncle al-ʿAbbās, from whom the ʿAbbāsid caliphs descended, as his successor, and cast his descendants as what one might call 'imams in exile' down to their open assumption of power. In principle, they thus rejected all the caliphs from the Prophet's death in 632 down to the ʿAbbāsid revolution in 750 as usurpers (though they were unwilling to say so in practice).[39] Not long after the Rāwandiyya's appearance there were people who proposed a compromise between the ʿUthmānī and the ʿAlawī positions: the rightly guided imams after the Prophet had been Abū Bakr, ʿUmar, ʿUthmān, *and* ʿAlī. This was the famous four-caliphs thesis which spread at great speed during the ninth century to become the hallmark of all those Muslims who 'stuck to communal unity' (*lazima al-jamāʿa*).

Jamāʿī *Muslims*

The Muslims who stuck to communal unity will be referred to in what follows as *jamāʿī* Muslims. The reference is to all those who refused to form separatist communities under present or future imams of their own even though they might regard the ruling dynasty as sinful – in effect all those who were not Shīʿites or Khārijites. By the eleventh century one would call them Sunnis. One cannot use that adjective, however, until they had coalesced as a single party endowed with a shared understanding of the Sunna of the Prophet and its implications. In the early centuries they were divided into hostile groups that had little in common apart from their high appreciation of communal togetherness, and for this reason there is no single word for them. They did form a single party for some fifty years, from the first civil war to c. 700, and in that period one can call them ʿUthmānīs. But then the Murjiʾites appeared, followed by Partisans of Ḥadīth and Muʿtazilites, while 'ʿUthmānī' came to mean different things. All these people remained something of a single party to their Shīʿite and Khārijite opponents thereafter too, but this did not give them a name that we can use. The Shīʿites and the Kharijites often called those who were prepared to live under sinful rulers 'Murjiʾites', at least from the ninth

39. Cf. below, 92f.

century onwards. But this is confusing in that the Murjiʾites were strictly speaking only one party committed to *jamāʿa* and that the Traditionalists, the other major party, resented being bracketed with them. Moreover, the Muʿtazilites were probably not included in the appellation; and even if they were, they shared with the Traditionalists the feature of not wanting to be: they called all *their* non-Shīʿite and non-Khārijite opponents 'Murjiʾites.'[40]

External observers could see that the various parties had something in common, but it was usually in a polemical vein that they grouped them together, and they always perceived their own parties as special. For this reason no term coined at the time is likely to help us. The use of the term *jamāʿī* was pioneered by Hodgson half a century ago, when Islamicists routinely spoke of Sunnis from the first civil war onwards, or even from the time of the Prophet. As the first to change established usage, he felt obliged to retain a reference to the Sunnis in his new expression, so he opted for *jamāʿī-sunnī*, regretfully noting that *jamāʿī* on its own would have been a better term.[41] Now that it is generally accepted that the formation of Sunnism was a protracted process, we can adopt the more accurate (and less cumbersome) form. *Jamāʿī* Muslims in this book are much the same people as the 'Murjiʾites' of the Shīʿites and the Khārijites, but they include Muʿtazilite adherents of the four-caliphs thesis, and from the eleventh century onwards I shall replace the expression with 'Sunnis', except when I wish to include the Muʿtazilites. When I have to use English terms, I shall translate *jamāʿī* as 'communitarian' or 'communalistic', refusing to sanction either by exclusive use since neither is very apt. The reader is asked to remember that in the context of this book a communitarian is the opposite of sectarian, not of a believer in individual rights; the term stands for somebody who wanted to keep the caravan together, not for somebody who wanted to shore up the family. Similarly, communalism in this book has nothing to do with shared property, local autonomy, or devotion to ethnic and cultural subgroups at the expense of the community as a whole; on the contrary, devotion to the community as a whole was precisely what commitment to the *jamāʿa* was about.

Present Caliphs

Initially, contemporary caliphs played the same role in the self-definition of the rival parties as those of the past. It was after all as a dispute about

40. Cf. Crone and Zimmermann, *Epistle*, 243.

41. Hodgson, *Venture of Islam*, i, 278. The better term is not in fact entirely without support in the sources; cf. YB, 352.15: its inhabitants are not Khārijites (*shurāt*) but rather *jamāʿiyya*.

contemporary claimants to the imamate that the first civil war had begun. Questions such as "what do you say about Muʿāwiya?" or "what do you say about ʿAbd al-Malik?" were meant to elucidate whether contemporaries regarded these caliphs as imams of guidance, and at first sight things continued unchanged after the second civil war. The notorious governor, al-Ḥajjāj, professed to believe not only in the unity of God and the messengership of Muḥammad, but also in obedience to the caliph al-Walīd I (705–15): "on this he would live, on this he would die, and on this he would be resurrected."[42] Adherents of the Umayyads continued to accept the caliphs of their own time as imams down to the end of the dynasty, and indeed beyond.[43] But for all that, it is clear that Muslim society was rapidly becoming too complex for the old fusion of the political and religious communities to be viable. In 744 civil war broke out again, provoked by the murder of the caliph al-Walīd II in 744 and continuing as the ʿAbbāsid revolution that toppled the Umayyads in 750. The third civil war was yet another *fitna*, or test, of the believers, but a good number of Muslims now held that the best reaction was to lock one's door and stay at home until the candidates for power had fought it out: to choose one's caliph was no longer to choose one's vehicle of salvation; the caliph was no longer an imam in the original sense of the word.

He thus ceased to matter for purposes of the genealogy of the community: he was a mere guardian of the community now, not a link in the history of the transmission of right guidance from the Prophet down to today. Most Muslims ceased to regard the Umayyads as such a link in the course of the Umayyad period and never really accepted the ʿAbbāsids in that role either; as they saw it, the transmission of right guidance had passed to the religious scholars. Only the Shīʿites continued to think that the ruler ought to be such a link, and would be if only he was chosen from among the rightful candidates. To the majority of Muslims, the debates about the genealogy of the community stopped involving the caliphs after 661, when the Umayyads took over.

The de-politicization of the community of believers

That the caliph had ceased to define the community is neatly illustrated by the contrasting reactions to the Arabian and the Andalusian withdrawals of allegiance to him, in 632 and 756 respectively. When Muḥammad died in 632, many Arab tribes stopped sending alms taxes to Medina. They did not all repudiate Islam, but they were branded as apostates (*murtadd*s) regardless, for they

42. Crone and Hinds, *God's Caliph*, 41.

43. Cf. Naṣr b. Sayyār's poem in Dīnawarī, 359; Tab., i, 2815.13; Azdī, 252.10; *EI*², s.v. 'ʿUthmāniyya'.

had ceased to be members of the Muslim community by their refusal to recognize Muḥammad's successor in Medina. A little over a century later, in 756, the ruler of al-Andalus, ʿAbd al-Raḥmān I, stopped acknowledging the ʿAbbāsid caliph as his overlord by omitting mention of him in the Friday oration. In principle the Andalusians had thus also ceased to be members of Muḥammad's community, and it would have been easy enough for the ʿAbbāsids to brand them as apostates. But it does not seem to have occurred to them, or for that matter anyone else, to do so. One could now be a member of Muḥammad's community without paying allegiance to Muḥammad's successor.

This point of view is also attested in the account, by the Kufan historian Sayf b. ʿUmar (d. between 786 and 809), of the Arab conquest of Iran. On the eve of the battle of Qādisiyya (between 635 and 637), according to Sayf, the Arabs assured the Persians that they had no wish to conquer their land, only to bring them to the truth; if the Persians would accept Islam voluntarily, the Arabs would go home, leaving them to rule themselves in alliance with Medina. "Choose Islam and we'll leave you alone on your land," they said; "we'll be loosely associated with one another, but your land will be yours and your affairs will be in your hands"; "we'll leave you with the Book of God and put you in charge of it on the understanding that you'll govern according to its laws. We'll leave your country and let you deal with its affairs as you please."[44] This is apologetic, of course: it is directed against charges by the conquered peoples that the Arab conquests were motivated by worldly ambitions rather than a desire to spread the truth.[45] But its interest here lies in the fact that by the later eighth century it was possible to imagine a world in which there were two sovereign Muslim states within the community of believers. If the Persians had not been so stubborn, according to Sayf, an Arab and a Persian polity would have coexisted in amity, ruled by a successor of Muḥammad and a Khusraw respectively, travelling along the same paths of truth without amalgamating in political terms. Others, too, were entertaining the idea of a Muslim world divided into a plurality of allied or federated states about this time.[46] There was only one community of believers, as all agreed even though they disagreed about its identity; but as most Muslims now saw it, it was defined by its beliefs and its religious leaders, not by its political leadership.

By fixing the number of rightly guided caliphs at four, mainstream Muslims laid down that religious guidance could never be concentrated in the head of state again (cf. chs. 11, 16). As noted, the Shīʿites disagreed. But one section of them, the so-called Imamis (or Ithna-ʿasharīs, 'Twelvers') declared

44. Tab., i, 2240, 2272, 2280, cf. 2271, 2273, 2284.
45. Cf. below, 374.
46. Cf. al-Aṣamm below, 68.

their imam to have gone into hiding in 874, thereby in effect laying down that the religious guide could never become a head of state again (cf. further below, ch. 10). Most Khārijites and all Shīʿites of the type known as Zaydīs continued to consider it possible to unite the two roles in a single man, but they never succeeded in taking control of the Muslim world at large and such imamates as they succeeded in establishing on the fringes were intermittent. Within two centuries of the conquests, the vast majority of Muslims thus found themselves ruled by caliphs whom they did not consider to be embodiments of right and wrong. They might grudgingly recognize them as legitimate, accepting them as what one might call quasi-caliphs – caliphs without the epithet of Rāshidūn (rightly guided)[47] – or they might positively denounce them as kings and tyrants, but either way they could not model themselves on them. For guidance to salvation they had to look elsewhere. Their religious fate thus ceased to be bound up with that of the ruler. Even quasi-caliphs could be righteous; the same was eventually found to be true even of kings. But one could not assure oneself of salvation by paying allegiance to them. In short, the community ceased to be in the nature of a caravan which travelled along a single path under the leadership of a single religio-political leader to a single destination. One still had to choose one's community, but one no longer did so by paying allegiance to a caliph.

The end of simplicity

By c. 800 the community of believers came in several rival versions and had at least two different types of leadership within each version, one political and the others religious. The proliferation of the types of leadership was not to stop there, for the caliphs soon came to coexist with kings and sultans, while the religious scholars soon came to coexist with philosophers and Sufis (mystics) too. The simplicity of Muḥammad's multi-purpose polity had gone.

It is sometimes said that the schisms over the imamate arose because the Prophet had made no provisions for the succession, but this is difficult to accept. For one thing, no serious disagreement arose over the succession until ʿUthmān was killed. For another thing, the Muslims were unlikely to retain their simple socio-political order and broad consensus on political and religious matters when the bulk of them left Arabia for the fleshpots of Egypt, Syria, Iraq, and Iran. The very fact that the imam represented their worldly and otherworldly interests alike meant that all clashes of interests were likely to display themselves in disputes about his identity and the nature of his office. It is to these disputes that we may now turn.

47. Cf. below, 139.

CHAPTER

3

THE UMAYYADS

As the Roman expansion had undermined the Roman republic, so the Muslim conquest of the Middle East destroyed the patriarchal regime in Medina. In both cases, civil war was followed by the emergence of an increasingly authoritarian monarchy. The Muslim counterpart to Augustus was Muʿāwiya (661–80), who moved the capital to Syria and founded the Umayyad dynasty (661–750), under whom the embryonic state founded by the Prophet acquired a more developed form. But the developments unleashed by the conquests continued to transform Muslim society, rapidly making the political organization of the Umayyads obsolete, their orientation outmoded, and the dynasty itself heartily disliked. Within three generations they had come to be denounced as impious survivors from the pagan past who had somehow managed to hijack the Islamic enterprise. They were ousted in the third civil war, more precisely that part of it known as the ʿAbbāsid revolution. But contrary to what many had hoped, the trend towards more authoritarian government was not reversed. A fully-fledged, if shortlived, empire emerged under the ʿAbbāsids (effectively 750–861; fainéance 861–1258). All the fundamental questions first raised under the Umayyads continued to be debated down to the effective end of the ʿAbbāsid empire some hundred years after the revolution.

Legitimacy

By what right did the Umayyads rule? An extraordinary amount of medieval Islamic political thought is devoted to legitimation of the dynasty in power, and this was so already in Umayyad times.

The Umayyads grounded their right to the caliphate in the legitimacy of ʿUthmān. He had been lawfully elected by consultation (*shūrā*) and unlawfully killed, indeed martyred; his Umayyad kinsmen and avengers had taken over his position as imam of guidance.[1] ʿAlī had never been a caliph, merely a rebel or imam of error whose family the idolatrous Iraqis continued to worship as the Israelites had worshiped the golden calf.[2] In short, the Umayyads were ʿUthmānīs who cast their accession as a Restoration: the royalists had won, the legitimate monarchy was back, the rebel interlude was over.

In addition, every Umayyad ruler was a man of unsurpassed merit (*al-afḍal*), indeed the best man alive (*khayr al-nās*):[3] so numerous poets from the time of ʿAbd al-Malik onwards assure us in the conviction that monarchy was government by the most virtuous individual. This was an idea with long roots. "Nothing can be found better than the rule of the one best man," as Herodotus had made the Persian emperor Darius (d. 486 BC) declare. A man far superior to everyone else would have to be obeyed as king, or alternatively ostracized, as Aristotle (d. 322 BC) said. "Among human beings the highest merit means the highest position," as the Stoic philosopher Seneca (d. 65) succinctly put it, voicing what had by then become a Hellenistic commonplace. It was still current in late antiquity, and not just on the Greek side of the border.[4] When the philosopher Paul the Persian dedicated a treatise on logic to the Persian emperor Khusraw I (531–79), he addressed him as the best of men (*ṭāvā de-gavrē*).[5] But what if a man initially rejected as inferior proved capable of making everyone obey him? One response would be to accept that he had the requisite merit after all and hence that his power was right. It appears to have been by some such reasoning from might to right that the Arabs came to terms with Muʿāwiya. It was certainly how the court poets tended to think: the sheer

1. Cf. Tab., i, 3243.5–12; Crone and Hinds, *God's Caliph*, 31f.; Nadler, *Umayyadenkalifen*, 65ff.

2. Crone, *Slaves*, 204, note 30; Tab. ii, 1774; Cook, 'Apocalyptic Chronicle', 27. Cf. also the attitude to ʿAlī in early ʿAbbāsid Syria (van Ess, *TG*, i, 70f.).

3. Crone and Hinds, *God's Caliph*, 30, notes 23, 24; Nadler, *Umayyadenkalifen*, 77, 145, 170, 175.

4. Dvornik, *Political Philosophy*, i, 175 (citing Herodotus, iii, 81), and index, s.v. 'best man', theory of; Aristotle, *Politics*, 1284a-b, cf. 1288a; Seneca, *Letters*, no. 90. Cf. also Themistius, *Risāla*, 34, 36/96f., 100, translated (if his it is) long after the idea had surfaced on its own in Islam.

5. Land, *Anecdota Syriaca*, iv, l = 1.

fact that the Umayyads had power showed that they deserved it; since God had indisputably raised them up, they had to have qualities which pleased Him.[6]

The fact that the Umayyads saw their power as decreed by God has often been taken by modern Islamicists to mean that they supported determinism against the doctrine of free will (known as Qadarism) in an effort to deprive their subjects of a right to resist: God having decreed that they should rule, there was nothing the believers could do about it.[7] But although it is undoubtedly true that the Umayyads were determinists, it has to be remembered that so were most of their enemies, be they Khārijites, Murjiʾites, or Shīʿites. Since the political debate took place within a generally determinist ambience, the Umayyads had no reason to give much thought to the relationship between divine omnipotence and human action for purposes of justifying their regime, nor do they seem to have done so. They simply took their success to mean that God was on their side.[8] "So long as He will have them to reign . . . kings are armed with authority from God," as Calvin said, meaning that a particular ruler was to be obeyed so long as he had the power to impose obedience.[9] "God helps the strongest," as a popular maxim quoted by Luther more succinctly puts it.[10] This is precisely what the Umayyads meant, and how early Muslims in general seem to have looked at things. The obvious determinist response was to deprive the Umayyads of their divine authority by defeating them, and a fair number of determinist rebels tried to do just that. God eventually helped the strongest by toppling the Umayyads at the hands of Khurāsānī revolutionaries whose views, if any, on determinism are unknown. But the fact that the Umayyads had expressed themselves in a determinist vein came in handy for the advocates of free will, who used it to discredit the determinist position, perhaps already in the Umayyad period and certainly in later times. This is what accounts for the modern impression that the Umayyads supported determinism in opposition to the doctrine of free will for political reasons.[11]

6. Compare the story in which Sulaymān takes the very misery of lepers to prove that they deserve it: God would not otherwise have inflicted such a fate on them (Conrad, 'First Islamic Hospital', 234f.).

7. Thus Goldziher, *Theology and Law*, 83f.; Watt, *Political Thought*, 38; 'God's Caliph', 570 (and elsewhere); van Ess, *Zwischen Ḥadīt und Theologie*, 181ff. (and elsewhere); but cf. now *TG*, i, 24. Further references in Murad, '*Jabr* and *Qadar*', 117.

8. Cf. Crone and Hinds, *God's Caliph*, 117f.; Crone and Zimmermann, *Epistle*, ch. 5; Nadler, *Umayyadenkalifen*, 194, 275; Murad, '*Jabr* and *Qadar*'.

9. Walzer, *Revolution of the Saints*, 38.

10. Luther, 'Secular Authority', 40.

11. Cf. al-Jubbāʾī in van Ess, *Anfänge*, 241f.; Zimmermann, review of *Anfänge*, 440f.

Dynastic succession

Shortly before his death Muʿāwiya designated his son Yazīd as his successor and made the leading men of the garrison cities pay allegiance to him. When Yazīd I died prematurely in 683, the Syrian chiefs chose Marwān I, from a different branch of the Umayyad house, as his successor; and Marwān I in his turn designated two sons as his successors, one as heir and one to spare. Though at times the presence of two heirs proved almost as problematic as none, this became standard practice for the rest of the Umayyad period. The Umayyads themselves took pride in their dynastic succession. As their court poets present it, ʿUthmān's election by *shūrā* showed that the founder of the lineage was legitimate while the hereditary nature of the caliphate thereafter showed that the Umayyads were highborn rather than upstart rulers.[12] But to the enemies of the dynasty, it was above all by their introduction of dynastic succession that the Umayyads condemned themselves.

How much resentment Muʿāwiya's designation of Yazīd actually aroused at the time is difficult to say: the main opposition seems to have come from Qurashīs in Medina (such as Ibn al-Zubayr and al-Ḥusayn) who found themselves excluded from consideration. But whatever the initial reaction, there is no doubt that the resentment grew thereafter. Automatic succession within a single family was quite rightly seen as a first step towards the imperial form of government which was to culminate under the ʿAbbāsids. The sources for the Umayyad period abound in calls for the election of the caliph, whether from among all Muslims, all Arabs, all Qurashīs, or all members of the Prophet's family, by consultation (*shūrā*). Indeed, when Yazīd III rebelled against al-Walīd II to ascend the throne himself in 744, he too called for *shūrā* and volunteered to step down if a more meritorious candidate could be found.

For all that, there are two puzzling problems here. First, the Umayyad mode of succession continued under the ʿAbbāsids, who sometimes designated one heir and sometimes two. The chroniclers accept this without demur, but nonetheless continue to blame the Umayyads in strident tones for their introduction of dynastic succession. Secondly, the Umayyad mode of succession was adopted by the Imami Shīʿites too, without the heir to spare; but in polemics against the Shīʿites, the Sunnis will insist, not that the Shīʿites are copying their mode of succession, but on the contrary that their own mode of succession is elective.

The secondary literature usually copes with these problems by postulating that succession in early Islam was elective and that this is what Sunni law

12. Crone and Hinds, *God's Caliph*, 31. Cf. also the Umayyad claims in Kumayt, *Hāšimijjāt*, no. 2:37.

preserves; hereditary succession was allegedly introduced by the Umayyads under Byzantine or Persian influence,[13] or alternatively by way of reversion to Arabian ideas,[14] in any case by way of departure from Islamic norms; the Sunnis learnt to live with it, but they always maintained a principled stance against it, which they displayed by insisting on the elective nature of their own system and condemning the Umayyads for changing it.

But this is not quite on target. It is certainly true that succession to high office in pre-Islamic Arabia was normally hereditary. Tribal chiefs, judges, and guardians of sanctuaries in pre-Islamic Arabia came from the same families for generations on end; the sources envisage Muḥammad's own tribe of Quraysh as hereditary guardians of the Kaʿba. Chiefs were not necessarily followed by their sons, however, still less was there a rule of primogeniture; rather, the most suitable candidate from the chiefly family would be 'elected', in the sense that the person capable of asserting his authority would be accepted. (God helped the strongest in pre-Islamic times as well.) There were not usually any formal procedures, though there cannot be much doubt that the pre-Islamic Arabs were familiar with *shūrā*, the practice of letting rival candidates come to an agreement among themselves on the basis of estimates (acquired by consultation) of their relative support.[15]

Another component of the explanation is undoubtedly off target, however: we do not have to await the Umayyads for the pre-Islamic mode of succession to reappear in Islam. In a sense, the very first Muslims could be said to have used it. Abū Bakr, ʿUmar and all six members of the *shūrā*, including ʿUthmān, were Qurashī emigrants to Medina. So too were all the contenders for the caliphate in the first civil war unleashed by ʿUthmān's death, including Muʿāwiya. Some Syrians are said to have liked the idea of ʿAbd al-Raḥmān b. Khālid b. al-Walīd as Muʿāwiya's successor: he too was a Qurashī, and the son of an emigrant to Medina.[16] So too were all al-Ḥusayn, Ibn al-Zubayr, and the men considered eligible for the caliphate in Syria at the time of Muʿāwiya's designation of Yazīd.[17] With the exception of the Khārijites, all northern Arabs continued to expect the caliph to be chosen from Quraysh thereafter,[18] and

13. Tyan, *Califat*, 243–8.

14. Watt, *Political Thought*, 39.

15. *EI*², s.v. Crone, '*Shūrā* as an Elective Institution'.

16. *Aghānī*, xvi, 197.

17. Ibid. xx, 212. A Syrian chief who said that they could easily find a replacement for Muʿāwiya specified that they could do so *fī qawmihi*, 'in his tribe' (Tab., ii, 144).

18. A north Arabian participant in the revolt of Ibn al-Ashʿath is admittedly said to have hoped that the latter would become caliph, but the reader is expected to find it absurd (Tab., ii, 1111). A late Christian source alleges that non-Qurashī Yazīd b. al-Muhallab

some had apparently formulated it as a doctrinal requirement by the mid-Umayyad period.[19] In short, it would appear that the Qurashī emigrants in Medina were regarded as the equivalent of a chiefly family. They were the only kinsmen that the Prophet had left after cutting his ties with Mecca (where many genealogically closer relatives of his remained), and they were the men with whom he had come to Medina. Within this group the caliph would be chosen by one traditional procedure or other: Abū Bakr was 'elected'; ʿUmar is said to have been nominated by Abū Bakr, which may have been an innovation, but he may also have succeeded simply because he was the obvious successor;[20] and the *shūrā* which he in his turn appointed was another pre-Islamic procedure.

Still, succession within a lineage is not quite what is normally understood by hereditary succession, and the lineage broadened to become an entire tribe as all Quraysh converted. But succession from father to son (or other close kinsman) appeared already in the first civil war. This war pitted Qurashī leaders against each other. Obviously, these men were not going to regard their rivals as candidates for the succession; on the contrary, both they and their followers would have a strong interest in keeping the office within their own house. Accordingly, when ʿAlī was killed, his followers elevated his son al-Ḥasan to the caliphate. Towards the end of his life Muʿāwiya similarly designated his son as his successor. All this was repeated in the second civil war, when sons reappear in their father's shoes on the Umayyad, the ʿAlid, and the Zubayrid side alike. And when Yazīd died a mere three years after his accession, the Syrian chiefs behind Muʿāwiya's regime reacted, like the Iraqi chiefs behind ʿAlī's, by elevating a kinsman of their deceased caliph to the throne, as has been seen.

Three points follow from this. First, in a sense the imamate could be said to have been conceived as a hereditary institution from the start, but heredity did not determine the heir and thus did not exclude election. The Arabs combined heredity and election in much the same manner as the Franks of Merovingian Gaul, with whom they were contemporary. Secondly, the Umayyads narrowed down the group within which it was hereditary to their

---

claimed the caliphate when he rebelled, but the claim is presumably wrong (Mārī b. Sulaymān, 65.16).

19. When Jazīran Khārijites considered an alliance with Muṭarrif b. al-Mughīra in 77/696f., they were up against the fact that the latter restricted the caliphate to Qurashīs: thus Abū Mikhnaf (d. 157/774) in Tab., ii, 984ff., and he may well be right, for the Shīʿite poet al-Kumayt (d. 126/743) also knew that the caliphate was restricted to Quraysh (he took it to mean that the Prophet's family must have the best right to it; *Hāšimijjāt*, no. 2:55).

20. Cf. Rotter, *Bürgerkrieg*, 7.

own family and replaced election within the group by designation, to be followed in this by the ʿAbbāsids and some of the ʿAlids. Thirdly, the Umayyads were not the first to attempt succession from father to son, as the ill-starred reign of al-Ḥasan shows; they were only the first to do so successfully. The reason why the sources continue to lambast them for their introduction of dynastic succession long after this institution had come to be taken for granted in its ʿAbbāsid form, or accepted as a positive article of faith by the Shīʿites, is not that people disliked the institution but rather that they disliked the Umayyads: the one point on which all enemies of the Umayyads could agree was that the imamate should never have been hereditary in *their* family.

So much for the first problem. As regards the second, the reason why the Sunnis describe themselves as adherents of election (*ikhtiyār*), as distinct from those who made the office hereditary (*mawrūtha*), is not that they were clinging to Islamic norms which had come to be violated in practice, but rather that they were trying to distinguish their own mode of succession from that of the Shīʿites .[21] In tenth-century Sunni theory succession rested on a combination of heredity (within Quraysh) and either election or designation. The authors of this theory accepted dynastic succession within the ʿAbbāsid family, even from father to son, without the slightest reluctance, whatever they might say about the Umayyads. They could not declare the imamate to be hereditary, however, without thereby appearing to agree with the Shīʿites that the imamate was a personal quality transmitted by descent rather than an office bestowed by the community.[22] Moreover, if the succession was hereditary in the narrow sense of passing from father to son, or other close kinsman, as a matter of principle, not just in mundane practice, then the caliphate had passed from the Prophet to his cousin, ʿAlī, and his descendants, even though others had taken it in actual fact, or alternatively it had passed to his uncle, al-ʿAbbās, and his descendants: in the former case all actual caliphs other than ʿAlī had been usurpers, in the latter case ʿAlī had been a usurper too, though all caliphs had been legitimate from the ʿAbbāsid revolution onwards. Since the Sunnis did not agree with either view they said that the imamate was elective within Quraysh. What they meant was, first, that Abū Bakr, ʿUmar, and ʿUthmān had been legitimate caliphs even though they were not members of the Prophet's family (i.e. the Hāshimites), and secondly, that the dynastic nature of the succession under the ʿAbbāsids was not of the slightest religious significance to them.

21. Similarly Mikhail, *Mawardi and After*, 21.
22. Cf. below, ch. 16, 226f.

The caliphal role

The Umayyads conceived their role as one of multi-purpose imams in the old style. As they saw it, the community of believers owed its legal existence to the imam, who guided it in what to us are both political and religious terms: he defended it against infidel enemies, sought to expand its domain, maintained internal order and formulated God's law as the ultimate authority on the righteous behaviour that the believers should seek to adopt. In the past, God had used prophets to convey His message; now He was using another type of agent to administer it. The caliph was God's deputy or vicar on earth (*khalīfat allāh fī arḍihi*) with all the fullness of power that this implied.[23]

Like the assumption that the ruler had to be the best of men, this idea seems to be rooted in Hellenistic conceptions. The king was living law (*nomos empsychos*), as people said from Hellenistic to Byzantine times; he ought to be sinless and perfect in argument and deed, a certain Musonius (d. c. 120) told a Syrian king. It was his duty to imitate God, so that his subjects could imitate him, as everyone agreed. "There is no need for any compulsion or menace . . . when they see with their own eyes a conspicuous and shining example of virtue in the life of their ruler," the moral philosopher Plutarch (d. after 120) explained.[24] The king had been fashioned on the model of his maker; he was the image of God, the archetype of the true king, as the pagans said and the Christians started agreeing when Constantine converted.[25] He was living law in the sense of embodying and exemplifying the law, not in the sense of overruling it. On the contrary, he had to be ruled by God's law in order to rule legitimately himself.[26]

All this was close to the Muslim conception, except that they did not usually believe in human images of God. It was as God's deputy (*khalīfa*), not as his image or 'after His likeness', that Adam had been created according to the Qurʾān;[27] and it was as God's deputy rather than His image that the caliph was expected to provide a model for imitation by his subjects. But like their Hellenistic predecessors, they saw their imam as living law and held him to display his legal insight, among other things, by adjudicating (cf. Q. 38:25). Like them, too, they saw the ruler's position as depending on his relationship with God,

23. Crone and Hinds, *God's Caliph*, ch. 3.

24. Dvornik, *Political Philosophy*, ii, 548, 552f.; Hunger, *Prooimon*, 58ff.

25. Ecphantus in Dvornik, *Political Philosophy*, i, 253; Beskow, *Rex Gloriae*, 263 (Eusebius); cf. also Baynes, 'Eusebius and the Christian Empire'.

26. Themistius in Dagron, 'Empire romain', 129ff.; Aalders, 'Nomos Empsychos', 322f. and note 28; Agapetos in Barker, *Social and Political Thought*, 59 (cap. 37); Henry, 'A Mirror for Justinian', 301; Dagron, *Empereur et prêtre*, 37.

27. Q. 2:20, paraphrasing Gen. 1:26.

that is, his moral rectitude: leadership was a reflection of personal virtue rather than an office. "It is not wealth . . . that makes a king, nor his purple cloak, nor his tiara and scepter . . . nor numerous hoplites and myriad cavalry; not though all men should gather together and acknowledge him for their king, because virtue they cannot bestow on him, but only power," as Julian the Apostate (d. 363) said. If a virtuous man seized power (*monarchia*), his virtue would at once make it lawful sovereignty (*basileia*), as the eclectic philosopher Plutarch had put it.[28] It was thanks to this line of thought that the debate about ʿUthmān had centered on his moral status rather than the relative rights of rulers and subjects. It is thanks to the same view of things that people would deny that the Umayyads were caliphs when they held them to be wrong, or that conversely the Shīʿites came to view their imam as the ruler even though he did not have any political power, or again (after the further injection of such ideas by means of translations) that the philosophers would insist that the true king was not "someone possessing a cavalcade, a retinue or a realm: what is meant, rather, is one truly deserving of kingship, even if nobody pays him any attention."[29] Of course, the ruler's moral status displayed itself above all in his treatment of his subjects, so people did indirectly discuss such rights as well. In fact, the relative rights of ruler and subjects figure prominently in the political debate of the Umayyad period, but only in the sense that whenever moral evaluations are spelt out in concrete terms, it turns out to be such rights that are involved.

It should be noted that court poetry also describes the Umayyad caliphs in terms that can only be characterized as messianic: they dispersed darkness, made the blind see, made the road plain, loosened burdens, healed sicknesses of the breast, slaked people's thirst, filled the earth with mercy, justice, and light; each one was a *mahdī*, a rightly guided deliverer from evil; some were even hailed as *the* Mahdi, the Redeemer.[30] There was a Hellenistic tradition for casting the ruler as a saviour (*sōtēr*), but it was not meant in a transcendental sense and is unlikely to account for the Muslim conception. The significance of the messianic overtones will be taken up in Chapter 7.

Exalted though his position was, the caliph was not credited with any personal sanctity, nor was his court dominated by elaborate ceremonial designed to assure people that they formed part of an eternal and 'profoundly correct' polity maintained directly by God.[31] He did fulfil a major cultic function as the leader, in person or through his governors, of the weekly Friday prayer, and

28. Dvornik, *Political Philosophy*, ii, 547, 662 (with oddly off-target comments).
29. Naṣīr al-Dīn Ṭūsī, *Ethics*, 192; cf. further below, ch. 14.
30. Crone and Hinds, *God's Caliph*, 36f.
31. Cf. Bowersock et al. (eds), *Late Antiquity*, s.v. 'emperor'.

also of the annual pilgrimage (usually delegated to members of his family). But he owed this function to his position as head of the community, which was seen as coming together in its entirety on these occasions and whose togetherness he symbolized, not to any personal magic or charisma (*baraka*). He had no physical inviolability, no special powers or healing touch, and no special ritual status either; on the contrary, he was subject to the same rules of purification, worship, and marriage as everyone else. He did play a prominent role in prayers for rain,[32] and the later Umayyad caliphs were the object of more extravagant claims than the first, in terms of their persons and their religious insight alike;[33] but by and large the caliph remained an ordinary human being in the Umayyad period. The redemptive overtones of his guidance notwithstanding, his role was conceived in a sober vein: as God's caravaneer, he kept the believers together in safety and order while leading them along the right path to their ultimate destination, no more and no less. The Umayyads constantly stressed the importance of sticking to the *jamāʿa*, the collective body or compact majority. "Satan is with the individual," as al-Walīd I reputedly said;[34] scattering, dispersing, going separate ways and following individual whims (for which there was a rich vocabulary) meant going astray and perishing. One stuck to the *jamāʿa*, and thus to the safe path, by obeying the Umayyad imams of guidance, who were way-marks and lodestars to their followers and who never tire of enjoining obedience (*ṭāʿa*) in their official letters.

The rise of the scholars

The manner in which the Umayyads fulfilled their duties as religious guides strikes the reader from a Christian background as odd. Contrary to what one would expect, they did not create a hierarchy of officials charged with the definition, maintenance, and dissemination of right belief or practice. The same was to be true of the Shīʿite imams, though the latter's formal role as religious guides was more pronounced than that of the Umayyads. But then the Christian church developed as a separate organization within the Roman empire; it

32. Ringgren, 'Some Religious Aspects of the Caliphate', 740 (where one line seems to suggest that the caliph was a factor behind fertility in general); cf. *EI*², s.v. 'Istisḳāʾ'.

33. Cf. *K. al-ʿUyūn*, iii, 101 (where Hishām is told that caliphs were immune to plague, without however being convinced); Crone and Hinds, *God's Caliph*, 56 (where the Marwānids are credited with superhuman insight and immunity against minor mistakes); Qadi, 'Religious Foundations', 250 (where the late Umayyad secretary ʿAbd al-Ḥamīd b. Yaḥyā credits them with *ilhām*, divine inspiration; compare Abū 'l-Jārūd on the Zaydī imam and Ibn al-Muqaffaʿ on the ʿAbbāsids, below, 104, 130f.).

34. Tab., ii, 1178.11.

modelled its own ecclesiastical hierarchy on the secular chain of command in the Roman empire, but it could not identify the two. Islam, by contrast, developed by taking over from the empire, imposing its own chain of command, and the idea that religious authority could be channelled through a separate hierarchy of offices does not appear to have occurred to the early Muslims. Rather, they seem to have assumed that since the imam was the best man of his time, everyone would automatically follow him of his own accord, as everyone had followed Abū Bakr and ʿUmar: one went where he went and did as he did, by following his kinsmen and governors and other local substitutes for him who were assumed to do as he did, too. There was no need for a separate hierarchy because right guidance was built into the power structure.

In line with this, the Umayyads saw themselves as guiding the community by exemplifying the law in everything they did, in person or through their governors and judges, rather than by issuing directives to a clergy. They did make explicit pronouncements on the law when they adjudicated disputes and answered questions submitted to them by petitioners; they also sent legal instructions to judges on particular questions from time to time, and issued edicts on legal questions of a public nature, such as ʿUmar II's famous edict on the status of converts and other fiscal matters. But they did not appoint ministers to represent them among their subjects at large.

The task of answering everyday questions thus fell to men outside the government apparatus. Obviously, people could not travel to the imam's residence every time they needed to know whether a particular form of prayer was valid, whether maintenance was owed to a former wife, whether a particular food could be lawfully eaten, or the like. They could turn to the governor, who was officially charged with teaching the religion,[35] or to his deputy, the judge; and no doubt they did, especially for questions with a public angle. But neither the governor nor the judge was a local minister intimately involved with the lives of his parishioners after the fashion of a village priest. Where such intimate familiarity was desired, people would turn to local friends and neighbours credited with a better understanding of the religion than the rest. The latter developed into local scholars. They would answer questions on the basis of what they remembered upright men in the past to have done, what appeared right to them, or by second-guessing the imam's views, meaning that they would devise their own solutions and attribute them to him. The Umayyad caliphs themselves would consult such scholars at times, regarding them as their memory bank, and they seem to have granted some of them official authorization to

35. This emerges from statements attributed to ʿUmar (Tab., i, 2740.14, 2742.2) and al-Aṣamm's image of the Prophet's governors (Ps.-Nāshi, §103).

issue legal responsa (*fatwās*).[36] Caliphs and scholars were not initially rivals. But this was to change when the Umayyad claim to legitimacy was rejected.

Umayyad mulk

The rejection of the Umayyads was commonly formulated as an accusation that they had perverted the caliphate (or imamate) by turning it into kingship (*mulk*). We do not know when this accusation first appeared. It is often directed at Muʿāwiya, who is said to have effected the transformation by designating his own son as his successor, or by introducing jails, bodyguards, forced labour and the like, or in ways unspecified.[37] But all these statements are clearly retrospective: the founder of the dynasty here stands for the Umayyads at large.[38] Since our sources were compiled in ʿAbbāsid times, it has been suggested that their hostility to the Umayyads reflects ʿAbbāsid prejudice against the fallen dynasty, but this is unlikely to be right: the hostility to the Umayyads is too pervasive in the sources to reflect the change of dynasty. More probably, the denunciation of the Umayyads as mere kings began in Iraq in the mid-Umayyad period, when Umayyad government became more openly authoritarian than it had been in Muʿāwiya's days and when scholars hostile to the regime emerged, to reject the Umayyad view of themselves as leaders of the vehicle of salvation.[39]

The equation of kings with oppressive rulers, which the reader has encountered before in this book, had both tribal and monotheist roots.[40] The pre-Islamic Arabs conceived of public life as an arena of competition between free men, who would fiercely resist the encroachments of others while trying to accumulate more power than everyone else themselves,[41] and their attitude to kings (*mulūk*, sing. *malik*) was correspondingly ambivalent. On the one hand, a king was an insufferable tyrant. "Since the time of ʿĀd we have thought well

36. Cf. Crone and Hinds, *God's Caliph*, 51f.; Dhahabī, *Taʾrīkh*, v, 185, where Yazīd b. Abī Ḥabīb (d. 128/745f.) is described as one of the three men appointed by ʿUmar II to give responsa in Egypt.

37. *Aghānī*, xvii, 357; YT, ii, 276 (cf. ʿAbd al-Malik b. Ḥabīb, *Taʾrīkh*, no. 343); BA, iv, a, 125; Goldziher, *MS*, ii, 31f.

38. Cf. Safīna's statement that "the Umayyads are the worst kings, and the first king was Muʿāwiya" (in Ibn Abū Shayba, xiv, no. 17854, and elsewhere).

39. Schacht, *Introduction*, 23 (followed by Lambton, *State and Government*, 47); Crone and Hinds, *God's Caliph*, 23.

40. Above, 7; Lewis, *Political Language*, 53ff.

41. For the coexistence of these attitudes, and an illuminating comparison with modern America, see Lindholm, 'Kinship Structure and Political Authority' and 'Quandaries of Command in Egalitarian Societies'; much of it also in *The Islamic Middle East*, 10ff.

of capturing kings, killing them and fighting them," a pre-Islamic poet boasts; "we will tell you of the days long and glorious when we rebelled against the king and would not serve him," another echoes. When the poet al-Ṭirimmāḥ al-Ṭāʾī advised al-Ḥusayn, in 680, to seek refuge the mountains of Aja, where "we held out against the kings of Ghassān, Ḥimyar, al-Nuʿmān b. al-Mundhir and everybody altogether," he was expressing himself in a wholly Jāhilī vein.[42] But on the other hand, a king was also somebody to be admired, for there was nothing more prestigious than being *muṭāʿ*, obeyed by others rather than obedient to them. The kings of Kinda, Ḥīra, and Ghassān were as respected and envied as they were resisted. 'King' could thus be a complimentary term no less than one of abuse. A pre-Islamic ruler hyperbolically identifies himself as "king of all the Arabs" in the famous Nemara inscription of 328, and the term often appears in a flattering vein in Umayyad court poetry, and indeed in other contexts in which it is not implicitly or explicitly contrasted with *imām* or *khalīfa*.[43]

The negative evaluation of kingship was further developed when the Arabs converted to Islam. This, one assumes, is when they came to equate it with the pursuit of private interests at the expense of public welfare (when kings enter a town, they corrupt it, as the Queen of Sheba notes in Q. 27:34, though curiously the exegetes make nothing of this verse). The Prophet identified God as king and reserved all power for Him, thereby rendering all human use of it illegitimate unless it was used for God's ends. God was practically synonymous with the community. He was perceived as a higher authority who had miraculously intervened to regulate the competition between selfish human beings by setting the rules of the game, and He stood for the interests that the believers had in common.[44] Wherever God had a claim to something, humans had none: this was why the idea of being governed by God struck the Muslims as so liberating. An imam or caliph was a ruler who recognized all power as God's and used it in accordance with His will, and government by such a person accorded with the wishes of his subjects, for all believers accepted God's rules. By contrast, a king would treat his power as his private property and use it to further his own individual interests (*ahwāʾ*, whims), which necessarily meant that he had to subjugate other people by force, depriving them of their freedom to act, inasmuch as their interests would conflict with his. "I am not a king who will

42. Abū Tammām, *Hamasae Carmina*, i/1, 195; ʿAmr b. Kulthūm in Arberry (tr.), *Seven Odes*, 205; Tab. ii, 304. Cf. also the Basran who boasted, in 684, of "how many a brutal and violent tyrant we have killed" (Tab. ii, 456); Athamina, 'Tribal Kings', 36f.

43. Beeston, 'Nemara and Faw', 3; also cited in Lewis, *Political Language*, 54; Tyan, *Califat*, 382f.

44. See further below, 393.

enslave you, only a servant of God who has been offered a trust," as ʿUmar is reputed to have said.[45] In short, *imāma/khilāfa* stood for theocracy, government by God, whereas *mulk* stood for autocracy, government by selfish, arbitrary, and shortsighted human beings.

Thanks to Islam, kingship came to be seen as both an infidel and a non-Arab institution. It must of course have been strongly associated with non-Arabs already in pagan times, by far the most famous kings being those of the Persians and the Byzantines; but non-Arabs were not branded as infidels in those days, and the Arabs themselves had been ruled by kings from time to time. The Muslim polity was however created without recourse to the institution, and the Muslims soon set out to defeat the kings of this world, with the result that kingship came to seem incompatible with both Islam and the Arab tradition. "Servants of God, a king in the Tihāma!," a pre-Islamic Meccan, here cast as a proto-Muslim, indignantly exclaims in a story of how a Qurashī tried to have himself accepted as client king on behalf of the Byzantines in Mecca.[46] "He has gone Christian!," the troops exclaim in equal indignation in a story of how the son of the conqueror of Spain was persuaded by his Visigothic wife to wear a crown.[47] It was with good reason that Muʿāwiya wore no crown.[48] Kingship was illegitimate human self-aggrandizement which the Muslims had come to eliminate.

On all this the Muslims of the Umayyad period were agreed. But God did not rule the believers directly, so who represented Him in the here and now? This was the question that became deeply contentious. The Umayyads claimed that they did, but their enemies held them to have forfeited their position by allowing private interests to override those of the community and generally allowing power to be used in the manner characteristic of the conquered nations before the coming of Islam. This was the force of the accusation that they had turned the caliphate into kingship – kingship like that of the Persians and Byzantines (*kisrawī*, *hirqalī/qayṣarī*), as some added.[49] But if the Umayyads had no right to the caliphate, who did, and with precisely what competence in matters of religious guidance? Was it lawful to rebel against the

45. Tab., i, 2368. Cf. also Ibn Saʿd, iii/1, 221 (B, 306f.), where ʿUmar is told that a caliph only takes what is due and spends it where it is meant to be spent, whereas a king oppresses people by arbitrarily taking from some and giving to others.

46. Fāsī, *Shifāʾ al-gharām*, ii, 171.-5.

47. *Akhbār majmūʿa*, 20; Ibn ʿIdhārī, *Bayān*, ii, 23f.

48. Cf. the Maronite chronicle in Hoyland, *Seeing Islam as Others Saw It*, 136.

49. *Aghānī*, xvii, 357; Jāḥiẓ, 'Fī 'l-nābita', in his *Rasāʾil*, ii, 10f.; cf. BA, iv, a, 125.17. Kisrā (Khusraw), Hirqal (Heraclius) and Qayṣar (Caesar) are here generic terms for the Persian and Byzantine emperors.

head of state to enthrone the deserving candidate, or should one put up with oppressive government for the sake of communal togetherness? And if right guidance was not to be found with the head of state, where was one to look for it? These were the questions that increasingly preoccupied people as the Umayyad period wore on, especially in Iraq, which had the largest concentration of Arabs outside Arabia without being the centre of power.

II

THE WANING OF THE TRIBAL TRADITION, c. 700–900

CHAPTER

4

INTRODUCTION

The political thought of the first two centuries after the conquests, the subject of the chapters that follow, was dominated by the tribal tradition of the conquerors, especially that of the northern Arabs, to whom Muḥammad and his first followers belonged. One of the most striking features of this tradition was its libertarian character: all adult males participated in political decision-making; nothing could be done without consensus. Modern scholars sometimes characterize the tradition as 'democratic'. But it was not libertarian, let alone democratic, in the modern style. For one thing, it owed its character to the absence of a state, not to constitutional devices; and the tribal attitude to kings was ambivalent, as has been seen.[1] For another thing, tribesmen did not see themselves as endowed with individual rights against the groups to which they belonged. If they resisted kings, they submitted to the tyranny of kinsmen.[2] There was an immense premium on helping fellow-tribesmen ('cousins'), staying together with them, deferring to the majority view, and respecting consensus. Kinsmen hung together so as not to hang separately.[3] In short, the tribal tradition was not just libertarian, in the sense of opposed to overweening rulers, but also communitarian (or communalistic), in the sense of strongly attached to communal unity and solidarity.[4]

1. Above, 44ff.

2. Cf. Gellner, *Conditions of Liberty*, 7f.

3. Cf. the story of al-Muhallab, a general of the mid-Umayyad period, who had a bundle of arrows brought to his sons on his deathbed: they could not break it, though they could break each arrow separately (Tab., ii, 1082).

4. Cf. Watt, *Philosophy and Theology*, 17.

Both the libertarian and the communitarian features are strongly in evidence in the political thinking of the Umayyad period, above all among non-Shīʿites. There was a general presumption that power and fiscal resources would be shared by informal means such as consultation, generosity, general accessibility of the caliph and his governors, and familiar forms of interaction between ruler and ruled. The tribesmen greeted the Umayyad concentration of power with endless demands for *shūrā* and calls for 'the Book of God and the Sunna of His Prophet', meaning the entrenched norms of Arab/early Muslim society; they accused the Umayyads of monopolizing the revenues (*fayʾ*), and squandering them on women, wine, song, and sumptuous palaces; they charged them with ignoring local interests and oppressing local populations (notably the Iraqis), with arresting, torturing, and killing people at will; they claimed that the Umayyads were reducing them to slaves; of one caliph, Yazīd I (680–3), they even said that he had forced defeated Medinese rebels to pay him allegiance on the understanding that they were slaves with whose lives and property he could do what he wished.[5] Of rebels there were many, for coming from a tradition of self-help, the early Muslims were generally activists. When systematization began, it was above all in Khārijism, Muʿtazilism, and Zaydism (below, chs 5, 6, 9) that activist attitudes were endorsed.

The behaviour of the ʿAbbāsids was not significantly different from that of the Umayyads, but they were more careful about their public image, and they changed the nature of the political opposition by coming to power in the name of Shīʿism. Like everyone else, the Shīʿites wanted to replace tyranny with right government, but they held right government to result from enthronement of the right lineage rather than the establishment of communal control, and the political debate now came to focus on the relative rights of ʿAlids and ʿAbbāsids rather than those of rulers and subjects (chs 7–10). The Khārijites and the Zaydīs withdrew to the periphery; libertarianism did make a striking appearance in the early ninth century with the Muʿtazilite anarchists, but their numbers were extremely small (ch. 6). The weightiest alternative to mainstream Islam and its ʿAbbāsid guardians was to be Imamism, also known as Ithnā-ʿasharite ('Twelver') Shīʿism (ch. 10).

But if libertarianism disappeared, communalism continued. Appeals to *jamāʿa* (communal unity and solidarity) were likewise extremely common in the Umayyad period.[6] The caliphs and their governors would endlessly invoke

5. Crone, '*Shūrā* as an Elective Institution', 17f.; Crone and Hinds, *God's Caliph*, 59ff., 130ff.; Crone, 'The Qays and the Yemen', 27f., 41; Sudayf in Ibn Qutayba, *Shiʿr*, 761; YT, ii, 199; Tab. ii, 233.1, 371.7, 475.9; Rotter, *Bürgerkrieg*, 50 (Yazīd).

6. Al-Muhallab fittingly meant his sons to see the merit of both *jamāʿa* and kinship solidarity (cf. above, note 3).

it in their demands for obedience; their subjects would do the same in polemics against sectarianism. The communal orientation was usually also strong among the sectarians themselves, as is clear from the importance they attached to *walāya* and *barāʾa*, association with co-religionists and dissociation from everyone else. Their aim was to establish a new community of believers fiercely loyal to one another, but they did have to break up the existing *jamāʿa* to do so. Most Muslims found this unacceptable. *Jamāʿa* was first formalized as a fundamental value by the Murjiʾites of the Umayyad and early ʿAbbāsid periods. We have met them already as the people who suspended judgement on the moral status of ʿUthmān and ʿAlī, the two key figures of the first civil war.[7] One reason why they refused to pass judgement is precisely that the question was extremely divisive. The Murjiʾites also deemed all self-declared Muslims to be believers, however unacceptable their behaviour might be: even grave sinners remained members of the community of believers, they said, rejecting the sectarian (above all Khārijite) habit of declaring them to be infidels who could be freely killed. This too was an attempt to keep the community together.[8] Thereafter *jamāʿa* was enshrined as a fundamental value in the system of the Traditionalists, who forbade revolt in the name of it. The pursuit of rightly guided government (*imāma*) and communal solidarity (*jamāʿa*) had proved to be mutually exclusive. Both the Khārijites and the Shīʿites deemed rightly guided government to be more important than communal unity (though they envisaged such government in antithetical veins). More precisely, they could not see how those who rejected their conception of right government could count as members of their community at all. The Traditionalists, sometimes known as proto-Sunnīs, were those who took the opposite view. Communal unity was more important than right government; and the community was formed by acceptance of the guidance left behind by the Prophet, not by any religio-political leader in the here and now (ch. 11).

7. Above, 27f.
8. See further below, 385ff.

CHAPTER

5

THE KHĀRIJITES

The most prominent enemies of the Umayyads were the Khārijites, also known as Ḥarūrīs and Muḥakkima. Their origins are quite obscure. They are identified as those who seceded from ʿAlī at Ṣiffīn in protest against his acceptance of the Syrian call for arbitration, but the story does not offer a satisfactory explanation of the issues between them and ʿAlī, and contrary to what is often said, it was not with reference to their departure from ʿAlī's camp that they were known as Khārijites ('those who go out').[1] It may have been because they assembled at Ḥarūrāʾ that they came to be known as Ḥarūrīs, but this does not tell us much, and though they were indeed known as Muḥakkima because they were given to shouting 'judgement belongs to God alone' (*lā ḥukma illā li'llāh*), nobody knows what they meant by it. To the Ibāḍīs, who are the only Khārijite sect to survive to this day, they merely meant that any rule laid down in the Qurʾān must be applied: humans cannot make their own decisions on questions settled by God. But this is too banal to explain the programmatic nature of the slogan. It was so obviously right that the Khārijites must have meant something special by it, as ʿAlī is said to have observed; in his view they meant that they did not want any government. But this does not appear to be correct either, except later in the case of the Najdiyya.[2]

1. It was a self-designation, probably coined with reference to Q. 4:100 (cf. Crone and Zimmermann, *Epistle*, 275).

2. BA, ii, 352, 361, 377; Mubarrad, *Kāmil*, iii, 938 (ed. Wright, 555); *Nahj al-balāgha*, 114; IAH, ii, 307. Other interpretations are proposed in Crone and Cook, *Hagarism*, 27, and Hawting, 'The Significance'.

One point is clear, however. Of the rebels against ʿUthmān, only the Khārijites retained a clear conviction that it had been right to kill him. The accounts of the first civil war abound in discussions of the question whether ʿAlī had been implicated in the killing (directly or by sheltering the killers) premised on the ʿUthmānī assumption that this would be deeply embarrassing if it were true.[3] But why should ʿAlī's followers accept the ʿUthmānī premise? Of course ʿAlī had been on the right side: "ʿAlī's killing of ʿUthmān was one of his greatest acts of obedience to God," as some Shīʿites continued to say in agreement with the Khārijites.[4] Where he had gone wrong was in accepting arbitration with people whom he should have fought until they either reverted to God's command or were killed (cf. Q. 49:9).[5] This was how the Khārijites saw it, and to them, ʿAlī's change of mind was paradigmatic of non-Khārijite behavior. Ṭalḥa and al-Zubayr had been among the fiercest critics of ʿUthmān while he was alive, yet they had demanded vengeance for him the moment he was killed;[6] adherents of the Zubayrids declared themselves to be enemies of the caliph ʿAbd al-Malik (685–705) in this world and the next as long as they thought him a loser, but they changed their tune the moment they heard that he was winning:[7] people were forever sacrificing their principles to the demands of power; only the Khārijites refused. One has to grant them that this was true. Relentless Sunnification notwithstanding, it was only in the twentieth century that the Ibāḍīs began to express doubts about their own participation in the much maligned killing of ʿUthmān.[8]

The Khārijites were originally concentrated in Kufa, where they survived into the ʿAbbāsid period, but their main home soon came to be Basra. In the second civil war the Basran Khārijites produced two sub-sects, the Azāriqa and the Najdiyya (or Najadāt), both of whom left Basra under their own Commanders of the Believers to fight holy war against the infidels, meaning the Muslims who refused to join them. The Azāriqa rampaged in Iran and disappeared after their suppression in 699; the Najdiyya were mainly active in Arabia; they were suppressed in 693, but survived for several centuries thereafter. In the third civil war two further sects made their appearance, that is the Ṣufriyya, who had adherents in the Jazīra and North Africa down to the tenth century or longer, and the Ibāḍiyya, who survive in Oman and North Africa to

3. Cf. Nagel, *Rechtleitung und Kalifat*, 157ff.

4. Jāḥiẓ, 'R. fī 'l-ḥakamayn', 436, §44.

5. Cf. the poem in Naṣr b. Muzāḥim, *Waqʿat Ṣiffīn*,[2] 513.1 (cited in Nagel, *Rechtleitung und Kalifat*, 159); Crone and Zimmermann, *Epistle*, 193.

6. Sālim, *Epistle*, II, 59.

7. Tab., ii, 821f.

8. Crone and Zimmermann, *Epistle*, 215.

this day. These four 'mother sects' were divided over the status of non-Khārijite Muslims, an issue that will be considered in chapter 21. The later Khārijite sects (for there were to be many more) diverged over other theological questions of no relevance to this book. All seem to have had much the same views on the imamate, however, though the Najdiyya were to develop a distinctive slant of their own.

Past and present imams

According to the Khārijites, Abū Bakr and ʿUmar had been true imams of guidance (a view that the Najdiyya were to modify, without however in any way wishing to belittle their righteousness). ʿUthmān and ʿAlī had also started as legitimate caliphs, but both had violated God's rules and so forfeited their status as caliphs and Muslims alike, and all their followers had likewise lost their membership of the community of believers. Thereafter all so-called caliphs had been kings and tyrants (*mulūk*, *jabābira*).[9] The only Muslims left were the Khārijites, and the only true imams after ʿUthmān and ʿAlī's forfeiture of their position were those of the Khārijites themselves.

A true imam was both a political leader and a religious guide. This being so, the Khārijites usually had to live without them, as a community of true believers under infidel rule. The Azāriqa and Najdiyya emerged by denying that this was lawful. What they meant was not that a community devoid of an imam was bereft of guidance, but rather that no saving community existed at all under infidel sovereignty. One had to separate oneself from the infidels, meaning that one had to move to an abode of emigration (*dār al-hijra*), there to establish a sovereign polity of one's own and wage holy war against the infidels left behind, as the Prophet had done when he emigrated from Mecca to Medina. It was in this spirit that the Azāriqa and Najadāt left Basra for western Iran and Arabia. The Ibāḍīs and the Ṣufrīs agreed that one had to establish a Muslim polity if one could, but denied that one forfeited one's status as a Muslim by living among the unbelievers. One had to affirm belief in the obligatory nature of the imamate and rebel in order to establish one if one could. It was not allowed to doubt God's command to "fight the insolent until they return to God's command" (Q. 49:9). But rebellion was not always possible, and in the meantime the believers could live under the kings of "their *qawm*", that is, non-Khārijite Muslims, following their own law as expounded by their own scholars. The Khārijites freely referred to their scholars and other

9. *Mulūk* was the more common term at first, *jabābira* won out in later Ibāḍī parlance (cf. ibid., 289).

righteous people as imams, but they never accepted as 'great imam' a person who was not head of state. Thus, unlike the Imāmī Shīʿites, they did not have a continuous line of imams.

The rules pertaining to the imamate

According to the Khārijites, there was only one criterion of eligibility for the office: merit. In itself this was not a startling proposition, given that the imam was generally equated with the most meritorious person of his time (*al-afḍal*); but their definition of merit was unusual in that it excluded considerations of descent. According to them, Abū Bakr and ʿUmar had been legitimate imams because they were the most pious and learned men of their time, no more and no less. The fact that they had been Qurashīs was irrelevant, for merit had nothing to do with ethnic origin or tribal membership. Quraysh had no special claim to the imamate over and above other Arabs (still less did the Umayyads or the ʿAbbāsids), and the Arabs had no special claim over and above non-Arabs. Any free, male, adult Muslim of sound body and mind was eligible as caliph, whatever his origins. Slaves were excluded from consideration (contrary to what is often stated),[10] and so were women. The claim that a Jazīran Khārijite by the name of Shabīb (d. 697) regarded women as eligible is doubtful, and in any case, he did not set a trend.[11] Women and slaves were, however, entitled, in some sects even obliged, to participate in holy war, and the sources frequently mention female warriors among the Khārijite troops. (The more established the Ibāḍīs became, the less they liked this.)[12]

If all free, male, adult Muslims were eligible for the caliphate, who were the electors? According to the Najdiyya, the election of an imam required "a unanimous choice by every single [free, male, adult] member of the community"; but their point was that this was impossible: no unanimity could be obtained that way.[13] That apart, the subject does not seem to have been discussed. The proposition that even a non-Arab could lead the community was, however, radical in the extreme, for the Arabs of the Umayyad period viewed the idea of deferring to a non-Arab in much the same light as would aristocrats the idea of taking orders from a serf. It was also more easily preached than practised. When the Azāriqa elected a non-Arab imam towards the end of their revolt,

10. Cf. Crone, 'Ethiopian Slave'; for an explicit Ibāḍī statement that the imam must be free, see Abū Isḥāq Ibrāhīm b. Qays, *Mukhtaṣar al-Khiṣāl*, 194.1.

11. Baghdādī, *Farq*, 89f.

12. Cf. Crone and Zimmermann, *Epistle*, 180f.

13. Crone, 'Statement by the Najdiyya Khārijites', 66f.

large numbers went off under an Arab imam of their own.[14] Nonetheless, the Khārijites meant what they said, and all the imams of the Ṣufrīs and Ibāḍīs in North Africa from the 740s onwards were non-Arabs.

Unlike all other Muslims, the Khārijites rejected hereditary succession outright, whether within a tribe or lineage or from father to son. The most meritorious candidate was elected by the community and retained his position for as long as he retained his superior merit. He was God's deputy on earth, or so at least according to the Ibāḍīs,[15] and he was entitled to unquestioned obedience as long as this was the case. If he erred, the believers should ask him to repent, that is, to mend his ways. If he did, all was well; if not, he forfeited the imamate. If he then refused to resign of his own accord, the believers were obliged to depose him by force and, if necessary, kill him, this being how they had dealt with ʿUthmān. Their account of ʿUthmān endorsed the lawfulness, indeed obligatory nature, of rebellion and tyrannicide.[16]

The Khārijite vision and its fate

The overall effect of the Khārijite tenets was to downgrade the position of the communal leader. He was not distinguished from the rest of the community by anything other than superior merit: he had no special tribal status, no sacred descent, no residue of Prophetic blood in his veins. He was just a man like any other, as the Ibāḍīs explicitly say.[17] If it is true that some Khārijites accepted women as imams, that too was meant in a downgrading vein. The vision is anti-authoritarian. The imam is slightly raised above the rest of the believers by his superior merit, but this is a difference of degree, not of kind, and he is easily reduced to an ordinary believer again. For it is the believers who elect him, and though they must obey him as long as his superior merit holds, it is also they who sit in judgement of him and who depose him if they deem his merit to have failed.

In practice, then, he can only rule by formulating the general consensus, much as tribal chiefs had done. The balance of power is in the community's

14. Mubarrad, *Kāmil*, iii, 1151f (ed. Wright, 686); IAH, iv, 204f. Compare the Najdiyya who, when Najda is losing control, affirm that they will only take commands from an Arab (BA, xi, 143). The followers of the Jazīran Khārijite Ṣāliḥ b. Musarriḥ, later classified as Ṣufrī, are presented as still taking for granted in 696 that candidates would be Arabs (Tab., ii, 986).

15. Cf. Crone, 'The Khārijites and the Caliphal Title', 85f. (correcting Crone and Hinds, *God's Caliph*, 12).

16. For an Ibāḍī account of the rules, see Abū 'l-Muʾthir in Kāshif, ii, 177f.

17. Abū 'l-Muʾthir in Kāshif, i, 157.9; Shabīb b. ʿAṭiyya in Crone and Zimmermann, *Epistle*, 246.

favour, and for this reason the Khārijites have been described as 'democratic'.[18] The Ibāḍīs did not see it that way: the imam represented God in their view, not the people, who merely had to obey. But since it was the people (in the form of the scholars) who decided whether he represented God or not, it was in practice through them rather than him that God displayed His will.

The Khārijites, then, did not cope with the imam's fullness of power by denying that he had religious authority. He was still authorized to settle questions of law and doctrine. He did of course do so in collaboration with scholars, and there was no sharp distinction between them: this is why living without an imam was perfectly possible as long as there were scholars. But he was the most meritorious scholar, just as he was the most meritorious statesman, so his authority overrode that of everyone else (as long as his superior merit held). There was no separation of powers. The Khārijites continued to see the imam as a multi-purpose leader presiding over a multi-purpose community. They merely cut him down to size, religious authority, political power and all.

For all its novel rejection of ethnic, tribal, and to some extent even gender distinctions, it was a conservative vision. As the Khārijites saw it, they were simply systematizing the principles behind the early caliphate in Medina, and so in effect they were: their beliefs fused Islam and the political egalitarianism of the Arab tribesmen. But the problem was precisely that the Muslims had ceased to be a small community of free tribesmen and that one could not rule a complex society stretching from what is now Pakistan to Portugal on the assumption that nothing had changed. Almost all Muslims of the Umayyad period regretted the loss of the old ways, and almost all were looking for a solution to the problem of how tyranny could be avoided. The Khārijite solution had considerable appeal in those days, even in high circles.[19] But on the crucial questions it dodged the issue. How can one ensure that a man receives unqualified obedience as long as he is meritorious without thereby depriving the community of the power it needs in order to depose him when he errs? Conversely, if it is up to the community to decide whether the imam is right or not, how can one ensure that it will obey his orders? Who, moreover, is to decide whether a ruler has erred or not, how is disagreement among the decision-makers to be resolved, and by what procedures is he to be removed? The Khārijites offered no answers to these questions.

More precisely, only the sub-sect of North African Ibāḍīs known as the Nukkār had something approaching a formal answer to these questions. The

18. E.g. Goldziher, *Theology and Law*, 172; Macdonald, *Development*, 23.
19. Cf. Mubarrad, *Kāmil*, iii, 949f. (W, 561f.).

Nukkār split off from the main body of Ibāḍīs in the 780s over the election of the second Rustumid imam in Tāhert, whom they would only recognize with the proviso that he was not to impose any decisions on people without the consent of a body of notables (presumably scholars and/or tribal leaders).[20] In other words, the compromise between the imam's need for unqualified obedience and the community's need for protection against tyrants lay in some kind of joint rule between the two. But the Ibāḍīs at large reacted to this eminently constitutionalist idea with horror. As they saw it, the community controlled the election and deposition of the imam, but had no share in ongoing government in between, for no real government would be possible at all if this were the case. Their solution was rather to rely on the informal distribution of power. The first Ibāḍī imam in Tāhert, the founder of the Rustumid dynasty, was an immigrant of Iranian origin chosen on the grounds that people would find it easy to obey him as long as he adhered to the truth because he was an outsider, and also easy to depose him if he should stray because he had no local tribe behind him.[21] Though the Nukkār split off after his death, everyone else apparently found the arrangement satisfactory: the imamate was continued in his family. In Oman the Ibāḍīs eventually developed a division of power between tribes who supplied electors and others who supplied imams, which had the same effect of putting shackles on the imam's power without subjecting him to formal constitutional restraints. (These tendencies in the direction of hereditary succession do not seem to have caused doctrinal problems.) As for who was to decide whether the imam had violated the law or not, the informal answer was scholars, notables, pious men. But the very fact that the answer was informal meant that there were no institutional procedures for singling them out or making them agree; and without such procedures, of course, they disagreed as much as anyone else.

The Khārijites, then, preserved communal participation in decision-making at the cost of restoring the disorder by which it had traditionally been accompanied. When Najda b. ʿĀmir, the founder of the Najdiyya, did various things of which his followers disapproved, his followers demanded that he repent, which he did. But then a group of them regretted having asked him to repent and told him, "We were wrong to ask you to repent, for you are an imam. We have repented of it, so now you should repent of your repentance, and demand that those who asked you to repent should repent (of having asked you). If you don't, we will separate from you." So he went out and

20. Rebstock, *Ibāḍiten im Maġrib*, 163ff. (*allā yaqḍī dūna jamāʿa maʿlūma*); cf. below, 278.

21. Cf. Ibn Ṣaghīr, 'Chronique', 9 = 63f. Compare the argument of Ḍirār and Ḥafṣ (below, 66).

(announced to the people that he) repented of his repentance. His followers then began to quarrel among themselves.[22] No wonder that some suspected the Khārijites of meaning 'no government' with their slogan 'no judgement except God's' (*lā ḥukma illā li'llāh*).[23]

The more complex Muslim society became, the less attracted it was by Khārijism, and by the early ʿAbbāsid period the sect was disappearing from the urban centres. It continued to flourish in the tribal countryside of the Jazīra, where it seems to have functioned as an ideology of social banditry down to the tenth century.[24] It also survived in various parts of Iran down to the Seljuq invasions, above all in Sīstān, where a famous imam by the name Ḥamza (fl. c. 800) established roving bands of Khārijites who kept the tax collectors of the ʿAbbāsids out of the Sīstānī countryside for some fifty years.[25] Above all, it flourished among the settled tribesmen of the Arabian peninsula and North Africa, where the imam's religious authority allowed for a measure of political organization over and above the tribes, as it had in Muḥammad's days, and generated a higher degree of literacy and learning than might otherwise have been expected. Ṣufrī and Ibāḍī imamates were established and re-established from the 740s down to the tenth century in the case of North Africa, while Ibāḍī imamates flourished on and off from the 740s down to the eleventh century in the Ḥaḍramawt, and down to the 1950s in highland Oman. In North Africa the imamate was hereditary in the Rustumid family (778–909), but in Oman it remained elective. In the period 794–893 the imams came from one set of tribes, with the electors drawn from another, but outright dynasticism does not seem to have prevailed for any length of time in Oman in the period covered by this book. The imamate established by Ḥamza in Sīstān was also elective.[26] The rulers of Oman are still Ibāḍīs today, but they rule as secular sultans of Oman and Mascat, not as imams, and they treat Ibāḍism as cultural heritage rather than as live religion.

Doctrinal modifications

Though they mostly had no imamate, the Ibāḍīs also experienced the opposite problem of having two, one in North Africa (the Rustumids, 778–909) and another in Oman (non-dynastic, 794–890). From time to time there was also an

22. Ashʿarī, 92.
23. Cf. above, note 2.
24. Robinson, *Empire and Elites*, ch. 5.
25. Madelung, *Religious Trends*, 54ff.; Bosworth, *Sīstān*, 37ff., 87ff.
26. *EI*², s.v. 'Rustamids'; Crone and Zimmermann, *Epistle*, 273, note 31, and appendix 2; Wilkinson, *Imamate Tradition*, 9, 203ff.

imamate in the Ḥaḍramawt of which little is known down to the eleventh century. Given that there was only one God, one community of believers and one imam, one would have expected the two (or even three) imams to denounce each other as infidels and imams of error, for they were well aware of each other's existence. But there was not in fact any rivalry between them. Initially, the imams in North Africa and Oman both deferred to the Basran leadership under which they had emerged, thereafter the physical distance between them was too great for them for either to have ambitions that impinged on the other; but relations remained friendly even when imamates in Oman and the Ḥaḍramawt coexisted. The Omanis coped by formally acknowledging that several imams could coexist, provided that their jurisdictions were separate and that they did not use the title *amīr al-muʾminīn*, Commander of the Believers, which was reserved for men who governed all the users of the *qibla* (i.e. all Muslims, Kharijite or non-Kharijite) after the fashion of Abū Bakr and ʿUmar. The response of the North Africans does not currently appear to be known, but unlike the Omanis and possibly all eastern Ibāḍīs, the North Africans certainly did not renounce the title *amīr al-muʾminīn*.[27]

The Sīstānī Ḥamza al-Khārijī (c. 800) is said also to have permitted the coexistence of two imams as long as disagreement prevailed and there were enemies to be fought.[28] We are not told why, but we know that he too allowed himself to be addressed as *amīr al-muʾminīn*.[29]

The Najdiyya

By far the most radical doctrinal modification was that introduced by the Najdiyya, who famously claimed that the law did not oblige the community to have an imam, only to live by the book of God.[30] We are not told when they adopted this doctrine, but there cannot be much doubt that they did so after the suppression of their revolt in 73/692f., when they had the choice between ceasing to be Najdites and modifying their doctrine. Having previously denied that one could be a Muslim under 'infidel' rule, they now accepted it. If there was no obligation to have an imam, there was also none to rebel in order to set one up: one could be a Najdite without committing oneself to emigration and holy war; one could live under illegitimate kings without endangering one's chances of salvation.

27. Crone, 'The Khārijites and the Caliphal Title', 86f. Cf. also Wilkinson, *Imamate Tradition*, 163–9.

28. Shahrastānī, *Milal*, 96.

29. Baghdādī, *Farq*, 77.-4, -2.

30. What follows is based on Crone, 'Statement by the Najdiyya Khārijites'.

But there was, or came to be, more to the Najdiyya's doctrine of the imamate: they denied that it had ever existed. They took as their starting point the widely accepted view that an imam was someone on whom everybody agreed, which they equated with unanimous choice by every single member of the community, and made the obvious rejoinder that no such agreement is possible. Even Abū Bakr had encountered opposition, as everyone knew: his election had been a kind of coup. It followed that the Companions had not actually elected an imam, but rather an ordinary leader (*raʾīs*). Certainly, he had been righteous, but it was wrong to claim (as did the Sunnis and many Muʿtazilites) that the Companions had established a legal duty to have an imam by their agreement (*ijmāʿ*) to elect one, for no imam had in fact been elected; and given that unanimous agreement was impossible, *ijmāʿ* could in any case never be a source of law. All believers were entitled to their own opinion on legal question on the basis of *ijtihād*, independent reasoning: all were "like the teeth of a comb" or "like a hundred male camels without a single female riding camel among them". This explained why unanimous agreement was impossible. It also showed that the imamate in the proper sense of the word was impossible. How could people defer to the opinions of someone no different from themselves?

By the time the Najdiyya were saying all this (probably the ninth century), their target was clearly religious authority: they did not want an imam to lay down the law for them, nor did they want to be bound by communal agreement. Every Najdite was a *mujtahid* entitled to his own opinion. They were perfectly willing to accept the desirability of government (in a hypothetical polity established by themselves): the *mujtahid*s were free to appoint a leader (*raʾīs*, *amīr*) to maintain internal and external order, provided that they would depose him, and if necessary kill him, if he strayed from the law. Here, as in Khārijite doctrine in general, the ruler is simply the community's agent. But he was *not* empowered to dispense law and doctrine, nor was anyone else. Everybody was responsible for his own road to salvation. Najdite Islam was a do-it-yourself religion.

Of all the libertarian visions that of the Najdites was the most extreme, and also the most retrogressive. The Najdiyya did not in principle recognize non-Najdites as Muslims (cf. below, chapter 21). To the question how the Muslims might avoid tyranny now that they had ceased to be a small community of tribesmen they responded by restoring them to freedom as a small community of Najdites. They could tolerate a high degree of intellectual freedom because their society was small, probably face-to-face and thus likely to have enjoyed a high degree of consensus; and they could countenance a high degree of political freedom because they did not in practice have any polity of their own. As a solution to the problem how all Muḥammad's followers might be kept together in religious and political terms without recourse to tyranny their vision had nothing to offer. They purchased their freedom by opting out of Muslim society at large and renouncing the reality of power. As we shall see, Imami Shīʿism carried the same costs, but whereas Shīʿism shorn of politics still offered a holy family for veneration and speculation, Khārijism without politics was an ideology without its heart: the regulation of power was what it was first and foremost about. It is possible that the Najdiyya survived into the eleventh century, though we do not know where; but it is not surprising that they disappeared.

CHAPTER

6

THE MUʿTAZILITES

Among the neighbours of the Khārijites in Basra were devotees of rationalizing theology (*kalām*) known as Muʿtazilites. They are said to have appeared in 720s, and at least one of their doctrines (regarding the status of the sinner) plainly has its roots in the Umayyad period. But they remain shadowy down to about 800, when they emerge as a loose association of diverse people and principles in Basra and Baghdad. Their school was systematized from the late ninth century onwards and flourished, above all in Iran, down to the mid-eleventh century. It suffered in the so-called 'Sunni revival' and disappeared altogether as a school in its own right after the Mongol invasion.

Unlike the Khārijites, the Muʿtazilites had neither a communal genealogy nor a law of their own, meaning that they did not form a complete saving vehicle. Some Muʿtazilites were ʿUthmānīs, as one would expect of Basrans who were not Khārijites; but most of them were fond of ʿAlī, and in Baghdad they were often Zaydīs (Shīʿites of the type described below, ch. 9).[1] All eventually accepted either the four-caliphs thesis or Shīʿite affiliation, probably in the course of the ninth century. This finalized their status as a mere school of thought rather than a sect of their own.

As Basrans by origin, if not always domicile, the early Muʿtazilites generally shared the libertarian outlook of the Khārijites.[2] All held the imamate to

1. The Baghdadi Muʿtazilites typically continued to deem ʿAlī more meritorious than the first three caliphs even after they had joined the four-caliphs consensus (cf. *EI*², s.v. 'ʿUthmāniyya', sec. 3).

2. For documentation of what follows, see Crone, 'Statement by the Najdiyya Khārijites', 71. For the libertarian outlook, see above, ch. 4, or the index/glossary.

be elective; most agreed that it must be awarded to the most meritorious candidate (the Baghdadi Muʿtazilites would accept a less meritorious man);[3] and many of them denied that merit had anything to do with ethnic or tribal membership: Arabs and non-Arabs, whether Qurashīs or other, were equally eligible.[4] Two ninth-century Muʿtazilites (Ḍirār and Ḥafṣ) famously added that a non-Arab imam would be positively preferable because he would not have any tribe to support him and might therefore be easier than an Arab to depose, much as the Ibāḍīs of North Africa had opted for a foreign imam on the grounds that he would be easier to depose. Like the Khārijites, the Muʿtazilites had no doubt that deposed he must be if he strayed from the law: one had to rebel against him if one could. In general, one had to take action, with the sword if necessary, when one saw the law being transgressed.[5] They were also at one with the Khārijites in that they retained the imam in his old multi-purpose role, casting him as a teacher of the law no less than a political leader.[6] But the most striking convergence between the two is that some Muʿtazilites, like the Najdiyya, held that the believers could manage without any imam at all.

The imamate as an optional institution[7]

A number of ninth-century Muʿtazilites, including al-Aṣamm (d. 816 or 817), al-Naẓẓām (d. between 835 and 845), Hishām al-Fuwaṭī (d. 840s?), his pupil ʿAbbād b. Sulaymān (d. 870s?), and the so-called Muʿtazilite ascetics (*ṣūfiyyat al-muʿtazila*), denied that the imamate was prescribed by the law. Unlike prayer or pilgrimage, it was simply a human convention that could be dropped if its utility was lost. With the possible exception of al-Naẓẓām, they all thought that its utility had in fact been lost, at least under prevailing conditions.

It had lost its utility by turning into tyranny. Kingship was forbidden in Islam, as the ascetics pointed out: other religious communities had kings who enslaved their subjects, but neither the Prophet nor the first caliphs had been

3. Meaning that they would accept Abū Bakr and ʿUmar as legitimate even though they held ʿAlī to have been the best candidate at the time.

4. To the references given in Crone, 'Statement by the Najdiyya Khārijites', 71, note 54, add Ashʿarī, 461; Jāḥiẓ in Madelung, *Qāsim*, 42.

5. For the North African Ibāḍīs, see above ch. 5, note 21. For the sword, see Ps.-Nāshiʾ, §108; Ashʿarī, 451; Cook, *Commanding Right*, ch. 9.

6. Ps.-Nāshi, §85; al-Aṣamm implies the same in §103, cf. Crone, 'Ninth-Century Muslim Anarchists', 18, note 59.

7. What follows is based on Crone, 'Ninth-Century Muslim Anarchists', to which the reader is referred for documentation.

kings; and if an imam were to develop into a king by ceasing to govern in accordance with the law, the Muslims would be legally obliged to fight him and depose him. But, they added, civil war split the community and led to more violation of the law without guaranteeing a better outcome, and imams did have a tendency to turn into kings; therefore the best solution was not to have them. Al-Aṣamm and, in slightly different ways, Hishām al-Fuwaṭī and ʿAbbād b. Sulaymān, took as their premise the fact that an imam was a person on whom all members of the community agreed: without such consensus, he would not be an imam at all. This was also the view of the Najdiyya, but unlike the Najdiyya, these Muʿtazilites did not infer that imams simply could not exist. What they said was rather that whereas the first caliphs had ruled with the requisite consensus, the community was now too large or too sinful for this to be possible. Like most Muslims, Al-Aṣamm seems to have accepted the ʿAbbāsids as quasi-imams, a pale reflection of the real thing, whereas Hishām, ʿAbbād and the ascetics held the Muslims to be living without an imam in actual fact; ʿAbbād, probably echoing Hishām, even declared that there never could be a genuine imam again. This was more than the others were willing to say, but whether a genuine imamate could exist again or not, it seemed impossible to have it now; hence it was better to do without central government altogether.

All these Muʿtazilites, then, were anarchists, if only in the simple sense of believers in the viability of a society from which the state had been removed. None of them condemned the state on principle. All held it to be a legitimate institution when its leadership was right, and all would have preferred to retain it under a proper imam. It was only kingship that they rejected on principle. But the imamate no longer seemed to be distinguishable from kingship. That was why it had lost its utility, or indeed turned positively unlawful.

Doing without the imam

All the Muʿtazilite anarchists put some thought into the question how one might manage without an imam, and above all who would apply the law and dispense the so-called *ḥudūd*, penalties of death, amputation or lashing which only a public authority could inflict; their very existence suggested that an imam was prescribed by the law. Their response varied. Hishām al-Fuwaṭī seems to have recommended straightforward recourse to self-help: the believers should take the law into their own hands when they could. Others thought that the leaders of households, districts, towns, and tribes might maintain the law and apply the *ḥudūd*. In other words, public power could be dissolved in favour of patriarchs and other local leaders (or what one might more idiomatically call domestic tyrants and local thugs). Still others came up with solutions which abandoned anarchism in favour of the state in a radically different form. Thus some (apparently the ascetics) proposed to retain a modicum of public power by electing temporary imams when legal disputes arose or crimes were committed, or when the enemy invaded; the imam would lose his position as soon as he had finished the job, just as an imam in the sense of prayer leader loses his authority the moment the prayer comes to an end. What they wanted was government by elected officials. Al-Aṣamm said that if you assembled people in sufficient numbers to minimize the danger of bias and collusion, then they could replace the imam for purposes of maintaining the law and applying the *ḥudūd*. In other words, he wanted government by assembly.

Al-Aṣamm had another idea, too: one could have several imams in different places at the same time. One imam for the entire community had been fine in the days of the first caliphs, he said, but nowadays there could no longer be real unanimity on any one man, and no real collaboration between the imam and local elites. Hence it would be better to have several imams, and this was perfectly lawful, not because the imamate was a human convention that one could do with what one liked (as one would have expected him to say), but rather because there was a good Prophetic precedent: the governors appointed by the Prophet in Arabia had in effect been independent imams; each one had collected taxes, maintained order, conducted defence and taught people the law. All had of course acknowledged the single imam above them, that is, the Prophet, but when the Prophet died, the inhabitants of each provincial centre had inherited the right to appoint their own governors. In short, each province was now entitled to elect its own semi-independent ruler. Differently put, Al-Aṣamm proposed to replace the unitary caliphate with a federation.

None of these proposals is spelt out in any detail. We are not told how the relationship between the leaders of households, districts, towns, and tribes should be envisaged, who would elect the temporary imams, whether there should be a single executive committee in the entire caliphate or on the contrary one in each province, or what would hold the federation together now that the Prophet had died. Nor are we told how the proposals might be implemented. It is nonetheless a remarkably inventive set of ideas, especially in view of the fact that its authors were not thinking in terms of a return to some putative original condition. Unlike Western anarchists, they had not been brought up on the idea that humans had originated without states, nor were they trained to see the many tribes around them as preserving a primitive condition of freedom. They had no assurance whatever from either real or imagined history that law, order and morality could be upheld in a society without coercive government. They simply reasoned their way to the conviction that it could.

For all that, their proposals were as backward-looking as those of the Najdiyya. Neither could accept that the Muslim polity had acquired dimensions so vast that political and intellectual egalitarianism had ceased to be viable: the Najdiyya preferred to keep their intellectual autonomy at the cost of remaining a tiny minority; the Muʿtazilite anarchists wanted their political participation back at the cost of sacrificing the imamate. But though it was possible to opt out of the wider community (*jamāʿa*), the *jamāʿa* itself could not be cleared of the authoritarian structures it had accumulated. Al-Aṣamm was right that the ʿAbbāsid empire was ripe for fragmentation, but not that participatory politics could be restored: the caliphate split up under military leaders who were simply miniature versions of the autocrats he wished to replace. Kingship had come to stay.

Later Muʿtazilites

According to the Imāmī scholar al-Mufīd (d. 413/1022), the Muʿtazilites were always reviling the Imāmīs for their belief in an absent imam, yet they themselves would freely admit that they had been without an imam since the time of ʿAlī and that this was unlikely to change in the foreseeable future.[8] In line with this the Muʿtazilite judge of Rayy, ʿAbd al-Jabbār (d. 415/1025), mentions as a matter of course that there was no imam in his own time. Quasi-caliphs did not count.[9] He did accept some imams after ʿAlī, and he was not an anarchist, for he held the imamate to be prescribed by the law: the *umma* was living without it because it was impossible to fulfil the obligation, not because the obligation could be denied.[10] But it is clear that the Muʿtazilites, or some of them, were still disinclined to come to terms with kingship.

8. McDermott, *al-Mufīd*, 123.

9. For quasi-caliphs, see the index/glossary.

10. *Mughnī*, xx/1, 50f.; xx/2, 145, 149f. (where he acknowledges al-Ḥasan, al-Ḥusayn, ʿUmar II, Yazīd III, Zayd b. ʿAlī, Muḥammad al-Nafs al-Zakiyya, and his brother Ibrāhīm); cf. IAH, ii, 309 where the Muʿtazilites only accept ʿUthmān, ʿUmar II, and Yazīd III of the Umayyads (later caliphs are not discussed); McDermott, *al-Mufīd*, 124; Madelung, *Qāsim*, 41. ʿAbd al-Jabbār's two-volume treatment of the imamate awaits a monograph.

CHAPTER

7

THE SHĪʿITES OF THE UMAYYAD PERIOD

Both the Khārijites and the Muʿtazilite anarchists restated the libertarian aspect of the tribal tradition in Islamic form. With the Shīʿites, by contrast, we encounter a thinking that can only be described as authoritarian. All Shīʿites held the imam to be something more than an ordinary human being and explained his special status in terms of his kinship with the Prophet. Yet Shīʿism also began among the conquerors, as has often been stressed, and the authoritarian style of thinking may well have tribal roots as well. For if the tribesmen of Arabia resisted kings, they also deferred to sanctity, as they showed when they accepted Muḥammad (and on many later occasions too). Early Shīʿism boiled down to the claim that power should be handed to a man of sanctity, defined as somebody more closely related to the Prophet than the Qurashīs originally seen as constituting his family. A kinsman of the Prophet was bound to be rightly guided: it ran in the blood. It is an odd idea to a modern reader, but it made sense in medieval times, and not only to tribesmen. In a world in which social roles were overwhelmingly allocated on the basis of descent it seemed self-evident that humans were replicas of their forebears: children everywhere tended to step into their parents' positions. The Shīʿites thought that things had gone wrong because the Prophet's descendants had not been allowed to step into his.

This does not of course explain why some tribesmen should have opted for leadership by a man endowed with hereditary sanctity while others rejected heredity altogether. The answer may be that Shīʿism has its roots in the tribal tradition of the southern Arabs rather than that of the northerners.[1] Shīʿism

1. Cf. Djait, 'Les Yamanites à Kufa', 165ff.

developed in Kufa, where a substantial part of the population hailed from South Arabia, whereas Khārijism developed in Basra, where the tribes were of northern, eastern, and mostly nomadic origin, and this is unlikely to be accidental. Precisely where its significance is to be sought is another question. One suggestion would be that South Arabians had a penchant for holy men. They certainly did in the nineteenth century, when descendants of the Prophet functioned as holy men who either mediated between the tribes (in Sunnī Ḥaḍramawt) or actually ruled them (in Zaydī Yemen). This pattern can be traced all the way back to the tenth century and it is generally assumed to be an islamized version of a pre-Islamic system. By contrast, no reverence for holy men as mediators or rulers is attested for north Arabia in either pre-Islamic or Islamic times.[2] That inherited patterns of authority played a role in the Yemeni espousal of the Prophet's family has been suggested before, in a different form.[3] But inherited patterns apart, it is also clear that the sheer marginality of the South Arabians in the new polity played a role in drawing them to ʿAlī, a potent symbol of victimhood, and this may well have been the most important factor in the early days.[4] As things stand, all explanations are in the nature of guesswork.

Hāshimite Shīʿism

The first Shīʿites, or ʿAlawīs, as they were more often called, were distinguished by their acceptance of ʿAlī rather than ʿUthmān as caliph, no more and no less.[5] They had no special views on ʿAlī's predecessors or on the succession after his death, nor were they set apart from the Muslims at large by other political convictions. But all this was to change in the Umayyad period. We may start with the succession.

When ʿAlī died in 661, his adherents chose his son al-Ḥasan as his successor, presumably because they had acquired a vested interest in the Hāshimite clan rather than because they held right guidance to be concentrated in the Prophet's lineage. Most of them seem to have accepted Muʿāwiya when

2. Crone, 'Tribes without Saints' (in preparation; meanwhile see *Meccan Trade and the Rise of Islam*, 184n. and 'Serjeant and Meccan Trade', 223ff.).

3. Cf. Watt in various publications, most recently his *Formative Period*, 43.

4. In Fusṭāṭ, which was settled by southerners without going Shīʿite, it was the southerners who dominated.

5. Cf. Nashwān, 180. Nashwān adds that Jāḥiẓ defined an early Shīʿite as somebody who gave priority to ʿAlī over ʿUthmān; this is only true if he meant someone who rejected ʿUthmān in favour of ʿAlī, not someone who simply held ʿUthmān to have been less meritorious than ʿAlī.

al-Ḥasan abdicated in the same year, disillusioned by al-Ḥasan's behaviour and probably inferring from Muʿāwiya's ability to make himself obeyed that he was the rightful imam.[6] But they had to think again when Muʿāwiya designated Yazīd as his successor and thereby made it clear that the office would be kept in the Umayyad family.

Like other opponents of Muʿāwiya's move, the ʿAlawīs could reject the monopolization outright, either to assert the rights of Quraysh at large (as did Ibn al-Zubayr), or to strike out heredity altogether (as did the Khārijites); alternatively, they could accept the monopolization with reference to a different clan. Many, perhaps most, ʿAlawīs opted for the first solution and thereby fell into the category of what this book calls 'soft Shīʿites', that is to say people who accepted ʿAlī rather than ʿUthmān as caliph (or who at least held that ʿAlī should have been caliph before ʿUthmān), but who continued to regard all Qurashīs as eligible for the caliphate. It was the natural stance for ʿAlawīs to adopt, given that they accepted the legitimacy of Abū Bakr and ʿUmar: for if the caliphate had not been reserved for the Prophet's family in the beginning, there was no reason to assume that it was so now. Soft Shīʿites were prominent in Kufa and elsewhere down to the ninth century, when they disappeared in the four-caliphs consensus. But it was the alternative solution that became characteristic of Shīʿism proper: the Umayyad reservation of the office for a single clan of Quraysh was accepted, but the clan was identified as Hāshimite rather than Umayyad. The Umayyads had no claim to the caliphate at all, it was asserted, nor did any other Qurashīs apart from the Hāshimites.

It should be noted that when early Shīʿites declared themselves loyal to the Prophet's family, they normally had the entire Hāshimite clan in mind, not just ʿAlī's family They probably did regard ʿAlī's family as special, for he had after all been caliph, and of the three Hāshimites who rebelled in the Umayyad period, al-Ḥusayn in 680, Zayd b. ʿAlī in 740, and ʿAbdallāh b. Muʿāwiya in 744–7, the first two were direct descendants of ʿAlī while the third was a descendant of his brother Jaʿfar (cf. charts 3 and 4).[7] But the Shīʿite poet al-Kumayt (d. 743) venerates all the Hāshimites in his *Hāshimiyyīt*;[8] and when non-Hāshimites rebelled in the hope of enthroning a member of the Prophet's family, they would simply call for *al-riḍā min āl rasūl allāh/banī Hāshim/ahl al-bayt*, 'the generally accepted member of the Messenger's kin/the Hāshimites/ the (holy) family', apparently meaning that a *shūrā* of Hāshimite candidates

6. Nawbakhtī, 21 (who belittles their number); above, 34f.

7. There was a similar sense among non-Shīʿites that descendants of Abū Bakr and ʿUmar ought to have pride of place in a *shūrā* for the election of the most meritorious Qurashī (cf. Crone, '*Shūrā* as an Elective Institution', 21).

8. Madelung, 'Hāshimī Shīʿism'.

should be convoked so that they could choose the most meritorious member from among themselves. Even ʿAlid rebels might call to *al-riḍā* rather than themselves, as ʿAbdallāh b. Muʿāwiya is said to have done.[9] There was no sense that any one Hāshimite lineage had a monopoly on the caliphate, let alone that there already was what one might call a counter-imam, or imam in exile. In short, by the later Umayyad period a real (as opposed to a soft) Shīʿite was somebody who held, not only that ʿAlī rather than ʿUthmān had been the legitimate caliph, but also that the Hāshimites rather than the Umayyads had a hereditary monopoly on the caliphate.

It was in the name of Hāshimite Shīʿism that the Khurāsānīs toppled the Umayyads. But by enthroning one branch of the Hāshimite house they willy-nilly excluded the other from power, thereby splitting the house into two; so the very success of the revolution subverted the creed in the name of which it had been conducted. Hāshimite Shiʿism died with the participants in the revolution.[10]

The appearance of rafḍ

Some Shīʿites took to claiming that the Prophet's kinsmen had *always* had a monopoly on the caliphate. The Prophet had designated ʿAlī as his successor at Ghadīr Khumm, they said, with the words "whoever accepts me as master, ʿAlī is his master too" (*man kuntu mawlāhu fa-ʿAlī mawlāhu*). ʿAlī was the Prophet's *waṣī*, legatee, and should have been accepted as caliph already when the Prophet died, not in 656. There was no room for non-Hāshimite caliphs at any time, past, present or future.

This was a radical view because it meant that Abū Bakr and ʿUmar had been usurpers on a par with the Umayyads, and moreover that the vast majority of Companions (all but six of them according to the Imamis) had fallen into error by following the usurpers: the Prophet's guidance had passed to the few who had remained faithful to ʿAlī, and from there to the few who were faithful to his family now. Adherents of this position were known as Rāfiḍīs, *rafḍ* being rejection of the venerable *shaykh*s Abū Bakr and ʿUmar as illegitimate rulers, not just of the controversial ʿUthmān.

Rafḍ seems to have emerged in the 680s, perhaps also in response to Muʿāwiya's designation of Yazīd. There is no sign of it in the (admittedly biased) accounts of Ḥujr b. ʿAdī, an ʿAlawī agitator executed by Muʿāwiya in 671f., or the revolt of al-Ḥusayn against Yazīd I in 680: both episodes involve

9. Crone, '*al-Riḍā*', 98 (Ibn Muʿāwiya).
10. See further below, ch. 8.

old-style ʿAlawīs versus ʿUthmānīs.[11] But ʿAlī is identified as the Prophet's legatee (*waṣī*) in the sources on al-Mukhtār, who rebelled in Kufa in 685–7;[12] and al-Mukhtār's 'Sabaʾiyya' (a derogatory term for Shīʿites) were duly accused of dissociating from "our righteous forebears", that is, the first caliphs and other Companions.[13] That "many Sabaʾiyya" (but not all of them) slandered Abū Bakr and ʿUmar is also mentioned by the Ibāḍī Sālim b. Dhakwān, here reflecting a source composed about 720.[14] A poem by the Shīʿite Kuthayyir ʿAzza (d. 723) repudiates Abū Bakr, ʿUmar, and ʿUthmān alike;[15] the first attestation of the Prophet's designation of ʿAlī at Ghadīr Khumm comes in the *Hāshimiyyāt* of al-Kumayt (d. 126/743),[16] and the first appearance of the term Rāfiḍī comes in the account of Zayd b. ʿAlī's revolt in 740, on which occasion it is supposed to have been coined.[17] The reliability of every one of these references can be queried, but taken together they hardly leave much doubt that Rāfiḍism had emerged by the later Umayyad period, and perhaps already by the middle.[18] The Kufan traditionist Layth b. Abī Sulaym (d. 760 or later) may just be right when he claims that the Shīʿites never thought of putting ʿAlī before Abū Bakr and ʿUmar when he was young (by which he meant that they were wrong now to do so);[19] but he must in that case have been very old when he died.

In the course of the Umayyad period, Shīʿism thus came to exist in two different forms, one expressing a greater degree of alienation than the other. According to the one, the community had remained rightly guided until the first civil war, when the ʿUthmānī majority went astray but many followed ʿAlī. According to the other, practically the entire community had gone astray

11. The accounts are biased in that they come overwhelmingly from Abū Mikhnaf, a soft Shīʿite who tendentiously claimed that Zayd's followers did not include any Rāfiḍīs (cf. below, 118).

12. E.g. Tab., ii, 611.1, 638.5, cf. 747.13 (here Ibn al-Ḥanafiyya rather than his father); BA, v, 218.11.

13. Tab., ii, 651.2.

14. Crone and Zimmermann, *Epistle*, 118 (Sālim, III, 97), 299.

15. Kuthayyir, *Dīwān*, i, 269; Tab., ii, 1699f., where Zayd is presented as rejecting Rāfiḍism.

16. Kumayt, *Hāšimijjāt*, 6:8–9; cf. Madelung, 'Hāshimī Shīʿism', 8.

17. Tab., ii, 1699f., where Zayd is presented as rejecting Rāfiḍism.

18. See further Nagel, *Rechtleitung und Kalifat*, 167ff.; van Ess, *TG*, i, 308ff.

19. Van Ess, *TG*, i, 237. Cf. also Damīrī in Goldziher, 'Beiträge', 444n., where an old-style Shīʿite (*min al-shīʿa al-ūlā*) is identified as a person who favoured the Prophet's family without denigrating the Companions; and compare ʿAbd al-Jabbār's chronology of heretical innovations: Khārijism appeared first, then *irjāʾ*, then free will, then *rafḍ* (*Tathbīt*, i, 24).

the moment the Prophet died, only a tiny number of Companions remaining faithful to ʿAlī until he finally became caliph.

Messianism

The Umayyad period was also characterized by strong messianic expectations, both among Shīʿites and *jamāʿī* Muslims (i.e. all those who did not opt out of the community by reserving their allegiance for current or future imams of their own). Only the Khārijites remained immune to them. But it was among the Shīʿites that such expectations were to play the greatest role.

The Muslim messiah is known as the *mahdī*, 'the rightly guided one'. The term may not have had any messianic or apocalyptic meaning by origin. It is said to mean no more than 'rightly guided' when it is applied to the Prophet, the caliphs in Medina, ʿAlī, al-Ḥusayn, and the general run of Umayyad caliphs.[20] It has however been suggested that Islam originated as an apocalyptic movement.[21] If this is correct, the chances are that all the many terms to do with right guidance had an apocalyptic and/or messianic meaning from the start. That would still leave the question how and why the term *mahdī* came to be singled out from the rest, but it would have the merit of explaining why descriptions of guidance by caliphs described as *mahdī* should have such strong redemptive overtones in Umayyad court poetry:[22] the Umayyads would be trying to assure their subjects that the politico-religious salvation promised by the first leaders of the movement had now been effected, even though the end of history was still to come. Like the ʿAbbāsid and the Fāṭimid caliphs, they would be institutionalized messiahs, bearers of routinized redemption.

If so, it will have been by way of resurgence of apocalyptic expectations that two Umayyad caliphs are described as *the* Mahdi in the sense of a unique figure whose coming had been predicted, not just as an institutionalized saviour. Sulaymān (715–17) was the Mahdi "predicted by priests and rabbis" according to the poet al-Farazdaq, who praised him for removing all grievances and making the crooked straight;[23] and ʿUmar II (717–20) was the Mahdi and "the scarred one" who would fill the earth with justice and who had been predicted

20. *EI*², s.v. 'al-mahdī'.

21. Donner, 'Sources of Islamic Conceptions of War', 43ff.; D. Cook, 'Muslim Apocalyptic and *Jihād*'; Arjomand, 'Islamic Apocalypticism' (the strongest case); cf. also his 'Messianism, Millenialism and Revolution'.

22. Cf. above, 41f. This presupposes that the apocalypticism was messianic, which Donner denies ('La question du messianisme'). I hope to return to the question elsewhere.

23. *Dīwān*, 327f.

in the Book of Daniel according to a number of sources.[24] It is generally agreed that this should be connected with the fact that the first Muslim century was about to come to an end. The Prophet is supposed to have predicted that "There won't be anyone left on the face of the earth after the year 100" or alternatively that "Every community has a term and the term for my community is 100 years";[25] either the whole world would be destroyed or the Muslim community would. This was so widespread a belief that even the Chinese got to hear about it: "As regards these Arabs, they are only supposed to be in power for a total of 100 years," the king of Samarqand told the Chinese emperor in 719 in an attempt to persuade him to lend him troops against them.[26] Sulaymān came to the throne in AH 96. It was a reasonable expectation that he would still be alive in AH 100, but he died in AH 99, so that it was ʿUmar II who ruled in the fateful year. This must be why both caliphs were expected to be *the* Mahdi. If the Muslim community was scheduled for destruction, the Mahdi's role may have been to defer the disaster ("God would not punish them while you were among them," as Q. 8:33 says to Muḥammad). At the very least he would have been expected to mitigate its everlasting consequences by reducing the sinfulness of the community. If people expected a disaster so total that not a single human being would be left on earth, the next event would presumably be the resurrection and the Day of Judgement, for mainstream Islam does not really have the notion of an intervening millennium on earth. In that case, too, the Mahdi's role would be to put things right in order to save the believers from everlasting torment. Sensibly, neither Sulaymān nor ʿUmar made public reference to the anticipated disaster, but Sulaymān stepped into the Mahdic role by making a grand attempt to conquer Constantinople, a task associated with the Mahdi in Ḥadīth.[27] Realizing that he would not make it to the year 100, he designated ʿUmar II as his successor, presumably because the latter was not just an Umayyad but also a kinsman and namesake of ʿUmar al-Fārūq. "We were telling each other that this matter will not come to an end until a man from ʿUmar's descendants with a mark on his face has taken charge of this community and followed the conduct (*sīra*) of ʿUmar," a report from ʿUmar's son ʿAbdallāh has it.[28] "You resemble ʿUmar al-Fārūq in respect of his *sīra*," the

24. Notably Ibn Qutayba, *Maʿārif*, 362; Ibn Saʿd, v, 243, 245 (B, 330f., 333); cf. also *EI*², s.v. 'al-Mahdī'.

25. Nuʿaym b. Ḥammād, *Fitan*, 418 (S, §§1448, 1486); cf. Bashear, 'Muslim Apocalypse', 90ff.

26. Hoyland, *Seeing Islam*, 331n.

27. "The hour will not come until the city of Qayṣar/Heraclius is conquered" (Nuʿaym b. Ḥammād, *Fitan*, 321 (§1318, cf. 318f./ §§1315ff.)).

28. Ibn Saʿd, v, 243 (B, 331).

poet al-Jarīr told ʿUmar II,[29] who stepped into the Mahdic role by doing his best to fill the earth with justice, above all by fiscal reforms.

Of ʿUmar II it was later said that he had been a *mujaddid*, a renewer predicted for the beginning of every century,[30] or that he had been rightly guided (*mahdiyyan*) without being the Mahdi.[31] Either way, he was something less than the apocalyptic redeemer, and communitarian (*jamāʿī*) Muslims took to denying that there was any such thing as a Mahdi at all: more precisely, the only Mahdi was Jesus, who would appear at the end of times to kill Antichrist and confirm the truth of Islam; he would not come to rule the Muslim community in a millennium before the resurrection.[32] Down to the twelfth century practically all messianism after the later Umayyad period was Shīʿite.[33]

The first Shīʿite to invoke the Mahdi was active in Kufa before ʿUmar II. His name was al-Mukhtār (d. 687), and his preaching is generally regarded as seminal without anyone knowing precisely how it is to be interpreted. He is said to be the first to have used the word in a messianic sense (on the assumption that it was not born with that sense), and he identified himself as the Mahdi's vizier (*wazīr al-mahdī*), presumably with reference to Q.29:20, where Aaron appears as the vizier of Moses. He took the two names to stand for prototypes. Moses stood for Muḥammad, and Muḥammad's part he took to be enacted now by Muḥammad b. al-Ḥanafiyya, a son of ʿAlī's (by a slavegirl) who lived in Medina and is said to have been wary of his claims. The sources do not have him claim that Ibn al-Ḥanafiyya actually was the Prophet, whether by return from the dead or reincarnation, but they make much of the fact that Ibn al-Ḥanafiyya bore the Prophet's name, Muḥammad, and tecnonym, Abū 'l-Qāsim. (Thanks to al-Mukhtār, this came to be a standard requirement for the Mahdi.) Presumably, then, he was a new Muḥammad in the same loose way in which ʿUmar II was a new ʿUmar.

Aaron, on the other hand, normally stood for ʿAlī,[34] but he clearly did not do so in al-Mukhtār's scheme of things. Aaron's part as vizier to Moses was

29. Cited in Crone and Hinds, *God's Caliph*, 114.

30. Cf. Friedmann, *Prophecy Continuous*, 95ff.; Landau-Tasseron, 'Cyclical Reform' (whose findings go well with Friedmann's, despite her arguments against it).

31. Thus Ṭāwūs in EI^2, s.v. 'al-Mahdī', col. 1231b.

32. Cf. EI^2, s.vv. 'al-mahdī', col. 1234a; 'ʿĪsā b. Maryam', col. 84b.

33. The main exceptions are the political redeemers who appeared in Syria after the ʿAbbāsid revolution under the name of 'the Sufyānī' (Madelung, 'The Sufyani'; 'Abū 'l-ʿAmayṭar').

34. A famous tradition has Muḥammad tell ʿAlī that their relationship was like that between Aaron and Moses (Momen, *Introduction*, 13).

enacted by al-Mukhtār himself. What was the pair to accomplish? There are passages in which al-Mukhtār calls his Mahdi *imām al-hudā* and "the best man on earth today", implying that he saw him as the imam who would inaugurate the Hāshimite dynasty.[35] But such passages are few and far between, and there is no mention of future rulers in his summons or oaths of allegiance, be it under the label of imam, *al-riḍā*, the Mahdi, or Ibn al-Ḥanafiyya's own name. The task with which al-Mukhtār repeatedly associated himself in his programmatic statements was vengeance for the Prophet's family and protection of 'the weak', accomplished by ruthless purges and (if by 'the weak' he meant non-Arabs) by the enrolment of slaves and freedmen in the rebel army.[36] What was to happen thereafter is never stated. One passage has his followers call adherents of the Zubayrids to "allegiance to the commander al-Mukhtār and to making this matter *shūrā* in the Messenger's family".[37] If the future ruler remained to be chosen, they can hardly have seen Ibn al-Ḥanafiyya as their imam, unless they regarded the *shūrā* as a mere formality to endorse his position.

Having purged Kufa of al-Ḥusayn's killers, al-Mukhtār ceremoniously paraded a new Ark of the Covenant (*tābūt*) around the town, in the form of an empty stool of ʿAlī's transported on a mule, and appointed South Arabian devotees of his to serve as its guardians. It was, he explained, the equivalent of the *tābūt* of the Israelites which had contained the legacy of Moses' and Aaron's families.[38] He also made obscure prophecies in rhymed prose, denying that he was a *kāhin* (soothsayer) and claiming rather to be the *fārūq*, presumably the Aramaic redeemer in whose role ʿUmar had once been cast.[39] According to later accounts, his followers credited him with revelations brought by Gabriel, or he claimed to be a prophet himself;[40] one passage has an adherent identify him as infallible (*maʿṣūm*).[41] Was trying to transfer the characteristics of the Mahdi to himself? In any case, his Mahdi seems to have been some version or other of the Prophet in an apocalyptic role, more precisely in that of apocalyptic avenger of his own family and other victims of the Umayyad regime, primarily the South Arabian tribesmen (many of them converts from

35. Tab., ii, 608 (= BA, v, 222), 611. The heresiographers take it for granted that al-Mukhtār saw Ibn al-Ḥanafiyya as ʿAlī's successor (e.g. Nawbakhtī, *Firaq*, 21).

36. On all this, see *EI*², s.v. 'al-Mukhtār'.

37. Tab., ii, 722.

38. Ibid., ii, 703; cf. BA, v, 242.

39. BA, v, 236.3.

40. Nawbakhtī, *Firaq*, 21; Ibn Ḥazm, *Faṣl*, iv, 184; similarly the Syriac Chronicle *ad* 1234 in Brock, 'North Mesopotamia in the Late Seventh Century', 64n.

41. Tab., ii, 628.3.

Judaism, all marginalized by their inclusion in a polity founded by northern Arabs) and the non-Arab captives of Kufa.[42] Whether the world, or at least the world as we know it, was to end is never stated, but one certainly gets the impression that a new era was to start. Unfortunately, the sources are such that nothing can be said for certain.

Things become a good deal clearer thereafter. By the 740s the Shīʿites had two quite different conceptions of the Mahdi. The first was the Mahdi as a bearer of routinized redemption, much like the caliph in power. Unlike his Umayyad competitor, this Mahdi had to be a member of the Prophet's family who bore the name of Muḥammad; and unlike him, he would have to conquer his throne. This made him more of a redemptive figure than ʿAbd al-Malik or Hishām, but not much more. For example, the Ḥasanid Muḥammad b. ʿAbdallāh (al-Nafs al-Zakiyya) is said to have been recognized as the Mahdi by leading members of the Hāshimite clan at a meeting held at Abwāʾ near Medina shortly before the ʿAbbāsid revolution.[43] Since one cannot elect a redeemer by committee, all they can have meant by this was that al-Nafs al-Zakiyya was the member of the Prophet's family destined to initiate Hāshimite rule and that they were prepared to pay allegiance to him on that basis. Having been deprived of the imamate by the ʿAbbāsids, al-Nafs al-Zakiyya duly rebelled at Medina in 762, along with his brother Ibrāhīm in Basra, calling himself Commander of the Faithful.[44] He bore the Prophet's exact name and studiously imitated the Prophet's behaviour, but he did so as a scholar familiar with the Prophet's *sunna*, not as Muḥammad *redivivus*, and apart from the fact that he was expected to initiate a new and better dynasty there was nothing messianic about his revolt.

The second Mahdi was of an altogether more dramatic type. He too was a member of the Prophet's family, but he was dead or (his death having been denied) in hiding. He would come back from the dead, or out of hiding, to wreak terrible vengeance on the enemies of the Prophet's family, possess the earth and fill it with justice, usually as part of the grand eschatological drama at the end of times. Sometimes he would revive the dead as well, or some of them. He was not usually expected to found a caliphal dynasty, as opposed to putting an end to the world altogether, or at least the world as we know it, but there were many variations on the theme. Unlike mainstream Muslims, the Shīʿites clearly had a notion of a millennium on earth before the Day of Judgement. They expected a change of fortune (*dawla*) and a resurrection of some of the dead (*rajʿa*), presumably meaning their saints, before the general

42. Cf. Djait, 'Les Yamanites à Kufa', 165, 168ff.
43. Nagel, 'Ein früher Bericht', 258f.
44. He is thus addressed, e.g., in Tab., iii, 201, 215, 218.

resurrection, as polemics of the late Umayyad or the early ʿAbbāsid period inform us.[45]

It was a characteristic of the second type of Mahdi that one could not have an imam while one awaited him. He was deemed to have taken the imamate with him when he died or went into hiding (though he could have deputies). Shīʿites often called him *al-qāʾim*, the standing one, a term also used in sectarian circles of the pre-Islamic Near East of saviour figures who would not 'taste death'.[46] He barely figures outside Shīʿism. It was probably by way of polemics against this figure that non-Shīʿites identified the Mahdi scheduled to appear at the end of times as Jesus, denying that there could be others.

However Ibn al-Ḥanafiyya may have been envisaged when he was alive, he became a Mahdi of this second type to some Shīʿites when he died. He had gone into hiding in a cave on Mount Raḍwā near Medina, they said, and he would not die, but would come forth one day to fill the earth with justice.[47] There were also Shīʿites who cast al-Nafs al-Zakiyya as the Mahdi in this sense, apparently even while he was still alive. They predicted that he would possess the earth and engage in feats such as reviving seventeen men with the great name of God; when he was killed, they angrily declared that he had not actually been al-Nafs al-Zakiyya but rather a demon impersonating him. Other Kufans denied that he had died, claiming that he was hiding in a cave from which he would come forth as the *qāʾim*, Mahdi, and imam.[48] One could be the Mahdi in different senses to different people, indeed one could be the Mahdi to some and something else to others: for while some Shīʿites claimed that Ibn al-Ḥanafiyya had gone into hiding, taking the imamate with him, others claimed that he had died, bequeathing the imamate to his son Abū Hāshim, who had passed it to a brother of his, or to another ʿAlid, or to an ʿAbbāsid.[49] This last claim is said to have been the ticket with which the ʿAbbāsids rose to power.

Ghuluww *('Extremism')*

Al-Mukhtār's revolt is the first occasion on which we see non-Arab converts play a major role in a Shīʿite movement; there were to be many thereafter. Since non-Arab Muslims were in general beginning to outnumber their Arab counterparts, this is not surprising, but their contribution to the development of

45. Van Ess (ed.), *Kitāb al-irǧāʾ*, §7; the passage is translated in Cook, *Dogma*, 11.
46. Crone and Cook, *Hagarism*, 165, note 49.
47. Cf. *EI*², s.v. 'Muḥammad b. al-Ḥanafiyya'.
48. Ashʿarī, 8f.; Nawbakhtī, *Firaq*, 53–5.
49. Nawbakhtī, *Firaq*, 27ff.

Shīʿism has attracted particular attention, partly because they rapidly seem to have developed a particular affinity for Shīʿism (cf. below, 84f.), and partly because many of them were carriers of highly distinctive ideas which gave them great visibility to contemporaries and modern scholars alike. The ideas in question were Gnostic.

Gnosticism is the name for a set of beliefs attested in the Near East from the first century AD onwards, and soon elsewhere as well. The beliefs rarely added up to a complete religion, but were rather in the nature of a code which could be spelt out in any religious language, or a virus which could attack any established religion and subvert it to its own ends. Where the code originated is a moot point, but the primary language in which it appeared was Judeo-Christian.

Whatever the language used, the code was spelt out in an innumerable variety of ways, reflecting small circles of sectarians devoid of overall leadership. The message was that the world was bad, that God (or the highest God) had nothing to do with its creation, that humans did not belong in it, and that they had to extricate themselves from it in order to get home. This was usually expressed in a cosmological myth depicting the creation of the world as the outcome of a cosmic error whereby divine light had been progressively encased in matter; human beings were sparks of the divine trapped in such matter, from which they must seek to escape to return to their divine origins, typically by a life of abstention leading to reincarnation in successively higher forms (the idea of bodily resurrection was disgusting). Most Gnostics operated with saviour figures, often cast as incarnations of the divine and/or prophets descending to awaken humans from their deep slumber by telling them where they came from and how they should return. One was saved by such knowledge (Greek *gnōsis*), or by following the bearer of knowledge, not by the law, which they usually dismissed as mere shackles chaining humans to the corporeal world. Gnosticism was nothing if not a religion of alienation, and in line with this its adherents were much given to flouting established values, partly by ritual violation of the law (for which its adherents became so notorious that one never knows how much truth there is to the reports) and partly by transvaluation of the key figures of the religion within which they were active: the serpent was sacred, Judas was a hero, and so forth.

In Egypt (where a large Gnostic library, collected by Christians, was found at Nag Hammadi in 1945), as also in Syria, the Christian church enjoyed the backing of the state; accordingly, Gnosticism had been largely suppressed there by the time of the Arab conquests. But it was still rampant in Iraq (where the Mandaeans are among its modern survivors) and in Iran. Here it flourished in a bewildering variety of forms, shading off into Jewish and Christian esotericism of other kinds at one end of the spectrum and, at the other, blending with originally pagan types of religiosity with which it shared the assumption that human beings could be incarnations or manifestations of the divine. It did not take long for Muslims to pick up the Gnostic virus. Almost invariably, it manifested itself within Rāfiḍī Shīʿism, a religion of alienation focused on a holy family easily cast by Gnostics as bearers of saving knowledge, spurned by the masses who were too deeply sunk in ignorance to recognize the truth. In its mixed, semi-pagan form, Gnosticism profoundly influenced what eventually became Imami Shīʿism. As the genuine article, it was a key ingredient in the grand religious synthesis known as Ismailism; and it also generated a profusion of small sects notorious for their belief in things such as the incarnation of God in human beings (*ḥulūl*), continuous prophethood, the transmigration of souls (*tanāsukh*), denial of the resurrection, antinomianism, and transvaluation (such as that Abū Bakr and ʿUmar were demons in rebellion against God, or that Gabriel was to be cursed for misdelivering the Qurʾān to Muḥammad rather than ʿAlī).[50] Some sects of this type still survive today (for example the ʿAlawīs of Syria). All sectarians of a Gnostic character, whether genuine or shading into something else, were dismissed by their many opponents inside and outside Shīʿism as *ghulāt*, or extremists.[51]

Gnosticism may conceivably have been a factor in the emergence of *rafḍ* itself, but there are no unambiguous signs of it in al-Mukhtār's revolt. It is however unmistakable in the teaching reported, with whatever degrees of reliability, for Bayān and al-Mughīra (both executed by Khalid al-Qasri, i.e. in the 730s), ʿAbdallāh b. Muʿāwiya (d. 747), and Abū 'l-Khaṭṭāb (executed after the ʿAbbāsid revolution). By the ninth century its influence was pervasive, especially in Iraq and Iran.

Imamate without caliphate

It seems to have been the Rāfiḍīs in general and the Ghulāt in particular who began to apply the title of imam to men who had never been, or even tried to become, caliphs. Thus a poem by Kuthayyir ʿAzza (d. 723), an extremist who is said to have believed in the transmigration of souls,[52] has it that there were

50. E.g. *EI*[2], s.vv. 'ghulāt', 'Ghurābiyya', 'Ḥulūl', 'Manṣūriyya', 'Mughīriyya', 'Khaṭṭābiyya', 'Tanāsukh'.

51. For a study of the term, see al-Qāḍī, 'Development of the Term *Ghulāt*'. The term *ghuluww* (extremism) could be used whenever people were felt to go too far, just as *taqṣīr* (falling short) could be used for the opposite, whatever the belief involved; cf. Modarressi, *Crisis*, 35f.; Daou, 'Conception', 54; and the Khārijite examples in Crone and Zimmermann, *Epistle*, 201.

52. *Aghānī*, ix, 4; he also believed in *rajʿa*.

four imams of Quraysh, ʿAlī and his three sons, meaning al-Ḥasan, al-Ḥusayn, and Muḥammad b. al-Ḥanafiyya. All four had indeed been associated with politics, but to a diminishing degree: whereas ʿAlī had been caliph till he died, al-Ḥasan had soon abdicated in favour of an Umayyad, while al-Ḥusayn had only rebelled and Muḥammad b. al-Ḥanafiyya had merely been named in somebody else's revolt. Yet Kuthayyir casts all four as the legitimate leaders of the community. As he sees it, the imam is defined by his personal quality (above all his descent), not by his political power.[53]

Other Ghulāt of the Umayyad period applied the title of imam to Hāshimites who had even less to do with politics than Kuthayyir's four. Thus various extremists are said to have applied it to Muḥammad al-Bāqir (d. 735 or earlier) and his son Jaʿfar al-Ṣādiq, two ʿAlid scholars devoid of political ambition who lived in Medina. Unlike Kuthayyir, however, these extremists clearly did not see their imam as a caliph in exile. Nor can they have seen him as a source of law, since they were as contemptuous of the law as they were of politics. In fact, they do not seem to have deferred to their alleged imam at all. What they meant was that Muḥammad al-Bāqir and/or Jaʿfar al-Ṣādiq were bearers of saving knowledge which the many sunk in ignorance wrongly assumed to be legal instruction, but which would liberate the few who recognized it so that they would be able to do what they liked – sin would no longer touch them. To know the imam as he really was one had to accept the claims of some self-appointed missionary, typically a local man of humble origin such as Bayān, said to have been a dealer in straw. The latter preached the good news about Muḥammad al-Bāqir to the Kufans and thereby formed a sectarian circle of his own.

Imām was only one out of many terms with which sectarians would pick out their object of veneration. Mahdi, prophet, incarnation of God, carrier of God's spirit, vessel of divine light, all these and many other terms were also used, apparently in an indiscriminate fashion. According to a poem by a Zaydī active in Iraq in the 740s-60s, some Rāfiḍīs said that Jaʿfar al-Ṣādiq was imam (or god) and others said he was a prophet,[54] but Abū 'l-Khaṭṭāb' followers said that Jaʿfar al-Ṣādiq and his precedessors were imams *and* prophets, messengers, and gods, casting Abū 'l-Khaṭṭāb as a prophet, too.[55] ʿAbdallāh b. Muʿāwiya's followers said that he was the imam, a prophet, God (*rabb*), divine light, or a carrier of God's spirit.[56] The followers of Bayān al-Nahdī said that

53. E.g. Baghdādī, *Farq*, 28.

54. Ibn Qutayba, *Taʾwīl mukhtalif al-ḥadīth*, 70f; Baghdādī, *Farq*, 240 (*ilāh* for *imām*), cf. van Ess, *TG*, i, 252f. for discussion and further references.

55. Ashʿarī, 10f.

56. Ibid., 6; Nawbakhtī, *Firaq*, 29.

Abū Hāshim was the imam, *qāʾim*, and Mahdi who would come back and/or that he was a prophet, and that Bayān was the imam and/or prophet after his death;[57] and so on. What mattered was that the imam, messiah, or divine incarnation was a conduit of supernatural knowledge that poured into the local missionary, or whose position the local missionary could be seen as taking over; either way, he served to authorize the local missionary to act as leader of a new cult. The local leader, too, would be known as imam, messiah, prophet or God, in much the same haphazard way.

In other words, the Ghulāt hijacked the term imam to apply it, alongside many other appellations, to their Gnostic saviour or other divine leader of the quasi-pagan type. They thus familiarized the Muslims with the concept of the imam as a spiritual guide who was fundamentally apolitical.

Non-Arabs and Umayyad Shīʿism[58]

It is often suggested in the older literature that there was a special affinity between non-Arabs and Shīʿism in Umayyad times. The reasons given are not always good, and the idea has long been out of favour, but the observation seems to be correct.

From the conquests onwards, converts of highly diverse origin had been brought together in a single polity, never having formed one before and having little in common apart from their belief in God and Muḥammad. They needed some way to translate this belief into legitimation of their newfound political unity. Since they shared their belief in God with most inhabitants of the Middle East, they usually looked for this legitimation in the Prophet: the Prophet had been and gone, but a caliph from his kinsfolk, whether identified as Quraysh or just the Hāshimites, continued to rule them in his place, seeing to the preservation of his message and the execution of his law. The immense importance ascribed to succession within the Prophet's descent group by Shīʿites and non-Shīʿites alike did not just reflect belief in the hereditary nature of merit and other human characteristics, strong though that was, but also the fact that this group provided a much-needed language in which the political unity of utterly diverse groups in utterly different places could be articulated.

The Umayyads were Qurashīs and thus kinsfolk of the Prophet in the wider sense. But they had come to power at a time when the polity consisted almost entirely of Arabs fresh from the peninsula and when God rather than the Prophet was seen as the source of the caliph's position. That God should

57. Nawbakhtī, *Firaq*, 30; Ashʿarī, 5f.

58. This section draws on and quotes from Crone, 'Wooden Weapons'; '*Shūrā* as an Elective Institution', sec. vi; '*Mawālī* and the Prophet's Family'.

have chosen the Arabs for His mission was an excellent answer to the question why Arabs should form a single polity: this was indeed why the Arabs had come together in the first place. But it did nothing for the rapidly growing number of non-Arab Muslims, to whom it assigned the position of mere clients of the master race.

On top of that there was massive prejudice against non-Arab Muslims. All colonial rulers tend to despise the natives they have overrun, and most non-Arab Muslims owed their membership of the Muslim community to capture and enslavement. In practice too, then, they were clients of the master race. They were classified as *mawālī*, clients (of their manumitters and/or the persons 'at whose hands' they had converted), and horror stories of their ill treatment in the Umayyad period abound. The sins of the Arabs were laid at the door of the caliphs, whose Arab orientation was perceived as related to their ill-treatment of the Prophet's family: the latter were assumed to be the true upholders of the universalist message of Islam; *mawālī* and Hāshimites were joint victims of narrow tribalism. Vengeance for al-Ḥusayn meant vengeance for the non-Arabs of Kufa already in al-Mukhtār's revolt,[59] and a Rāfiḍī account of Umayyad policy dating from shortly after the ʿAbbāsid revolution endorses this view. Included in the book of Sulaym b. Qays, it presents ʿUmar and Muʿāwiya as so prejudiced against *mawālī* that they would have preferred to kill them en masse, on the grounds that they were natural allies of the Prophet's family. Muʿāwiya is made to declare that if it had not been for Abū Bakr and ʿUmar, "we and this entire nation would have been *mawālī* of the Hāshimites", and he instructs his governor of Iraq to apply all the humiliating rules that ʿUmar had supposedly devised regarding marriage, inheritance, stipends, appointments, blood-money, and so forth to keep the *mawālī* in their place; but the reader knows it to have been in vain, for ʿAlī had predicted that non-Arabs would come with black banners from Khurāsān to kill the Umayyads under every star.[60]

It was not just *mawālī* who found the Umayyads constricting. Muslim society was fast outstripping the colonial organization they had devised in the aftermath of the conquest and which they could only tinker with thereafter if they were not to alienate the people on whom their power rested. The Umayyad realm was a loose federation of semi-autonomous provinces increasingly dominated by Syrian soldiers of tribal origin who struck most other Muslims as insufferable. It had no capital to symbolize Islamic unity, no centre that could be envisaged as the wellspring of Muslim power, no magnet drawing people together from all over the Muslim world, and no pan-Islamic

59. Crone, 'Wooden Weapons', 176.
60. Sulaym, *Kitāb*, 739ff.; tr. Crone, '*Mawālī* and the Prophet's Family'.

aristocracy: all it had was provincial magnates, local notables, tribal chiefs, sectarian leaders, scholars of greater or lesser renown, and Syrian soldiers everywhere. The more diverse the caliphate became in ethnic and cultural terms, the more people hankered for a focus, to find it in the Prophet; and the more important the Prophet became, the more the Umayyads looked like survivors from the Jāhilīyya.

CHAPTER

8

THE ʿABBĀSIDS AND SHĪʿISM

The Umayyads fell in 750 to rebel troops from eastern Iran, more precisely Khurāsān. The troops had been recruited by Iraqi dissidents who named themselves and their Khurāsānī followers *Hāshimiyya*, adherents of Hāshim's descendants, and who called for allegiance to the *riḍā* of the Prophet's family. The sources claim that the term *al-riḍā* was a mere cover for an ʿAbbāsid, but it seems more likely that it stood for a Hāshimite to be elected by *shūrā*. (For the Hāshimite clan, the reader may consult chart 3; for its ʿAbbāsid branch, chart 5.) The main candidate of the *Hāshimiyya* seems to have been the ʿAbbāsid known as Ibrāhīm *al-imām*, whose election they may indeed have regarded as a foregone conclusion: to that extent, the sources may be right when they claim that *al-riḍā* was a mere cover name. Ibrāhīm died in the jail of the last Umayyad caliph, and attempts to get a *shūrā* of Hāshimites together after the conquest of Iraq came to nothing when the ʿAlids refused to participate.[1] It was impatient generals who elected Abū 'l-ʿAbbās (750–4), the first ʿAbbāsid caliph. The revolution had raised strong messianic expectations of the apocalyptic type in Khurāsān. Like al-Mukhtār, the Hāshimiyya saw the Mahdi as an avenger, and they too associated him with a vizier who organized the movement on his behalf.[2] The first caliph, Abū 'l-ʿAbbās, duly styled himself *al-mahdī* to indicate that the world had now been filled with justice. His regnal name al-Saffāḥ was apparently also messianic, and his successors

1. Crone, 'al-Riḍā'; cf. Ibn Shahrāshūb, *Manāqib*, iv, 249f., for categorical Imāmī statements that Abū Salama (or Abū Muslim) offered the caliphate to Jaʿfar al-Ṣādiq and other ʿAlids.

2. I.e. Abū Salama, *wazīr āl Muḥammad*, who led the movement from Kufa.

certainly assumed messianic names (al-Manṣūr, al-Mahdī, al-Hādī, al-Rashīd) to ram home the message that a blessed era (*dawla mubāraka*) of exceptionally righteous imams had now begun.[3]

The blessed era was focused on Iraq, henceforth the centre of the caliphate. Here the second ʿAbbāsid caliph, al-Manṣūr (754–75), built Baghdad; it served as the headquarters of the Khurāsānī troops and the Iraqi bureaucrats on whom ʿAbbāsid power rested, and rapidly developed into a cultural capital attracting talent from all over the Muslim world. There had been nothing like it in Umayyad Syria. For all that, the ʿAbbāsids found it difficult to maintain control of their possessions. They were not able even to attempt to recover Spain, which seceded under an Umayyad prince in 756; by 800 they had given up trying to rule North Africa directly; and in 811 a dynastic dispute between two sons of Hārūn al-Rashīd (786–809) resulted in yet another civil war, which in the end cost them their direct control of Khurāsān. The victorious son was al-Maʾmūn (813–33), who was governor of Khurāsān when the civil war broke out and who initially tried to rule the entire empire from there, spurning the capital of his predecessors and completing his break with the past, in 816, by designating an ʿAlid as his successor. But Egypt, Syria and Iraq sank into chaos, the Baghdadis elected a counter-caliph, so either al-Maʾmūn had to renounce the rest of the ʿAbbāsid empire or else he had to return to Baghdad. He chose to return, abandoning his plans for an ʿAlid successor and eventually also his control of Khurāsān, which soon after his return to Iraq acquired autonomy under a hereditary dynasty closely allied with the caliphal house. Back in Iraq, al-Maʾmūn set about repairing the foundations of his authority, and in the last year of his reign he set up a famous, but ultimately unsuccessful, inquisition intended to bring the religious scholars under his control (cf. below, ch. 11). His successor, al-Muʿtaṣim (833–42) tried to repair the foundations of his power in a very different way, by building up a retinue of freed slaves, mostly of Turkish origin, with which he hoped to make himself independent of other wielders of power, whether military (such as the commanders of the Khurāsānī troops brought to Iraq by al-Maʾmūn) or civilian (such as the scholars). But al-Muʿtaṣim's second successor, al-Mutawakkil (846–61), was assassinated by the Turkish slave soldiers, and thereafter they took over. This marked the effective end of the ʿAbbāsid empire, though the ʿAbbāsid caliphs stayed on, sometimes recovering limited power of one kind or another, down to 1258.

3. Crone, *Slaves*, 65; Dūrī, 'al-Fikra al-mahdiyya', 124; Lewis, 'Regnal Titles'.

Legitimacy

One of the major difficulties the ʿAbbāsids had to confront was that their very rise to power had undermined the ideology by means of which they had risen. The revolution had been conducted in the name of Hāshimite Shīʿism. In principle, it had thus vindicated the rights of the entire Hāshimite clan, and the revolutionaries may have had visions of caliphs drawn from whatever branch of the clan produced the best candidate at any given time. But it goes without saying that the first caliph, whoever he was going to be, would try to keep the caliphate in his own family, so that loyalty to him would rule out allegiance to the rest of the Hāshimite clan. As it happened, the first caliph was an ʿAbbāsid. All lovers of the Prophet's family now had to decide whether to side with him or with the other Hāshimites, known as the Ṭālibids after ʿAlī's father. (See charts 3 and 6.) Faced with this choice, a fair number of Khurāsānī generals drifted to the ʿAlid side, and in 762 the ʿAlid Muḥammad b. ʿAbdallāh (al-Nafs al-Zakiyya) dealt a mortal blow to Hāshimite Shīʿism by rebelling along with his brother against the caliph al-Manṣūr, claiming the throne as the Mahdi.[4] Henceforth one belonged to either ʿAlī's party (*shīʿat ʿAlī*) or that of the ʿAbbāsids (*shīʿat banī 'l-ʿAbbās*).

It is this split which accounts for the common modern idea that the ʿAbbāsids had cheated in the revolution: they were not Shīʿites at all, it is said; they merely duped the adherents of ʿAlī into supporting their cause. But this rests on the assumption that already before the revolution a Shīʿite was a supporter of the ʿAlids to the exclusion of other members of the Prophet's house, so that the slogan '*al-riḍā* from the Prophet's family' would normally be taken to refer to an ʿAlid: in other words, the leaders of the revolution actually had an ʿAbbāsid in mind, but they attracted followers of the ʿAlids by keeping silent about this fact. Most Islamicists probably see it this way. Up to the ʿAbbāsid revolution, however, there is no reason to think that the Prophet's family meant anything other than the entire Hāshimite clan, after which the movement in Khurāsān was named. As the Muʿtazilite ʿAbd al-Jabbār (d. 1025) explains, 'At that time the Hāshimites were united, without disagreement or splits. The descendants of al-ʿAbbās, ʿAlī, and ʿAqīl and Jaʿfar [ʿAlī's brothers], and all the other Hāshimites, were in agreement. They only came to disagree when sovereignty and kingship passed to the ʿAbbāsids, in the days of Abū Jaʿfar al-Manṣūr, when well-known events took place between him and his Ḥasanid kinsmen.'[5]

4. Cf. above, 79.
5. ʿAbd al-Jabbār, *Tathbīt*, i, 17.

Once the Hāshimite clan had split, however, there is no doubt that the revolution made ʿAlid Shīʿism a greater problem to the central government than it had been under the Umayyads, for by vindicating the rights of the *ahl al-bayt* the Abbāsids had inadvertently put wind in the sails of the ʿAlids: revolts on behalf of the ʿAlids increased, and there was much more official persecution of the ʿAlids, too. The demise of Hāshimite Shīʿism left the ʿAbbāsids in an ideologically weak position vis-à-vis the ʿAlids (or for that matter all Ṭālibids, but the ʿAlids overshadowed the rest): why was it descendants of al-ʿAbbās rather than ʿAlī who ruled? The new caliphs urgently needed to explain how they came to have a better right to the throne than their ʿAlid cousins.

This was more easily said than done, for ʿAlī was a magnetic figure whom the Hāshimiyya regarded as the only legitimate caliph to have ruled before the revolution. When a kinsman of the first ʿAbbāsid caliph made the inaugural speech on the latter's behalf in Kufa in 750, he told the Kufans that "there has not been any caliph/imam among you since the Prophet died, apart from ʿAlī b. Abī Ṭālib and this Commander of the Faithful who is behind me/the one standing among you (i.e. Abū 'l-ʿAbbās)".[6] In line with this, the caliph al-Mahdī (775–85) is credited with citing to a Khārijite the Prophet's statement that "whoever accepts me as master, ʿAlī is his master too";[7] and the testament of a prominent leader of the revolution who died in 785 declared ʿAlī to be the Prophet's legatee (*waṣī*) and heir to the imamate after him (*wārith al-imāma baʿdahu*). On this occasion, however, al-Mahdī is said to have disapproved of *rafḍ* (rejection of the first caliphs as usurpers),[8] and he is presented as doing so elsewhere as well,[9] including in a variant version of the above story in which another dying veteran of the revolution asks him to show favour to his son; here the caliph objects that the son "is on the wrong track and at odds with our views and yours: he slanders the two *shaykh*s Abū Bakr and ʿUmar and speaks

6. Tab., iii, 37.8; MM, vi, 55 (iv, §2279). Another version has, "no caliph has ascended this pulpit of yours since the time of the Prophet apart from the Commander of the Faithful ʿAlī b. Abī Ṭālib and the Commander of the Faithful ʿAbdallāh b. Muḥammad (i.e. Abū 'l-ʿAbbās)" (Tab., iii, 33.4; cf. YT, ii, 420; Azdī, *Mawṣil*, 124). This could simply mean that ʿAlī and Abū 'l-ʿAbbās were the only caliphs to have led the prayer in Kufa (the Umayyads who had done so being rejected as kings), but here too the prima facie sense is Rāfiḍī.

7. Azdī, *Mawṣil*, 238. He may simply have meant that the Khārijite was wrong to speak ill of ʿAlī, understanding the tradition in the non-Rāfiḍī sense in which *jamāʿī* Muslims would explain it in polemics against Shīʿites. But it is a striking statement even so, for *jamāʿī* Muslims did not usually cite the tradition of their own accord.

8. Tab., iii, 532, on al-Qāsim b. Mujāshiʿ al-Tamīmī.

9. Cf. the story in which the Kufan judge Sharīk b. ʿAbdallāh al-Nakhaʿī is accused of *rafḍ* (Wakīʿ, *Akhbār al-quḍāh*, iii, 155f.).

ill of them" – to which the dying veteran replies that "he is adhering to the stance we stood for and that we called to when we rebelled".[10]

If ʿAlī was the Prophet's legatee, the ʿAbbāsids needed an account of how the imamate had passed from him to them. They solved this problem by postulating that ʿAlī had been succeeded by his son Ibn al-Ḥanafiyya, the Mahdi of al-Mukhtār, who had passed the imamate to his son; this son, the aptly named Abū Hāshim, had then bequeathed it to the ʿAbbāsids during a visit to Syria; he had been poisoned by the Umayyads, and when he realized what had happened to him, he was in a hurry to settle his affairs: the ʿAbbāsids lived at al-Ḥumayma in southern Syria and so were within reach, whereas the ʿAlids resided in Medina.[11] (See chart 6.) The trouble with this story was not that it was painfully contrived (many modern Islamicists have managed to believe it), but rather that it acknowledged the ʿAlids as the primary claimants to the caliphate and sought to counter them by manipulation of an obscure figure associated with extremists. In a world teeming with ʿAlids of scholarly renown and lofty descent from ʿAlī and the Prophet's daughter Fāṭima, the claim that a minor member of the family descended from a mere slave girl had alienated its collective rights by a semi-accidental bequest was not likely to carry general conviction. Abū Hāshim was a hero to the Ghulāt, who probably found it deeply significant that he sprang from a union of ʿAlī with a non-Arab slave woman, and in whose circles he was invoked as a transmitter of divine power to various local leaders of humble origin, sometimes by bequest of the imamate, sometimes by other means.[12] The story of his bequest to the ʿAbbāsids was all too reminiscent of attempts to elevate some lowly non-Arab to authoritative status, and any normal nose could discern the waft of claims to divinity, prophecy, omniscience, and the like with which such attempts tended to be associated. The armies of the new dynasty did in fact include many who construed Abū Hāshim's bequest as a transfer of divine powers to their ʿAbbāsid imam.[13] It has even been suggested that the entire Hāshimite movement in Khurāsān was founded and led by adherents of such ideas.[14] But however the original relationship between the Ghulāt of Iraq and the movement in Khurāsān

10. Tab., iii, 537, on Abū ʿAwn ʿAbd al-Malik b. Yazīd.

11. Nawbakhtī, *Firaq*, 29f., 42f.; *EI*², s.v. 'Abū Hāshim' (Moscati); Sharon, *Black Banners*, 84f., 121ff. (treating it as historical).

12. Nawbakhtī, *Firaq*, 28ff.

13. Ibid., 46; cf. below, 94f.

14. Thus Lewis in *EI*², s.v. "Abbāsids', col. 15. Both Lewis and Sharon (*Black Banners*, 84) take the name of the Hāshimite movement to refer to Abū Hāshim rather than Hāshim, the ancestor of the Hāshimite clan (cf. Nawbakhtī, 46, *Firaq*, with reference to extremist devotees of the ʿAbbāsids).

is to be envisaged, the ʿAbbāsids could not base their claim to the caliphate on extremist ideas.

Consequently, they tried to give up on ʿAlī altogether. They had inherited the caliphate from their own ancestors, they said: the Prophet had bequeathed the imamate to his uncle al-ʿAbbās, not to his cousin ʿAlī, and thereafter it had passed to al-ʿAbbās' descendants until it reached Abū 'l-ʿAbbās, the first ʿAbbāsid caliph. The essence of this argument first appears in al-Manṣūr's correspondence with the rebel ʿAlid, Muḥammad al-Nafs al-Zakiyya (if it is authentic). Al-Manṣūr here stresses the many virtues of al-ʿAbbās, notably that he enjoyed the privilege of providing water for the pilgrims in Mecca (known as the *siqāya*) and converted early to Islam, unlike Abū Ṭālib, the Prophet's other uncle and progenitor of the ʿAlids; and it culminates in the ringing statement, regarding al-ʿAbbās, that "the legacy of the Prophet is his, the caliphate is in his descendants, and there is no nobility or merit in either Jāhiliyya or Islam, in this world or the next, which al-ʿAbbās has not inherited and passed on to his descendants".[15] But it is al-Mahdī rather than al-Manṣūr who is singled out as the sponsor of the ʿAbbāsid claim to the caliphate by inheritance (*wirātha*) from al-ʿAbbās, as opposed to by bequest (*waṣiyya*) from Abū Hāshim;[16] or it was one Abū Hurayra al-Rāwandī who proposed the doctrine of inheritance in the time of al-Mahdī.[17] Either way, it was now postulated that the imamate had passed from the Prophet to al-ʿAbbās, and from there to the latter's descendants down to the revolution. (See chart 6.) This fits the information that al-Mahdī tried to de-emphasize ʿAlī's rights to the caliphate towards the end of his life, but not that he tried to do so by recognizing Abū Bakr and ʿUmar, for in principle the doctrine of inheritance from the ʿAbbāsid ancestor defined *every* caliph up to the first ʿAbbāsid caliph as a usurper, as the Imami Shīʿite heresiographer al-Nawbakhtī gleefully points out.[18] But in practice the doctrine seems to have been taken to mean that the ʿAbbāsids had an irrefutable claim to the caliphate in terms of ancestral merit which did not preclude acceptance of Abū Bakr and ʿUmar, or for that matter ʿAlī himself, though it did preclude acceptance of the ʿAlids. Quite how this was achieved is unclear. The chances are that the doctrine of *wirātha* was seen as a claim to political leadership alone, not to the transmission of the Prophet's guidance. If

15. Tab., iii, 212, 214f. For a discussion of the correspondence, see Nagel, 'Ein früher Bericht', 247ff.

16. Nawbakhtī, *Firaq*, 43, cf. 42 (compare also Baghdādī, *Uṣūl*, 284f.); Qummī, *Tafsīr*, 65f.; AA, 165.

17. Ps.-Nāshiʾ, §47; Kaʿbī in ʿAbd al-Jabbār, *Mughnī*, xx/2, 177.

18. He credits al-Mahdī with an explicit identification of Abū Bakr, ʿUmar, ʿUthmān, and ʿAlī as usurpers (*ghāṣibūn mutawaththibūn*).

so, the many Muslims of a communitarian (*jamāʿī*) persuasion likely to have been cheered by al-Mahdī's disapproval of ʿAlid *rafḍ* will no doubt have had the courtesy to overlook the faulty nature of his compromise.[19]

For all that, one caliph, the above-mentioned al-Maʾmūn (813–33), went to the other extreme of giving up on the ʿAbbāsids. He had come to power by defeating and killing his brother, the reigning caliph al-Amīn (809–13), who was backed by the descendants of the original revolutionary troops in Baghdad, including the Rāwandiyya. This made ʿAbbāsid legitimism and Baghdad alike problematic for al-Maʾmūn, and it was in part for that reason that he stayed in Khurāsān and designated an ʿAlid as his heir, claiming that this ʿAlid was the most meritorious man of the time. The ʿAlid was ʿAlī b. Mūsā, imam of the Imāmī Shīʿites (below, ch. 10), whom al-Maʾmūn must have hoped to rally to his side. He gave the ʿAlid the name of al-Riḍā, credited himself with a new mission (*al-daʿwa al-thāniya*)[20] and changed the official colour of the dynasty from black to green, in effect doing a rerun of the Hāshimite revolution with a new and better end: this time the *riḍā* raised up by the Khurāsānīs came from the right branch of the Prophet's house. How the succession was to be organized thereafter is not specified, possibly because al-Maʾmūn expected the world to come to an end, as a Shīʿite source claims.[21] In any case, the ʿAbbāsid establishment in Baghdad was outraged, the ʿAlid conveniently died, probably with a little help, and al-Maʾmūn went back to Baghdad, where he reverted to black though he remained a devotee of ʿAlī.[22]

All in all, the ʿAbbāsid position from the 780s onwards seems to have been that they recognized Abū Bakr and ʿUmar as legitimate caliphs whether or not they held ʿAlī to have been the most meritorious man at the time of the Prophet's death, but rejected ʿUthmān and the Umayyads, deeming the caliphate to belong to the Prophet's family from ʿAlī onwards. There was little to distinguish their position from that of the milder Zaydīs, as will be seen (cf. ch. 9), though the ʿAbbāsids were behaving more like Imami Shīʿites when they cast themselves as inheritors of the imamate from al-ʿAbbās. But with or without the inheritance doctrine, they insisted on their own membership of the Prophet's family, claiming that since they rather than the ʿAlids had conducted the revolt against the Umayyads, the caliphate now belonged to them. Here, too, they parted company with the Zaydīs, for though the latter also took the

19. According to Nawbakhtī and Qummī, the adherents of the *wirātha* doctrine kept their loyalty to their first imams secret, since they were reluctant to impute infidelity to their forebears (*aslāf*), or it was only in secret that they would brand them as unbelievers.

20. Cf. Arazi and Elʿad, 'Epître', i, 29, 50.

21. Madelung, 'New Documents,' 343, 345f.

22. Cf. *EI*², s.v. 'al-Maʾmūn'.

imam to activate his rights by revolt, they did not usually deem him to have any rights unless he was an ʿAlid (or at least a Ṭālibid), nor did they think that the imamate would henceforth belong to the rebel's descendants.[23] The ʿAbbāsids eventually parted company with all Shīʿites in a more decisive way by recognizing ʿUthmān as the third rightly guided caliph, thus ending up in the four-caliphs camp along with the vast majority of their subjects. Presumably, this happened in the ninth century, but the process awaits documentation.[24] The one and only stable component of their position from beginning to end was that they were *ahl al-bayt* who had rendered themselves deserving of the imamate over and above all other kinsmen of the Prophet, whether ʿAlids or plain Qurashīs, by bringing about the blessed *dawla*.

Iranian Ghulāt

Throughout the first century of their caliphate the ʿAbbāsids were plagued by problems caused by the Ghulāt in the revolutionary armies, partly in Iraq and further west, but more particularly in Iran. The architects of the revolution had recruited a large number of Iranians whose native religious language was a mish-mash of Zoroastrian, Manichean, and Buddhist idioms and who, once they became Muslims, were prone to casting their imams as divine saviour figures. In Iraq the secretary Ibn al-Muqaffaʿ noted with concern that the Khurāsānī troops included groups led by extremist leaders (*raʾs mufriṭ ghālin*); many commanders, he said, spoke in a manner suggesting that the caliph could make the mountains move and that people would pray with their backs to the *qibla* if he so commanded; there were people who professed to obey their imams without enquiring into what constituted obedience and disobedience to God on the grounds that they were not authorized to sit in judgement of those endowed with knowledge.[25] All this was dangerous, Ibn al-Muqaffaʿ said; relying on people who might not share one's view was like riding on a lion. For this reason he hoped that the caliph would draw up a concise catechism or creed free of *ghuluww* for the leaders of the army to memorize.[26]

23. Cf. below, 99f., 106.

24. The four-caliphs thesis is said to have been adopted already by al-Manṣūr, which cannot possibly be correct (e.g. Zubayr b. Bakkār, *Muwaffaqiyyāt*, 199, no. 113; TB, x, 55.-6). We are also told, again on Zubayrid authority, that al-Rashīd is said to have inquired about the legitimacy of denigrating ʿUthmān, to be told that Shīʿites, Khārijites and other innovators engaged in it whereas the people of *jamāʿa* defended him (Tab., iii, 749). That al-Rashīd should have adopted the *jamāʿī* view, as the reader is obviously expected to infer, is again unlikely (differently Zaman, *Emergence*, 56–9).

25. *Ṣaḥāba*, 194.8, 195.3, 196.8 (P, §§, 10, 12, 14).

26. Ibid., 194 (P, §§10–11).

The men described by Ibn al-Muqaffaʿ (who also knew the army to contain adherents of the opposite and equally dangerous view that the imam had no greater authority than anyone else)[27] are said by others to have taken Abū Hāshim's bequest to mean that their imam was God (*allāh*), that nobody who did not know him knew God, that those who did know him would not be touched by sin, that he knew everything, including their inner thoughts, that Abū Muslim was a prophet sent by al-Manṣūr, and the like.[28] They seem to have expected some kind of ultimate event to take place at the end of the 750s. Around that time, black-clothed Iranians in northern Syria are reported to have sold their possessions and jumped naked from the city walls in the expectation of going to heaven; others at Dābiq, also in northern Syria, proclaimed the caliph's son (*sic*) to be divine and went to Iraq, where they entered Basra by force to take money and captives;[29] in Baghdad still others publicly proclaimed al-Manṣūr to be divine, identified two Khurāsānī generals as incarnations of Adam and Gabriel, and proceeded to circumambulate al-Manṣūr's palace.[30] Al-Manṣūr is said to have commented that he preferred heretical obedience to orthodox disobedience,[31] but he wisely had the heretics suppressed. Apart from being deeply offensive to normal Muslim sensibility, their behaviour was dangerous in that they were taking it upon themselves to define what the caliph was, claiming to know better than the caliph himself, much as other Ghulāt were doing to Muḥammad al-Bāqir and Jaʿfar al-Ṣādiq about the same time. The fact that the caliph sent troops against them in no way convinced them that they were wrong. "Al-Manṣūr is our lord," they responded (according to their descendants), "He is killing us as martyrs, just as He killed His prophets and messengers at the hands of whoever He wanted . . . that is His right, He may do what He wants with His creatures."[32] Being divine is not an advantage if it is for other people to define your divine intentions.

This incident was soon over and done with, and thereafter the Rāwandiyya in the caliph's troops seem to have kept their exaltation of the ʿAbbāsids under control. In the meantime, however, Abū Muslim's troops had been disbanded, Abū Muslim himself having been assassinated by al-Manṣūr in 754, and the now unemployed soldiers went on to stir up revolts in Iran, where the

27. Ibid., 196 (P, §13).

28. Nawbakhtī, *Firaq*, 30, 46f., where they are first called Rāwandiyya, next spuriously distinguished as two separate groups called Hāshimiyya and Rāwandiyya.

29. Theophanes, AM 6250, 6252 (tr. Mango and Scott, 595, 597).

30. Tab., iii, 129ff., where the Rāwandiyya incident is dated AH 136, 137, or 141 (the last being 758f., the year under which it is narrated).

31. Ibid., iii, 132.

32. Nawbakhtī, *Firaq*, 47.

commotion rapidly spread. The leaders of these revolts came from, and recruited their followers in, the same kind of milieu as that from which the Rāwandī troops in Syria and Iraq had been drawn, that is to say village Iran and its local cult societies; and they too invoked the authority of – or identified themselves as – divine incarnations, prophets, imams, or messiahs in a mixture of Shīʿite and pre-Islamic religious idioms. Unlike the Rāwandiyya, however, they used such Islamic idiom as they had mastered *against* the Muslims.[33] Their creeds were wild and woolly, but the supernatural was potent stuff, as the Prophet himself had demonstrated when he transformed backwoods Arabia into the greatest power on earth by claiming to be in contact with God. The Muslims had good reason to be alarmed: had the prophets succeeded, Iran would have been lost to them. In an orderly world the supernatural had to be carefully channelled and wrapped in insulating material, like electricity today, so as not to galvanize people who were meant to be politically inactive or run through live wires carelessly left behind by those who had used it to make power for themselves. Ghulāt everywhere tended to be religious amateurs drawn from the semi-literate world of villagers or petty urban people (such as smiths, watchmen, grocers, or tailors), and their tinkering with the wires of the supernatural was more often than not ineffective. The Iranian prophets too were eventually suppressed. But it was not until 838 that the last of them, Bābak, was defeated in Azerbayjān, and many of the religious communities they had founded survived for centuries.

The ʿAbbāsid contribution[34]

Though the ʿAbbāsids owed some of their worst problems to the fact that they claimed membership of the Prophet's house, this was also the source of their greatest success: they made the political unity of the Muslims meaningful again. As Hāshimites, the ʿAbbāsids were not perceived as Arabs at all, but rather as a sacred lineage elevated above all ethnic, tribal, regional, and local divisions.[35] Unlike the Umayyads, they rapidly came to be seen as endowed with personal sanctity;[36] they were more closely linked with the sanctuary

33. For the past twenty years or so it has been customary to recast the Iranian prophets as members of the Iranian elite and to deny or belittle their anti-Arab/Muslim animus. My reasons for not going along with this will be set out, I hope, in another publication.

34. This section is based on Crone, '*Shūrā* as an Elective Institution', 26ff.

35. Cf. Crone, 'Wooden Weapons', 180.

36. Cf., in very broad brush-strokes, Al-Azmeh, *Muslim Kingship*, 154ff.

too.[37] As beneficiaries of a revolution they swept away the remains of the conquest federation, replaced the tribally orientated Syrians with Khurāsānīs sanctified by their services to the blessed *dawla*, and built Baghdad, a highly visible and immensely magnetic centre of power and culture. The caliphate thus became a truly supra-ethnic polity, a political organization in which people could have a sense of belonging wherever they might hail from and with which they could identify. This was the great achievement of the ʿAbbāsids which secured them survival, in however debilitated a form, down to 1258; and this, one would assume, is what modern scholars really have in mind when they say that the ʿAbbāsids 'granted equality' to Arab and non-Arab Muslims.

The political idiom[38]

Changing though their relationship with Shīʿism was, the ʿAbbāsids endowed it with a near monopoly on the idiom of political protest. Before the revolution, the debate between rulers and ruled had centered on communal rights and generally accepted norms. Now it came to focus on entitlement to the imamate: was it by descent, bequest, designation, unsurpassed virtue, activism, or a mixture of all these things that the imam merited his unique position? Libertarianism lost its appeal. Where the Khārijites wanted autonomy, participation, and consensus even if it meant sacrificing the *jamāʿa*, the majority now wanted political unity under a leader aligned with the divine even at the cost of political freedom. This is probably why the ʿAbbāsids were rarely denounced as kings even though they were worse autocrats than the Umayyads. Khārijism, highly attractive to many in the Umayyad period, was now reduced to a marginal status; and though it was precisely under the ʿAbbāsids that Muʿtazilite anarchism appeared, it was both shortlived and confined to small circles. Umayyad legitimism persisted in Syria, but even that came to be cast in a Shīʿite idiom, and the many demands for *shūrā* with which the Umayyads had been confronted came an abrupt end: the ruler had to be a member of the *ahl al-bayt*; other Qurashīs had ceased to matter as candidates. The Sunnis stuck to the formulation that the caliphate belonged to Quraysh because they had enshrined it in Ḥadīth and needed it to preserve the legitimacy of the first three caliphs, not because they wished to keep Zubayrids or other Qurashīs in

37. The Umayyads tended to assign the leadership of the pilgrimage to a member of their own family, but the early ʿAbbāsids invariably did so, with the sole exception of al-Maʾmūn who briefly appointed an ʿAlid; and some ʿAbbāsid caliphs led the pilgrimage in person time and again (cf. the annual entries in Khalīfa b. Khayyāṭ, *Taʾrīkh*, or the list in MM, ix, 54ff. (v, §§3630ff.), with the ʿAlid in years 204, 205).

38. What follows is based on Crone, '*Shūrā* as an Elective Institution', sec. vi.

reserve as candidates. In practice there could not be any question of replacing Hāshimites with Qurashīs more distantly related to the Prophet, only with Hāshimites more closely related to him. To the vast majority of Muslims, in short, the alternative to ʿAbbāsids was ʿAlids.

CHAPTER

9

THE ZAYDĪS

The ʿAbbāsids forced the Shīʿites to put their own house in order. The imamate had been restored to the Prophet's house, the new caliphs said, but what if one disagreed? A clear alternative to the *shīʿat banī 'l-ʿAbbās* was needed, and the Zaydīs were the first to develop it.

The Zaydīs were named after Zayd b. ʿAlī (d. 740), a great grandson of ʿAlī who mounted an unsuccessful revolt against the Umayyads in Kufa in 740.[1] For the first hundred years or so after Zayd's death, and to some extent even thereafter, the Zaydīs should be envisaged as a multiplicity of small circles formed around teachers whose doctrines were sufficiently similar on certain points to constitute a trend, not as a party defined by a single set of shared beliefs. In the broadest possible sense, the term 'Zaydīs' may have included soft Shīʿites, that is people who accepted ʿAlī rather than ʿUthmān as caliph in the past without deeming the Hāshimites to have an exclusive right to the caliphate thereafter (though they might well have a preference for them).[2] Such people were rapidly being absorbed into the great majority, however, be it thanks to what one might call the ʿAbbāsid version of Zaydism[3] or to the attractions of the four-caliphs thesis. Zaydīs are usually envisaged as Shīʿites of a somewhat harder variety.

As such they had in common the fact that they vested the caliphate after ʿAlī's death in the Ṭālibid branch of the Hāshimites to which ʿAlī belonged (see chart 3), but that still left room for a variety of stances. For example, there were

1. Cf. *EI*[1], s.v.

2. This is probably the sense in which Ibn Isḥāq held most *muḥaddithūn* to have been Zaydīs (Ibn al-Nadīm, *Fihrist*, 227.10; cf. 226.-4). Compare also below, notes 20–4.

3. Cf. above, 93f.

some who accepted the entitlement of all Ṭālibids, not just ʿAlī's own descendants, and others who limited the candidates to ʿAlī's descendants by Fāṭima, – the Ḥasanids and Ḥusaynids.[4] All Zaydīs in the classical sense were of the latter variety, but they still did not have a unified stance. Of the several groups known to have emerged in the eighth century, the two most important ones were the Batrīs (or Butrīs) and Jārūdīs, of which the former were 'weak' Zaydīs, the latter 'strong,' as the Imāmīs were to put it, meaning that the former accepted Abū Bakr and ʿUmar as legitimate caliphs whereas the latter were Rāfiḍīs.

Until the emergence of Imami Shīʿism (on which below, ch. 10), it would seems that the word Zaydī was applied by preference to weak Zaydīs (in addition to the soft Shīʿites mentioned above). Thus Abū Mikhnaf excluded the Jārūdīs from the ranks of Zayd's followers in his account of Zayd's revolt on the grounds that they rejected Abū Bakr and ʿUmar: in his view, such Rāfiḍīs belonged with the Shīʿites who came to be known as Imamis. He was being tendentious, but al-Jāḥiẓ (d. 868f.), who had no axe to grind, similarly held Shīʿites to be either Zaydīs or Rāfiḍīs. He characterized the former as those who would accept an inferior person (such as Abū Bakr or ʿUmar) as caliph, that is they were what we would call Batrī Zaydīs (or even soft Shiʿites), and he implicitly identified the Rāfiḍīs with the Imamis.[5] Apparently, a Rāfiḍī Zaydī was a contradiction in terms to him. Yet that is precisely what the Jārūdīs were. Presumably it is because the Jārūdīs were activists that they ended up by merging with the Zaydīs rather than the Imamis (who were quietists, as will be seen). They must in fact done so already by al-Jāḥiẓ' time, for classical Zaydism is generally held to have emerged with al-Qāsim b. Ibrāhīm (d. 246/860), a prolific writer who was a Jārūdī even though he was not much of an activist.[6] Since Batrī Zaydīs, like their even softer peers, were susceptible to the attractions of the *jamāʿī* fold, later Zaydism was largely, but not wholly, Jārūdī in nature.

4. For the former, known as the Ṭālibiyya, see Madelung, *Qāsim*, 47n. One would assume Abū 'l-Faraj al-Iṣbahānī (d. 356/967), author of *Maqātil al-Ṭālibiyyīn*, to have been a Zaydī of this variety.

5. For Abū Mikhnaf, see below, 117f. (he has the Rāfiḍīs opt for Jaʿfar al-Ṣādiq as imam). For Jāḥiẓ, see his 'Istiḥqāq al-imāma' in his *Rasāʾil*, iv, 207.5, 210ff.

6. Madelung, *Qāsim*, 144f. Abrahamov strangely denies his Jārūdism ('Ḳāsim,' 92ff.), though his own account leads to the same conclusion (cf. 89f.). Note that the Zaydīs include both Jārūdīs and Batrīs in Ps.-Nāshiʾ (§§64–8), probably the work of the Muʿtazilite Jaʿfar b. Ḥarb (d. 236/850), as proposed by Madelung, 'Frühe muʿtazilitische Häresiographie?'

The first caliphs

As regards the past, both the Jārūdīs and the Batrīs said that ʿAlī had been the most meritorious man (*al-afḍal*) in his time, meaning that he ought to have been the caliph from the start. The Jārūdīs duly declared Abū Bakr and ʿUmar to have been usurpers (and ʿUthmān too, of course, but that went without saying). By the third/ninth-century they even claimed that the Prophet had implicitly designated ʿAlī as his successor.[7] By contrast, the Batrīs adopted the newfangled idea to the effect that it was lawful to recognize a less meritorious man (*al-mafḍūl*) as caliph when there were good reasons to do so. Abū Bakr and ʿUmar had in their view been legitimate imams even though they were inferior to ʿAlī. The Prophet had not designated a successor, implicitly or otherwise; so the community had not gone astray, let alone turned infidel, by electing the first two caliphs. Some Batrīs dissociated from ʿUthmān, or even declared him an infidel, with reference to the last years of his reign, others suspended judgement on him.[8] Both the Rāfiḍī and the non-Rāfiḍī views are represented in later Zaydism.[9]

Singling out the imam

As regards the present, both parties said that after ʿAlī's death the imamate was reserved for his offspring by Fāṭima. According to the Jārūdīs, the Prophet had designated ʿAlī, who designated al-Ḥasan, who designated al-Ḥusayn, or alternatively the Prophet had designated all three, but thereafter designation came to an end. As for the procedures thereafter, the Jārūdīs would seem originally to have held that the candidate had to be chosen by *shūrā* within the family and that he had to activate his rights by rebelling: this was how Muḥammad al-Nafs al-Zakiyyya had emerged as the imam.[10] But they soon dropped the

7. The Prophet had designated him *bi'l-waṣf* or by a *naṣṣ khafī* rather than *jalī* (cf. Madelung, *Qāsim*, 45; van Ess, *TG*, i, 257f.; Daou, 'Conception', 79n.).

8. Nawbakhtī, *Firaq*, 9; Ps.-Nāshiʾ, §68; Ashʿarī, 69, cf. 68 and Kaʿbī in ʿAbd al-Jabbār, *Mughnī*, xx/2, 184 on the followers of Sulaymān b. Jarīr al-Raqqī, a Batrī to all intents and purposes, even though he is credited with a school of his own (Madelung, *Qāsim*, 61ff.).

9. Cf. Kohlberg, 'Some Zaydī Views on the Companions', 92ff.; Haykel, 'Order and Righteousness,' 185ff.

10. Cf. above, 79. I take this to lie behind the odd formulation in Nawbakhtī, *Firaq*, 19: "henceforth it was *shūrā* among their offspring, so whoever among them rebelled and was qualified for the imamate, he would be the imam" (similarly Ashʿarī, 67; Nashwān, *Ḥūr al-ʿīn*, 155). All Zaydīs recognized al-Nafs al-Zakiyya as a legitimate imam.

requirement of family agreement, presumably because there were too many Ḥasanids and Ḥusaynids for them to come together in a *shūrā*, so their classical position was that any learned and meritorious descendant of al-Ḥasan or al-Ḥusayn who rebelled thereby became caliph.[11] Either way, the community had no say in the matter.[12] The Batrīs denied that ʿAlī had been designated. Some accounts have them declare that the first caliphs were elected by *shūrā*, meaning by the community,[13] but with the exception of Sulaymān b. Jarīr al-Raqqī, they did not actually think that the community had anything to do with it either: according to them, too, any qualified candidate who rebelled thereby became imam.[14] This was also how the later Zaydīs saw it: any Ḥasanid or Ḥusaynid endowed with legal learning, piety, courage, and political ability who called for allegiance to himself with a view to taking over government thereby became the imam.[15] The view that he had to be more learned, pious, and generally meritorious than everyone else persisted: were anyone other than the most virtuous (*al-afḍal*) to seize power, Zaydī government would become mere kingship. But it was not unanimously accepted.[16]

There was however an interesting slant to the Jārudī position on the imam's learning and to the Batrī position on his descent. As regards the imam's learning, Abū 'l-Jārūd, the founding father of Jārūdism, is said to have argued that Ḥasanids and Ḥusaynids were so numerous that it would be impossible to establish which one of them was the most meritorious at any given time. Hence they must all be equally meritorious. Babies or old men, all had complete knowledge of the religious precepts brought by the Prophet, and all had the same virtues once they were grown; for this reason any one of them who rebelled became the imam.[17] Among the later Zaydīs this doctrine appears to have been completely forgotten. Not even the Prophet had been born with learning, they would point out in polemics against Imāmīs.[18]

11. Heresiographers such as Ps.-Nāshiʾ (§66) and Abū Tammām (94 = 90) duly omit the reference to *shūrā*.

12. Al-Hādī ilā 'l-Ḥaqq, *Aḥkām*, i, 462; cf. Qāsim b. Ibrāhīm's polemics against *ikhtiyār* (Madelung, *Qāsim*, 142; Abrahamov, 'Ḳāsim', 89ff.).

13. Thus Shāh Sarījān and al-Ḥajūrī in Madelung, *Qāsim*, 60.

14. Nawbakhtī, *Firaq*, 51; Abū Tammām, *Heresiography*, 93 = 89. Sulaymān b. Jarīr (cf. above, note 8) said that the imam was elected by *shūrā* and that two men sufficed for the election (Ashʿarī, 68; Kaʿbī in ʿAbd al-Jabbār, *Mughnī*, xx/2, 184).

15. E.g. ʿAlawī, *Sīrat al-Hādī*, 27; Strothmann, *Staatsrecht*, 104f.

16. Strothmann, *Staatsrecht*, 62, 71f. and 71, note 2, with al-Qāsim, al-Uṭrūsh, and the sect known as the Muṭarrifiyya in favour of *al-afḍal*.

17. Ps.-Nāshiʾ, §67; Nawbakhtī, *Firaq*, 49f.

18. Strothmann, *Staatsrecht*, 68.

As regards the Batrī doctrine on descent, it was impossible to accept Abū Bakr and ʿUmar as legitimate caliphs without granting that non-ʿAlids were, or had once been, eligible for the imamate, if only as inferior candidates (sing. *al-mafḍūl*). Some said that their eligibility had come to an end,[19] but al-Ḥasan b. Ṣāliḥ b. Ḥayy (d. 167/784), a founding father of Batrism, is reported to have acknowledged all Qurashīs as candidates,[20] or even all Qurashīs and non-Qurashīs alike,[21] though he had a preference for Fāṭima's offspring.[22] A grandson of Zayd b. ʿAlī by the name of Aḥmad b. ʿĪsā agreed that a person of manifest righteousness would be eligible even if he did not descend from al-Ḥasan or al-Ḥusayn, without specifying whether he had to be a Qurashī or not;[23] and al-Jāḥiẓ claims that some Zaydīs rejected the genealogical principle altogether, crediting ʿAlī with superior merit regardless of his kinship with the Prophet, which makes it difficult to see how they could justify a continued preference for ʿAlids as imams (if indeed they had one).[24] Perhaps they held, like the Caspian imam Abū Ṭālib al-Nāṭiq (d. c. 1033), that if the imam had been designated, descent was not a consideration whereas under other circumstances he must be a descendant of al-Ḥasan or al-Ḥusayn.[25] It is at all events unclear why this doctrine should have mattered so much. In seventeenth-century Yemen, too, there were Zaydīs who claimed that the imam could be of any origin. The Khārijite connotations of their statements notwithstanding, they were harbingers of Sunnification, and what they actually meant was probably that the imam could be any Qurashī; they simply could not say this because to the locals 'Qurashīs' conjured up 'Umayyads' (i.e. enemies of God).[26] But the earlier statements

19. Thus Sulaymān b. Jarīr (Ps.-Nāshiʾ, §69).

20. Ibn Ḥazm, *Faṣl*, iv, 92f., citing a book by Hishām b. al-Ḥakam and noting that al-Ḥasan b. Ḥayy cites Muʿāwiya and Ibn al-Zubayr as authorities.

21. MM, vi, 24f. (iv, §2257); cf. van Ess, *TG*, i, 250, who rejects it.

22. He wrote a book called *K. imāmat wuld ʿAlī min Fāṭima* (Ibn al-Nadīm, *Fihrist*, 227).

23. Madelung, *Qāsim*, 52.

24. 'Maqālat al-zaydiyya wa'l-rāfiḍa' in his *Rasāʾil*, iv, 311ff. (ʿAli was superior in terms of time of conversion, abstention from worldly things, religious insight and readiness to fight in defence of Islam, these being the only criteria of merit), 317 (they do not consider *qarāba* or *ḥasab* a source of entitlement to the imamate and are only one among several Zaydī schools). As noted by Nagel (*Rechtleitung und Kalifat*, 393, 396), their argument is similar to that of Bishr b. al-Muʿtamir, the founder of the Baghdadi school of Muʿtazilites and a well-known Zaydī.

25. Strothmann, *Staatsrecht*, 104 (line 5 of the Arabic section).

26. Haykel, 'Order and Righteousness', 42, on Aḥmad b. al-Ḥasan al-Jalāl (d. 1084/1673); cf. 223ff. on the Umayyad connotations and in general on Sunnification; add Maqbalī (d. 1108/1696) in Crone, 'Ethiopian Slave', 64.

must have had a different import, which cannot be established without knowledge of their context, currently unknown.

The nature of the imamate

Both the Jārudīs and the Batrīs saw the imam as a religious guide. According to Abū 'l-Jārūd, the law (*al-ḥalāl wa'l-ḥarām*) was what the Prophet's family declared it to be. The Prophet's family knew everything the Prophet had brought; indeed, whoever became an imam would apparently know more than the Prophet, for as new problems arose the imam would receive the solution to them by *ilhām*, divine inspiration. The community by implication knew nothing except insofar as they had it from the Prophet's descendants: ordinary people relied exclusively on Ḥadīth from them. This was a typically Rāfiḍī view. The Batrīs by contrast said that religious knowledge was dispersed in the community: the Companions had not gone astray; they had passed on the Prophet's teaching to the Muslims at large, and both ordinary people and the ʿAlids had a share in it; one could learn from both. The Batrīs would transmit Ḥadith from authorities other than the Prophet's family, and where no precepts were known to exist, they would rely on *ijtihād* and *ra'y*, independent reasoning and sensible opinion.[27] It was on the whole the Jārūdī view that won out in later Zaydī doctrine, though there is no trace of *ilhām* in it. All learning was acquired from books, by hard work; and as the books piled up, the imam's freedom of decision was limited by the consensus of his forebears. But he was still the most learned descendant of the Prophet at the time, or at least he was learned enough to count as a *mujtahid*; and unlike the ʿAbbāsid caliph and *jamāʿī* scholars, he presided over a legal system devised by members of the Holy Family.[28]

Learning did not suffice to make a *khalīfat allāh*, however.[29] He needed political power too. The vast majority of Zaydīs agreed that nobody could be recognized as imam without making a *daʿwa* and *khurūj*, summoning people to allegiance and marching out to fight.[30] One was not obliged to obey a man who merely sat at home, neither commanding nor forbidding, as the Zaydīs liked telling the Imāmīs; such a man was just an authority on legal matters (*imām al-ḥalāl wa'l-ḥarām*). One recognized the imam by the fact that he

27. Ps.-Nāshi', §67; Nawbakhtī, *Firaq*, 50; cf. Madelung, *Qāsim*, 48ff.

28. Strothmann, *Staatsrecht*, 68ff.

29. The Zaydīs accepted the title, cf. al-Hādī ilā 'l-Ḥaqq, *Aḥkām*, i, 462.3; Ibn al-Wazīr, *Hidāyat al-afkār*, fol. 217b (unknown to Crone and Hinds, *God's Caliph*, 18 and note 63 thereto; I owe both references to Michael Cook).

30. Cf. Shāh-Sarījān and Jushamī in Madelung, *Qāsim*, 144, 188f.

commanded good and prohibited evil, an expression almost synonymous with the forcible establishment of righteous government in Zaydī usage: the rebel who died at Fakhkh in 786 was said to have died commanding good and prohibiting evil; any offspring of the Prophet's who commanded good and prohibited evil was God's caliph on earth; if an imam claimed not to have been ordered to wage holy war, apply the *ḥudūd*, resist the oppressors and command good, what *had* he been ordered to do?, as a thirteenth-century Yemeni imam rhetorically asked.[31] In short, there could be no such thing as an imam who did not engage in government.

The Zaydīs thus did not have a continuous line of imams from the Prophet to their own time. More often than not, they had to live their entire lives under illegitimate rule. This was possible as long as they recognized that loyalty (*walāya*) to the imam, should he appear, was a fundamental duty. The imamate was a fundamental principle of the religion (*aṣl al-dīn*) on a par with the unity of God; without the imamate the religion would turn into Jāhiliyya again. But what this meant was that Islam would disappear if the institution did not exist as a moral obligation, not that all Muslims would die a pagan death for lack of allegiance to an imam in their own time. The law remained valid even under illegitimate government.[32]

Other developments

In 864 the Ḥasanid al-Ḥasan b. Zayd succeded in establishing a Zaydī statelet in Ṭabaristān. Neither he nor his brother and successor seems to have claimed the imamate, except perhaps in the limited sense of imams 'who call for the imam eliciting consent (*al-imām al-riḍā*).'[33] The title of imam was however adopted by al-Ḥasan al-Uṭrūsh (d. 917), who established himself among the Daylamīs and the Gīlīs on the Caspian coast, adopting the regnal name of al-Nāṣir li'l-Ḥaqq. There continued to be a Zaydī imamate in the area down to 1126, with imams appearing sporadically thereafter. Another imamate was established in Yemen in 897 by Yaḥyā, known as al-Hādī ilā 'l-Ḥaqq (d. 911), to continue, on and off, down to 1962. (The Caspian Zaydīs survived down to the

31. Cook, *Commanding Right*, 232ff. and note 39; al-Qāsim b. Ibrāhīm (who was however more interested in the imam as an authority on law and doctrine than as a ruler) in Madelung, *Qāsim*, 143 (cf. 150); Ps.-Nāshi', §66, on the Jārūdīs; Nawbakhtī, *Firaq*, 51, on the Batrīs.

32. Strothmann, *Staatsrecht*, 90ff.; Madelung, *Qāsim*, 142; Abrahamov, 'Ḳāsim', 88; Zayd (attrib.), *Majmū'*, 236 (no. 853), cited in Cook, *Commanding Right*, 228.

33. Cf. Madelung, *Qāsim*, 154f.

sixteenth century, when they accepted Imami Shīʿism at the hands of the Safavids; the Yemeni highlanders are still Zaydīs today.)

The foundation of these states did not generate more orderly rules of succession, for they were not really states, though one has to call them that for purposes of shorthand; rather, they were areas in which the Zaydī rules of the game were generally acknowledged. The acknowledgement of the rules meant that imams kept appearing, but no attempt was made to develop a governmental apparatus which had to be passed on from one to the next. Some imams were followed by sons or brothers, but each imam occupied a position that began and ended with himself.[34] A Zaydī state in the proper sense of the word only developed under the Qāsimī imams of Yemen (1598–1851), under whom dynastic succession made its appearance too; but the more these imams came to resemble traditional Muslim rulers, the more they distanced themselves from their Zaydī heritage, to rely on Sunnified scholars, and it was in Sunni terms that their dynastic succession came to be justified.[35]

The establishment of the Caspian and Yemeni imamates did however mean that the Zaydīs, like the Khārijites, passed from the problem of having no imam to that of having two. It was impossible for the two 'states' to ignore each other. There was much interaction between them; they even recognized the same imam on two occasions.[36] But though there could be several imams in the restricted sense of callers to *al-riḍā* (or *muḥtasib* imams, as the later Zaydīs called righteous rulers who fell short of the full imamate),[37] there could only be one imam in the sense of the most meritorious (*al-afḍal*), for one claimant would invariably know more than the other, the ninth-century al-Qāsim b. Ibrāhīm had explained; and even if one denied that the imam had to be the most meritorious, ʿUmar had said that two swords could not fit into a single scabbard.[38] There was much acrimonious discussion of who was, or had been, the imam at a particular time. But the Yemeni al-Manṣūr bi'llāh (d. 1003) squarely acknowledged that two imams could coexist, even in the same land as long as they were not actually in the same town.[39]

Their activism notwithstanding, the Zaydīs were not immune to messianic dreams. There were Jārūdīs in Kufa, Khurasan, the Caspian coast and perhaps

34. Cf. Strothmann, *Staatsrecht*, 52ff.

35. For all this, see Haykel, 'Order and Righteousness'.

36. They were united under the Daylami imam Abū Ṭālib al-akhīr (d. 520/1126) and the Yemeni imam ʿAbdallāh b. Ḥamza al-Manṣūr (d. 614/1217) (Madelung, *Qāsim*, 209f., 216).

37. Strothmann, *Staatsrecht*, 94ff. The term was eventually adopted by the Ibāḍīs too (cf. Wilkinson, *Imamate Tradition*, 161f.).

38. Madelung, *Qāsim*, 143f.; Abrahamov, 'Ḳāsim', 90n.; Strothmann, *Staatsrecht*, 98ff.

39. Madelung, *Qāsim*, 196. Compare Shahrastānī, *Milal*, 115 (echoed in Ījī, *Mawāqif*, viii, 353.-6).

elsewhere who cast their martyrs as saviour figures destined to come back to fill the earth with justice.[40] A Yemeni imam by the name of al-Ḥusayn al-ʿAyyānī, who took the regnal name of al-Mahdī li-dīn allāh (d. 1013), was also believed to be the Mahdi who would fill the earth with justice. When he died, his brother and successor refrained from adopting the title of imam because he expected the Mahdi to come back, and the Yemenis who shared his view formed a sect known as the Ḥusayniyya which survived into the fourteenth century.[41] But to the vast majority of Zaydīs, the imam could no more be absent than he could sit quietly at home. A fourteenth-century scholar debited the very idea of an absent imam to al-Maʾmūn, who had supposedly invented it to keep the living members of the Prophet's family inactive.[42]

The Zaydī vision

Zaydism may be described as the Shīʿite answer to Khārijism in that it was activist and retained the imam in his archaic role of multi-purpose leader, so that it worked best in tribal environments. Differently put, it was how political participation and autonomy could be preserved on the premise that the ruler had to be of the *ahl al-bayt*. In the Zaydī view there was no reason to submit to wrongful government in order to keep the community together, as the *ahl al-sunna wa'l-jamāʿa* said,[43] for knowledge of right and wrong was not to be found in the community, or at any rate not in the community to the exclusion of the Prophet's family; nor did one have to abstain from action in order to protect the imam from danger, as the Imamis said, for the Prophet's family was large and potential imams were not in short supply. It was the insistence that the greatest religious authority must be head of state which kept the Zaydīs distinct. Without it, the Batrīs turned into Sunnis, the Jārūdīs into Imamis.

Unlike the Khārijites, the Zaydīs made no attempt to belittle the imam in relation to the community. The Zaydī imam is distinguished from the believers he rules by his special descent. He has Prophetic blood in his vein and this is a difference of kind, not of degree. In the early Jārūdī vision his learning is also of a different kind, all members of the Prophet's family being born with it, and though this idea was abandoned, holy descent and holy knowledge continued to go together. The *sayyids*, as the descendants of the Prophet came to be known in Yemen, were religious specialists and government servants, being

40. MM, vii, 117 (iv, §2800); Ashʿarī, 67.

41. Madelung, *Qāsim*, 199ff. (I have followed his vocalization of the *nisba*, sometimes differently given).

42. Strothmann, *Staatsrecht*, 63f.

43. Cf. below, 135f.

genealogically predestined for literacy; the tribesmen (*qabīlī*s) were mostly illiterate agriculturalists and warriors who relied on the *sayyid*s for instruction, mediation, spells and such other religious services as they might require, though the tribes did produce learned men too.

Khārijism located religious authority within the tribes and formally empowered the scholars to elect and depose its bearer, whereas Zaydism located it outside the tribes and lacked formal rules regarding election and deposition: the imam manifested himself; the scholars' oath of allegiance was declarative rather than constitutive of his imamate. If he could not make himself obeyed, he was not the imam: he was free to abdicate, and he could also be defeated, but he could not otherwise be deposed.[44] Whether there is a structural reason for the victory of the one in Oman, the other in Yemen is unknown. It was certainly associated with different behavior. Zaydī imams took their learning far more seriously than their Ibāḍī counterparts. A fair number of ʿAlid rulers in the Caspian refrained from adopting the title of imam for lack of the requisite learning. A twelfth-century Yemeni claimed it in a limited sense because he only knew a third of the Qurʾān by heart. One Caspian candidate whose learning was found to be defective was given a crash course before he received allegiance.[45] There is no parallel to this in Ibāḍī Oman or North Africa. Many Zaydī imams were outstanding scholars, Ibāḍī imams rarely were: they simply relied on the scholars, much as the Yemeni imams were to do after the Sunnification of their regime.[46]

On the other hand, the Ibāḍīs would split over the election and deposition of imams in a manner unknown to the Zaydīs. The election of the Rustumid imam ʿAbd al-Wahhāb in North Africa in 171/788 was contested by the Nukkār, who dissociated from him and split off as a sect of their own. The deposition in 886 of the imam al-Ṣalt b. Mālik on grounds of senility split the Ibāḍīs of Oman into two hostile parties, forcing everyone to dissociate from either the deposed imam or his successor, though it miraculously stopped short of producing rival sects.[47] In principle the Zaydī imams could have generated comparable splits, for obedience to them was also conditional on their being right. "If we fulfil our obligations to you, you must fulfil yours to us; if we don't, you owe us no allegiance," the rebel at Fakhkh declared after outlining his programme in 786. "If I contravene what is in it (the Qurʾān) by so much as a single letter, you have no duty to obey me; rather, it is your duty to fight

44. Strothmann, *Staatsrecht*, 61, 63.
45. Madelung, *Arabic Texts*, 322 and *Qāsim*, 210.
46. For the Sunnified pattern, see Haykel, 'Order and Righteousness', 75, 78ff.
47. Cf. Wilkinson, *Imamate Tradition*, 166ff., 175f., et passim.

me," al-Hādī said in his *daʿwa* about a century later.[48] But of Zaydī tribesmen turning against their imam to depose or dissociate from him there does not appear to be any example (though there certainly are of imams abdicating). Descendants of noted imams often refused to recognize the *daʿwa* of more successful claimants, establishing petty dynasties of their own, and the political history of Zaydī Yemen is dominated by struggles between rival contenders.[49] But no doctrinal parties ensued from them. All claimants seem merely to have waxed and waned in accordance with their popular support, and such sects as appeared in Zaydī Yemen had nothing to do with the rights and wrongs of the contenders for power.

The Zaydīs held on for longer than the Khārijites in the Muslim heartlands. Like so many other residual groups, they were probably swept away by the Mongols. But Zaydism was no better suited as a political programme for the heartlands than its Khārijite counterpart. Its conception of the imam's office was too personal, its mode of succession too disorderly, and its activism too impracticable once an imperial state apparatus had developed. Even without these apparent defects the Zaydī imam was a poor alternative to the Umayyads and ʿAbbāsids as far as the problem of tyranny was concerned: he claimed the same political and religious competence as the former and buttressed it with descent more sacred than that possessed by the latter. Had a Zaydī imam succeeded in conquering the entire Muslim world, he would have proved no easier to bear than al-Maʾmūn (who practically was one). As a political doctrine, Zaydism owed its protracted appeal in the heartlands to the widespread belief in the hereditary nature of righteousness. The ʿAbbāsids enthroned by the Hāshimite revolution had proved no better than the Umayyads, but then they were not ʿAlids, and one could still hope that an ʿAlid would be different. The hope eventually faded. The unpalatable truth was that the price of civilization was submission to tyrants. The alternative was tribalism, with or without religious beautification.

48. Abū 'l-Faraj, *Maqātil*, 450.4; van Arendonk, *Débuts*, 123n.
49. Cf. Haykel, 'Order and Righteousness', 24f., 79.

CHAPTER

10

THE IMAMIS

Like Zaydism, Imamism crystallized in the course of the eighth and ninth centuries, but it only acquired its classical form of Twelver Shīʿism in the tenth and early eleventh. (It could to that extent have been covered in part III of this book rather than here.) Unlike Zaydism, it was not a doctrine for export to the tribal world. It developed in Kufa, Qumm and Baghdad, and to a lesser extent in Medina, where its imams resided until 848, and it reflected the spiritual needs of townsmen who had come to terms with their own exclusion from politics; indeed, it could almost be defined as de-politicized Shīʿism. All in all, it differed from Zaydism in four major ways.

First, it was uniformly Rāfiḍī. All Imamis believed ʿAlī to be the Prophet's legatee (*waṣī*), claiming that the Prophet had publicly designated him as his successor and branding the first three caliphs as usurpers. They would routinely vilify these caliphs (especially the first two) as well as the many Companions who had followed them, branding all of them as infidels or hypocrites.[1] Secondly, where the Zaydīs held all ʿAlī's offspring by Fāṭima to be eligible for the imamate, the Imamis narrowed down the candidates to a single line of Ḥusaynids within which the office was passed down by bequest (*waṣiyya*), also known as designation (*naṣṣ*), from father to son, except that al-Ḥasan had been succeeded by his brother al-Ḥusayn. Thirdly, their imam was an apolitical figure. He owed his position to designation, not to revolt, and his imamate was not invalidated by political impotence. All the imams ought to have been caliphs and Commanders of the Believers, but only ʿAlī had actually

1. Cf. Kohlberg, 'Some Imāmī Shīʿī Views on the *Ṣaḥāba*'.

held this position (for which reason he is always known as *amīr al-muʾminīn*, Commander of the Faithful, in Imami sources); al-Ḥasan and al-Ḥusayn had enjoyed some political importance too, but all the remaining imams were mere imams of *al-ḥalāl wa'l-ḥarām*, as the Zaydīs contemptuously put it, mere authorities on right and wrong. Fourthly, the religious role of the imam was far greater in Imamism than in Zaydism. As the Imamis saw it, humans would be doomed without a spiritual guide, but God had not left them in the lurch, for the world was not, and never would be, without an imam: even if there were only two people on earth, one of them would be the imam.[2] Unlike his Zaydī counterpart, the imam was divinely protected against error (*maʿṣūm*) and thus an infallible guide to Islamic law and doctrine. Indeed, to many he was the key to the secret meaning of things, the pillar of the universe, and the axis of the creation. But for the Prophet and his family, God would not have created either the heavens or the earth, Paradise or Hell, Adam or Eve, the angels or anything else, it was said.[3] Recognition of the imams was a prerequisite for salvation according to all. The imams were gates to God; they were like Noah's Ark: whoever boarded was saved, whoever did not was drowned.[4]

The formation of Imamism

The history of Imamism as a separate branch of Shīʿism is generally assumed to start with Muḥammad al-Bāqir (d. c. 735) and Jaʿfar al-Ṣādiq (d. 765), whom the Imamis count as their fifth and sixth imams respectively and who generally figure as such in the secondary literature too. But though there cannot be much doubt that both men played a major role in the development of Shīʿism,[5] it only seems to have been after Jaʿfar al-Ṣādiq's death that one can speak of the Imamis as a separate sect. Both men were celebrated scholars. Being ʿAlids, they were regarded by most Muslims as particularly qualified to transmit Prophetic Ḥadīth, and by most Shīʿites as potential candidates for the caliphate, but this did not make them different from other members of the Prophet's family who took to scholarship. The Imamis, however, postulated that both had been imams in actual fact, for all that neither had enjoyed political power or even tried to obtain it. Both had been what one might call imams in exile: imams without a political role, but still with political rights. What is more, the Imamis said, there had been an unbroken succession of such imams in exile from the Prophet's death until their own time (except that one of them,

2. E.g. Nawbakhtī, *Firaq*, 90.
3. Ibn Bābawayh, *Iʿtiqād*, 138 = 95 (ch. 35).
4. Ibid., 139 = 96 (ch. 35).
5. Hodgson, 'How did the Early Shiʿa become Sectarian?'.

ʿAlī, had become the imam in power after waiting for twenty-four years). It was this concept of a single line of hereditary imams, whether in exile or in power, that marked off the Imamis from other Shīʿites. Precisely how and when it appeared is still uncertain, but a preliminary sketch may be attempted.

Saviour-scholars

In the mid-eighth century the idea of apolitical imams was current only among the Ghulāt, to whom 'imam', 'prophet', 'mahdi', 'god', and the like were so many terms for the same thing, as has been seen. The Ghulāt were carriers of a wide range of ideas, mostly Gnostic, but shading off into Jewish and Christian esotericism on the one hand and pagan ideas of cosmic kingship on the other, and all operated with a superhuman saviour figure. It seems to be this figure which lives on in the Imami imam, fused with a scholarly model.[6] According to the Imamis, the imam is the bearer of saving knowledge, and all those who do not recognize him will perish; but what the imam knows is the Qurʾān and Ḥadīth, two sources available to everyone. The two propositions are not so contradictory as they seem at first sight, for the Imamis did not think that the Qurʾān and Ḥadīth were really available to everyone: their true wording had been lost and/or their true interpretation was not something that ordinary humans could work out for themselves; this was why the imams were indispensable. But even so, the tension between the two propositions was (and has remained) considerable. To some Imamis, the imams were simply 'righteous and pious scholars' (*ʿulamāʾ abrār atqiyāʾ*), who differed from ordinary scholars only in that they had perfect mastery of Muḥammad's legacy and were divinely protected against error (*maʿṣūm*).[7] Even that was sometimes denied,[8] making it difficult to see what distinguished them from the scholars that Sunnis would call imams. Most Imamis understandably wanted the imams' knowledge to be commensurate with the central role ascribed to them and so endowed them with supernatural knowledge of all kinds, such as knowledge of the future and of all languages, including those of animals, claiming that they had books in which everything was written down, that angels talked to them, and so on. Some credited them with understanding of the esoteric meaning of the Prophet's teaching and cast its hidden message as the real key to salvation. There was always a tendency to veer into *ghuluww*.

6. Cf. above, 81. The material in Amir-Moezzi, *Divine Guide in Early Shiʿism*, is more reminiscent of cosmic kingship ideas than of Gnosticism.

7. Thus Hishām b. al-Ḥakam, al-Faḍl b. Shādhān, and other *mutakallims* (Daou, 'Conception', chs 1–5), including Ibn Qiba (Modarressi, *Crisis*, 124, cf. 30 for the phrase).

8. Modaressi, *Crisis*, 42.

The Imami leadership consistently opposed attempts to credit the imams with prophetic or divine status, but that apart, their views on the nature of the imams' knowledge have remained divided to this day.[9]

It was probably thanks to the input from the Ghulāt that there could be such a thing as an apolitical imam, for to everyone else an imam who neither ruled nor claimed a saving role was just a great scholar, like the founders of Sunni legal schools. One would assume the reception of this input to have been effected between c. 730 and 800, for it was in that period that extremists were casting Muḥammad al-Bāqir and Jaʿfar al-Ṣādiq (and al-Manṣūr) as imams, prophets, mahdis, and manifestations of the divine, for all that their objects of veneration seem to have regarded themselves as straightforward scholars, not as saviours of any kind. That the two ʿAlids saw themselves as ordinary scholars is not a view commonly found in the modern literature, but there is much to commend it. According to the Sunnis, both al-Bāqir and al-Ṣādiq had *jamāʿī* (in later terminology, Sunni) pupils, who included luminaries such as al-Awzāʿī, Abū Ḥanīfa, Sufyān al-Thawrī, Shuʿba b. al-Ḥajjāj, Mālik and Ibn Jurayj.[10] This suggests that the teachers were differently perceived by their *jamāʿī* and their Rāfiḍī pupils: the former regarded them simply as distinguished jurists and transmitters; the latter saw them as the sole transmitters of the Prophet's legacy or as imams, mahdis, prophets or divine incarnations, in any case the only source of religious guidance in their time.[11] But this in its turn presupposes that the teacher had not committed himself to a sectarian view of his own position, for if he had seen himself as the sole source of religious guidance (not to mention as divine), he would have been known to his followers as the leader of a sect which regarded all *jamāʿī* Muslims as doomed to perdition. This was hardly something that he could have kept secret from his other pupils, and it defies belief that *jamāʿī* Muslims should have sought religious instruction from such a man.

Sunnī dictionaries of traditionists routinely include entries on Muḥammad al-Bāqir and Jaʿfar al-Ṣādiq, predictably claiming that both of them disowned *rafḍ* and soberly listing the Companions and Successors from whom they (especially al-Bāqir) transmitted Ḥadīth, implying that neither of them saw the Prophet's family as the sole transmitters of the Prophet's legacy.[12] How much truth there is to this is impossible to say. What one can say is that the case is

9. Ibid., 50f.

10. Ibn Ḥajar, *Tahdhīb*, ii, 103; ix, 350; cf. Lalani, *al-Bāqir*, 101f., with more names.

11. Cf. Modarressi, *Crisis*, 29f.

12. Ibn Ḥajar, *Tahdhīb*, ii, 103; ix, 350f. Bāqir is presented as a Medinese jurist like any other, while opinions are divided over the permissibility of adducing Jaʿfar's traditions. Mūsā al-Kāẓim and ʿAlī al-Riḍā are more marginal.

similar to that of Jābir b. Zayd (d. c. 720), whom the Ibāḍīs claim as their founder while the Sunnis list him as one of theirs, claiming that he disowned Ibāḍism. It is only of Jābir's successors that we can say with some certainty that they were leaders of a sect of their own.[13] The disagreement over al-Bāqir and al-Ṣādiq seems likewise to signal separation in the next generation. The concept of the imam as an apolitical figure dispensing saving knowledge of a severely scholarly type is fully attested in the work of Hishām b. al-Ḥakam (d. c. 800).[14]

Counter-caliphs

Just as Jaʿfar al-Ṣādiq seems to have regarded himself as a straightforward scholar rather than an imam in the sense of saviour, so he seems to have stuck to the scholarly role without claiming to be the imam in the sense of ruler. Two of his sons (ʿAbdallāh al-Afṭaḥ and Mūsā al-Kāẓim) supported the revolt of the Ḥasanid Muḥammad b. ʿAbdallāh, posthumously known as al-Nafs al-Zakiyya, the Mahdi who proclaimed himself *amīr al-muʾminīn* in Medina in 762.[15] They clearly cannot have regarded their father as the legitimate caliph of the time. One would infer that he himself did not do so either. It is on grounds of prudence that he is said to have counselled against participation in al-Nafs al-Zakiyya's revolt,[16] not on the grounds that al-Nafs al-Zakiyya was trying to usurp his role, and there is no evidence that he regarded his sons as traitors. He is also said to have refused to participate in a *shūrā* for the election of a caliph after the Hāshimite (in retrospect ʿAbbāsid) revolution, and his general reluctance to get involved in politics is well known. In what sense was he an imam, then? He plainly had all the right qualifications for the imamate, to Shīʿites and *jamāʿī*s alike, and he could have found plenty of people to fight for him if he had stepped forward to claim the imamate. People were tearing their hair out at his refusal to do so.[17] But the fact is that he did not. In retrospect, this seems to mean that he was an imam who refused to get involved with political power, but there cannot be much doubt that at the time it meant that he was no imam at all. The Zaydīs must be right when they assert that he shared their view of the imamate and did not claim it "in the way that the Imamis mention".[18] In fact, the Imamis themselves preserve a Zaydī-type statement by him

13. Cf. Crone and Zimmermann, *Epistle*, 302, 303, 305.

14. Daou, 'Conception', ch. 1.

15. Abū 'l-Faraj, *Maqātil*, 277. For his name, cf. Q. 18:74: "why have you killed an innocent soul (*nafsan zakiyyatan*)?".

16. Ibn Bābawayh, *ʿUyūn*, i, 310.-4.

17. Above, 87, note 1; Modarressi, *Crisis*, 7f.

18. Ibn Qiba, 'Naqḍ kitāb al-ishhād', §20. There are also Imami statements in which Jaʿfar seems to deny that he is the imam (Modarressi, *Crisis*, 8 and note 23 thereto).

in response to the ʿAbbāsid revolution: go home, he told people who consulted him about how to react, "until you see that we have *agreed on* a man"; only then were they to wield arms on the family's behalf.[19] Though the transmitters may not have noticed it, this statement (preserved because of its quietist message) is by a person who presumed there to be no imam at the time.

In short, all Shīʿites in Jaʿfar al-Ṣādiq's time would seem still to have been of either the Zaydī or the extremist type. The former operated with a large pool of candidates for the imamate (all Hāshimites, all Ṭālibids, all ʿAlids, or all descendants of al-Ḥasan and al-Ḥusayn) and held the imam to be singled out by revolt in combination with superior learning and/or agreement within the family, i.e. by *shūrā* (as attempted after the Hāshimite revolution and as claimed for al-Nafs al-Zakiyya); they saw the imam as a pious and learned sovereign, not as an apolitical saviour. By contrast, the extremists would pick out individuals such as Ibn al-Ḥanafiyya, Muḥammad al-Bāqir, Jaʿfar al-Ṣādiq or al-Manṣūr with reference to divine choice of one kind or another and see them as spiritual saviours, with or without casting them as political rulers as well. Jaʿfar and his circles would seem to have seem Shīʿites of the first type. But the views characteristic of the second type were clearly exerting a pull, and it is not just in the conception of the imam that we see it: the Imamis call other Muslims the *ʿāmma*, the common people, and themselves the *khāṣṣa*, the elite, thereby revealing a conception of themselves as the enlightened few within a community, after the fashion of Gnostics, as opposed to a community in their own right, with their own law and political leader, after the fashion of the Zaydīs or Khārijites.

Jaʿfar's son, Mūsā al-Kāẓim (the seventh imam of the Imamis) does seem to have regarded himself as an imam to be, for unlike his father, he was politically active. First he participated in al-Nafs al-Zakiyya's revolt and next he began to levy regular contributions from his adherents, presumably to collect funds for a new revolt. Many expected him to be the Mahdi destined to inaugurate ʿAlid rule.[20] Others expected his younger brother Muḥammad to be that person.[21] The ʿAbbāsids were sufficiently worried by Mūsā's activities to throw him into jail, where he died in 799. No revolt was ever staged, but the network of agents (*wakīl*s) continued to operate, presumably on the grounds that the revolt would soon be staged by Mūsā's son, ʿAlī (the future al-Riḍā). Mūsā thus turned his followers into a religious community with its own sovereign-to-be, its own taxes, and its own hierarchy of administrators, who had nothing to gain from political activities likely to ruin their lucrative positions and who took to

19. Nuʿmānī, *Ghayba*, 131.
20. Modarressi, *Crisis*, 10, 13f.
21. Cf. van Ess, *TG*, i, 326; iii, 151; below, note 23.

providing religious services in the name of the imam, both locally and at the imam's residence, in order to ensure that the local constituencies remained willing to pay.[22] The more obvious it became that the sovereign-to-be would remain apolitical, the more strongly his saving role had to be stressed to justify his existence, allowing the second model to play a greater role. In short, it seems to be from Mūsā's time onwards that the Imamis acquired sectarian organization in the name of a politically quiescent saviour-scholar. Whereas Mūsā had supported al-Nafs al-Zakiyya's bid for the caliphate, neither his successor, ʿAlī al-Riḍā, nor his other sons seem to have been among those who joined other people's rebellions; and when another son of Jaʿfar al-Ṣādiq, the above-mentioned Muḥammad, rebelled in Medina in 815, adopting the caliphal title and expressing the hope that he would be Mahdi and *qāʾim*, his supporters were described as Jārūdīs, that is Zaydīs, suggesting that activist Rafiḍīs and Imamis had parted ways. [23]

It has to be stressed that the Imamis were only some among many Shīʿites who counted Jaʿfar al-Ṣadiq among their heroes. According to the Muʿtazilite heresiographer Abū 'l-Qāsim al-Balkhī, also known as al-Kaʿbī (d. 319/931), the biggest and most important section of the Jaʿfariyya were the Fuṭḥiyya (or Afṭaḥiyya), – those who held that Jaʿfar's imamate passed to his son ʿAbdallāh al-Afṭaḥ and that the imamate came to an end when ʿAbdallāh died shortly thereafter.[24] One may well wonder whether these and other Shīʿites who allegedly stopped the imamate almost as soon as it had been formed actually operated with imams in the Imami sense at all. It seems more likely that Jaʿfar was just a great scholar to them, deserving of particular reverence because of his Prophetic descent, but not a saviour figure.[25] Under pressure to recast him and others as saviours, they will have kept themselves free of them by recourse to the idea that the imamate that everyone was foisting on Jaʿfar had passed to ʿAbdallāh and disappeared with him. But however this may be, the sectarian organization developed by Mūsā proved capable of survival when ʿAlī al-Riḍā was succeeded by a minor, who was succeeded by a minor in his turn. Just as the imam was no longer required to wield political power, so he did not really have to be an adult scholar any more, his work having been taken over by central and local hierachies of scholars and administrators. There was, in fact, no need for the imam to be present at all.

22. Modarressi, *Crisis*, 12ff.
23. Abū 'l-Faraj, *Maqātil*, 538f; Mufīd, *Irshād*, 432f.
24. Balkhī in ʿAbd al-Jabbār, *Mughnī*, xx/2, 181.1.
25. Cf. Modarressi, *Crisis*, 54f., on the Nāwūsiyya.

The caliphal mode of succession

If it was the Gnostic or semi-pagan input that allowed for an apolitical imam, it was the caliphal mode of succession by a combination of heredity and designation/bequest (*naṣṣ/waṣiyya*) that allowed for a stable sect. Unlike the Zaydīs and the *ghulāt*, the Imamis had a sovereign at all times, without requiring the candidate for the imamate to rebel and without recourse to the postulates of divine revelation, divine incarnation, or metempsychosis with which *ghulāt* would single out their saviour figures.[26] The continuous imamate also gave them a neat communal genealogy showing how right guidance had been transmitted from the Prophet to their own time. (See chart 4.)

All Rāfiḍīs accepted that the Prophet had designated ʿAlī as his successor, and all saw al-Ḥasan and al-Ḥusayn as recipients of a *waṣiyya* from the Prophet or ʿAlī, too. But there the sequence ended according to the Jārūdīs,[27] and the Kaysānīs merely added Ibn al-Ḥanafiyya.[28] That apart, the idea of bequest is attested in attempts to legitimate non-ʿAlid imams: Abū Hāshim is supposed to have bequeathed the imamate to the ʿAbbāsids and others; various ʿAlids are supposed to have bequeathed it to local *ghulāt*. But the interest here is in the transfer, not in continuous sequences. The first complete sequence of apolitical imams outside Imamism comes in the presentation by or under al-Mahdī (775–85) of al-ʿAbbās' descendants as imams from the death of the Prophet to his own time. The sequence culminates in caliphs whose claim to power it is meant to legitimate; it is not really concerned with the transmission of guidance, as noted already.[29] By contrast, the Imami sequence is concerned with the transmission of guidance and displays no real interest in claims to caliphal power. For all that, it is a reasonable guess that al-Mahdī's sequence was meant to counter a Shīʿite one. "There must necessarily be a man in his place . . . designated (*manṣūs ʿalayhi*) by the previous imam," al-Nawbakhtī says on the basis of an earlier Imami source, almost certainly Hishām b. al-Ḥakam (d. c. 800).[30]

There is corroborating evidence for this in Abū Mikhnaf's account of Zayd b. ʿAlī's revolt. According to this historian, a Kufan who died in 774, Zayd came to Kufa in 739, between four and six years after Muḥammad al-Bāqir had died. Had there been a regular succession of imams from father to son, Jaʿfar

26. But supernatural knowledge does figure among the signs whereby the imam may be known in some works (e.g. Mufīd, *Irshād*, 443).

27. Cf. above, 101.

28. Cf. Kuthayyir, above, 82f.

29. Cf. above, ch. 8, 92f.

30. Nawbakhtī, *Firaq*, 17.

al-Ṣādiq would have taken over, but the Kufans did not apparently have an imam; they reacted to Zayd's arrival by paying allegiance to him when he decided to rebel. According to Abū Mikhnaf, however, some of them abandoned Zayd when he refused to dissociate from the first two caliphs and accepted Jaʿfar al-Ṣādiq as their imam instead, claiming that he had a better right to the position after his father's death.[31] This is tendentious: as noted already, Abū Mikhnaf was a Zaydī of the soft or weak variety who did not want his hero to have anything to do with Rāfiḍīs.[32] But he was clearly familiar with Rāfiḍīs who cast Jaʿfar al-Ṣādiq as their imam in an apolitical sense on grounds of dynastic legitimism. He does not mention designation, nor does he credit his Rāfiḍīs with the view that one imam had taken over from the other ever since the Prophet's death. But if the Kufan Rāfiḍīs endowed one line of ʿAlids with a sole right to the imamate, this will soon have been supported with a claim to the effect that the line in question had always possessed it. Once again, then, the evidence takes us to Mūsā al-Kāẓim's time.

The ghayba

The de-politicization of the Imamis culminated in the disappearance of the imam in the late ninth century. The eleventh imam died in 874, almost certainly childless. He had a brother who was more than willing to succeed him, but the Imami leadership fiercely resisted his claims, invoking the doctrine that the imamate was not supposed to pass from brother to brother after al-Ḥasan and al-Ḥusayn. The deceased imam had an infant son who had gone into hiding (*ghayba*), they claimed. When the son failed to appear within the normal lifespan of a human being, it came to be agreed that he would remain in hiding until the end of time, when he would return as the Mahdi. It followed that his name was Muḥammad.[33] The Imamis thus became Twelver-Shīʿites.[34] Initially, the imam was held to communicate with the believers through intermediaries known as *safīr*s, but the lines of communication were cut off (as people saw it) in 941. This marked the end of the 'lesser *ghayba*' and the beginning of 'the greater *ghayba*' in which Imamis still find themselves today. The imam could still appear to the believers in dreams, and he was believed to move around invisibly among them, but nobody could claim to work on his orders. The Imamis thus made themselves wholly innocuous in political terms: they no longer had an imam to enthrone, and no political action could be presented as

31. Tab., ii, 1699f.
32. Cf. above, 74, note 11. Similarly van Ess, *TG*, i, 311.
33. Cf. Arjomand, 'Imam *Absconditus*', 10f.
34. Cf. Kohlberg, 'From Imāmiyya to Ithnā-ʿashariyya'.

ordered by him. At the same time, messianism was neutralized by incorporation as a doctrine about a future so indeterminate that it had no bearing on the present. All mahdis were problematic, if live because they would embroil the community in bloodshed and suppression, if dead or absent because their adherents would await their return instead of allowing the imamate to continue. The Imamis now ruled out the first scenario by officially opting for the second.[35]

In Imamism as in Sunnism, religious leadership passed to scholars. More precisely, the leadership of scholars became undisguised, for how far the imams had ever possessed it is open to doubt. There were no ʿAlid scholars before Muḥammad al-Bāqir and Jaʿfar al-Ṣādiq, and their ability to secure acceptance for their views was no greater than that of any other scholars; in fact, it must have been less, for they were objects of speculation rather than a source of instruction to the many who credited them with supernatural knowledge. The *wikāla* instituted by Mūsā al-Kāẓim was used largely or wholly for the collection of funds rather than doctrinal policing. Two of the imams after him were minors; and of these, the first died young, while the second ended up under house arrest in Samarra, where his son remained, to die as the eleventh imam. All in all, then, they can hardly have functioned as ultimate leaders in practice. The imams (or their staff) did occasionally send directives to local scholars, but they do not seem to have taken it upon themselves to issue encyclical letters for the settlement of controversial issues or definition of the faith on a regular basis. In practice, then, Imamism had always been dominated by local scholars who maintained doctrinal unity by reading each others' treatises, engaging in polemics, studying with each other, and developing a general consensus, much as did their *jamāʿī* counterparts. This was formalized when the imam disappeared.

Imamism after the ghayba

The disappearance of the imam greatly eased relations between the Imamis and the powers that be. In effect, the Imamis had adopted the Christian solution of leaving politics to Caesar, who thereby acquired a certain legitimacy of his own. Things improved even further in the mid-tenth century, when western Iran and Iraq came to be ruled by the Būyids (945–1055 in Iraq), for the Būyids, who hailed from Daylam on the Caspian coast, were Shīʿites themselves.

35. Cf. Momen, *Introduction*, 75; Sachedina, *Islamic Messianism* (though one may disagree with the view, p. 1, that "the essence of Shiʿite Islam is a chiliastic vision of history"); Arjomand, 'The Consolation of Theology'; and 'Ǧayba' in *Enc. Iran.*

Originally they were almost certainly Zaydīs, but they veered to Imamism under exposure to it in Iraq, so that for the first time the Imamis experienced the pleasure of having political backing. The Būyids patronized Imami scholars, officially celebrated Imami festivals, and rebuilt Imami shrines. On the basis of ambivalent formulations used by al-Ṭūsi (d. 1066) it has been suggested that the Imamis repaid the Būyids by accepting the concept of a just ruler who was not the imam.[36] But neat though this would be in view of the parallel with Christianity, it does not seem to be correct. As far as the jurists were concerned, Caesar ruled because things had gone wrong, not because he had been authorized to do so by the founder of the faith.[37] He remained a *sulṭān jāʾir*, an illegitimate ruler,[38] meaning a ruler who did not derive his authority from God or the Prophet and whose government thus could not embody divine law and morality, however pious or observant of the law he might be.

His power was profane, then.[39] But it was not profane in the neutral sense of 'secular' or 'not sacred'. There was something positively wrong about it. It is true that the Būyids and other kings sympathetic to Imamism did not claim the imam's position (unlike the Umayyads and the ʿAbbāsids), but there was no way round the fact that they owed their presence to a violation of God's order. The reader may retort that so too did Christian kings, according to the churchmen of medieval Europe. But in their view, the violation had taken place back in Paradise, not on the earth as we know it. It was human nature as such that had been corrupted according to them, not a specific polity in the recent history of the Christians themselves; the kings that God raised up by way of punishment and remedy for the violation were thus perfectly legitimate. The Imamis might have found things easier if they had accepted some such view, for example in the form of the Gnostic diagnosis of a cosmic mistake behind the human condition. But this would have been difficult to square with the conviction that a sacred order had prevailed under the Prophet, and briefly also under ʿAlī. The fact that it did not prevail now reflected the errors of recent history, not the human condition. To the Imami jurists, kings were thus fundamentally illegitimate.

36. Madelung, 'Treatise', 30; Sachedina, *Just Ruler*, 100ff.

37. It was the imam's function to "lead troops, fight oppressors, administer legal punishments (*ḥadd*), protect the boundaries, see that justice is done to the oppressed", but oppressive people prevented him from doing so, as a treatise ascribed to the Sharīf al-Murtaḍā (d. 436/1044) puts it (Sachedina, 'Treatise on the Occultation', 120f.).

38. The term is not an assertion of practical wickedness, only of legal status, as Calder rightly notes ('Legitimacy and Accommodation', 99).

39. Cf. Calder, 'Judicial Authority', 105.

They were not necessarily wicked, however, and even if they were, one had to put up with them, for even government in contravention of God's law was better than none. "People must necessarily have a profane ruler (*sulṭān*) when the imams of justice are absent," as the Imami secretary Ibn Wahb, writing in or after 335/946f., declared; "for if they lacked both such a ruler (*al-sulṭān*) and imams they would eat one another." Even wrongful rulers did more good than harm, he added, citing ʿAlī as saying that "government (*imāra*) is indispensable, whether pious or profligate".[40] The Umayyads had been profligate, but they had conquered lands, distributed the booty, defended the borders, and kept the roads safe, as Ibn Abī 'l-Ḥadīd explained.[41] One could even work for such a regime according to some, for Joseph had worked for Pharaoh.[42] But Pharaonic legitimacy was at best expedient; it could never be *sharʿī*, and there were times when non-cooperation was best: if the Umayyads had not found people to work as secretaries, tax collectors and soldiers for them, they would not have been able to deprive the imams of their rights, as a tradition credited to Jaʿfar al-Ṣādiq put it.[43]

When the last imam went into hiding, some held that the public order based on the Sharīʿa had practically ceased to exist: all the imam's functions had lapsed, so that there was no moral basis for holy war (other than of the purely defensive type), the collection of taxes, the application of the public penalties (*ḥudūd*), or the conduct of public worship.[44] Some did hold the imam's functions, or some of them, to have passed to others, but they saw them as having passed to the scholars, not to the kings. As deputies of the imams, the scholars were in a position to bestow *sharʿī* legitimacy on kings, but the legitimacy thus acquired by secular government was borrowed.[45] Unlike the scholars, kings could not validate their status with reference to the Sharīʿa in their own right. In the long run, their jurisdiction was undermined by the transfer of the imam's powers to the scholars, as the Ṣafavids and their successors were to find in modern times.

40. Ibn Wahb, *Burhān*, 403.-6; cf. *EI*², supplement, s.v. 'Ibn Wahb'. This eminently *jamāʿī* view is first credited to ʿAlī by Abū Mikhnaf (BA, ii, 377, cf. 352, 361, against the Khārijite *lā ḥukma illā li'llāh*, taken to mean 'no government'). It later appears in the famous Imāmī anthology of ʿAlī's sayings, the *Nahj al-balāgha* (probably compiled c. 400/1000), 114, no. 40, quoted in IAH, ii, 307, where ʿAlī also enumerates some functions of the ruler. For a variant version, see Ibn Abū Shayba, *Muṣannaf*, xv, no. 19101 (*K. al-fitan*).

41. IAH, iii, 209.

42. Madelung, 'Treatise', 22 = 25.

43. Newman, *Formative Period of Twelver Shīʿism*, 175.

44. Below, 289ff.

45. Cf. Calder, 'Legitimacy and Accommodation', the best treatment of the question.

The happy condominium between the Imamis and their Būyid rulers came to an end with the Seljuq invasions, for the Seljuqs, who entered Baghdad in 1055, were Sunnis; and though the Mongols who occupied Baghdad in 1258 extended favours to the Imamis, the Imamis never again had political support on a major scale until the Ṣafavids turned Iran into a Shīʿite country by political decree in the sixteenth century. This development was to change the nature of Imamism, including its political doctrines, culminating in Khomeini's doctrine of government by the most eminent jurist. But all that lies far beyond the scope of this book

The Imami vision

Imamism is a much more complicated belief-system, developed over much longer periods and reflecting much more differentiated societies, than either Khārijism or Zaydism. Like all complex systems of thought, it can be played in many ways. One hesitates, then, to offer something so simple as a summary of 'the Imami vision'. But some obvious points can be made.

Imamism hugely widens the gulf between the imam and his followers. There was only one family, indeed one lineage, from which he could come forth, and only one individual who could be him at any given time. After the *ghayba* he could no longer be begotten at all. He was created of a special substance, endowed with divine light, divinely inspired (*mufahham*), protected against error (*maʿṣūm*), possessed of knowledge over and above that possessed by ordinary human believers, and eventually not a member of the ordinary human world at all. The gulf between the imam and his devotees is replicated in that between the Imamis and other Muslims. The former were *al-khāṣṣa*, the elite; the latter were *al-ʿāmma*, the masses, made "from the stinking mud of hell".[46] The imams were the possessors of knowledge and their followers were those who had acquired it; the rest of humanity were "scum".

The Imami solution to Muḥammad's multipurpose polity was thus to elevate the imam to a religious importance so overwhelming that he ceased to have anything to do with politics; politics was left in the hands of kings and amirs. The Imamis tended to separate the sacred and the profane, as Calder observes. But as seen already, this did not allow for an autonomous sphere of politics, for the fact that the imams ought in principle to have ruled stood in the way of full endorsement of the powers that be.[47] Of *sharʿī* government there were only two shortlived examples in Imami history, the Prophet's ten

46. Kohlberg, 'Imam and Community', 32.
47. Calder, 'Judicial Authority', 107; above, 120.

years in Medina and ʿAli's five years as caliph in Kufa. The century of Būyid rule was quasi-legitimate and stimulated sufficient interest in government for the Sharīf al-Rāḍī (d. 1012) to include a letter of political advice in his celebrated compilation of ʿAlī's sayings and writings, the *Nahj al-balāgha*.[48] But illegitimacy was so fundamental a fact about political power that until the Ṣafavids created an Imami state, the Imamis did not generally devote their thought to how to organize, manage, or change it, but rather to how to live with it. If their imams were about salvation, their politics were about accommodation. This showed itself in three fundamental values.

The first is quietism. In principle the pre-*ghayba* Imāmīs were committed to the overthrow of the usurpers, and hopes for a political redeemer sometimes ran high, as has been seen. But in practice the Imamis can be defined as those Shīʿites who renounced political action. Hishām b. al-Ḥakam (c. 800) laid down that it was forbidden to rebel without the imam's permission. Unauthorized revolt would endanger the imam's life, the Imamis said; what they actually meant was that it would endanger the community. No imam after al-Ḥusayn led or authorized a revolt, and when the twelfth went into hiding, revolt became doctrinally impossible.[49] To the Zaydī charge that imams sitting at home were just legal authorities, or worse, effete cowards sponging off the believers instead of getting up to fight the oppressors,[50] the Imamis responded that it was wrong to court self-destruction. People exposed themselves to unlawful danger when they went out in "a small band without experience of war or military training . . . to meet an army trained in war who control the land, who are killing people, who are numerous, well armed, well-equipped, and who have supporters a hundred times more numerous than their troops among the common people, convinced that anyone who attacks them can be lawfully killed".[51] The Imamis were in a state of truce with their non-Shīʿite opponents, they said.[52] Shīʿites hankering for political action had to abandon the Imami fold for Zaydism or (from the late ninth century onwards) Ismailism. To be an Imami was to know that power was beyond reform.

The second fundamental value is *taqiyya*, precautionary dissimulation. Muslims are allowed to hide or deny their faith under conditions of danger. A few activists rejected it, notably the Azāriqa, who saw it as a cowardly way of evading one's duty to fight for the truth. Most Khārijites and Sunnis accepted

48. The letter is translated in Chittick, *Anthology*, 68ff. See further below, 152, note 23.
49. Ashʿarī, 58; Ṭūsī, *Nihāya*, 297.2.
50. Cf. above, 105, note 31; ʿAlawī, *Sīrat al-Hādī*, 27f.
51. Ibn Qiba, 'Naqḍ kitāb al-ishhād', §61.
52. Cook, *Commanding Right*, 257.

it, if only under certain circumstances. But only the Imamis made it central to their faith. "Nine tenths of faith is *taqiyya*," Jaʿfar al-Ṣādiq is reputed to have said.[53] Like political inactivity, *taqiyya* was enjoined as crucial for the protection of the imam's life, and again its key function was to shield the Imamis themselves from attack when they left the relative safety of their own quarters: "in concealment and silence lies security and protection for him and for us," as one Imami statement has it.[54] Being suspected of Shīʿism could have nasty consequences in staunchly Sunni areas. Imamis who saw the imams as possessors of esoteric knowledge also enjoined *taqiyya* to protect their secret wisdom from exposure to the uncomprehending masses (including their own co-religionists), who might pervert it or denounce it as heretical.[55]

Finally, the Imamis developed their own conception of martyrdom, above all with reference to al-Ḥusayn's death at Karbalāʾ in 680. A martyr (*shahīd*) was a person killed in holy war against infidels. A Sunni martyr died at the hands of non-Muslims, typically on the winning side and certainly on that of the solid majority, so that no sense of tragedy or pathos attached to his fate: he was a hero rewarded by Paradise. The infidels against whom Shīʿite and Khārijite martyrs fell, on the other hand, were usually 'people of the *qibla*' (i.e. other Muslims), and the Shīʿites and Khārijite martyrs themselves typically fell on the losing side, as members of an oppressed minority. Yet no sense of tragedy or pathos attaches to Khārijite martyrs either: they were staunch heroes who would flinch at nothing in the path of God, not tragic victims of a vitiated world in which the forces of evil always win. The same is true of Zaydī martyrs. But to the Imamis, a martyr was indeed a victim of an evil world, like al-Ḥusayn, whose fate was a tragedy eliciting profound emotions of grief and pity, and a sense of sinfulness in the survivors. The so-called Penitents reportedly left Kufa to let themselves be slaughtered by Umayyad troops by way of atonement for their failure to assist al-Ḥusayn;[56] and later Shīʿites were to re-enact his martyrdom with self-flagellation, turning the violence they might have applied to the external world against themselves. Like Christianity, Imamism was a religion that saw salvation as lying with the losers.

53. Kulīnī, *Kāfī*, ii, 217; cf. Newman, *Formative Period of Twelver Shīʿism*, 157f.
54. Nawbakhtī, *Firaq*, 91.
55. Kohlberg, 'Taqiyya in Shīʿī Theology and Religion'.
56. *EI*², s.v. 'Tawwābūn'.

CHAPTER

11

THE ḤADĪTH PARTY

Scholars had appeared within all parties, in all Muslim settlements, in the course of the Umayyad period. By the late Umayyad/early ʿAbbāsid period some of them had come to form a party of their own under the label *aṣḥāb al-ḥadīth*, 'adherents of Ḥadīth/reports', or 'Ḥadīth party', or, as the term is more commonly translated, 'Traditionalists'. Initially they seem to have been concentrated in Iraq and the Ḥijāz, but they soon spread to Khurāsān, Egypt, and elsewhere.

The adherents of Ḥadīth believed that the Prophet's practice (*sunna*) could be recovered from *ḥadīth*, 'traditions', that is short statements reporting the Prophet's solutions to legal or doctrinal problems as they had arisen in his time. Most *aṣḥāb al-ḥadīth* were active compilers, teachers, and transmitters of such reports (*muḥaddithūn*, 'traditionists').[1] In the late Umayyad period *ḥadīth* reporting the practice of the Prophet, as opposed to that of a Companion or later figure, had great rarity value. They also had great popular appeal, for

1. Some Islamicists use the same word (usually 'traditionists') to translate *muḥaddithūn* (transmitters of Ḥadīth) and *aṣḥāb al-ḥadīth* (believers in Ḥadīth as a source for the Muslim way of life). It has to be said that the entire terminology is unfortunate. Ḥadīth is labelled 'tradition' because it is something handed down from the past, but one normally associates tradition with customs rather than reports, and a traditionalist is normally someone attached to venerable institutions, not someone who holds right practice to be revealed in a certain type of literature. On both counts the terminology invites confusion between Ḥadīth (the literary genre) and Sunna (the practices that the genre illustrates). The Traditionalists were, moreover, radicals when they first appeared. The terminology is however too entrenched in the literature to be changed.

they were typically transmitted orally, with just one transmitter per generation in the chain of authorities (*isnād*) attached to them, so that hearing one was almost like hearing the Prophet himself. The Muslim world was soon to be flooded with reports from the Prophet, but initially, Prophetic traditions were in the nature of relics, which also induced a sense of direct contact, and the social prestige accruing from the possession of such treasured items was great. "If I were a bean-seller, you would think nothing of me – without these traditions we would no better than greengrocers," as the Kufan al-Aʿmash (d. 148/765) reputedly said.[2] The traditionists would travel far and wide to find their relics, display them with pride, pass on as many of them as they could, or alternatively hoard as many as they could in their private collections, and inevitably they would also traffic in fakes and heavily restored items. (This, incidentally, is *not* why the authenticity of Prophetic ḥadīth is disputed by many Islamicists, though participants in the debate often convey this impression by casting the debate as one about 'fabrications'.)[3]

Not all scholars who worked with Ḥadīth had the same views on politico-religious or theological questions at first: some were Shīʿites, others Murjiʾites, some believed in predestination, others in free will. But boundaries hardened in the ninth century. Some Traditionalists henceforth worked as members of Shīʿite sects; others died out (believers in free will henceforth expressed themselves in *kalām*, rationalizing theology, alone); and still others grouped together as *aṣḥāb al-ḥadīth*. Another name for this last group was *ahl al-sunna wa'l-jamāʿa*, roughly 'adherents of right practice and communal solidarity', or *ahl al-sunna* for short. This was a flattering self-description which many groups were to adopt without necessarily meaning very much by it. As used by the Ḥadīth party, however, it appears to have been programmatic.

Sunna

Everyone knew that religious guidance was to be found in the Qurʾān and the Sunna, that is to say in the Book and the example set by upright men in the past (*al-salaf*). Looking in the Qurʾān was easy enough, but how was the Sunna to

2. Khaṭīb, *Sharaf aṣḥāb al-ḥadīth*, 135, no. 320.

3. The assumption of the sceptics is rather that relics are never authentic, whether accepted as such or not by those who revere them. Traditions from the Prophet only begin to appear about a century after his death as ammunition in debates about law and doctrine: even if they had a starting point in something the Prophet actually said or did, they had undergone so many changes in the course of transmission that unless the contrary can be shown, they are best treated as evidence for the debates in which they were used rather than for the views of the figures to whom they were traced.

be found? The general assumption in the Umayyad period seems to have been that one knew the Sunna too primarily from the Qurʾān: whatever the Qurʾān commanded was what the Prophet and other upright men must have done; tradition supplied the context in which they had done it.[4] One could also infer the Sunna from the practice of upright people in the present, for whatever they did must always have been right; the Sunna was good communal practice. There was a scattering of Ḥadīth from and/or about the Prophet and later righteous figures, but it seems only to have been in the later Umayyad period that such reports began to proliferate.

The adherents of Ḥadīth said that the Sunna was what the Prophet had said and done as recorded in Ḥadīth. It was not the example of upright men in general, only of one of them, and it was not to be found in the Qurʾān or communal practice, but rather in a particular type of (initially oral) report about his rulings. Many would use Ḥadīth from the Companions and later authorities as well, but all held, or soon came to hold, that Prophetic tradition overruled all other non-Qurʾānic data when available; and all would stop short of using *raʾy*, individual judgement, dismissing it as arbitrary opinion. Their point was that all guidance was sealed in the past. The Prophet had been the last window onto God's will. The window was now shut for ever, not only in the sense that there would be no more scriptures, but also in the sense that there could be no further sources of Sunna. Contrary to what adherents of the Umayyads and the Hāshimites claimed, no living being had, or ever would have, special access to God: the imam was no exception. And contrary to what everyone else said, no living beings could be presumed to perpetuate the Prophet's Sunna merely because they were upright, pious, learned, or clever: the scholars were no exception. All humans depended entirely on the book and other records that the Prophet had left behind for their authority. Some believers were endowed with better memories, higher reliability, and greater learning than others, but these were differences of degree, not of kind. This is not to deny that they were of vital importance: scholars knew so much more than other believers that they assumed the position of clergy in relation to them. But nobody had a private line to the truth any more, let alone a monopoly on it. All were equidistant from God.

This was the Traditionalist thesis, and it was a radical pruning exercise. It left no room for juristic reasoning, rationalizing theology or (when it appeared) philosophy, let alone for ongoing revelation or other forms of supernatural knowledge after the Prophet's death as claimed by new prophets, Umayyad or Shīʿite imams, or (when they appeared) Sufi saints. What was on

4. This is the still how the Prophet's Sunna is identified by the Ibāḍī Sālim (later second/eighth century?) (Crone and Zimmermann, *Epistle*, 28f.).

the other side of the window could only be known from *samʿ*, authoritative information going back to the days when the window was open, meaning the Qurʾān and Prophetic Ḥadīth.

It followed that religious authority rested entirely on knowledge (*ʿilm*) of the Qurʾān and Prophetic Ḥadīth, not on high office, descent from the Prophet, superior reasoning, or (when they appeared) claims to special friendship with God. This had radical implications in socio-political terms. The truth was dispersed among the believers at large; the greengrocers of Kufa were more authoritative than the caliph if they had Ḥadīth to offer along with their beans. It was perfectly possible for a caliph to possess religious knowledge too: ʿUmar II was remembered (rightly or wrongly) as having tried to follow the Sunna in the Traditionalist sense. But the caliph was no different from any other Muslim in this respect, and knowledge of the Qurʾān and Ḥadīth could never be concentrated in a single man, for anyone who cared to study them was free to do so. This was the doctrine by which the adherents of Ḥadīth cut the imam down to size. He was not endowed with a divine fullness of power, only with the authority to regulate matters of this world. As successor of the Prophet, commander of the believers, and executor of Islamic law, he still occupied a position of central importance to the religion, but he was not authorized to define it.

It was at the hands of the Ḥadīth party that the caliphs and the scholars became rivals. Like the Khārijites and Shīʿites, the early Ḥadīth scholars were hostile to the Umayyads, in Kufa as soft Shīʿites and Murjiʾites, in Basra and Medina as ʿUthmānīs. But unlike the Khārijites and other Shīʿites, they all came to subscribe to a thesis which implied that *no* caliph, legitimate or otherwise, could claim religious authority any more. Whether this implication was apparent already in the Umayyad period is hard to say. Thanks to the general undatability of Ḥadīth, all aspects of Traditionalist history before c. 800 are highly uncertain, and it was only in the mid-ninth century that a caliph put their thesis to the test (as will be seen). But it was probably in the later Umayyad period that the Traditionalists rejected the title *khalīfat allāh* for its connotations of religious authority (lacking in other grandiloquent titles such as 'shadow of God on earth'), claiming that Abū Bakr and ʿUmar had repudiated this version of the title in favour of *khalīfat rasūl allāh*, successor of the messenger of God.[5] 'Deputy of God' was a title suitable only for the prophets of whom it was used

5. Cf. Crone and Hinds, *God's Caliph*, 20; above, 18, 43f. The ruler was God's shadow (*ẓill allāh*) in the sense that God provided shade (i.e. protection) through him (cf. Goldziher, 'Ombre de Dieu', 133f.). Later it was often taken to cast him in grander terms as a reflection of God (cf. below, 153, note 30), but it does not figure in disputes over religious authority.

in the Qurʾān, they said,[6] studiously avoiding identifying the Qurʾānic *khalīfa* as the head of state;[7] or alternatively, they belittled the significance of the title, claiming that any Muslim who commanded right and forbad wrong was God's deputy on earth.[8] At some point it was decided that the caliph was, or ought to be, a *mujtahid*, one endowed with sufficient legal learning to exercise independent judgement. If this was meant as a concession to the caliph, it was not much of one, for it reduced his voice to one among many: like other scholars endowed with the requisite learning, he was entitled to interpret the law, but he had no special prerogatives by virtue of his office. More probably, however, it was just meant to ensure that he was properly educated in the law so that his day-to-day decisions would remain within its bounds: the idea was that he would be able to interpret it for his own day-to-day purposes, much like a judge, not that the decisions he reached on the basis of *ijtihād* would have legislative force.[9]

If Islam had been born with an ecclesiastical hierarchy, the adherents of Ḥadīth would have had as many obstacles to overcome to get their way as the Protestants of Reformation Europe, meaning that they might well have failed. But since the Umayyads had never developed an official hierarchy for the dissemination of their views, there was not much they could do about the scholars' withdrawal of recognition of their authority, except in matters of direct relevance to government. They did have some leverage on judges and other government appointees, but no Traditionalist scholar accepted judicial appointment if he could avoid it. Clashes were most likely to arise in the field of public ritual and taxation, where the scholars had to defer to the authorities. For the rest, people continued to consult the scholars, who would no longer consult the caliphs or ascribe their views to them.[10]

6. Thus ʿUmar II in Ibn ʿAbd al-Ḥakam, *Sīrat*, 46.

7. Qāḍī, 'The Term "Khalīfa"', i, 409, 411 (with this and an alternative interpretation).

8. Cook, *Commanding Right*, 38. The idea that all humans are deputies of God on earth by virtue of their descent from Adam (identified as *khalīfat allāh* in Q. 2:30) seems first to be attested in tenth-century philosophical circles (Rāghib, *Dharīʿa*, 91f.; cf. Idris, 'Is man the Vicegerent of God?'). Early exegetes who identified man as *khalīfa* saw humans as successors of the angels, the *jinn*, or earlier generations, not as deputies of God (cf. Qāḍī, 'The Term "Khalīfa"', 398ff).

9. For a different view of the relationship between scholars and caliphs, see Zaman, *Emergence*, ch. 3. For an example of caliphal *ijtihād*, see below, 225, note 33.

10. According to Ibn Ḥazm, the Medinese accepted legal decisions from/attributed to Umayyad caliphs as late as Yazīd II, Hishām and al-Walīd II, but the last Umayyad caliph to figure as an authority on law in a non-polemical context is Hishām (Crone and Hinds, *God's Caliph*, 47f., cf. 45).

The Aṣḥāb al-Ḥadīth *and the ʿAbbāsids*

The ʿAbbāsids came to power as imams entitled to unquestioned obedience in both religious and political terms. When the Prophet died, the knowledge which God had revealed to him passed to his family (*ʿitra*, *ahl bayt*) in the order of genealogical proximity (*al-aqrab fa'l-aqrab*), not to anyone else, the leaders of the Hāshimite movement in Khurāsān are represented as agreeing in 129/746; the Prophet's family were the fount of religious knowledge and the recipients of the Prophet's legacy (*maʿdin al-ʿilm wa-aṣḥāb mīrāth rasūl allāh*); nobody would want to transfer their obedience from them to other members of his family (*ʿan ahl al-bayt ilā ghayrihim min ʿitrat al-nabī*), and the recipients of the Prophet's legacy could not be gainsaid.[11] Religious knowledge is here concentrated in the Prophet's inner family, as the Rāfiḍīs saw it, not dispersed in the community.[12] A similar concept of the imam's knowledge is attested in Ibn al-Muqaffaʿ, a secretary who began his career in the service of the Umayyads. As noted before,[13] he was worried by extremism among the Khurāsānī troops. Many officers spoke as if the imam could change the *qibla* and make mountains move, he said; some saw the imams as entitled to unconditional obedience, saying that it was not for their followers to sit in judgement on their orders, while others went to the opposite extreme of seeing the imams as no more authoritative than anyone else. The one extreme here is clearly Shīʿite *ghuluww*, the other seems to be something close to Najdite Khārijism. By way of solution Ibn al-Muqaffaʿ asked the caliph to draw up a catechism for the officers to memorize, containing everything they needed to know. In another context he asked him to codify the law as well: from among the mass of conflicting rules in current use the imam was to ratify the ones he deemed best on the basis of divine inspiration (*ra'yahu alladhī yulhimuhu allāh*), and all later imams were to do the same.[14] His own moderate view of the imam's knowledge would thus seem to be that also attested for the late Umayyad secretary ʿAbd al-Ḥamīd b. Yaḥyā and the Zaydī Abū 'l-Jārūd: all three credited the imam with a divine inspiration that made him the ultimate arbiter of right and

11. Tab., ii, 1961. Rāfiḍī though it is, it must have been written or revised with the doctrine of al-ʿAbbās' inheritance in mind; cf. the polemical reference to other members of the Prophet's family and the invocation of genealogical proximity (*al-aqrab fa'l-aqrab*, a common expression in connection with agnatic succession, in which an uncle, i.e. al-ʿAbbās, would exclude a cousin, i.e. ʿAlī).

12. Cf. above, 104.

13. Above, 94, notes 25, 26.

14. *Ṣaḥāba*, 194–8, 208 (Pt, §§10–18, 36).

wrong.[15] This suggests that the view was widespread. It was certainly shared by the devotees of the ʿAbbāsid house known as Rizāmīs.[16]

But the ʿAbbāsids do not seem to have made much use of their special knowledge. As far as law is concerned, they appear to have recognized the scholars' monopoly from the start. As regards theology, the caliph al-Maʾmūn (813–33) did try to assert his religious authority, but not along the lines recommended by Ibn al-Muqaffaʿ. In the last year of his reign he instituted a famous inquisition (*miḥna*) designed to ensure that all judges, jurists, and well-known traditionists subscribed to the doctrine of the createdness of the Qurʾān, which had been propounded by rationalist theologians.[17] Contrary to what is often stated, the measure was not an attempt to impose Muʿtazilite theology. For one thing, the doctrine of the createdness of the Qurʾān was not unique to the Muʿtazilites, and though al-Maʾmūn appointed a Muʿtazilite as chief prosecutor, he was not a Muʿtazilite himself; his mentor seems to have been the Murjiʾite Bishr al-Marīsī. For another thing, al-Maʾmūn only picked a single tenet for his inquisition, not a complete system, so he was not trying to impose any one system at all.[18] What his choice of a single, highly controversial rationalist doctrine shows is that the *miḥna* was in the nature of a gauntlet flung at the Ḥadīth party. It was not an attempt at permanent, institutional control of people's beliefs. In fact, ordinary people were not targeted at all, presumably because they were expected simply to follow their leaders. But it did attempt to force everyone in a position of authority to accept a tenet derived from the rationalist theology favored by the courtly elite, and thus to concede that the ultimate authority in matters of faith was the caliph.

The *miḥna* was a failure. Some adherents of Ḥadīth bowed to pressure, others staunchly resisted, most famously Ibn Ḥanbal, but either way the scholars were too amorphous for the caliph to get a grip on them, and it was clear where popular sympathy lay. The inquisition was phased out on the accession of al-Mutawakkil (847–61). Splendidly arrayed courtiers would now wade through the puddles on the streets of Ibn Ḥanbal's humble quarter to lavish unsolicited favours on the spokesman of populist traditionalism.[19] It was effectively the

15. Above, 42, note 33; below, 104.

16. Ps. Nāshiʾ, §54: the community had to have recourse to the imam whenever disagreements arose about religion, for God would make him think of the right solution and inspire him with knowledge of it.

17. Cf. *EI²*, s.v. 'miḥna'.

18. Van Ess, *TG*, iii, 157, 176ff., 178f. Other tenets cropped up later (such as the denial that God would be visible to humans in the next world), but they never gained much prominence.

19. Cook, *Commanding Right*, 112 and note 248 thereto.

end of the caliph as a religious authority in his own right. The overriding authority which the Rāshidūn had possessed, and which the Umayyads had continued to claim for themselves, was now seen as dispersed in the community and expressed in scholarly agreement (*ijmāʿ*).[20]

Contrary to what one might have expected, however, the scholars did not proceed to draw up a clear line of demarcation between their own and the caliph's jurisdiction. In fact, no definition of the two spheres of competence was ever attempted, at least not in the period covered in this book. The dividing line between the two jurisdictions remained not just fuzzy, but studiously unexplored. As a result, the role of later caliphs in the definition of orthodoxy depended less on theory than on politics. As allies of the Ḥadīth party they could, and did, take a leading role; as allies of others they were resisted, in so far as they tried.

For example, when al-Mutawakkil abolished the inquisition, he made Ḥadīth transmission prevail (*aẓhara 'l-riwāya fī 'l-ḥadīth*), ordering people to refrain from disputation and to practice *taqlīd* (blind acceptance),[21] giving rich rewards to transmitters and jurists, and telling them to relate traditions in refutation of the Muʿtazilites and Jahmites.[22] For good measure he demolished the tomb of al-Ḥusayn and prohibited visits there, flogged to death a hostel-owner accused of defaming Abū Bakr, ʿUmar, and their daughters, meted out the same treatment to an Iranian pseudo-prophet in Samarra and to one of his followers, beheaded and burnt a Christian convert to Islam for reverting to Christianity, imposed a profusion of discriminatory rules on *dhimmī*s, and had an Egyptian Sufi sent in fetters to Baghdad for interrogation.[23] It was a good demonstration of what could be done under the Traditionalist rules. By contrast, al-Muʿtaḍid did not get far with his attempts, such as they were, to replay the role of al-Maʾmūn. In 284/897 he decided to have Muʿāwiya publicly cursed. Al-Maʾmūn had planned to do the same back in his days as a quasi-Shīʿite imam, and al-Muʿtaḍid now ordered the document drafted for al-Maʾmūn to be fetched and rewritten for his own use. We are given the complete text of the new version. It identified the Prophet's family as purified by God to serve as the fount of wisdom, the heirs of prophethood, and the locus of the caliphate, explicitly telling people that "God has guided you through us; we are

20. Thus Crone and Hinds, *God's Caliph*, 93f. Differently Zaman, *Emergence*, ch. 3.

21. Tab., iii, 1412.16; MM, viii, 303/v, §3456.

22. Ibn al-Jawzī, *Muntaẓam*, ed. ʿAṭā and ʿAṭā, xi, 207 (year 237). He did not appoint partisans of ḥadīth as judges (Melchert, 'Religious policies'), but then it was well known that their hostile attitude to human reasoning made them unsuited for that position (cf. Māwardī, *Aḥkām*, 111/67 = 74f.; Abū Yaʿlā, *Aḥkām*, 63).

23. Tab., iii, 1389f., 1394, 1407, 1424ff., 1434; *EI*², s.v. 'Dhū 'l-Nūn Abū 'l-Fayḍ'.

the ones who preserve God's command among you; we are the heirs of the messengers of God and the upholders of God's religion," and assuring them that "as long as you obey God's caliphs and imams of guidance you are on the path of faith and piety".[24] In short, it espoused a Rāfiḍī rather than *jamāʿī* concept of religious knowledge. Al-Muʿtaḍid prepared for the publication of this document by banning story-tellers and other people from the streets and Friday mosques of Baghdad, forbidding people to gather for disputation and ordering the water carriers of Baghdad to stop invoking God's mercy on Muʿāwiya. It would clearly have been an uphill battle, and he soon decided to leave Muʿāwiya alone.[25]

In 408/1017 the caliph al-Qādir resumed the alliance with the Traditionalists, more precisely the Ḥanbalites of Baghdad. He prohibited the discussion and teaching of Muʿtazilism, Rāfiḍī Shīʿism and other things, and in the following years he periodically summoned jurists, preachers and other notables to hear and sign long statements in support of Traditionalism which eventually came to be known as the Qādirī creed.[26] His measures were highly influential, not least because the powerful Turkish ruler, Maḥmūd of Ghazna, cast himself as the executor of caliphal policies. By contrast, the caliph al-Nāṣir (575–622/1180–1225) remained an eccentric when he made a last attempt to recover religious authority for the caliph. He presented himself as a cross between a Shīʿite imam and a Sufi *shaykh*, and claimed to lead a mission of guidance (*daʿwa hādiya*) destined to unite Sunnīs and Shīʿites. Unlike al-Maʾmūn and al-Muʿtaḍid, he played the populist card, too, by denouncing the sciences of the Greeks, burning libraries and destroying philosophical literature.[27] But his successors did not continue his efforts in such time as they had left before 1258, when the Mongols put an end to the caliphate.

In practice, then, the caliphs continued to play a role in the definition of orthodoxy, but only as the powerful (or at least prestigious) arm of the scholars, not as a divinely inspired institution set up to guide them. As the spearhead of popular forces they could be highly influential; as leaders of an elite institution appointed to control such forces they had failed. In other words, the Traditionalists had successfully reduced the caliph to a purely executive role. They defined orthodoxy and he enforced it, or made others do so.

24. Tab., iii, 2166ff.

25. Ibid., iii, 2165–78; Ibn al-Jawzī, *Muntaẓam*, ed. ʿAṭā and ʿAṭā, xii, 371f. (year 284). Ibn Taghribirdī places the action against story-tellers and others in 279/892, claiming that al-Muʿtaḍid also had booksellers undertake under oath not to sell any books of disputation (*jadal*) or philosophy (*Nujūm*, iii, 80).

26. Makdisi, *Ibn ʿAqīl et la résurgence*, 299ff; more briefly, id., *Ibn ʿAqil*, 8ff.

27. *EI*², s.v. 'al-Nāṣir', §§5, 7, and the literature cited there. Cf. further below, 249f.

Jamāʿa

As the Traditionalists saw it, the Prophet's guidance was dispersed in the community when he died, for he had passed his knowledge to his Companions, who passed it on to the next generation (known as the Successors), who passed it on to their pupils, and so on. Given this dispersal, it was by sticking together that the Muslims preserved his legacy. This was the doctrine with which the Traditionalists rationalized the intense feeling of communal loyalty that so many Muslims had evinced from the beginning. People had to stick together, lonesomeness was bad, from whatever angle one looked at it. "May God preserve us from isolation (*al-waḥda*)! The Prophet cursed anyone who spends the night alone," as an eleventh-century diarist wrote, shocked by the news that a lady of high social standing had died on her own without anybody knowing about it.[28] It was not just at the level of the family that togetherness was a virtue. Just as kinsmen had to hang together in order not to hang separately, so *jamāʿa* (communal unity) had to be preserved against *furqa* (schism) at all cost.[29] In practice the Traditionalists were often seen as schismatics themselves, not least for their habit of denouncing people who did not agree with them as infidels.[30] But that was a habit they shared with others. Their commitment to communal unity went beyond that of others, with three major consequences.

Companions

First, all the Companions had to be accepted as rightly guided, so that their warring adherents could be reconciled. It took the *aṣḥāb al-ḥadīth* a while to reach this conclusion, for how could one declare one's loyalty to all the Companions when they had fought each other? If ʿUthmān had been a rightly guided caliph, ʿAlī could hardly have been one as well. Conversely, if ʿAlī had been a rightly guided caliph, how could Companions such as Ṭalḥa, al-Zubayr or Muʿāwiya have been right to fight him? In the Umayyad period one had to choose between these caliphs. Many adherents of Ḥadīth, perhaps most of them, were ʿUthmānīs, not in the sense of adherents of the Umayyads but rather in that of people who held the rightly guided caliphate to have ended with ʿUthmān. But others were soft Shīʿites.[31] At one extreme, then, the devotees of Ḥadīth shaded off into into Rāfiḍīs and at the other extreme they blended with the Murjiʾites, who suspended judgement on all the participants

28. Makdisi, 'Autograph Diary', II, §24.
29. Cf. the story cited above, note 3; Nagel, *Rechtleitung und Kalifat*, 259ff.
30. Cf. below, ch. 21, 'Muslims as Infidels'.
31. *EI*², s.v. ʿUthmāniyya', §2; van Ess, *TG*, i, 235ff.; Ibn al-Nadīm, above, 99, note 2.

in the first civil war. Only their boundaries with the Khārijites were perfectly clear.

It is not known when or where it was first proposed that one should recognize both ʿUthmān *and* ʿAlī as rightly guided caliphs, and accept that all the Companions who had followed them had been rightly guided too, but it was in the course of the ninth century that the four-caliphs thesis spread in Iraq. As for how one could possibly remain loyal to all the participants in a mortal conflict, the answer was that one should suspend judgement on the rights and wrongs of it, not in the sense that one should neither affiliate to nor dissociate from the participants as the early Murjiʾites said, but rather in the sense that one should affiliate to all of them, on the grounds that it was not for later generations to sit in judgement on people so favoured by God as the Companions. One should not dwell on their disputes or read about their quarrels. Only God knew the ultimate truth about them. Both sides had exercised independent judgement (*ijtihād*), it was also said, and those who do so are always right, in the sense that God will reward them for their efforts even if He deems them to be wrong in their views (humans cannot tell whether a result reached by *ijtihād* is ultimately true or not). With this explanation the ʿUthmānī Traditionalists accepted ʿAlī as rightly guided while the soft Shīʿites accepted ʿUthmān, and the Murjiʾites accepted both as rightly guided instead of suspending judgement on them. The Muʿtazilites, who had mostly been soft Shīʿites, generally accepted the four-caliphs thesis too. By the end of the ninth century practically all Muslims who were not outright Shīʿites or Khārijites seem to have accepted the new, broad genealogy of the *umma*.[32]

Quietism

Just as one should not engage in sectarian arguments about the first civil war, so one should refrain from participation in divisive conflicts over the leadership of the community in the present. The proper response to oppressive government was to endure it. Given that guidance was dispersed, it was more important to keep the community together than to ensure that its ruler was just. Internal fighting was worse for the community, in terms of lives, property, and violations of the law, than tyranny could ever be; and even oppressive rulers were divinely ordained. Indeed, some said, they were raised up in order to punish the believers for their sins (which was also how the Christians of medieval Europe normally explained them). Hence one was not to take up arms against

32. Ps.-Nāshiʾ, §§109–11, 114; van Ess, *TG*, ii, 439, 478; *EI*², s.v. ʻʿUthmāniyyaʼ, §3; Crone and Zimmermann, *Epistle*, 229f.

them, but rather to endure their oppression with fortitude, limiting oneself to passive resistance if one was ordered to disobey God.[33] One was to wage holy war under the leadership of the caliph "whatever his acts might be", perform the Friday prayer behind any ruler whether pious or reprobate, endure whatever justice or oppression he might dispense, and not rebel with the sword against the amirs even if they were wrongful, according to the creed of the *ahl al-sunna wa'l-jamāʿa* presented by Ibn ʿUkāsha in Basra in 225/839f.[34] "Prayer behind every believer, whether pious or reprobate, is valid," others agreed.[35] The Prophet had said that one was to obey the ruler "even if he be an Ethiopian slave".[36] "Commanding right and prohibiting wrong is indeed a fine thing, but it is no part of the normative custom *sunna* to take up arms against your ruler (imam)," as a Companion of the Prophet was believed to have said.[37] "What do you say about a person who commands good and prohibits evil, with the result that people follow him and rebel against the *jamāʿa*?," Abū Muṭīʿ asked Abū Ḥanīfa, who is here cast as a quietist; he replies that it is wrong, on the grounds that it would cause greater evil than abstaining.[38]

Some held that one should even fight rebels (*bughāt*) whether the ruler they had rebelled against was righteous or not. First one should command them to do good and avoid wrongdoing, and next, if they did not respond, one should do battle against them: one would place oneself in the righteous party thereby even if the imam was a wrongdoer, they said.[39] According to others, however, one should only fight rebels if the ruler was just: this was the view of al-Shāfiʿī (who was not quite a Traditionalist himself, but the legal school that bears his name is generally counted as such). Not even al-Shāfiʿī said that one should join the rebels if the ruler was a wrongdoer, however.[40] The standard Traditionalist view was that if a revolt broke out, one should remain neutral, abstain

33. Cook, *Commanding Right*, 52f. For the ruler as punishment, see Abū Yūsuf, *Kharāj*, 82 (no. 24); Ḥasan al-Baṣrī with reference to Ḥajjāj in Ibn Saʿd, vii/1, 120 (B, 164); the exegetes *ad* Q. 6:65, where Ibn ʿAbbās identifies *ʿadhāban min fawqikum* as evil rulers (also in Māwardī, *Adab al-dunyā*, 139); Ṭurṭūshī, below, 156, note 43.

34. Ibn ʿAsākir, *Taʾrīkh madīnat Dimashq*, ix, 300f, s.v. 'Umayya b. ʿUthmān'.

35. Maghnīsāwī, *Sharḥ al-fiqh al-akbar*, 27; tr. Wensinck, *Creed*, 192 (Fiqh Akbar II, §13); Abū Yūsuf, *Kharāj*, 83 (no. 26): "Obey every amir, pray behind every imam, and do not slander any of my Companions."

36. Cf. Crone, 'Ethiopian Slave'.

37. Cook, *Commanding Right*, 52. The second half is also cited in Abū Yūsuf, *Kharāj*, 83, no. 27.

38. Abū Muṭīʿ, *al-Fiqh al-absaṭ*, 44; in Cook, *Commanding Right*, 8.

39. Abū Muṭīʿ, *al-Fiqh al-absaṭ*, 44; Bidaʿiyya in Sālim, *Epistle*, III, §§106–13; cf. Crone and Zimmermann, *Epistle*, 243ff.

40. Abou El Fadl, 'Islamic Law of Rebellion', 173.

from fighting and recognize the winner as caliph, provided that he was a Qurashī, or at least a Muslim. "It is part of their doctrine, and also that of other *aṣḥāb al-ḥadīth*, that they will treat as imam in every age whoever has established control over the domain (of Islam), provided that he is a man who formally professes the religion (*yantaḥilu ism al-milla*), and they deem it obligatory to pray behind him and conduct holy war under him and allow him to apply the *ḥudūd* penalties," a Muʿtazilite writing (probably) before 850 observed with reference to Kufan and Basran traditionists, adding that they had a profusion of Ḥadīth in support of this view.[41] One widely cited tradition was to the effect that in civil war (*fitna*) the person who sat quietly was better than the one who stood up, who was better than the one who walked, who was better than one who rode. "Be the servant of God who is killed rather than the one who is the killer," another said. "We are with the winners," as Ibn ʿUmar (a favourite mouthpiece of ʿUthmānī traditionists) was reputed to have declared.[42] People who separated from the *jamāʿa* died a pagan death, according to a Traditionalist version of the statement that "whoever dies without allegiance to an imam dies a pagan death."[43] The classical Ḥadīth collections abound in quietist traditions.

The attitude of the Ḥadīth Party struck the Ibāḍī Shabīb b. ʿAṭiyya (c. 760s) as absurd: these people doubted God's injunction to "fight the insolent until they return to God's command"; they deemed the *jamāʿa* to lie with their kings even though they admitted that these kings abandoned the book of God, the Sunna of the Prophet, and the example of the rightly guided caliph; they held that "God will strengthen this religion with men who have no share in afterlife"; how anyone could say such things was beyond him.[44] There were also *jamāʿī* scholars who disagreed with the Ḥadīth party here. For example, most early Murjiʾites, probably including Abū Ḥanīfa, were activists who 'believed in the sword.'[45] There were even adherents of the Ḥadīth party who favoured the idea of rebelling in the days of the inquisition, though Ibn Ḥanbal was not among them. There was no warmth whatever in his own attitude to the caliph, but his obedience to him was total as long as he was not forced to disobey God.[46]

41. Ps.-Nāshiʾ, §112.

42. For these and other quietist traditions, see Ps.-Nāshiʾ, §19; Ibn Qutayba, *Mukhtalif al-ḥadīth*, 4; Abū Yaʿlā, *Aḥkām*, 7; Crone and Zimmermann, *Epistle*, 247.

43. E.g. Muslim, *Ṣaḥīḥ*, v, 21 (*K. al-imāra, bāb al-amr fī luzūm al-jamāʿa*), with other quietist traditions.

44. Crone and Zimmermann, *Epistle*, 245–8.

45. Ibid., 236ff.

46. Cook, *Commanding Right*, 107, 113.

Quietism made sense because the imam no longer determined the believers' otherworldly fate. One did not go where he went or expect to prosper with him in this world and the next if he was rightly guided, to perish with him if he was not. All aspects of the law, be they ritual, fiscal, commercial or other, remained valid regardless of the ruler's moral status as long as he remained a member of the Muslim community. No believer who lived by the law was harmed by the ruler's sinfulness, just as no believer who transgressed the law would benefit from the ruler's justice.[47] "The imam is (just) a shield behind which one fights and seeks shelter. If he orders fear of God and justice he gets the reward for it, and if he does otherwise he gets the blame."[48] God, the real ruler of the community, was represented in the here and now by the Qurʾān and the Sunna of His Prophet, not by the caliph, as numerous exegetes went out of their way to show in their interpretation of Q. 4:59 ("O you who believe, obey God, the Messenger and those in command among you"). Just as they had refused to equate the Qurʾānic *khalīfa* with the caliph, so they refused to read this verse as an injunction to obey the head of state. "Those in command among you" (*ūlū 'l-amr*) were the scholars, they insisted; some held them to be commanders of expeditions sent out by the Prophet, but the obvious interpretation that they were caliphs was avoided, though the Khārijites and the Shīʿites took it for granted that the verse enjoined obedience to the imams.[49] Even if the *ūlū 'l-amr* were commanders, al-Shāfiʿī said, the explanation was that the Arabs at the time of the Prophet needed injunctions to obey, but the obedience enjoined upon them was not absolute; and if they disagreed with their commanders, both parties were to submit their dispute to God and the Prophet (Q. 4:59; 33:36).[50] One way or the other, then, the verse endorsed the supremacy of the Book and the Sunna. Rulers were merely appointed to protect the community against external and internal enemies, appoint judges, patronize scholars, and so forth: this was how they served as shields. They did not function as waymarks and sources of light along the paths to salvation any more. Only the Rāshidūn had been such lodestars.

47. Ibn Baṭṭa, *Profession de foi*, 67f. = 127ff.

48. Abū Yūsuf, *Kharāj*, 79 (no. 17); similarly 82 (no. 24); and compare 83 (no. 28), where Abū Bakr cites Q. 5:105, on how "he who goes astray does not harm you as long as you are rightly guided".

49. Cf. Ṭabarī, *Tafsīr*, *ad* 4:59 (where his personal opinion accords with the classical Sunni quietist view); Crone and Zimmermann, *Epistle*, 152 (*ad* Sālim, *Epistle*, II, 38); ʿAlawī, *Sīrat al-Hādī*, 22; Ṭūsī, *Tibyān*, iii, 236; Nuʿmān, *Himma*, 38 (session 1); above, note 7.

50. Shāfiʿī, *Risāla*, 79f. = 112ff.

Only the Rāshidūn, in other words, had been caliphs and imams in the full sense of the words; after them there was kingship.[51] But the adherents of Ḥadīth did not usually call the ʿAbbāsids kings, for this would amount to a denial of their legitimacy as humble shields and serve to invite rebellion. In Traditionalist terminology all holders of the caliphal office were caliphs and imams, just not in the same sense. Any Qurashī who established himself as caliph was caliph, but there had only been five caliphs, as a summary of al-Shāfiʿī's position puts it.[52] This sounds confusing, but the meaning is perfectly clear. al-Shāfiʿī's five were true caliphs, holders of *khilāfat al-nubuwwa* (the fifth was ʿUmar II); the rest were quasi-caliphs, holders of *khilāfat al-mulk*, or what Sanhoury calls 'irregular caliphs'[53] – in short, the normal caliphs of real life. The first three successors of the Prophet had been true caliphs because they were Companions of the Prophet who ruled in his city of Medina and enjoyed universal acceptance: it was on those grounds that the ʿUthmānīs deemed the true caliphate to have come to an end with the death of ʿUthmān. The addition of ʿAlī as the fourth spoilt the beauty of this argument and made it difficult to exclude Muʿāwiya, for both he and ʿAlī were Companions who had ruled outside Medina after unanimity had come to an end. But then compromise solutions are usually messy. ʿAlī was accommodated as the last rightly guided caliph,[54] whereas Muʿāwiya retained his status as ordinary caliph or king, except to an extreme wing of mostly Baghdadi devotees of Ḥadīth. Other Traditionalists merely said that one had to respect Muʿāwiya as a Companion. The only Umayyad caliph they were prepared to consider as rightly guided was ʿUmar II, who had followed the Prophet's Sunna in the only way possible for somebody who had not been his Companion, that is by looking for it in Ḥadīth. But though he appears on al-Shāfiʿī's list as the fifth, he was too different in kind from the first Rāshidūn to be generally admitted.

51. A widely cited tradition had the Prophet predict that the caliphate would only last for thirty years (*khilāfat al-nubuwwa thalāthūn sana/al-khilāfa thalāthūn ʿāman thumma yakūnu baʿda dhālika mulk*; cf. Wensinck et al., *Concordances*, s.v. 'khilāfa'; also MM, v, 7 (iii, §1765); Ibn Kathīr, *Nihāya*, xiii, 172.6, year 656, obituary of Mustaʿṣim).

52. ʿAbbādī, *Ṭabaqāt*, 17. Compare al-Bāqillānī, who wrote books in defence of the imamate of the ʿAbbāsids, but only included the four Rāshidūn in his *Tamhīd* (Ibish, *Al-Baqillani*, 10, 15, 131f.).

53. Sanhoury, *Califat*, 82, 210ff. et passim.

54. Some added al-Ḥasan (thus Masʿūdī and Ibn Kathīr above, note 51).

Communal consensus

Every single scholar (*ʿālim*) was fallible, but collectively they united all the guidance dispersed in the community and thus could no more go astray than the Prophet himself: "my community will never agree on an error," as the Prophet was believed to have said.[55] Communal agreement (*ijmāʿ*) was thus the ultimate test of the validity of doctrines, not endorsement by the ruler.

Ijmāʿ is classically described as the third source of law, but it was only a source in the sense that it put doctrinal constructions to the test, eliminating some, endorsing others and thereby adding a new layer of accepted views, on which the next generations could build. Like most Muslim institutions, it was entirely lacking in formal procedures. It did not generate any synods, conciliar movements, proclamations of what had been agreed, official creeds, or the like. Nor, it should be added, was it used as an argument for the participation of scholars, let alone the masses, in the election of rulers or other political decision making. It was not a political doctrine at all, except in the sense that it reduced the ruler's voice to one among many as far as the validation of doctrines was concerned.

The Traditionalist vision

Unlike most of the political visions considered so far, that of the *aṣḥāb al-ḥadīth* had the merit of being realistic. The Traditionalists did not believe that complex society could manage without government. They found it deeply troublesome that government tended to be synonymous with tyranny, but they were not prepared to abandon civilization for the world of tribes, and they saw no other way of avoiding it. Since all rulers tended to be wrongful there was no point in engaging in deeply destructive civil war to replace one with another: tyranny had to be accepted as a fact of life. What one could do was to save the moral foundations of social life by withdrawing it from government control.

The Traditionalists thus sacrificed the political autonomy of the first Muslims in order to preserve their social solidarity. It could also be said that they came to terms with two different kinds of tyranny, the ruler's in the political sphere and that of the community in religious matters. They would have been astonished by Ibsen's famous claim that "the compact majority is always wrong" (an eminently Rāfiḍī sentiment).[56] In their view it was precisely with the great majority (*al-sawād al-aʿẓam*) that the truth was always to be found.

55. E.g. Ibn Abū Shayba, *Muṣannaf*, xv, no. 19039.
56. Cf. Kohlberg, 'In Praise of the Few'.

Individuals and petty groups setting off on their own would perish: wolves only took animals that strayed.[57] One reached one's destination by travelling in serried ranks along the well-trodden paths of earlier generations. The community could still be envisaged as a caravan, but it was now guiding itself.

57. Ibn Ḥanbal, *Musnad*, v, 196; cf. Nagel, *Rechtleitung und Kalifat*, 260f.

III

. . .

COPING WITH A FRAGMENTED WORLD

CHAPTER

12

INTRODUCTION

Of all the visions developed in the first two centuries it can be said that their starting point is monotheism in combination with the tribal conceptions of the Arab conquerors. By the tenth century, this was no longer the case. Back in the early days the Arabs were conquerors who set the cultural tone, and as it happened, the cultural traditions of the Syriac and Aramaic-speaking Jews and Christians who were their neighbours in Syria and Iraq blended imperceptibly with their own. The other native traditions, above all the Greek and the Persian, were not absent, but it was only after the ʿAbbāsid revolution that they began to influence high cultural thinking on a major scale, and it was only in the tenth century that they acquired a dominant role.

The main topics of debate also changed. In the first two centuries, the key issue in political thought was tyranny and how to avoid it, whether by reducing the imam's power or on the contrary by sanctifying it. The debate reflected the relentless transformation of autonomous tribesmen into miserable subjects, which was all the more painful in that the victims were acutely conscious of what was happening to them and resisted with all the means at their disposal. By the end of the ninth century the transformation was a *fait accompli*. To most people, the ruler was now a remote figure, as inevitable, tyrannical, and uncontrollable as the weather with which he was sometimes compared.

The ruler was particularly difficult to control because military and political power had been handed to outsiders. Muslim society, though highly differentiated in socio-economic terms, did not include a landed aristocracy or gentry (from whom the governors, generals, and other high officials of premodern empires were normally drawn); nor did the peasants, who formed some eighty percent of the population at a rough guess, supply the soldiers of the imperial armies (again in contrast with other empires). From the ninth century onwards, the main armies consisted of recently converted slaves and freedmen imported from tribal populations and other peoples outside the Muslim world, supplemented with free, homeborn troops of varying importance who were usually dominated by tribesmen as well. It was from their ranks that generals and governors and other high officials were drawn. Educated Muslims could still participate in central government as secretaries and other bureaucrats, and many of them had experience of courts, having been patronized there. But they had no power independently of the ruler to whom they owed their position. All in all, it was clear that arbitrary government had come to stay, and political thought shifted to other issues.

At the same time there was a distinct secularization of the political order. From the ninth century onwards, the political fragmentation of the Muslim world transferred power from the caliph to men who styled themselves amirs, kings, or sultans, first in the provinces and eventually in the capital itself. Government was now in the hands of rulers who were not successors to the Prophet, merely wielders of brute force, and who did not rule the Prophet's polity, merely an arbitrary section of it which they had taken over by force of arms. Devoid of legal status and moral significance, they were rulers of the type that the Muslims had initially seen themselves as called upon to eliminate, and though they learnt to live with them, they could never see them as intrinsically Islamic. Their rise coincided with the transfer of military power to a foreign elite of slave soldiers and mercenaries, who could never become as intimately linked with Islam as the holy warriors and devotees of the Prophet's house on whom the polity had rested in Umayyad and early ʿAbbāsid times, though people came to take them for granted too. In principle, the actual conduct of politics was still based on the law, however profane the new rulers and their servants, but even that was becoming difficult to maintain. In short, government had separated from religion, not in the sense that it had ceased to have anything to do with religion, but rather in the sense that it had acquired autonomous existence. It was no longer a mere branch of religion.

Meanwhile, a new elite had risen on the civilian side, in the form of educated laymen. In the first two centuries of Islam, the vast majority of educated people, poets apart, were scholars trained in sciences connected with the Islamic revelation in some way or other, such as Qurʾānic exegesis, Ḥadīth, jurisprudence, theology, philology, genealogy, or Arabian antiquities. Political thought was dominated by religious scholars (*ʿulamāʾ*) and theologians (*mutakallims*). But by early ʿAbbāsid times this was rapidly changing thanks to the growth of cities, the influx of converts, and the expansion of the court, and in the next three centuries the intellectual pioneers were what one might call professionals: secretaries, administrators, physicians, astrologers, and scientists, in short people who owed their position to the mastery of non-*sharʿī* learning. It was first and foremost educated laymen who cultivated the Persian and the Greek traditions, and they were also prominent among those who wrote on government in the tenth and eleventh centuries. Their influence waned after the Seljuq conquests, and though they never disappeared, religious scholars and theologians predominated again towards the end of the period covered in this book.

From the ninth century onwards the increasing complexity of Muslim society generated a new interest in the spiritual dimension of religion, and by the tenth century one of the key questions of political thought had come to be how the law and the social and political order based on it were to relate, not just to each other, but also to a spirituality far transcending social and political institutions. The main participants in this debate down to c. 1100 were the philosophers, the Ismailis, and the Sufis inside and outside Sunnism. Thereafter it became clear that the Sunnis were winning, and the main debate was within Sunnism itself.

CHAPTER

13

THE PERSIAN TRADITION AND ADVICE LITERATURE

The Persian tradition was deeply alien to the early Muslim thought world. In religious terms it took the form of Zoroastrianism, a dualist or indeed polytheist religion which had no prophet or scripture (it took a while for Zoroaster and the Avesta to be adapted to those roles),[1] which expressed itself in mythology and priestly ritual, and which endorsed the oddest of marriage rules and burial customs. Manichaeism struck the Muslims as much more intelligible, for although it used Zoroastrian names, its conceptual world was Judeo-Christian and its message Gnostic. Thus it was usually against Manichaeism rather than Zoroastrianism that Muslim polemics against dualist religions were directed.[2] In political terms, the Iranians glorified the very kingship that the early Muslims regarded as offensive to God, calling their emperor by the blasphemous title of King of Kings (*shāhānshāh*) and taking pride in their deeply inegalitarian socio-political organization. Even their language was unintelligible, being Indo-European rather than Semitic.

For all that, the Persian tradition rapidly became a key component in Islamic culture. The Arabs conquered the Sasanid empire in its entirety, and eventually subdued the independent principalities of eastern Iran as well, so that the Iranians had no Iranian refuges to flee to. They formed the single largest ethnic group in the caliphate. They were also the only conquered people to have possessed an imperial polity and culture of their own, and they

1. "We have no *kitāb nāṭiq* and no *nabī mursal*" (an Iranian in Tab., ii, 1636, year 120/738). Compare the use of the word *majūs* to mean pagan.

2. Cf. Monnot, *Penseurs musulmans et religions iraniennes*, pp. ix, 102ff.

were subdued complete with their aristocracy, the main bearers of their political ideals. Their political tradition was moreover strongly represented not just in Iran itself but also in Iraq, where the Sasanid capital had been located and where the local Christians had participated in the running of the imperial administration, so all in all, it is not surprising that their political thought rapidly came to affect the Muslims. It reached even the Umayyads in distant Syria, where the caliph Hishām (724–43) ordered the compilation and translation into Arabic of a book about Persian kings.[3] But it was after the ʿAbbāsids moved the capital to Iraq that Persian culture began to resurface in earnest.

Mirrors for princes[4]

Literature of advice (Arabic *naṣīḥa*) was much appreciated in Iran and elsewhere in the Middle East, where it had been cultivated since ancient times, and it retained its popularity in Islam. It often took the form of a 'testament' (*waṣiyya*), that is to say advice passed by a father to his son, or by an older man to a member of the next generation, on his deathbed or on some other momentous occasion. Much advice literature in Sasanid Iran was addressed to kings and touched on problems of government, usually in a moralizing vein. Such works of advice are dubbed 'mirrors for princes' by modern Islamicists, and mirrors were produced in great quantities in the Muslim Middle East down to the nineteenth, or even the early twentieth, century.[5] The name of the genre is borrowed from medieval European history (Latin *specula regis*). It casts the advice as a mirror in which the prince would look at himself and try to improve his appearance, and this idea is encountered on the Muslim side too, even though the term itself is not. "A loyal man may serve one as a mirror: by regarding him one may straighten one's habits and character," as an eleventh-century Turkish work puts it.[6]

Mirrors overlapped with wisdom literature, works of etiquette, religious instruction, and above all ethics. Governance (*siyāsa*) was often said to be of three types: of the self (i.e. ethics), of the household (i.e. economics in its

3. Masʿūdī, *Tanbīh*, 106.

4. For surveys, see Lambton, 'Islamic Mirrors for Princes'; Fouchécour, *Moralia*; Leder, 'Aspekte', and the works listed in Danishpazhouh, 'Bibliography on Government and Statecraft', 214ff.

5. Lambton mentions one composed in 1909 ('Islamic Mirrors for Princes', 420).

6. Yūsuf, *Wisdom*, 222. On this work, see Dankoff's introduction and Inalcik, 'Turkish and Iranian Political Theories'.

original sense of household management), and of cities/the masses (i.e. politics).[7] All mirrors spoke at length about the moral ideals to which the ruler should aspire; many included at least a modicum of political advice as well, and a few discussed governance of all three types. Whatever their focus, all made heavy use of proverbs, aphorisms, and other sententious statements, of which there were also separate collections. Some mirrors, if one can call them that, are just compilations of aphorisms and/or anecdotes on the theme of rulership. But they could also take the form of historical chronicles, epic or didactic poetry, or collections of entertaining stories, or so at least in Persian.

Some mirrors were written by rulers for their sons.[8] More commonly the authors were courtiers, usually secretaries; but some were religious scholars. Though they wrote for kings (and sometimes viziers), it is clear that their readers were drawn from the entire educated elite. Their wisdom was general rather than technical even when they displayed a strong interest in statecraft. "This book is suitable for all and sundry, but more especially to kings," as the Turkish mirror cited above proclaims.[9] Modern readers sometimes marvel at the popularity of the genre, for although it includes some masterpieces (especially in Persian), many mirrors are banal and formulaic. But the same can be said of modern advice literature, which is also widely read ('how to succeed at business', 'how to achieve happiness', 'how to preserve your marriage', and so on). A steady stream of banalities seems to be what one gets when there is a strong market for concrete advice without anyone actually having any to give.

All mirrors for princes treat government as a domain of its own. They usually exhort the ruler to piety and remind him of the judgement to come, and some are very homiletic. Their key aim is always to make the king (or other reader) reflect on himself. But insofar as they touch on government, they see it as a fundamentally secular domain – something which should be regulated by religion, but which does not form part of it. They appeal to authorities such as Sasanid kings, Greek philosophers, and sages of all kinds, not just the Prophet, Companions, and religious scholars; and their sense of justice is usually expedient rather than *sharʿī*. Their ultimate concern in matters of government is

7. These were the three branches of practical philosophy as defined by Aristotelians (cf. *EI*[2], s.v. 'tadbīr'). For their appearance in mirrors, see al-Wazīr al-Maghribī, *Kitāb al-siyāsa*, 56; *NM* (M), 113, 159, 193 (captions); Ibn Abī 'l-Rabīʿ, *Sulūk*, 81ff.

8. Thus the *waṣiyya* of Ṭāhir, the *Pandnāme* of Sübüktegin, the *Qābūsnāme* of Kay Kāʾūs.

9. Yūsuf, *Wisdom*, 259. Compare the title 'The Book of Counsel for Kings and Every Rich Man and Beggar' borne by one Arabic version of Pseudo-Ghazālī's *NM*, which even a Shīʿite scholar such as Ibn Ṭāwūs had in his library (Crone, 'Did al-Ghazālī Write a Mirror for Princes?', 175; Kohlberg, *A Medieval Muslim Scholar at Work*, 373f.).

with what works. The aim of statecraft is prosperity, stability, and satisfaction in this world. What happens in the next is for other books to discuss.

The main works

Political advice first appears in the form of short testaments (*waṣiyya*s) reputedly addressed by early caliphs to their successors or governors.[10] A Greek input was added in the later Umayyad period, when a secretary of the caliph Hishām (724–43) by the name of Sālim edited a translation of letters supposedly sent by Aristotle to Alexander the Great on the topic of government. These were widely read, and one of them formed the basis of the *Sirr al-asrār*, a work of political and other advice which gained huge popularity in medieval Europe under the title of *Secreta Secretorum*. A couple of other Greek pieces were translated later, notably the *Oikonomos* of Bryson (second century AD?) on household management, and a letter by Themistius (d. c. 388) to Julian the Apostate on government.[11] But the mirror genre rapidly came to be dominated by the Persian tradition. By the tenth century, Persians were associated with governance to such an extent that the Egyptian Ibn al-Dāya felt compelled to defend the Greeks against charges of inferiority in this field, which he did by offering three new testaments allegedly extracted (at least according to their title) from "the allegories of Plato's Republic".[12]

Persian works had begun to flood the market after the ʿAbbāsid revolution. The famous secretary Ibn al-Muqaffaʿ (d. c. 140/757) translated the ultimately Indian collection of animal fables, *Kalīla wa-Dimna*, and composed two new works of ethico-political advice, the *Adab al-kabīr* and the *Yatīma*.[13] (He is also famed for his epistle *al-Risāla fī 'l-ṣaḥāba*, but this work offers concrete advice on how to deal with a specific historical situation, not perennial wisdom, so one would not call it a mirror.) Several testaments by Persian kings were made available by unknown translators,[14] and numerous new works were

10. Cf. Tab., i, 2740ff.; Ibn Saʿd, iii/1, 245f. (B, iii, 339) (ʿUmar to his governors and to his successor); BA, iv a, 13, 186; Jāḥiẓ, *Bayān*, ii, 131 (Muʿāwiya to Ziyād and to Yazīd); Tab., iii, 443ff., 1136ff. (al-Manṣūr to al-Mahdī, al-Maʾmūn to al-Muʿtaṣim).

11. See the bibliography, s.v. Grignaschi, Manzalaoui, Ryan and Schmitt, Plessner, Themistius.

12. Ibn al-Dāya, *K. al-ʿuhūd al-yūnāniyya*, 3f. Their alleged Platonic derivation is not mentioned in the text.

13. The *Adab* is extant, the *Yatīma* lost except for quotations. ʿAbbās, 'Naẓra jadīda', 555ff, thinks they are two parts of the same work and shows the *Adab al-ṣaghīr* not to be by Ibn al-Muqaffaʿ.

14. Ibn al-Nadīm, *Fihrist*, 377 = 739f.; cf. ʿAbbās (ed.), *ʿAhd Ardashīr*; also Grignaschi, 'Quelques spécimens de la littérature sassanide'.

composed by Iranians writing in Arabic. Ṭāhir, the founder of the Ṭāhirid dynasty in eastern Iran, wrote a *waṣiyya* to his son ʿAbdallāh on the latter's appointment as governor;[15] the latter's son in turn, ʿUbaydallāh b. ʿAbdallāh b. Ṭāhir, wrote a *Risāla fi'l-siyāsa al-mulūkiyya* which is lost.[16] Several other works on *siyāsa* were composed in the ninth century without surviving.[17] Sasanid books of courtly etiquette (sing. *āʾīnnāme*) were also translated and adapted for caliphal use,[18] and one such adaptation survives in the *Book of the Crown (Kitāb al-tāj)* which has been falsely ascribed to al-Jāḥiẓ.[19]

Among the mirrors written thereafter down to the Mongol invasion which are both extant and published one may mention those in Arabic by al-Wazīr al-Maghribī (d. 418/1027), al-Thaʿālibī (d. 429/1038), al-Māwardī (d. 450/1058), al-Murādī (d. 489/1096), al-Ṭurṭūshī (d. 520/1126), and Ibn Abī 'l-Rabīʿ (c. 650/1250?), plus works falsely ascribed to al-Thaʿālibī and al-Māwardī.[20] The best known Persian works are by Kay Kāʾūs b. Iskandar (wrote 475/1082f.), Pseudo-Ghazālī (sixth/twelfth century?),[21] and (Pseudo?-) Niẓām al-Mulk (d. 485/1092).[22] But there were many more. As mentioned already, there is also an early mirror for princes in Turkish, the *Kutadgu Bilig* of Yūsuf Khāṣṣ Ḥājib, composed in 463/1069f.

The genre was overwhelmingly *jamāʿī*, eventually Sunni. The Imamis and the Ismailis did know a letter of political advice credited to ʿAlī,[23] and the Ismaili judge al-Nuʿmān composed a *Kitab al-himma fī ādāb atbāʿ al-aʾimma* which resembles a mirror, but it is a mirror for subjects rather than for princes

15. Cf. Bosworth, 'Early Arabic Mirror for Princes'.

16. Ibn al-Nadīm, *Fihrist*, 131 = 256f.

17. Cf. *EI*², s.v. 'Sahl b. Hārūn' (Zakeri); F. Rosenthal, 'Abū Zayd al-Balkhī on Politics', 295f. For the possibility that one of Abū Zayd's works survives under a false ascription, see the bibliography, s.v. 'Pseudo-Māwardī'.

18. One such is said to have been translated by Ibn al-Muqaffaʿ (Ibn al-Nadīm, *Fihrist*, 132 = 260).

19. Its real author is probably a courtier by the name of Muḥammad b. al-Ḥārith al-Taghlibī/Thaʿlabī who died in 250/864 (Schoeler, 'Kitāb al-Tāǧ').

20. See the bibliography, s.vv.

21. The first half of this work is by al-Ghazālī, but not a mirror; the second half is a mirror, but cannot be his (cf. Crone, 'Did al-Ghazāli Write a Mirror for Princes?').

22. For a discussion of its authenticity, see Glassen, *Mittlere Weg.*, 122ff.; Simidchieva, '*Siyāsat-nāme* Revisited'.

23. For the Imami version, see above, 123, note 48. For the Ismaili version, see Nuʿmān, *Daʿāʾim*, i, §1464ff.; tr. G. Salinger, 'A Muslim Mirror for Princes'. There is a comparison of the two versions in Qāḍī, 'Fāṭimid Political Document', who argues that the Imami version is secondary. But note the corrective in Danishpazhouh, 'Bibliography on Government and Statecraft', 215ff., and, on a different point, Halm, *Reich/Empire*, ch. 3, note 72.

inasmuch as it is the former who are meant to look in it and improve their ways. It does not seem to have had any imitators. When Ismailis wrote on kings, they did so as philosophers, not as purveyors of commonsense wisdom (except in so far as the genres merged). Imamis employed by Sunni rulers wrote as if they were Sunnis themselves.[24]

Kings

A century after an Arab had been killed in Spain for putting on a crown, understood as a sign that he had gone Christian, the ʿAbbāsid caliphs were bestowing crowns on favourite members of their Khurāsānī troops in Iraq without anyone accusing them of having gone Zoroastrian. By the mid-tenth century most of the independent rulers who had taken over from the caliphs were using the royal title officially. The Būyid rulers of Iraq (945–1055) even took to calling themselves 'King of Kings' (*shāhānshāh, malik al-mulūk*), and other rulers were soon to follow suit.[25] Mirrors often use the terms 'imam' and 'king' interchangeably and apply them to any kind of ruler, whether caliph, amir, or sultan, but it is normally with amirs and sultans rather than the caliph that they are concerned.

All mirrors are extravagant in their high praise of kings, whom they see as belonging to a special class of human beings, of the same rank as prophets.[26] God had singled them out and placed them in charge of the rest of mankind, endowing them with divine effulgence (*farr-i izadī*), and ennobling their essence by allowing them to receive a reflection of the Divine essence.[27] They shared their very appellation of king with God.[28] "All men are made of earth, water, fire and air, but this king descends from the purest Sasanian stock," as the tenth-century Persian poet Rūdakī said in praise of a Sīstānī king.[29] Kings were God's deputies and His shadow on earth;[30] the righteous ones among them were proof of God's existence (so that mankind could not plead

24. Thus al-Maghribī (on whom, see *EI*², s.v.).

25. Busse, 'The Revival of Persian Kingship'; Madelung, 'Assumption of the title Shāhānshāh'.

26. Cf. Marlow, 'Kings, Prophets and ʿUlamāʾ', 106.

27. *NM* (G), 45; cf. *QN*, 196; Thaʿālibī, *Ādāb al-mulūk*, 29; Dāya, *God's Bondsmen*, 395.

28. *NM* (M), 62; Afḍal al-Dīn Kirmānī in Fouchécour, *Moralia*, 433.

29. *Mādar-i may*, verse 40, in *Tārīkh-i Sīstān*, 320.1 = 261.

30. Thaʿālibī, *Ādāb al-mulūk*, 52, 136 (§§73, 366), cf. 29; Māwardī, *Tashīl al-naẓar*, 202; *NM* (M), 51; *NM* (G), 77; Dāya, *God's Bondsmen*, 395, 409; Fakhr al-Dīn al-Rāzī and Afḍal al-Dīn al-Kirmānī in Fouchécour, *Moralia*, 426–8, 433. (For the meaning of the king as God's shadow (*ẓill allāh*), see above, 128, note 5).

ignorance of Him, *ḥujja ʿalā khalqihi*);[31] one could have neither religion nor this world without them.[32] Charles I's statement that "a subject and a sovereign are clean different things" would have struck all of them as entirely correct.[33]

Like the Muslims of the first centuries, the mirror writers assume the highest position and the highest merit to go together: kings were the noblest, the most intelligent, and the most meritorious of people; the general run of kings were more intelligent and virtuous than the most select of their subjects.[34] Like imams, they were object of imitation for their subjects.[35] But there were no legal qualifications for royal office, such as Hāshimite, Qurashī, or Arab descent, for kings could not be elected: God raised up whomsoever He willed (cf. Q.3:26). Nor could they be deposed: that too was for God, who would transfer their kingship to another house when they acted tyranically and disobeyed His law.[36] If a king paid no heed to justice, his subjects would rebel, his kingdom would be laid waste, and his fortune would turn: this piece of wisdom, current already in the third millenium BC, was still valid.[37]

Obedience

The people that God would raise up against wrongdoing kings were typically foreign generals and tribal chiefs rather than their subjects, whose duty, as the mirrors see it, was simply to obey whoever proved to be in charge. In practice, this was more easily said than done. It might be possible to endure oppressive rulers, but some kind of action had to be taken when warlords or tribal invaders threatened a city, more often than not without a ruler or governor being within reach. Maḥmūd of Ghazna (d. 1030) allegedly preferred his subjects to adopt a passive role even when they were on their own. When, in 1038, the inhabitants of Nishapur decided to surrender to the Seljuqs, deeming it impossible to hold out against them, the *qāḍī* of Nishapur supported this decision with a story of Maḥmūd's reaction to a similar event in the past. The

31. Thus already Rūdakī in praise of the ruler of Sīstān, verse 39 (cf. the reference above, note 29); similarly *NM*(M), 52.

32. Thaʿālibī, preface to his *Ghurar*, xlvii.4 (*fa-lā dīn illā bihim wa-lā dunyā illa maʿahum*).

33. Cited in Walzer, *Regicide and Revolution*, 17. The statement was made on the scaffold.

34. Thaʿālibī, *Ādāb al-mulūk*, 32, 63 (preface and §114).

35. *NM* (M), 71.1.

36. *NM* (G), 46; *SN*, chs 1, §§1–3; 6, §3; 49, §§1–2; Ibn al-Balkhī in Lambton, 'Internal Structure', 205.

37. Driver and Miles, *Babylonian Laws*, i, 5.

inhabitants of Balkh had resisted when the Qarakhānids occupied Balkh, he said, with the result that the city had been damaged; and when Maḥmūd reoccupied it, he castigated the Balkhīs for having taken to arms in defence. "What have subjects to do with war?" Maḥmūd had said; "it was natural that your town should be destroyed and that they should burn down the property belonging to me, which used to bring in such revenues." He had gone so far as to declare that the Balkhīs ought to pay him an indemnity for the losses, but he had forgiven them on condition that in future they would submit to whoever proved stronger at any given moment. The people of Nishapur duly did so now. They also saw to it that the story of Maḥmūd's reaction was included in the official despatch to the reigning sultan, Maḥmūd's son and successor, Masʿūd, on whom it had what one assumes was the desired effect: he refrained from punishing the inhabitants when he reconquered the city.[38] Squeezed between rival powers, the people of Nishapur had to survive by their wits, and it seems unlikely that the *qāḍī*'s story was entirely accurate. "The sultan is far away; we can justify our conduct to him later," another notable had said, taking it for granted that surrendering was contrary to the sultan's wishes. Maybe the trouble with the Balkhīs' action was only that they had lost: when the inhabitants of Rayy clubbed together and successfully beat off the Būyids, thinking that they would be better off under Masʿūd, they were praised for it.[39] In any case, the locals had their own lives and property to think of when they were invaded, and whether they surrendered or resisted depended on their chances of holding off the enemy, in Nishapur as elsewhere.[40]

The mirrors do not discuss the finer points of the duty of obedience. Reflecting the ruler's point of view they merely stress it, with the problem of tyranny rather than external invasion in mind. Of the strong tension between activism and quietism characteristic of legal and theological writings on the imamate there is little trace in this literature. Mirrors routinely invoke the Qurʾānic verse, "O you who believe, obey God, the Messenger and those in command (*ulū 'l-amr*) among you" (4:59), as an injunction to obey rulers, seemingly unaware that many religious scholars had gone out of their way to avoid this interpretation of the verse.[41] The twelfth-century *Sea of Precious Virtues*, clearly written by a religious scholar, stands out by affirming that no

38. Bosworth, *Ghaznavids*, 253, citing Bayhaqī, *Tārīkh*, 729.

39. Bayhaqī, *Tārīkh*, 44f. (drawn to my attention by Mohsen Ashtiany).

40. Cf. Paul, *Herrscher, Gemeinwesen, Vermittler*, 117ff., for a good discussion of the whole issue.

41. Thus already Ps.-Jāḥiẓ, *Tāj*, 2 = 27; also *NM* (M) 53; *NM* (G), 45, 104f.; Ibn Abī 'l-Rabīʿ, *Sulūk*, 78; and many others; cf. also Marlow, 'Kings, Prophets and the ʿUlamāʾ', 108. Cf. above, 138.

obedience is due to a ruler who acts against God and the Prophet; but even this work stresses that "we do not consider it permissible to draw the sword against a wrongdoing and unjust ruler so long as he does not oppose the faith or (commit) impiety".[42] A tyrannical ruler had to be endured as a punishment for sins, as al-Ṭurtushī said.[43] He might inflict some damage, but the same was true of rain, cold, and other things, which nonetheless did good as well, and on balance God did more good than bad through him, as authors of the most diverse kind agreed.[44] God had created the king to be such that "all men in the world are obliged to hold themselves in servitude and submission to him", Kay Kāʾūs reminded his son; the king had to treat his subjects in such a fashion that they would not "take out the ring of slavery from their ears", Niẓām al-Mulk agreed.[45] Still, one should not go so far as to deify kings after the fashion of the pre-Islamic Persians and others.[46]

Governance

Most mirrors think of governance (*siyāsa*) as the art of staying in the saddle. The king must ensure that his underlings do not conspire against him, that brigands, robbers, rebels, and heretics do not evict him, that foreign rulers do not invade his lands, that nobody fleeces his sheep, and that generally speaking he is always in control. It required endless vigilance. The mirrors offer advice on bodyguards, armies, viziers, secretaries, tax-collectors, boon companions, wives, nobles, and commoners, or on some of these things, usually with a view to how they should be managed: keep your bodyguard mixed to ensure that they stay loyal, recruit military units of diverse ethnic origin so that some can be played off against others;[47] always choose people of noble birth for important positions;[48] treat nobles with love, the common people with a mixture of

42. Meisami, *Sea*, 223, 254; cf. Lambton, 'Islamic Mirrors', 430.

43. Lambton, 'Islamic Mirrors', 424. Cf. above, 135f.

44. Ibn Qutayba, *ʿUyūn*, i, 3f., and Thaʿālibī, *Ādāb al-mulūk*, 57 (§99), both citing Ibn al-Muqaffaʿ's *Yatīma*; Māwardī, *Adab al-dunyā*, 137.14; al-Maʿarrī in Nicholson, 'Meditations', no. 115; Ibn Wahb, above, 121, note 40; Fakhr al-Dīn al-Rāzī, *K. al-arbaʿīn*, 328 and *Jāmiʿ al-ʿulūm* in Lambton, *State and Government* 135.

45. *QN*, 196; *SN*, ch. 42, §21, in Lambton, 'Dilemma', 59 (Darke opts for the milder "ring of service"). Subjects appear as slaves already in Ps.-Jahiz, *Tāj*, 76 = 105.

46. Thaʿālibī, *Ādāb al-mulūk*, 36–8 (§§11–17).

47. *QN*, 230; Murādī, *Ishāra*, 125.

48. E.g. *NM* (G), 86.

carrot and stick, and the lowly with measures inducing fear;[49] never follow the advice of women or allow them to take charge;[50] study history to learn from the experiences of past kings; know your heretics and all their wiles;[51] above all, keep yourself informed. "It is most important that you should keep yourself well-informed about the condition of the army, their pay and daily allowance," the Turkish ruler of Ghazna, Sübüktegin (d. 387/997), told his son, insisting that "every night before you have said your night prayer, you should have obtained detailed information about your country".[52] "It is incumbent upon the ruler to enquire into the condition of the subjects and the army," Niẓām al-Mulk concurs, lamenting the disappearance of the old intelligence and postal system (*barīd*) and recommending the use of spies in every conceivable disguise. The king must enquire into the condition of his appointees "in secret and in public" so as to stop them oppressing his subjects, he said; everyone who had an important office had to have somebody over him to report on him in secret.[53] One had to be on one's guard against foreign powers too. "You should always keep spies to bring you news of foreign kingdoms and armies and of distant cities," Sübüktegin advised. One should find out everything there was to know about neighbouring kings, including their drinking habits and sexual preferences, others agreed.[54] But the key problem was getting the king's own officials to obey. If the king's command was ineffectual and his appointees ignored his writ, he was no different from anyone else and ruin would overwhelm his state.[55]

People keeping company with kings should also be circumspect, as many mirrors say. Never contradict a king, never feel safe with your patron, beware of everyone in power.[56] "If you are being fattened by someone, you may expect very quickly to be slaughtered by him," as the *Qābūsnāme* puts it. Remember

49. Thus, e.g., Buzurjmihr in Iskāfī, *Luṭf al-tadbīr*, 4; Ibn Wahb, *Burhān*, 421 (citing Ps.-Aristotle); Murādī, *Ishāra*, 155; Anūshirwān cited by others in Rosenthal, 'Abū Zayd al-Balkhī on Politics,' 294 and note 32.

50. *SN*, ch. 42, §1, with illustrations in the rest of the chapter; *NM* (G), 171f.; Ps.-Thaʿālibī, *Tuḥfat al-wuzarāʾ*, 92; Meisami, *Sea*, 295; cf. the Prophet in Ibn Qutayba, *ʿUyūn*, ii, 1. The destructiveness of female wiles is the major theme of the *Sinbādhnāme* of the twelfth-century al-Ẓāhirī al-Samarqandī (Fouchécour, *Moralia*, 421–3).

51. Thus esp. Niẓām al-Mulk, *Siyāsatnāme*, who has much on the *bāṭinī* menace (ch. 46). Thaʿālibī is also concerned to warn rulers against Ismailis (*Ādāb al-mulūk*, 168ff., §§458ff.).

52. Nazim, '*Pand-Nāmah*', 616, 620 = 625, 627. Cf. Ṭāhir in Tab., iii, 1055.

53. *SN*, 27 = 42; Lambton, 'Dilemma', 56, 63; cf. also Najm al-Dīn Rāzī in Lambton, 'Justice', 112f.

54. Nazim, '*Pand-Nāmah*', 620 = 627; *QN*, 214, 231ff.; *SN*, ch. 21, §2.

55. *QN*, 228.

56. Cf. Richter, *Fürstenspiegel*, 8f., on Ibn al-Muqaffaʿ's *Adab al-kabīr*.

that money gained in government service is "more easily dissipated than the dust on the surface of the world"; never display your wealth to the world, but make sure that you pass some of it to your friends. If you become a boon companion, keep your eyes off the rulers' slaves. If you become a secretary, "commit no forgery for a trivial object but (reserve it) for the day when it will be of real service to you." If you become a vizier, go wherever the king goes: "do not leave him alone, lest your enemies in your absence find the opportunity for slandering you . . . contrive that the people in close attendance upon him shall be your spies, informing you of every breath that he draws."[57] Be righteous, fulfill your duties conscientiously, never be a traitor, but don't trust anyone and keep your ears to the ground.

Justice

If the mirrors view people in power with distrust and suspicion, they generally depict the masses as defenceless sheep. Only nobles and heretics are seen as potential rebels. Nobles are particularly dangerous when their circumstances are straitened: one should fear the noble when he is hungry and dominated, the ignoble when he is sated and in control, as Ibn al-Muqaffaᶜ and others said, advising the ruler to look into the poverty of the good and the noble among his subjects (*al-akhyār, al-aḥrār*) and remedy it. Ṭāhir gives the same advice to his son. A tenth-century ruler of Umayyad Spain is said to have made a point of seeking out impoverished nobles in Cordoba in order to assist them.[58]

But as far as the common people were concerned, it was the king's fundamental duty is to ensure that justice prevailed. "The masses need only three things," the caliph al-Manṣūr is reputed to have said; "if someone is appointed to look into their laws so that justice is done among them, to make their roads safe so that they need not fear by night or day, and to strengthen their frontiers and outlying lands so that the enemy will not come upon them, then I will have done those things for them."[59] Justice consisted in doing things in accordance with the rules, allowing people their due, taking only what they owed, and making sure that nobody else robbed them either. A just king compensated people for the losses they suffered as a result of his incompetence. Ziyād b. Abīhi, Muᶜāwiya's governor of Iraq, told the Iraqis that they need not lock their doors at night and that he would pay them compensation for any loss

57. *QN*, 191, 192f., 194, 209, 214.

58. Ibn al-Muqaffaᶜ, *al-Adab al-kabīr*, 116 (with numerous parallels in ᶜAbbās, 'Naẓra jadīda', 544; add Murādī, *Ishāra*, 155); Tab., iii, 1058.12; Ibn Wahb, *Burhān*, 423.-4; Marín, 'Muslim Religious Practices', 884 (al-Ḥakam II).

59. Tab., iii, 422.

they incurred.[60] When a woman informed Maḥmūd of Ghazna that she had been robbed of her possessions while travelling through Kirmān, he initially responded that the place was too remote for him to do anything about it. "What kind of shepherd are you if you cannot protect the sheep from the wolves?" she feistily replied, "look at me in my weakness, all alone, and you with all your army and power." Moved to tears, Maḥmūd duly paid her compensation and promised to deal with the matter.[61]

Preventing authority from being abused was even more important than putting down robbers. The just ruler did not use public money for private purposes,[62] did not display partiality to high-ranking litigants against unknown ones, did not allow his underlings to fleece his subjects, and redressed the grievances of everyone who had been wronged by his officials. There was a special court for the redress of such wrongs (*maẓālim*), and mirrors often stress that the ruler should attend it in person, or generally make himself available to the masses.[63] The Sasanid kings would make themselves available to the public on the days of Mihrijān and Nawrūz and hear petitions from everyone, without debarring anyone.[64]

The Sasanids were wise, we are commonly told, for justice led to prosperity. For one thing, giving people what was rightfully theirs kept them prosperous and easy to manage, whereas injustice caused peasants to leave, so that the revenues diminished, leading to political decline.[65] "If you do not possess money, gold or wealth, nobody will obey you," as Sübüktegin told his son; "no person will ever obey another like himself, except when he is in want and you provide for him."[66] For another thing, kings were believed to have a decisive influence on the natural order. They were like wellsprings determining the purity or impurity of the streams flowing from them. "If the king intends justice, plenty and blessings appear in his domains." Rain would come at the due time, springs and streams would fill up, crops would grow abundant, the roads would be safe, and the kingdom would prosper. But if the king intended injustice, famine and barrenness would appear. The rains would fail, famine and

60. *NM* (G), 79; cf. Abū Hilāl al-ʿAskarī, *Awāʾil*, ii, 38 (fol. 165a).

61. *SN*, ch. 10, §2. Cf. Plutarch, *Lives: Demetrius*, 42.

62. *NM* (G), 68 (where ʿUmar extinguishes a candle paid for by the treasury the moment a slave comes to discuss domestic matters), 69.

63. *SN*, ch. 3; ch. 6, §6; ch. 48, §3; *NM* (G), 95f.; Ibn al-Jawzī, *Shifāʾ*, 67; Meisami, *Sea*, 82, 295.

64. Ps.-Jāḥiẓ, *Tāj*, 159ff. = 179ff.; *NM* (M), 211f.; almost identically in *SN*, ch. 6, §§2–3, and *NM* (G), 102f.

65. *QN*, 229; *NM* (G), 56.

66. Nazim, '*Pand-Nāmah*', 615 = 624. Compare Murādī, *Ishāra*, 156: people are your slaves as long as they have needs you can fulfil and your enemies as soon as they don't.

shortages would follow, highway robbery and unlawful killing would make their appearance, and the kingdom would be ruined.[67] With or without repercussions on the natural order, right religion and political stability went together.[68]

A kingdom depended on wealth, for without wealth one could not maintain an army; and wealth could only be acquired by good government, which in its turn was synonymous with justice, as countless mirrors said.[69] This was where the wisdom of the Persian kings displayed itself: they knew that the greater the prosperity of their realm, the longer they would rule.[70] They survived for four thousand years because they ruled justly, never perpetrating any injustice or oppression.[71] Even Pharaoh had avoided injustice: this was why God allowed him to remain in power.[72] By contrast, the Umayyads fell because they were preoccupied with pleasures and delegated their affairs to others, who pursued their own interests, with the result that the subjects were oppressed, their livelihood was destroyed, the treasury was emptied, and the troops stopped obeying because they were no longer paid.[73] Kingship could survive unbelief, but it could not survive injustice.[74]

The eleventh-century Persian mirrors abound in vivid stories of people who abuse their authority: judges who appropriate money deposited with them, governors and other officials who appropriate land and other property they have set their eyes on, despoiling widows, peasants, and impoverished fishermen, soldiers who rape women, high dignitaries who do not repay their debts to merchants, viziers who oppress everyone and slam their victims into jail, getting away with it because they have the king's confidence, and so on. People travel long distances to have their cases heard, from Azerbaijan to Ctesiphon in one story, from Nishapur to Ghazna in another, only to be denied access or to find on their return that the verdict in their favour cannot be

67. Lambton, 'Islamic Mirrors for Princes', 424, 432, 435, 438f., citing the *Sea*, Ṭurṭūshī and Fakhr al-Mudabbir. See also Al-Azmeh, *Muslim Kingship*, 157, and, in general, Crone, *Pre-Industrial Societies*, 47f.

68. Lambton, 'Justice', 100.

69. Nazim, '*Pand-Nāmah*', 614f. = 624; Inalcik, 'Turkish and Iranian Political Theories', 4ff.; Sadan, 'A "Closed-Circuit" Saying on Practical Justice', 330ff.

70. *NM* (G), 56; cf. *SN*, ch. 5, §3.

71. *NM* (G), 46.

72. Lambton, 'Islamic Mirrors for Princes', 435, 437, citing the *Sea* and Afḍal al-dīn Kirmānī.

73. Iskāfī, *Luṭf al-tadbīr*, 12 (another version in Shayzarī, *Nahj*, 76).

74. *SN*, ch. 2, §1; *NM* (G), 46; Afḍal al-dīn Kirmānī in Lambton, 'Islamic Mirrors for Princes', 437; cf. Sadan, '"Community" and "Extra-Community"', 108ff.; cf. below, 361f.

enforced, whereupon they set off again for the capital.[75] That people's lives were ruined by such things is openly acknowledged, but of course things always come out right in the anecdotes. In Niẓām al-Mulk the happy endings are told with a particularly cloying sentimentality reminiscent of the tone with which modern media will report, say, the successful airlifting of a child from a war-torn area for a lifesaving operation as if it somehow made up for all the atrocities of war. The unexpected rescue of an old woman or other hapless victim from official oppression similarly allows Niẓām al-Mulk to wipe a pious tear off his cheek and to reassure himself and his readers that everything is really all right. As a polished man of wealth and power, he did not actually like all these uncouth people crowding the streets around the *maẓālim* court: it did not look good that there should be so many complainants. "The doors must be closed to such crowds," he said, suggesting ways of keeping the numbers under control.[76]

Moral advice

All mirrors devote much attention to moral advice. They often seem to be written on the assumption that political problems could be solved by moral precepts.[77] Their function was to serve as medicine against the inevitable maladies of absolute power, not by a change of the political system, but rather through an inner conversion of the prince, as Dagron observes in connection with the Byzantine variety of the genre.[78] Moral perfection was a key desideratum in a ruler in that virtue was required for justice. Besides, the moral outlook of kings was generally assumed to affect that of their subjects. Under the influence of philosophy some even went so far as to define *siyāsa* as "the guidance by kings and *imāms* of their subjects . . . to praiseworthy and acceptable actions and strong ways", thereby giving secular rulers the guiding role that the Sunni caliphs had lost.[79] But even if one disagreed, it was obvious that at the very least kings needed self-control in order not to harm their subjects. That the ruler must first learn to govern himself had been a common theme in Greek advice literature,[80] and it remained prominent in Islam. "Unless the king first be truly king of himself, he cannot properly exercise kingship over others," as

75. *SN*, chs 3–13, is about little else, but see esp. ch. 4, §§5–21.

76. Ibid., ch. 49, §1. Compare Niẓāmī ʿArūḍī's attitude to peasants seeking redress in the *Chahár Maqála*, anecd. 6.

77. Cf. Nagel, *Staat und Glaubengemeinschaft*, ii, 95f.

78. Dagron, *Empereur et prêtre*, 38.

79. Qudāma, *Kharāj*, 427; cited in in Rosenthal, 'Abū Zayd al-Balkhī on Politics', 297.

80. Dvornik, *Political Philosophy*, ii, 540, 543, 668, 713.

a thirteenth-century mystic put it.[81] One could think of reason as the husband, the self as the wife, and the body as the house they shared: reason had to keep the self under control, so that it looked after the body as a well-controlled wife looked after the house; everyone knew what damage a dominant wife could do.[82] In more down-to-earth terms, the king should learn to keep his temper, remain calm and collected, listen before taking action, abstain from intoxicating drinks, or at any rate from drinking too much, and keep his eyes and hands off his subjects' women.[83] (If he had to sin, "at least let it be with a good wine . . . and a beautiful partner," Kay Kāʾūs counselled.)[84] All in all, the king should be just, truthful, respectful of the law, forbearing, forgiving, charitable to people known and unknown, a good horseman, courageous, intelligent, and attentive to the lessons of the past. He should also be generous and neither hoard nor economize. It helped to have a perfect physique and good looks.

Overall

Few institutions in Islamic history provoked such conflicting views as kingship, and few were the object of such rapidly changing attitudes. Shortly before the ʿAbbāsid revolution the Ibāḍī Shabīb b. ʿAṭiyya had affirmed that "intelligent people know that the imam is just an ordinary Muslim".[85] This was indeed what he had been at first, to *jamāʿī* Muslims and Ibāḍīs alike. Since this view of him was enshrined in Ḥadīth and other normative literature, everyone with a modicum of education had the wherewithal to deflate the puffed up picture of the ruler presented in the mirror literature, and some actually did so from time to time. According to the poet al-Maʿarrī (d. 449/1058), amirs and kings were just servants of the people they ruled, or mere hirelings, like hired slaves (the ultimate insult). "In terms of obligation to fulfil the laws and observe Islam the imam is like any other obligated person (*mukallaf*)," the jurist al-Juwaynī (d. 478/1085) observed in a more straightforward vein; "he is merely a device for making people obey the Sharīʿa." But al-Maʿarrī's delight in stripping emperors of their illusory clothes was unusual, and al-Juwaynī was being brutal because he was discussing an emergency situation.[86] By their time, neither caliphs nor kings were normally regarded as ordinary humans.

81. Dāya, *God's Bondsmen*, 412.

82. Shayzarī, *Nahj*, 76.

83. E.g. Yūsuf, *Wisdom*, 50; Meisami, *Sea*, 298; *QN*, 218, 222

84. *QN*, 62.

85. In Kāshif, *Siyar*, ii, 358.7.

86. Maʿarrī in Nicholson, 'Meditations', nos. 117–19; Juwaynī, *Ghiyāth*, §488. Cf. below, 234ff.

Down to the mid-Umayyad period the caliphs are presented as being addressed and regarded in much the same way as everybody else. But special rules regarding conversation with, or in the presence of, the caliph are said to have been laid down under the caliph ʿAbd al-Malik (685–705).[87] The tone in official correspondence certainly becomes more formal; statements about the caliphs' minds and bodies become more grandiose,[88] and by the early ʿAbbāsid period the caliph's person had come to be regarded as sacred. By the tenth century the caliph had become a veritable "epiphany of sublimity", as Al-Azmeh calls it: one kissed the ground before him, perhaps the hem of his cloak or, for the privileged, his hand or foot; Saladin even kissed the ground where he had received caliphal greetings.[89] It was not just caliphs who ranked high on the scale of sublimity: kings did too, with similar effects. As usual, there were some who protested. Ibn Ḥazm, for example, noted that the Umayyads had not obliged people to kiss their hands or their feet; the Fatimid caliph al-Ḥākim forbade it, declaring it to be a Byzantine practice unseemly in Muslims; al-Ghazālī declared prostrating to the ruler and kissing his hand to be a grave sin.[90] But all courts worth the name now had elaborate ceremonial designed to emphasize the ruler's grandeur, and all those who worked in, or were patronized by, courts had to come to terms with it. The sanctity of the first caliphs had lain in their perfect fidelity to *sharʿī* morality, not in any external pomp or ceremony, but then they had only existed in the ideal past. What prevailed now was kingship of a universal type: half brutal power and half theatre.

The theatre owed something to the fact that rulers had come to be credited with a cosmic role, in the sense that they were believed to influence the regularities of nature. Natural disasters would ensue if caliphs were killed, it was held, though there was plenty of experience to disprove it. Both caliphs and kings were seen as having special access to the sources of life, health, energy, and well-being, in short of all the pagan desiderata which the great salvation religions had reduced to secondary importance.[91] The basic assumption behind these ideas is that the regularities of nature depended on a moral order which it was the duty of the king to maintain. "When rulers act wrongly, the heavens dry up," a saying ascribed to the Prophet had it.[92] The assumption was

87. Ibn al-Ṭiqṭaqā, *Fakhrī*, 167 (C, 97) = 118.

88. Cf. above, 42, note 33.

89. Al-Azmeh, *Muslim Kingship*, 140f.

90. Ibn Ḥazm in Ibn ʿIdhārī, *Bayān*, i, 63.-2; Halm, 'Treuhändler Gottes', 58; Laoust, *Politique de Ġazālī*, 99.

91. Of kings, see above, 159f.; of caliphs, see Goldziher, *MS*, ii, 64; Sperl, 'Islamic Kingship and Arabic Panegyric', 23f. (with the ancient Near-Eastern antecedents). Cf. also l'Orange, *Cosmic Kingship*.

92. Māwardī, *Tashīl al-naẓar*, 247 (*idhā jārat al-wulāt qaḥaṭat al-samāʾ*).

pagan, not only in the sense that it pre-dated the rise of monotheism and placed a high premium on well-being in this world, but also in the sense that it idolized a single human being in a manner that Sunnis were normally quick to disown. Of course, many monotheists also believed the maintenance of moral order to be crucial for the proper functioning of the natural world, but they identified the moral order as God's law and, in the Islamic world at least, had mostly blamed misfortunes such as drought and earthquakes (or political reverses) on collective sins rather than those of the king alone. Numerous Shīʿites had objected when their imams were cast in a cosmic role, and some continued to do so. Yet the Sunnis do not seem to have been worried when similar ideas began to be attached to their rulers. Altogether, the changing conceptions of kingship testify to the fact that the sharp separation between God and man characteristic of monotheism was disappearing. Zoroastrianism, Gnosticism, and Neoplatonism (pagan or Christianized) had all conceived of divinity as graded – as a light ranging from unbearable intensity to a mere spark, for example – rather than as something concentrated in a single point. Now that most of the pre-conquest population found itself within Islam, this view of things was returning.

Speaking of the patterns of royal aggrandizement common to the centralized monarchies of early modern Europe, Walzer observes that "It is as if every king until the revolution preened himself before the same magic mirror and saw the same gratifying images: himself God's deputy, head and soul of the body politic, sole knower of the mysteries of state, father of his subjects, husband of the realm, healer, peacemaker, sovereign lord."[93] Many other kings looked at themselves in that mirror, too, including those of the medieval Muslim world. They did not usually see the images of father or husband,[94] nor did Muslim kings have a healing touch, whereas they did have a decisive effect on the natural order that the kings of early modern Europe seem to have lacked. But both saw their rulers as God's deputies on earth and His image or shadow. God had raised them up and there was something divine about them, even though one should not go so far as to deify them. To early Muslims, kings were usurpers of God's power. To later Muslims, by contrast, they typified it.

93. *Regicide and Revolution*, 9.

94. The closest one gets to it is statements to the effect that the ruler will handle the affairs of his subjects "as fathers handle the affairs of their children" (Juwaynī, *Ghiyāth*, §382).

CHAPTER

14

THE GREEK TRADITION AND 'POLITICAL SCIENCE'

The Greek tradition was less opaque to the early Muslims than the Persian, having long been Christian, but its role in Islamic culture was nonetheless more marginal, largely thanks to the fact that the Arabs only succeeded in conquering the eastern provinces of the Byzantine empire. Greeks were poorly represented in the caliphate. The metropolitan elite remained outside it, and their number was limited even at a provincial level, for many Greeks left Syria and Egypt when the Arabs took over: unlike the Persians, they still had an empire to go to. Of the educated men, Greek or non-Greek, who stayed behind, few were as steeped in imperial culture as their Persian and Persianized counterparts in Iraq, who had the Sasanid capital at their doorstep. Facility in Greek was of course required for a career in the local bureaucracies, and Syrian bureaucrats did play a role in the transmission of Greek political ideas under the Umayyads: it was a secretary of the caliph Hishām (724–43) who translated the Pseudo-Aristotelian letters to Alexander into Arabic.[1] But the Syrian contribution was limited, and the Egyptians do not seem to have contributed at all. Paradoxically, it was overwhelmingly in Iraq, not in the former Byzantine provinces, that Greek learning resurfaced, and it did so in response to caliphal demand rather than pressure from Greek or Hellenized converts. What the translators made available was moreover the legacy of the ancient Greeks (*al-yunāniyyūn*, literally the Ionians), not the culture of the contemporary Byzantines (*al-rūm*, literally the Romans). Philosophy did survive in Byzantium, where it formed part of the training of a civil servant, but it was classified as

1. Cf. above, 151.

'external learning' in contrast with Christian theology, and professional philosophers had all but disappeared by the time of the Arab conquests.[2] The intellectual orientation of seventh-century Byzantium is best illustrated by the book that the Arabs are said to have found during a campaign near Constantinople in the reign of Muʿāwiya: it was an apocalypse attributed to Daniel and concerned with celestial omens.[3] If the story is true, it will have been the first Greek work that the Muslims translated.

The translations

The translation of Greek works began in earnest shortly after the ʿAbbāsid revolution and continued down to the tenth century, sponsored by caliphs, princes, courtiers, and other learned laymen. The original impetus was a desire for scientific and technological know-how, whether Indian, Persian or Greek. Philosophy (*falsafa*) only began to be made available on a systematic basis in the mid-ninth century, when al-Kindī (d. c. 252/866), tutor to a son of al-Muʿtaṣim, assembled a large circle of translators, scholars, and thinkers for that purpose.[4]

The bulk of the philosophical translations were of Aristotle. Given that late antique and Islamic philosophy alike are often described as Neoplatonist, this may come as a surprise to the reader, but Neoplatonism as taught in Athens (till 529) and Alexandria (till c. 610) was actually Platonizing Aristotelianism. The bulk of the curriculum, after lengthy introductions, was devoted to Aristotle, and the Neoplatonist philosophers wrote extensive commentaries on his works, held to be in fundamental agreement with Plato's.[5] This predominance of Aristotle continued in Islam. With the exception of the *Politics*, of which only some excerpts were known, all Aristotle's extant works (and numerous spurious items) were translated, usually in full. By contrast, only some of Plato's works were made available, usually, perhaps always, in epitomes of late antique provenance made by amateurs such as doctors (above all Galen). These amateurs had emerged as the main bearers, along with astronomers/astrologers, of philosophical ideas in the Greco-Roman world when the number of professional philosophers dwindled, and they retained

2. Burstein, 'The Greek Tradition', 49.

3. Hoyland, *Seeing Islam as Others Saw It*, 330.

4. Endress, 'The Circle of al-Kindī', esp. 64f.; cf. Gutas, *Greek Thought, Arabic Culture*, 30ff.

5. Cf. Sorabji (ed.), *Aristotle Transformed*. I do not know what sense to make of Mahdi, *Alfarabi and the Foundation of Islamic Political Philosophy*, 34.

this role in Islam.[6] Of Plotinus (d. 269f.), the founder of Neoplatonism, the Muslims had only a paraphrase of extracts from the *Enneads* mistitled 'The Theology of Aristotle' (*Uthūlujiyya Arisṭāṭālis*), and the works of Iamblichus (d. c. 325) do not seem to have reached them at all. They did better with Porphyry (d. c. 305) and Proclus (d. 484).[7] Of philosophers before Plotinus, the above-mentioned Galen (d. c. 200) and the Aristotelian Alexander of Aphrodisias (fl. early third century) were well represented; a couple of works by Plutarch were also translated. But the pre-Socratics, Cynics, Stoics, Sceptics, and other minor schools were known only from collections of wise sayings, doxographies, and histories, except insofar as their doctrines had passed in the general culture of the pre-Islamic Near East, and from there to the Muslims.[8]

The first Muslims to write on political subjects under philosphical influence were al-Kindī (d. c. 252/866), al-Sarakhsī (d. 286/899), and Abū Zayd al-Balkhī (d. 322/934).[9] But their works (all lost) seem to have had greater affinities with advice literature and ethics than with the branch of learning known as *al-ʿilm al-madanī*, for which the literal translation is 'the science relating to the city (in the sense of polity)', or more idiomatically, 'political science.' The founder of that science was al-Fārābī (d. 339/950), active in Baghdad, Egypt, and Syria. Among the best-known philosophers influenced by him are Ibn Sīnā (d. 428/1037), active in eastern Iran, and Ibn Bājja (d. 533/1139), Ibn Ṭufayl (d. 581/1185f.), and Ibn Rushd (d. 595/1198), all active in Spain. Philosophical thinking about governance also flourished among the Ismailis, who had taken up the subject independently of al-Fārābī: the main thinkers here are Abū Ḥātim al-Rāzī (d. 322/934), Abū Yaʿqūb al-Sijistānī (probably d. after 360/971), and the Brethren of Purity (wrote second half of fourth/tenth century).[10]

A historian of mainstream Islam is apt to dismiss all philosophers as marginal (except in so far as they had other strings to their bows), for mainstream Islam was shaped by religious scholars, who were prone to rejecting philosophers and Ismailis alike as heretical. One does not often encounter the philosophers or their 'political science' in sources written by these scholars. In fact,

6. Brague, 'Note sur la traduction arabe de la *Politique*', with discussion of earlier views; Rosenthal, 'On the Knowledge of Plato's Philosophy', 392f.; Endress, 'The Circle of al-Kindī', 51f.

7. *EI*², s.vv. 'Buruḳlus,' 'Furfūriyūs'.

8. Gutas, 'Pre-Plotinian Philosophy in Arabic'.

9. Rosenthal, 'Abū Zayd al-Balkhī on Politics', 287ff., 296. For a helpful overview of the sources and an excellent bibliography, see Daiber, 'Political Philosophy'.

10. Cf. further below, ch. 15. Daiber, 'Political Philosophy', 848f., sees the Ismailis as first and Fārābī as working under their influence (cf. further below, note 70).

one does not often encounter al-Fārābī anywhere at all.[11] But after al-Fārābī's time, attempts to fuse philosophy with the religious sciences began to be made, notably by al-ʿĀmirī (d. 381/992) and Rāghib al-Iṣfahānī (c. 400/1010),[12] and though some rejected such efforts as attempts to undermine Islam from within,[13] there can be little doubt that the appeal of philosophy widened. Even religious scholars and theologians took to reading it, be it for purposes of instruction or refutation. By far the most famous theologian to study philosophy was al-Ghazālī, who was in effect a philosopher himself. He rejected key parts of its metaphysics as incompatible with Islam, and at a popular level he rejected the entire metaphysical edifice, but even at a popular level he insisted that nothing was wrong with mathematics, natural science (some specific doctrines apart), logic, or for that matter writings on governance (*siyāsiyyāt*); on the contrary, he said, some of it was positively useful.[14] For all that, people continued to condemn philosophy as a whole, now out of ignorance and now on suspicion that one thing would lead to another. To call a man a philosopher (*faylasūf*) was still to brand him as a heretic or infidel.[15] (Hence it was by preference under the label of wisdom [*ḥikma*] that philosophy was cultivated.) But the absorption of Greek philosophical ideas into general Muslim culture continued. It was particularly in Iran that the two heritages flowed together, and above all in works written in Persian (a language in which people felt freer to depart from established norms). But the amalgamation of the heritages can also be seen in works written in Arabic, in Iran and elsewhere. The extent to which the philosophers contributed to political thought outside their own circles should become clear in chapter 17. Meanwhile, it may be noted that political thought of *falsafa* origin appears in a greater or lesser state of domestication in works by secretaries and courtiers such as Qudāma b. Jaʿfar (d. 337/948), Ibn Wahb al-Kātib (wrote c. 335/946), al-Bayhaqī (d. 470/1077), and Niẓāmī ʿArūḍī (d. after 547/1152),[16] in mirrors for princes such as that by

11. The only near-contemporary source to mention him is the Shīʿite Masʿūdī (d. 345/956); cf. Stern, 'Al-Masʿūdī and the Philosopher al-Fārābī'.

12. Cf. *EI*², s.vv. (the former in the supplement).

13. Rowson, *Muslim Philosopher*, 2ff., citing Tawḥīdī, *Imtāʿ*, ii, 13–23.

14. Cf. his summary in his *Munqidh*, 20ff. = 32ff. On Ghazālī's attitude to philosophy important work is being done by F. Griffel.

15. Cf. Ḥassan-i Ṣabbāḥ in Hodgson, *Assassins*, 44.

16. Cf. Hiyari, 'Qudāma b. Ǧaʿfars Behandlung der Politik'; Heck, *Construction of Knowledge*, ch. 5; *EI*², Suppl., s.v. 'Ibn Wahb'; Meisami, *Historiography*, 81ff.; Niẓāmī ʿArūḍī, *Chahár Maqála*, 10ff.

the otherwise unknown Ibī Abī 'l-Rabīᶜ (wrote c. 650/1250),[17] and in the work of a heavyweight theologian such as Fakhr al-Dīn al-Rāzī (d. 606/1209).[18]

'Political Science'

What the philosophers called 'political science' (*al-ᶜilm al-madanī*) formed part of practical philosophy, traditionally divided into ethics (*akhlāq*), household management (*siyāsat/tadbīr al-manzil*), and politics (*siyāsat al-mudun, siyāsa ᶜāmmiyya, (ᶜilm madanī*). All three branches concerned themselves with the male aspiring to be in control, of himself in the first case, of his women, children and slaves in the second case, and of his co-religionists in the third. In the third case, however, the control was envisaged as intellectual. 'Political science' did not have much to do with what we know by that name today. Rather, its focus was on what Pico della Mirandola (d. 1494), the Florentine Neoplatonist, called the 'dignity of man' (and to most *falāsifa*, this really did mean the male half of the species): man rising above the limitations imposed by his self and others, trying to elevate himself to the rank of the angels. Altogether, it is Renaissance Platonism that the reader should have in mind as the comparable phenomenon in Europe, not the medieval Latin political thought inspired by Aristotle's *Politics*.[19]

As the philosophers saw it, man's highest aim was to seek intellectual and moral perfection, by study and self-control, in order to purify his rational soul and enable it to survive the death of his body, so that he would live for ever as pure soul in blissful contemplation of the truth. This view was tied to an understanding of ultimate reality different from that of traditional Islam. It was the moral implications of metaphysics as understood by the philosophers, and for this reason it is often with metaphysics that books on *(ilm madanī* will start. Of the thirty-four chapters that make up al-Fārābī's book on the virtuous city (*al-madīna al-fāḍila*), for example, twenty-five are concerned with God, cosmology, the soul, the intellect, virtue, and happiness; only the last nine are concerned with the communal setting in which virtue might be achieved.[20] His *Siyāsa madaniyya* ('Political/Communal Governance') is similarly organized. It is also at the end of his exposition of metaphysics that Ibn Sīnā places his chapter on communal organization and government in his *Shifāʾ* ('Healing') and *Najāt* ('Salvation'). Similarly, it was at the end of

17. Cf. Brockelmann, *GAL*, *Suppl.* i, 372, noting the influence of Ibn Buṭlān and Bryson. There is also much Themistius in this work.

18. On whom cf. *EI*², s.v.

19. For a good account, see Hodgson, *Venture of Islam*, i, esp. 418f., 433ff.

20. Rosenthal, 'Politics in the Philosophy of Al-Farabi', 158f.

expositions of theology (*kalām*, *uṣūl al-dīn*) that the imamate was traditionally discussed. In philosophy as in theology, the 'political' chapters explain what the vision through the window meant for humans seeking to live intellectually and morally upright lives as social beings.

Christians, Jews, and Muslims in the period covered in this book all saw the aim of human life as living in accordance with a great truth about ultimate reality and the moral code with which it was associated. All focused their attention on the nature of this reality and code, seeking to discover and disseminate the true and the right, and all took an interest in government first and foremost for its ability to assist or obstruct this endeavour. In their capacity as religious scholars, philosophers, missionaries, clergymen, or rabbis, they had a professional interest in the government of human minds, or, as they would put it themselves, the government of souls, not in that of bodies, which was not under their control even when the coercive machinery that we call the state was their own. But a great deal of what they said about the true and the right had implications for the distribution of power even when it was not thought about the state. This is certainly true of 'political science'. For if the philosophical version of the view through the window was right, it would follow that it was the philosophers who ought to be revered as the most authoritative spokesmen of the truth and the attendant code. That was precisely what al-Fārābī held them to be.

Al-Fārābī[21]

Al-Fārābī was an Aristotelian who saw Aristotle through the Platonizing filter of the late Greek tradition. On the subject of 'political science' he went further, however: here his key source of inspiration was actually Plato himself. It part this may be because Aristotle's *Politics* was unavailable to him (he certainly made heavy use of Aristotle's *Nicomachaean Ethics*); but it was hardly for that reason alone.

Plato had written on politics in a utopian vein, discussing the ideal polity on the assumption that a polity was something which could be created by *fiat* on the basis of a design drawn up in advance. This assumption, which is so striking a feature of early Greek political thought, reflected the Greek colonizing experience. From c. 750 BC onwards the Greeks founded new settlements in Anatolia, southern Italy, and eventually in the Near East as well. Each colony was planned by a founder (*oikistēs*), who identified its site, divided the land

21. For an introduction, see Mahdi, 'Alfarabi'; *Enc. Iran.*, s.v. 'Fārābī' (Gutas, Mahdi, et al.).

into plots for the settlers, and held autocratic powers during the period of foundation; and each received a written code of law drawn up for it by a law-giver (*nomothetēs*), who might be identical with the founder. By Plato's time the Greeks had long been thinking of polities as human inventions and discussed the best form of government in the context of new colonies. Plato's *Republic* is a thought experiment for a colony so ideal that even Plato granted that it was unlikely ever to be realized. He explored more realistic constitutions in his *Laws* and *The Statesman* without entirely abandoning his ideal.[22]

Plato died in the fourth century BC. By the fourth century AD, the colonizing movement had receded to the remote past, the city states were no longer polities, just cities, and the imperial government to which they had long been subjected had turned autocratic. Accordingly, political thought now went into administrative manuals and advice to rulers rather than blueprints for the best constitution; philosophy had come to concern itself with man in the abstract rather than with man the citizen, and its focus was on the ethical systems whereby he could control his inner life.[23] Though the philosophers of late antiquity were not as indifferent to politics as used to be thought,[24] it was usually educated layman rather than professional philosophers who would speak of constitutions and vaunt the Platonic philosopher king, in speeches, encomia, and advice for kings.[25] Al-Fārābī reversed this trend: a professional philosopher, he read Plato mainly for the political thought that his predecessors had come to regard as secondary.

The reason why al-Fārābī was fascinated with this thought is not that he had an interest in political experimentation. Rather, Plato's political thought was attractive to him because it seemed to share a number of Muslim presuppositions.[26] As it happened, Islam had itself begun as a colonizing venture: the Prophet and his followers had migrated to Medina where the Prophet had founded a new polity and promulgated a new law. Moreover, the early Greeks shared the early Muslim view that membership of a particular polity (the city state in their case, Muḥammad's *umma* in that of the Muslims) was a

22. For all this, see Dawson, *Cities of the Gods*, chs 1–2, esp. 22, 71ff.

23. Burstein, 'The Greek Tradition', 34f.

24. The field has been transformed by the work of O'Meara (see the bibliography).

25. Thus Dio Chrysostom, Themistius (a professional court philosopher), Synesius (Dvornik, index), Agapetus (in Barker, *Social and Political Thought*, 56f.; Henry, 'Mirror', 295), and, not least, the anonymous dialogue on political science (*peri politikēs epistēmēs*) from Justinian's time, which speaks of the philosopher king and 'the true king' in terms reminiscent of Fārābī (book v, ch. vii, in Barker, *Social and Political Thought*, 71; cf. also O'Meara, 'The Justinianic Dialogue').

26. Mahdi, 'Alfarabi', 161.

precondition for human perfection/salvation. This gave al-Fārābī the bridge between the two thought worlds he wished to connect. He deduced that Islamic history had two faces, the familiar one to be found in Muslim history books and another to be found in Plato, in which one could read of the Prophet as the lawgiver (*wāḍiʿ al-nāmūs*), the Sharīʿa as the law (*nāmūs*) or constitution (*sīra*, *siyāsa*), the Muslim community as his polity (*madīna*), and, not least, of the philosophers as the true legatees of its founder. In short, Plato enabled al-Fārābī to domesticate and legitimate philosophy as a Muslim science, while at the same time making a daring bid for philosophical leadership of the Islamic world. This was the project to which he returned time and again throughout his career.

Philosophy and religion

The two thought worlds that al-Fārābī wished to connect are conventionally known as philosophy and religion, but it would be more accurate to call them two different types of religion (or alternatively two different types of philosophy). For the final goal of philosophy was knowledge of God, or knowledge of 'things human and divine' and 'assimilation to God insofar as attainable for man', as every student at Alexandria was told.[27] Neoplatonists were moreover prone to envisaging ultimate knowledge of God as mystical union with Him. Al-Fārābī was not a Neoplatonist, and there is no hint of mysticism in his work,[28] but philosophy was certainly a religion to him too. It was a religion without revelation, however: humans could reason their way to the ultimate truth without supernatural help. It was this conviction that put philosophy on a collision course with religion, if by religion one means revelation which had to be taken on trust.

They had in fact already collided by the time he wrote. The physician and philosopher Abū Bakr al-Rāzī (d. 313/925) had dismissed revealed religion as false. There was only one saving truth, he had said, namely that of philosophy, and it was accessible to all men, elite and masses alike. God had given all humans the ability to find their way to salvation by *ilhām*, literally divine inspiration, here meaning something like instinct: animals and humans alike knew what was good or bad for them by virtue of it. Prophets were impostors who impressed people with their tricks and sleights of hand. In the same vein, an earlier philosopher, al-Sarakhsī (d. 286/899), had written a book on "the secrets of the charlatans", meaning the prophets,[29] while the rationalist

27. Westerink, 'Alexandrian Commentators', 343, 344, 346.
28. Differently Corbin, *Philosophie islamique*, 225f.
29. Rosenthal, *Saraḫsī*, 51.

theologian Ibn al-Rāwandī (d. c. 245/860 or 298/912) had argued, behind the cover of the brahmans, that the miracles claimed by prophets were mere tricks and that revealed law should be rejected: either it accorded with reason, in which case it was superfluous, or else contradicted it, in which case it was wrong.[30]

Al-Fārābī did not want religion and philosophy to collide, so he had either to identify them or to subordinate the one to the other. In effect he did both. He said that both philosophy (*falsafa*) and religion (*milla*) gave you the truth, but that they did so in different versions, designed for different audiences. Philosophy, which had existed before religion, led you to things as they really were by means of proofs based on demonstration (*burhān*); religion represented the abstract truths of philosophy in symbols, images and similes that everyone could understand and secured acceptance for them by persuasion (*iqnāʿ*). For example, religion would describe the void as water or darkness.[31] The relationship he postulated was rather like that between professional and popular science today. It is the same truth that they postulate, but professional science rests on mathematical demonstration, whereas popularizers resort to analogies, similes, and images drawn from the reader's everyday experience; the reader of popular science cannot actually check the arguments, but he can be swayed by the author's powers of persuasion. (The big difference, of course, is that science has no saving role at either level and that accordingly, popularizers today do not have to operate with metaphors set in advance by organized religion, but can choose whatever they like.) According to al-Fārābī, those who dismissed revealed religion as false were ignorant of its symbolic nature.[32] He did not think that all religions were equally good at representing the truth,[33] but neither did he think that one alone had got it right. There were many ways of depicting the ultimate truth in symbolic and allegorical form. All were approximations, none gave you access to things as they really were. It was only philosophy which allowed you direct knowledge of ultimate reality.

Unlike religion, philosophy was unchanging. It always led you to the same universal truth wherever or whenever it was pursued, for ultimate reality never changed. But religions were designed for particular segments of humanity at particular places and times, so they came in many different versions and changed as one lawgiver abrogated his predecessor's version in favor of his own. Every lawgiver knew the absolute truth, but used religion to get elite and

30. Kraus, 'Beiträge', 97 = 111 (no. 3).

31. Fārābī, *Taḥṣīl*, §56 = §55.

32. *MF*, ch. 17, §6.

33. Cf. Fārābī, *Kitāb al-ḥurūf*, §147 (pp. 153f., tr. in Berman, 'Maimonides, the Disciple of Alfārābī', 175f.).

masses together in a polity. Without religion there would be no polity and no salvation for the masses. But religion only offered a relative truth, and it was only by means of philosophy that one could escape from relativism.

It is al-Fārābī's belief in the universal nature of philosophy that accounts for his strangely context-free presentation. He names no names, apart from those of Plato and Aristotle, and hardly ever gives concrete examples of the religions, polities, constitutions, or other phenomena he describes. Unlike the Brethren of Purity or Ibn Rushd, he never explicitly identifies the lawgiver as the Prophet: one is free (indeed strongly encouraged) to envisage him as Muḥammad, but one can also identify him as Moses or any other prophet familiar to Islam, or as a past or future philosopher. By the same token one is prevented from objecting when al-Fārābī's model cannot be squared with the Islamic past as known from the history books. Al-Fārābī did implicitly confront the historical record of Islam in one of his works: if a nation receives a religion without knowing that it is a reflection of philosophy, he says, and philosophy only arrives later, then the result may be that there is religious opposition to philosophy.[34] But no names are named here either. Whether or not Muḥammad preached philosophy behind the façade of popular religion is never stated. It is also rare for al-Fārābī to use Muslim terminology, and when he does, he typically replaces the familiar sense with a philosophical one. *Jāhilī* means ignorant, not of Islam, but rather of the nature of true happiness as defined by the philosophers. *Jihād* is war in defense of the perfect polity, again as defined by the philosophers, and not of the Muslim community. A *malik* is a king in a new sense to which political power is incidental. Here and elsewhere, al-Fārābī is using Muslim terminology to familiarize the reader with new concepts, much as astrophysicists do when they apply everyday terms such as 'big bang' or 'black hole' to unfamiliar cosmic phenomena (with such success, in their case, that their usage has become primary).[35] Sometimes he confuses his reader by using a word in its familiar sense as well. He is always operating at two levels, the familiar and the philosophical, and he will flit backwards and forwards between the two, leaving it to the reader to work out exactly where he is, in part no doubt for reasons of precaution: the philosophers have to speak in riddles (*rumūz*) to filter out unworthy readers (such as hostile rulers and the mob), as he said, resuming a theme dear to the hearts of the late antique philosophers.[36] This is not to say that he saw philosophy as an

34. Ibid., §149 (p. 155, tr. in Berman, 'Maimonides, the Disciple of Alfārābī', 176f.); cf. Zimmermann, *Al-Farabi's Commentary*, cxiv, note 1.

35. Cf. Kraemer, 'The *Jihād* of the *Falāsifa*', 293.

36. Fārābī, *Talkhīs*, 4 and *Jamʿ*, 84 = 64, on Plato; cf. Plotinus on Plato in Wallis, *Neoplatonism*, 17; others on Aristotle in Westerink, 'Alexandrian Commentators', 343 (I, 9).

esoteric discipline or that he wrote in a code that only initiates could understand, so that the real meaning of what he is saying has to be sought between the lines.[37] On the contrary, he speaks loud and clear on general points. But it is impossible not to sense a certain wariness when it comes to spelling out the concrete implications. What with his refusal to give examples, his flitting from one level to another, and the peculiar Arabic he constructed for philosophical use,[38] he is a difficult author to get into. The novice feels utterly disorientated by the absence of familiar landmarks, the high level of abstraction, and the cumbersome phraseology. Al-Fārābī would probably have responded that this is entirely as it should be.

Philosophy and religio-political organization

Al-Fārābī was greatly indebted to the late antique philosophers for his view of religion as a popular version of philosophy.[39] As pagans, the philosophers had had to come to terms with Greek mythology, found in their revered Homer and elsewhere; thereafter, they had had to explain the relationship between philosophy and Christianity, sometimes as Christians trying to retain their philosophical beliefs (there were Christian Platonists already by the second century), and sometimes as pagans trying to accommodate the Christian world around them (the professional philosophers remained pagans down to the mid-sixth century). Whatever their religious affiliation, Platonists routinely combined philosophy with competing belief systems by distinguishing between two levels of truth. All peoples interested in metaphysics were assumed to operate with a high truth for the few (such as monotheism in a polytheist environment, rationalism in one of revealed religion) and to disseminate a vulgar version for the common people, expressed in myths, riddles, symbols, and allegories which the common people would take at face value, but which the philosophers would see as pointing to higher things.[40] It was not just to screen the truth from the masses that the philosophers would speak in myths and riddles: they would also do so to educate them, at the level appropriate to them. Plato, Aristotle, and other philosophers had all used myth to

37. The thesis of Leo Strauss, followed by Mahdi and his students, notably Butterworth and Galston.

38. Cf. Zimmermann, *Al-Farabi's Commentary*, xlviiiff., cxxxiff.

39. See, for example, O'Meara, 'Religion as Abbild der Philosophie'; cf. Fārābī, *Taḥṣīl*, §56 = §55, where he presents his own views as simply those of the ancients.

40. Clement of Alexandria, *Stromata*, V, 4, 21, 4; V, 7, 41.1; et passim; Origen, *Contra Celsum*, I, 12; Julian the Apostate, Sallustius, Proclus, and Hierocles in O'Meara, 'Religion als Abbild der Philosophie', 346ff. 3 and note 29.

convey the truth to the common people, according to the Neoplatonists. The Hebrews, too, had told stories as if they were myths, though practised minds could see their hidden meaning, according to Eusebius, bishop of Caesarea (d. 340); and when Moses prescribed the law for them, he formulated some of it in the form of symbols which contained a direct image of the divine realities. This was very much how the Muslim philosophers saw their philosophical predecessors and Muḥammad as having proceeded, too.[41] In antiquity the relationship between the two levels was sometimes perceived as effortless, sometimes as tense, and there were also some who rejected the lower level as outright fraud. All these positions reappeared in Islam (and again in post-Renaissance Europe).[42]

But on one crucial point the Neoplatonist philosophers left al-Fārābī in the lurch. Though some of their views on the subject of government may have come in useful to him,[43] they had no reason to think deeply about the relationship between their philosophy and the Roman empire in which they were trying to keep it alive. Both were pagan by origin. It was the Christians who had to think hard about the relationship between their own 'philosophy' and the empire, having started out indifferent or hostile to it; and if al-Fārābī received any assistance on this topic, it will have been from them rather than the pagan Neoplatonists that he received it. Already Philo of Alexandria (d. after 41), a Hellenized Jew much read by Christians, had cast Moses as the philosopher king envisaged by Plato.[44] Eusebius similarly presented Moses as a lawgiver (*nomothetēs*) who gave the Jews a constitution (*politeia*), that is a religious law which kept their crude natures under control while at the same time pointing to the ultimate truth in symbolic form.[45] And according to a dialogue on 'political science' by a sixth-century Byzantine official,[46] God had

41. Cf. above, note 26; Eusebius, *Praep. Evang.*, vii, 8, 38; xii, 4, 2; xii, 19,1; Abū Ḥātim al-Rāzī, *Aʿlām*, 107; *RIS*, iv, 122.6, 132.3, 157.ult.; Ibn Wahb al-Kātib, *Burhān*, 137f. (In historical fact, Plato did use myth, but to convey difficult ideas to his disciples, not to educate the masses or to screen the highest truth from them.)

42. See the riveting discussion by Assmann, *Moses the Egyptian*, esp. chs 3–4.

43. Notably their concept of philosophy as including the care of inferiors, of legislation as the outcome of contemplative union with the divine, and of philosopher kings as councillors to kings (cf. O'Meara, 'Neoplatonist Conceptions of the Philosopher King', 281ff., 286f).

44. Runia, 'God and Man in Philo,' 54.

45. Eusebius, *Praep. Evang.*, book vii, ch. 9.1; below, 324.

46. Cf. Barker, *Social and Political Thought*, 63ff.; O'Meara, 'The Justinianic Dialogue'. Only fragments survive. The work, known as *Peri politikēs epistēmes*, is presumably identical with the dialogue on politics (*peri politikēs*) mentioned by Photius.

devised political science as a divine form of discipline by which mankind, living in a colony (*apoika*) sent out by Him from on High, could return to the mother-city, so that "the only sort of polity possible – the only way for the whole of the human race to attain salvation – is that . . . philosophical and political authority should . . . be united".[47] This was also al-Fārābī's view. With or without help from such thinkers, he saw that Plato's ideal city was a polity spawned by philosophy just as Muḥammad's *umma* was a polity spawned by Islam. He deduced that Plato's city and Muḥammad's *umma* were the two faces of the same saving community and that the philosophers had ultimate responsibility for its guidance.

The virtuous city

Al-Fārābī starts his account of the virtuous city by noting that man cannot live without cooperation: nature has designed him for life in a 'city' (*madīna*), here meaning simply a community. This was a well-rehearsed cliché,[48] but he strikes out on his own by observing that humans can cooperate for a variety of aims. They may form a city merely to procure the necessities of life, for example (he called such a city *al-madīna al-ḍarūriyya*). They may also aim for something over and above survival, in which case some aims will be better than others. People who cooperated for morally indifferent or reprehensible aims, such as power, wealth, or pleasure, formed imperfect cities of various kinds. By contrast, people who cooperated for the highest aim, that is, true happiness (*al-saʿāda fī 'l-ḥaqīqa*) – meaning happiness as understood by the philosophers – formed a virtuous polity (*madīna fāḍila*). True happiness, according to al-Fārābī, was intellectual and moral perfection in this world and immortality of the rational soul in the next. Ultimate happiness (*al-saʿāda al-quṣwā*), which popularizers called Paradise, consisted in eternal contemplation, as pure mind, of ultimate reality. This could only be attained by philosophers. But there were lower degrees of happiness for those who accepted the guidance of the chief and achieved the virtue appropriate to their rank in the order of existence.[49] All

47. In Barker, *Social and Political Thought*, 72, 74; cf. O'Meara, 'The Justinianic Dialogue'. The tone of this work strongly supports Barker's translation of *sōtēria* as salvation. By contrast, where Alcinous (c. 150) identifies politics as concerned with the care of the city and its *sōtēria* (translated 'salvation' in O'Meara, 'Aspects', 65f.), Dillon takes it to mean no more than 'preservation' (*Handbook*, 2, §3, cf. the comments at p. 60).

48. Cf. below, 259ff., 341.

49. *SM*, 81f. = 37f.; *Taḥṣīl*, §49 = 43. What people engage in here are not 'political activities' (*pace* Galston, 'Theoretical and Practical Dimensions', 101), merely activities suitable for them as members of a community.

others were either annihilated when they died or destined to suffer eternal psychic pain.[50]

The founder of a virtuous city was a person endowed with an exceptional set of outstanding characteristics (twelve given by nature and six acquired by training), which enabled him to achieve contact with the active intellect (*al-ʿaql al-faʿʿāl*). God inspired him through the medium of the active intellect, as al-Fārābī also put it. This was the mechanics behind prophethood. The inspiration (*waḥy*) activated his own acute intellect, as well as his imaginative power, enabling him to combine the role of philosopher, capable of understanding God's ordering of the universe, with that of religious preacher, able to formulate his philosophical insights in language that the masses can understand. Such a man, the first or ultimate chief (*al-raʾīs al-awwal*),[51] was imam, king, philosopher, and prophet alike. In short, he was Plato's lawgiver and the prophet of the Islamic tradition rolled together.[52]

So far, al-Fārābī has simply amalgamated two traditions, but he had to answer three further questions to bring the philosophical picture into line with that of Islam. First, as regards the territorial extent of the perfect polity, Plato had simply taken it for granted that it would be a city state. al-Fārābī agreed that it could be a city, but added that it could also comprise an *umma*, presumably meaning a community such as that of Islam, and that it might also encompass the entire inhabited earth. This aligned the virtuous city with the Islamic ideal, but he may have found support for universalism in Pseudo-Aristotle as well.[53]

Secondly, Plato had not considered the question whether several virtuous cities could exist at the same time (he considered it unlikely that even one might be created). To al-Fārābī, however, the fact that the truth had to be translated into different symbols and metaphors for different people meant that there could be several virtuous nations and cities which all pursued the same kind of philosophical happiness under different religious umbrellas.[54] But the philosophers in all these virtuous polities would really form a single elite. It

50. *MF*, ch. 16, §§7–10; cf. Fakhry, *Islamic Philosophy*, 126ff.; Davidson, *Alfarabi, Avicenna, & Averroes, on Intellect*, 56–8.

51. The expression is defined in terms of authority in *SM*, 79.3 ("the first leader in absolute terms is the one who does not need any man to lead him in any respect at all"), but it often seems to be used in a chronological sense as well.

52. Rahman, *Prophecy in Islam*, 11ff.; Davidson, *Alfarabi, Avicenna, & Averroes, on Intellect*, 58ff. Compare Plotinus in O'Meara, 'Neoplatonist Conceptions of the Philosopher King', 281 (where the union is with the One rather than the active intellect).

53. *MF*, ch. 15, §2; cf. Bielawski and Plezia, 'Lettre d'Aristote à Alexandre', xi, 5–8 (p. 16 of the Arabic text); Stern, *Aristotle on the World State*.

54. *SM*, 85f. = 41.

may happen, he says, that there are several 'kings' (i.e. philosophically perfected people) at the same time, either in a single city or in several nations (*umam kathīra*); either way, they will function as a single king thanks to the identity of their aspirations and aims.[55] One senses that this was the very form that he hoped the future would take: all educated people would form a single, universal elite united by philosophy above the confessional barriers, while underneath the masses would pursue their own religious cults led by their diverse religious personnel, very much as had been the case (presumably unknown to al-Fārābī) in the world of the Greek philosophers themselves.

Finally, Plato did not give his city a history, but al-Fārābī had to sketch its further evolution to align it with the *umma*. After the founder there would be other leaders, he said. These leaders might be other outstanding men similar to the first leader in all respects. As true kings and pious imams, all would be living law: all could change and modify the legislation of their predecessors as they saw fit, for all would embody the same soul.[56] As usual, he gives no examples, but the reference must be to either a sequence of great philosophers in the same ideal polity (such as Socrates, Plato, and Aristotle) or a succession of prophets giving changing religio-political embodiment to the same eternal truth (such as Moses, Jesus, and Muḥammad). Whatever the answer, al-Fārābī notes that it was not a common mode of succession, for it was rare for all the qualifications required in the *ra'īs al-awwal* to be united in a single man. If no such individual was available, the city might be ruled by a less outstanding chief, who would govern by modelling himself on the leader or leaders before them. The laws that he or they had laid down would in that case have to be written down and memorized, and all new law would have to be derived from it by means of juristic science (*fiqh*). A ruler of this second type was called a *ra'īs* or *malik al-sunna*, a chief or king in accordance with the law.[57] One would assume the rightly guided caliphs of Medina and other righteous rulers of the Muslim world to fall into this category. But the various qualities that went to make a first chief might also be dispersed in many people; if so, they could take the place of the first chief and rule as a team. This was how al-Fārābī understood aristocracy (*riyāsat al-afāḍil/al-akhyār*): a virtuous regime in which several philosophically trained people managed things together, perhaps as king, vizier, military leader, and advisers, though he does not say precisely how.[58] In one of his works he also has a plurality of *ru'asā' al-sunna*, 'leaders

55. Ibid., 80.-5 = 37.
56. *Milla*, 49f (§8); *SM*, 80f. = 37.
57. *Fuṣūl*, §54/58; *Milla*, 50 (§9); *SM*, 81.4 = 37; *MF*, ch. 15, §13 (where he is just called *al-ra'īs al-thānī*).
58. *Fuṣūl*, §54/58; *MF*, ch. 15, §14.

in accordance with the law', to rule as a team in lieu of the single *malik al-sunna*, but they do not recur elsewhere.[59]

The ideal ruler behind all these variations is a true king (*al-malik fī 'l-ḥaqīqa*), meaning a philosopher whose understanding surpassed that of everyone else, so that everybody would follow him, or ought to follow him, while he himself followed nobody. Whether he rose to prophetic gifts or not, he was the source of right guidance, not its recipient. When such a man existed, he ought to rule in political no less than intellectual terms, for it remained axiomatic that monarchy ought to be government by the most excellent individual.[60] But like the Shīʿite imam, the true king was king and imam even if he did not rule: he was king by virtue of his mastery of the royal craft whether he actually practised it or not, as al-Fārābī said; it was not his fault if his contemporaries failed to appreciate his merits.[61] How could he be said to be meritorious if nobody saw him as such? al-Fārābī does not answer this question. Like most people at the time, he probably thought of excellence as an objective quality which existed independently of its observers. It was there even if people could not see it because he could see it himself. In other words, the philosopher king whom nobody recognized was a private philosopher with a high opinion of his own worth.

Al-Fārābī may have seen himself as such a king-in-truth (*al-malik fī 'l-ḥaqīqa*), or he may have credited himself with only some of the qualities required for government, so that he was destined to rule with others. Either way, he was adamant that the philosopher had to make his influence felt in the public arena. Theoretical virtue was not enough, one had to exercise one's craft to reach perfection, he said.[62] Since he also said that the king was king by virtue of his mastery of the royal craft whether he actually practised it or not, he seems to be contradicting himself, but the inconsistency lies entirely in his metaphors. What he meant was simply that true power was intellectual rather than material (one was king whether one ruled or not) and that the philosophers must seek to bring their intellectual influence to bear on the material world (one had to exercise one's craft). The philosophers should teach, advise, write, and seek to convert rulers to the cause of philosophy, in short strive to obtain the public place they deserved. The knowledge of the philosopher who did not teach was vain.[63] And rulers should patronize them, consult them and defer to them, as they did to the *ʿulamāʾ* and *mutakallim*s whom al-Fārābī

59. *Fuṣūl*, §54/58.
60. Cf. above, 34f.; below, 226.
61. *Fuṣūl*, §29/32; *Talkhīṣ*, 8 = 88; *Taḥṣīl*, §64 = 62 (cf. Plato, *Republic*, 489b).
62. *Fuṣūl*, §25/28.
63. *Taḥṣīl*, §57 = 56.

regarded as his subordinates. The ultimate spiritual directors of the Islamic world were the philosophers.

In his view, no polity could flourish without some attention to the philosophers' directives. If the ruler lacked all the characteristics of a true king, the only way his polity could avert destruction was by attaching a philosopher to him; and if no philosopher could be found, the polity was bound to perish.[64] It has been inferred that al-Fārābī saw the Muslim community of his own time as in serious danger of dissolution and assigned to philosophy the task of rescuing it: "Only by true philosophy, the true religion could be saved."[65] But this seems unlikely. He must of course have been aware that the Muslim world was in a parlous state, politically speaking, but he did not think of philosophy as a mere instrument in the service of political restoration (a project which does not seem to have preoccupied him at all), nor is it obvious that he regarded Islam as the only true religion. Rather, his doomsday talk sounds like wishful thinking: contemporary rulers had better patronize philosophy or else!

Imperfect cities

Imperfect cities were societies in which people pursued morally indifferent or reprehensible aims. Like their virtuous counterpart, they are singled out by a particular belief about the ultimate good, not a particular distribution of power. The corrupt constitutions familiar from Plato's *Republic* and the commentators on it are bracketed as ignorant (*jāhilī*): they pursued aims such as honour (*karāma*), wealth (*yasār*), domination (*taghallub*), freedom (*ḥurriyya*), pleasure (*ladhdha*), or the bare necessities of life, which they mistakenly regarded as the best. To these regimes al-Fārabī kept adding new ones, which were not *jāhilī*, but rather perverse in that they knew the nature of true happiness, or had once known it, but had forgotten or changed or suppressed it. His final statement on the subject enumerated the erring (*ḍālla*), changed (*mubaddala*), and corrupt (*fāsida*) cities, all clearly monotheist societies which failed to grant philosophy its proper role, as well as 'weeds' (*nawābit*) and pseudo-philosophers suffering from spiritual diseases such as scepticism and relativism who were found within the virtuous city itself.[66]

Al-Fārābī clearly meant to capture the spiritual errors of his own time with his new forms of imperfection, and as he modified his early views, the virtuous and the imperfect cities ceased to be discrete entities. Originally, he had envisaged the *madīna fāḍila* as a real polity, like Muḥammad's in Medina

64. *MF*, ch. 15, §14.
65. Endress, 'Defense of Reason', 21.
66. Cf. Mahdi, 'Alfarabi'.

(except that there could be several), and ruled that the virtuous man in a city bereft of philosophical leadership had to emigrate to one such polity in order to be saved (*wajabat ʿalayhi al-hijra ilā al-mudun al-fāḍila*); if no virtuous polity existed, the virtuous man had to live like a stranger in this world, which would reduce his chances of salvation, for salvation depended on the perfection of virtue, and a virtuous constitution enabled both the ruler and the subjects to achieve a greater degree of virtue than was attainable elsewhere.[67] Just as a Muslim had to live with other Muslims under Muslim rule in order to achieve salvation, so a philosopher had to live with like-minded people under philosophical government to reach ultimate happiness. Here the correspondence between Muḥammad's *umma* and its philosophical counterpart is perfect.

But there is also something archaic about this correspondence, for by al-Fārābī's time the Muslim *umma* was not a polity any more, nor was Muslim government synonymous with religious guidance. It is true that many scholars required or recommended emigration (*hijra*) within the realm of Islam when people lived in lands where wrongdoing prevailed, to avoid participating in it.[68] But that the highest truth could be pursued in a variety of political frameworks had been known ever since the secession of al-Andalus; by now, people were even debating whether one could pursue the highest truth in isolation rather than through communal life.[69] In the Muslim heartlands, only the Shīʿites still conflated political governance and religious guidance. This is one reason why it is sometimes conjectured that al-Fārābī was a Shīʿite by background or sympathy.[70] (Another is that both he and the Shīʿites saw the imamate as a personal characteristic rather than an office, so that its possessor retained it whether he actually ruled or not.) But though the similarity between the two conceptions of the imam certainly helps to explain why Shīʿites found al-Fārābī's ideas congenial, what it reflects in al-Fārābī's case is probably not Shīʿism, but rather his presentation of philosophy as the other side of the message preached by the Prophet, cast as a true king and living law.

67. *Fuṣūl*, §§84, 88/89, 93; cf. Socrates in *Falsafat Aflāṭūn*, 19 = 64; and Plato in *Jamʿ*, 83.

68. Thus Abū Ḥanīfa, Mālik, Abū 'l-Layth al-Samarqandī, Ḥalīmī, and others on the *jamāʿī* side, al-Qāsim b. Ibrāhīm among the Zaydīs (Cook, *Commanding Right*, 75, 229 [note 15], 309, 313, 341, 361f., 380 [note 169], 384).

69. Cf. above, 30f; below, 362.

70. Thus for example Walzer, *Farabi on the Perfect State*, esp. 5, 442; Najjar, 'Farabi's Political Philosophy and Shīʿism', 62; Corbin, *Philosophie islamique*, 223; Guerrero, 'Compromiso político' (Imami). Daiber ('Ismaili Background' and 'Political Philosophy', 848f.; cf. also Corbin, *Philosophie islamique*, 225ff.) postulates Ismaili influence, not Ismaili sympathies, but others have seen sympathies too (cf. Guerrero, 'Compromiso político', 464f., 474f.). For criticism, see Mahdi, 'Al-Fārābī's Imperfect State', 705ff.; Lameer, *Al-Fārābī and Aristotelian Syllogistics*, 286.

Al-Fārābī modified his position, however. There is no obligation to make a *hijra* in his later works. He did reiterate that "happiness is not attainable in every city",[71] but for all that we hear of virtuous people who follow the rules of the first chief even though they live in a state of dispersal, because they have not yet formed a polity or because their city has broken up, as al-Fārābī explains; either way, they are strangers in their own land, but they are virtuous, good, and happy (*al-fāḍilūna wa'l-akhyār wa'l-suʿadāʾ*) without having to emigrate in order to perfect themselves, forming a spiritual aristocracy and a single soul regardless of their separation in space (or for that matter time).[72] Virtuous people who lived in corrupt polities were like chimeras, having the head of one species and the legs of another, he said; the same was true of vicious people living in virtuous polities. The former ought to emigrate if a virtuous city came to be created.[73] But virtuous people *could* live in corrupt regimes without losing their virtue, even if they were forced to act corruptly at times: they had to practise a combination of external conformity and internal resistance.[74] Conversely, even perfect cities had 'weeds' and pseudo-philosophers among their inhabitants. In other words, the more al-Fārābī thought about it, the more difficult he found it to endow truth and falsehood with separate political embodiments. In real life there would always be a mixture of both wherever one was. The virtuous city was not so much a polity as a brotherhood.

Philosophy thus ceased to be a political prescription. It did not have to create a saving polity for itself any more; a fraternity of like-minded men would do. Either al-Fārābī did not need the legitimating bridge any more or else he realized that the philosophers were not going to make it as the official elite. When it came to it, only revealed religion (*milla*) was a prescription for a polity such as that founded by the Prophet; philosophy transcended it. It was by accepting a *milla* that the philosophers lived in a socio-political community, however imperfect, but the city they formed themselves was a purely spiritual community above it. However dispersed they might live, in whatever degree of subjection to *jāhilī* or corrupt rulers, they could cooperate as devotees of philosophy, forming a single soul and occupying the same rank (*martaba*) in the next world, to live for ever after in jubilant contemplation of the divine.

71. *MF*, ch. 15, §3; taken by Galston to say the opposite (*Politics and Excellence*, 175f., in polemics against E. Rosenthal).

72. *SM*, 80 (reading *yudabbirūna*) = 37; *MF*, ch. 16, §1.

73. *Milla*, 55f. (§14, a).

74. *MF*, ch. 16, §11. Contrast Ghazālī, according to whom emigration was unnecessary as long as one was not compelled to participate in wrongdoing, but clearly prescribed if one could not stay away from it (Cook, *Commanding Right*, 432).

The philosopher king as the new model of perfection

Even without a public role, the philosopher prophet had his attractions: what he offered was a new ideal for the educated layman to aspire to. All Muslims tried to imitate the Prophet. What al-Fārābī offered was a radically new version of the Prophet holding out the promise that whoever perfected himself in intellectual and moral terms would rise to the level of king, or to that of prophet in some low-key sense. Even a king-in-truth (*al-malik fī 'l-ḥaqīqa*) was likely to fall short of prophetic gifts, but unlike the common mass of people, he would be his own master.

Plato had said that divine wisdom and control should come from within, if possible; failing that it must be imposed from outside, but reasonable individuals did not need the guidance of the lawgiver.[75] In other words, as al-Fārābī commented, good and virtuous men did not need laws: the *nawāmīs* and *sunan* were only for crooked characters.[76] The *sharīʿa* was the medicine of the sick, as one of the Brethren of Purity put it; having taken the medicine or never been sick, one was ready for philosophy, for whereas prophets treated the diseased, philosophers treated the healthy;[77] and "when the power of the lawgiver is added to the intelligence of rational and good men, they do not need a chief to lead them or to order them, forbid them, restrain them or impose decisions on them, for the intelligence and power of the lawgiver takes the place of the imam and chief."[78] What the Brethren of Purity were saying was that if one internalized the wisdom and power of the philosopher-prophet-king, one could in effect become him – maybe not on one's own, but at least together with like-minded people, as a member of a philosophical brotherhood.

This was the beguiling attraction of philosophy. Its rationalist portrayal of the universe and the place of the human soul in it enabled a man to transcend the restrictions that organized religion imposed on individuality, to escape from the world of conformity, and to pursue salvation as an individual unfettered by the petty demands of local jurists, scholars, neighbours, family, and children, tied down by nothing except the limits of his own intellect. The burden of the social obligations that a medieval Muslim had to bear for the sake of general welfare and public propriety far exceeds anything imaginable by a modern Westerner. "In infancy he is under the discipline of his parents; when grown up, and in the prime of life, under the restraint of the teacher and professor; and when a mature man, under the restraint of the ruler, unable to

75. *Republic*, 590d; *Laws*, 875c–d.
76. *Talkhīṣ*, 41.21.
77. Maqdisī in Tawḥīdī, *Imtāʿ*, ii, 11; cf. *RIS*, ii, 325.11 = *Case*, 157.
78. *RIS*, iv, 137; cited in Netton, *Muslim Neoplatonists*, 99.

dispense with his reform. When will this person free himself from the restraint of men?": thus Ibn ʿAqīl, a religious scholar who had submitted to the restraint of men in his youth by publicly abjuring his Muʿtazilite convictions.[79] It was not by means of philosophy that Ibn ʿAqīl sought freedom, but it did commend itself as the solution for a great many people who, though educated, did not owe their livelihood to religious knowledge: secretaries, administrators, doctors, astronomers/astrologers, and other courtiers and professional men. Endowed with an all-round education, trained in the handling of information, and typically handsomely rewarded for their professional services, they were not inclined to turn to jurists, theologians, or other religious scholars for instruction on what to believe or what they should try to make of themselves. They wanted control of their own lives. Freedom from political rulers was difficult to achieve. The philosophers never advocated their abolition: chaos would prevail without them, for most people needed rulers even if they themselves did not. Some said that a true philosopher should live as an ascetic, imitating Socrates by avoiding kings and all the luxury and dissimulation that went with them.[80] But in practice it was overwhelmingly on the patronage of courts that philosophers depended for their livelihood, be it as bearers of practical skills such as medicine or as court philosophers (professional philosophers holding teaching posts at educational institutions never made their appearance in the medieval Islamic world). So philosophy did not usually free a man from the demands of rulers. But it did hand the keys of salvation to the individual philosopher himself.

This was the fact to which al-Rāzī gave such powerful expression when he rejected organized religion altogether. Al-Fārābī toned it down: organized religion was necessary, if only for socio-political and educational purposes. Those who had achieved intellectual and moral perfection could dispense with it. They could and, according to some, should continue to display their allegiance to Muslim society by participating in the public rituals (such as prayer and fasting), but they did not actually need them. Like Plato's guardians, they could live not just without rulers/judges, but also without doctors, according to Ibn Bājja, if the polity were organized along ideal lines: for not only would perfect amity prevail among them, they would also eat the right things.[81] The science of communal governance (*siyāsa madaniyya*) was a utopian enterprise

79. Makdisi, *Ibn ʿAqīl*, 167 (here with reference to people who fail to live by reason, not to himself).

80. Cf. the charges levelled at Rāzī, who did not imitate Socrates in this respect (*Sīra*, 309 = 322).

81. Ibn Bājja, *Tadbīr*, fol. 166a–b = 126; reiterated by Ibn Rushd, *Commentary on Plato's 'Republic'*, 37 = 137; rooted in Plato, *Republic*, 404f.

exploring "the dispositions of soul and character which each member of a social organization must have in order for them completely to dispense with *al-ḥukkām* (rulers, judges)", as Ibn Khaldūn puts it.[82] Unlike the ninth-century anarchists, the devotees of 'political science' never envisaged a society in which government was abolished altogether, for this presupposed that everyone could acquire all virtues, which was impossible. If all men could become philosophers, evil would indeed be eradicated from human life and there would be no need for the constraint of the law, according to a Roman emperor as presented by the fourth-century Themistius; but people were not made that way (it was on that ground that Proclus and others ruled out the possibility of a good and virtuous democracy).[83] If all men attained virtue, all would become masters, and there cannot be masters without followers, as Ibn Rushd put it.[84] But all men of intellectual ability could become imams unto themselves in spiritual and moral terms, or even something resembling prophets; the only people in a position to dominate them would be the wielders of brute force.

Philosophy, then, was a new way of bidding for freedom. But it was only suitable for highly educated men who did not owe their livelihood to religion, and it struck the Muslims at large as deeply offensive, partly because its adherents espoused views at variance with Muslim doctrine on questions to do with bodily resurrection, divine providence and the eternity of matter, but more particularly because they held ultimate reality to be accessible to human reason and treated revealed religion as its socio-political handmaiden, a utilitarian institution of lesser truth value than the rational deductions of the philosophers themselves. To most Muslims the philosophers came across as arrogant, as well as utterly abstruse; and contrary to what al-Fārābī hoped, the philosophers never succeeded in inserting themselves above the *mutakallim*s and *ʿulamāʾ* as leaders of Muslim society. The common people remained beyond their control, and more often than not deeply hostile to them as well. Al-Fārābī had hoped for a society in which the official religion was philosophy, widely diffused by means of rhetoric[85] and generally accepted as the iron structure behind revealed religion, which the vast majority would continue to cultivate in public and private alike. What later philosophers had to accept, by contrast, was a society in which revealed religion was the only official truth and educated people cultivated philosophy in private. Christianity had reduced

82. *Muqaddima*, 335f. = ii, 138 (first noted by D. Gutas).

83. Themistius in Dagron, 'Empire romain', 129f. (drawn to my attention by Claudia Rappe); Proclus below, ch. 17, note 105; similarly Dio Chrysostom, 'Peri basileias', third oration, 47.

84. *Commentary*, 69 = 189f.; cf. also 22f. = 113.

85. Cf. Daiber, 'The Ruler as Philosopher', 10.

philosophy to an esoteric doctrine already in late antiquity, and al-Fārābī's efforts notwithstanding, this is what it remained in Islam. It soon exhibited a strong tendency to coalesce with other esoteric belief systems, notably Ismailism and Sufism.

After al-Fārābī

All the major philosophers who wrote on 'political science' after al-Fārābī were deeply influenced by him, but all treated philosophy as an esoteric truth for the few, not as the public elite culture that al-Fārābī had hoped it could become. Some accepted his spiritualization of the virtuous city. The Brethren of Purity (wrote c. 350/960), for example, saw themselves as forming one together with their readers, in whatever degree of dispersal they might live, in whatever degree of subjection to corrupt rulers.[86] Others, notably Ibn Sīnā (Avicenna, d. 428/1037), equated the ideal city with the Muslim community, abandoning al-Fārābī's vision of a universal elite united by philosophy above the confessional barriers. Ibn Sīnā's lawgiver is clearly Muḥammad (and, implicitly, him alone); Islam is (again implicitly) identified as the only acceptable popularization of the highest truth; and the *sharīʿa* is analysed as the perfect embodiment of philosophical insight.[87] The common people had won, not only in the sense that Islam had retained its status as the only true revelation, but also in the sense that it was better not to tell them that the revelation had a philosophical counterpart: it annoyed them to hear philosophers treat their cherished symbols as mere signposts to higher things, Ibn Sīnā said. So although he rose to the vizierate, a position beyond al-Fārābī's wildest dreams, he did not use it to establish institutions for the teaching of philosophy or generally to make propaganda for his view of the truth.

Ibn Sīnā's discussion of 'political science' (which is short) starts with a demonstration that humans cannot manage without a lawgiver prophet and proceeds to an analysis of what this lawgiver must do and why, in a new style of analysis best described as functional sociology: prayer, pilgrimage, and holy war serve as regular reminders of God and afterlife, indispensable for social control; placing the right to divorce in the hands of the male and keeping women secluded secures the permanence of marriage; prescribing acts of worship that can only be performed in the caliph's presence heightens the latter's importance; enslaving Turks, Blacks, and other inhabitants of unfortunate climes is sensible in that such people are natural slaves incapable of virtue, and

86. Cf. Fakhry, *Islamic Philosophy*, 165f.; Kraemer, 'The *Jihād* of the *Falāsifa*', 305n.

87. This is what causes the impression that his philosophy is more realistic than Fārābī's (cf. Galston, 'Realism and Idealism in Avicenna's Political Philosophy').

so on.[88] Throughout the analysis, he is writing as a social scientist interested in the way in which religion helps to make societies work, not as a theologian concerned with the way in which religion holds out the prospect of other-worldly salvation. For it was philosophy that held out the prospect of salvation to him. Revealed religion was simply how it was translated into social organization. In short, al-Fārābī's two-tiered concept of religion generated a philosophical approach to the higher level of religion and a sociological approach to the lower. (The second approach was to culminate, many centuries later, in the work of Ibn Khaldūn.)

Brilliant though Ibn Sīnā's analysis is, it also conveys a sense of somewhat smug satisfaction with the existing order. Al-Fārābī was a troubled man with a mission who had had to learn philosophy from Christian teachers and who worked on the margins of high society to secure acceptance for his discipline. But to Ibn Sīnā everything was easy. The son of wealthy Ismaili parents (though not an Ismaili himself), he was tutored in philosophy by a private teacher as a child and moved on to a glittering career as a court physician and vizier to a succession of rulers. Immensely gifted, he was the sort of man who could, and would, set about mastering a major discipline in a couple of days merely to put a critic in his place. The world was agreeably arranged for his comfort. Politics did turn his circumstances upside down from time to time, landing him in jail or forcing him to flee, but this was a common price for a politically active life, especially for a man so given to advertising his own brilliance. His only serious problems as a philosopher were that he never had enough time to write and that he could not write freely lest it be misunderstood by the masses. It "is not proper for any man to reveal that he possesses knowledge he is hiding from the vulgar. Indeed, he must never permit any reference to this," he said, meaning that it would undermine their religious beliefs.[89] This would be bad for the social order and also for the philosophers, for vulgar people were apt to take violent action against them. He refers to the need for secrecy in other works as well.

There was nothing smug about Ibn Bājja, the Latin Avempace (d. 533/1138), the first of three Andalusians to cultivate 'political science'.[90] He too rose to the rank of vizier, but for all that he saw the philosopher as a loner. In principle, it was only by cooperating that humans achieved the highest good; in practice, people seeking moral perfection had to isolate themselves (mentally and/or physically) because all cities were corrupt. The philosophers

88. Ibn Sīna, *SI*, *x*. Cf. Marmura, 'The Islamic Philosophers' Conception of Islam,' 98f. and 'Avicenna's Theory of Prophecy', 172f.

89. Ibn Sīna, *SI*, *x*, 443 = 100f.

90. Cf. *EI*², s.v. 'Ibn Bādjdja'.

were 'weeds', he said, using the word to mean any kind of people at odds with their fellow-citizens, whether corrupt members of a virtuous polity (as in al-Fārābī) or virtuous men who had sprouted in a corrupt one (the usage he prefers).[91] That the philosopher was a loner is also the moral of the celebrated philosophical tale, *Ḥayy b. Yaqẓān* by Ibn Ṭufayl (d. 581/1185f.), in which the philosopher withdraws to the desert island on which he has grown up after an unsuccessful attempt to join a polity organized on the basis of revealed religion.[92]

Ibn Rushd

By far the most important thinker in al-Andalus for our purposes was Ibn Rushd (Averroes, d. 595/1198), who shared al-Fārābī's view of the relationship between revealed religion and philosophy: both were avenues to God; there was no conflict between them, as he showed by working both as a jurist (and indeed judge) and as a philosopher who wrote vigorous responses to al-Ghazālī's attack on philosophy.[93] (In fact, it was primarily as a jurist that he was remembered in the Islamic world; his main legatees as far as philosophy is concerned were the Jews and Christians of Latin Europe.) He agreed with Ibn Sīnā that philosophy was only for a few, who had to keep quiet about it and conform externally: to attack revealed religion was attack social life.[94]

Like al-Fārābī, Ibn Rushd was an Aristotelian who had to make do with Plato for purposes of political science, but in his case it was only because he could not find a translation of Aristotle's *Politics* that he did so.[95] The most striking feature of his commentary on Plato's *Republic* is his unflinching acceptance of Plato's proposals regarding communism and women and its attempt to relate the Greek constitutions to Islamic history, past and present. As he developed it, 'political science' was indeed about political organization.

91. Ibn Bājja, *Tadbīr*, fols 166bf = 127f.; cf. Marmura, 'The Philosopher and Society', 317f., and, at greater length, Harvey, 'The Place of the Philosopher'; Leaman, 'Ibn Bājja on Society and Philosophy'.

92. Cf. *EI*², s.v. 'Ibn Ṭufayl'; Marmura, 'The Philosopher and Society'; Fradkin, 'The Political Thought of Ibn Ṭufayl'. For an English translation of the tale, see Goodman, *Hayy ibn Yaqzan*.

93. Cf. *EI*², s.v. 'Ibn Rushd'. On his political thought, see Butterworth, 'Politischen Lehren' and *Philosophy, Ethics and Virtuous Rule*.

94. Fierro, 'Legal Policies of the Almohad Caliphs', 242f.

95. Ibn Rushd, *Commentary*, 22 = 112.

Communism

To Ibn Rushd as to other philosophers, the virtuous city was a society devoted to the pursuit of ultimate happiness. One of the beauties of such a society was that it subordinated the individual to the collective good: the parts here existed for the sake of the whole, as the different organs existed for the sake of the body they made up; there was a sense of common purpose. In a tyranny there also was a single, overriding aim, however misguided, but this was not true of all regimes, and certainly not of democracy (*siyāsat al-jamāʿiyya/al-ḥurriyya*). Here the whole existed for the sake of the parts. The unity of such a society was accidental inasmuch as the different households of which it was composed did not have a common conception of the highest good, but were free to pursue whatever they took it to be. Government reflected the will of the subjects rather than virtue. Societies of this kind were mere 'household cities' (*al-mudun al-manziliyya*).[96] As described so far, the contrast sounds rather like that between the modern liberal West, in which the public domain is also a utilitarian sphere divorced from people's conceptions of the ultimate aim of life, and, say, Mao's China, in which there was a single public good for the sake of which the polity existed and to which all citizens were meant to subordinate their lives. But whether Ibn Rushd would have acknowledged this as a valid example or not, what he actually meant by democracy was a society in which the public sphere had turned into a private playground for big men, whose competition for power tended sooner or later to result in the establishment of tyranny: the privatization of public power and revenues was common to both regimes. Magnate families who plundered the masses had been characteristic of Iran and were also found "in many of these cities of ours"; most of the cities "today" were democratic, he said.[97] It was against this dissolution of the sphere of collective interest by private households that he endorsed Plato's abolition of the household for the guardians of the city (i.e. rulers and soldiers). People with access to public power should not have private property or wives and children of their own; rather, their lives should be collectivized: they should live together, eat together, and share their women and children, on a highly regimented basis (for eugenic purposes). This would promote love among them and ensure that their only interest would be the furtherance of the public good.[98]

96. Ibid., 45, 83f. = 151, 212–14 and *Compendio de Metafísica*, §39; Butterworth, *Philosophy, Ethics and Virtuous Rule*, 76.

97. *Commentary*, 84 = 214.

98. Ibid., 54, 56–8 = 167, 169–73, See further below, 346f., 349f.

The transformation of regimes

To Ibn Rushd, the lowest form of common life was that pursued by *al-mudun al-ḍarūriyya*, societies which pursued nothing but the bare necessities of life, but democracy merely added the fulfilment of private desires, the first thing to spring to people's minds.[99] In one of the several developmental sketches found in his commentary on Plato's *Republic* he observes how a 'necessity society' in which everyone fights for himself may turn into a society in which kings collect taxes to pay for the troops, and in which democracy (as he understands it) appears to obtain. In agreement with al-Fārābī he concedes that since all conceptions of the highest good could be represented in a democracy, adherents of virtue could also spring up in it. He infers that democracy could develop into a virtuous polity: it could abolish itself.[100] It could in fact develop into anything. But usually it degenerated into tyranny, the worst of all imperfect regimes because it aimed at the aggrandizement of a single man and reduced everyone else to slaves.[101] The best of the imperfect polities was timocracy (*madīnat al-karāma*), especially when the distribution of honour was hierarchical, he says, again in agreement with al-Fārābī, because such a polity aimed at characteristics and actions that were virtuous at first sight.[102] Timocracy was "frequently found among us", he says; one could understand Plato's comments on the transformation of virtuous governance into timocracy by considering that the Arabs began with virtuous governance (or at least they modelled themselves on it, as he cautiously puts it), then Muʿāwiya transformed it into timocracy (not, as one might have expected, a tyranny). Similarly, the first Almoravid ruler had modelled himself on governance based on the law, but under his son the constitution became timocratic, with an admixture of love of wealth (characteristic of oligarchy); and under his grandson the constitution became one of pleasure, whereupon it perished.[103] The Almoravids fell because the governance of their opponents (i.e. the Almohads) resembled that based on the law, though they had apparently turned timocratic too.[104]

99. *Commentary*, 84 = 214.

100. Ibid., 83f., 93 = 213f., 229f. Cf. Fārābī, *SM*, 100f. = 51 (echoing Plato, *Republic*, 557–8).

101. *Commentary*, 85, 94, 96 = 215, 232, 235, with government in Cordoba before and after 540/1145 as illustration.

102. Ibid., 81, 82, 91 = 209, 211, 225; cf. Fārābī, *SM*, 93.13–94.2.

103. *Commentary*, 82, 89, 92 = 211, 223, 227.

104. Ibid., 92 = 227, cf. 89 = 223 (where, after mentioning Muʿāwiya's transformation of quasi-virtuous governance into timocracy, he adds that "such seems to be the case with the constitution that exists now in these islands").

Ibn Rushd was not the first to try to identify the classical constitutions with contemporary regimes: Ibn Sīnā had noted that "the constitution found in our land is a mixture of tyranny, oligarchy, timocracy and a remnant of democracy; in so far as there is an element of aristocracy [i.e. a virtuous regime] in it, it is extremely small."[105] But Ibn Rushd was the first to think deeply about the transformation of constitutions with reference to historical evidence. His commentary on Plato's *Republic* may not have been widely read: the Arabic original is lost; the work only survives in a Hebrew translation (and a Latin one made from the Hebrew). But Ibn Khaldūn's theory of the rise and fall of dynasties clearly owes much to it.

'Political science' in Iran

At the hands of Ibn Rushd, al-Fārābī's *ʿilm madanī* came close to 'political science' in the modern sense. At the hands of Yaḥyā al-Suhrawardī (d. 587/1191), by contrast, it was wholly interiorized. In his work the corporeal world in which we live our everyday lives is reduced to a mere stage-set, a cardboard front ceded without further ado to the kings and sultans of this world, mere wielders of brute force (who made use of that attribute to execute him). All the real action is in the world of images or archetypes, an invisible realm between this one and the next reminiscent of the Zoroastrian *menok*, a spiritual image of the world known as *ʿālam al-mithāl*. The true rulers are those who have freed themselves from the shackles of their bodies in the here and now and who inform mankind of sacred knowledge: prophets, kings, philosophers, sages, pillars of the universe. Their powers over the natural world in al-Suhrawardī's vision far exceeded that popularly ascribed to ordinary kings: they could raise earthquakes and tempests, ruin entire nations, cure the sick, sate the hungry, make wild beasts obey; some could ascend to the light and appear in any form they liked, or, with further light bestowed on them, walk on the water, fly in the sky, and traverse the earth. Even clear revelation might be given to them (as to Muḥammad and, some said, to al-Suhrawardī himself). Everyone could acquire the intuitive, visionary knowledge that would give them wisdom, divine power, and the special light of Iranian kings, for every soul had a portion of God's light, a little or a lot. This had also been Abū Bakr al-Rāzī's view, though he had put it differently. He had inferred that there was no such thing as prophets. Al-Suhrawardī's view was rather than we can all become prophets, though he prudently reserves the word for those who were specifically charged (*maʾmūr*) by God.[106]

105. Ibn Sīnā, *Rīṭūrīqā*, 42.
106. Ziai, 'Source and Nature of Authority' and in *EI*², s.v. 'al-Suhrawardī'.

Al-Suhrawardī's philosophy was an amazing synthesis of Zoroastrian, Greek, Gnostic, and Muslim concepts (both Sunnī and Shīʿite) of great visionary power and striking imaginative beauty, and like all spiritual systems which hand the keys of salvation to the individual, it was above confessional divisions. But it was much too esoteric to be concerned with mundane government. Al-Suhrawardī remarks that government was not normally enlightened, and it has been conjectured that he saw himself as destined to reform it as councilor to the prince who patronized him, a son of Saladin's in charge of Aleppo. But although it goes without saying that general adoption of his religious system would greatly have affected the external world, his attention was too strongly focused on the inner lives of humans for his thought to count as political.

The unenlightened nature of contemporary government was also remarked on by Bābā Afḍal (d. 610/1213f.), a philosopher from Kāshān sometimes, but probably wrongly, identified as an Ismaili. Among his many works is *Sāz u pīrāya-yi shāhān-i purmāya* (The Accoutrements and Ornaments of Worthy Kings), in which the role of the king, the perfect man, is to enable his subjects to achieve full actualization of their intellect, but which displays no interest in government in the normal sense of the word.[107] The same could be said of the *Akhlāq-i Nāsirī* (Naṣirean Ethics) by the philosopher and scientist Naṣīr al-Dīn Ṭūsī (d. 672/1274), an Imami who converted to Ismailism and back again, and who wrote the *Ethics* in his Ismaili phase. Devoted to all three branches of practical philosophy, ethics, household management, and politics, it is both a work of 'political science' in the tradition of al-Fārābī, who is quoted and paraphrased at length, and a mirror for princes (of the ethical rather than the managerial type).

The philosopher king

Some readers of 'political science' from al-Fārābī to al-Suhrawardī and Bāba Afḍal will have a curious sense of déjà vu: the perfect king sounds familiar, just not from Plato. Even in al-Fārābī he looms much larger than he does in either Plato himself or the later Platonist philosophers. No doubt, this reflects al-Fārābī's need to build bridges: Plato's philosopher king grew in stature because he was fused with the Prophet. But the very fact that such a fusion seemed possible suggests that something had happened to him already before al-Fārābī, for there really is not much in the *Republic* itself to remind the reader of prophets. It is on turning to Eusebius, bishop of Caesarea (d. 340), that one

107. Nasr, 'Afdal al-Din Kashani', 255; Chittick in *Enc. Iran.*, s.v. 'Bābā Afẓal-al-Dīn'; cf. the translated portion in Chittick, *Heart of Islamic Philosophy*, 178ff.

recognizes the ultimate source of his growth. When the emperor Constantine converted to Christianity, the Roman empire had to be endowed with a positive role in the religion it had so far tried to suppress, and Eusebius responded by turning to that amalgam of ancient Near Eastern, Iranian and Greek ideas which goes under the name of Hellenistic kingship (because it is mainly from Greek sources of the Hellenistic period onwards that we know it).[108] The Hellenistic king, attested in diverse forms and varying shades of humanity and divinity, was a supremely virtuous man endowed with a fullness of power over all things spiritual and material. As Eusebius cast him, he was the image of the supreme God, a copy of divine perfection, the representative (*hyparchos*) of God on earth, a bearer of divine light and carrier of the divine name (of king), a replica of the *logos*, a philosopher and an interpreter of God's word whose earthly court was an image of the divine realm and whose task it was to lead men back to the knowledge of God. Only the distinction of being living law (*nomos empsychos*) was denied him.[109] Eusebius's picture of Constantine contributed substantially to the view of the emperor in Byzantium, where he was occasionally cast as living law as well.[110] It was as such a supremely virtuous emperor of the Hellenistic type that Plato's philosopher king came to be understood. "There has been revealed in our age that time of felicity which one of the writers of old prophesied as coming to pass when either philosophers were kings or kings were students of philosophy," Agapetus told Justinian; "pursuing the study of philosophy, you [Justinian] were counted worthy of kingship; and holding the office of king, you did not desert the study of philosophy."[111] "A man who is a philosopher king and a king-philosopher, after the manner of the doctrine of Plato . . . will naturally seek, to the best of his power, to act as king in the manner of Him whose copy and image he is – otherwise he would not be a true king, but would only bear idly an empty name," as the dialogue on 'political science' from Justinian's time declares.[112]

It was on the same reservoir of Hellenistic kingship ideas that al-Fārābī drew for the naturalization of philosophy in the Islamic world, assisted by the

108. Compare the situation in the field of law: it is mainly from late Roman sources that the amalgam of ancient Near Eastern, Iranian, and Greek law which goes under the name of 'provincial law' is known.

109. Dvornik, *Political Philosophy*, ii, 616–22, and the sources cited there. For kings sharing their name with God, see also above, 153, note 28.

110. Hunger, *Prooimion*, 117ff. The formulaic identification of the ruler as 'the best of men' does not seem to have made it to Byzantium.

111. Barker, *Social and Political Thought*, 56f., with reference to Plato, *Republic*, 473d. For a survey of the use of this passage in late antique and Byzantine literature, see Praechter, 'Antikes in der Grabrede des Georgios Akropolites', 482f.

112. Barker, *Social and Political Thought*, 71.

fact that these ideas had already contributed to the Muslim conception of the imamate, perhaps from the start, certainly from the Umayyad period onwards, and most obviously in its Imami Shīʿite form.[113] They surfaced in the Persian mirrors too, and played a role in Sufi notions of the perfect man as well. They are in fact so ubiquitous and multifarious that they are difficult to trace in any meaningful way in the present state of research. (We need an Islamicist version of Dvornik's book on early Christian political philosophy, which starts where it should, in the ancient Near East, and ends with Justinian, but which does not consider the Syriac and Aramaic literature of such importance to cultural developments after the Arab conquests.) What can be surmised in the present state of research is that al-Fārābī and his successors created their version of the philosopher king by reading the Hellenistic king as they knew him from their own tradition back into Plato and Aristotle.

Like the early imam, the philosopher king expressed a hankering for power so true and morally right that it must be absolute: everyone would have to subordinate his own interests to it; indeed, every righteous person would fall into line with it of his own accord and model his own life on the superior example; only perverted people would be able to resist it. The deep longing for such morally meaningful government is one of the most striking characteristics of medieval Islamic political thought. The Prophet and the caliphs in Medina exemplified it, or the Prophet and ʿAlī did. Power proved corrupt in real life, morality had to be removed from the hands of the caliph, or the imam had to be removed from this world. But no sooner had this operation been accomplished than the absolutist vision returned, in the form of Ismailism, philosophy, and the extremely high evaluation of kingship in Iranian literature.

Unlike the other absolutist visions, however, that of the philosophers was never put to the test in communal practice. No philosopher king ever ruled in real life, nor was there a kingdom in which the philosophers were openly accepted as the spiritual leaders of the Muslim world, except perhaps in the case of the Ismailis: their *dāʿī*s were carriers of philosophical ideas even though they did not see themselves as philosophers, and there were times when they were rulers too. Elsewhere, however, the philosophers' bid for pre-eminence failed, for obvious reasons. By the time they appeared, the religious scholars had long been established in that role, while the slot for rationalist thinking about religion had been taken by the theologians (*mutakallim*s). The educated laymen among whom the philosophers recruited their adherents were limited in number, since by and large it was only at the court that there was a demand

113. When the Umayyads and their successors applied the title *khalīfat allāh* to themselves, they were expressing their claims to the ancient Near Eastern tradition of 'divine kingship', as Morris quite rightly remarks (*The Master and the Disciple*, 207, note 214).

for them; and though secular rulers often patronized philosophers, they did not need their political thought as ammunition against the caliph, as they did against the pope in Latin Europe. Ordinary people had no use for their learning, which they would dismiss as nonsense on stilts or infidel poison. By contrast, religious scholars were in demand everywhere, as preachers, teachers, prayer-leaders, legal experts, administrators of charitable foundations, go-betweens, and more besides. That a small number of philosophers should succeed in imposing control over so well-established an elite was clearly a forlorn hope.

Accordingly, it was only in the individual that moral absolutes and power could come together. It was in any case at the individual level that the vision of rising to the level of the angels had always had its strongest appeal. Just as every Muslim who ordered right and prohibited wrong was God's caliph on earth, so every Muslim who polished the mirror of his soul could hope to become a philosopher king unto himself, or even something resembling a prophet.

CHAPTER

15

THE ISMAILIS

Ismailism first came to the attention of the authorities in 891, when villagers from the countryside of Kufa were reported to have been infected by a new heresy.[1] By then, as it turned out, lower Iraq had hosted an Ismaili mission for some sixteen years while other missions had sprung up, or were fast appearing, in Baḥrayn, Iran, Yemen, India, Syria, Egypt, and North Africa, and even in Baghdad itself. Where was it all coming from? The answer proved to be from Salamiyya in Syria, where a family, originally from al-Ahwāz in Khuzistan, was directing a grand movement to take over the Muslim world in the name of a new creed. By the time the ʿAbbāsids discovered this, the leader of the sect, the fourth member of the family to hold the leadership, had fled. He reappeared in 909 in what is now Tunisia as ʿUbaydallāh al-Mahdī, founder of the Fatimid dynasty which ruled North Africa before moving to Egypt, where they held sway from 969 until 1171, when Saladin removed the dynasty.[2]

THE EARLY DOCTRINE AND ITS ADHERENTS

The believers

The founders of Ismailism were probably breakaway Imamis. Practically all the early missionaries were Imami Shīʿites by origin, as were many of their converts. Their first mission, in lower Iraq, is said to have begun in 261/874 or

1. Tab., iii, 2124ff.
2. Cf. Halm, *Reich des Mahdi* (English tr. *Empire of the Mahdi*).

three years later,[3] either way not long after the eleventh imam of the Imamis had died without an apparent successor (in 260/874). One missionary explicitly identifies the occultation as the key factor behind his conversion.[4] The early Ismailis often jeered at the Imami belief in a hidden imam. "We are not like the stupid Rāfiḍa who call to somebody absent or awaited," as a supporter of the Baḥrayn Ismailis seized by the Abbasid authorities said in 315/927f.[5] The Ismailis did not feel their own Mahdi to be hidden, though he was absent and awaited too, for he was just about to return and had a spokesman in the here and now, initially the leader of the sect in Salamiyya (known as the *ḥujja*, proof). One could take political action on behalf of the Ismaili imam whereas the twelfth imam was wholly out of human reach whether one believed him to exist or not, like Jesus after his ascension to the Christians.[6] It was apparently the complete depoliticization of Imamism that caused the Ismailis to break away.

In social terms the Ismailis came from the most diverse milieux. The first converts were peasants and other villagers (in lower Iraq and north-western Iran). Others were settled tribesmen (in Yemen and North Africa), bedouin (in the Syrian desert and to some extent Baḥrayn), brigands (in Kirman), educated urbanites (in Iraq) and, from c. 900 onwards, local rulers and their courtiers (in Iran and India). These people must have envisaged the messianic age in very different terms, but as long as they all attached their hopes to the same imminent event, the missionaries could cater to the local needs of their particular constituencies without traducing the overall unity of the movement.

Cosmology

The doctrine to which the early converts committed themselves was a peculiar mixture of Gnostic beliefs and militant messianism. The Gnostic input was apparent above all in a cosmology which explained the origin of the world in terms of a cosmic fall. When God spoke the word 'be' (the Qur'ānic *kun*), His command acquired existence as an independent being, Kūnī. Unable to see God, who is beyond reach of the senses and indescribable in any terms familiar to humans, Kūnī thought that he was god himself. His arrogance caused six

3. Ibn Rizām in Ibn al-Nadīm, *Fihrist*, 238 = i, 464; Akhū Muḥsin in various works listed in Daftary, *Ismāʿīlīs*, 606, n.123. The Imami claim that already al-Faḍl b. Shādhān (d. 260/873f) had written a refutation of the Qarāmiṭa is probably mistaken (*pace* Daftary, *Ismāʿīlīs*, 117).

4. Ibn Ḥawshab in Nuʿmān, *Iftitāḥ*, 33ff.

5. Miskawayh, *Tajārib*, i, 181.-5 = iv, 204f.

6. Cf. Abū 'l-Fawāris, *Imāma*, 104r (ch. 14).

dignitaries (*ḥudūd*) to come forth from God, whereupon Kūnī realized his mistake and testified to the unity of God. At God's command, Kūnī then created *qadar*, meaning '(God's) power' or 'determination'. The names of Kūnī and Qadar added up to seven letters between them, and God created everything through them. God, 'the creator of the creators' (*bāriʾ al-abriyāʾ*), is not directly responsible for the making of this world, then. The implication is that but for Kūnī's mistake the world would not have come into existence.[7]

It cannot be said that the implication is clearly brought out in the one relatively full account of the myth to survive, dating from the time of al-Muʿizz (953–75). Many Ismailis had by then replaced, or overlaid, the myth with a Neoplatonist cosmology of an intellectually more upmarket kind, but even the earliest Ismailis were bent on subduing the earth rather than escaping from it. The most striking feature of the oldest texts to have come down to us is not hatred of the world but rather messianism and a Kabbalistic delight in numbers and letters as the key to the secret meaning of things: as *yāʾ* is the last letter of the word *al-mahdī*, so the Mahdi will be the last of the speaker prophets and imams; since *yāʾ* is also the last letter of the alphabet, he will not bring a new law; the Qurʾānic reference to "seven nights and eight days" (Q.69:7) shows that he will come after a sequence of seven imams, as the eighth; and so on.[8] Such letter and number speculation is also found in later works, including those of a Neoplatonist bent.

Human history

The Gnostic input is also apparent in the Ismaili account of history from the creation till the end. There would be a total of seven eras (*adwār*, sing. *dawr*); the current era was the sixth. Each era was opened by a prophet known as a *nāṭiq* (speaker). The prophet was followed by an executor (*waṣī*), or foundation (*asās*), who was followed in his turn by six imams known as 'completers' (*mutimmūn*), making seven imams in all; or alternatively, the executor was counted as a separate figure followed by seven completer imams. A full sequence of prophet, executor and completers exhausted an era. (Since an era had to be at least a thousand years long to make sense in astrological terms it was soon granted that there could be intervals (*fatarāt*, sing. *fatra*) between the

7. Abū ʿĪsā al-Murshid in Stern, *Studies*, ch, 1. For the origin and meaning of the Gnostic elements, see Halm, *Kosmologie und Heilslehre* and 'Cosmology of the pre-Fatimid Ismāʿīliyya'.

8. *K. al-rushd*, 198f. = 43.

imams.)[9] The seven speaker prophets were usually identified as (1) Adam, (2) Noah, (3) Abraham, (4) Moses, (5) Jesus, and (6) Muhammad, to be followed in the future by (7) Muḥammad b. Ismāʿīl. Each prophet was really the same person in a different manifestation: Muḥammad was the sixth Adam.[10] But they were not manifestations of God, only emissaries of His. Their executors were (1) Seth, (2) Shem, (3) Ishmael (Ismāʿīl),[11] (4) Aaron, (5) Simon Peter, and (6) ʿAlī; the seventh speaker prophet would not have an executor. The seven completer imams who followed the executor were usually left unnamed until the authors reached Muḥammad's era,[12] in which they were (1) al-Ḥasan, (2) al-Ḥusayn, (3) ʿAlī b. al-Ḥusayn, (4) Muḥammad al-Bāqir, (5) Jaʿfar al-Ṣādiq, and (6) Ismāʿīl, who formed a heptad together with ʿAlī, the executor; or alternatively they formed a heptad with Muḥammad b. Ismāʿīl, on the principle that the last imam of one era would return as the first person to appear in the next. After Muḥammad b. Ismāʿīl, the last speaker (*nāṭiq*), history would come to an end. (For a schematic presentation, see chart 7.)

The relative roles of the prophets and imams reflected the Ismaili conviction that God's message to mankind could be read at two different levels, the one plain, literal and exoteric (*ẓāhir*, 'external'), the other spiritual, metaphorical, and esoteric (*bāṭin*, 'inner'). For example, the plain meaning of the injunction to go on pilgrimage was that the believers must travel to Mecca to circumambulate the house of God located there, but the spiritual or inner meaning was that the believers must betake themselves to the imam, the true house of God.[13] It was only by following the inner meaning that one could be saved: the law in the plain meaning of the word was mere shackles and chains,[14] mere regulations of a socio-political kind. (In principle they meant the revealed law in its entirety, but in practice their concern was really with the *ʿibādāt*, ritual law.) The external meaning of the revelation had been brought by the speaker prophets. Some held that there had been no law in Adam's era, but thereafter each *nāṭiq* had inaugurated a new era by bringing a law which

9. Cf. Sijistānī, *Ithbāt*, 192f. (The concept was familiar already to Abū Ḥātim al-Rāzī, d. 322/934, cf. Stern, *Studies*, 38; Madelung, 'Imamat', 104). Sijistānī nonetheless says that the world can never be without an imam, manifest or hidden (*Iftikhār*, 70).

10. Jaʿfar b. Manṣūr al-Yaman (attrib.), *K. al-kashf*, 98.1 (G, 97), cf. 'the first Adam' on the previous page; Pines, 'Shiʿite Terms and Conception', 172; Halm, *Kosmologie und Heilslehre*, 20.

11. Or Isḥāq (Isaac) in external reality (*fī 'l-ẓāhir*) and Ismāʿīl in inner truth (*fī 'l-bāṭin*).

12. Only the *K. al-Fatarāt* names all of them, cf. Halm, *Kosmologie und Heilslehre*, 31ff.

13. E.g. Sijistānī, *Iftikhār,* 128.

14. Nawbakhtī, *Firaq*, 63f.

superseded that of his predecessor (if any). The inner meaning of the revelation, which never changed, was elucidated by the executor and the completer imams, who expounded it by allegorical interpretation (*taʾwīl*). Since salvation lay in knowledge of the inner meaning, it would follow that the prophets were subordinate to the imams who brought the saving knowledge, or worse, that the prophets were emissaries of malign powers seeking to chain mankind to this world.[15] But here as so often the Ismailis seem to have shied away from the implications of their Gnostic heritage. They shared the normal Muslim evaluation of the prophets as the best of all human beings. The earliest Ismailis, or some of them, even seem to have cast ʿAlī as one: he had taken over from Muḥammad as messenger, they said.[16]

It was thanks to their high valuation of the inner meaning of things that the Ismailis were called Bāṭinīs by their opponents (their favourite self-appellation was *ahl al-ḥaqq*, the people of the truth). They responded by calling their opponents *ahl al-ẓāhir*, a term with much the same connotations as 'flat-earthers' today.

The future

Muḥammad b. Ismāʿīl would inaugurate the seventh and last era. Like his predecessors, he would abolish the law of the era he had come to terminate, but he would not bring a law of his own, for he would come as the Mahdi and *qāʾim* who would make the inner, spiritual meaning of things directly accessible to all. The shackles would fall away; there would be no more prophets, law or imams to interpret it. Organized religion would wither away and so, by implication, would the socio-political order based on it; history would come to an end: the pure spirituality of Adam's Paradise would be restored. But first the Mahdi would conquer the earth and subdue the infidels. For the Ismailis were politicized Gnostics who expected to participate in a last apocalyptic round of violence before their messiah put an end to power and authority altogether. In the last resort their combination of Gnostic beliefs and political ambitions was a source of incoherence, as will be seen. In the short run it made them highly dangerous to other Muslims, whom they regarded as infidels devoid of legal protection.[17]

Like the scheme proposed by Joachim of Fiore (d. 1202) of three world historical eras inexorably leading to the messianic age, or for that matter that proposed by Marx, the Ismaili scheme of seven eras served first and foremost to

15. Cf. Halm, *Kosmologie und Heilslehre*, 20f.
16. Nawbakhtī, *Firaq*, 61; cf. Madelung, 'The Account', 55.
17. Nawbakhtī, *Firaq*, 64. For *takfīr*, see below, 385ff.

predict that the revolution was imminent. Since all imams of the sixth era had been and gone, it was plain that the seventh era was about to begin. One had to make sure that one would find oneself on the right side in the future conflagration, as a soldier on the Mahdi's side rather than on that of the infidels doomed to perdition.

Exactly when the new era would start was uncertain. Since turns of centuries were traditionally held to inaugurate new eras, some proposed that the Mahdi would come in the year 300 (corresponding to 912f.).[18] By then, the movement had already split up, but it was in preparation for this year that the Ismailis of Iraq pooled their property and moved to an abode of emigration (*dār al-hijra*), where they exchanged their life as downtrodden villagers for one as soldiers on the Mahdi's behalf;[19] about the same time, a section of the Ismaili community in Yemen took to ritual violation of the law.[20] But no Mahdi appeared in either place. Astrology yielded an alternative date of 316/928.[21] In that year the Ismailis of Baḥrayn, joined by Iraqi co-religionists, made what they expected to be the final attack on Iraq, carrying banners inscribed with Q. 28:5, "We desire to show favour to those considered weak on earth, and to make them imams and heirs."[22] In the following year the Baḥrayn Ismailis demonstrated that the external rites of Islam had come to an end by slaughtering pilgrims in Mecca and removing the black stone. By then, many Iraqis had gone to Baḥrayn to be present when the messiah came,[23] and this time he did indeed come. In 319/931 the Ismailis of Baḥrayn recognized a Persian captive as the Mahdi and acknowledged all the radical implications of their doctrine. Their Mahdi was identified as a manifestation of God, not just as His emissary; he cursed the prophets as malign deceivers; and he engaged in ritual violation of their *ẓāhirī* law in as shocking and outrageous a manner as possible, with much recourse to Zoroastrian ideas.[24]

18. ʿAbd al-Jabbār, *Tathbīt*, 381; cf. Halm, *Reich*, 225/*Empire*, 250.

19. Ibn al-Dawādārī, *Kanz*, vi, 50 (read 296 for 276), 53 (where 299 is correct); Halm, *Reich*, 51ff./*Empire*, 47ff. (placing it before the break with Salamiyya).

20. ʿAlawī, *Sīrat al-Hādī*, 394f. (year 297); Halm, *Reich*, 178f./*Empire*, 194f. (year 299); cf. also Geddes, 'Apostasy of ʿAlī b. al-Faḍl'.

21. Bīrūnī, *Āthār*, 213 = 196f.; Kennedy, 'The World Year Concept in Islamic Astrology', 38 (dating the conjunction to 928); Madelung, 'Fatimiden und Bahrainqarmaṭen', 80 (also 316/928)/48 and note 254 (redated to 296/908).

22. Thābit b. Sinān, *Akhbār*, 53; Ibn al-Jawzī, *Muntaẓam*, vi, 215f.

23. ʿAbd al-Jabbār, *Tathbīt*, ii, 381.

24. On all this, see Halm, *Reich*, 225–36/*Empire*, 250–64.

The great schism and the rise of the Fatimids

Going back to the 870s, one can see that in the long run the diverse constituencies were likely to fall apart. If the leaders in Salamiyya allowed the Mahdi to arrive, the single hope by which they were united would be replaced by conflicting and generally unrealistic expectations of what the Mahdi was meant to do; and if the leaders kept deferring the arrival of the Mahdi, the single hope would weaken as his return became as indeterminate an event as that of the twelfth imam in Imamism or the second coming of Jesus in Christianity. Since the Ismailis seem to have owed their existence to dissatisfaction with the Imami preference for the latter option, it is not surprising that they opted for the former. Shortly before the year 900 the new *ḥujja* Saʿīd b. al-Ḥusayn, later known as ʿAbdallāh or ʿUbaydallāh al-Mahdī, declared the Mahdi to be himself. But, strangely, he did so in a manner which practically guaranteed that the movement would split.

Contrary to what one would have expected, he did not simply declare himself to be Muḥammad b. Ismāʿīl. He declared himself to be the Mahdi *as opposed to* Muḥammad b. Ismaʿīl. More precisely, he said that Muḥammad b. Ismāʿīl had been a mere cover name of no significance in itself. Neither Ismāʿīl nor his son had been imams. Rather, the imamate had passed from Jaʿfar al-Ṣādiq to the latter's son ʿAbdallāh (al-Afṭaḥ, normally assumed to have died childless), and from him to his descendants, who had lived in disguise as mere *ḥujja*s in Salamiyya and from whose ranks it had been known that the Mahdi would eventually emerge. (See chart 4.) Now that he had emerged, there was no further need for cover names or other forms of disguise.[25]

Why did ʿUbaydallāh al-Mahdī refuse to play Muḥammad b. Ismāʿīl? The answer may lie in the fact that the latter was a real person who had left real descendants outside the Ismaili movement; one of them, known as Sharīf Akhū Muḥsin, wrote a refutation of Ismailism from which the bulk of our information on its early phase derives. It probably did not help that the leaders of the movement (known as *ḥujja*s) had lived for a long time in Salamiyya, where they had been known as descendants of ʿAqīl b. Abī Ṭālib and where people both inside and outside the movement had seen the future ʿUbaydallāh grow up. He plainly was not Muḥammad b. Ismāʿīl in the straightforward, *ẓāhirī* terms by which most of us evaluate information. But why should that have mattered to Bāṭinīs? Whatever the answer, ʿUbaydallāh's revision of the doctrine had the merit (from a *ẓāhirī* point of view) of filling the gap between Jaʿfar al-Ṣādiq and the Mahdi with imams of normal life spans; but by upgrading the leaders in Salamiyya to imams he ruined both the elegance and the predictive value of the

25. Madelung, 'Imamat', 65ff.; Daftary, *Ismāʿīlīs*, 125ff.

cyclical history, for the number of imams in Muḥammad's era now exceeded the normal seven, and he grossly violated the doctrine by changing the Mahdi's name and descent. Perhaps he thought that a messiah was a messiah whatever his precise name or ancestry: all that mattered was whether he could deliver the goods. The Kutāma Berbers who conquered North Africa for him may have agreed, but the vast majority of Ismailis certainly did not. The constituencies in Iraq, India, Iran, and Baḥrayn fell away, leaving the Fatimids with the Kutāma Berbers and Syrian tribesmen. Henceforth there were two forms of Ismailism, the Fatimid version followed by the subjects of ʿUbaydallāh and his descendants, and the pre-Fatimid form (often called Qarmaṭī in the modern literature) of those who retained the old doctrine.[26]

We do not know what the adherents of the old doctrine got up to in Iran or India in the years set for the Mahdi's arrival, but some of them would appear also to have produced a Mahdi of their own, for a former missionary by the name of al-Kayyāl presented himself in Transoxania as the *qāʾim* charged with the abrogation of Muḥammad's law in 295/907f.[27] But the Ismailis of Iran and India were eventually won back by the Fatimids, who readmitted Muḥammad b. Ismāʿīl as the Mahdi (or more precisely the first manifestation of the Mahdi) under al-Muʿizz (953–75) and adopted descent from him as well. Yemen was also recovered for Fatimid Ismailism. But Fatimid Ismailism itself changed character as it came to preside over an increasingly complex polity, and the mountaineers within the movement gradually rejected the Egyptian leadership to form small communities of their own: the Druzes broke away in the 1020s, to survive in the Syrian mountains; the Nizārīs broke away in the 1090s, to survive in northern Iran (eventually also in Syria); and the Ṭayyibīs broke away in Yemen in the 1130s. The Egyptian state itself was hard to distinguish from a Sunni sultanate by the time it finally fell in 1171. It is descendants of the Yemeni, Syrian, and Iranian breakaways and their Indian converts who are the Ismailis of today. (See chart 8.)

ISMAILI POLITICAL THOUGHT

For practical purposes all Ismaili political thought is Fatimid, partly because most pre-Fatimid literature is lost and partly because pre-Fatimid Ismailism was so focused on the Mahdi that all it had to offer on the political front was

26. Strictly speaking, the term 'Qarmaṭī' (pl. Qarāmiṭa) only applies to people converted by Ḥamdān and ʿAbdān Qarmaṭ and his missionaries; but as it happens, most of them remained adherents of the old doctrine. The sources extend the term even further by using it indiscriminately of all Ismailis.

27. Cf. *EI*², s.v. 'al-Kayyāl'; Crone and Treadwell, 'Ismailism at the Sāmānid Court'.

a messianic fantasy to the effect that the world was about to be turned upside down. In practice it was the old believers rather than the Fatimids who engaged in daring political experiments, impelled by their messianic expectations, but they did not write about their thoughts. The only non-Fatimid Ismailis to commit some political thought to paper (or at least the only ones whose thought survives) were Abū Ḥātim al-Rāzī and al-Nasafī, Iranian missionaries active before the Iranian constituencies were recovered by the Fatimids, and the Brethren of Purity (Ikhwān al-Ṣafā), a pseudonym for a group of tenth-century littérateurs in Basra who produced a collection of epistles exploring all aspects of learning known at the time. (The Brethren were not affiliated to any Ismaili community and their Ismaili allegiances are sometimes disputed.) But none of them takes us back to the earliest phase before the split.

Fatimid Ismailis, on the other hand, had three major questions to answer: first, why did government (i.e. the imamate) and law continue even though the Mahdi was meant to put an end to both? Secondly, given that government continued to be necessary, why were the Fatimids rather than other claimants entitled to exercise it? And thirdly, given that the Ismaili community of believers was not identical with the Fatimid polity, just what was the purpose of this polity?

Why did government continue?

Government continued, according to ʿUbaydallāh (909–34) and his successors, because the messianic age had not actually come yet. The sixth era was still in progress. By way of playing for time he initially identified the real saviour as his son rather than himself. The latter had the right name (Muḥammad b. ʿAbd/ʿUbaydallāh) and *kunya* (Abū 'l-Qāsim) and was officially given the title 'al-Qāʾim' soon after the establishment of the Fatimid state. ʿUbaydallāh himself had merely been a mini-mahdi. There would be many Mahdis, he said, citing Jaʿfar al-Ṣādiq.[28] His son al-Qāʾim (934–46) also proved to be a mini-Mahdi. As long as the final redeemer was absent, government would be exercised by his deputies (*khulafāʾ*), a felicitous idea which allowed the Fatimids to call themselves caliphs in the normal style. The fact that there were meant to be only seven imams in each era was no objection, ʿUbaydallāh was quoted as saying, for the seven imams were recurring types like the days of the week: there could be any number of them before the coming of the Mahdi.[29] Some, including the Iranian Abū Yaʿqūb al-Sijistānī, proposed that there would only be seven *khulafāʾ* before he came, to match the seven completer imams.[30] But

28. Hamdani, 'On the Genealogy', Arabic text 12f.
29. Ibid., Arabic text 14.
30. Sijistānī, *Wellsprings of Wisdom*, tr. Walker, §30 and *Iftikhār*, 127, cf. 72, 128.

since the *khulafāʾ* included ʿUbaydallāh al-Mahdī's three predecessors in Salamiyya, now seen as imams and deputies in hiding, this only allowed for four Fatimid caliphs (cf. chart 9), which was not going to suffice: the fourth caliph was al-Muʿizz (953–75), who duly argued against *tawqīt*, determination of the time of the coming of the Mahdi, as reported to him by the missionary in India.[31] A more cautious formulation was that there would be seven, or in any case many, heptads of imams. God had favoured Muḥammad with 'the seven repeated ones (*mathānī*)' (Q. 15:87), as al-Qāḍī al-Nuʿmān explained in the time of al-Muʿizz. That idea, too, is found in al-Sijistānī's work.[32] The seventh imam of the last heptad would be the Lord of the Resurrection, but when would that be? Al-Nuʿmān dropped various hints, some pointing to al-Muʿizz, his patron under whom the Fatimids conquered Egypt, and others to "the successor of his successor" (who proved to be al-Ḥākim).[33] Writing under al-Ḥākim (996–1021) against heretics who claimed that the resurrection had come, the chief missionary al-Kirmānī stressed that there might be any number of imams: thirty-five, fifty-nine, a hundred.[34] (Cf. chart 7.) Fatimid government might go on for ever. But a chief judge writing under al-Mustanṣir (1036–94) expected this caliph to be the *qāʾim* on the grounds that the first seven Fatimid imams had now completed a set of *mathānī*: al-Mustanṣir was the eighth, and also the nineteenth imam since the Prophet, a significant figure since it consisted of 7 plus 12; so now God would conquer the world for him. But the physical world, government, and law would continue.[35]

If the final redemption was receding into the distant future, there was consolation in the fact that salvation had started already in the past. According to al-Nuʿmān, the *qāʾim* had first manifested himself in Muḥammad b. Ismāʿīl; he was still at work in his rightly guided deputies, and he would manifest himself again in the last of these caliphs, the eighteenth, who would preside over the end of the corporeal world as his *ḥujja*. Then the *qāʾim* would appear in his final manifestation in the world of stars to sit in judgement over mankind, abrogate all laws, seal the era of works, and rise to the World Soul, whence he would rule a Neoplatonist version of Adam's Paradise.[36] In short, redemption

31. Stern, 'Heterodox Ismailism', in his *Studies*, 259ff.

32. Nuʿmān, *Asās al-taʾwīl*, in Madelung, 'Imamat', 84; Malījī, *al-Majālis al-mustanṣiriyya*, 30; Sijistānī, 'Tuḥfat al-mustajībīn', 153 (*sabʿa bi-sabʿa min al-khulafāʾ*); cf. Sijistānī, *Ithbāt*, 4 (where it is unclear whether the *mathānī* are recurrent), 193 (*aʾimma kathīrīn*).

33. Madelung, 'Imamat', 85, 87f.

34. Kirmānī, 'al-Risāla al-wāʿiẓa', 143; cf. Daftary, *Ismāʿīlīs*, 218 and note 155 thereto. Kirmānī clearly counts al-Ḥākim as the seventeenth.

35. Malījī, *al-Majālis al-mustanṣiriyya*, 30f., 32, 36f.; Daftary, *Ismāʿīlīs*, 218f.

36. Nuʿmān in Madelung, 'Imamat', 88f.; Daftary, *Ismāʿīlīs*, 177f.

had started in the past and would be completed in the future, but did not greatly affect the here and now, much as in Christianity.

This being so, humans were in need of imams providing spiritual and political guidance. These imams were of the Imami type. They were instituted by God and succeeded by designation from father to son. There could be no question of an elective caliphate. The ʿAbbāsid caliphs were not imams, partly because they were *ṭulaqāʾ* (i.e. descended from a man whom the Prophet could have enslaved after his conquest of Mecca), and partly because they had been elected by the community rather than God.[37] Nor of course could the imam be deposed. He was God's deputy (as well as the Mahdi's), the gate to God, a link between Him and mankind, infallible,[38] and endowed with superhuman knowledge. He knew "the secrets of God without having been taught", as a poet put it.[39]

The law

Unlike the Ismailis of Iraq and Baḥrayn, the Fatimids never tried to abrogate the law, nor do their Berber supporters seem to have expected them to do so. The Kutāma did come to doubt ʿUbaydallāh's claim to be the Mahdi, but not because he left the law in place. In 298/911 some of them raised up a Mahdi of their own and "wrote a book containing a *sharīʿa*, claiming that it had been revealed to him":[40] what the rebels wanted was a community of their own based on a new revelation, not a purely spiritual religion.[41]

Antinomianism did come to the fore in the cities, however. In 309/921 two hundred people were arrested in Qayrawān, Tunis, and Beja for openly declaring forbidden things to be permitted and signalling that a new dispensation had arrived by eating pork and drinking wine in Ramaḍān. They included a slave dealer of whom it is implied that he regarded ʿUbaydallāh al-Mahdī as a manifestation of God. It took a while before ʿUbaydallāh took action against them, but they were suppressed on the grounds that the *ẓāhir* and the *bāṭin* between them constituted the true religion.[42] That was now the official line. Charged by

37. Abū ʾl-Fawāris, *Imāma*, 83v, with further argument against the elective caliphate in ch. 3. It is more commonly the Umayyads who are taunted as *ṭulaqāʾ*, freedmen.

38. Cf. Jaʿfar b. Manṣūr al-Yaman, *Asrār al-nuṭaqāʾ*, 248, 255, 257 (I, 83, 94, 96 = 278, 291, 292).

39. Ibn Hāniʾ in Canard, 'L'impérialisme des Fatimides', 161.

40. Ibn ʿIdhārī, *Bayān*, i, 166f., on the basis of a source probably also reflected in the *ʿUyūn wa'l-ḥadāʾiq*, iv/1,162 and Ibn Ẓāfir, *Akhbār*, 10. Differently Nuʿmān, *Iftitāḥ*, 273.

41. On all of this, see Halm, *Reich*, 148–62/*Empire*, 159–76 (relating Nuʿmān's stereotyped accusations to the practice of guest prostitution).

42. Ibn ʿIdhārī, *Bayān*, 185f.; Halm, *Reich*, 222ff./*Empire*, 247ff.

al-Muʿizz with the creation of a specifically Ismaili legal system, the judge al-Nuʿmān (d. 363/974) compiled a manual of Ismaili law and wrote an interpretation of its inner meaning, but he affirmed the importance of legal observance in both works: the *ẓāhir* was incomplete without the *bāṭin*, and the obverse was equally true; it was not enough merely to know the imam.[43] That external observance and inner understanding alike were required for salvation remained the standard Fatimid doctrine. It actually made for greater consistency, given the Ismaili veneration of the lawgiver prophets, the founders of socio-political order.

There was more antinomianism in the east. In Baḥrayn the first attempt to abolish the law, by the Persian captive, ended in tears, but a second attempt must have been made later, for Baḥrayn had acquired a new political organization and abolished ritual worship by 1056, when it was visited by the Ismaili Nāṣir-i Khusraw: the locals did not pray, but there was a mosque for visitors.[44] Elsewhere in the east, the antinomianism was bookish.

To bookish people, the key question was why one had to worship God by physical acts seemingly devoid of spiritual meaning. The practical value of ablutions, prostrations, fasting, alms-giving, pilgrimage, and holy war was obvious for anyone to see: they kept people clean, exercised their bodies, kept bad thoughts away, induced a spirit of humility, inured against hardship, counteracted laziness, distributed income, secured the defence and expansion of the Islamic world, and so on.[45] But what did that have to do with the ineffable? As the Brethren of Purity saw it, the law was one of the five forces that reduced free and noble human beings to a slavery from which the only escape was death; one had to endure the hunger of fasting, the physical fatigue of prayer, the cold water of ablutions, the battle against avarice when alms had to be paid, the toil of going on pilgrimage and waging holy war, and the pain of forgoing forbidden pleasures – all this because communal life was impossible without it.[46] The diverse interests of human beings were such that they could not live together without coercion and external commands.[47] But al-Sābiq and al-Tālī (alias Kūnī and Qadar) did not worship God in so prosaic a manner, bound by legal fetters and bonds, as al-Sijistānī said; rather, they praised and

43. Nuʿmān, *Daʿāʾim*, i, 53f. and *Taʾwīl al-daʿāʾim*, i, 53f (sic); cf. also Madelung, 'Imamat', 89.

44. Nāṣir-i Khusraw, *Travels*, 87ff. (also in Lewis, *Islam*, ii, no. 26). Cf. further below, 325.

45. Sijistānī, *Ithbāt*, 55, 179.17; *RIS*, ii, 306f. = Goodman, *Case*, 156f. (abbreviated and faulty in places); Ghazālī, *Munqidh*, 48 = 79.

46. *RIS*, iii, 306ff.

47. Abū Ḥātim al-Rāzī, *Aʿlām*, 111; Sijistānī, *Ithbāt*, 176. Cf. further below, 251f.

worshipped God by natural impulse (*gharīza*).[48] So also do the animals in a famous fable told by Brethren of Purity, in which humans are told that they needed the fetters and bonds of organized religion because they were sick.[49] Unlike the animals, they could no longer manage with natural religion. According to al-Sijistānī, ritual law had been introduced to remind souls united with human bodies to worship God, to divert their attention from this world, keep them in a state of gratitude, and help them avoid envisaging Him in terms of qualities derived from this world without falling into the other extreme of reducing him to an abstract principle; but when the Mahdi and Qa'im came it would no longer be necessary to express things in the limiting medium of speech: things would return to pure thought, and so the bonds and fetters could be removed.[50] The Qa'im would bring spiritual resurrection (*qiyāma*), as later Ismailis said. According to al-Sijistānī, he would not abrogate all of the law, for no society could do without the prohibition of homicide and theft or laws of marriage, sale and other contracts; that part of the law was rational (*ʿaqlī*), he said, equating the rational with the universal (and, as we might say, the natural). But ritual law was conventional (*waḍʿī*)[51] and differed from one religious community to the next; law of this type would disappear again.[52]

Like the philosopher Abū Bakr al-Rāzī, then, the Ismailis dreamt of a world without organized religion, tired now of its authoritarian character, now of its social demands, and now of its intellectual limitations. Some of them went so far as to claim that mankind had originated without it. According to al-Nasafī (d. 330s/940s), supported by Abū Yaʿqūb al-Sijistānī, there had been no law in Adam's era, the longest of the six.[53] As far as the original state of mankind was concerned, they thus agreed with Abū Bakr al-Rāzī: down to the Flood, humans did indeed know God without revelation, religion without law, the truth

48. Sijistānī, *Ithbāt*, 175.

49. *RIS*, ii, 324ff. = Goodman, *Case*, 156ff.

50. Sijistānī, *Ithbāt*, 175ff.

51. The text wrongly has *waṣfī*. Al-Sijistānī also distinguishes the two as *muḥkam* and *mutashābih*, defined as indispensable and dispensable for the well-being of the world (*Ithbāt*, 178). For a discussion, see Pines, 'Shīʿite Terms and Conceptions', 232f.

52. Sijistānī, *Ithbāt*, 177ff. The chapter strangely ends by describing the disappearance of the law as a process of corruption. A similar idea is credited to al-Zanjānī, one of the authors of the *Rasā'il Ikhwān al-Ṣafā*: the fact that the canonical penalties have ceased to be applied, that unlawful taxes are collected, and that the law is being violated in other ways shows that the era of Muḥammad is coming to an end (ʿAbd al-Jabbār, *Tathbīt*, 355f.; tr. Stern, 'New Information', in his *Studies*, 159). But the idea hardly fits in al-Sijistānī (similarly Pines, 'Shīʿite Terms and Conceptions', 234). The whole chapter seems to be somewhat lacking in clarity and coherence, possibly due to later revision.

53. Madelung, 'Imamat', 102f., 106f.

without social and political discipline, spirituality without hierarchy, and salvation by individual effort alone.

To Abū Ḥātim al-Rāzī (d. 322/924), however, this was too close to Abū Bakr al-Rāzī's position for comfort. According to him, mankind had lived under external commands from the start of its earthly existence,[54] for organized religion was required for social and political order. "It is by these laws that elite and masses alike are governed and that the affairs of the world are maintained, for the welfare of the world in this life can only be achieved by compulsion, coercion and domination," he said, sounding rather as if he were speaking of secular law.[55] The prophets had played so great a role in the governance of mankind, what with their protection of lives and property, their defence of the weak against the strong, and their management of things in general, that one would have to respect them even if one rejected their miracles and denied their prophetic status, he insisted, sounding as if the religious element was of secondary importance yet again.[56] In line with this, he repeatedly stressed that salvation lay in the inner meaning.[57] Behind the polemics, then, he too was close to Abū Bakr al-Rāzī's position: people needed laws and got them in a religious form which he, like Abū Bakr al-Rāzī, deemed to be lacking in saving value. But whereas Abū Bakr al-Rāzī dismissed the religious element as fraudulent, Abū Ḥātim al-Rāzī insisted on its reality. The laws brought by the prophets came from God, not from the prophets themselves, and their institutions formed an indispensable part of religion even if they had no saving role in themselves, as disciplinary measures and vessels in which the saving meaning was carried. There was apparently no other way in which this meaning could be conveyed to human beings in their present state. Abū Ḥātim would clearly have had an easier time if he had credited the external acts with a saving role in themselves. That was what the judge al-Nuʿmān did, and it seems eventually to have been accepted by the eastern Ismailis as well.

For all that, antinomianism flared up again in the Fatimid realm under the caliph al-Ḥākim (386–411/996–1021), when the founders of what came to be known as the Druze religion declared al-Ḥākim to be a manifestation of God. "Your resurrection (*qiyāma*) has taken place, your era of concealment (of the inner meaning) has run its course," the missionary al-Akhram proclaimed to the Ismaili community in 408/1017. The law was now empty shells and otiose

54. Ibid., 103f.

55. *Aʿlām*, 110f.

56. Ibid., 89.17. Similarly the anonymous Ismaili, possibly al-Muʾayyad (d. 470/1078), against Ibn al-Rāwandī in Kraus, 'Ketzergeschichte', 109 = 118.

57. *Aʿlām*, 110.13, 112.2 (*maʿānīhā . . . allatī fīhā al-najāt*; *mā fīhi najātuhu min al-maʿānī*).

material.[58] "Our Lord has completely abrogated the *sharīʿa* of Muḥammad," Ḥamza al-Labbād declared.[59] This, as it proved, was Ismailism suited for Syrian mountaineers defining themselves out of Muslim society. Another set of mountaineers, mainly in northern Iran, but also in Syria, accepted the 'New Mission' founded in the 1090s by Ḥasan-i Ṣabbāḥ, who ensconced himself in the fortress of Alamūt and broke with the Fatimids over the succession in 487/1094. His followers, known to the Crusaders as 'the Assassins', were committed to the destruction of Seljuq power, and having no armies, they resorted to what we now call assassination. In 559/1164 the great-grandson of Ḥasan-i Ṣabbāḥ, the chief missionary (later imam) Ḥasan II, declared the resurrection (*qiyāma*) to have come and formally abolished the law by breaking the fast and drinking wine in a new 'Festival of the Resurrection' on the seventeenth of Ramaḍān. But by comparison with events in Baḥrayn it was a very decorous affair. The initiative came from the missionary; there were no long drawn-out expectations, eagerly followed predictions, no feverish pitch, and no excesses either. They returned to the law at the order of another leader in, or soon after, 607/1210.[60]

Why this particular dynasty?

Granted that there would be more than seven imams in the present era, why were the Fatimids entitled to the imamate? The answer was simple enough: because they descended from the particular son of Jaʿfar al-Ṣādiq to whom they deemed the imamate to have passed. But their attempt to document their claim to the requisite ancestry was neither simple nor consistent. As *ḥujja*s in Salamiyya they had claimed descent from a brother of ʿAlī's by the name of ʿAqīl; as imams they claimed descent first from Jaʿfar al-Ṣādiq's eldest son, ʿAbdallāh, and thereafter from Ismāʿīl (cf. chart 4); and they were forever adjusting the names and positions of the 'imams in hiding', as the *ḥujja*s in Salamiyya came to be known.[61] The Sunnis denied their claims to ʿAlid status altogether, asserting that they descended from one Maymūn al-Qaddāḥ; for good measure they identified the latter as a descendant of the third-century Syrian Christian known to the Greeks as Bardesanes and to the Muslims as Ibn

58. Kirmānī, 'al-Risāla al-wāʿiẓa', 142, 145; cf. Madelung, 'Imamat', 121; Bryer, 'Origins of the Druze Religion (part I)', 68.

59. Bryer, 'Origins of the Druze Religion (ch. 3)', 250.

60. Hodgson, *Assassins*, 148ff., 217ff.

61. Consequently, most Ismaili sources omit the names of the imams between Jaʿfar al-Ṣādiq (or Ismāʿīl or Muḥammad b. Ismāʿīl) and the Fatimids, subsuming them as the 'later' or 'hidden imams' and resuming the names with ʿUbaydallāh.

Dayṣān.[62] The result of all these manoeuvres was a dense fog which long caused the study of the Fatimids to be dominated by the problem of "the birth certificate of the first Fāṭimid ruler", as one scholar noted in disgust.[63] The issue mattered enormously to contemporaries. Medieval Islamic political thought is much concerned with the legitimation of particular dynasties, and as far as the Shīʿite imamate was concerned, legitimacy rested on descent, not because monarchic claims to particular lands were transmitted by heredity, as in Europe, but rather because the monarch's special relationship with God was thus passed down. The question of the imam's birth certificate has been unravelled by Madelung with great acuity from a mass of confusing information,[64] but the reader of this book can dispense with the details.

What was the purpose of the Fatimid state?

The Fatimids were originally meant to conquer the entire world, or at least the entire Muslim world, before abolishing the *ẓāhir*. They began well enough by conquering North Africa in 909, Egypt in 969, and from there pushing into Syria, while also establishing control of the Ḥijāz, Yemen, and Multān (in India). But they ground to a halt in Syria, and in 1041 they lost North Africa. With or without North Africa, what was the purpose of Egypt as a polity in its own right, if it could no longer be seen as simply a stepping stone to Baghdad?

The Fatimids never really answered this question. As Shīʿites they found it self-evident that humans needed a spiritual guide. Why did the guide need to have political power? They treated that as self-evident too. The Prophet had ruled people in both political and religious terms, and so had ʿAlī, so this was obviously right. Humans must have prophets and imams "to keep people under control in this world and lead them in their religious affairs", as Abū Ḥātim al-Rāzī said.[65] Even the *ahl al-ẓāhir* agreed that the imam had originally combined both powers. This was a pan-Islamic heritage, and no Ismaili could see that there was anything to explain.

But by the tenth century it was only in marginal communities such of those of the Khārijites and Zaydīs that the pan-Islamic heritage was still alive. In the heartlands the multi-purpose imam was out of date. The *ahl al-ẓāhir* now operated with imams in two senses, that is to say rulers who had no claim to religious authority on the one hand and scholars who had no claim to political leadership on the other. In practice the Imami Shīʿites lived with the same

62. For a survey of the problem, see Daftary, *Ismāʿīlīs*, 108ff.
63. Shaban, *Islamic History*, ii, 188.
64. Madelung, 'Imamat', 69ff.
65. *Aʿlām*, 9.7.

division, since the one and only person entitled to power of both types had gone into hiding until the end of time. Of course, it was precisely because this person had gone into hiding that the early Ismailis took action. What they initially wanted, however, was not to restore the imamate, but rather to speed up the great Mahdic transformation of the world. They moved forward the end of history in the hope of doing away with imams of every kind.

But just as twentieth-century communists vested all economic resources in the state in the expectation that it would wither away, only to find that they had massively increased its power, so the Ismailis vested all authority in the Mahdi in the belief that he would abrogate it, only to find that they too had thereby lent enormous strength to the very institution they wished to remove. Far from having abolished the imamate, they had restored it in its multi-purpose form.

The new multi-purpose imam went well enough with the tribal environment in which the Fatimids rose to statehood, but not with their other domains or spheres of influence. To most Ismailis, it seems mainly to have been as a spiritual figurehead that he made sense. He, and only he, knew the ultimate meaning of things; without him, one had no access to the *bāṭin*: however closely the Ismailis identified the inner meaning with philosophy, they never agreed with the philosophers that one could reason one's way to the ultimate truth unaided. All saving knowledge came from the imams; their guidance encapsulated the entire moral and cognitive sphere that separated humans from animals, as al-Naysābūrī said, putting paid to the idea that humans had the innate ability to save themselves: mankind would have neither wisdom nor virtue but for the imams.[66] One had to cling to them to benefit from the ongoing redemption, and to be wholly saved when the Lord of the Resurrection came. The earthly hierarchy over which the imams presided reflected that of the spiritual world. One had to model oneself on the occupants of this hierarchy to ascend along the ladder of salvation in the hope of approaching the rank of the imam himself.

But what were spiritual leaders of such profound significance to mankind doing as rulers of Egypt? Their case was not comparable with that of the Prophet. He, too, was a figure of profound significance for mankind who had ruled a small part of the earth, but his polity had made sense because it was a community of believers, a saving vehicle headed by the saving figure himself. By contrast, the Fatimid polity only overlapped with the Ismaili community of believers. Most Egyptians were Sunnis; most Ismailis lived outside the Fatimid state, under non-Ismaili rulers. What then was the polity for?

66. Naysābūrī, *Imāma*, 41.

The fact of the matter is that nobody knew. The missionaries could have cast the Fatimid polity as a saving vehicle by requiring all converts to emigrate to the imam's domain. Back in the early days of the Ismaili mission, the believers had indeed moved to abodes of *hijra* in which to prepare for the coming of the Mahdi,[67] and the sense that the imam's residence was a *dār al-hijra* was still alive under the Fatimids. Thus the tenth-century Jaʿfar b. Manṣūr al-Yaman tells us that all the prophets and imams had sent out missionaries to establish abodes of *hijra*, where they would later join them, or else they had established such bases themselves. This was how they had taken to fighting their opponents, for it was wrong to rebel without an abode of emigration of one's own.[68] But Jaʿfar does not think of *hijra* as a radical departure from a doomed society to a community of the saved, for he also calls the triumphant return to the metropolis a *hijra*,[69] and he takes it for granted that one could be an Ismaili outside the imam's polity. He does rhetorically ask, "have you not been commanded to stay with the imams wherever they are?"[70] but he is not speaking of a prerequisite for salvation. When the missionaries revealed the imam's name and whereabouts to their converts, he says, "those who could would travel to him", while those who could not "were ordered to live in hiding and secrecy and to move about on earth until the moment of the manifestation came"; the poor and the powerless (*al-mustaḍʿafūn*) who were unable to leave were excused.[71] The anonymous *Kitāb al-kashf* felicitously explains *hijra* as a form of pilgrimage.[72]

In practice, future missionaries would normally visit the imam, or even take up residence at his abode, and one of them explicitly says that he came to Egypt as an emigrant (*muhājiran*).[73] But ordinary Ismailis rarely seem to have visited Fatimid North Africa or Egypt, let alone to have emigrated there on a permanent basis, despite the persecution to which they were often exposed in their native lands. Al-Naysābūrī explains that they were the imam's army abroad,[74] presupposing that the imam's polity was simply a platform for further conquest. This is of course precisely what a *dār hijra* normally was, but if

67. For the abodes of *hijra* set up wherever a mission began, see Halm, *Reich*, 55ff./*Empire*, 51ff. It is only in Iraq that we see an entire community move to one on the eve of the coming of the messiah.

68. Jaʿfar, *Asrār al-nuṭaqāʾ*, 233–6, 238f., 247, 248f., 251, 254f., 257, 259, 263.

69. Ibid., 237 (Muḥammad's conquest of Mecca), 255 (of Abraham's conquest of his ancestral *ḥaram*).

70. Ibid., 240 (against Imamis).

71. Ibid., 260.

72. *K. al-kashf*, 111.4.

73. Walker, *Kirmānī*, 17.

74. Naysābūrī in Stern, 'Cairo as the Centre of the Ismāʿīlī Movement', 438.

one could be saved outside it, what was the purpose of Fatimid Egypt once the expansion had ground to a halt?

The Ismailis could not answer this question because they had originated as Gnostics whose messiah was expected to abolish law and politics, not to sanctify them. As devotees of philosophy they could have played around with al-Fārābī's political ideas, and some eventually did: Naṣīr al-dīn Ṭūsī cast the imams as rulers of the virtuous city in his *Naṣirean Ethics* (c. 633/1235). But by then the Fatimids no longer existed; the reference was to the Nizārī imams at Alamūt, and the virtuous city that Ṭūsī placed them in was not a concrete polity, but rather the world.[75]

In fact, the Ismailis had trouble seeing themselves as forming a polity at all. Like the Imamis they were always speaking of the imam rather than the *umma*: both applied the metaphor of Noah's Ark to the imams, not to the saving community in which the believers travelled, for example.[76] But the Ismailis were far more given than the Imamis to seeing themselves as a spiritual elite rather than a complete community. They did sometimes identify themselves as the only Muslims left in Muḥammad's *umma*, but they still thought of the *umma* as the totality of Muslims, not as one constituted by themselves.[77] What they were was rather the enlightened few who did not share the beliefs of the *ʿāmma*, the vulgar masses.[78] Al-Sijistānī even spoke of *al-ʿawāmm min al-umma*, the (non-Ismaili) masses of the (shared) community.[79] There was not really any Ismaili community at all, except at the local level: the missionary administered his flock in religious and worldly terms alike, much as Christian clerics and rabbis administered the *dhimmī*s. Here the multi-purpose nature of the community made sense. But it did so precisely because most Ismailis were living like *dhimmī*s, in communities of their own under non-Ismaili rule, and would continue to do so whether the Fatimid caliphate existed or not.

The key question left unanswered by the Fatimid Ismailis was the relationship between political organization and salvation. They rehearsed the familiar arguments: without an imam, chaos would prevail, the weak would have no protectors, whereas the imam defended the believers against their religious and worldly enemies alike; without him, no two of them would survive.[80] But the

75. Madelung, 'Naṣīr al-Dīn Ṭūsī's Ethics', 95–7.

76. Naysābūrī, *Imāma*, 73; Malījī, *al-Majālis al-mustanṣiriyya*, 57; cf. above, 111, 115f.

77. Jaʿfar, *Asrār al-nuṭaqāʾ*, 243.-7, 260.14.

78. Abū Ḥātim al-Rāzī in Stern, *Studies*, 36; Nuʿmān, 'al-Risāla al-mudhhiba', 30.14; Jaʿfar, *Asrār al-nuṭaqāʾ*, 261.2.

79. People who reject the Ismaili view of the imam as a God-given guide are *al-ʿawāmm min al-umma*, "the masses of the community"; and the disagreement *fī 'l-umma*, "in the community", is caused by its failure to raise up the rightful imams (Sijistānī, *Iftikhār*, 70f.).

subjects of kings plainly did survive in this world, whatever fate awaited them in the next; indeed, it was under kings that most Ismailis were living. Whoever died without allegiance to an imam might well die a pagan death, as the Ismaili literature often stresses, but one could give such allegiance to the Fatimid imam anywhere in the Muslim world. Did people living under Fatimid rule have a higher chance of salvation? The literature never says so. Ultimately, it seems not to have mattered much who held power in the here and now.

When the Egyptian stepping stone to world conquest proved to be a permanent abode, it lost its point. More precisely, it came to function as what one might call the Ismaili Vatican: an area from which the pontiff directed his followers wherever they might be found, and which for historical reasons he actually ruled, but which barely overlapped with the community of believers and played no role at all in their salvation. It merely enabled the pontiff to avoid dependence on other rulers and increased the prestige of his cause.

Egypt was of course too big a country to be relegated to Vatican status, and this soon caused political government to develop in a direction quite different from that of the pontiff's spiritual leadership. Daylamī mercenaries, black African slaves and Turkish *ghilmān* eclipsed the original Berber troops; the bureaucracy was largely run by *dhimmī*s; four, possibly five, viziers of Fatimid Egypt were Christians, while three were recently converted Jews. All in all, from the reign of al-ʿAzīz (975–96) onwards, both military and civil government effectively ceased to represent the Ismaili cause. Ismailism and political government parted ways. Significantly, it was Sunnis (Ibn Zūlāq, al-Musabbiḥī, al-Quḍāʿī) rather than Ismailis who wrote historical accounts of the Fatimids in Egypt, for to the Sunnis, the Fatimids looked much like any other Egyptian dynasty, except for their elaborate missionary and educational institutions and the ritual displays they went in for in the capital.[81] But their failure to endow the polity with Ismaili meaning eventually affected the pontiff's spiritual leadership as well. Under al-Ḥākim (996–1021) non-Ismailis began to receive religious office: a Ḥanafī was appointed chief judge; a former retainer, possibly freedman, of the Būyid ruler ʿAḍud al-Dawla was appointed chief missionary;[82] and under al-Mustanṣir (1036–94) a Sunni became chief judge and chief missionary, as well as vizier.[83] At the same time the political

80. Naysābūrī, *Imāma*, 45, 52; similarly Sijistānī, *Iftikhār*, 71.

81. Cf. Halm, *Traditions of Learning*; Sanders, *Ritual, Politics, and the City*.

82. Walker, *Kirmānī*, 7f., where the judge, Ibn Abī 'l-ʿAwwām, is identified as Ḥanbalī on the basis of Ibn Ḥajar, *Rafʿ*, 610; similarly Lev, *State and Society*, 136f. But Maqrīzī's claim (in Lev, 137n.) that he was a Ḥanafī is both intrinsically more plausible and confirmed by the fact that he wrote a book on the virtues of Abū Ḥanīfa (Ibn Ḥajar, *Rafʿ*, 612.5). The retainer was Khatkīn al-Ḍayf al-ʿAḍudī.

establishment, likewise often headed by non-Ismailis, displayed increasing indifference to the spiritual branch that it was meant to serve: in 1041 the Zīrid governor of North Africa began a long drawn-out transfer of allegiances from the Fatimids to the ʿAbbāsids; in 1070–2 the governor of Alexandria tried similarly to restore Egypt to ʿAbbāsid allegiance; in 1094 the Armenian soldier and vizier al-Afḍal caused large numbers of Ismailis outside Egypt to split off by elevating al-Mustaʿlī rather than Nizār to the imamate; in 1131 al-Afḍal's son Kutayfāt tried to substitute the Mahdi of the Imamis for the Fatimids; and in the 1160s a former vizier seeking to oust his rival called upon the Sunni Nūr al-Dīn to intervene in Egypt. In 1171 Saladin, a commander in the service of Nūr al-Dīn, put an end to the Fatimid imamate.[84]

In the last resort, then, the odd mixture of Gnostic/Neoplatonist beliefs and political messianism curdled. This is hardly surprising. It is more surprising that there should have been such a mixture at all, and its existence testifies to the extraordinary impact of Muḥammad's career on the Middle East: even Gnostics came to see religious state formation and conquest to be the way out of their problems, for all that their key interest was in individual enlightenment. Ismaili conversion stories typically tell of young men in search of the truth who are picked out by sharp-eyed missionaries and subjected to difficult tests which they must pass to qualify for admission to the spiritual elite, much like Tamino in Mozart's masonic opera, *The Magic Flute*. The missionaries are not trying to convert communities. "The Ismāʿīlī *dāʿī* does not give a public sermon, does not address himself to the multitude. His mission is to discover, from individual to individual, those in whom he can detect the spiritual aptitude to respond to the *daʿwa*," as Corbin observes with reference to two such stories.[85] The young men join a spiritual brotherhood, not a community. Communal demands and family obligations are precisely what they leave behind.

For all that, the young men set out to conquer the world for the truth they have found, stirred by the prospect of adventure and heroic deeds. Here the story ought to have ended, and of course that is precisely what they initially expected. The everyday political responsibilities they acquired did not fit their creed. It was only for the villagers and tribesmen in the movement that apocalyptic politics worked, and they worked for them precisely because their outlook was communal: Baḥrānīs and Berbers alike succeeded in dramatically changing their collective lives. But the educated youths in search of individual

83. Lev, *State and Society*, 137 (al-Yāzūrī).

84. EI², s.vv. 'Fāṭimids'; 'al-Muʿizz b. Badīs', col. 483a; 'al-Mustanṣir', col. 731; 'Shāwar'.

85. Corbin, 'The Ismāʿīlī Response', 83; cf. also Cyclical Time, 130ff., on the quest of the imam.

enlightenment might have done better in the long run if Ismailism had been without political ambitions, as it was to the Brethren of Purity and as it is today. What their ambitions brought them was a polity which was neither a brotherhood nor a community of believers and which ended up by destroying the spiritual organization it was meant to support.

CHAPTER

16

THE SUNNIS

The Sunnis have their roots in, and derive their name from, the partisans of *ḥadīth* who came to prominence in the ninth century under the name of *ahl al-sunna wa'l-jamāʿa*. It is probably safe to say that by the end of the ninth or the beginning of the tenth century the majority of Muslims had come to accept their political convictions. Numerous though the Shīʿites were in those centuries, most Muslims were neither Shīʿites nor Khārijites; and most of those identifiable in negative terms could now also be identified in positive terms as accepting the four-caliphs thesis and holding communal togetherness to be more important than rightly guided leadership. But the adherents of communal togetherness (*jamāʿa*) were still divided over theology and law. They disagreed not only over concrete doctrines, but also over the rules by which doctrines were to be derived and explained. The partisans of *ḥadīth* concentrated all authority in God and His prophet: what came from them was authoritative information of super-human origin (*samʿ*) which had to be taken on trust, just as it stood (*bilā kayf*), whether or not it made sense in terms of such rationality as humans possess. The jurists (*fuqahāʾ*) and theologians (*mutakallims*), both of whom had begun their system-building before the traditionalists appeared on the scene, maintained that one could not answer questions about either the law or the articles of faith without employing human reasoning (which the jurists initially called *raʾy*, sensible opinion, thereafter *qiyās*, analogy, while the theologians spoke of *naẓar*). And the philosophers (to whom *qiyās* meant syllogism) insisted that all answers had to be based on human reasoning alone. The Sunnis are the members of the *jamāʿa* who reached a compromise, or at least an agreement to disagree, on these questions.

How and when this agreement was reached is still unknown, but the answer seems to be the tenth to eleventh centuries as far as law is concerned, somewhat later in the case of theology (insofar as the conflict between Traditionalism and *kalām* was ever resolved). When the dust had settled after the Mongol conquests, the Sunnis appear with great clarity as those who belonged to the Ḥanafī, Mālikī, Shāfiʿī, or Ḥanbalī legal schools, and who accepted the creeds associated with these schools, be it in Traditionalist form or in that of Ashʿarite or Māturīdite theology. In this chapter I shall take the existence of the Sunni community for granted. Neither the Muʿtazilites nor the philosophers were partners to the Sunni agreement, but in terms of political thought the Muʿtazilites were sufficiently close to the Sunnis (unless they were Shīʿites) to be treated together with them. When Muʿtazilites and Sunnis are treated together I shall refer to them as *jamāʿī* Muslims.

The caliphs and their masters

The classical Sunni statements of the doctrine of the imamate were formulated in the tenth and eleventh centuries, when the fortunes of the caliphate were at a low ebb. For practical purposes the caliph had not ruled since 861, a short period of restoration apart, and in the tenth century it looked as if he was going to be removed altogether. A new caliphate was proclaimed in 909 in North Africa by the Ismaili Fatimids, who conquered Egypt in 969, as has been seen; in 929 the Umayyad ruler of Spain declared themselves to be caliphs too; and in 945 Iraq was conquered by Shīʿite soldiers of fortune from the Daylamī highlands on the Caspian coast. The Būyids or Buwayhids (945–1055), as the new rulers were called, seem originally to have been Zaydīs, but they veered towards the Imami camp after their arrival in Iraq; in any case they were Shīʿites. Many expected them to abolish the ʿAbbāsid caliphate in favour of the ʿAlids, but they could not have done so in accordance with either Zaydī or Imami rules,[1] and it would have led to trouble with Sunni Muslims while at the same time circumscribing their freedom of action.[2] As mercenaries, they were used to keeping their religious convictions private, so they allowed the ʿAbbāsid caliphate to continue.

They did however treat the caliphs badly, partly by deposing and blinding them at will, and partly by keeping them practically penniless.[3] When the

1. The Imāmī imam was in hiding; the Zaydī imam obtains his position by making a *daʿwa* and *khurūj*, not by being enthroned by others.

2. Cf. Ibn al-Athīr, *Kāmil*, viii, 452f. (yr 334).

3. They had no religious motive (*bāʿith dīnī*) to respect them, as Ibn al-Athīr points out, ibid.

caliph al-Muṭīʿ was asked to supply funds for the holy war against the Byzantines in 362/972f., he denied that he had any obligations in respect of either holy war or pilgrimage on the grounds that he was under other people's control (*maḥṣūr*) and barely had enough to live on. "All you allow me is mention of my name on the pulpit," he said, volunteering to abdicate (as in fact he did in the following year).[4] One Būyid ruler, ʿAḍud al-Dawla (d. 372/983), even omitted the caliph's name from the Friday oration for two months.[5] The Būyids openly favoured the Shīʿites, giving them appointments, allowing them to celebrate their festivals, and paying handsome sums to Shīʿite poets and littérateurs. They also insulted the caliph by adopting the Persian title of *shāhānshāh* (king of kings) and treating him as if he were a mere high priest in their service.[6] All in all, the ʿAbbāsids "are not seen and no attention is paid to their opinion", as the geographer Maqdisī (better known as al-Muqaddasī) observed in c. 985.[7] Al-Bīrūnī, writing c. 1000, cites astrologers as saying that the caliphate was now a matter of religious creed (*amr dīnī iʿtiqādī*) rather than worldly power (*lā mulkī dunyāwī*), by which they seem to have meant, not that the caliph only had religious authority now (since he had none of that either), but rather that he only had religious significance: to mainstream Muslims, he still represented the community of believers founded by the Prophet.[8]

Things improved in some respects with the rise of Turkish rulers in the east, first the Ghaznavids and next the Seljuqs. Unlike the Iranians, the Turks were not known to have had a period of pre-Islamic grandeur, and initially most of them became Muslims by enslavement for military use: to be a Turk in the Muslim world was thus to be a nobody. Maḥmūd of Ghazna (388–421/998–1030) resolutely cast himself as an Iranian king, tracing his descent to the Sāsānid house and patronizing Persian poets; but the only safe way to legitimate oneself as a Turkish ruler was by services to Islam, preferably capped by caliphal recognition. Maḥmūd accordingly presented himself as a loyal supporter of al-Qādir (381–422/991–1031), which suited al-Qādir because the Būyids were on the wane and he was attempting a come-back with the support of the Baghdadī Ḥanbalites.[9] Maḥmūd received official appointment as ruler of Khurāsān in 389/999, along with the title Yamīn al-Dawla,[10] and

4. Hamdānī, *Takmila*, 211.
5. Ibish, *Al-Baqillani*, 45.
6. Busse, *Chalif und Grosskönig*, 420ff. and 'The Revival of Persian Kingship'.
7. *Aḥsan*, 131.2.
8. *Āthār*, 132 = 129. They compare the caliph with the Jewish exilarch.
9. Above, 133.
10. Bosworth, *Ghaznavids*, 46.

proceeded to hammer wealthy infidels in India and to kill Ismailis, Muʿtazilites and other heretics at home.

The Seljuqs, who arrived in Baghdad in 1055, were tribal leaders whose ability to defeat the Ghaznavids came as a shock and whose rapacious followers inflicted great damage on the Muslim world. They too supported the caliph in return for legitimation, and they made life easier for him by rarely setting foot in Baghdad. But the first sultan, Tughril Beg (d. 455/1063), caused deep embarrassment by asking for an ʿAbbāsid princess in marriage (somewhat like an African chief asking for the hand of a Victorian princess); Malikshāh (d. 485/1092) had a plan for evicting the caliph in order to have a Seljuq winter capital in Baghdad; and relations with the caliph were tense at other times as well.[11] Nonetheless, the Seljuqs went down in history as saviours of Islam, thanks to the Sunni effort to see the bright side of things. Apart from sweeping away the last remains of the Shīʿite Būyids, they dealt a mortal blow to the Ismaili statelet in Baḥrayn, and defeated the Byzantines at Manzikert in 1071, putting a decisive end to their recovery of northern Syria and placing a question mark over the very survival of Byzantium by enabling Turkish tribesmen to pour into Anatolia. For all of this, the scholar al-Juwaynī said, it was worth putting up with a bit of wanton destruction at home.[12] Al-Juwaynī's pupil, al-Ghazālī, also cast the Turks as a blessing for Islam.[13] But the Seljuq empire was shortlived. After the death of Malikshāh in 1092 it fell apart under different branches of the family, and eventually under other Turks. In eastern Iran the Seljuqs lasted down to 1194. In Syria they were on the way out already when the first Crusaders arrived in 1097. The many petty dynasties that faced the Crusaders here were eventually to be replaced by the Ayyūbids, a dynasty with many branches founded by Saladin (d. 589/1193), famed as the conqueror of Egypt from the Fatimids and of Jerusalem from the Crusaders. It was slave soldiers of the last Ayyūbids who halted the western advance of the Mongols at Ayn Jālūt in 658/1260.

*Constitutional law (*al-aḥkām al-sulṭāniyya*)*

This was the situation in which constitutional law came to be written. Until then, the imamate had been covered, not in legal handbooks,[14] but rather in

11. Makdisi, 'The Marriage of Ṭughril Beg' and 'Les rapports entre calife et sulṭân'; Bosworth, 'Political and Dynastic History', 101.

12. *Ghiyāth*, §§492ff., esp. 496, 499f.; cf. Nagel, *Festung*, 278f.

13. Below, note 93.

14. *Pace* Gibb ('Al-Mawardi's Theory', in his *Studies*, 151). The chapters on *imāma* that one does find in *fiqh* works are about prayer leadership, not the 'great imamate'.

works of *kalām* and *uṣūl al-dīn*, where it continued to be treated thereafter too, usually at the end and almost always with some comments on how the subject did not really form part of theology. The imamate had originated as part of the faith and had thus fallen to the theologians, but they no longer knew why. In the Būyid period the main theologians to deal with the subject were ʿAbd al-Jabbār (d. 415/1025), al-Bāqillānī (d. 403/1013) and al-Baghdādī (d. 429/1037), all three in polemics against Shīʿites. After the Seljuq invasions the main authors were al-Mutawallī (d. 478/1085), al-Juwaynī (d. 478/1085), al-Bazdawī (d. 493/1099), al-Ghazālī (d. 505/1111), al-Nasafī (d. 537/1142), al-Shahrastānī (d. 548/1153), Fakhr al-Dīn al-Rāzī (d. 606/1209), and al-Āmidī (d. 631/1233).

But thanks to the Shāfiʿite al-Māwardī (d. 450/1058) the imamate now came to be treated as a legal topic as well. Al-Māwardi collected the rules pertaining to all aspects of government – the imamate, vizierate, taxation, judgeship, holy war, the treatment of rebels, market inspection, and more besides – from a variety of genres and put them together in a single book, which he called *al-aḥkām al-sulṭāniyya*, the ordinances of government, or more idiomatically, constitutional law. It was presumably because the constitution was now an endangered species that he set out to conserve it: all he says in his preface is that he collected the rules in a book of their own to make it easier for people in power to study them, and that this was in compliance with the wishes of someone who could not be disobeyed (usually taken to be the caliph). He may even have intended his collection as a blueprint for a caliphal restoration, as is often claimed.[15] At all events, he was a brilliant synthesizer who excelled at concise and orderly presentation of a mass of conflicting views. A contemporary of his, the Ḥanbalite Abū Yaʿlā Ibn al-Farrāʾ (d. 458/1065), is the author of a similar work, probably by reworking al-Māwardī's for Ḥanbalite use,[16] and al-Māwardī's work rapidly came to be treated as authoritative.[17] It has tended to dominate modern Islamicist discussions of the imamate too. But al-Juwaynī mercilessly criticized al-Māwardī as a mindless compiler in his *Ghiyāth al-umam*, an unusual work best characterized as a socio-political *What to do in an Emergency*,[18] and al-Juwaynī's pupil al-Ghazālī also had a vision of his own. We may start by considering the generally accepted rules.

15. The idea was first proposed by Gibb, 'Al-Mawardi's Theory', 152f.

16. Though the original work is normally assumed to be Māwardī's, rightly in my view, the problem awaits systematic treatment (cf. Little, 'A New Look at *al-Aḥkām al-Sulṭāniyya*').

17. Cf. the list in Mikhail, *Politics and Revelation*, 59f.

18. *Ghiyāth*, §§209, 303, cf. also §45.

The classical rules[19]

Like the *aṣḥāb al-ḥadīth*, the Sunnis saw the imamate as a surrogate institution, a second-best substitute for prophecy, not as the alternative form of divine agency that it had been to the Umayyads.[20] Again like the ḥadīth party, they deemed the proper title of the caliph to be *khalīfat rasūl allāh*, successor of the Messenger of God[21] (though by now there must have been something ritualistic about their opposition to *khalīfat allāh*), and they held the legitimate caliphs in the past to have been Abū Bakr, ʿUmar, ʿUthmān, and ʿAlī, deeming them to have been the most meritorious persons of their time in that order. The Umayyads were only kings, as they said, meaning that they were quasi-caliphs, and the same was true of the ʿAbbāsids, though it was customary to speak more politely about them: their actions could not be adduced as legal precedents.[22] The Muʿtazilites went further in that they did not regard the ʿAbbāsids as caliphs at all.[23] But whether there was a current caliph or not, the institution was obligatory when it was possible to establish it (*maʿa 'l-imkān*).[24]

The candidate

The caliph had to be a free, male, adult member of Quraysh. The genealogical requirement, first formulated as Sunni doctrine by Ibn Qutayba, was assumed to have been laid down by the Prophet in the Ḥadīth "the imams are of Quraysh".[25] Countless books affirm it. But the books often read like insurance policies without the small print, in the sense that they will state the rules without qualifications even though the qualifications are sometimes such as to undermine the rules altogether. As far as the requirement of Qurashī descent

19. For beginners, there is a useful translation of the relevant section from Baghdādī's *Uṣūl* in Gibb, 'Constitutional Organization', 7ff. At a specialist level, see the richly documented study by Dumayjī, *al-Imāma al-ʿuẓmā*.

20. Cf. Nagel, *Rechtleitung und Kalifat*, et passim.

21. Cf. Crone and Hinds, *God's Caliph*, 21, note 86.

22. Above, 139. Cf. Juwaynī, *Ghiyāth*, §206: in his opinion it was lawful for the caliph to designate his son as successor in his opinion, but this could not be decisively proved for lack of precedent, for the imamate had turned into *mulk* after the first four (who only designated peers, not sons).

23. Cf. above, 69, notes 8–10.

24. The expression is Juwaynī's (*Ghiyāth*, §15). Similarly ʿAbd al-Jabbār, *Mughnī*, xx/1, 51. For further attestations, see Dumayjī, *al-Imāma al-ʿuẓmā*, 45f.

25. Ibn Qutayba, *K. al-ʿarab*, 374.6. Adherents of the rule were to find many more reasons for it, cf. the battery of proof-texts and arguments available to Dumayjī, who vigorously defends it (*al-Imāma al-ʿuẓmā*, 265ff.).

was concerned, the small print often said that if the worst came to the worst, one could dispense with it. The requirement of Qurashī descent had no grounding in either tradition or reason, al-Bāqillānī opined.[26] According to al-Juwaynī, it was merely meant as a mark of respect for the Prophet's house. In practice, he said, nobody had ever claimed the caliphate without real or alleged Qurashī descent, but as a legal requirement it rested on surmise (*ẓann*) rather than decisive proof, and if the only competent candidate was a non-Qurashī, he was to be accepted.[27] Many agreed, adducing the Prophetic tradition to obey even an Ethiopian slave (originally meant in a quietist vein) in support of their position.[28]

The caliph also had to be free of physical and mental handicaps, in part for practical reasons, but possibly also because it was felt that only a perfect specimen could serve as the community's link with God. The same idea was found in Byzantium, where mutilation was used to disqualify candidates for the throne. By the tenth century, the same method was used in the Islamic world: three caliphs of the Būyid period were blinded rather than killed when they were deposed.[29]

Further, the caliph had to be a man of probity (*ʿadāla*),[30] scrupulous observance of the law (*waraʿ*), and sufficient knowledge of the law to practise independent reasoning (*ijtihād*).[31] The eleventh-century Ibn al-Simnānī explained this last requirement as meaning that he had to know the law well enough to "resolve ambivalent cases, guide those in error, give responsa to those who asked for them, and adjudicate between disputing parties": here the imam seems to be envisaged as a teacher again, perhaps under Muʿtazilite influence.[32] On a less ambitious plane he needed to know the law so as to be allowed the discretion required for political decision making.[33] He did not have to be infallible, as the sources will say to the great merriment of modern readers

26. Dumayjī, *al-Imāma al-ʿuẓmā*, 275.

27. *Ghiyāth*, §§106–9, 438–9; cf. also his *Irshād*, 240 = 359; Hallaq, 'Caliphs, Jurists and the Saljūqs,' 38f.

28. Crone, 'Ethiopian Slave', 63ff.; add Simnānī, *Rawḍat*, i, §40 (some *aṣḥāb al-ḥadīth*).

29. Al-Muktafī, al-Qāhir, and al-Muttaqī.

30. Sufficiently to be accepted as a witness in court (e.g. Baghdādī, *Uṣūl*, 277; tr. Gibb, 'Constitutional Organization', 9).

31. Dumayjī, *al-Imāma al-ʿuẓmā*, 248, with dissenting voices at p. 250.

32. Simnānī, *Rawḍa*, i, §35. For the Muʿtazilite view of the imam as a teacher, see above, 66, note 6; for the Muʿtazilite who taught him *kalām*, see below, note 97.

33. For a concrete example, see Nasawī, *Sīra*, 52, where the Khwārizmshāh accuses the Caliph al-Nāṣir of keeping members of the ʿAbbāsid family in jail for so long that they were procreating there: the response is that if the caliph's *ijtihād* led him to conclude that the incarceration of some would benefit all, then their incarceration was justified.

(were infallible people in plentiful supply?); it is of course simply the scholars' way of saying that unlike the Shīʿites, they did not credit him with infallibility.[34] Finally, he had to have a talent for war and government.[35] But did he have to be the most meritorious man in his time? Under normal circumstances, yes, but were exceptions allowed? Some denied it, on the grounds that an imam who was not the most meritorious person would be a mere king (in the sense of a usurper).[36] But most now conceded it, meaning that Qurashī descent was not a prerequisite, or that the candidate could be inferior in other ways, at least when the alternative was civil war.[37]

In reality, nobody can have believed that the ʿAbbāsids were anywhere near the most meritorious men of their time, or even qualified at all in terms of the more concrete requirements, but then they were not real caliphs. True caliphs were models to be imitated, the ideal to which one should see imperfect reality as aspiring: it is such caliphs that the jurists normally describe. The ʿAbbāsids were just caliphs in the realm of imperfect reality who played by the rules with sufficient overt fidelity to be accepted as approximations to the ideal. Unlike the Būyids, they could at least be seen as reflections of that ideal.

The succession

Like all rulers, the caliph was raised up by God: all power came from God, who gave it and took it away as He pleased (Q. 3:26). But what was the specific method whereby this particular kind of ruler was singled out? The Sunni answer was election, which a modern reader is apt to misunderstand. When the Sunnis say that the caliphate (or imamate) is elective, they simply mean that it is an office to be filled by the community, not a personal quality with which God has singled out a particular person above all others. Nobody was born an imam; one could not acquire the position without being chosen by someone

34. Baghdādī, *Farq*, 341.6, with extended arguments in *Uṣūl*, 277–9; Bāqillānī, *Tamhīd*, 182.4, also with arguments (cf. Ibish, *Al-Baqillani*, 99f.); Nasafī in Macdonald, *Development*, 314; Rāzī, *Arbaʿīn*, 433ff. Cf. also the arguments in the Muʿtazilite ʿAbd al-Jabbār, *Mughnī*, xx/1, 75.10.

35. Dumayjī, *al-Imāma al-ʿuẓmā*, 259ff.; also Nasafī in Macdonald, *Development*, 314.

36. Thus Ashʿarī in Baghdādī, *Uṣūl*, 293; followed by most Ashʿarites according to Bazdawī, *Uṣūl*, 188.14 (no. 61); similarly Jāḥiz in Māwardī, *Aḥkām*, 9/8 = 7.

37. Thus Qalānisī, another Ashʿarite, followed by most Shāfiʿites according to Baghdādī, *Uṣūl*, 293; by most Sunnīs according to Bazdawī, *Uṣūl*, 188 (no. 61); similarly most jurists and theologians in Māwardī, *Aḥkām*, 9/8 = 7. Cf. also Juwaynī *Ghiyāth*, ch. 6 (§§242ff.); ʿAbd al-Jabbār, *Mughnī*, xx/1, 215–33 (with much scholastic detail); Dumayjī, *al-Imāma al-ʿuẓmā*, 296ff.

else (*ikhtiyār al-ghayr*).[38] Some Iraqis thought that if there only were one qualified candidate, he would automatically become the caliph,[39] and others agreed that this would be so if he took the position by force.[40] But leaving aside the question of the usurper, most jurists and theologians held that although the electors would be obliged to choose the only qualified candidate, the imamate could not be established without them, just as the position of judge could not be acquired without appointment.[41] Even the most meritorious man on earth would not be the imam without a contract of allegiance (*ʿaqd al-bayʿa*). In other words, the pledge of allegiance was constitutive of the imamate, not merely declarative of it, and the imamate was established by a contract between two parties, not by unilateral declaration. The two parties to the contract were the candidate and the community, represented by the man who made the formal handclasp ratifying the agreement. All this is what the Sunnis had in mind when they identified themselves as adherents of election (*ikhtiyār*) in polemics against the Shīʿites.

How one came up with the person to be offered the contract of allegiance was another question. The fact that the candidate owed his office to election by the community (*ikhtiyār min al-umma*)[42] did not mean that the community played any role in singling him out, though there were some who held that it should. What it meant was simply that someone had to pick a candidate from the pool of princes if the caliph had not designated a successor himself. That the caliph could do so was fully accepted, on the grounds that Abū Bakr had designated ʿUmar. (Contrary to what is sometimes said in the Islamicist literature, there was no attempt to disguise the hereditary nature of the ʿAbbāsid caliphate.[43]) Either the caliph designated a successor or else it was up to electors to choose and enthrone one. Some held that electors were required to ratify the succession even when a successor had been designated, or at least when they had designated a son.[44] But who then were the electors? Known as *ahl al-ḥall wa'l-ʿaqd* (the people of loosening and binding) or as *ahl al-ikhtiyār* (electors), they are envisaged as scholars and other men of eminence,[45] and there

38. ʿAbd al-Jabbār, *Mughnī*, xx/1, 250.10.

39. Māwardī, *Aḥkām*, 9f/8 = 7.

40. Thus Juwaynī, *Ghiyāth*, §453; Ghazālī, *Iqtiṣād*, 238.

41. Māwardī, *Aḥkām*, 9f/8 = 7.

42. For this expression, see for example Baghdādī, *Uṣūl*, 279.-5; MM, vi, 25 (iv, §2257).

43. See, for example, Binder, 'Al-Ghazālī's Theory of Islamic Government', 231; cf. above, 39; Juwaynī above, note 22.

44. Māwardī, *Aḥkām*, 13 /10 = 9, on the Basrans.

45. The sources refer to them by terms such as *ahl al-siyar wa'l-ṣalāḥ wa'l-ʿilm* (ʿAbd al-Jabbār, *Mughnī*, xx/1, 256.16), *ʿulamāʾ min ahl al-tadbīr* (Bazdawī, *Uṣūl*, 18.10), *ahl al-ijthād wa'l-waraʿ* (Baghdādī, *Uṣūl*, 281); *afāḍil al-umma* (Bāqillānī, *Tamhīd*, 179).

were some who required them to be *mujtahids*,[46] but for the most part, it is simply taken for granted that their identity would be obvious at any given time. In practice they were usually generals and/or viziers. There is much interest in the minimal number of them required for a valid contract. The most radical view was that all potential electors in all provinces ought to participate in an election, which sounds like a bid for representative government, with the scholars as electors on behalf of their local constituencies. One would have liked to know more about the arguments used by its adherents, but the sources report it without further information, to dismiss it as impracticable.[47] Others merely said that all scholars at the imam's residence should participate,[48] or that forty was the minimum.[49] Most said that the requisite number was five, four, three, or two,[50] or just one, on the grounds that there was no fixed number and that it took just one person to make a contract with another.[51]

Deposition and the problem of rebellion

If the imam had to be the most meritorious person (*al-afḍal*) of his time, it would follow that he had to be deposed if he lost his superiority, for example if somebody more meritorious made his appearance. In that vein a Zaydī imam assured his followers that he would step down if he knew someone better qualified than himself.[52] To him as to other Shīʿites, the imamate was a quality that inhered in people, not an office that had to be filled: the more meritorious person would actually be the imam whether one recognized him as such or not. This seems to have been how most early Muslims conceived the imamate, but one could not run an orderly polity on that basis, and perhaps for this reason all Sunnis decided against it. If the imam had to be the most meritorious person when he was chosen, he retained his office even if he lost his superiority thereafter.[53]

46. See the discussion in Juwaynī, *Ghiyāth*, §74ff.

47. Dumayjī, *al-Imāma al-ʿuẓmā*, 174ff.; Crone, '*Shūrā* as an Elective Institution', 38.

48. Thus Qalānisī in Baghdādī, *Uṣūl*, 281.7 (tr. Gibb, 'Constitutional Organization', 11).

49. Thus some Shāfiʿites with reference to the number required for a valid Friday service (cf. Juwaynī, *Ghiyāth*, §83).

50. Dumayjī, *al-Imāma al-ʿuẓmā*, 176ff.

51. Ashʿarī in Baghdādī, *Uṣūl*, 280f.; in Bazdawī, *Uṣūl*, 189; Bāqillānī, *Tamhīd*, 179; Juwaynī, *Ghiyāth*, §85; Dumayjī, *al-Imāma al-ʿuẓmā*, 177f.

52. Van Arendonk, *Débuts*, 234 (al-Hādī, c. 900).

53. Bāqillānī, *Tamhīd*, 186f. But according to him a caliph who was *mafḍūl* at the time of his election would indeed have to be replaced. Similarly Ghazālī, *Iqtiṣād*, 239, on the imam lacking in *ijtihād*, provided that it could be done without fighting.

But how low could he sink? He could not renounce Islam and still retain his position: on that there was universal agreement. Nor could he continue in office if he suffered serious physical disability such as the loss of sanity, sight or hearing, or was captured by enemies without immediate prospect of release.[54] No such cases seem to have arisen in practice, except in the sense that three caliphs of the Būyid period were blinded for that very purpose and that all caliphs of this period could be construed as captured (a construction implicitly rejected by al-Māwardī, as will be seen). But what happened if he lost his probity? This was more controversial.

According to the Khārijites, ʿUthmān had been deposed (by being killed) for his violations of the law; they upheld the right, or indeed duty, of the community to depose and, if necessary, kill a morally reprobate ruler, as has been seen. The Sunnis denied that ʿUthmān had done wrong, or that he had done so sufficiently to warrant deposition, but that still left the question what one should do with a ruler who did. An Umayyad caliph, al-Walīd II (d. 744), had been deposed for his immoral behaviour, again by being killed, and this was endorsed by the Muʿtazilites, who agreed with the Khārijites that the community was obliged to remove a wrongful ruler.[55] But the Sunnis generally held that whereas immorality (*fisq*) disqualified a candidate from election, he was not to be deposed for it if he developed it after his accession.[56] Armed revolt led to civil war, a source of worse disorder, bloodshed and immorality than anything a ruler could inflict, and was forbidden.[57] A quasi-caliph did not matter enough at the level of either everyday life or future salvation for such sacrifices to be worth it. One should admonish him, preach Hell-fire to him and refuse to obey him whenever he ordered something in disobedience to God, but for the rest one should put up with his oppression; the Prophet had laid down that one had to obey even an Ethiopian slave.[58] Conflicts between competitors for power were of interest only to the competitors themselves. "We are with the winners," as the Ḥanbalites said.[59]

This should not be taken to mean that the Sunnis were spineless supporters of the powers-that-be. What it does mean is that they attached enormous

54. Dumayjī, *al-Imāma al-ʿuẓmā*, 468ff.

55. Cf. above, 66, note 5; Bazdawī, *Uṣūl*, 191, with an amusing story. The Muʿtazilites accepted Yazīd III, the killer of al-Walīd II, as a legitimate caliph (above, 69, note 10).

56. Bāqillānī, *Tamhīd*, 187.2, on what has been transmitted *ʿan aṣḥābinā*. Nasafī in Macdonald, *Development*, 314.

57. Bazdawī, *Uṣūl*, 192, nos. 65–6, citing Abū Ḥanīfa (cf. Cook, *Commanding Right*, 8); cf. the review of the statements for and against in Dumayjī, *al-Imāma al-ʿuẓmā*, part iii (pp. 465ff.).

58. Bāqillānī, *Tamhīd*, 186.

59. Ibn Ḥanbal citing Ibn ʿUmar in Abū Yaʿlā, *Aḥkām*, 24.3.

importance to communal togetherness, and this they showed in their treatment of rebels too. The Qur'ān prescribes draconian penalties for "those who wage war against God and His Messenger, and strive to spread corruption on the earth" (5:33). The Umayyads took this verse to be about rebels. As heirs to a long *jamāʿī* tradition of reading the Qur'ān in an anti-authoritarian vein, however, the jurists refused to equate God and His Messenger with the state; as communitarians, they took God and His Messenger rather to stand for Muslim society; and those who waged war against them they took to be brigands. As far as rebels were concerned, they invoked Q. 49:9f., which does not refer to the state at all, but merely lays down that whenever two parties of believers fight each other, the party acting wrongfully (*baghat*) must be fought, though peace must be restored with justice and fairness as soon as possible since the believers are brothers. On the assumption that Muslim society was headed by a legitimate imam, the jurists labelled rebels with a cause *bughāt*, wrongdoers, and elaborated the law regarding their treatment on the basis of ʿAlī's generous treatment of the Khārijites and other opponents in the first civil war.[60]

Rebels against the regime were not enemies of God, however misguided, but rather fellow-Muslims who had gone astray and should be brought back into the fold as soon and as gently as possible: this was the Sunni position. There were some who would not fight fellow-Muslims at all, invoking a Prophetic statement to the effect that "fighting a believer is unbelief (*qitāl al-mu'min kufr*)", but this was going too far, al-Qurṭubī said: if one always had to stay at home when conflicts broke out, it would be impossible to apply any *ḥudūd* penalties or combat any falsehood, he reported al-Ṭabarī (d. 310/923) as observing; the verse clearly prescribed that the wrongdoing party must be fought; if one did not, profligate people would gang up against the Muslims and prevail.[61] But one should treat them in accordance with the generous rules.

'Bear the ruler and spare the rebel': that is how one might summarize the Sunni view. But just as one could go too far in one's willingness to spare the rebels, so one could go too far in one's readiness to tolerate the ruler in the opinion of some. Thus al-Bāqillānī knew of many people (*kathīr min al-nās*) who believed that a wrongdoing and oppressive caliph should be deposed.[62]

60. Abou El Fadl, 'Islamic Law of Rebellion', i, 40ff., 53ff., 60ff. and 'Irregular Warfare and the Law of Rebellion', 151ff.; cf. also Sālim, *Epistle*, II, 53, and the commentary thereto, where ʿUthmān applies one of the draconian penalties to the rebels against him with explicit invocation of 5:33.

61. Qurṭubī, *Jāmiʿ*, xvi, 317 (cf. Abou El Fadl, 'Islamic Law of Rebellion', i, 53, slightly out of focus).

62. *Tamhīd*, 186.5.

Al-Māwardī and al-Juwaynī knew of them too: there were theologians (*uṣūliyyūn*, probably Muʿtazilites) and jurists who argued that a reprobate imam would forfeit his office in the same way as a madman, the latter explained.[63] When an imam turned oppressive and amassed property, it was the duty of religious leaders (*ahl al-dīn*) and the Muslims at large to depose him and replace him by another, the Ḥanafī jurist Ibn al-Simnānī (d. 493/1100) declared; this was how the Muslims had customarily dealt with those who abandoned the right path, he claimed.[64] But how was the deposition to be effected? According to al-Māwardī, some held that the imam would recover his position without renewal of the contract of allegiance if his behaviour improved.[65] His deposition was purely moral, then; one simply stopped regarding him as the caliph until he was deemed worthy of the title again. But others held that a new contract of allegiance would be required to restore him to office, implying that he had been ousted. They do not discuss the procedures for his removal, however.[66] Al-Juwaynī does report some as holding the electors (*ahl al-ḥall wa'l-ʿaqd*) to be responsible for his deposition,[67] but this probably meant no more than that the electors had to declare him deposed. Again, it is left unclear who was responsible for the actual removal of the wrongdoer.

According to al-Juwaynī himself, one had to tolerate a certain amount of immoral behaviour in the imam, for he had to keep the company of rough soldiers and handle large sums of money, neither of which was conducive to piety. However, there came a point where a wrongdoer would have to be stopped, and here one would have to remember the importance of getting one's priorities right. If it was likely to be more costly, in terms of human lives, to remove the wrongdoing imam than to put up with him, then it would be better to leave him in place. (Al-Juwaynī's pupil, al-Ghazālī, was to argue the same with reference to an oppressive sultan.)[68] If not, the electors should depose him and set up another: it was the new imam who would be responsible for the actual removal of his predecessor, who should be treated as a rebel if he refused to step down.[69] Elsewhere, however, al-Juwaynī seems to envisage the electors

63. Juwaynī, *Ghiyāth*, §142. For Māwardī, see below, note 66.

64. *Rawḍa*, i, §517. For the name and dates of this author, see the bibliography, s.v. 'al-Simnānī'.

65. Māwardī, *Aḥkām*, 26/17 = 17. Here two kinds of immorality are considered, inability to control one's passions and the adoption of suspect doctrines. Only the former necessitated deposition according to the Basrans.

66. Ibid.; he was in this camp himself.

67. Juwaynī, *Ghiyāth*, §143.

68. For al-Ghazālī, see his *Iḥyā'*, ii, 115.-3; above, note 53; Hillenbrand, 'Al-Ghazālī's View on Government', 90.

69. Juwaynī, *Ghiyāth*, §§145–59, 183. Cf. below, 235.

themselves as taking up arms against the wrongdoing imam (or sultan: the term here is *walī al-waqt*, 'the ruler of the time', which would cover both). If the ruler engaged in wrongdoing and oppression and did not respond to moral admonition, the electors should stop him even if it meant going to war with him, he said in a brief discussion of the duty to command right and prohibit wrong.[70] He does not mention deposition here, however. The reason why the Sunnis legalized deposition without explaining how it was to be achieved is probably that they wanted to have their cake and eat it. There had to be a point where even a quasi-caliph (not to mention a mere king) forfeited his position, but it was best not to specify where and how, so as not to create an obligation to take action.

The political unity of the umma

By the eleventh century the community founded by the Prophet had split into several sects and several polities alike. To an adherent of *jamāʿa*, this was deplorable and had to be countered by compromise. The four-caliphs theory had been such a compromise, designed to unite as many believers as possible in a single community. Al-Māwardī (d. 1058) now presented another compromise to preserve it as a single polity.

Al-Māwardī's first problem was that the caliph who embodied the political unity of the believers was not in control of himself any more, but rather confined (*maḥṣūr*), as the caliph al-Muṭīʿ had said of himself.[71] Was there a caliph at all, then? Al-Māwardī gives the reader a choice.[72] There were two ways in which an imam's freedom could be restricted, by wardship (*ḥajr*) or by captivity of various kinds, subsumed as brute power (*qahr*); as a ward the imam would retain his office, and as a captive he would lose it once it was clear that there was no hope of release. Al-Māwardī does not say which category the caliph of his time fell into, nor is his formulation so loaded that the result is a foregone conclusion, but whereas capture was a possibility considered by other authors,[73] wardship seems to be a category unique to al-Māwardī, who probably introduced it precisely because he needed a rubric under which the caliphs of the Būyid period could be legitimated. He did after all work for two such caliphs himself.

70. Juwaynī, *Irshād*, 370; cited in Cook, *Commanding Right*, 346.

71. Above, note 4.

72. Māwardī, *Aḥkām*, 30ff. (19ff.) = 20f.

73. Cf. Bāqillānī, *Tamhīd*, 186.-5; Juwaynī, *Ghiyāth*, §§164, 171, both affirming that a captured imam unlikely to regain his liberty must be replaced.

Even if the caliph retained his office, however, he did not actually rule the lands of Islam. Al-Māwardī solved this second problem by casting all local rulers as his potential governors. There were two kinds of governors, he said: by appointment and by usurpation (*al-istīlā'*). The latter were local rulers who had established themselves by force and whose position the caliph had regularized by formally appointing them to their positions (such as the Būyids, the Ghaznavids or even the Seljuqs, who took over from the Ghaznavids in eastern Iran in 1040 and to whom al-Māwardī was sent by the caliph as ambassador in 1042 and 1044; but he does not give examples). Regularization was highly commendable, he said, and should be practised as far as possible, though there were obviously cases where it could not be done (e.g. the Fatimids and the Spanish Umayyads who claimed to be caliphs themselves). This stratagem secured a fair measure of political unity, if only in formal terms.[74]

Al-Māwardī's *imārat al-istīlā'* has become notorious in the Islamicist literature because Gibb found it deeply shocking: it brought down the entire edifice of the law, he declared in sweeping and faintly hysterical terms for which he has often been castigated.[75] His reaction is peculiar, for what could be more common in history than the recognition of usurpers? It was by casting the barbarian polities of Europe as subordinate kingdoms (*regna*) within the empire (*imperium*) that Christians such as Isidore of Seville (d. 636) maintained the theoretical unity of the Roman empire.[76] In al-Māwardī's opinion the legalization of usurpers, far from bringing down the edifice of the law, helped to preserve its provisions (*qawānīn al-sharʿ*), partly by keeping the caliphate going and the Muslims united and partly by ensuring that public authority remained valid in the provinces in question, so that the decisions and judgements (of governors and *qāḍī*s) retained their legality, the canonical taxes could be collected, and the penalties known as the *ḥudūd* could be imposed.[77] What al-Māwardī recommended was moreover what had long been practised. It simply had not been codified as law before.

74. Māwardī, *Aḥkām*, 47, 66ff./30, 33f. = 32, 36f.

75. Gibb, 'Al-Mawardi's Theory', 164 and 'Constitutional Organization', 19; Mikhail, *Politics and Revelation*, 43; Al-Azmeh, *Muslim Kingship*, 254f., note 85 (in a tone not unlike Gibb's own).

76. Morall, *Political Thought*, 18; cf. the *Cambridge History of Medieval Political Thought*, 230, where the idea is a commonplace already by Isidore's time. For Gibb's reaction, see also below, 255.

77. Māwardī, *Aḥkām*, 67f. (34) = 36. For the assumptions behind the statement, see below, ch. 18.

Saving the umma*: al-Juwaynī*

Al-Māwardī's solution was undermined by the further Seljuq advance: as conquerors who reunited the Islamic world from Transoxania to Syria, the Seljuqs were much too powerful to masquerade as governors.[78] In 447/1055 the first of them, Ṭughril Beg, received the titles of sultan and king of kings (*shāhānshāh*) from the caliph; in 449/1058 he was formally appointed to all the lands placed by God in the caliph's charge and graced with the title of 'King of the East and West'; and in 454/1062 an official letter identified him as 'The great *shāhānshāh*, King of the East and West, the Reviver of Islam, Deputy of the Imam and Right Hand of God's Caliph, the Commander of the Faithful'.[79] In short, the sultan had now formally replaced the caliph as the political ruler of the *umma*, by the caliph's own agreement.

The second Seljuq sultan, Alp Arslān, died in 465/1072, leaving a minor son, Malikshāh, and for the next twenty years the real ruler was neither the caliph nor the sultan, but rather the vizier Niẓām al-Mulk. This was when al-Juwaynī (d. 478/1085) wrote his *Ghiyāth al-umam*. Dedicated to Niẓām al-Mulk and written in a florid language strangely at odds with its steely mode of thought, it confronted the legal and practical problems arising from a situation in which, as al-Juwaynī saw it, there was no imam at all. The ʿAbbāsid caliphate no longer counted as one; here al-Juwaynī had reached a Muʿtazilite position. But that was only half the problem, for he could foresee even greater disasters ahead: *mujtahid*s might disappear, and jurisprudence itself might be completely forgotten one day. Unlike the Muʿtazilites, he felt obliged to come up with practical proposals. His message, formulated in "allusions to the lord of the time and foremost man of his age", was that Niẓām al-Mulk should rescue Islam by taking over the imamate himself.[80]

The imamate, he said, existed to keep people together on the shared basis of Islamic law. This could not be done without power, and the key quality required in an imam was *kifāya*, the ability to take care of people and to get things done, or competence for short. He stressed this point time and again. All other qualities were dispensable, if not to the same degree. The least important was Qurashī descent, which had no bearing on governmental ability. *Ijtihād* did affect the imam's ability to make decisions, and al-Juwaynī did not

78. If the Ghaznavids had not been so far away, the same would probably have been felt to be true already of them; they certainly liked to see themselves as the caliph's protectors rather than his governors (cf. Nagel, 'Urspünge der Religionspolitik', 244f.).

79. *EI*², s.vv. 'al-Ḳāʾim'; 'Ṭoghril (I) Beg'; Ibn al-Jawzī, *Muntaẓam*, viii, 223 (where 'Commander of the Faithful' refers to God's Caliph, not Ṭughril himself).

80. Hallaq, 'Caliphs, Jurists and the Saljūqs', 39; Nagel, *Festung*, esp. 293–9 (with a briefer treatment of Juwaynī in his *Staat und Glaubensgemeinschaft*, vol. ii).

like the idea of an imam who had to consult scholars first, for competence included the ability to act on one's own (*istiqlāl*). Nonetheless, the requirement of *ijtihād* could also be dropped if the worst came to the worst.[81] Even probity and scrupulous observance of the law (*waraʿ*) could be abandoned as long as the imam's immorality (*fisq*) did not stand in the way of proper decision-making. But an imam whose immorality caused him to neglect the fundamental aims of government would have to be deposed, for it would be better for people to be left leaderless than to follow such a wrongdoer;[82] and an imam who failed to secure obedience for himself would likewise have to be deposed, for he fell into the same category as one who had been captured without prospects of release, that is, he lost his office.[83] This was clearly the category in which al-Juwaynī took the ʿAbbāsid caliph to fall.

How then was deposition to be effected? Al-Juwaynī envisages three possibilities. First, the caliph could be declared deposed by the men who had elected him, the *ahl al-ḥall wa'l-ʿaqd*, as already discussed. If it was easy for them to set up a new imam with the right qualities, they should do so. He would be charged with the removal of his iniquitous predecessor; if the latter resisted, he should be treated in accordance with the rules concerning rebels (*bughāt*) set out in the law books; and if it would be more costly in terms of lives and suffering to remove the wrongdoer than to endure him, then one should leave him in place (without acknowledging him as caliph).[84]

This gives us the second situation: the electors can do nothing, either because they cannot find a new imam with the right qualities or because it would be too costly for the new imam to remove his predecessor, whose wrongdoing is such that it would be better for people to be left leaderless. At this point one would deem people to be living without someone engaged in upholding the truth (*al-qiyām bi'l-ḥaqq*), and it was with this emergency in mind that he wrote his *Ghiyāth*.[85] The imam of his time was not a terrible wrongdoer; rather, he was a nonentity whom nobody obeyed, but the result was the same. Without somebody to restrain people and keep them on the paths of truth, society would fall apart, he thought.[86] How then were people to cope when there was no imam? (*ʿinda khuluww al-zamān ʿan al-aʾimma*)? They would have to apply God's law on their own, he said; if the worst came to the worst,

81. *Ghiyāth*, §§113ff., 440. It is difficult to avoid the impression that he contradicts himself here.

82. Ibid., §§151f.

83. Ibid., §§164f., 177, 463.

84. Ibid., §155–7 (cf. above, note 69).

85. Ibid., §153.

86. Ibid., §19. For this conviction, very common at the time, see below, 270.

they would have to manage without *muftī*s qualified as *mujtahid*s, too, such jurists having disappeared as well.[87]

But there was a third possibility: somebody might take action without being either one of the electors or someone enthroned by them. Al-Juwaynī did not have ordinary people in mind: private individuals (*al-āḥād*) were not allowed to rebel, he said; all sorts of evils would ensue if they did.[88] But if a powerful man (*rajul muṭāʿ*) endowed with many followers would arise commanding good and prohibiting wrong (*muḥtasiban*), then he should go ahead, for although private individuals were not normally allowed to use arms in the performance of the duty to command good and prohibit wrong, they were indeed permitted to do so when rescuing others in emergencies (such as attempted robbery or murder). A fortiori, they were allowed to do so when it was Islam itself that had to be rescued.[89] Again, the same clearly applied if the problem was an incompetent ruler rather than an immoral one. No doubt, al-Juwaynī added, "our lord, the cavern of the nations, and user of both sword and pen" would be able to take the hint.[90] In short, al-Juwaynī allowed the caliphate itself to be acquired by usurpation.

Al-Juwaynī's argument suffers from the weaknesses that a powerful man might simply be a private individual who had used arms to build up a position of strength, and that most people who rebelled claimed to do so for the sake of Islam in some way or other, so that the difference between his *āḥād* and his *rajul muṭāʿ* was less than obvious. In effect, he prohibited revolt, yet applauded it when it was conducted for purposes that he approved of and was likely to be successful. Or, as one could also put it, he prohibited it to some would-be rescuers of Islam while allowing it to others on the grounds that the person who *truly* wanted to rescue Islam, and had the wherewithal to do it, could dispense with the normal rules. The judge of true intentions was al-Juwaynī himself. In other words, the distinction between legality and illegality seems to lie entirely in his personal convictions.

For all that, his diagnosis was right. It was to the profane power of barbarian invaders, not to Muḥammad's successor, that the Muslims owed their partial unification and recent victories against external and internal enemies. Such power was now too massive and too dominant a presence to be dealt with by perfunctory legitimation. Translated into the idiom of medieval Europe, al-Juwaynī was saying that the *majordomus* should proclaim himself king (as Charlemagne's father had done in medieval Gaul); translated into the idiom of

87. *Ghiyāth*, §153.
88. Ibid., §163.
89. Ibid., §§163, 478–81, 484f. and *Irshād*, 370.1 (Cook, *Commanding Right*, 346).
90. Ibid., §§166, 483. By 'cavern' (*kahf*) one would assume him to mean refuge.

medieval Japan, he was saying that the *shogun* should take over the position of emperor. More precisely, he was saying that the deputy of the *majordomus* or *shogun* should do so, for what he was hinting seems to be that Niẓām al-Mulk should assume the position of caliph himself, not that he should set up Malikshāh as such. Either way, he was secularizing the caliphate.[91] But Niẓām al-Mulk did not act on al-Juwaynī's advice, and the invaders themselves began to split up after his death in 485/1092. What then was the solution?

Saving the umma*: al-Ghazālī*

Al-Ghazālī accepted most of his teacher's premises. In fact, there are strong echoes of the *Ghiyāth* in his *Faḍā'ih al-bāṭiniyya* (also known as the *Mustaẓhirī*), his first work on the subject, though he mentions neither al-Juwaynī nor his books by name. Like al-Juwaynī (and many others, in fact), he held that people left without an imam would perish in internal disunity and conflict.[92] The imamate existed for the unification of people and the defence of their religious community. For this purpose the imam needed military power (*shawka*), and such power was now supplied by the Turks, who were beloved by God and working for His cause, however terrible their behaviour might be.[93]

Al-Ghazālī's caliph

Al-Ghazālī also agreed with his teacher that most rules regarding the imamate rested on mere surmise (*ẓann*) rather than categorical proof in the Qur'ān and Ḥadīth, meaning that there was room for much rethinking;[94] but he did believe that there was one authoritative statement (*naṣṣ*) on the subject, namely the Prophetic statement that "The imams are of Quraysh", generally understood as a prescription rather than a simple description. Unlike his teacher, he did *not* think that Qurashī descent was dispensable.[95] He was ready to accept al-Juwaynī's imamate by usurpation, but only if the usurper was a Qurashī.[96]

91. Cf. Hallaq, 'Caliphs, Jurists and the Saljūqs', 30; Nagel, *Festung*, 303f.

92. *Faḍā'iḥ*, ch. 9, esp. 106f. and *Iqtiṣād*, 236 (summarized in Laoust, *Politique de Ġazālī*, 236f.). Cf. below, ch. 17, 270.

93. *Faḍā'iḥ*, 113; cf. Hillenbrand, 'Al-Ghazālī's Views on Government', 83f. Cf. Juwaynī, above, note 12.

94. *Faḍā'iḥ*, 119 (in the discussion of the imam's *'ilm*); Hallaq, 'Caliphs, Jurists and the Saljūqs', 30ff.

95. *Faḍā'iḥ*, 119.2; cf. 112, where he paraphrases Juwaynī, *Ghiyāth*, §108, on how all past claimants have been Qurashīs, treating it as further evidence rather than a concession.

96. Cf. above, note 40.

This seemingly minor disagreement reflects a fundamental difference between them. To al-Juwaynī, the imam was first and foremost a political and military leader whose descent had no bearing on his competence; to al-Ghazālī, he was first and foremost a religious figurehead singled out by sacred descent. According to al-Ghazālī, the imam also had to be distinguished by scrupulous observance of the law (*warac*), and he really ought to have learning to the level of *ijtihād*, but this requirement could be relaxed: here al-Juwaynī and al-Ghazālī agreed. But whereas al-Juwaynī was thinking of a military commander who consulted jurists for lack of personal knowledge when major decisions had to be taken, al-Ghazālī had in mind a religious figurehead who was meant to embody the law in everything he did and who would have to do so by constant consultation with jurists. Both would have preferred an imam who could work out right and wrong for himself, but again for different reasons. Al-Juwaynī wanted an effective ruler: this was why the current caliph did not qualify. Al-Ghazālī wanted a legitimate imam: this was why the current caliph *had* to qualify. The requirement of learning to the level of *ijtihād* had to be relinquished for reasons of necessity (*ḍarūra*), al-Ghazālī said, for if it was not, the current caliph, al-Mustaẓhir (487–512/1094–1118), would fall short of the qualifications for the imamate, and so would the caliphs before him.

In al-Ghazālī's view, one needed a legitimate imam in order to have a valid public sphere. Most authors on the imamate, he said, wrote in a vein implying that there was no lawful caliph today and that past periods had also been without one. This was presumably a reference to Muᶜtazilites such as ᶜAbd al-Jabbār as well as his own teacher, and he was not the only scholar to be worried by views of this kind. A Muᶜtazilite by the name of al-Karkhī (d. 478/1085f) is reported have argued, much as al-Ghazālī was to do, that the requirement of learning would have to be relaxed since there would not otherwise be a legitimate imam any more. In al-Karkhī's view the imam had so many other things to do that he could not master the law without neglecting his governmental duties; all one could require was that he be a man of discernment, intelligence, and good judgement.[97] The reason why al-Karkhī relaxed the requirement, however, is that he wanted an imam who was both legitimate and effective, much as did al-Juwaynī. By contrast, al-Ghazālī did not think of the imam as a ruler at all. In his view the reason why one needed an imam was that the absence of such a figurehead would mean that all public offices (*al-wilāyāt*) were invalid, that God's rights and *ḥudūd* could not be effected, and that all dispositions regarding lives, sexual relations and property would be void, for "judges owe their authority to their appointment by the imam (*maṣdar*

97. Simnānī, *Rawḍa*, i, §37, on his teacher Abū ᶜAlī Muḥammad b. Aḥmad b. al-Walīd (al-Karkhī).

al-quḍāh tawliyat al-imām); if the imamate is void, their appointment is also void, their authority dissolves, and they become private individuals (*iltaḥaqū bi-āḥād al-khalq*)."[98] The carpet of the law would be rolled up in its entirety, as he put it.[99] He expresses himself in similar terms in his *Iqtiṣād* and, more briefly, the *Iḥyā'*: if there were no caliph, all public appointments (*wilāyāt*) would be invalid, marriages would not be lawfully contracted, all the dispositions of all officials in all parts of the Muslim world would be void, and all humans would be engaging in forbidden acts. There were only three possible ways of handling the problem, he says: one could prohibit marriages and other dispositions requiring judges, which was impossible; or one could declare the forbidden marriages and other dispositions to be valid by overriding necessity (*ḍarūra*); or one could declare the caliphate itself to be valid on grounds of overriding necessity. Once more, he deems relaxation of the requirement of *ijtihād* to be the only acceptable solution.[100]

Al-Ghazālī seems unduly perturbed by the idea of the imamate being vacant. In principle, of course, everyone agreed that all legitimate power flowed from the imam, so that all public offices would be void in his absence, including those of judges. One of the advantages of recognizing usurpers as caliphal governors was precisely that it ensured the validity of official appointments and legal judgements made in the areas under their control, as al-Māwardī had said.[101] But al-Ghazālī does seem to go to extremes. For a start, he appears to overstate the need for judges. They were indeed required to contract marriages on behalf of orphans and other girls without guardians (according to the schools which did not allow women to contract marriage for themselves), and this must be what al-Ghazālī has in mind.[102] It is possible that all marriages were normally concluded with the assistance of judges in his time;[103] but in strict law neither marriage contracts nor commercial transactions required judges for their validity, and it was likewise by custom rather than legal requirement that retaliation for killing and wounding was dealt with by public authorities rather than the victim's kin, as al-Ghazālī's own teacher had pointed out.[104] It was only the *ḥudūd* penalties that could not be applied in

98. *Faḍā'iḥ*, 105 (opening of ch. 9).

99. Ibid., 105.

100. *Iqtiṣād*, 239f.; *Iḥyā'*, ii, 115f., with reference to the *Mustaẓhirī* in both.

101. Above, note 77.

102. Compare Juwaynī, *Ghiyāth*, §557, on the impossibility of closing the door of marriage for women without guardians at a time without a *sulṭān*. (He solves the problem by assigning the duty to an influential scholar.)

103. Cf. Ibn Sīnā, *SI*, *x*, 10, 452 = 108: the lawgiver must prescribe acts that cannot be completed without the imam's participation, e.g. marriage.

104. Juwaynī, *Ghiyāth*, §553.

the absence of an imam (whether in the sense that no imam existed or that he was in hiding).[105]

Even if judges were indispensable, moreover, the Muslim world had been ruled by kings and sultans for so long that people had in practice come to think of judges as deriving their authority from them, and/or from the community at large.[106] In fact, al-Ghazālī shared that view himself, if only by recourse to *ḍarūra*: "Every judge appointed by a powerful man (*ṣāḥib shawka*) can make valid judgements, because of overriding necessity," he conceded in his *Wajīz*.[107] ʿAbd al-Jabbār incidentally remarks that if the imam could not appoint governors and judges, the community could do so by way of deputizing for him (*niyābatan ʿanhu*);[108] in the same vein al-Māwardī says that a local community could appoint its own judge on an interim basis if there happened to be no imam at the time;[109] and it was precisely by tracing the authority of judges to the community rather than to the caliph that the Ḥanafī al-Kāsānī (d. 587/1189) eliminated the problem two generations after al-Ghazālī.[110] By then, the Mālikī al-Māzarī (d. 536/1141) had gone so far as to rule that the verdicts of judges appointed by *infidel* rulers in Sicily were authoritative.[111] Yet al-Ghazālī continued to speak as if all public offices would be void for lack of a valid caliph.

Finally, if al-Mustaẓhir absolutely had to be legitimate, why did al-Ghazālī not simply deem him to be a *mujtahid* irrespective of fact? Earlier caliphs such as the soldier al-Muʿtaṣim (d. 227/842) or the pleasure-seeker al-Muqtadir (d. 294/908) can hardly have possessed the requisite learning, yet nobody seems to have questioned their legitimacy on those grounds. There were obviously Muʿtazilites who regarded them, and most other caliphs past or present, to be illegitimate, but their precise grounds for doing so are unknown. The Sunnis who accepted them must have deemed such caliphs to be *mujtahids* by virtue of their office or alternatively else regarded the requirement of learning as unimportant. Yet al-Ghazālī writes in tones so alarmist than he sounds like a

105. See further below, ch. 18.

106. Niẓām al-Mulk blithely identifies judges as the deputies of kings, adding that they are the deputies of the caliph too (*SN*, ch. 6, §6 (59f. = 46). Pseudo-Māwardī, *Naṣīḥa*, 51.3, identifies kings rather than caliphs as God's deputies and the executors of His *aḥkām* and *ḥudūd*.

107. Tyan, *Organisation judiciaire*, i, 258 (citing the *Wajīz*, ii, 143).

108. *Mughnī*, xx/1, 51.

109. Cf. the end of the chapter on judges (*Aḥkām*, 128/76 = 86); noted in Tyan, *Organisation judiciaire*, i, 222.

110. Sanhoury, *Califat*, 168f., citing the *Badāʾiʿ*, vii, 16. Compare the sixteenth-century Ramlī cited in Tyan, *Organisation judiciaire*, i, 223: the judge was a representative of both the sultan and the collectivity.

111. Abou El Fadl, 'Islamic Law and Muslim Minorities', 151.

Shīʿite (or a first-century Muslim) to whom dying without allegiance to an imam was tantamount to dying as a pagan. God's rights (*ḥuqūq*) would remain unfilfilled, the entire carpet of the law would be rolled up, he says, though he plainly does not think that ritual law (except perhaps for the Friday prayer) would be invalidated. One would not guess from his account that Khārijites, Imāmīs, Zaydīs, and Muʿtazilites had long debated how to cope without an imam or that Sunnis had now begun to do so too, let alone that his own teacher had devoted a whole book to the question.[112]

It is hard to avoid the suspicion that al-Ghazālī had been affected by the Ismailism he wrote against and the attractions of which he understood all too well. What he wanted was some counterpart to the Ismaili imam; without it, he seems to have felt, Sunnism would not be a real alternative. Since the Ismaili imam was by now identified first and foremost as an infallible source of religious instruction (*taʿlīm*), a caliph endowed with genuine learning was required for purposes of counterbalance, and al-Mustaẓhir clearly did not possess such learning. "You cannot claim that *this* requirement is fulfilled," as al-Ghazālī has a hypothetical opponent declare.[113] Possibly, the Ismaili stress on *taʿlīm* had also affected the Muʿtazilites: it was well before al-Ghazālī that al-Karkhī tried to save the legitimacy of current imams by relaxing the requirement of learning; it was eight to nine years before al-Ghazālī's first statement on the subject that al-Karkhī's pupil defined the issue as *ijtihād* in a maximal sense and denied that one could have an imam without it (though he did not spell out the implications for the current caliph); and other Muʿtazilites of the eleventh century are well known to have been among those who declared the imamate to be vacant.[114] In other words, it would seem that the Ismailis caused other people to focus their attentions on a requirement that they might otherwise have dismissed as a mere formality. Under pressure from extreme adherents of the view that the imam was a source of religious instruction, *jamāʿī* Muslims were now forced either to abandon the requirement of learning or else to see to it that it was actually observed: the only other option was to concede that their imam was as illegitimate as their opponents declared him to be. Under such pressure it cannot have taken al-Ghazālī long to decide that the requirement had to be abandoned. In his later works he explains that learning

112. Cf. also al-Karkhī's Ḥanafī pupil Ibn al-Simnāni, who explicitly asked what would happen to the law if there was neither an imam nor a righteous usurper, described in terms reminiscent of Juwaynī's (Simnānī, *Rawḍa*, i, §§113–15).

113. *Faḍāʾiḥ*, 118 (*lā yumkinukum daʿwā wujūd hādhihi 'l-sharīṭa*).

114. See above, note 97, on al-Karkhī; note 32 on his pupil, Ibn al-Simnānī, who completed his work in 479/1086 (as stated in his *Rawḍa*, iv, p. 1520); above, 69, on the Muʿtazilite view of past caliphs.

to the level of *ijtihād* belonged in the rubric of *mazāyā 'l-maṣāliḥ*, desiderata over and on top of the basic requirements of welfare – mere icing on the cake, as we might put it – and that it would be absurd to reject the entire cake for lack of icing.[115] The cake he wanted to keep was clearly a communal life that continued to be valid by Islamic law.

The role of the imam in the validation of the community will be discussed in detail in Chapter 18. Here it will suffice to say that there were three views on what would happen to the community if there ceased to be an imam. The first was that it would cease to exist altogether, not in the sense that it would fall apart (though it might do that as well), but rather in the sense that it would lose its moral footing. It would turn into a haphazard collection of human beings who merely happened to live together, instead of being a community of believers set apart by their devotion to God's law. The saving vehicle would disappear; the abode of Islam would be indistinguishable from that of unbelief; everyone would die as a pagan. The imam of the Imami and Ismaili Shīʿites retained this role in al-Ghazālī's time, with the result that he could not be allowed to disappear. One way or the other he existed, if only in hiding; the true community was constituted by his followers.

The second position was that a community without an imam would continue to exist, but that it would lose its public sphere. All public functions would be suspended: there would be no Friday prayer, no collection of taxes, no missionary *jihād*, no judges, and no execution of the *ḥudūd*; or all these functions might still be fulfilled, but they would not have any validity. One would however still be able to live an upright life along with other Muslims by following the law in the regulation of one's private life, avoiding the powers that be to the best of one's ability. In effect, one would live as if under non-Muslim rule. This was the view of the Imamis and Ismailis (on the understanding that the imam actually existed even if he was not present), and also of the Zaydīs, Muʿtazilites, and (probably) Khārijites, as well as at least some Sunnis, such as the Ḥanafī Ibn al-Simnānī.[116] Al-Māwardī also adhered to this view, if only up to a point.[117] But the Sunnis typically avoided the problem by never getting into a situation in which no imam existed, first by acknowledging every caliph as the legitimate imam even if he fell short of rightly guided status and next by accepting secular kings in the imam's role, or by deeming the legitimacy of public life to depend on the community rather than its leader. There had however long been ascetics and Sufis who were prone to seeing

115. *Iqtiṣād*, 239; *Iḥyā'*, ii, 116. Compare Juwaynī's view that everything over and above competence is *fī ḥukm al-istikmāl wa'l-tatimma lahā* (*Ghiyāth*, §449).

116. Cf. above, note 112.

117. Cf. above, notes 77, 109; below, 293.

public life (or even the Muslim community altogether) as invalidated by the transgressions of the quasi-caliphs, and there were many more who took this view when government fell to the Seljuqs and their ill-behaved followers.

The third view was that the community would continue to exist in the absence of an imam and that it would even retain its public life, or some of it, because the imam's functions, or some of them, would devolve to the jurists: they would take over the convocation of the Friday prayer, the collection of taxes, and perhaps other functions too. This was a new idea propounded on the Imami side by al-Mufīd (d. 413/1022) and al-Ṭūsī (d. 459/1067), and on the Sunni side by al-Ghazālī's teacher al-Juwaynī (d. 478/1085) in his *Ghiyāth*.

Al-Ghazālī's tone is so alarmist that one initially takes him to adhere to the first position, but what he actually outlines is the second view, without ever mentioning the third, though he must have known it well enough. In other words, he identifies himself as a Sunni of an unusually imamocentric type: neither kings nor jurists would do in the imam's role; quasi-caliph though he was, al-Mustaẓhir had to be legitimate. One would assume his alarmism to reflect the fact that the moral basis of public life was now under attack from both outside and inside the Sunni camp, from the Ismailis against whom he wrote his *Mustaẓhirī* on the one hand, and from the ascetics and Sufis to whom he set out the rights and wrongs of the public order in his *Iḥyā'* on the other.[118]

Caliph and sultan

Al-Ghazālī's caliph had a novel feature in that he was not meant to rule his followers in political terms. Unlike the Ismailis, or for that matter his teacher, al-Ghazālī acknowledged that the Muslims now belonged to two different communities, one religious and the other political, one the *umma* and the other the secular kingdoms into which it was divided. The *umma* had been founded by the Prophet on the basis of his law and was still headed by one of his descendants: this was the community of believers or congregation to which all Muslims (as seen by al-Ghazālī) belonged, the Sunni version of the catholic (all-embracing, 'big-tent') church; and this was the community that the caliph represented. But as subjects the Muslims were now distributed in ephemeral kingdoms headed by profane rulers, to whom they paid their taxes and on whose armies they relied for such security as they had. This was the community or communities (*regna* in medieval European parlance) represented by the sultan(s). Al-Ghazālī would clearly have preferred to live without this duality, but unlike his teacher, he saw that it had come to stay. Al-Juwaynī had still

118. For the latter, see below, 348.

thought of the imam as the leader of a community that was both political and religious: it was for this reason that he wanted to replace the titular caliph with a real ruler. The Ismailis also thought of the imam as the head of a community that was both political and religious: what they wanted was a rightly guided imam in charge of both spheres. Al-Juwaynī's solution amounted to secularization of the community of believers, while that of the Ismailis left the Turkish invaders out of the picture, or alternatively required their military power to be sanctified. Al-Ghazālī found the only solution to lie in a division of labour.

The division of labour proposed by al-Ghazālī was quite simple: the secular ruler supplied the power, the caliph supplied the moral purpose for which power was to be used. Differently put, the caliph was now head of the religious community alone. This was the only community to matter in moral terms, for unlike the ephemeral kingdoms into which it was divided from time to time, it was the community in which one travelled to eternal salvation. But it lacked military power. The imam needed such power (*shawka*), al-Ghazālī said, so he had to collaborate with a secular ruler or, as he terms it, a strongman (*dhū shawka*), who would set him up. If there was a single powerful man commanding general obedience, the candidate became imam by virtue of receiving allegiance from him. If there were several, they would have to come to an agreement and the same would apply. The key point was that the military ruler or rulers should lend their power to the imam, by undertaking to serve as his executives.[119]

Al-Ghazālī calls this undertaking *tafwīḍ*, delegation,[120] a startling term in that it acknowledges upfront that the power came from outside the religious institution. The term is more commonly used of the imam's delegation of power to his underlings, such as viziers and governors, but al-Ghazālī did not try to present the Seljuqs as owing their power to the caliph. On the contrary, the caliph owed his power to the Seljuq ruler and paid him back by legitimating his position. "Public authority (*al-wilāya*) today follows nothing but military power (*al-shawka*). Whoever receives allegiance from the holder of military power is caliph (*fa-man bāyaʿahu ṣāḥib al-shawka fa-huwa al-khalīfa*)," as he said in his final statement on the subject; "and whoever exercises independent power while obeying the caliph as regards the Friday oration and the coinage, he is the sultan whose decision and judgement must be carried out in the provinces"; "the public authority of the sultans in the distant lands who pay allegiance to the caliph is effective (*al-wilāya nāfidha li'l-salāṭīn fī aqṭār al-bilād al-mubāyiʿīna li'l-khalīfa*)."[121] Sometimes al-Ghazālī envisages the

119. *Iqtiṣād*, 238; *Faḍāʾiḥ*, 110; cf. Lambton, 'Internal Structure', 207.
120. *Iqtiṣād*, 238.2 and elsewhere.
121. *Iḥyāʾ*, ii, 116. 1, 6.

strongman as paying allegiance to a candidate chosen by the electors; at other times, he casts the strongman as the elector himself. One elector would do provided that he was powerful and not opposed by anyone who mattered, he says. When ʿUmar gave allegiance to Abū Bakr, his imamate was contracted by virtue of that one allegiance alone, because the Muslims in general followed; Abū Bakr would not have become caliph if they had resisted or been divided.[122] To the reader accustomed to thinking of the caliph as a ruler, al-Ghazālī seems to be saying that one needed a ruler (ʿUmar) in order to acquire a ruler (Abū Bakr). Why not make do with the first? But the first ruler is just a person who happens to be powerful, like the Seljuq sultan. It is his role that ʿUmar illustrates as elector of Abū Bakr. The second ruler is the properly constituted imam, elected to serve God's purpose by keeping the Muslims together on the right path, a man of Qurashī descent and other characteristics which as it happened ʿUmar had also possessed, but which the sultan could never acquire.

The Seljuqs had arrived as wielders of brutal and destructive power without anything that counted as a moral purpose from the point of view of the world they overran. The best one could do was to tame them, to put their power to constructive use and give them a positive role by harnessing them to the cause of Islam. It was in that spirit that al-Juwaynī had lauded them for their services to Islam against the Byzantines and the Qarāmiṭa of Baḥrayn, for naive he most certainly was not, and he will not have taken it for granted that it was with the intention of pleasing God that they had embarked on the campaigns in question; rather, he was habituating them to the idea that they had a moral role to play.[123] Al-Ghazālī, too, is engaged in the task of taming them. His strongman is a brute enrolled in the service of Islam. Like the Byzantine emperor, the brute elects a man of God to serve as the moral leader of the community; and like the Byzantine patriarch, the moral leader rewards the brute who has chosen him by legitimating his military power. Communal life thus continued to be based on the service of God under properly constituted authorities, now two rather than one. Both political *and* moral anarchy were avoided.

Al-Ghazālī pays no attention to the question how the strongman, or the two or three strongmen who divided up the community between them, might emerge. *Their* power cannot be regulated by humans, he says; that is up to God.[124] Political power is left to chance, in other words. The only constitution

122. *Faḍāʾiḥ*, 110.
123. Cf. above, note 12.
124. *Faḍāʾiḥ*, 110f.

that interests al-Ghazālī is that of the religious community, the congregation. His concern is not with the political realm, only with moral life.

Secular government and society

Like his teacher, al-Ghazālī is quite brutal about the nature of *shawka*. His tone has been deemed to be frank, realistic, disillusioned, and even cynical, and so it is, but not quite as normally understood.[125] He is indeed realistic in his open confrontation of the fact that the caliph was no longer the ruler and in his admission that al-Mustaẓhir lacked learning to the level of *ijtihād*, but contrary to what is often implied, he should not be seen as sacrificing his principles and selling out to Seljuq might, suppressing his scruples in order to legitimate a secular government for which there was no room in the classical doctrine. On the contrary, he devotes page after page to the legitimacy of the *caliph*, not the sultan, whose status he either takes for granted or settles in a couple of lines with reference to his recognition of the caliph. He does speak in cynical tones about secular government. The reason why he does so, however, is not that he is sacrificing his scruples in order to accommodate it, but on the contrary that he is putting it in its place: *shawka* is mere muscle power, mere brute force, and there is nothing exalted or elevated about it, though one cannot do without it. Far from selling out to secular power he is going out of his way to belittle its moral significance.

Political and military government was secular. It had been seized by foreigners, but it was not worth crying over it, let alone removing the caliph for it, whether in favour of an Ismaili imam or a secular leader such as Niẓām al-Mulk: this seems to be the message. The moral foundation of the community was guaranteed by the caliph, not by the king, and the caliph did not need to be a secular ruler himself; conversely a secular ruler could not guarantee the moral foundation. All that a secular ruler had was coercive power, and contrary to what the Ismailis and Neoplatonists said, coercive power had no place on the ladder of salvation. One was *not* to envisage the relationship between religion and government after the fashion of, say, the courtier Niẓāmī ʿArūḍī (d. after 547/1153), who saw the king as forming a continuum with the imam, the Prophet and God.[126] Unlike the caliph, the king was *not* the leader of the community founded by Muḥammad, or his representative, just a crude soldier

125. Gibb, 'Constitutional Organization', 19 (but contrast 20); von Grunebaum, *Medieval Islam*, 168; Lambton, *State and Government*, 110; Lewis, *Political Language*, 101; Hillenbrand, 'Al-Ghazālī's Views on Government', 85f., 90 (where he is also deemed to engage in pious dishonesty).

126. Niẓāmī ʿArūdī, *Chahár Maqála*, 20f.

given to self-indulgence, abuse of power, misuse of funds and other violations of the law. One did *not* gain virtue by frequenting the courts of kings or working for their cause. On the contrary, one should avoid the company of rulers (*ṣuḥbat al-sulṭān*), as so many ascetics and *aṣḥāb al-ḥadīth* had said.[127] But though secular government was ugly, oppressive, and immoral, there was no question of managing without it. Oppressive rulers had to be left in place if they were too powerful to be removed without civil war;[128] and one had to be grateful to God for raising up the brutes who took it upon themselves to provide some minimal order in allegiance to the caliph. But the power they exercised had no positive moral meaning in itself. It was only as a sword wielded on behalf of Islam that it acquired value. The only legitimacy the secular ruler could hope for was instrumental, as a mere tool of the religious institution.

What deeply worried al-Ghazālī was not the legitimacy of secular government, but on the contrary that of Muslim society. When he discusses the validity of public offices, his concern is not for the sultan, but for all the ordinary Muslims who might find themselves unable to marry, divorce, conduct business and otherwise pursue their daily lives on a lawful basis. He wants the caliph to be legitimate to ensure that *they* can live in accordance with God's will. He displays the same concern for the moral status of Muslim society in his discussion of the question whether one could cross bridges built by rulers, handle the coins they issued, or accept money from them. Here as there, the question is how far the community could be said still to be based on the law: had the public order which distinguished the abode of Islam from that of unbelief survived the transfer of power from Muḥammad's descendant to barbarian invaders? His answer was that it had, as long as the invaders recognized the caliph and thus allowed their power to be used in the service of the law again. One *could* use their coins, cross their bridges and accept money from them, provided that one had a legal title to it.[129] But one could not rely on the invaders to enforce the law in more than a basic sense. It is private individuals that al-Ghazālī sees as the main performers of the duty to command right and prohibit wrong, allowing them to use force where necessary.[130] In short, the caliph and the community over which he presided represented Islamic morality; the best the barbarian rulers could hope for was to serve it.

127. *Iḥyā'*, ii, 124f.; cf. Lambton, *State and Government*, 314f.
128. *Iḥyā'*, ii, 115.-2 (tr. in Gibb, 'Constitutional Organization', 19)
129. *Iḥyā'*, ii, book 4, ch. 5, esp. 115ff.
130. Below, ch. 18, 302.

Umma and state

Al-Ghazālī was the first clearly to articulate the fact that the Muslim world had developed something similar to the division between state and church in medieval Europe. There were now two types of community, one of believers and another of subjects. The former was pan-Islamic (the *umma*), the latter usually took the form of a plurality of kingdoms. The one was intrinsically holy, the other secular. God had "given one power to the prophets and another power to king; and He has made it incumbent on the people of the earth that they should submit themselves to the two powers", as the historian Bayhaqī (d. 470/1077) observed in terms recalling the famous statement by Pope Gelasius (d. 496) on the two powers, the authority (*auctoritas*) of popes and power (*potestas*) of kings, by which this world was ruled.[131] The scholars had to obey the sultan in everything that fell under his authority just as the sultan had to obey the scholars in everything that came within their jurisdiction, al-Juwaynī was reported to have said,[132] raising the question what the precise division of labour between them was. Al-Ghazālī's praise of the Turks has been interpreted as a veiled warning to the caliph not to interfere in the sultan's sphere,[133] and there were certainly others who explicitly told him not to do so. "If the caliph is the imam, his constant occupation must be prayer . . . There is no sense in the caliph's interference in the affairs of ephemeral earthly rule. This is the business of sultans," the guardian (*atabeg*) of the last Seljuq sultan, Ṭughril III (d. 590/1194), is reported to have declared,[134] voicing sentiments with which most European kings of the same period would have agreed. There were two kinds of government, one external and the other internal; kings and their deputies were in charge of the former while the latter fell to the *ʿulamāʾ*, as we are told by Fakhr al-Dīn al-Rāzī said (to whom the caliph barely existed, except as a moral ideal).[135] All were operating with a division between secular and spiritual government reminiscent of that in Europe.

But there were two major differences. First, the caliph had no ecclesiastical machinery within the kingdoms into which the Muslim community was divided, only an amorphous body of scholars who might or might not look to him for guidance. When there was tension between him and a political ruler, it was usually because he was trying to recover his own former position as

131. Cited in Bosworth, *Ghaznavids*, 63; cf. Gelasius in the *Cambridge History of Medieval Political Thought*, 288f.

132. Cited by ʿAlī Iṣfahānī in Marlow, 'Kings, Prophets and the ʿUlamāʾ', 118f.

133. Hillenbrand, 'Al-Ghazālī's View on Government', 86.

134. Rāwandī in Barthold, *Turkestan*, 372; in Lewis, *Political Language*, 47f. The statement was directed against the caliph al-Nāṣir.

135. Fouchécour, *Moralia*, 426.

political ruler, not because he was using the local scholars to collect funds or execute directives on behalf of a separate religious agency. The coexistence of caliph and sultan, in other words, led to political competition of the normal kind, not to attempts at ever-sharper definitions of the relationship between their jurisdictions. Secondly, the scholars and kings of the Islamic world ruled the believers/subjects on the basis of the same law, the Sharīʿa, not, as in the Latin West, on the basis of two different legal systems, canon law and Roman or common law, devised by different sets of authorities. So from that point of view, too, the cards were stacked against a sharp separation of the two spheres of government on the Islamic side of the fence.

Al-Nāṣir and ʿUmar al-Suhrawardī

Tension between the caliph and a secular ruler came to a head with the accession of al-Nāṣir (575–622/1180–1225), a caliph determined to recover his fullness of power. By his time, the Seljuq sultanate had collapsed completely, leaving behind a profusion of minor dynasties, notably the Ayyūbids in Syria and Egypt, and the Ghūrids and Khwārizmshāhs in eastern Iran. Al-Nāṣir cast himself as the ultimate ruler of the Muslim world, aided and abetted by his court theologian al-Suhrawardī, with a modicum of success everywhere except in the case of the Khwārizmshāh, who emerged as his chief rival.

ʿUmar al-Suhrawardī, not to be confused with 'the Suhrawardī who was killed' (*al-S. al-maqtūl*), was a Sufi. Of Sufism it can be said that it began in the ninth century, though its roots stretched far back in the pre-Islamic Near East, and that it had a bearing on public life from the start in the sense that it counselled withdrawal from this world, but that it had not so far meshed directly with thought about government. This is what it came to do now. Al-Suhrawardī cast al-Nāṣir as an intermediary (*wāsiṭa*) between man and God, claiming that God had singled out His caliph for the highest perfection a Sufi could attain and that the caliphate was deputyship of God on earth to lead mankind to God.[136] He thus reinvested the caliphate with religious authority, clearly with a view to justifying a political come-back, by casting the caliph as a Sufi *shaykh* on whom all Sufis had to model themselves, all Muslims being his disciples. Given that the caliphate had developed in isolation from Sufism, it was an apt way of endowing it with significance in an increasingly Sufi world, but one may of course wonder how seriously it was taken.

136. Hartmann, *an-Nāṣir*, 112ff., Al-Nāṣir duly called himself *khalīfat allāh ʿalā kāffat ahl al-islām* in an inscription at ʿArafa (*RCEA*, ix, no. 3435, cf. Lewis, *Political Language*, 46).

If al-Suhrawardi's ideas were grandiose, al-Nāṣir's methods were bizarre, and his general behaviour behind the sugary façade was brutish.[137] He tried to restore his position of primacy by enrolling other rulers in chivalric organizations, pigeon clubs, and shooting associations, of which he secured a monopoly by outlawing all except his own. He did his best to control education and culture, too, and spied on everyone. Saladin dutifully requested a document of investiture from him, as did some Seljuqs in Anatolia. But the Khwārizmshāh Tekish (d. 1200) clashed with him in Western Iran, on which both had designs, and Tekish's successor Muḥammad (d. 1220) turned up the temperature by declaring al-Nāṣir to be deposed and setting up an ʿAlid anti-caliph. In 1217 he marched on Baghdad, but snowstorms in Kurdistan forced him to turn back.[138] Meanwhile al-Nāṣir, repeatedly ignoring requests by the Ayyūbids for help against the Crusaders, was rumoured to be inviting the Mongols to take action against Muḥammad.[139] In 656/1258 the Mongols sacked Baghdad and killed the last Abbasid caliph, al-Mustaʿṣim. The reaction awaits a study, but the sources are not exactly brimming over with grief.

Western Islam and Sunni mahdism

The Seljuq unification had stopped short of Egypt, let alone North Africa and al-Andalus. Egypt was recovered for eastern Islam by Saladin in 1171, but North Africa and al-Andalus continued to have their separate history, dominated by two great reformist movements, the Almoravids (al-Murābiṭūn) and the Almohads (al-Muwaḥḥidūn). The Almoravids were Ṣanhāja Berber tribesmen from the southwestern Sahara united by the scholar ʿAbdallāh b. Yāsīn (d. 450/1058). They reached Morocco after Ibn Yāsīn's death, founded Marrakesh in 454/1062 and crossed over to al-Andalus in 479/1086, to rule it down to 541/1147. The Almohads who succeeded them were Maṣmūda Berbers from the Atlas mountains in Morocco who were united by the scholar Ibn Tūmart (d. 524/1130). They captured Marrakesh from the Almoravids in 542/1147 and occupied the rest of North Africa as well as al-Andalus soon thereafter. In the early thirteenth century, their North African possessions fell to new dynasties, and by the middle of the century they had lost the whole of al-Andalus, apart from Granada, to the Christians. It was when the first of these two Berber movements was petering out that Sunni Mahdism rose to political importance.

137. Ibn al-Athīr, *Kāmil*, xii, 440 (year 622), describing him as abhorrent. Ibn al-Jawzī wrote a *dhamm al-imām al-Nāṣir* (Hartmann, *an-Nāṣir*, 117).

138. For all this, see Barthold, *Turkestan*, 372f., 402f.; *EI*², s.v. 'Khʷārizmshāh'.

139. *EI*², s.v. 'al-Nāṣir' (A. Hartmann, who likes him a good deal better than did Ibn al-Athīr).

From the later Umayyad period down to the end of the Fatimid caliphate, Mahdism had been an overwhelmingly Shīʿite phenomenon. There may well have been equal interest in the Mahdi as an eschatological figure in *jamāʿī* and Shīʿite circles; both certainly wrote about him. But it was only to Shīʿites that he was of political significance. When *jamāʿī* Muslims produced messianic leaders, they were marginal figures, and they did not usually call themselves the Mahdi, as opposed to 'the Sufyānī', 'the Qaḥṭānī', or the like, with reference to different apocalyptic models.[140] By contrast, Shīʿite Mahdism generated the ʿAbbāsid revolution, the Ismaili movement, and numerous minor Mahdis in between. With the failure of Ismailism, however, it was played out. From now onwards it was primarily the Sunnis who put the idea to political use.

The first to do so was probably Ibn Tūmart, the leader of the Almohad movement in North Africa who has gone down in history as "the well-known Mahdi and the infallible imam" (*al-mahdī al-maʿlūm wa'l-imām al-maʿṣūm*). The mahdic role may however have been bestowed on him posthumously by his successor, ʿAbd al-Muʾmin (d. 558/1163), under whom the Almohads conquered al-Andalus; and the first Sunni to make a bid for power as the Mahdi may in that case have been Ibn Qasī, a Sufi rebel in al-Andalus who struck coins with the legend "God is our Lord, Muḥammad is our prophet, and the Mahdi is our imam" in 539/1144, using a formula also found on undated Almohad coins.[141] Whoever may have been the first, their conception of the mahdic role comes across as strikingly different from that of the Shīʿites. None of them predicted (or was posthumously made to predict) an imminent, total, and violent transformation of the world; none of them declared the resurrection to be imminent, be it in the literal or a spiritual sense; and it was not with a view to being on the right side in a coming cataclysm that any of them took to fighting. The Almohads did see themselves as making a drastic break with the past, but there does not seem to have been anything apocalyptic about it: Ibn Tūmart was the Mahdi in the sense of a reformer rather than a redeemer. This is true of most Sunni Mahdis, for they were usually tribesmen and thus orientated towards external organization rather than inner spirituality even when they were Sufis. Salvation lay in strict application of the law, the strengthening of organized religion, and the perfection of collective affairs, not in the spiritual redemption of individuals. Doing God's will meant getting people into line, making them obey, suppressing internal strife, and setting about

140. Fierro, 'Le mahdi Ibn Tûmart', 119 and 'al-Aṣfar Again'; Cobb, *White Banners*, ch. 4; Madelung, 'The Sufyāni' and 'Abū 'l-ʿAmayṭar'.

141. Cf. Fierro, 'Le mahdi Ibn Tûmart', esp. 109f. (the earlier Mahdis in al-Andalus were caliphs using the title in the old style as a caliphal epithet; cf. 116f.; above, 75). For the formula used on the coins, see also Crone and Zimmermann, *Epistle*, 254ff.

subduing the infidels. In short, it meant returning to the model of moral puritanism and military activism represented by the Prophet and the Rāshidūn.

One may well ask why such a restorer should call himself the Mahdi. The answer seems to be that only as the Mahdi would he be authorized, and indeed expected, to take action against the political and religious leadership of his time. Religious authority is notoriously dispersed in Sunni Islam. Every scholar has much the same authority as any other, and though some are more persuasive than others, they cannot depart from the consensus in major ways without thereby losing their scholarly credentials. Moreover, revolt against the powers that be was condemned. By what authority could Ibn Tūmart claim the right to overturn the Almoravid establishment, itself established in the name of religious reform? One answer was by means of the Mahdi, who offered a way of concentrating religious authority again. As far as Ibn Tūmart's Berber followers are concerned, it may not have mattered very much what role he claimed as long as it made him a holy man of some kind or other, but Ibn Tūmart was a genuinely learned man with supra-local ambitions who had to justify himself and the new elite he created in the eyes of the wider world, or maybe it was his successor who felt the need to do so when he conquered al-Andalus.[142] Either way, Ibn Tūmart was the Mahdi in a new reformist sense of someone who guided the believers to God's path, or in other words to His law (*al-mahdī ilā sabīl allāh*), and whose mahdic status conferred infallibility on his legal reasoning (*ijtihād*).[143] He does not seem to have set a trend as far as infallibility is concerned, but of Mahdis there were to be plenty after him, especially in his own North Africa, but also elsewhere.

The king as caliph

When Ibn Tūmart died, his successor, ʿAbd al-Muʾmin, styled himself *khalīfa* and *amīr al-muʾminīn*; it was the only title that made sense for a successor to the Mahdi.[144] It aligned them with the Umayyad caliphs of al-Andalus, but contributed to the devaluation of the caliphal title, which was to be adopted by a variety of minor dynasts after the ʿAbbāsid caliphate was suppressed by the Mongols.

In the east, caliphal epithets were bestowed on secular rulers well before the Mongols, but not yet as actual titles. Kings appear as *khalīfat allāh* and/or God's shadow on earth in mirrors already from the eleventh century

142. Fierro, 'Le mahdi Ibn Tûmart', 115.
143. Ibid., 112f. and 'Legal Policies of the Almohad Caliphs,' 232f.
144. Compare the successor to the Mahdi in nineteenth-century Sudan.

onwards.[145] Unlike the Latin assertion that "the king is emperor in his own territory", the claim that the king was caliph in his own kingdom was not meant as an assertion of sovereignty. Sometimes the intention was simply to stress that the ruler must be obeyed: "the king is God's caliph in His lands, and his caliphate will not be right if he is opposed," al-Māwardī said, quoting a saying that came to be attributed to Aristotle.[146] More commonly, the intention was to educate the king by means of flattery. One presented him as having achieved a state of moral perfection in the hope that he would respond by actually trying to achieve it: only the righteous ruler was God's proof (*ḥujja*) and shadow on earth, al-Bīrūnī explained; but if he was just, al-Kirmānī added, he was caliph "even if he was an Ethiopian slave".[147] Every man who commanded good and prohibited wrong was God's caliph on earth according to the jurists, and every man could also aspire to the position of true king, imam, and God's caliph on earth according to the philosophers, since that position rested on mastery of the royal craft (as they understood it), not on the possession of power.[148] But it was of course particularly important for the actual wielders of political power to acquire the intellectual and moral perfection involved; and when they did so, their combination of power and perfection raised them above all others. The ruler who had acquired both knowledge and justice possessed one of the ingredients of prophethood, according to Ibn al-Balkhī (c. 500/1100).[149] In the opinion of Dāya, God had made David His caliph on earth, instructing him to rule with justice (cf. Q. 38:26), to show not only that kingship is *khilāfa* of God and that justice is of its essence, but also that kingship over men may be joined to the rank of prophethood; He thereby gave the lie to kings who claimed that the duties of kingship in this world left them unable to cultivate their religion.[150] It was as a king who had risen to prophethood that Niẓāmī depicted Alexander in his *Iskandarnāme*.

The application of the caliphal title to kings, accepted as counterparts to prophets, testifies to a progressive blurring of distinctions between rulers of the Islamic, the Iranian, and the Greek traditions. It is about the same time that the different literary genres devoted to these rulers began to merge. Constitutional law came to be rehearsed in mirrors for princes, which in their turn came to include accounts of the king drawn from the philosophers, frequently with an input of Sufism too, so that it is often difficult to tell where the reference is

145. Cf. above, 153.
146. Māwardī, *Tashīl al-naẓar*, 202 and the editorial note thereto.
147. Bīrūnī, *Aẓlāl*, 8 = 45; Kirmānī in Fouchécour, *Moralia*, 433.
148. Above, 128f., 180; ʿĀmirī, *Iʿlām*, 155.2; Ṭūsī, *Ethics*, 192.
149. Lambton, 'Justice', 100. For the king as God's *ḥujja*, see also above, ch. 13, 153f.
150. Dāya, *God's Bondsmen*, 397–9; cf. Marlow, 'Kings, Prophets and the ʿUlamā'', 107f.

to the historical caliphate, where to contemporary kings, and where to real rulers as opposed to moral ideals. In the Iranian east the secular ruler fell heir to all three political traditions – the monotheist, the Persian, and the Greek. Fakhr al-Dīn al-Rāzī's *Jāmiʿ al-ʿulūm*, a Sunni work originally written in Arabic, is an early example of this synthesis; a more famous example is Naṣīr al-Dīn Ṭūsī's *Nasirean Ethics* (*Akhlāq-i nāṣirī*), which is Shīʿite and written in Persian.[151]

The Sunni way

The merger of the caliphal and the royal titles also testifies to what one might pick out as the single most striking difference between Sunni political thought on the one hand and that of the Khārijites and Shīʿites on the other: the Sunni determination to keep the present legitimate. All three parties believed that moral ideals and power politics had coincided in the Prophet's Medina and all had to confront the fact that they did not do so anymore. What were they to do about it? The Khārijite answer was that one had to get the two together again by fighting wrongful rulers until they saw the light or were eradicated, or at least until one had a rightly guided polity of one's own. As has been seen, this and the Zaydī equivalent rapidly ceased to carry conviction outside the tribal fringes. The Imami answer, by contrast, was that morality and power could never come together again: one had to choose between them. People pursuing power had too many short-term interests in this world to care for what was true and right, so the best one could do was to leave politics to the wrongdoers and seek to live an upright life in an apolitical community of one's own. God and Caesar were kept apart, not because this was viewed as a positive good (as in the modern West), but rather because it was the best one could do in the circumstances.

The Adherents of Ḥadīth sometimes came very close to the Imami view. Ibn Ḥanbal and his associates, for example, also saw political power as irredeemably corrupt and tried to live an upright life in an apolitical community of their own. But there was no denunciation of the rulers as usurpers, and no veneration of the losers either, in their case. Instead, there was cold recognition of the fact that the rulers one had were the best one was ever going to get. God would never replace or abolish them, nor did God approve of those who spent their lives weeping over the political oppression of the righteous. Rulers certainly had to be avoided, but they also had to be accepted as legitimate.

151. On which, see above, 193, 215; cf. also Fouchécour, *Moralia*, 443, on Sirāj al-Dīn Urmawī's *Laṭāʾif al-ḥikma* (completed in 655/1257 and modeled on Fakhr al-Dīn Rāzī, discussed in Marlow, 'Kings, Prophets and the ʿUlamāʾ').

It might be thought that Ibn Ḥanbal merely described as half full a glass that the Imamis described as half empty, but this reflects a fundamental difference between their attitudes. Where the Imamis tried to separate moral ideals and political reality, the Sunnis were trying to keep the two together by stretching the principles to keep reality within their domain. The caliph was really a king: the Sunnis accepted him as quasi-caliph. Upstart rulers usurped the position of caliphal governors: the Sunnis responded by casting them as caliphal governors. The caliph himself lacked a crucial qualification for office: the Sunnis recognized him as legitimate with reference to overriding necessity. Kings usurped the position of the caliph: the Sunnis responded by encouraging them to see themselves as incumbents of the caliphate. The caliphate disappeared: the Sunnis responded by extending the title of caliph or imam to rulers of any kind.

It is this constant stretching of basic principles that Gibb found so shocking in al-Māwardī and which comes across as cynicism or pious fraud to some Western scholars of al-Ghazālī. It also shocked, or rather disgusted, the Khārijites and Shīʿites, to whom the Sunnis came across as unprincipled people ready to pay allegiance to any tyrant and oppressor. Like modern Westerners, the Shīʿites and Khārijites thought of moral principles as rules by which people were to be judged, so that some would pass and others fail. To the Sunnis, by contrast, the moral principles were in the nature of nets which had to be cast wide to ensure that everybody was caught in them. If the nets had to be enlarged to encompass sinful rulers, so be it. Compromise was always better than conflict: everyone stayed together, and those caught in the net might sooner or later learn to abide by the rules of their own accord.

Differently put, the Sunnis reacted to power by trying to tame it, by bringing it into the house in the hope that it could be domesticated. It did not really make much difference whether the rulers were their own caliphs or barbarian invaders. It was only against infidels that the barriers went up, excluding the possibility of compromise.

IV

. . .

GOVERNMENT AND SOCIETY

CHAPTER

17

THE NATURE OF GOVERNMENT

As seen in Chapter 1, early Muslims tacitly assumed humans to have originated in a politically organized society based on revealed law, and to have recreated such a society whenever God sent them a messenger with a new law. In the ninth century they began to enquire into their own presuppositions. Why do humans live social lives? Must their societies be based on religious law brought by a prophet or might man-made law and morality suffice? Could one manage without a monarch? Must government be monarchic, or indeed autocratic, or could alternative forms of political organization be envisaged? Their answers mostly, though not always, endorsed the assumptions with which they had started out, but they did so with a plethora of explicit argumentation which often raised new questions and which continued beyond the period considered in this book. The debate was dominated by philosophers, *mutakallim*s, and Shīʿite thinkers rather than by religious scholars from the Sunni camp, but the latter accepted many of the ideas it produced. Since the arguments are scattered in works of the most diverse genres and the study of them is still in its infancy, what follows is merely a preliminary survey.

Why do humans live in societies?

Most educated persons in the Near East before the rise of Islam knew the answer to this question, ultimately from Aristotle and other Greek philosophers. "Because of the arts and sciences and the useful things to which they lead, we have mutual need of one another, and because we need one another we come together in one place in large numbers," as Nemesius of Emesa (c. 400) explained in a widely read treatise on human nature (which was eventually translated into Arabic too); "to this human assemblage . . . we give the name of city (*polis*), for man is a naturally sociable animal (*politikon zōon*). No single person is in all ways self-sufficient."[1] Most educated persons in the Near East gave the same answer after they had become Muslims. It is first encountered in al-Jāḥiẓ (d. 255/869), the first Muslim author known to have considered the question: it is in the nature of humans that they need one another and must cooperate to survive, he says, adding "God, exalted is He, has not created anyone who is able to fulfil his need on his own."[2] The Muslims could soon read the same in Arabic translations of Greek works, which they rapidly took to citing.[3] Humans must come together to cooperate, especially as they also need to associate in order to live virtuous lives, al-ʿĀmirī (d. 381/992) declared, paraphrasing Aristotle; exceptions would be in the nature of gods or beasts.[4] "For this reason it is said that man is sociable by nature (*al-insān madanī bi'l-ṭabʿ*)," Rāghib al-Iṣfahānī (c. 400/1010) observed.[5] The same argument was used in varying versions, now with and now without the Aristotelian tag that man is a social animal (*ḥayawān insī/madanī*), by the philosophers al-Rāzī (d. prob. 313/925),[6] al-Fārābī (d. 339/950),[7] Ibn Sīnā (d. 428/1037),[8] and Ibn Rushd (d. 595/1198),[9] the secretary Qudāma b. Jaʿfar (d. prob. 337/948),[10] the polymath al-Bīrūnī (d. 440/1048),[11] the religious scholar Fakhr al-Dīn al-Rāzī (d. 606/1209),[12] the Shīʿite Muʿtazilite Ibn Abī 'l-Ḥadīd (d. prob. 655/1257),[13] the Ismaili philosopher Naṣīr al-Dīn Ṭūsī (d. 672/1274)[14] and, after our period, by authors as diverse as Ibn Taymiyya (d. 728/1328)[15] and Ibn Khaldūn (d.

1. Nemesius, §52 = 243.
2. *Ḥayawān*, i, 42ff.
3. Plessner, *Bryson*, Arabic text, 146f.; Themistius, *Risāla*, 28f./90; cited in Ibn Abī 'l-Rabīʿ, *Sulūk*, 78f. Cf. also Plato, *Republic*, 369bf, and the Aristotelian passages in the next note.
4. ʿĀmirī, *Saʿāda*, 150 (cf. Aristotle, *Politics*, 1253a, 1278b). For the question whether ʿĀmirī is really the author of this work, see the bibliography s.v.
5. *Dharīʿa*, 374. Adam had to perform a thousand tasks to eat bread, as Naṣīr al-Dīn Ṭusī says (*Ethics*, 189).
6. Rāzī, *al-Ṭibb al-rūḥānī*, 105f. = 88f. (ch. 17).
7. Fārābī, *MF*, ch. 15, §1; cf. *Taḥṣīl*, §16 = §18.
8. Ibn Sīnā, *SI, x*, 441 = 99.
9. Ibn Rushd, *Commentary*, 22 = 113.
10. Qudāma, *Kharāj*, 432f.; cf. also Māwardī, *Adab al-dunyā*, 135f. *Tasḥīl al-naẓar*, 97.
11. *Jawāhir*, 6f. = 6. His deathdate is placed later by some.
12. Rāzī, *al-Mabāḥith al-mashriqiyya*, ii, 523; cf. also Lambton, *State and Society*, 132f.; Fouchécour, *Moralia*, 426, on his *Jāmiʿ al-ʿulūm*, ch. 56.
13. IAH, *Sharḥ*, xvii, 49f.
14. *Ethics*, 189f.
15. *Al-Ḥisba fī 'l-islām*, 4 = 20.

808/1406).[16] It was also a popular argument in medieval Europe. It does not impress a modern observer, for occupational specialization comes late in the development of civilization: simple societies have little or no division of labour, except by age and sex. Producing a loaf of bread is indeed beyond the ability of a single person wholly on his own, as the literature often says, but it is not beyond the capacity of a household, and there the division of labour may stop. Even Ibn Khaldūn, who had a strong sense of the differences between simple (tribal) and complex (urban) societies in North Africa, overlooked this objection, however, and the traditional explanation had the merit of stressing the cooperative nature of society. Rāghib al-Iṣfahānī interspersed his account of the division of labour with Prophetic dicta on the solidarity of the believers.

Why must human societies have law?

Though the need for cooperation meant that humans had to live in societies, their nature was such that that they could not do so without some kind of restraint. God had imprinted a desire for good things on all humans, and indeed animals, an epistle credited to al-Jāḥiẓ says; He has implanted a desire for self-preservation in people, as al-Māturidī (d. 333/944) put it.[17] Humans were competitive, brutish, swayed by strong desires, and avaricious too: unlike animals, they were for ever hoarding things they did not need. Left to their own devices they would ruthlessly pursue their own interests and diverse passions, engage in constant rivalry and strife without affection or altruism, ignorant of their true interests in this world and the next, and thus bring about their own ruin.[18] "There is nothing as social by nature and as anti-social by corruption as the human race," as St Augustine had put it.[19] This was the Muslim view entirely, except that they did not usually credit the anti-social streak to later corruption. But whether humans had been created deficient or were corrupted at some later stage (by Adam's fall,[20] Cain's murder of Abel,[21] or the like),

16. *Muqaddima*, 46f. = 89ff.

17. 'Al-Maʿāsh wa'l-maʿād' in his *Rasāʾil*, i, 102f.; Māturīdī, *Tawḥīd*, 177.

18. In addition to the references in the previous note, see the Zaydī view in Jāḥiẓ, 'Maqālat al-Zaydiyya wa'l-Rāfiḍa' (also known as 'Bayān madhāhib al-shīʿa') in his *Rasāʾil*, iv, 318f.; al-Qāsim b. Ibrāhīm in Madelung, *Qāsim*, 14; Abrahamov, 'Ḳāsim', 85; Abū Ḥātim al-Rāzī, *Aʿlām*, 110f.; Juwaynī, *Ghiyāth*, §19; Ghazālī, *Iqtiṣād*, 236; Ṭurṭūshī, *Sirāj*, 41f.

19. In Markus, *Saeculum*, 95.

20. *RIS*, iv, 166; cf. ii, 21; iv, 18.

21. Thus Bīrūnī, who also debits the envy and rivalry to the mixture of contradictory elements in human nature (*Jawāhir*, 6f., 24 = 6, 26).

practically all medieval Muslims envisaged life in what Westerners call the state of nature as nasty, brutish, and short.[22]

The idea of human life in its unmodified form as lacking in morality, co-operation, and social cohesion had long roots in the ancient world. It had however once been balanced by a countervailing belief to the effect that the original state of mankind was a golden age of freedom and innocence which had lasted until avarice caused coercion and inequality to appear. This view, promoted above all by the Stoics, fused with the biblical story of the Fall and went on to a long career in European political thought, where it placed a question mark over the necessity of states.[23] In the hugely popular *Roman de la Rose* (c. 1270), for example, Jean de Meun tells of how people had once lived in mutual amity, without agriculture, work, private property, rulers, marriage, or other restraints on free love until a host of vices, including covetousness, appeared: this was when human nature turned so nasty that a ruler had to be elected for the maintenance of order.[24] But though a strikingly similar concept of a golden age was current in India, it is not clear that there was an Iranian version as well,[25] and in its Greek form, the myth seems to have lost prominence in the eastern Mediterranean before the rise of Islam. Al-Bīrūnī, it is true, knew it from the astronomical poem of Aratus of Soli (d. 240 BC) and compared it with the Indian version of the myth; but he wrote as a scholar, not as somebody to whom the myth was alive.[26] As live tradition it may be reflected in the Brethren of Purity, who tell a story of how humans lived carefree lives in mutual love like a single family until they started hoarding; but this story is meant to illustrate the divine world from which we have fallen (thereby becoming human), not a primitive stage of human history that we have lost, that is, its import is Neoplatonist or Gnostic, not socio-political.[27] Elsewhere, too, there are suggestions

22. The parallel with Hobbes's Leviathan is drawn in Pines, 'La loi naturelle et la société', 167; implicitly, also in Al-Azmeh, *Muslim Kingship*, 115f. There is no Arabic term for 'the state of nature'. It is evoked with statements like 'if people were left on their own' (i.e. without divine intervention), or 'If God left them alone with their natures'.

23. For all this, see the references given in Crone, 'Ninth-Century Muslim Anarchists', 6–8.

24. Cf. Milan, 'The Golden Age and the Political Theory of Jean de Meun'; George, 'Jean de Meung and the Myth of the Golden Age'; also Cohn, *Pursuit of the Millenium*, 195f.

25. Cf. Crone, 'Zoroastrian Communism', 459.

26. Bīrūnī, *Hind*, 192.12 = 383 (ch. 43); cf. Sachau's comments *ad. loc.*, and Lovejoy and Boas, *Primitivism and Related Ideas in Antiquity*, 34ff. (Aratus), 433ff. (Indians).

27. *RIS*, iv, 37f.; cf. ii, 326 = Goodman, *Case*, 157, where the animals pick out human avarice and hoarding of superfluous things as one reason why humans need religious laws; Abū Ḥātim al-Rāzī, *Aʿlām*, 188, where the contrast between animals and humans in this

that the Brethren of Purity and other early Ismailis thought in terms of an aboriginal state of human innocence, especially when they speak of law and government as punishment,[28] but they never explicitly state that mankind had once been free of their many vices, and they do not focus on this question in what survives of their debate regarding the existence or otherwise of law in Adam's era.[29] If the concept was there, it certainly was not prominent. In short, the Muslim view of aboriginal life was overwhelmingly that of Hobbes, without any admixture of positive views of the state of nature.

Unlike Hobbes and other contract theorists, however, the Muslims usually saw the state of nature as having come to an end thanks to divine intervention rather than human action: God in His mercy sent a Prophet with a law, to found a polity. Differently put, the social contract was with God, not with a human being. Without God's law, there could be no civilization, indeed humans would not survive at all, as Shīʿites above all were prone to claiming.[30]

Why must the law be God-given?

Hobbes took it for granted that humans can devise moral and legal codes on their own. How then did the Muslims explain their conviction that God had to send a prophet with a law in order for social order to appear? There were two answers to that question.

No natural law

The first explanation was that no human had the right to impose obligations on other people. Nobody was authorized to tell anyone else what to do or what to believe, be he a ruler, parent, husband, schoolmaster, or even a prophet: God was the only source of legal/moral obligations; before revelation, humans had lived in a state of fundamental non-obligation (*barāʾa aṣliyya*).[31] Nobody had

---

respect is one reason why humans must have imams. Compare the role of *Āz*, covetousness, in Mazdak's vision of the abolition of private property and pair-bonding (Crone, 'Kavad's Heresy,' 28; add Firdawsī's presentation in Davis, *Epic and Sedition*, 30).

28. Cf. above, 200, 201; below, 356, on the animal fable.

29. Cf. Madelung, 'Imamat', 102–4, 106–8, where al-Nasafī does broach the question, but the argument does not make sense.

30. The reason why God had made humans dependent on prophets instead of implanting a religious instinct in them (contrary to Abū Bakr al-Rāzī's claims) is that self-sufficient humans would fight one another to death; "if it were not for religion and the laws of the Prophets . . . people would perish" (Abū Ḥātim, *Aʿlām*, 190). Similarly Jāḥiẓ, 'Maʿāsh wa'l-maʿād', 103f.

31. Thus Ghazālī in Laoust, *Politique de Ġazālī*, 153f. (citing the *Mustaṣfā*).

the right to inflict punishments on anyone else either; only God could do so.[32] For only God could determine what was right and wrong or, as medieval Muslims preferred to put it, what was permitted and forbidden. Without revelation, humans would not have any morality or law at all.

The expression 'before revelation' (*qabla wurūd al-sharʿ*) with which people examined the nature of obligations did not refer to a historical stage. Nor, strictly speaking, does the Western concept of 'the state of nature', though there has been a strong tendency to envisage it as such. Both expressions stand for thought experiments in which human nature is imagined in the raw, stripped of divine guidance in the one case, of civilization in the other. The Muslim thought experiment focused on the moral status of human acts whereas the Greek experiment focused on the moral nature of humans themselves, but the issue was the same: how far was morality natural, how far conventional? Like other Ashʿarites, al-Ghazālī subscribed to the view that it was entirely conventional, in the sense of established by God: no human act had any moral value in itself; all acts were good or bad only because God had defined them so to us. It followed that humans could not have an inner moral compass, or any "law written in their hearts" (Rom. 2:15), enabling them to live moral lives on the basis of their own unaided reason. All morality took the form of positive law enacted by God.[33] Humans might still be able to devise rules of their own (the possibility is not discussed in the context of this debate, which was not directly concerned with socio-political organization); but such rules would not be moral, nor would they lead to otherworldly salvation. According to this view of things, in short, it was only by divine intervention that humans could escape from their amoral state of nature. "For when the religion of God was taken away, they lost also the knowledge of good and evil," as the church father Lactantius (d. c. 320) says in his account of how the golden age (here envisaged as an age of perfect monotheism) came to an end. "Thus community-living perished among men, and the compact of human society was broken."[34] This was how the causal connection between God, morality/law and human society was envisaged in Islam as well.

Human abilities insufficient

The second explanation was a modified version of the first, reshaped as a direct answer to the question why societies had to be based on laws brought by prophets. It did not claim that human actions have no moral value in them-

32. ʿAbd al-Jabbār, *Mughnī*, xx/2, 152.13.
33. Cf. Reinhart, *Before Revelation*, 70ff., et passim.
34. Lactantius, *Divine Institutes*, v, 5.

selves: certain things were indeed intrinsically good or bad. But humans did not know what was best for them or how to achieve it, according to this argument. Only God could supply the wisdom, the authority, and the sanctions required for a community based on true morality.

As regards wisdom, people were not intelligent enough to know what was best for them in this world, let alone the next. They needed a superior intelligence to tell them. It was thanks to divine intervention that they had acquired their knowledge of right and wrong, and also of many other things: how would they have worked out the difference between edible and poisonous substances, for example, without perishing in the attempt? How could they have known about agriculture? Prophets were not just founders of polities, but also culture heroes.

As regards authority, people were too similar to submit to one another. They were always competing, for ever thinking that they had a better right to power and wealth than anyone else. They needed a superior authority to defer to. It was thanks to divine intervention that some were raised above others, boosted with divine authority, as everyone knew from the story of the rise of Islam: it was by divine intervention that government had been created for the egalitarian tribesmen of Muḥammad's Arabia.[35]

Finally, as regards sanctions, humans needed a strong incentive to submit, and again, the solution lay with God, who had instituted otherworldly rewards and punishments.[36] "We know that people cannot defend themselves against their own natures or act contrary to their desires except by a strong deterrent, the long-term threat of eternal punishment over and on top of punishment in the here and now," al-Jāḥiẓ has the Shīᶜites say.[37] God had instituted Paradise and Hell as the carrot and the stick (*al-targhīb wa'l- al-tarhīb*), and without them society would go to rack and ruin, he (or somebody mistaken for him) says in another epistle.[38] Ibn Sīnā agreed, with implicit reference to the phases of Muḥammad's career: the lawgiver prophet should start by telling the masses that they had a maker who had prepared eternal rewards and punishments for them; this would make them obey. Next the lawgiver should institute acts of worship that would constantly remind them of this; and finally he should regulate the social and political aspects of his polity.[39] Religion diverted people

35. Cf. Bīrūnī, below, 285.

36. Cf. Jāḥiẓ, 'Maqālat al-Zaydiyya', 318ff. and 'al-Maᶜāsh wa'l-maᶜād', 102ff.; Māturīdī, *Tawḥīd*, 177ff.; Māwardī, *Aᶜlām al-nubuwwa*, 49; Ibn Sīnā, *SI*, *x*, 441 = 91; Fakhr al-Dīn al-Rāzī, *Muḥaṣṣal*, 176.

37. 'Maqālat al-Zaydiyya', 320.

38. Jāḥiẓ, 'al-Maᶜāsh wa'l-maᶜād', 104.

39. *SI*, *x*, 442ff = 100ff.

from their desires and turned their hearts away from their selfish wishes "until it comes to dominate their innermost soul and exercise restraint on their conscience, supervising their soul in its inner solitude, and giving it sincere advice in its misfortunes", al-Māwardī said in a good description of internalization.[40] In short, religion enabled people to suppress selfish inclinations incompatible with communal existence, as Durkheim was to say centuries later in the West.

But whereas religion has formed part of all human societies, prophets have not, and medieval Muslims were well aware of this fact. How then had societies without prophets come to live by what the societies in question considered to be right and wrong? One might have expected the answer that they too owed them to belief in the supernatural, for people obviously did not need prophets in order to believe in gods, cosmic order, or an afterlife. But this would have implied that any religion, even paganism, could supply social and political organization, however misguided it might be. The philosophers did in fact hold this to be the case, and al-Bīrūnī seems to have thought so, too.[41] But it was not wise to air this opinion openly; and besides, many Muslims, like many Christians, had trouble seeing paganism as a religion at all. When they declared all kingdoms to be based on religion, the reference was to monotheist religion.[42] Insofar as pagans were perceived to have laws, they were assumed to have devised them of their own, by conscious legislation rather than imperceptible development. On the rare occasions on which the problem of non-prophetic laws was openly confronted, the alternative to revelation was human reason, whether in the form of common sense or philosophy, not religion of other types.

Human and divine wisdom compared

Thus al-Jāḥiẓ tells a story in which a commander of the Umayyad period meets with the Turkish *khāqān* to compare their respective laws, to find that they agree on some things and disagree on others. "You are a people who trace your laws to what reason permits and what seems to be a good idea," the commander concludes, "but we think that we are not fit to manage the servants (of

40. *Adab al-dunyā*, 136.

41. It is implied by al-Fārābī's theories (above, 173) and explicitly stated by the philosopher in Judah Halevi, *Radd*, 5 = 34 (I, §1), while Bīrūnī had no trouble seeing the religious basis of socio-political organization in India in his *Hind* (esp. chs 9–10); and he dispassionately notes the similarity between Muslim, Zoroastrian, and pagan Tibetan and Turkish ways of invoking religion to single out the ruler in his *Jawāhir* (24f. = 26, cf. below, note 128).

42. Thus *NM* (M), 67; cf. Abū Yaʿqūb al-Sijistānī, above, 13, note 20.

God)." Only God knew the true nature of things that was hidden to people.[43] Al-Jāḥiẓ' intention here is not to idealize the Turks as people who followed reason of their own accord, without the need for punishment, for the Turkish laws discussed include the penalties for theft, murder, and cutting off people's ears and noses. Nor is he trying the opposite, to depict them as amoral, for as a Muʿtazilite, he took it for granted that reason could provide moral guidance, and his commander speaks with respect of the Turkish laws. Al-Jāḥiẓ' position is simply that revealed law is better, not because otherworldly sanctions had a good effect on social order (which is not discussed) or even because revelation provided for otherworldly salvation (the discussion is only about this world), but rather because revealed law was rooted in supernatural wisdom: its institutions were intrinsically better in his view. But he evidently did not assume revelation to be the only option. Humans could devise their own rules on the basis of common sense.

Similarly, philosophically inclined Iranians held their ancestors to have instituted kingship by deducing its necessity from the anti-social nature of human beings and enthroning Gayomard (the first, or almost first, man on earth): government here owes its existence to a social contract of the Hobbesian type, and the result is a virtuous polity based on philosophy.[44] If people would follow rational laws, they would not need prophets to bring them law, as Aristotle's father was supposed to have said.[45] We do not know whether Ibn al-Rāwandī, al-Sarakhsī, al-Rāzī and others who rejected prophethood considered the socio-political implications of their own views; but if they did, they must similarly have held that society could be based on human reason, or indeed that it *was* so based.

Nonetheless, the assumption that only a prophet could bring a law suitable for the organization of a society was rarely challenged in our period. People only saw the cases which confirmed it. Thus it was noted that several African peoples lacked both religion and socio-political organization, whereas the Nubians and the Abyssians had something in the nature of both, which fitted the theory in that they were Christians thanks to their former proximity to Byzantium.[46] It was not noted as a problem that India and China had complex societies of the most sophisticated kind, which did not fit the theory in that no

43. 'Manāqib al-turk' in his *Rasāʾil*, i, 80f.; tr. Walker, 692; cited in Pines, 'La loi naturelle et la société', 185n.

44. MM, ii, 106f (i, §531).

45. Pines, 'La loi naturalle et la société', 184n., citing ʿĀmirī, *Saʿāda*, 178.8.

46. Cf. Iṣṭakhrī, *Masālik*, 4, penult. (drawn to my attention by Adam Silverstein).

prophets had been sent to either them or their neighbours.[47] One has to go all the way to Ibn Taymiyya for a straightforward statement that polities did not have to be based on religion,[48] and all the way to Ibn Khaldūn for a refutation of the view that they did have to be thus based. Most people had acquired government without receiving either prophets or books, according to Ibn Khaldūn, which showed that laws suppressing selfish inclinations could be devised by reason and imposed by force. Such rational governance (*siyāsa ʿaqliyya*) could be either of the philosophical type which had been practised by the ancient Iranians (i.e. under Gayomard), but which was not otherwise encountered in history, or of the selfish type practised by all rulers nowadays whether they were Muslims or not. God had however made manmade law unnecessary for the Muslims by means of that which the Prophet had instituted and the caliphs had upheld, and this was preferable because a divine law served both this world and the next.[49] The type actually practised was simply a perversion. In short, Ibn Khaldūn agreed with al-Jāḥiẓ: revealed law was not indispensable, but it was certainly better.

Why does the law necessitate rulers?

Granted that human society owed its existence to the division of labour and that it had to be regulated by a revealed law, why did there have to be rulers? Could one not live by the law alone? One would have expected this to be a much debated question, given that the Muslims traced their spiritual ancestry to stateless Arabia. Ancient observers had commented on the political freedom of the northern Arabs, now in a negative and now in a positive vein; the Arabs had boasted about it in their poetry themselves; and the specialists in Arabian antiquities who collected their poetry along with their stories about tribal wars (*ayyām al-ʿarab*) were clearly impressed by it too: before the rise of Islam the northern Arabs (Muḍar, Nizār), and above all the Prophet's tribe Quraysh, had been *laqāḥ*, free people who did not obey any kings or pay any taxes, they tell us with pride.[50] But as seen already, neither the pre-Islamic Arabs nor the tribesmen who continued to inhabit the peninsula after the conquests were regarded as a model of inspiration or imitation for Muslims as far as political organization was concerned.[51] The scholars who did field work in the desert

47. Cf. the striking example of Sijistānī above, 13, note 20.

48. *Al-Ḥisba fī 'l-islām*, 4 = 20: people without divine books or religion obey their kings in matters they think will serve their worldly interests.

49. *Muqaddima*, 48, 212f., 241f. = i, 93, 389f., 448f.; cf. above, note 44, and ch. 1, 13f.

50. Cf. the attestations in *Wörterbuch*, s.v. '*laqāḥ*'.

51. Cf. above, 7, 68.

were philologists eager to record the language of the bedouin, assumed to be the purest version of Arabic, not utopianists seeking inspiration in tribal organization. Pious people without an interest in pre-Islamic lore assumed the pre-Islamic Arabs to have lived in a state of ignorant barbarism (*jāhiliyya*), fighting each other and generally exemplifying the anti-social side of human beings, except insofar as the Qurashī guardians of God's house had preserved some monotheism among them; and the later bedouin were effectively living in the Jāhiliyya too, as people who crossed paths with them knew all too well. For political models one looked to Medina, where the Prophet had worked.[52]

This is not to say, of course, that the tribal tradition contributed nothing to Islamic political thought. On the contrary, as seen already, it dominated the thinking of the first two centuries and is discernible behind most libertarian and communitarian thinking in classical Islam. But it owes its overriding importance to the facts that it was islamized in Medina and that the conquerors were tribesmen whose values went into the foundations of Islamic culture, not to a memory of tribal organization as a model of admiration and imitation in its own right. A fourteenth-century work does preserve an undatable argument in favour of doing without rulers in which the bedouin are invoked as an example, but this is very unusual.[53] Since the Muslims did not have a notion of an aboriginal state of freedom and innocence, they were not inclined to credit members of simple societies with the preservation of virtues they had lost, after the fashion of the Greeks, whose fascination with Scythians and other tribal peoples (Arabs included) did not reach them; and the many tribal peoples they encountered in the course of their conquests did not strike them as any better than their own. Ibn Khaldūn did admire the Turks for their preservation of the martial values once possessed by the Arabs, but the Turks in question were Muslims serving as soldiers in the Middle East, not tribesmen back in their pagan arcadia. The Persian tradition did say that the earth had been devoid of kings, whether Persian or other, every now and again from the death of Gayomard onwards, but it did not say so in an anarchist vein.[54] Had one asked how people coped in the periods without kings, the answer would probably have been *amruhum shūrā*, that is, that they settled their affairs by consultation, a Qur'ānic expression which came to stand for anarchy in the sense of chaotic conditions.[55]

In short, there was no question mark over the need for rulers in the Islamic tradition, the Khārijite and Muʿtazilite anarchists notwithstanding. The

52. Cf. below, 318f.
53. Ījī, *Mawāqif*, viii, 347.
54. Ḥamza, *Ta'rīkh*, 14f. (G, 10).
55. E.g. Ghazālī, *Faḍā'iḥ*, 106.ult.

normal answer to the question whether one could live without rulers was that one could not, and this seemed so obvious that many argued directly from the anti-social nature of humans to the need for rulers, without first explaining how social life generates a need for law. For those who wanted the full argument, however, the explanation was that bringing together the diverse natures and ambitions of humans in a single society created a need for rules, which in their turn created a need for somebody to uphold the rules. There had to be a ruler to apply the law, to judge, and to maintain order with the sword, which induced fear and deterred the wrongdoer, for people would not obey the law of their own accord: just as somebody had to teach them the law, so somebody had to reward and punish them for their obedience or disobedience to it, in this world as well as the next.[56]

One needed both religion and government for an orderly society, then: without religious injunctions to obey, the ruler's authority would be weak; and without a ruler to enforce the laws of the religion, people would abandon them; this was why Ardashīr said that religion and government were twins.[57] The ruler on his own was better placed to enforce the law than either religion or reason on their own because selfish desires tend to overwhelm moral intentions, al-Māwardī noted; "God restrains (people) more through the *sulṭān* than through the Qur'ān," as the Prophet had said.[58] Without a king, sultan, or imam, people became disorganized, power passed to whoever was in a position to take it, chaos prevailed, trust disappeared, and the community disintegrated, just as flocks perish without a shepherd.[59] "Civil strife results when there is no imam to take charge of people."[60] Moreover, political leadership was natural, as was clear from the subordination of the body to the soul, of women to men, of slaves to the free, and of children to adults, al-ʿĀmirī said, crediting his views to Aristotle.[61] Al-Jāḥiẓ also found it natural: even animals have leaders that they follow.[62] By contrast, the Ismaili Abū Yaʿqūb al-Sijistānī held political leadership to be unique to humans because he equated it with

56. E.g. Qudāma, *Kharāj*, 436; ʿĀmirī, *Saʿāda*, 179, 185.2, 186f., citing Plato, Aristotle, and Ps.-Aristotle's *Fī siyāsat al-mudun*, §3.1; Ghazālī, *Iqtiṣād*, 236f.; Shahrastānī, *Nihāya*, 490 = 155; Abrahamov, 'al-Ḳāsim ibn Ibrāhīm', 86.

57. *ʿAhd Ardashīr*, §4 (p. 53); cited in countless works, e.g. Qudāma, *Kharāj*, 436; Ibn Wahb, *Burhān*, 401.

58. Māwardī, *Adab al-dunyā*, 137.6. The saying (not always attributed to the Prophet) is also adduced in Ibn ʿAbd Rabbih, *ʿIqd*, i, 7.6; Qudāma, *Kharāj*, 440.13; Juwaynī, *Ghiyāth*, §19; Ghazālī, *Qisṭās*, 90.-5; Naysābūrī, *Imāma*, 86, and no doubt elsewhere.

59. Jāḥiẓ, 'al-Nisāʾ' in his *Rasāʾil*, iii, 149–51.

60. Ibn Ḥanbal in Abū Yaʿlā, *Aḥkām*, 19.

61. *Saʿāda*, 187f.

62. 'Al-Nisāʾ', 150; cf. Dio Chrysostom, 'Peri basileias' (third oration), §50.

religious leadership, which animals did not have: unlike humans, they were equal because they all had the same instinctive knowledge of the basic things that animals needed to know.[63]

How do we know rulers to be prescribed by the law?

All these rational considerations apart, one could of course settle the question by an appeal to authority: the law made it obligatory for Muslims to have an imam, as everyone except for the Najdiyya and the Muʿtazilite anarchists agreed. But appeals to authority merely took you back to reason, for how was the imamate known to be a legal duty?

Many Muʿtazilites said that it was known from reason (*ʿaql*), meaning from considerations of the kind just reviewed, or from both reason and supra-rational authority (*sharʿ*, *samʿ*, also translated 'revelation').[64] But according to the Traditionalists and the classical Sunnis, and many Muʿtazilites too, the obligation rested exclusively on supra-rational authority.[65] By this they did not usually mean that the obligation was grounded in the Qurʾān or Ḥadīth (though some found evidence for it there as well), but rather that it rested on *ijmāʿ*, the consensus of the community, starting with the agreement of the Companions to have the institution.[66] This may sound like a retreat from reason, and so it was, in the sense that there comes a point where particular ways of doing things can no longer be explained in terms of universal rationality: secularists will then shrug their shoulders and say that this is how we happen to do things, while believers will point to their books or sacred persons and say that this is how God happens to have instructed us. Revelation typically works to justify the particular, as Ismailis, philosophers, Sufis, and others who distinguished between organized religion and the universal truth above it all had occasion to note. Reason could demonstrate that humans needed government of some kind or another; it could not demonstrate that they needed it in the particular form of the imamate: it was only on the basis of supra-rational authority that the specific form of government enjoined on the Muslims was known to be

63. *Ithbāt*, 174; Abū Ḥātim, *Aʿlām*, 185. Cf. also below, 336f.

64. Cf. IAH, ii, 308, on Jāḥiẓ, the Baghdadis, and Abū 'l-Ḥusayn (reason); Madelung, *Qāsim*, 143; Ījī, *Mawāqif*, viii, 345 (reason and revelation).

65. Thus ʿAbd al-Jabbār, *Mughnī*, xx/1, 17ff., 41, and the Basrans in IAH, ii, 308. It is identified as the position of most Muʿtazilites in Rāzī, *Muḥaṣṣal*, 176.9 and *Arbaʿīn*, 426.

66. Cf. Juwaynī, *Ghiyāth*, §§17–18, and again §66 (in the context of election vs. designation), cf. Nagel, *Festung*, 298f.; Shahrastānī, *Nihāya*, 478ff. =150f. In Māwardī, *Aḥkām*, 4 (5) = 5, those who ground the obligation in revelation adduce Q. 4:59 and a quietist tradition.

indispensable for human welfare, as Ibn Khaldūn said, summarizing earlier arguments.[67]

On these arguments, humans could see government to be in their interest, but God could see further and added instructions that they could not have worked out on their own. This line of reasoning rested on the assumption that there was a basic congruence between human needs and the ultimate nature of reality. The Greek philosophers, firm believers in that congruence, had called it providence. But what basis could there possibly be for such wishful thinking? On purely rational grounds we might well infer that God wished to destroy His creatures, as al-Juwaynī said; there was no way in which we could second-guess His views. Since He allowed the world to be without prophets at times, it would have been reasonable to infer that He also permitted people to go without imams at times, but He did not. All this went to show that it was only on the basis of revelation that we knew the imamate to form part of God's law.[68] In Abū Yaʿlā's formulation it *had* to be on the basis of revelation that one knew it, for one could not know whether anything was obligatory, indifferent, permitted, or forbidden on the basis of reason at all.[69]

Al-Juwaynī's outlook was in line with the worldview of ancient Mesopotamia, which confronted the moral arbitrariness of the universe with extraordinary openness.[70] But this was much too austere for the Rāfiḍīs. The Imamis accepted the providential nature of ultimate reality and claimed the imamate to be indispensable in terms of reason and revelation alike. This was also the Ismaili position, except that they put it in even more extravagant terms: the imamate was obligatory by nature, reason, considerations of governance (*siyāsa*), revelation and custom, in every religion and community.[71]

Why must government be monarchic?

Granted that we must have rulers, why could there only be one ruler at a time? Could one not have several, be it in the form of joint rulers forming a council,

67. Ibn Khaldūn, *Muqaddima*, 212 = i, 389f.; cf. above, note 49; Māwardī, *Adab al-dunyā*, 138 and *Aḥkām*, 3f./5 = 3, where reason does not even demonstrate the need for government, only for fairness and justice in mutual dealings.

68. Juwaynī, *Ghiyāth*, §§20–5; cf. Nagel, *Festung*, 297.

69. *Aḥkām*, 19. Cf. Reinhart, *Before Revelation*, 24 (where the same position is reported for his *Muʿtamad*), 33ff., on his ambivalent *ʿUdda*.

70. Cf. Beaulieu, 'Theodicy, Theology, Philosophy: Mesopotamia'. It was not only in Juwaynī that it lived on; cf. Cook on the bleak conception of the relationship between man and God in Islam (*Muhammad*, 83).

71. Naysāburī, *Imāma*, 28f.

or semi-autonomous rulers forming a federation, or even wholly independent rulers dividing the Islamic world between them? Some Muʿtazilites considered the first two options and endorsed them, as has been seen.[72] But the vast majority of scholars rejected all three options without much attempt to distinguish between them. There was nothing wrong with the idea of several rulers from a rational point of view, ʿAbd al-Jabbār said, but authoritative instruction (*samʿ*) was against it.[73] Some adduced the Qurʾānic statement that heaven and earth would go to ruin if there were several deities (21:22): it stood to reason that a plurality of human rulers would have a similarly dire effect.[74] Others marshaled Ḥadīth: the Prophet was on record as having said, "when allegiance is given to two commanders, kill the second";[75] and when the Prophet died, the Companions rejected the Anṣār's proposal that they and the Muhājirūn should have a leader each.[76] "Two amirs: the people have perished!" as Ibn ʿAbbās reputedly exclaimed on hearing of the appointment of two leaders by the rebellious Medinese in 63/682f.[77] One leader would be able to disobey the other;[78] there would be rivalry and strife between them, even having several viziers was dangerous: too many cooks spoil the broth or, as the Arabic version of the proverb went, too many sailors caused the ship to sink.[79] For all that, there were some who disagreed.

Several imams

Al-Aṣamm's idea of a federation was never fielded again, but a plurality of caliphs, each fully autonomous in his own sphere, was occasionally deemed acceptable. In 929 the amir of al-Andalus, ʿAbd al-Raḥmān III, declared himself to the caliph. Absurd though it must have sounded to most Muslims in the east, many Ashʿarites were ready to accept him as such, presumably as an antidote to the Fatimids, who also claimed the caliphate. They proposed that there could be several imams if their domains were separated by a barrier obstructing

72. Cf. above, 68.
73. ʿAbd al-Jabbār, *Mughnī*, xx/1, 243.
74. Thus Qudāma, *Kharāj*, 437; also cited in Abū 'l-Fawāris, *Imāma*, ch. 8.
75. Ibn Ḥazm, *Faṣl*, iv, 88.12; cf. Kāshif, *Siyar*, ii, 266.
76. Adduced in Jāḥiẓ, 'Jawābāt', in his *Rasāʾil*, iv, 290f.; ʿAbd al-Jabbār, *Mughnī*, xx/1, 244.
77. Khalīfa, *Taʾrīkh*, 290.5.
78. ʿAbd al-Jabbār, *Mughnī*, xx/1, 244.8.
79. Jāḥiẓ, 'Jawābāt', 204f.; 'Nisāʾ', iii, 149, 151 (nos. 10, 11); Ps.-Thaʿālibī, *Tuḥfat al-wuzarāʾ*, 53.

cooperation between them, such as for example the sea.[80] If there could be two prophets in the same community, as there was in the time of Moses and Aaron, or even three, as hinted in Q. 36:14, a fortiori there could be two or more imams, they said.[81] This view unsurprisingly proved popular with Spanish and Maghribī scholars,[82] though the Spanish Ibn Ḥazm affirmed the classical position,[83] and it gained sufficient currency for the Fatimid missionary Abū 'l-Fawāris (d. 411/1021) to find it necessary to explain why it was not allowed to have two or more imams when distances required it.[84] Most Sunnis rejected it, too.[85] Of those who accepted it, some were outraged when the Karrāmiyya accepted ʿAlī and Muʿāwiya as equally legitimate imams in their separate domains. ʿAlī had been imam in accordance with the *sunna* and Muʿāwiya imam in violation of it (*ʿalā khilāf al-sunna*), the Karrāmiyya said, and the followers of each had been obliged to obey. Al-Baghdādī marvels at an alleged duty to obey *fī khilāf al-sunna*, though the Sunnis operated with just such a duty themselves: even al-Maʾmūn had to be obeyed, as Ibn Ḥanbal had said. But al-Maʾmūn had just been a quasi-caliph whereas ʿAlī was a real imam, someone whose acts embodied God's law so that everyone had to follow him.[86] There could perhaps be two quasi-caliphs at the same time, but real caliphs could not coexist, be it with each other or with quasi-caliphs.[87]

A plurality of kings and sultans was a different matter. This was what the Muslims had come to have in actual fact, but it was the leadership of the religious community, the church, that preoccupied them. The issue was whether more than one leader of this community (more than one pope, in the terminology of medieval Europe) could be acknowledged under exceptional circumstances in which some believers were isolated from the rest – the question

80. Baghdādī, *Uṣūl*, 274 and *Farq*, 341; Ashʿarī and Isfarāʾinī in Juwaynī, *Ghiyāth*, §257; Juwaynī himself favoured this view in his *Irshād*, 425, but not in his *Ghiyāth*, 258ff. (summarized in Hallaq, 'Caliphs, Jurists and the Saljūqs,' 35).

81. Simnānī, *Rawḍa*, i, §§56f. (Isfarāʾinī and some Shāfiʿites); for Juwaynī's view that one cannot argue from prophets to imams, see above, note 68.

82. Ibn Khaldūn, *Muqaddima*, ed. Quatremère, i, 348 = i, 393. The section is missing in the Beirut edition.

83. *Muḥallā*, ix, 360 (§1771).

84. Abū 'l-Fawāris, *Imāma*, ch. 8. His reply was "one God, one imam".

85. Cf. Sanhoury, *Califat*, 120ff.; cf. also Bāqillānī, *Tamhīd*, 180; ʿAbd al-Jabbār, *Mughnī*, xx/1, 244f.; Simnānī, *Rawḍa*, i, 58, and the discussion in Māwardī, *Adab al-dunyā*, 138f.

86. For this distinction, see above, 139.

87. Baghdādī, *Uṣūl*, 274f.; Shahrastānī, *Milal*, 85; Ibn Ḥazm, *Faṣl*, iv, 88, where the same view is said to been held by Abū 'l-Ṣabbāḥ al-Samarqandī (on whom, see van Ess, *TG*, ii, 562f.). For Ibn Ḥanbal, see above, 137.

to which the Zaydīs and Ibāḍīs had already given a positive answer, and which some Sunnis now answered in the affirmative too.[88] The fact that secular rulers had divided the Muslim world between them was also problematic, as has been seen, but it did not affect the religious unity of believers as long as the upstart rulers were willing to cast themselves as servants of the caliph. There was no question of recognizing them as ultimate rulers of the believers' souls. One could perhaps elevate one of them to the position of caliph, along the lines suggested by al-Juwaynī. One could also think away the caliph altogether. This would leave a plurality of de facto sovereigns in the political sense, but they still would not be sovereigns of the particular fragment of the religious community that happened to be in their charge. The religious community would simply be acephalous. Perceptions changed when the caliph disappeared in actual fact, but the secular kingdoms (*regna* in the terminology of medieval Europe) never succeeded in breaking up the religious community so as to turn each kingdom into a sovereign church of its own.

Conciliar government

So much for independent rulers. The conciliar model also found occasional adherents after al-Aṣamm. Thus al-Fārābī acknowledged that it was difficult to find a man endowed with all the characteristics desired in a virtuous ruler. If two men possessed the characteristics between them, they should rule together; and if the characteristics were dispersed in many men, then they should jointly form the government. He took that to be what the Greeks had meant by 'aristocracy' (*riyāsat al-akhyār*), as has been seen.[89] ʿAbd al-Jabbār may be arguing against this proposal when he says that the Companions had insisted on a single imam even though they knew that every candidate lacked qualities present in others: for example, Abū Bakr was strong in religion, but not physically, whereas it was the other way round with ʿUmar.[90] Al-ʿĀmirī also argued against the conciliar idea, on the grounds that one or the other had to be the superior if the arrangement were to work.[91] But it was accepted by Ibn Sīnā and Ibn Rushd, who agreed with al-Fārābī that the common aim would cause the rulers to function as a single soul.[92] The Brethren of Purity similarly held that when

88. Cf. above, 61f., 106.

89. Fārābī, *Fuṣūl*, §54/58 (reproduced in Naṣīr al-Dīn Ṭūsī, *Ethics*, 216, and in Ibn Rushd, *Commentary*, 80 = 208) and *MF*, ch. 15, §§12–14 (pp. 247ff.); above, 179f.

90. ʿAbd al-Jabbār, *Mughnī*, xx/1, 243.14.

91. *Saʿāda*, 194f.; cf. Arberry, 'Arabic Treatise on Politics', 15f.

92. Ibn Sīnā, *Rīṭūrīqā*, 41 and *SM, viii*, 62f. (*siyāsat al-akhyār*); Ibn Rushd, *Metafísica*, §39 (*madīnat al-akhyār*).

the forty-six qualities required in a prophet were dispersed in the community rather than united in a single *khalīfa*, the members of the community could cooperate to preserve and implement the law;[93] but they were talking about the distribution of intellectual and moral perfection rather than power: the aristocratic regime (*dawlat ahl al-khayr*) that such a group of people represented was their own brotherhood.[94] There is a stronger sense of concern with real power in Ibn Sīnā's discussion of aristocracy, and even more so in Ibn Rushd's, but it was still highly theoretical, and none of their suggestions had any political effect. The Qarāmiṭa did set up government by a family council in eleventh-century Baḥrayn, but their institution was rooted in the local tradition rather than in the views of the philosophers.[95] The local notables who jointly ruled Seville in the 1020s and Cordoba in the 1030s seem to have done so by default, and they were soon replaced by monarchs.[96]

Why must the ruler have absolute power?

Most medieval Islamic political thought proceeded from the assumption that power could only be delegated, not shared. This was so whether the ruler was seen as designated by God or elected by humans, by however great or small an electorate. He received it in full or lost it in full, even according to the Ibāḍīs. There was no halfway house. Presumably, this conviction reflected the fact that political power was fragile, all the surface grandeur notwithstanding: government had to be absolutist merely to survive. At all events, the view was deeply entrenched. Obviously, the ruler had to delegate most of his power to others, and he was strongly encouraged to consult, both in order to obtain expert views and to learn about the wishes of his subjects (in the sense of the elite). It was well known that it was difficult for him to ascertain their needs, especially in distant provinces.[97] The early ʿAbbāsid caliphs had surrounded themselves

93. *RIS*, iv, 125 (tr. in Netton, *Muslim Neoplatonists*, 102).

94. Ibid., iv, 125 (tr. in Netton, *Muslim Neoplatonists*, 102); cf. iv, 187.-4.

95. Cf. Nāṣir-i Khusraw, *Travels*, 87. Following Lewis, the translator takes the kinship of the six brothers to have been metaphorical, but it seems more likely that the number is symbolic (seven with the absent Mahdi). Two Julandā brothers were joint rulers of Oman in the time of the Prophet (Tab., i, 1686; Ibn Ḥazm, *Jamhara*, 384.14; Ibn Saʿd, i/2, 18 [B, i, 262], where one is singled out as the king); and two Julandā brothers are also said to have ruled Oman when al-Ḥajjāj sent an expedition to subdue it (Sālimī, *Tuḥfa*, i, 74; cf. Hamidullah, 'Règne conjoint', 101f., which aims to prove that it is lawful).

96. Stern, 'Islamic City', 33ff.; Wasserstein, *Party-Kings*, 139; Fierro, 'The *Qāḍī* as Ruler', 79, 106.

97. See, for example, the stress on equal favours to the near and the remote in Yazīd III's accession speech (Tab., ii, 1835.6), Ibn Abī Duʾād's insistence that distant subjects had the

with formally appointed companions who served as spokesmen of his subjects (*alsinat raʿiyyatihi*), according to Ibn al-Muqaffaʿ,[98] and it was perhaps in an effort to secure better representation of local interests at the centre that some scholars argued that all potential electors in all provinces ought to participate in the election of the caliph.[99] But once elected, the caliph was free to ignore all the advice he received. The consensus was that he could not be made answerable to anyone apart from God.

God was assumed not to call the ruler to account until the Day of Judgement, or at least not until he was dead, but why should He wait so long? If He could be represented in the here and now by a ruler who executed the law, He could also be represented by monitors who would call the ruler to account for his performance. The modern argument (used by conservative Muslims against democracy) that Muslims are ruled by God, not by the people, was alien to medieval Muslims because it rests on a tacit assumption that God can only display His will through the state – an abhorrent idea to the religious scholars, who had gone out of their way to disprove it. As they saw it, Muslims were not ruled by God as opposed to the people, but rather by God in the sense of the people, or more precisely in that of the community. The ruler represented both God and the community because they were two sides of the same coin; and it was precisely because the imam was the "representative and agent of the community" (*wakīl li'l-umma wa-nā'ib ʿanhā*) or "the agent of the Muslims" (*nā'ib ʿan al-muslimīn*) that he had to be deposed when he was guilty of wrongdoing, according to those who held that an oppressive ruler must be removed.[100] It was the scholars who formulated the law that the imam was meant to execute; by their own account, it was also they who elected and deposed him on behalf of the community. One would have thought that there was only a short step from all this to the view that the scholars should also monitor his performance, for example by forming independent councils authorized to signal when the rules had been breached, to strike out illegal decisions, and to block their execution.

Small though the step may seem, however, there were few who took it. In Khurāsān on the eve of the ʿAbbāsid revolution a rebel by the name of al-Ḥārith b. Surayj forced the Umayyad governor to set up a commission charged with

same claim to al-Muʿtaṣim's attention as those close by (Tab., iii, 1326), and al-Aṣamm's explanation of the need for several imams (Crone, 'Ninth-Century Muslim Anarchists', 18).

98. Ibn al-Muqaffaʿ, *Ṣaḥāba*, 213 (P, §44); cf. Zaman, *Emergence*, 83n., showing that the institution survived at least until al-Muʿtaṣim.

99. Cf. above, 228.

100. Bāqillānī, *Tamhīd*, 184.-5; Simnānī, *Rawḍa*, i, §517. On the equation of God and the community, see further below, 393f.

the task of nominating sub-governors and drawing up the rules and norms (*siyar*, *sunan*) they were to follow. Some of the members were scholars, the others are unknown. Al-Ḥārith's aim was to reduce the governor's control of local appointments and procedures rather than to monitor his performance, but the key point is that he tried to place institutional limits on the governor's power. Whether the commission actually got to work is unclear, and the idea did not survive the ʿAbbāsid revolution.[101] Some forty years later, as we have seen, a participant in the election of the Ibāḍī imam ʿAbd al-Wahhāb (c. 164/780) in North Africa would only endorse ʿAbd al-Wahhāb's election on condition that the latter "would not take any decision except in the presence of a specified group (*dūna jamāʿa maʿlūma*)": ʿAbd al-Wahhāb would have to rule in concert with a council. This proposal struck the other members of the electoral committee as monstrous, and their negative view was endorsed by the Ibāḍī leadership in Basra: the election of ʿAbd al-Wahhāb was valid and the condition was void.[102] Al-Aṣamm considered replacing the ruler altogether with a council of scholars, as has been seen.[103] Who would have monitored them? Maybe he thought that there was safety in numbers. In any case, after him there is silence for a long time. Neither the Sunnis nor the philosophers who accepted the possibility of a plurality of rulers were motivated by dislike of absolutism, and though the merits of consultation continued to be praised, the idea of imposing control on the ruler seems to have been abandoned.

It was briefly resumed in Almoravid Andalus, however, when a certain Ibn ʿAbdūn, writing around 500/1100, proposed that the judge should supervise a number of government functions, including tax-collection and the vizier's administration. He also expected the judge to serve on a consultative body along with other jurists and worthy men with whom the ruler (*al-raʾīs*) would meet on a regular basis, and he required the judge to consult with other jurists in the performance of his own juridical functions too. His primary concern seems to have been with the local government of his own Sevilla. Like al-Ḥārith b. Surayj, he was interested in practical reform of the world on the ground, not in grand moral visions, and his ideas were remarkably concrete; they were presumably meant for replication in other cities, including the capital. But whatever notice the Almoravids may have taken of them, he was also like al-Ḥārith b. Surayj in that his ideas were swept away along with the political landscape he wanted to reform by a revolution, in his case the Almohad conquest.[104]

101. Crone and Hinds, *God's Caliph*, 108; Crone, 'Shūra as an Elective Institution', 24–6.

102. Above, 59f.

103. Above, 68.

104. Ibn ʿAbdūn, 'Risāla', 4.ult., 7, 9, 14f. = 7, 13, 18, 29ff.; Fierro, 'The Qāḍī as Ruler', 109f. (and cf. Marín, '*Šūrā* et *ahl al-Šūrā* dans al-Andalus').

No libertarian Greek heritage

In this connection it may be noted that the Muslims did not inherit a republican or democratic tradition from the Greeks. How much difference it would have made if they had is difficult to say, but in any case, Plato was an authoritarian thinker, and what the Muslims knew of Aristotle's political views seemed to go the same way. They inferred that the virtuous polity could have either a single ruler (*malik, imām, ra'īs*) or several (the *akhyār, afāḍil*), the former being kingship and the latter aristocracy; either way the power of virtue was absolute. The Muslims did not know that the Greeks had lived in cities in which sovereignty was vested in popular or aristocratic assemblies rather than in kings, or that the Romans had begun by expelling their kings to be ruled by such assemblies down to the time of Augustus. Their Greek history reduced to Alexander the Great and his immediate successors, and their Roman history began with Augustus (because Jesus was born under him). Of Alexander they had interesting things to say: he was the greatest king on earth, indeed a prophet, who eventually renounced power altogether;[105] or alternatively, he was a mere hooligan who conquered for the sake of it, without bothering to devise any proper administration of his domains, in order to satisfy his own ambition rather than the demands of truth (unlike the Prophet).[106] Augustus, by contrast, was just a name to them. But whatever their views on these pivotal figures, they missed out on the republican city states which had preceded them. The word *polis*, arabized as *madīna*, they took to mean a politically organized society of any kind, or just a society, or even just a city in the normal sense of the word, not a self-governing city state. Had they known the concept, they might have applied it to pre-Islamic Mecca (as modern historians sometimes do), though it was actually stateless. Given that Muḥammad rejected Mecca for a theocracy in Medina, it would not necessarily have endeared the notion to them, but in any case the concept did not reach them.

They did learn about democracy, but they knew it as a regime of imperfection, since this was how Plato and Aristotle described it, and also how the Neoplatonists saw it.[107] In fact, of the three forms of constitution the worst

105. Cf. Bürgel, 'Krieg und Frieden im Alexanderepos Nizamis'.

106. Bayhaqī (finding the Ghaznavids superior) in Meisami, *Historiography*, 83f., cf. Abū Ḥātim al-Razī, *Aʿlām*, 89, where the ephemeral nature of Alexander's achievement is contrasted with the Prophet's.

107. Proclus, *Alcibiades*, 255; Iamblichus in O'Meara, 'Aspects', 71.

was democracy (*riyāsat al-ʿawāmm*), Aristotle says in the Arabic translation of his *Nichomachean Ethics*, though this is not what he says in the original.[108] The democratic city (*al-madīna al-jamāʿiyya*) was one in which "the aim of its people is to be free (*aḥrāran*), each one of them doing what he wishes without restraining his passions in the least", al-Fārābī observed, characteristically equating freedom with licentiousness rather than participation in political decision-making.[109] Nobody was subjected to any restraint, but rather each did whatever he wanted, within the limits of the law, Ibn Rushd observed.[110] It was a constitution under which people were equal: in the *siyāsat al-ḥurriyya* the chief would be slapped for every slap he gave. Nobody had any merit over anyone else, so that the virtuous and the vile had the same rights in respect of offices, honours, and punishments, and power was obtained by chance rather than by virtue. The leadership in *al-dīmūqrāṭiyya* went to whomever they happened to agree on.[111] It was an absurd idea to philosophers convinced that the distribution of political power ought to reflect gradations of virtue. On top of that, democracy was a regime without a common purpose, as Ibn Rushd observed; it allowed every household to pursue whatever it regarded as its highest goal, typically (then as now) material goods: on this ground he deemed most cities of his own time to be democratic.[112] As has been seen, this absence of a common purpose was its greatest demerit in Ibn Rushd's opinion, for the beauty of the ideal city lay precisely in its tight coordination of everyone for the pursuit of a single aim, ultimate happiness (as in the communist regimes of the twentieth century). But it was also where the escape from democracy lay, for the freedom with which everyone was left to pursue their own ideas meant that adherents of every conceivable regime could be found it democratic cities, including virtuous people. As Ibn Rushd saw it, they might eventually succeed in replacing democracy with a Virtuous City of the tightly coordinated kind.[113] Freedom always includes the option of putting an end to freedom (as we

108. *Akhlāq*, 293.ult.f. (translated in Rosenthal, *Classical Heritage*, 112), corresponding to 1160a of the original, where the worst of the three is timocracy. It seems to be a mere slip on the part of the translator.

109. Fārābī, *MF*, ch. 15, §17 (p. 256) and *SM*, 99 = 50; cf. Najjar, 'Democracy in Islamic Political Thought'.

110. Ibn Rushd, *Commentary*, 83f. = 212f.

111. Fārābī, SM, 99 = 50; Ibn Sīnā, *Rīṭūrīqā*, 37; Ibn Rushd, *Khaṭāba*, 136; ed. Aouad, 1, 8, 1; 1, 8, 3 (*ad* Aristotle, *Rhetoric*, 1365b; *Arabic Version*, i, 40.24, where it is described as a regime in which public offices were distributed by lot).

112. Above, 190.

113. Ibn Rushd, *Commentary*, 83 = 212f.; cf. Fārābī, *SM*, 100f. = 51 (where no transformation seems to be envisaged).

might say, though they never put it that way). The Virtuous Polity was both authoritarian and totalitarian.

The Sharīʿa as a constitution

The perfect polity of the scholars was a good deal more liberal than that of the philosophers in that the scholars regarded all rulers as subject to the law rather than sources of it. "Islamic government is neither tyrannical nor absolute, but constitutional . . . in the sense that rulers are subject to a certain set of conditions in governing and administering the country," as Khomeini put this point.[114] But he was a revolutionary. Pedantic scholars have to observe that although one could well characterize the Sharīʿa as a constitution, it does not follow that government based on it was constitutional.

The Sharīʿa was, or rather included, a constitution in the broadest sense of the word: a set of rules that allocated functions, powers, and duties among the various agencies and offices of government and defined the relationship between them and the public.[115] Al-Māwardī's *aḥkām sulṭāniyya* is a collection of such rules. But a constitution in this sense of the word is simply a frame of government or political order: a set of rules which organize, but do not restrain, the exercise of power. In order for the rules to yield constitutional government they have to include restraints, normally identified as a bill of rights and institutional devices for securing their observance.[116] The Sharīʿa does not include a bill of rights, let alone of rights perceived as common to all mankind, but it could still be said to guarantee personal freedoms for Muslims and people under their protection, and to seek to restrain arbitrary power.

Of course, words such as 'rights' and 'freedoms' are Western, but medieval Muslims certainly had a concept of both. They tended to view human relations in terms of duties, however, and they did not think that membership of the human species conferred any rights or duties in itself. Rather, rights and duties were conferred by God on His servants. It followed that there was no concept of human rights in the modern sense. Infidels had no legal existence except insofar as they were protected by Islamic law, as *dhimmī*s or *mustaʾmin*s (roughly permanent and temporary residents).[117] When the jurists spoke of human rights (*ḥuqūq al-ādamiyyīn/al-ʿibād*), they meant the claims that individuals had on each other, not rights vested in human beings by virtue of their human nature. The opposite of human rights were God's rights (*ḥuqūq*

114. E.g. Khomeini, *Islam and Revolution*, 55.
115. Cf. Finer, 'Notes Towards a History of Constitutions', 17.
116. Sartori, 'Constitutionalism', 856f.
117. Cf. below, 358.

allāh), meaning the claims that the Muslim community as represented by the ruler had on them. The distinction is close to that between civil and public (including criminal) law today. For example, certain penalties were owed to humans, meaning that they were carried out only if the aggrieved party demanded it.[118] The offenses were seen as private. Other penalties were duties owed to God, meaning that they had to be carried out whether anybody demanded it or not (thus the so-called *ḥudūd*). They were crimes against God, or in other words the Muslim community, not against individual Muslims. Penalties apart, God's claims included the canonical taxes, holy war, ritual worship such as prayer and fasting, and other things, such as the duty of giving advice to the ruler (or so at least according to an Ibāḍī scholar). There were also institutions which involved duties to humans and God alike.[119]

It was under the heading of 'human claims' that the lives, property, personal freedom, family relations, and commercial transactions of Muslims and *dhimmī*s were protected. One might call them 'civil rights' if this did not imply a consciousness of rights against the state which is not present in the sources. One could certainly call them 'civil claims'. The jurists discuss them from the point of view of dealings between private people, not between private people and the state, and no special attention is paid to them in works on constitutional law such as al-Māwardī's. For all that, the law was perfectly clear that the lives, property and internal relations of the subjects were sacrosanct as long as they observed the law themselves. The jurists paid less attention to public law, but they did cover subjects such as taxation, the conduct of holy war, the suppression of rebels, the punishment of criminals, and the appointment of judges. It certainly cannot be claimed that they gave no guidance on matters of government.[120] The law left much to the discretion of rulers, but its letter was often detailed and its spirit was unmistakably protective of the believers. It is for this reason that one can call the Sharīʿa a constitution in the fuller sense of the word. Nobody could, or did, have any doubt that most of what rulers did was illegal.

But the constitution was not enforceable. Allied with scholars, the ruler could compel his subjects to live by the law in respect of ritual worship, family relations, commerce, and inheritance (insofar as compulsion was needed). But whether they were allied with scholars or not, the subjects could not com-

118. Thus Māwardī, *Ahkām*, 390/229 = 249, on *qadhf* (one of the *ḥudūd* that were human rather than divine claims in his view).

119. Milliot, *Introduction à l'étude de droit musulman*, §196; Johansen, 'Eigentum, Familie und Obrigkeit', 386f., 409ff. and 'Sacred and Religious Elements in Hanafite Law', 289f, 299ff; Muḥammad b. Maḥbūb in Kāshif, *Siyar*, ii, 249.13.

120. *Pace* Finer, 'Notes towards a History of Constitutions', 18.

pel their ruler to observe the law in the exercise of government. The ruler had agents backed by force among his subjects, the subjects did not normally have any among the wielders of political power. There is a remarkable exception in eleventh-century Samarqand. In 488/1095 the inhabitants of this city, "both officers and subjects", agreed to kill Aḥmad Khān, a local dynast who ruled as a subordinate of the Seljuqs. They suspected him of heresy, seized him, and put him on trial in a court of jurists and judges, who condemned him to death on charges of Ismailism and apostasy; or, according to another version, the jurists and judges first met with leaders of the army and issued a *fatwā* declaring it licit (or obligatory) for anyone to kill Aḥmad, and next, when he was caught, put him on trial and condemned him to death again.[121]

The key to the subjects' power here is clearly their alliance with the leaders of the army. The result was a noteworthy attempt to handle power by lawful procedures. Military commanders did not usually stage trials or solicit *fatwā*s before killing a ruler; nor, for that matter, did rulers normally bother to stage trials in order to jail, kill, or seize the property of their commanders or civilian subjects. There is a famous exception in the caliph al-Muʿtaṣim (833–42), who found it prudent to have his powerful general, the Afshīn, convicted of apostasy before having him killed.[122] The generals in Samarqand now found it necessary similarly to dispose of Aḥmad Khān by lawful means (perhaps because he had an overlord who might have punished them). We do not know whether the charges they brought against him were seriously meant, let alone true, or merely a pretext, though the latter seems more likely: Aḥmad Khān was oppressive (*qabīḥ al-sīra*) and extortionate, and it was the second time that the Samarqandīs tried to rid themselves of him. The first time they wrote to the Seljuq sultan Malikshāh, inviting him to take control of Samarqand, which he duly did, but he reinstated Aḥmad Khān some years later, and this was when they brought charges against him; Aḥmad Khān flatly denied them.

But though the trial is unlikely to have been fair, it does give us a glimpse of what one might call constitutional government. It is typical, however, that the charges were of apostasy, not of illegal appropriation of other people's goods. No medieval Muslim ruler, or for that matter governor or general, is on record as having gone to trial for having killed, tortured, jailed, or robbed innocent Muslims, though a fair number of Sunni jurists held that the imam should be deposed for such crimes, as has been seen.[123] Violations of this kind were apparently too commonplace; many jurists denied that the ruler could be

121. Ibn al-Athīr, *Kāmil*, x, 243f. (year 488), cf. 171ff. (year 482) for the pre-history; Narshakhī, *Bukhārā*, 236f.; Barthold, *Turkestan*, 339.

122. Cf. *EI*², s.v. 'Afshīn'.

123. Above, 228ff.

deposed for them; to secure the removal of extremely powerful people only the ultimate charge would do: loss of status as a Muslim. Remarkable though it is in retrospect, moreover, the episode did not attract much attention at the time. Only two historians report it, one dispassionately and the other outraged by the Samarqandīs' behaviour: how strange that people of Sunna and Jamāʿa who hold Q.4:59 ("Obey the messenger and those in authority among you") to refer to kings should nonetheless rebel against kings, as the latter exclaims.[124]

Aḥmad Khān had clearly managed to alienate most members of the elite, including his own army. Elsewhere, too, it happened that people agreed to remove a ruler by inviting another to take over. But most rulers managed to retain sufficient support to go on oppressing the powerless. When such rulers violated what we would call the civil rights of its subjects, all the subjects could do was to turn to the state itself, petitioning the ruler for justice in the special court for the redress of grievances (*radd al-maẓālim*). It was a poor substitute for the independent councils with which al-Ḥārith and the North African Ibāḍī had wanted to restrain government. Al-Māwardī tells an edifying story in which a woman in rags accuses the caliph's own son of usurping her land and wins the case.[125] This was how things ought to be; between them, the divine authority of the law and the personal virtue of the ruler would ensure that justice won out even when this flew in the face of the immediate interests of the ruler. One could not call this constitutional government even if virtue did occasionally win out, or always, as it is said to have done under the Rightly Guided Caliphs or ʿUmar II. Rather, it was government by appeal to the ruler's conscience. With no authoritative devices for signaling breach of the rules, and no official mechanisms for the imposition of sanctions either, attempts to enforce the rules inevitably led to mutual recriminations and civil war.[126] It was precisely because sustained attempts to enforce the rules always led to civil war that most people eventually decided to live with such government as they had.

Political illusion tricks

Once it was accepted that government had to be absolutist, and indeed that rulers needed more power than they actually had, there was some interest in how they went about creating the illusion of possessing it. Humans are competitive because they are similar, al-Bīrūnī observed; all descend from the same ancestors and have much the same size and shape, so there is no obvious rea-

124. Narshakhī, *Bukhārā*, 237. For the verse and its interpretation, see above, 138, 155f.
125. *Aḥkām*, 144/85 = 95,
126. Cf. Finer, 'Notes Towards a History of Constitutions', 18f.

son why any one of them should lord it over others; everybody thinks he has a better right to wealth and power than everyone else. The difference between one man and another "is not so considerable as that one man can thereupon claim to himself any benefit to which another may not pretend as well as he", as Hobbes was to put it six centuries later in unwitting agreement with al-Bīrūnī.[127] The trick, then, was to make one person seem quite unlike the rest. For a start, one could declare rulership to be the monopoly of a single tribe, al-Bīrūnī observed, or of a particular individual within it, with reference to some celestial genealogy or divine designation after the fashion of the Sāsānids with their Kisrās, the Muslims with their limitation of the imamate to Quraysh, the Tibetans with their belief that their *khāqān* descended from the sun, and the Turks with their myth about their king emerging from a cave. Next there were ways of magnifying the physical presence of the ruler: tall palaces, spacious courts, raised seats, thrones, crowns, other headgear, arm-extensions, and more, all symbolizing elevated ambition and extended power. It was also important to think of adornments conveying an impression of great wealth, and so beautiful as to sway the hearts of the beholders. For the rest, the ruler had to seem to know more than anyone else about what was going on, be it locally or far away, among the elite or among the masses, for which purpose he needed to devise clever means of communication.[128] Abū Yaʿqūb al-Sijistānī had a strong sense that coins and public prayers served to disseminate awareness of the ruler's power, though it was only the association of the ruler's name with the Prophet's on and in them that he singled out as significant.[129] Ibn Sīnā laid down that the lawgiver prophet must magnify the position of his successor by prescribing acts of worship that can only be performed in his presence, adding that the legislator must also see to it that the ruler is involved (via the judge) in fundamental social acts such as marriage.[130] Here as elsewhere, the philosophers were sophisticated sociologists of religion.

127. *Leviathan*, ch. 13, 1.

128. Bīrūnī, *Jawāhir*, 24ff. = 26ff. For another sociological explanation of the limitation of the imamate to Quraysh, see Ibn Khaldūn, *Muqaddima*, 115ff. = i, 399ff.

129. *Ithbāt*, 174.

130. Ibn Sīnā, *SI*, *x*, 452 = 108.

CHAPTER

18

THE FUNCTIONS OF GOVERNMENT

What services did medieval Muslims expect from the state? Religious scholars often answer the question in the form of lists of the ruler's *sharʿī* functions (i.e. those required by the Sharʿīa), along the lines of "the Muslims must have an imam to execute their laws, apply their *ḥudūd*, despatch their armies, marry off their (female) orphans and distribute the booty (*fayʾ*) among them".[1] But such lists are too concise to be meaningful to a modern reader, and they do not mention any non-*sharʿī* functions, nor do they say what would happen to the *sharʿī* functions if the imam disappeared. What follows is an attempt at a fuller answer.

SHARʿĪ DUTIES

Validation of the community

A modern Westerner would answer the question of what government is for by starting with internal order and external defence, but medieval Muslim scholars never did, for government to them was first and foremost about the

1. Baghdādī, *Uṣūl*, 271. Or "there must be an imam to execute their laws, apply their *ḥudūd*, protect and guard their territory, despatch their armies, distribute their booty and alms, deal with their disputes and their marriages, supervise their communal prayers and feasts, do justice to the oppressed and exact vengeance from the oppressor, set up judges and governors in every area, and send Qurʾān-readers and missionaries to every area" (Shahrastānī, *Nihāya*, 478 = 151).

maintenance of a moral order, a law. It is with the moral order that we shall have to start as well, then.

The early Muslim community was constituted by allegiance to its imam (originally the Prophet, thereafter the caliphs). Without this leader, there was no saving vehicle in which to travel along the legal highways revealed by God: the law would not be in use; differently put, it would be suspended. If the imam was replaced with another type of ruler, the result would be the same, for whereas any kind of ruler would do for the avoidance of anarchy, only an imam would do for the avoidance of amorality. Without him, such community as existed would not be based on Islamic law. All the social and political arrangements of the Muslims would cease to be distinguishable, in legal as opposed to de facto terms, from those of infidels. The abode of Islam would merge with that of unbelief.

Initially, then, it would seem that the first and foremost role of the imam was to validate the law on which the Muslim community was based. The *umma* and the imamate thus went together: neither could exist without the other. But this is not how things remained. From the first civil war onwards an increasing number of Muslims deemed the head of state not to be an imam any more. They would rebel on behalf of real imams when they could, but this was not always possible, and all went through periods in which they had no imam at all. How then could they hope to be saved?

It is difficult to find an answer to this question. The early Khārijites and Shīʿites formed communities by affirming their loyalty (*walāya*) to imams of guidance in the past, dissociating from all imams of error and their supporters in the past and present, and accepting the obligation to establish a true imam as soon as circumstances would allow it. This seems to have sufficed, in the sense that it was only in terms of public law that the community merged with the abode of unbelief (*dār al-kufr*). In the absence of an imam the sectarians had no legitimate Friday service, courts, army, or other emblems of political organization, but for the rest the law remained valid, or so they seem to have assumed. They must in that case have operated with a distinction between the private and public aspects of the law, but they do not seem to have thought too deeply about it, for if one could live a morally upright life without political organization of one's own, what would be wrong about living in *dār al-kufr*?

The parallel between the Umayyad polity and *dār al-kufr* was brought into the open in the second civil war, when Khārijite extremists deemed life in this polity to be incompatible with Muslim status: if all non-Khārijites were infidels, they said (and all Khārijites agreed that this was so), then there was not and could not be a Muslim polity unless the Khārijites left to establish one themselves, and all Khārijites who refused to leave the abode of *kufr* were infidels. Their emphasis was on physical separation as a rightly guided community rather than the establishment of a rightly guided leader, but they clearly saw the two as going together: they made their *hijra* from the garrison cities to establish imamates of their own. This had the merit of consistency. Other Khārijites responded that Muḥammad had lived for ten years in Mecca, which was *dār al-kufr* at the time, or that in fact no imam was necessary for a valid community, since the imamate had never truly existed, or that other Muslims were only infidels in the sense of hypocrites.[2] But if hypocrites sufficed to validate the community, why did one have to rebel against them to establish another when one could? Again, it is hard to find an answer.

It was not just the Khārijites who preferred not to think too hard about the problem. The Andalusians never explained how they could claim to be Muslims, and indeed to live in a politically organized society with Friday prayer, courts, armies and so on, when their Umayyad governor stopped paying allegiance to the ʿAbbāsid caliph without adopting the status of imam himself.[3] By what avenues did the Zaydīs, who explicitly declared all precepts of the law to flow from the imamate,[4] reach the position that the law was valid whether there actually was an imam or not as long as people acknowledged the imamate to be prescribed by the law (so that it was for purely practical reasons that none existed)?[5] We do not know. As late as the tenth century, *jamāʿī* Muslims retained a feeling that there would be no Islamic community and no (public) law without the caliph, though they did not often say it.[6] The only imams, apart from the Prophet, whom they unanimously deemed indispensable for purposes of putting communal life on a moral basis were by then the first four. For the rest, the imamate was obligatory in the sense that one had to establish it when it was possible to do so, not in the sense that one would die as a pagan if circumstances forced one to live without it. They must have reached this position early, for nobody seems to have questioned that the Andalusians were Muslims, nor do the Muʿtazilite anarchists seem to have found it necessary to explain that one could remove the imam without suspending the law and dissolving the Muslim community thereby. But opinions seem to have developed stealthily, as if people were ashamed of them. The

2. Thus the Bayhasiyya, Najdiyya, and Ibāḍiyya respectively.

3. For their resolute silence on their ruler's (and thus also their own) status, see Fierro, 'Adopción des título califal', 36.

4. Strothmann, *Staatsrecht*, 5.

5. If there was an imam and one did not know him, one died as a pagan; if there was none, the imam was the Prophet, the Qur'ān and the Commander of the Faithful (i.e. ʿAlī), and one escaped a pagan death by knowing the doctrine of the imamate (al-Hādī ilā 'l-Ḥaqq, *Aḥkām*, i, 466f.; cf. also Strothman, *Staatsrecht*, 91).

6. Cf. Nagel, *Festung*, 35.

same is true of opinions on the parallel question whether one could or could not live in the abode of unbelief (*dār al-kufr*).[7]

Only the Rāfiḍī Shīʿites opted for an explicit assertion that the validity of the law depended on the imam. When he disappeared, his continued existence in hiding ensured that the world was not totally drained of morality, so that the Muslim (i.e. Imami) community continued to exist even though public law was a dead letter in his absence. By then, the tight concatenation of the imam and the law characteristic of Shiʿism must have come across as an aberration rather than a strong formulation of what had once been a shared view.

Validation of public worship

Whether or not a saving vehicle existed without the imam, his presence (or that of his governor or other deputy) was required for the validation of the Friday and the festival prayers in Umayyad times.[8] This was also the view of the Zaydīs,[9] Imamis,[10] Ismailis,[11] Ḥanafīs,[12] and Ibāḍīs.[13] It was for that reason that the Baghdadis would smash pulpits and declare that "they had no prayers" (*lā ṣalawāt lahum*) when they found al-Muqtadir (d. 932) too useless to count as their caliph.[14] The Shāfiʿites held it more suitable for the Friday prayer to be validated by judges rather than governors, or so at least according to al-Māwardī.[15] Since judges were also delegates of the caliphs, this did not make much difference in juristic theory, but other Shāfiʿites freed the Friday prayer

7. Such views as survive from the first four centuries are notable for their ambivalence, as Abou El Fadl points out ('Islamic Law and Muslim Minorities,' 148f.). Cf. further below, 359ff.

8. Crone and Hinds, *God's Caliph*, 33, citing Jarīr.

9. Strothman, *Staatsrecht*, 5n., cf. 97 (a *muḥtasib* imam did not suffice).

10. Ṭūsī, *Nihāya*, 103.

11. When the Ismaili missionaries lost touch with their imam, they said that they had "no prayer, no fasting" (Ivanow, 'Istitār al-imām', 93 = 158).

12. Māwardī, *Aḥkām*, 65/33.8 = 35; Baghdādī, *Uṣūl*, i, 272.9 (the Iraqis); ʿAbd al-Jabbār, *Mughnī*, xx/1, 48.9; Calder, 'Friday Prayer and Juristic Theory', 37. Compare Ibn Ḥanbal, who counted ʿAlī's leadership of the prayer among the proofs that he had been caliph (Zaman, *Emergence*, 169f.), and Ibn Sīnā, according to whom the lawgiver must prescribe worship which can only be performed in the caliph's presence (*SI*, *x*, 452 = 108).

13. Imams were needed, among other things, "to hold our prayers", as the Ibāḍīs of North Africa said when they elected Abū 'l-Khaṭṭāb (Ibn Ṣaghīr, 'Chronique', 9); if you depose the rightful imam, the new imam's *jumʿa* will be invalid (Bisyānī in *Kāshif*, ii, 186). The Ibāḍīs of Jerba had no Friday prayer due to the absence of the just imam, al-Tijānī noted in 706/1306 (*Riḥla*, 127).

14. Ḥamza al-Isbahānī, 153, 154 (G, 202f., 204).

15. Māwardī, *Aḥkām*, 65/33.7 = 35.

from its association with government altogether. It was customary, according to al-Juwaynī, for the imam to supervise events which served as an external emblem (*shiʿār*) of Islam, such as the Friday prayer and the pilgrimage, and he ought indeed to pay attention to anything involving large numbers, but in law, people were free to organize the rituals themselves.[16] According to the Ḥanafī Ibn al-Simnānī, all duties that fell on the believers as individuals, such as ritual prayer and alms, continued whether there was an imam or not. Whether he included the Friday prayer under this heading, not just the daily five, he does not say.[17]

Jamāʿī scholars who deemed the validity of the Friday prayer to depend on the presence of the ruler, in person or through his governor, held his presence to have the requisite effect whether he was morally upright or not;[18] but Shīʿites would not pray in the Friday mosques of illegitimate rulers,[19] and the Imāmīs ceased to have a public Friday service when their twelfth imam went into hiding.[20] This briefly changed under the Shīʿite Būyids, when al-Mufīd (d. 413/1022), followed by his pupil al-Ṭūsī (d. 459f/1066f), postulated that the imam had delegated his authority to the jurists: they were permitted to conduct the Friday and the Festival service on his behalf, provided that they could do so without getting into trouble.[21] But later scholars such as Ibn Idrīs al-Ḥillī (d. 598/1202) disagreed.[22] There was no Friday prayer in early Ṣafavid Iran; to conduct it was to identify oneself as a Sunni.[23]

In al-Juwaynī's opinion, no physical act of worship required validation by the imam.[24] That the pilgrimage remained valid regardless of the moral status of the ruler is explicitly affirmed by the Ḥanbalī Ibn Baṭṭa and the Zaydī

16. Juwaynī, *Ghiyāth*, §§289f., 553; cf. Shīrāzī in Calder, 'Friday Prayer and Juristic Theory', 41.

17. Simnānī, *Rawḍa*, i, §114; cf. §115.

18. Ibn Baṭṭa, *Profession de foi*, 67 = 127; cf. Lewis, *Political Language*, 101.

19. Already under the Umayyads we are told that the adherents of ʿAlī would stay away from Friday service and other public prayers (Tab. ii, 234); such absence counts as a sign of *rafḍ* in a Prophetic tradition cited in *SN*, ch. 41, §14.

20. There were no Friday prayers in Qumm in Būyid times until Rukn al-Dawla forced the Qummīs to rebuild and use Friday mosque (Muqaddasī, *Aḥsan*, 395). Kulīnī (d. 329/940f.) has the imams make provisions for performance of the Friday prayer by oneself, or prayers in lieu of it (Newman, *Formative Period of Twelver Shīʿism*, 168, 170).

21. Mufīd, *Muqniʿa*, 811; Ṭūsī, *Nihāya*, 302, cf. 107. For Mufīd on the law during the *ghayba*, see also Arjomand, 'The Consolation of Theology', 562f.

22. Ibn Idrīs, *Sarāʾir*, i, 302ff.

23. *Enc. Iran.*, s.v. 'jumʿa.'

24. Juwaynī, *Ghiyāth*, §§289f. (cf. above, note 16).

Majmūʿ,[25] and everyone else seems to have taken it for granted. As regards fasting in Ramaḍān, only the Ismailis held it to be suspended in the absence of the imam, presumably because they relied on him to announce its beginning and end, calculated by astronomers.[26] Other Muslims simply relied on the appearance of the new moon, which did not require expert knowledge. (This did not prevent the Mālikī al-Wansharīsī from adducing the fast of Ramaḍān among the ritual obligations that Muslims would be unable to fulfil if they stayed on in al-Andalus after the fall of Granada in 1492: without imams and their deputies, the sighting could not be accomplished, he declared, urging them to leave.)[27]

Finally, obligatory alms (*zakāh*, *ṣadaqa*) remained payable to any ruler whatever his moral status according to some Sunnis, but here there were dissenting voices, above all (though not only) among the Shāfiʿites: obligatory alms on gold, silver, and easily hidden things kept at home could or should always be paid directly to the recipients, listed in Q. 9:60, the dissenters said, rather than to officials (who would violate the privacy of the home); and the same was true of obligatory alms in general when the collectors were unjust, or even when they were not, according to some.[28] In the absence of a ruler of any kind, everything to do with public money would have to be managed by the scholars, according to Juwaynī, who does not explicitly mention alms. According to Ibn al-Simnānī, *zakāh* would continue to be payable because it was a duty which fell on the believers as individuals, whereas the imposition of *jizya* would stop because the duty did not fall on them, but rather on the imam.[29]

The Ibāḍīs and some Imamis also held that people could disburse the alms directly to the recipients, at least if there was no legitimate imam or one could not rely on the money reaching him.[30] What happened if one gave one's alms to a wrongful ruler, voluntarily or under duress? The Ibāḍīs and some Imamis said that one would have to pay them again, assuming that there was someone to pay them to. But there were also Imamis who said that it was lawful to pay them to rulers such as the Umayyads, and that they were not in any case to be

25. *Profession de foi*, 67 = 128, cited in Lewis, *Political Language*, 101; Zayd (attrib.), *Majmūʿ*, 236, no. 853.

26. Above, note 11; cf. Walker, *al-Kirmānī*, 35.

27. Wansharīsī, *Miʿyār*, ii, 138f.

28. Ibn Baṭṭa, *Profession de foi*, 67 = 128; cited in Lewis, *Political Language*, 101; Aghnides, *Theories of Finance*, 296ff.; Māwardī, *Aḥkām*, 209/121 = 135. There were even some who held that one could kill unjust collectors, cf. below, note 93.

29. Juwaynī, *Ghiyāth*, §560; Simnānī, *Rawḍa*, §§114f.

30. Cf. Bisyānī, *Mukhtaṣar*, 93; Newman, *Formative Period of Twelver Shīʿism*, 166f.

paid twice.[31] The Zaydīs and Ismailis held that (the true) *zakāh* was suspended in the imam's absence,[32] and so apparently did some Imamis, on the grounds that ordinary believers lacked the knowledge to hand it directly to the rightful recipients, and that three of the categories of recipients listed in the Qur'ān presupposed political organization: the Imami al-Mufīd and his pupil al-Ṭūsī brushed aside these objections, arguing that *zakāh* was payable to the jurists, who did have the requisite knowledge, and that the three problematic categories were simply suspended.[33]

*Execution of the law (*tanfīdh al-aḥkām*)*

Executing the law was the essence of the imam's *sharʿī* functions. It was to implement the moral and legal rules (*sunna*, *ḥukm*, *ḥudūd*, *farāʾiḍ*, *ḥuqūq*) brought by the prophets that God had raised up caliphs, as al-Walīd II said in 744.[34] All lists of the imam's functions mention this duty, and all the functions listed separately can be seen as subdivisions of it. In the early days the caliph would execute the law in person by adjudicating in person, and whether he did so or not, it was generally agreed that only the imam (or a delegate of his) could appoint judges.[35]

It followed that if there was no imam, people would have "no judgements (*aḥkām*)", as the Umayyad poet Jarīr put it.[36] One would have make do with *ṣulḥ*, private agreement or settlement out of court.[37] The Imamis had no courts capable of enforcing their decisions even back in the days when their imams were present, and their traditions sternly warn the believers not to use the courts of the opponents, telling them to submit their dispute to a traditionist or jurist and accept his judgement of their own accord.[38] When al-Mufīd,

31. Muḥammad b. Maḥbūb to the North Africans in Kāshif, *Siyar*, ii, 230f. (where the wrongful officials are Ibāḍī, not Sunnī); Ṭūsī, *Nihāya*, 185; Newman, *Formative Period of Twelver Shīʿism*, 174, 177.

32. Cf. Qāsim b. Ibrāhīm in Strothmann, *Staatsrecht*, 5n; Abrahamov, 'al-Ḳāsim', 86; not even a *muḥtasib* imam could collect them (Madelung in *EI*², s.v. 'imāma'); Nuʿmān, *Daʿāʾim*, i, 263f.

33. Mufīd, *Muqniʿa*, 252; Ṭūsī, *Nihāya*, 185; Calder, 'Zakāt in Imāmī Shīʿī Jurisprudence', 469.

34. Tab., ii, 1759ff.; tr. Crone and Hinds, *God's Caliph*, 121ff.

35. Ibn al-Muqaffaʿ, *Ṣaḥāba*, 197f. (P, §17); Sanhoury, *Califat*, 168ff.; Ṭūsī, *Khilāf*, v, 343.6. Cf. above, 238ff., on Ghazālī.

36. Above, note 8.

37. Cf. ʿAbd al-Jabbār, *Mughnī*, xx/1, 53f.

38. Kulīnī, *Kāfī*, vii, 410–12; Madelung, 'Authority in Twelver Shiism', 166, citing Ibn Bābawayh; Newman, *Formative Period of Twelver Shīʿism*, 180f.

followed by al-Ṭūsī, proposed the theory of delegation to the jurists (*tafwīḍ*), they affirmed that it was up to the jurists to take over the functions of *qāḍī*s.[39] Al-Ṭūsī added that a person appointed by the wrongful regime should try to use his position to apply Imami law; under duress he might even apply the law of the opponents, but only as long as it did not cause him to take lives: *taqiyya* (dissimulation under duress) could not legitimate unlawful killing.[40]

On the Sunni side al-Māwardī agreed that there could be no execution of the law (and also no collection of taxes) in a community without an imam, whereas an imam raised up by rebels would in his opinion validate its execution in the rebel community: he did not deem the (mostly Sunni) subjects of the Fatimid caliphs to be living in sin, one infers, though he does not mention any examples.[41] Here as elsewhere, the idea is that the public domain is created by God, the only power capable of overruling private interest, and that God has to be represented in the here and now by a single person, a deputy. But al-Juwaynī argued along the same lines as al-Mufīd and al-Ṭusī that the scholars could take over the execution of the law in the absence of a such a deputy: they could marry off women without marriage guardians and administer the property of orphans, for example.[42] Al-Ghazālī, his star pupil, disagreed, as has been seen: all transactions dependent on judges would be invalid in his view, or alternatively validated by overriding necessity (*ḍarūra*) alone, for the sultans to whom most judges owed their appointments had no moral right to appoint them unless they were authorized to do so by the caliph. Later Sunnis solved the problem by tracing the authority of the sultan to the community, thus reversing the original relationship between the community and its head, and/or by seeing the sultans as imams themselves.[43]

Execution of the ḥudūd

The modern state is often held to be an agency for the maintenance of internal order and the conduct of external defence distinguished by its monopoly on the right to use violence, where violence means force of the type required for physical damage, imprisonment or death: people may still slap their

39. Mufīd, *Muqniʿa*, 811.5; Ṭūsī, *Nihāya*, 301. The view was affirmed again in the Ṣafavid period, cf. Calder, 'Judicial Authority in Imāmī Shīʿī Jurisprudence,' 105.

40. Ṭūsī, *Nihāya*, 302.

41. Māwardī, *Aḥkām*, 95/59 = 65; cf. Mikhail, *Politics and Revelation*, 23 (wrongly having Māwardī speak of the religious duties in general); Abou El Fadl, 'Islamic Law of Rebellion', ii, 205f.

42. Juwaynī, *Ghiyāth*, §557–8.

43. Above, 238ff.

children (if only just), but in most countries they may not bear arms (except by special licence), and nowhere may they physically injure, detain or kill other people, except in self-defence (narrowly defined). If the state were to lose this monopoly, it would not simply be sharing a function with, or ceding a function to, private citizens; rather it would cease to be a modern state. Contrary to what one might have expected, given the level of violence they had to tolerate, some medieval Muslim jurists operated with similar notions, or so at least al-Juwaynī. Private individuals (*āḥād al-nās*) were not allowed to unsheath weapons against each other or their rulers, or only in self-defence and the rescue of others, he said, adding that this did not apply if there was no government. (Using arms against infidels was also another matter.)[44] Many jurists disagreed, as will be seen. There was, however, complete unanimity that the imam had a monopoly on the right to use force in one key area.

The area in question was that of the *ḥudūd*, penalties prescribed in the Sharʿīa which resulted in physical damage (by lashing), mutilation (by amputation) or death (by stoning or decapitation).[45] That only the imam could apply or authorize the application of these penalties to free persons was affirmed by all Muslims with rare exceptions, such as the ninth-century anarchists, to whom they were a major problem.[46] Many jurists went further by crediting the imam with a monopoly on all punishments, including discretionary flogging (*taʿzīr*), torture, imprisonment, and banishment, which are not prescribed in the Sharʿīa;[47] but only of the *ḥudūd* can it be emphatically said that if he ceded them to others, he would cease to be the imam, or alternatively the penalties would cease to be *ḥudūd*. They were penalties for fundamental transgressions of the moral code which held society together and had to be inflicted by a representative of God, that is to say a representative of collective interests, because there would not otherwise be anything to distinguish them from private vengeance. If everyone had the right to kill or maim other people, there would be no legal order to uphold: power would lose its moral

44. *Ghiyāth*, §§163, 479f., 485f., 554 and *Irshād*, 370.1 (Cook, *Commanding Right*, 346).

45. The penalties are classically identified as those for unlawful sexual relations (*zinā*), false accusations of such relations (*qadhf*), highway robbery (*qaṭʿ al-ṭarīq*), theft (*sariqa*) and wine-drinking; but many others count as *ḥudūd* in medieval works, including those for apostasy, blasphemy, and homicide; and there are times when *ḥadd* seems to mean capital punishment.

46. Cf. above, 67f. ʿAbd al-Jabbār knew of Medinese jurists who would allow all individuals to perform them on behalf of an imam unable to do it himself (*Mughnī*, xx/2, 155). For the question whether slave owners could perform them on their slaves, see Johansen, 'Mise en scene du vol,' 46; Naysābūrī, *Imāma*, 67.

47. Cf. Cook, *Commanding Right*, 268, note 103 (Murtaḍā), 342, note 21 (Ḥalīmī); Naysābūrī, *Imāma*, 67.5.

purpose, anarchy would prevail;[48] and one would be back in the proverbial *man ʿazza bazza* ('whoever has power takes the spoils') which had prevailed in the Jāhiliyya. The Imamis added a consideration likely to appeal to modern opponents of capital punishment: one needed infallibity to impose such penalties.[49] But with or without infallibility, the authority behind them had to be public.

Consequently, the imam's monopoly on the *ḥudūd* is frequently affirmed in the literature, whether Sunni,[50] Muʿtazilite,[51] Shīʿite,[52] or Ibāḍī.[53] Since the *ḥudūd* could not be applied by unauthorized people without ceasing to be *ḥudūd*, they could not be executed in the imam's absence. This was the problem that the ninth-century anarchists had struggled with. When the twelfth imam went into hiding, the Imamis duly declared the *ḥudūd* to be suspended, pending his return.[54] Not all held the suspension to be total, however. A tradition in al-Kulīnī allows self-help in the case of unlawful sexual relations, as long as the penalty was carried out in secret.[55] Several jurists of the Būyid period tried the alternative method of ruling that if an Imami official employed by a wrongful ruler was in a position to apply the *ḥudūd* in accordance with Imami law, then he was authorized (or even obliged) to do so, for he would in fact be acting on behalf of the true imam and should think of himself as doing so.[56] This ruling reflected the fact that the wrongful rulers at the time were Shīʿites; living under Sunnis, thirteenth-century jurists tended to disagree with it.[57] Al-Mufīd and al-Ṭūsī held that the jurists were allowed to apply the *ḥudūd* even without holding office, by delegation from the imams, when they were able to do so, as within their own households: they were authorized

48. Cf. Naysābūrī, *Imāma*, 67, explaining what is implicit elsewhere.

49. Cf. Ṭusī, *Mabsūṭ*, vii, 41.6, cited in Sachedina, *Just Ruler*, 100f. It was also ʿAbd al-Jabbār's understanding of the Imami position (*Mughnī*, xx/1, 74).

50. Baghdādī, *Uṣūl*, 272.7. As he observes, some held that slave owners could impose them on their slaves (cf. above, note 46).

51. ʿAbd al-Jabbār, *Mughnī*, xx/1, 41, 74, noting that if there is no imam, the *ḥudūd* must be suspended (*lā budda min suqūṭ al-ḥudūd*); Mānkdīm in Cook, *Commanding Right*, 215.

52. Below (Imami); Strothmann, *Staatsrecht*, 5n, cf. 97 (Zaydī); Naysābūrī, *Imāma*, 67 (Ismaili: not even slave owners).

53. Bisyānī and Muḥammad b. Maḥbūb in Kāshif, *Siyar*, ii, 197f., 239.

54. Murtaḍā in Sachedina, 'Treatise on the Occultation', 124, and other Imamis in Madelung, 'Treatise', note 25; similarly ʿAbd al-Jabbār, *Mughnī*, xx/1, 74f., on the Shīʿites.

55. Newman, *Formative Period of Twelver Shīʿism*, 177f.

56. Murtaḍā in Madelung, 'Treatise', 23 = 26, with other Imamis in note 25; Mufīd, *Muqniʿa*, 810; Ṭūsī, *Nihāya*, 301, 302.

57. Thus Ibn Idrīs and Muḥaqqiq al-Ḥillī; cf. Calder, 'Legitimacy and Accommodation', 96f.; Madelung, 'Treatise,' note 25.

to apply the penalties to their own wives, children, and slaves.[58] Here their attempt to save public authority ended up as an endorsement of self-help, if only for jurists, and perhaps only in their capacity as domestic tyrants. It was in any case a far cry from the infallible public authority that had once been required for the task, and it was too much for Ibn Idrīs al-Ḥillī: it was only to his slaves that a man could apply the *ḥudūd* in his view.[59]

According to al-Mufīd, people who took it upon themselves to kill blasphemers and other apostates 'out of anger on God's behalf', would be free to do so, apparently whether the imam was present or not.[60] His Muʿtazilite contemporaries agreed, though only if there was no imam, or so ʿAbd al-Jabbār insists.[61] The people in question should probably be envisaged as applying verdicts formulated by the jurists rather than acting on their own accord; in other words, the reference is to laymen acting as the jurists' henchmen. This was a role which laymen were often encouraged to take, by *jamāʿī* and Shīʿite jurists alike (and which became infamous in the West when Khomeini used it to deal with Rushdie). "Anyone who meets him and kills him is acting on my order," as an early ʿAbbāsid judge declared with reference to an alleged crypto-Manichean (*zindīq*).[62] The occasions on which scholars acted as rabble-rousers against theologians and philosophers are legion. As long as the decision was reached in accordance with the law (as formulated by them), they did not mind appealing directly to the community for execution. It was how outlawing functioned in medieval Europe too.

Authors connected with the government, however, were well aware of the overriding importance of reserving the infliction of physical punishment to the state and its officials. A model letter of appointment instructs a military commander "not to apply a *ḥadd* or a rule concerned with retaliation, whether involving loss of life or limb, without asking the Commander of the Faithful for his opinion and awaiting his reply".[63] A military commander should always execute major physical punishments himself, or at the most delegate it to a close associate, according to a military treatise.[64] Anyone who beheaded,

58. Mufīd, *Muqniʿa*, 810 (the imams *qad fawwaḍū al-naẓar fīhi ilā fuqahāʾ shīʿatihim maʿa 'l-imkān*); Ṭūsī, *Nihāya*, 300f., clearly on the basis of Mufīd.

59. Ibn Idrīs, *Sarāʾir*, ii, 24.

60. Mufīd, *Muqniʿa*, 743, with reference to blasphemers (*man sabba rasūl allāh aw aḥad min al-aʾimma*). They are deemed to be outlaws on the ground that they are apostates, so the rule presumably applied to other apostates as well.

61. ʿAbd al-Jabbār, *Mughnī*, xx/2, 156.1, 8.

62. Wakīʿ, iii, 265.4; cf. van Ess, *TG*, iii, 34, on Saʿīd b. ʿAbd al-Raḥmān al-Jumaḥī and his victim, Ḍirār.

63. Thus Qudāma, *Kharāj*, 45.

64. Harthamī, *Mukhtaṣar*, 17.

mutilated, castrated or otherwise punished anyone else without the king's permission, "even his own servant or slave", should be punished according to Niẓām al-Mulk, "so that others may take warning and know their places".[65] What then would happen if there were no imam? Al-Juwaynī avoids the issue, but Ibn al-Simnānī concedes that the *ḥudūd* would have to be abandoned.[66]

Jihād

Holy war was one of several types of warfare regulated by the jurists. Al-Māwardī called the other types 'wars of public welfare' (*ḥurūb al-maṣāliḥ*), by which he meant the suppression of apostates (*murtaddūn*), rebels (*bughāt*) and brigands (*muḥāribūn*).[67] Only *jihād* will be treated in detail in this book. The main account will come in Chapter 21; what follows is concerned only with the relationship between the imam and holy war.

If one could have a valid community while temporarily deprived of an imam, one was also entitled to defend it by force of arms: defensive warfare remained legitimate whether there was an imam or not according to all (though not all counted such warfare as *jihād*, except in the case of emergencies).[68] But the legitimacy of *jihād* in the sense of warfare for the spread of Islam was more problematic. The only reason why Muslims were entitled to invade the lands of other people to impose their own government on them was that they were doing God's will, and this was not self-evident if they were led by sinners. Companions are sometimes said to have had their names removed from the military roll after the death of ʿUmar or that of ʿUthmān, or whenever they took right guidance to have come to an end,[69] and the question how far it was lawful to participate in *jihād* under sinful rulers was hotly debated. A negative answer implied that the activity was suspended, not because it had ceased to be obligatory, but rather because circumstances made it impossible for the obligation to be discharged.

The *ahl al-sunna wa'l-jamāʿa* took the view that *jihād* could and should be waged behind the ruler of the time whatever his moral status; the activity

65. *SN*, 98 = 76 (ch. 11, §4).

66. *Rawḍa*, §115.

67. Māwardī, *Aḥkām*, ch. 5 (caption and introduction); cf. Sarakhsī, *Mabsūṭ*, x, 2, where the generic term for all types of licit war is *siyar*. On wars against rebels and brigands, see Abou El Fadl, 'Irregular Warfare and the Law of Rebellion', and 'Islamic Law of Rebellion'.

68. *Jihād* and border defence appear as different rubrics (nos. 5 and 6) in Māwardī, *Aḥkām*, 23/16 = 16; similarly Abū Yaʿlā, *Aḥkām*, 27; Juwaynī, *Ghiyāth*, §§308–10. The idea that *jihād* was primarily defensive is of apologetic origin and did enter juristic writings in medieval times (though one does encounter it elsewhere, cf. below, 382.).

69. Crone, 'Qays and Yemen', 40, note 223.

derived its validity from the law, which was validated in its turn by communal agreement, not by him, and whether he was sinful or upright was of no consequence to anyone except himself.[70] Nor would the duty be suspended in his absence, for it was imposed on the community, not on him. Holy war was a *farḍ kifāya*, a collective obligation, and such obligations could not be suspended.[71] If those who normally fulfilled them stopped doing so, they would devolve to others and eventually become individual obligations (sing. *farḍ ʿayn*) on everyone until somebody fulfilled them again.

A collective duty was not primarily a duty for the state. But given his role as the upholder of the law on the one hand and the vast resources at his disposal on the other, the ruler was naturally expected to take a leading role in the organization of holy war. He was in effect all Muslims in a single person, or the agent of their community (*nāʾib ʿan jamāʿatihim*), as eleventh-century jurists put it.[72] But did the imam, when there was one, have an actual monopoly on the conduct of war, in the sense that only he could authorize the inception and termination of campaigns? The answer may once have been yes. All the other items on the standard lists of the imam's duties are activities that only he could perform or authorize others to undertake, and Ibn al-Muqaffaʿ (d. c. 757) explicitly says that only the imam was entitled to obedience in matters of "starting campaigns and marching back (*al-ghazw wa'l-qufūl*), collecting and distributing (booty) . . . and fighting the enemy and making truces with him".[73] Sunnis often express themselves in similar terms.[74] For all that, the Sunnis held that laymen were free to initiate campaigns on their own.

Participation in *jihād* was highly meritorious for everyone, and civilians would often join the official campaigns as volunteers (*mutaṭawwiʿa*) or go to live on the frontier for extended periods, attaching themselves to fortified settlements of a private nature known as *ribāṭs*. The jurists make it clear that such volunteers would often set off in small raiding parties, now from the regular army and now "from a town in Syria or elsewhere",[75] to campaign in enemy territory on their own, without permission from the imam or his representative.

70. ʿAbd al-Razzāq, *Muṣannaf*, v, nos. 9610–13; Ibn Baṭṭa, *Profession de foi*, 67 = 127; Ibn ʿUkāsha, and others, above, 136, 137; Mālik in Talbi, *Émirat aghlabide*, 417n. (also in Mottahedeh and Sayyid, 'Idea of Jihād', 26, who link it with the debate over the obligatory nature of *jihād*); Sarakhsī, *Siyar*, i, 160, no. 161. Similarly Zayd b. ʿAlī, *Majmūʿ*, 236, no. 853: the dominance of the wicked does not invalidate holy war.

71. Cf. Juwaynī, *Ghiyāth*, §553.

72. Ibid., §307; Sarakhsī, *Siyar*, i, 189.

73. *Saḥāba*, 197f. (P, §17).

74. Hamidullah, *Conduct of State*, §312 (Abū Yūsuf, Māwardī); Baghdādī, *Uṣūl*, 272; cf. also the Muʿtazilite Mānkdīm (d. 425/1034) in Cook, *Commanding Right*, 215.

75. Abū Ḥanīfa in Ṭabarī, *Ikhtilāf*, 79.

They do not condemn the practice. They do have their reservations about it with reference to the safety of the participants, the maintenance of military discipline, or the problematic status of the booty (could they keep it, or was the imam entitled to his fifth?).[76] The Mālikīs said that if the imam had prohibited fighting for the sake of general welfare, then nobody was allowed to fight unless attacked (in which case no permission was needed to fight back).[77] But no school prohibited unauthorized campaigns outright. "We allow volunteers in holy war to penetrate the land of obdurate infidels on their own, though it is better that they should do so at the initiative of the imam," as al-Juwaynī observed.[78] The question how the imam was supposed to enforce truces and otherwise manage relations with the enemy if the frontier population was out of control does not seem to attract attention, perhaps because unauthorized expeditions were usually too small to make much difference. When a religious scholar who campaigned with great success against the Turks in Ṭāhirid Khurasan was denounced by envious people, the ruler accused him of "going out and gathering this army around you and disobeying the assistants of the government". Perhaps he had overstepped the limit by gathering so large an army, or maybe his detractors had accused him of rebellious intentions (he was released when the ruler was convinced of his loyalty).[79] In any case, private warfare was lawful as long as it was *jihād*.

The Khārijites held *jihād* to be highly meritorious whether they had an imam or not, but how they explained its validity in his absence is unknown.[80] The Shīʿites, on the other hand, held that *jihād* in the sense of missionary warfare could only be waged under the imam's banner; nobody was to participate

76. Abū Zayd al-Qayrawānī (d. 386/996) in Bredow, *Heilige Krieg*, Arabic text, 18ff. (drawn to my attention by Christopher Melchert); Ṭabarī, *Ikhtilāf*, 78f; Qaffāl, *Ḥilya*, vii, 657: Abū Ḥanīfa prohibited unauthorized expeditions unless they were at least ten men strong; al-Awzāʿī allowed the commander to punish or forgive men who went off on their own as he wished; the Shāfiʿites disliked expeditions undertaken without the imam's permission because of the risk, but did not hold them to be forbidden whatever their strength; the Mālikīs said that troops were not allowed to undertake unauthorized expeditions whereas people along the frontiers could do so if a good opportunity arose and it would take too long to await the imam's permission.

77. Bredow, *Heilige Krieg*, Arabic text, 20.1.

78. *Ghiyāth*, §486.

79. Dhahabī, *Nubalāʾ*, xi, 34 (drawn to my attention by Christopher Melchert). The scholar was Aḥmad b. Ḥarb (d. 234/849). Compare Ibn al-Athīr, vi, 361, year 205, where an earlier volunteer is suspected of rebellious intentions because he has gathered a large army on his own initiative in order to fight Khārijites.

80. Cf. Crone and Zimmermann, *Epistle*, 281. Sālim tells people going out to holy war to appoint 'imams' for the duration.

unless he was summoned by him or his representatives: thus the Imamis, Ismailis, and Zaydīs alike.[81] The activity was suspended in his absence. "When no imam is manifest and nobody appointed by the imam is present, it is not allowed to fight holy war against the enemy, for *jihād* with imams of injustice or without an imam is an error for which the agent incurs sin," al-Ṭūsī said; there could be "no fighting to make them (namely the unbelievers) adopt Islam", only to protect the Muslims, and no sojourn in military settlements along the frontier unless the warfare was defensive, until the coming of the Mahdi.[82] It would have entailed mixing with and taking orders from the opponents. Al-Mufīd did think that Imamis holding office on behalf of illegitimate rulers could, indeed must, wage *jihād* against infidels and sinners alike, and that the community had to assist them.[83] But al-Ṭūsī omitted holy war from the functions delegated by the imam to the jurists, be it with or without appointment from the wrongful regime. Later scholars also held missionary *jihād* to be suspended, though here as so often the coming of the Ṣafavids caused them to rethink.[84]

Commanding right and forbidding wrong

Islamic law obliged its adherents to intervene when they saw other believers engage in sinful behaviour and to persuade them to stop, or even to force them to do so if they could. This was called 'commanding right and forbidding wrong' (*al-amr bi'l-maʿrūf wa'l-nahy ʿan al-munkar*), and it was often compared with holy war: like *jihād*, it was a call to Islam backed by force where necessary; fighting sinners and fighting infidels were much the same.[85] Some saw government in its entirety as a type of 'commanding right and prohibiting wrong',[86] presumably on the grounds that the ruler's function was in essence

81. For the Imamis, see the next note. For the Ismailis, see Nuʿmān, *Daʿāʾim*, i, 264.7; Naysābūrī, *Imāma*, 66 (no *jihād* except under his banner, no expedition unless sent by him or his representative); cf. also Abū 'l-Fawāris, *Imāma*, 7 = 25 (85v). For the Zaydīs, see Strothmann, *Staatsrecht*, 5n., 97, cf. 96n. (the *muḥtasib* imam can use the sword in the performance of *al-amr bi'l-maʿrūf*). Differently Zayd b. ʿAlī (attrib.), *Majmūʿ*, 236, no. 853, but this manual played no role in classical Zaydī law.

82. Ṭūsī, *Nihāya*, 290f; cf. Kohlberg, 'Imāmī Shīʿī Doctrine of *Jihād*', 79ff; Sachedina, *Just Ruler*, 110f. There is no reason to think that defensive warfare was ever regarded as suspended.

83. *Muqniʿa*, 810.

84. Kohlberg, 'Imāmī Shīʿī Doctrine of *Jihād*', 81f.

85. Cook, *Commanding Right*, 198, note 21 (Masʿūdī), 341 (Ḥalīmī).

86. *Al-salṭana hiya hādhā*, as Ḥalīmī says in Cook, *Commanding Right*, 342n.; cf. Juwaynī, *Ghiyāth*, §113.

to apply the law, but Sunni lists of the ruler's functions do not normally mention it.

The duty was usually (though not always) seen as collective, and the ruler for his part fulfilled it by appointing a *muḥtasib* (censor and market inspector) who would patrol the streets with armed assistants to ensure that people obeyed the law in public, for example, by attending Friday prayer, fasting in Ramaḍān, abstaining from wine, and observing the rules regarding relations between the sexes. What people did in the privacy of their own homes was their own business as long as their actions did not affect others, directly or indirectly (e.g. by their behaviour coming to be known). But the existence of a public censor notwithstanding, it was meritorious, or even obligatory, for private citizens to take the duty of enforcing public morality upon themselves when they were able to do so. As in the case of *jihād*, the question arose as to how far they had to act under the imam's control. Since performers of the duty normally took spontaneous action at the sight of what they deemed to be wrong, rather than responding to *fatwā*s issued by the learned, the jurists now had to consider the wisdom of allowing laymen to trespass on not only the imam's territory, but also their own.

The earliest material is dominated by the problem of the sinful behaviour of rulers rather than that of fellow-citizens, and the key issue is the legitimacy of revolt: may one use the sword against the wrongdoing of caliphs and governors?[87] The answers became increasingly negative with the passage of time, and by the ninth century only the Muʿtazilites, the Khārijites, and the Zaydīs said that one could.[88] There remained the question how far one should attempt to rebuke them (given that one might risk one's life thereby): most scholars said that it was not obligatory, and not necessarily even meritorious, especially in public.[89]

How far could private individuals go in their action against the wrongdoing of their fellow-citizens, then? Some scholars would prefer them not to do anything at all. Thus al-Ḥalīmī (d. 1012), a Shāfiʿite jurist, held the performance of the duty to be so closely related to the infliction of punishments that it would be better for the ruler, in his case the Sāmānid amir, to take it over by appointing an upright and learned man in every town and village to execute it. If the ruler did nothing, the duty devolved onto the scholars, he said, though he allowed upright laymen to intervene when the law involved was simple.[90]

87. Cf. Cook, *Commanding Right*, chs 2–3.

88. Cf. ibid., chs 9, 10, 15.

89. Cf. Cook's own summary in his *Forbidding Wrong*, ch. 7.

90. Cook, *Commanding Right*, 342f.; there is also a Prophetic tradition prohibiting lay performance (p. 43, note 56), and Maʾmūn is said to have done the same (p. 71).

Other scholars agreed that the common people should stick to simple cases, or they preferred them just to disapprove 'in their hearts', without taking any action; and many of them placed the use of violence, or at least armed violence, in the ruler's hand, forbidding it to laymen or requiring them to obtain the ruler's permission.[91] Even the Ḥanbalites came around to this view. In the early tenth century they were notorious for their street violence in Baghdad, led by the rabble-rouser al-Barbahārī: in a famous incident in 935 they raided private homes, poured away wine, broke musical instruments, beat up singing girls, thrashed men unable to convince them that the women or young boys with them were lawful companions, and organized assaults on Shāfiʿite scholars, causing first the chief of police and next the caliph himself to intervene. But thereafter their relationship with the government warmed, and by the time we reach ʿAbd al-Qādir al-Jīlī (d. 1166) and Ibn al-Jawzī (d. 1200), the ruler's permission had come to be required for the use of violence in performance of the duty.[92]

But there were some notable exceptions, especially in the Shāfiʿite school,[93] and above all in al-Ghazālī (d. 1111), who authorized private individuals to take up arms in fulfilment of the duty, to collect armed helpers (*aʿwān*), and even to form troops (*tajnīd al-junūd*). He insisted that unjust rulers had to be endured, but he saw their subjects as direct executors of Islamic law, bypassing government officials. This was too extreme for most. His discussion of *al-amr bi'l-maʿrūf* was enormously influential, but few later scholars shared his vision of every Muslim as his brother's keeper, equipped with permission to use force in the maintenance of the public morality that had once been, and in principle still was, a key concern of the state.[94]

Outside the Sunni ranks, the Zaydīs, the Khārijites (insofar as they wrote about it) and the Muʿtazilites held laymen to be free to use armed violence when it was needed, as one would expect, though one Muʿtazilite would only grant them this right in the absence of a legitimate imam (whose monopoly would otherwise be infringed).[95] The Imamis were closer to the Sunni position. They were often accused of declaring *al-amr bi'l-maʿrūf* to be suspended in the imam's absence, but the accusations were false; in fact, they affirmed its

91. Cf. Cook's summary in his *Forbidding Wrong*, ch. 3, §§91–6.

92. Cook, *Commanding Right*, 117f., 138, 140.

93. Thus Qaffāl (d. 976) and Kiyā al-Harrāsī (d. 1110) held it lawful to kill offenders; the latter (inspired by the Muʿtazilite al-Jaṣṣāṣ) singled out collectors of illegal taxes as legitimate targets. Māwardī permitted the recruitment of (armed?) assistance in one work, though he forbade it in another (Cook, *Commanding Right*, 341, 344f., 347).

94. Cook, *Commanding Right*, 431, 441, 456ff.

95. Cook, *Forbidding Wrong*, ch. 3, §§94, 96.

continuing validity. Indeed, they sometimes went so far as to affirm the right of private individuals to use force in the course of its performance; but the majority, including al-Mufīd and al-Ṭūsī, ruled it out by requiring the permission of the (absent) imam for killing, wounding, or for the use of violence of any kind.[96] This is in line with the quietist nature of the sect, but they must have been motivated by a concern for internal order as well, for like al-Ghazālī, they could have authorized laymen to use force against each other without thereby authorizing revolt against wrongful rulers. Empowering private individuals to use force on a spontaneous basis in everyday life was however to invite chaos, and particularly dangerous in a community living under alien authorities.

*Preservation of the religion (*ḥifẓ al-dīn*)*

It was the imam's duty to maintain orthodoxy (right belief) and orthopraxy (right behaviour) among his subjects. The *muḥtasib* played a key role in both. He secured observance of the law in public, as seen already. He also checked on beliefs propagated in public. "If an innovator appears or a holder of suspect views goes astray, the imam should explain and clarify the correct view to him, and make him undergo the penalties appropriate to him, so that the religion may be preserved from flaws and the community preserved from error."[97] The *muḥtasib* was to ensure that people performed their ritual duties. He was also authorized to test religious teachers and correct anyone engaging in false interpretation of the Qurʾān, the transmission of bad traditions, and the dissemination of doctrines contrary to the scholarly consensus. If the culprit repented, no further action was needed; if he persisted in his ways, the censor was to pass him on to the ruler.[98] It was the ruler's duty to examine him and either make him repent or execute him, according to jurists and mirror writers alike.[99] There is plenty of attestation of the procedure in practice, sometimes with the judge taking *muḥtasib*'s role. Most culprits were probably denounced by their neighbours or colleagues, or brought to the attention of the *muḥtasib* or the *qāḍī* by an outraged mob. They included Muʿtazilites, dualists, materialists, philosophers, Sufis, Shīʿites, would-be prophets, deviant Qurʾān reciters, and

96. Cf. Cook, *Commanding Right*, 270, note 116, 266ff.

97. Māwardī, *Aḥkām*, 23/15 = 16. Similarly Abū Yaʿlā, *Aḥkām*, 27.

98. Māwardī, *Aḥkām*, 408ff., 415ff./243ff., 247ff. = 263ff., 268ff.; Abū Yaʿlā, *Aḥkām*, 287ff., 292f.

99. Shahrastānī, *Nihāya*, 478; Ps.-Ghazālī, *Naṣīḥa*, 59f., where the culprit may also be exiled.

blasphemers. Active hunts for heretics on the part of the government, though not unknown, were rare,[100] and there was little prying into people's homes.

Some authors recommend more active steps to secure orthodoxy: the ruler should send out missionaries and Qurʾān readers to every area under his control.[101] But though the government would eliminate heretics, it does not often seem to have engaged in internal missionary activity.

Fiscal services

The imam was expected to collect and distribute three taxes, the poll-tax (*jizya*), land-tax (*kharāj*), and tithe (*ʿushr*, often called *ṣadaqa*). If there was no imam, they could not be lawfully collected. Generally speaking, this was both the Sunni and (until the Safavid period) the Imami position, with the usual disagreement over who or what the imam was: one paid one's taxes to the ruler whether he was righteous or not, according to the Sunnis, but there could be no such thing as an unrighteous imam for the Shīʿites.[102] The imam was also entitled to a fifth of all moveable booty (*khums*), but he was not supposed to collect any other taxes. In practice he always did. Attempts to suppress uncanonical impositions (*mukūs*, sing. *maks*) are a constant feature of Islamic history.[103]

Two of the above-mentioned taxes, the poll-tax and land-tax, were classified as *fayʾ*, revenues from immobile booty. This had interesting implications for people's view of them. When the Arabs conquered the Middle East, we are told, they distributed moveable spoils (*ghanīma*) among themselves as they went along and considered doing the same with land taken by force (all such land having passed into the ownership of the conquerors), but decided to leave it in the hands of the original occupants in return for taxes. The government administered these immobile spoils on behalf of the conquerors who were their real owners and passed them their income in the form of stipends. Who then were the owners when the first generation of conquerors died? The children of the actual participants in the conquest of the lands involved, all Arab soldiers in the garrison city administering them, or all free Muslims there? By the ninth century it was agreed that the *fayʾ* was the common property of all Muslims regardless of whether they were descendants of the conquerors or of

100. The best known example is al-Mahdī's hunt for 'dualists' (cf. Chokr, *Zandaqa*).

101. Juwaynī, *Ghiyāth*, §282; Shahrastānī, *Aqdām*, 478. Compare Ḥalīmī's vision of official enforcement of orthopraxy, above, note 90.

102. Māwardī, *Aḥkām*, 55 /34 = 36; Simnānī, *Rawḍa*, i, §115; Ibn Baṭṭa, *Profession de foi*, 67 = 128; Madelung, 'Shiite Discussions of the Legality of the *Kharāj*'.

103. Cf. Aghnides, *Theories of Finance*, 376ff.

later arrivals, and whether they were Arabs or non-Arabs, settled people or bedouin, male or female, slaves or free: all that counted was membership of the Muslim community. By then the debate was academic in the sense that only a tiny number of Muslims were registered for payment of stipends, but it established the fundamental principle that public revenues should be spent in the interests of all, not of rulers or privileged groups.[104] "There is no doubt that the treasury belongs to the Muslims while you spend much of it for yourself," as Hārūn al-Rashīd's wife tells her husband in a story told by Niẓām al-Mulk, "they are quite justified if they complain about you."[105] When al-Ghazālī renounced his chair in Baghdad and gave away most of his wealth, he justified his retention of enough to maintain himself and his children on the grounds that the revenues from Iraq (which had been conquered by force) were earmarked for good works, since they were a pious foundation (*waqf*) for the Muslims; such money was absolutely clean, he claimed (many, especially Sufis, will have disagreed).[106] Just as conquest had established a sense of common ownership of land in many early Greek communities, so it created a sense of common ownership of the proceeds of land in that of the Muslims.

The imam was also expected to strike coins, but this function did not achieve *sharʿī* status, though it was an unquestioned monopoly of his and of well-known symbolic significance too: the very first thing a rebel claiming sovereign status would do was to strike coinage of his own.[107]

NON-SHARʿĪ DUTIES

Internal security

Most lists of the imam's *sharʿī* functions mention that the ruler must defend the community against external enemies (whether or not they count it as *jihād*),[108] and some add that he must suppress evildoers, but this is mostly treated as self-evident, given his responsibility for the execution of the law. One has to turn to the non-legal literature to find internal safety spelt out as a fundamental desideratum in its own right, often with reference to the roads. Ensuring the safety of the roads was one of the three things that the common people really wanted government for according to al-Manṣūr, and one of the

104. Madelung, 'Has the *Hijra* come to an End?', 236f.
105. *SN*, 192 = 145 (ch. 40, §5).
106. *Munqidh*, 38 = 61 (Watt's translation is not entirely right here); cf. below, 348.
107. *EI*², s.v. 'sikka'.
108. Cf. above, note 68.

two tasks that rulers were appointed for according to Ibn al-Jawzī; both singled it out along with external defence.[109] It is also one of the duties mentioned in practically every mirror for princes.

Roads, bridges, inns, walls, mosques, and other infrastructure

The construction of roads, as opposed to their safety, rarely figures among the services expected of rulers,[110] but the building of bridges, mosques, *madrasas*, and fortified centres (*ribāṭs*), is often mentioned. The imam had to budget for such activities under the rubric of general welfare according to al-Ghazālī.[111] A proper king would build underground canals, bridges across great waters, inns along the highways, fortifications, and new towns, and would restore ruined villages and farms to cultivation, according to Niẓām al-Mulk.[112] Muslim kings and governors often did so, generating the question how far it was permissible to use their bridges and other amenities when they were oppressors.[113] Headmen and other notables often did so as well.[114] Insofar as there was a formal division of labour, the treasury was responsible for the upkeep of the water supply, mosques and defensive walls in a particular locality when funds were available, but the responsibility devolved to the local men of means when the treasury was empty, or so according to al-Māwardī. The local men would need the ruler's permission to destroy buildings of importance to all, such as the city walls or the Friday mosque, but ordinary mosques were private.[115]

109. Above, 158; Ibn al-Jawzī, *Talbīs*, 129 = IV, 172.

110. But "Greek rulers were always building level roads through difficult territory, filling hollows, cutting through high mountains and banishing fear of them," the eleventh-century Mubashshir b. Fātik said in an account in which the Greeks typify the good old days (Rosenthal, *Classical Heritage*, 35); and Transoxanian nobles were famous for their upkeep (Ibn Ḥawqal, *Ṣūrat al-arḍ*, ii, 466.20).

111. *Faḍāʾiḥ*, 118 (ch. 9, under the rubric of *waraʿ*).

112. *SN*, 12f. = 10 (ch. 1, §3). Compare the budget in *Tārīkh-i Sīstān*, 31f. = 21f.; the Greek kings who in the good old days "were always constructing various kinds of bridges, erecting strong walls, building aqueducts and diverting rivers" (Rosenthal, *Classical Heritage*, 35); and Māwardī, *Tashīl al-naẓar*, 214, 279 (bridges, water supply, safe roads).

113. Ghazālī, *Iḥyāʾ*, ii, 125.21 (mosques, *ribāṭs*, bridges, watering provisions). For the worries, see below, 348.

114. Thus notables of Transoxania (Ibn Ḥawqal, *Ṣūrat al-arḍ*, ii, 466.21), the headman in *SN*, 197 = 149 (ch. 40, §14).

115. *Aḥkām*, 411f./245f. = 266; discussed in Aghnides, *Theories of Finance*, 350ff.

Poor help, disability pensions, famine relief

Helping the poor was a *sharʿī* duty fulfilled partly by the government and partly by private individuals. It was the ruler's duty to distribute the obligatory alms, paid once a year by all adult Muslims, to the poor and the indigent, slaves buying their freedom, debtors, travellers, holy warriors, collectors of the alms, and 'those whose hearts have been conciliated' (i.e. enemies placated by financial largesse), these being the recipients mentioned in the Qurʾān, 9:6; and he also had to distribute the fifth (*khums*), which was collected from moveable spoils taken in warfare and similar windfalls (such as mines and treasure troves), and which the Qurʾān, 8:41, assigns to God and His Messenger (represented by the ruler), kinsmen (understood as the Messenger's), orphans, indigent people, and travellers.[116] But the ruler might, and frequently did, assign further funds to charity, for the imam had to help every needy Muslim he heard of. The same was true of private people: the wealthy were guilty of sin if they neglected the poor among them.[117]

In the early centuries there seems to have been a conception of a system of regular government support for the poor and the invalid. This conception was rooted, not in the institution of obligatory alms or the fifth, but rather in the stipend system of the Umayyad period. Registered soldiers disabled in service would receive an invalidity pension, and some sources claim that similar provisions were made for the disabled and poor in general in Umayyad times. Thus al-Walīd I allegedly assigned payments, in cash or kind (*arzāq*), to the poor, the blind and the crippled (or lepers), or he supplied the blind with guides, giving servants to cripples, and paying pensions to all disabled people with pensions so as to spare them the need to beg.[118] Others say that it was al-Walīd II who gave money and clothes to the blind and cripples, supplying the latter with servants.[119] Still others say that it was ʿUmar II who did so.[120] There were also some who held the ʿAbbāsid caliph al-Mahdī to have been the first to give stipends to the poor, the maimed (or leprous) and others,[121] though he defends the absence of funds for such people in another story: a Byzantine

116. Cf. Aghnides, *Theories of Finance*, 207ff., 407ff., 461ff. In Imāmī law the *khums* was an income tax payable to the imam, who was meant to distribute it to the Qurʾānic recipients.

117. Juwaynī, *Ghiyāth*, §338f.

118. YT, ii, 348; Tab., ii, 1196.3; *ʿIqd*, iv, 424.4 (in Syria only?). For the hospitals with which he is also credited by Yaʿqūbī and others, see Conrad, 'First Islamic Hospital?'.

119. Tab., ii, 1754.5 (in Syria only), 1799.14; Ibn Ḥamdūn, *Tadhkira*, i, no. 1102.

120. Tab., ii, 1367.12; Ibn al-Jawzī, *Sīrat ʿUmar b. ʿAbd al-ʿAzīz*, 154f.

121. Sadūsī, *Ḥadhf*, 12 (adds foundlings); Ibn al-Athīr, *Kāmil*, vi, 57, yr 162 (adds prisoners).

emissary who came to Baghdad saw cripples begging on a bridge on his way to al-Ruṣāfa and commented that the ruler (then al-Manṣūr) ought to do something about them; a secretary said that the revenues did not suffice for that, but al-Mahdī hotly denied this; according to him, the reason why the caliph did nothing was that he did not want to monopolize merit making: his subjects too should have a chance to gain rewards by giving to beggars. Needless to say, the Byzantine accepted his point.[122] This story takes us away from the Umayyad stipend system, but all seem to envisage the funds as coming from the taxes in general, not just from the obligatory alms or the fifth, and those reflecting the stipend system rest on the conviction that the *fayʾ* was communal property. Precisely how much truth there is to them is debatable, but they do testify to a concept of what one might call a welfare state.

The idea persisted, too. "Give pensions from the treasury to the blind," Ṭāhir b. al-Ḥusayn, the governor of Khurasan, advised his son in 206/821f. when the latter was appointed to the governorship of Raqqa. The son was also advised to provide assistance to noble houses fallen on hard times,[123] to look after the poor and destitute in general, to be careful not to overlook victims of oppression unable to complain to him and wretches ignorant of how to claim their rights, and to assign pensions to victims of calamities and the orphans and widows they leave behind "in imitation of the Commander of the Faithful".[124] Similar advice is given in an Imami and Ismaili testament.[125] Both al-Fārābī and Ibn Sīnā assigned funds to cripples in the ideal city.[126]

The ruler was also expected to provide help on a one-off basis, especially in times of famine. Pseudo-Aristotle told Alexander to examine the state of the weak ones in his realm, to assist them with funds from the treasury when they were starving, and to store up grain for distribution in years of drought.[127] The ruler should store up food supplies for a year in every region for emergencies

122. Zubayr b. Bakkār, *Muwaffaqiyyāt*, 68f.; Jahshiyārī, *Wuzarāʾ*, 133; Ibn Ḥamdūn, *Tadhkira*, ix, no. 637.

123. Cf. above, 158, note 58.

124. Tab., iii, 1058.14, 1059.2, 5. At 1054.14 he could be taken to say "Grant all Muslims a share and portion of your *fayʾ*", by emendation of the word *niyyatika* to *fayʾika* (thus the *Addenda et Emendanda*, followed by Bosworth in *The History of al-Ṭabarī*, xxxii, 119 [though differently in 'Arabic Mirror', 36]; also in Ibn Khaldūn, *Muqaddima*, 340.-5 = ii, 148). But it is not entirely convincing: the *fayʾ* was not "your *fayʾ*", nor were the normal words for a share in it *ḥazz* or *naṣīb*.

125. IAH, xvii, 85f.; tr. Chittick, *Anthology*, 77; Nuʿmān, *Daʿāʾim*, i, no. 1478; tr. Salinger, 'A Muslim Mirror for Princes', 37.

126. Fārābī, *Fuṣūl*, §62/66; Ibn Sīnā, *SI*, *x*, 447 = 104, condemning the suggestion that incurable people should be killed.

127. *Sirr al-asrār*, 81f.

and move grain to needy provinces, Ibn al-Dāya advised.[128] Pseudo-Ghazālī stresses that the ruler was obliged to help his subjects when they fell into poverty and distress, especially in times of drought, specifying that he had to supply food and financial help alike, and stop oppression, since they would otherwise leave and thereby deplete his treasury.[129] (Peasants were not legally tied to the land.) Al-Juwaynī advised rich people to store up grain for a year and give the rest to the needy, for it fell on them to look after poor people overlooked by the imam; if burying the dead was a collective duty, a fortiori the same was true of preserving the lives of the poor.[130] In practice, rulers did sometimes help communities stricken by disaster with measures such as the remission of taxes, importation of food, and charitable payments. Ensuring that everyone had enough to eat was after all a good way of keeping the subjects orderly.[131] Devastating famines are nonetheless reported from time to time, and generally speaking, private charity seems to have played a far greater role than government measures in the alleviation of poverty and misfortune.

Medical services

Ṭāhir's letter of advice to his son, which was published to immense acclaim, included the statement, "Set up establishments (*dūran*) for sick Muslims where they can find shelter, and appoint custodians who will be kind to them and physicians who will treat their illnesses. Comply with their desires as long as it does not lead to the treasury being squandered."[132] The lepers, cripples, and blind to whom al-Walīd I, ʿUmar II, al-Walīd II, or al-Mahdī were reputedly the first to assign stipends are not said to have received medical treatment, except in the claim, probably false, that al-Walīd I founded a hospital.[133] But from the late ninth century onwards hospitals were all the rage, and the money for them seems often to have come from the treasury. By the reign of al-Muʿtaḍid (d. 289/902) one had been founded at public expense in Baghdad.[134] By 304/916f. there may have been five. In 306/918 the pagan court physician Sinān b. Thābit added another two in the name of the caliph al-Muqtadir and his mother; in 311/923 the vizier Ibn al-Furāt founded one as well. So too did

128. Ibn al-Dāya, *ʿUhūd*, 34.-9, 35.-8.
129. *NM*(G), 101.
130. *Ghiyāth*, §338–42.
131. Cf. *Sirr al-asrār*, 82.5, and the dialogue between a Byzantine and a Persian king cited in Kraemer, *Philosophy*, 19.
132. Tab., iii, 1059.
133. Conrad, 'First Islamic Hospital?'.
134. Cf. below, note 150.

the Būyid rulers Muʿizz al-Dawla in 355/965 and ʿAḍud al-Dawla in 371/987.[135] There were hospitals in tenth-century Basra,[136] Shīrāz, and Rayy; the inhabitants of tenth-century Nishapur asked for one, but were told by their governor that it was more than the treasury could bear, or maybe he did build one after all.[137] Hospitals had also been established in Mecca and Medina by the early tenth century, and a tenth- (or eleventh-) century Zaydī imam composed a manual for censors instructing them, in words similar to Ṭāhir's, that the hospital (*dār al-marḍā*) should have a skilled physician and that the expenses should be charged to the treasury, if it could bear it.[138] In the western Muslim world it seems to have taken longer for hospitals to appear.

All the hospitals of the tenth and eleventh centuries were founded by members of the ruling elite, and like the libraries and other public amenities to which Iraqis above all were treated in the tenth and eleventh centuries, they must have been a function of the competition for power in the politically fragmented and highly unstable world of the time. Why the competitors should have chosen to advertise their status in terms of hospitals, as opposed to some Muslim version of bread and circuses or, as in the Seljuq period, *madrasa*s is another question. But hospitals did have the advantage of giving the philosophers (who often made a living as doctors) a much-needed populist face.

There was more to the medical craze than hospitals. At a time of much sickness in Iraq, ʿAlī b. ʿIsā, 'the good vizier' (d. 334/946), wrote to the pagan court physician Sinān b. Thābit suggesting that some doctors be assigned the task of treating the inmates of prisons, who were bound to be riddled with diseases "in view of their numbers and the harshness of their whereabouts". This done, ʿAlī b. ʿĪsā despatched another note, saying that there must also be sick people who went without treatment in the Sawād, the countryside of southern Iraq, so would Sinān send a mobile medical team to tour this area? Sinān complied. The team soon encountered the problem that not all the inhabitants of the Iraqi countryside were Muslims. Sinān inquired whether Jews were to be treated too, adding that in his own hospital treatment was given to Muslims and Christians alike. The answer was that it was certainly right to treat *dhimmī*s, and cattle too, but Muslims came first, *dhimmī*s second, and

135. Mez, *Renaissance*, 377; *EI*², s.v. 'bīmāristān'.

136. Tanūkhī, *Nishwār*, viii, no. 102 = no. 81.

137. *EI*², s.v. 'bīmāristān'; Muqaddasī, 300, 430; Ibn Bābawayh, *ʿUyūn*, ii, 286, no. 12. The governor was Ḥamawayh b. ʿAlī.

138. *EI*², s.v. 'bīmāristān'; Serjeant, 'Zaidī Manual', 30.16, identifying the imam as al-Nṣīr li'l-Ḥaqq (d. Daylam, 304/917).

animals last.[139] Whether these justly famous services continued beyond the tenure of the good vizier is unknown.

In 319/931, however, the death of a patient by medical misadventure caused al-Muqtadir to instruct his censor to prevent doctors in Baghdad from practising unless they had been authorized by the same Sinān b. Thābit, who was instructed to examine them. No fewer than 860-odd doctors are said to have shown up for the test.[140] A similar story is told of the caliph al-Mustaḍīʾ (566–75/1170–80) and his Christian court physician Ibn al-Tilmīdh.[141] In Fāṭimid Cairo the court physician Ibn Riḍwān (d. 453/1061) would have liked more state control of doctors along these lines. "I shall tell you some stories about these doctors, their deceit and ignorance, so that you will be wary of them," he told his reader. "The government (*al-sulṭān*) might look into their affairs and prevent anyone from making a living by this profession unless he is skilled, and single out the best of them for the rest to emulate."[142] This was also the view of the Aleppan doctor al-Shayzarī (d. 589/1193) and the peripatetic ʿAbd al-Laṭīf al-Baghdādī (d. 629/1231), who both had dealings with Saladin. According to al-Shayzarī, the ancient Greeks had set up a chief physician in every city for the examination of doctors and ongoing quality control; doctors were required to provide written accounts of the treatment they prescribed and to give copies to their patients' relatives so that if a patient died, the chief physician could decide whether the doctor was at fault and, if he was, order him to pay compensation.[143] According to al-Baghdādī, good practices still prevailed in Constantinople, where people took proper care that only competent physicians were allowed to practise by holding medical examinations and imposing the Hippocratic oath on the candidates, or so at least until the Franks conquered the city (in 1204), he said.[144] Back in the good old days, Greek rulers had also supported the development of new drugs, and tested them before releasing them, according to the eleventh-century al-Mubashshir b. Fātik; public funds were always available for that.[145] But nowadays was a different story. In the absence of a chief physician it was the *muḥtasib* who had to

139. Ibn al-Qifṭī, *Ḥukamāʾ*, 193f.

140. Ibid., 191f.

141. Ibn Abī ʿUṣaybiʿa, *ʿUyūn*, i, 261f.

142. Gamal and Dols, *Medieval Islamic Medicine*, 24 = 123. Goitein, *Mediterranean Society*, ii, 247, claims that there was a licensing system for doctors in Egypt, adducing Ibn Riḍwān (in Ibn Abī Uṣaybiʿa); perhaps it was ʿAbd al-Laṭīf al-Baghdādī he had in mind (cf. below, note 147).

143. Shayzarī, *Nihāyat al-rutba*, 97ff.

144. Stern, 'Collection of Treatises by ʿAbd al-Laṭīf', 60.

145. Rosenthal, *Classical Heritage*, 35.

test the competence of doctors, armed with books by Galen, Paul of Aegina, Ḥunayn b. Isḥāq, and others, according to al-Shayzarī; he would administer the Hippocratic oath to them.[146] No such procedures are mentioned by al-Baghdādī. According to him, one needed a certificate signed by a leading man (or men) of the profession to practise as a physician in Cairo, Damascus, or Baghdad, but chaos prevailed in Aleppo, where he was writing.[147] All in all, rulers seem to have found it more attractive to found hospitals than to maintain control of doctors or their drugs.

Education, culture

Children learnt to read and write on the basis of the Qurʾān in elementary schools (sing. *kuttāb*) run by a single teacher. Higher education in subjects recognized as valid by the religious scholars took place in private homes or in mosques, where one would join a circle (*ḥalqa*) of pupils around a particular scholar; from the tenth and eleventh century onwards one could also study in *madrasa*s, residential colleges attached to mosques which specialized in law. For more rarified subjects such as philosophy (including science) one studied in private homes or on one's own, though one could also be attached to a hospital for the study of medicine. Most teachers charged a fee, and living expenses also had to be met. Schoolteachers were usually hired and paid by parents, and neither the Umayyad nor the ʿAbbāsid caliphs seem to have concerned themselves with education at so elementary a level, but later rulers sometimes did.[148] According to the Ḥanbalite Abū Yaʿlā (d. 1066), the imam was obliged to provide basic religious instruction for his subjects, women included, and to make public funding available to both teachers and pupils; this, he said, was more important than waging *jihād*.[149] Even so, it was more commonly to higher education that subsidies went. Mosques, *madrasa*s and hospitals were usually paid for by *waqf*s, charitable endowments established by the ruler and other members of the elite with funding from private sources or the treasury, though some were maintained directly by the treasury.[150] The

146. Shayzarī, *Nihāya t al-rutba*, 98ff.

147. Stern, 'Collection of Treatises by ʿAbd al-Laṭīf', 60; cf. Goitein, *Mediterranean Society*, ii, 247, for the certificate.

148. Nūr al-Dīn supplied elementary education for orphans (Elisséeff, 'Document contemporain,' 138; cf. Talmon-Heller, 'Religion in the Public Sphere', 54).

149. Abū Yaʿlā, *K. al-amr bi'l-maʿrūf*, fol. 114b (I owe this reference, along with a xerox of the passage, to Michael Cook).

150. Cf. *EI*², s.v. 'waḳf'. The caliph al-Muʿtaḍid paid the running expenses of the Ṣāʿidī hospital directly out of the treasury, at 450 dinars a month (Busse, 'Hofbudget', 29), and the

great libraries in which the Muslim world abounded in the tenth and eleventh centuries were usually also financed by charitable endowments. They were public in the sense of open to all. Many served learning of a type that the religious scholars disliked (notably philosophy and various types of Shīʿism), but no teaching seems to have gone on in them.

What rulers and other magnates did above all, however, was to patronize poets, scholars, littérateurs, and philosophers and other men of learning once their education was completed. No list of the ruler's *sharʿī* duties mentions this function directly, but it was implicit in 'preservation of the religion': as the army guarded the religion with their swords, so the scholars guarded it with their arguments and proofs, and the imam had to ensure that both were adequately funded, as al-Ghazālī said.[151] Besides, rulers needed religious scholars, jurists, poets, littérateurs, and, when they were thus inclined, philosophers for their own advice, edification and entertainment; and they also liked to have some control of what was being said, not only in the sense that poets and chroniclers could have great propaganda value, but also in the sense that they needed to gauge, and where necessary to influence, intellectual trends in order to stay on top. As patrons of learned men, rulers had a greater say in the shaping of the cultural orientation of Islam than anyone quite realized, not only because the court conferred wealth and prestige on those who frequented it, but also because some branches of learning depended on patronage for their very survival. Religious scholars could always find some source of income or other, however lowly, because they served needs common to all Muslims; but poets might find it more difficult to make a living, and only the elite found at courts appreciated the services of philosophers and *mutakallim*s (who reacted to the competition for scarce resources by being at each others' throats).

Conclusion

All in all an amazing number of services were supplied by the ruling elite at various times. It was, however, rare for all of them to be supplied at the same time, for the costs were high and political stability was low. Of the Būyid ruler ʿAḍud al-Dawla (d. 372/983) we are told that he swept Baghdad clear of thieves, restored order in the troubled deserts of Arabia and Kerman, provided a quick news-service, dug wells on the pilgrim routes, constructed cisterns, and built a wall around Medina, renovated the half-ruined Baghdad, built mosques and

---

undated budget in *Tārīkh-i Sīstān*, 32 = 22, assigns 10,000 dirhams a year to hospitals. The upkeep of prisons is considerably more costly in both budgets.

151. *Faḍāʾiḥ*, 117 (ch. 9, on *waraʿ*).

bazaars, repaired the bridges over the great canals, put railings on the bridge over the Tigris and appointed guards to it, made the wealthy repair dilapidated weirs, redug canals that had silted up and built mills along them, repaired dams and transferred people to the land thus reclaimed, established a richly endowed bazaar in Fars and made arrangements for the cultivation of fruits there, and introduced the cultivation of indigo in Kerman. On top of that, we are told, he loved learning and gave stipends to theologians, jurists, philologists, physicians, mathematicians, and engineers, as well as to preachers and muezzins, and built a huge library in Shīrāz. He also founded a hospital in Baghdad, made provisions for the poor and the strangers who lived in mosques, and gave away much money in charity. His governors engaged in similar deeds.[152] Or so we are told. One certainly would not characterize this as minimal government, which was what rulers normally dispensed in the medieval Islamic world or indeed in pre-modern times in general.[153] But in return he is said to have extorted money in every conceivable way, and there may have been less to the result than advertised. People would complain, the vizier Ibn Saʿdān (373–5/983–5) was told, of interference with their lives and property, disturbance of their tranquillity, and confiscation of their homes and land; they would lament that money was counterfeit, taxes doubled, business slack, soldiers and police swaggering about, mosques in ruins, hospitals desolate, enemies rabid, and more besides, quite apart from all the things they did not dare to say for fear of the whip.[154] What people really wanted rulers to supply was more and better government at lower cost, without violence or oppression. It sounds familiar.

152. Summarized from Mez, *Renaissance*, 25–7.

153. Goitein, 'Minority Selfrule', 102; Crone, *Pre-industrial Societies*, 49f., 57.

154. Tawḥīdī, *Imtāʿ*, iii, 88, quoting his teacher (who was patronized by ʿAḍud al-Dawla), in Kraemer, *Philosophy*, 252.

CHAPTER

19

VISIONS OF FREEDOM

In practice, government was more often than not both weak and oppressive: weak in the sense that it could not get much done, oppressive in the sense that rulers would freely sacrifice the lives and property of their subjects in order to stay in power and keep some semblance of order. It was normal for members of the elite, scholars included, to spend time in jail; most high-ranking governors and generals died violent deaths; and torture, assassination, poisoning, confiscation, and extortion were matters of routine. Yet the desire for freedom remained. Not that medieval Muslims used that term. They did speak of political oppression as enslavement,[1] but they did not call the opposite freedom, for the choice as they saw it was not between slavery and freedom, but rather between slavery to other human beings and slavery to God. No humans had the right to impose obligations on other humans, whether they were rulers, masters, fathers or husbands, or for that matter prophets; only God could do so.[2] To be governed in accordance with God's rules was to be protected from other people's arbitrary desires (*hawā*). In other words, it was to live as an autonomous person under the law, which is also how political freedom has traditionally been understood in the West. Living in accordance with God's rules was what most Muslims desired. In practice, however, this freedom only

1. Above, 45f., 52; for post-Umayyad examples, see Ps.-Nāshiʾ, §83 (of non-Muslim regimes); ʿĀmirī, *Iʿlām*, 175 (of the Persians); Marín-Guzman, 'ʿUmar ibn Ḥafṣūn', 194 (of al-Andalus).

2. Ghazālī in Laoust, *Politique de Ġazālī*, 153f. (citing the *Mustaṣfā*).

obtained in the sphere of life untouched by the state. The law controlled the details of daily life, but not the institutions of power.[3]

Keeping up appearances

People typically coped with this situation by keeping quiet about it, not just in the negative sense of avoiding involvement, but also in the positive sense of trying to draw a veil over the ugly things that went on. Most chroniclers write in a dispassionate tone and deliberately unspecific terms about the misdeeds of rulers even when they are not patronized by them. Embarrassing episodes are passed over lightly, or dropped altogether; criticism tends to be muted, indirect, or very general. In part, of course, this was because open criticism was dangerous, but the restraint seems to hold even when it would have been safe to speak out. (I have to stress, though, that no systematic work has been done on this.) Ibn al-Athīr comes across as unusually outspoken when he bluntly characterizes the policies of the caliph al-Nāṣir as detestable and supplies some illustrations of what he means. But even he speaks in terms too general for a modern historian to reconstruct exactly what al-Nāṣir did.[4] Some people were actually paid to criticize rulers – thus preachers of hellfire sermons and mirror writers, for example. But they too tended to speak generically, concentrating on standard sins and describing them in formulaic terms, using past figures as examples. Here again there are exceptions, especially Persian works such as the *Siyāsatnāme* and the *Qābūsnāme*. Though they too use past figures as examples, their accounts of the ways in which power was abused are extremely vivid, in no way flattened by the moralizing purpose for which they are told. But the overall impression is one of restraint. By contrast, people were happy to use vituperative language of people regarded as heretics. But their abuse also tended to be formulaic. The prevalent attitude seems to have been that all the terrible things people said and thought were only to be discussed insofar as they could be used for moral edification, preferably in unspecific terms that would not shock the pious or give ideas to the impious. For the rest, it was better not to delve into them.

It is not just in connection with rulers that this attitude is apparent. Turning a blind eye to other people's failings was in general a virtue, as indeed was covering one's own. He who covered the shame of a believer (*man satara muʾminan*) would receive the same consideration from God, according to a Prophetic tradition; such a person was like someone who rescued a female

3. Gellner, *Conditions of Liberty*, 26f.; cf. Crone, *Slaves*, 81, on the moral gap (referring to the same contrast, though widely misunderstood).

4. See the reference given above, 250, note 137.

infant buried alive.[5] "Cover me, cover me," a hapless secretary implored of God in a graffito left on a mountainside, describing himself as dressed in rags, afraid, in flight, and oppressed. The dishonour he wished to hide may simply have been poverty.[6] "May God see to it that (the faults of) Muslim youths are covered," an eleventh-century scholar wrote in his diary, grieved by the news that a young man had had a hand and a foot amputated for theft.[7] Whatever the type of dishonour involved, nothing would have been more distasteful to medieval Muslims than the modern Western idea of publicly revealing one's inner weaknesses in all their concrete detail, or of exposing other people's inability to live up to public norms, or washing dirty linen in public. "Most of what is known about people has to be left unsaid because of the importance attached in the religious law to preventing slander," as al-Ghazālī observed, adding that this was so even when the information could be verified.[8] For one thing, drawing attention to other people's failings was bad for social solidarity. The believers were supposed to stick together and support one another: helping the morally weak to remain respected members of the community was one way in which one did so (provided, of course, that no innocent parties were wronged thereby). For another thing, shared norms are undermined by repeated disclosure of how easy it is to violate them, and how often it is done. Keeping up appearances is a good way of enforcing them, for if everybody speaks as if the norms are generally accepted and observed, those who find it difficult to abide by them, or who positively dislike them, will perceive themselves as lone misfits who must try their best to conform so as not to be ostracized. "A sin that is kept secret only harms the person who has committed it, but if it becomes public and is not denounced, it harms people in general," as a tradition says.[9] Of such protection of public norms by silence and dissimulation (hypocrisy in popular parlance) there was much in the medieval Muslim world, some of it under the name of *taqiyya*, but most of it just by way of a general tendency to conform. Dissimulation was also called for in the form of flattery in polite society, where one could not get on without mouthing praise apt to make even American hype sound mild. Not all forms of dissimulation enjoyed a high moral status, but covering up one's own and other people's failings certainly did. Nakedness, physical or moral, was repulsive. Hidden sins were no less odious for being hidden, but as long as they did not affect third parties, they were between the sinner and God alone. Once things were into the

5. Cook, *Commanding Right*, 44 and note 61.
6. Abū 'l-Faraj al-Iṣbahānī (attrib.), *Ghurabā'* , §63.
7. Makdisi, 'Autograph Diary', III, §104.
8. *Iqtiṣād*, 244.
9. Cited by Ibn Taymiyya, *Siyāsa*, 167; tr. (slightly differently) Peters, *Jihad*, 50.

open, they had to be reproved and punished, by fellow-Muslims and/or by rulers, but it was better if it did not have to come to that.[10]

Most of the failings of rulers were all too public, of course, but one could still keep quiet about them. Not even scholars were obliged to speak up like Old Testament prophets against the iniquities of kings likely to respond by cutting off their heads.[11] The danger apart, it went against the grain of authority, and also against the desire to keep the community clean; bad though the ruler might be, he was still its guardian. Just as one did not take guests into the private quarters of one's home or violate the privacy of one's neighbours, so one did not throw dirt at one's own king, or not unless one was a zealot. If there was filth to dispose of, it was into the quarters of heretics and infidels that it should be cast.

Puritan reformism

Nonetheless, the urge to reform imperfect reality never disappeared. It was kept alive by a great utopian vision of enormous influence from early times until today, that of Medina in the time of the Prophet and the Rāshidūn, the rightly-guided caliphs.

Medieval Muslims did not write utopias in the sense of imaginary travel accounts or other descriptions of ideal societies which do not exist, such as Iambulus' *City of the Sun* or Thomas More's *Utopia*, nor did they often use exotic peoples or noble savages to illustrate social and political ideals. As noted before, they were not given to seeking ideals outside their own civilization at all.[12] But they did place a golden age right at the beginning of their own history, and their numerous accounts of this age add up to a detailed utopia of great emotive power. It was a primitivist utopia, both in the sense that it presented the earliest time as the best and in the sense that it deemed a simple, society to be the most virtuous.[13] In patriarchal Medina, we are assured, things were right because society was small, simple and poor. Government was minimal, wholly just, and without any kind of oppression or violence, except of course against evildoers. There were no palaces, wide courts, crowns, thrones, head or arm extensions such as those described by al-Bīrūnī, no jails or doorkeepers, no taxes, confiscations, or forced labour, and no differences between elite and commoners: everybody lived much like everyone else. ʿUmar's attire was a torn old shirt, which he preferred to a new one offered to him by the

10. Cook, *Forbidding Wrong*, ch. 5.

11. Ibid., ch. 7, sec. 2.

12. Above, 269.

13. Cf. Lovejoy and Boas, *Primitivism and Related Ideas in Antiquity*, ch. 1.

bishop of Ayla; and even in extreme heat he would personally count the camels sent to Medina as tax, wrapping a bit of clothing around his head.[14] "How blessed and how golden would be the condition of human affairs if, throughout the whole world, meekness and devotion and peace and innocence and fairness and temperance and faith should tarry!" as the Latin church father Lactantius (d. c. 320) wrote with reference to the golden age of the Stoic tradition. "There would not be need of so many and such various laws for ruling men, when the one law of God would suffice unto perfect innocence. Nor would there be need of prisons or the swords of guards and the terror of punishments, when the healthfulness of the heavenly precepts infused into human hearts would instruct men willingly to do the works of justice."[15] This is precisely how the patriarchal period went down in the Sunni tradition: all obeyed the law of their own accord. It was the time when the Muslims had all the virtues of tribesmen and none of their vices, for thanks to Islam there was no feuding, no factionalism, and no disorder, just austerity, solidarity, and total devotion to the truth.

This ideal polity, we are told, was ruined by the misdeeds of ʿUthmān, under whom the tribal bias in favour of kinsmen resurfaced, and/or by the conquests, which exposed the tribesmen to massive wealth and foreign ways. ʿUmar wept at the sight of the booty from the battle of Qādisiyya, explaining that no people had ever been given such wealth without developing mutual hatred and enmity.[16] The Persians and the Byzantines marvelled at his tattered clothes and at his habit of distributing the treasures of the earth among his people instead of storing them up; when somebody suggested to him that it might be a good idea to store up this wealth, he had replied that this was a suggestion made by the devil, predicting that the money would be a trial (*fitna*) for his successors.[17] He had also warned his subjects against the comfortable lifestyle of the Persians.[18] Muslims warriors had ridden their horses over the cushions of the Persians at Qādisiyya, shredding their silken covers with their swords and voicing egalitarian sentiments which inflamed the Persian masses.[19] But for all their efforts to combine the simplicity of Medina with possession of the world, the rightly guided polity with its egalitarian fraternity vanished.

14. Tab., i, 2522f., 2736f.

15. Lactantius, *Divine Institutes*, v, 8. Cf. also Al-Azmeh, 'Utopia and Islamic Political Thought', 15f.

16. *NM* (M), 68.

17. ʿAbd al-Jabbar, *Tathbīt*, ii, 328f.

18. Cf. Morony, *Iraq*, 262; add Jāḥiẓ, *Bayān*, iii, 23f. (against stirrups).

19. Tab. i, 2270ff.

This image of a simple society nourished by prophetic revelation and the virtues of the desert was irresistible to non-Shīʿite Muslims. It was above all ʿUmar, the hero of *jamāʿī* Muslims and Khārijites, who epitomized it. It is scattered all over the sources, in accounts of the Prophet, chronicles, epistles, mirrors, and above all in Ḥadīth, much of it canonized as Islamic law. It lies at the heart of Arabism, the belief that the Arabs and their heritage occupied a special place in Islam. Its essence could be defined as puritan reformism.

Puritan reformists called for the restoration of the law (*iḥyāʾ al-sunna*) and a return to the ways of the pious ancestors (*salaf*), seeing the law as a set of liberating rules, a constitution to be invoked against tyrants, corrupt officials, and other abusers of power (including foreign powers), not as a system of control imposed by clerics. It was not always against tyrants that their call was directed, however. Like commanding right and prohibiting wrong, of which it was a collective version, reformism might focus on the moral improvement of Muslim society on its own, without attention to the government, or even in alliance with it.

Sometimes, however, attempts were made to force rulers to observe the law. It is a striking characteristic of such attempts, as of commanding right in general, that they usually address the head of state as a private individual rather than a king, in the sense that the habits he is told to abandon are those pertaining to a life of luxury rather than those specific to political decision-making: wearing silken clothing, drinking wine, listening to music, and the like, as opposed to jailing political opponents, confiscating other people's property, executing people without due cause, tolerating corrupt officials, and so forth.[20] It is puritannical attitudes that drive the activity.[21] The only malpractice specific to rulers regularly singled out in reformist movements is the collection of uncanonical taxes (*mukūs*).

Rebels of the Umayyad period had regularly denounced the tyrannical ways of Umayyad rulers, too, if not usually to their face. What the Ibāḍī Abū Ḥamza (c. 130/747) held against the Umayyads, for example, was not just their dissolute habits, though they did not escape his hostile attention, but also that "they arrest on suspicion, make decrees capriciously, kill in anger, and judge by passing over crimes without punishment . . . (saying), 'This land is our land, the property is our property, and the people are our slaves'".[22] A year or two earlier, when the military commander al-Kirmānī took over the government of

20. Cf. Cook, *Forbidding Wrong*, ch. 7, sec. 1.

21. Ibid., ch. 9, sec. 5.

22. In Crone and Hinds, *God's Caliph*, 132. Compare Tab., ii, 266, where Ibn ʿAqīl denounces the bloodthirsty ways of Ziyād to Ibn Ziyād; ii, 624, where a follower of al-Mukhtār tells the Kufans that their hands and feet have been cut off, their eyes blinded, their

Khurāsān claiming to want only the Book of God, a daring scholar promptly asked him whether it was in the Book of God to tear down houses and seize wealth.[23] But when Sufyān al-Thawrī assumed the role of Old Testament prophet in relation to al-Mahdī (d. 169/785), it was only the caliph's luxurious style of pilgrimage, contrasted with the frugal practice of ʿUmar, that he castigated;[24] and apart from the usurpation of the property of orphans, there is not a single political item among the malpractices that Ibn Tūmart (d. 524/1130) is reported to have denounced in his encounter with the Almoravid ruler, against whom he was soon to rebel as the leader of the Almohad movement.[25]

Puritan reformism did not often inspire revolt, given that the victims of oppressive government were typically lacking in military power and that the Sunnis disapproved of rebellion. Down to c. 500/1100 a rebel with a cause (as opposed to a participant in mere power games) was more often than not a heretical tribesman, such as a Zaydī in Yemen, a Khārijite in North Africa, the Jazīra or Oman, or an Ismaili in North Africa, Baḥrayn, or the Syrian desert. He was usually a tribesman thereafter too, but he ceased to be a heretic. The Almoravids mark the first appearance of reformism as an ideology for the mobilization of militant tribesmen in Sunni Islam, the role it played again under Ibn Tūmart's Almohads. It was thanks to Ibn Tūmart that the Mahdi became a puritan reformist, too.

The outcome of such movements (of which there were more after the end of the period covered in this book) was typically government with greater military strength, but not usually less autocracy. On the contrary, those who seize power by force everywhere tend to be more autocratic than the tyrants they overthrow, since a very high degree of coordination from the top is needed to carry out the venture: what rebels claim is a version of emergency power, a well-known destroyer of civil rights. Insofar as the new rulers were felt to be more bearable, it was only because their state structures initially retained some of the simplicity of their tribal homeland. But the changes they wrought rarely lasted for more than about a hundred years, as Ibn Khaldūn observed. Within three generations or so, he noted, the conquest elite would be thoroughly undermined by the luxuries of urban life so that a fresh set of tribesmen would

---

bodies hung on tree trunks; ii, 999, where Muṭarrif denounces ʿAbd al-Malik and al-Ḥajjāj in words that recur in Abū Ḥamza's speech.

23. Tab., ii, 1930, where it is Muqātil b. Ḥayyān who asks him; cf. 1933, where it is Ibrāhīm (al-Ṣāʾigh), on whom see Cook, *Commanding Right*, ch. 1.

24. Cook, *Commanding Right*, 65.

25. The accounts are summarized in Bourouiba, *Ibn Toumart*, 45ff.; further references in Cook, *Commanding Right*, 458, note 226.

oust it. (A modern reader would not stress the role of luxury so much: with or without it, tribal ties were unlikely to survive under the new conditions. But luxury had a prominent role as a solvent of virtue already in Plato's *Republic*, and it went beautifully with the history of early Islam.) Within a century or so, Ibn Khaldūn said, the dynasty would be ripe for destruction, new tribesmen would take over, and so it was bound to go on, except insofar as slave soldiers were an alternative: the Turkish tribesmen imported as slaves were a substitute for a tribal conquest elite, he acutely remarked.[26]

Ibn Khaldūn's argument rested on the assumption that tribesmen (whether settled or nomadic) on the periphery of politically organized societies, or 'cities', as he calls them in the tradition of the philosophers, would always be stronger in military terms than people ruled by states: non-tribesmen could not be effective soldiers. A Roman or a Chinese would have been astonished by this assumption; in their version of the argument, the disintegration of the tribal conquest elite would have been followed by a resumption of imperial government, not by another tribal conquest. But given that military power had been handed to tribesmen and slaves in the Muslim world, Ibn Khaldūn was right. Dynasties rarely did last for more than a hundred years, whether by origin they were tribal or servile or something else again: the point is that whatever it was that held them together, it was usually something that set them apart from the world they ruled and which was accordingly doomed to dissipate in contact with their far more numerous subjects.[27] In short, political power in the medieval Muslim world tended to be a wasting asset. So too did such reduction of autocratic oppression as was experienced from time to time.

No amount of abstention from wine, silk, luxurious food, grand palaces, or the like could restore the simple nature of the society in which the Rāshidūn had been active and on which the libertarian aspect of government had rested. The substitute for tribal virtue would have had to be formal organization, but the evolution of government in the first two hundred years had been such that this was not possible: state and society had parted ways. There were times when they came closer again, above all in holy war against infidels, when they pursued the same aim, on the basis of the same religious law. But by and large people had to accept that the Sharīʿa was only the constitutional law of everyday life, not of the government appointed for its protection.

26. Cf. Crone, *Slaves* (devoted to the same theory), 89ff. and the references given there.

27. Mamluk Egypt (1250–1517) is the major exception. But then, some attempts at heredity notwithstanding, every generation of rulers and soldiers was freshly imported here.

Antinomianism

There was another road to freedom, however, of a diametrically opposed kind. The alternative to reform was escape. The escape could be literal: peasants would respond to oppression by fleeing from their land; merchants would respond to it by moving from one state to another; and one Arab tribe, the Banū Ḥabīb, responded to Ḥamdānid oppression by leaving the Jazīra with their families, slaves, and livestock for the Byzantine empire.[28] (Injustice was harder to bear than unbelief, as everyone knew.) Other people left their homes to become wandering ascetics, mendicants, hermits, inmates of Sufi lodges, or holy warriors in fortified settlements where they could fight real infidels regardless of what went on at home. But the escape could also be effected in the spirit alone. It was common for medieval Muslims to cultivate detachment: the true believer was a stranger to this world. And some dreamed of ultimate freedom in the form of escape from all external commands, by transcending or abolishing the law along with all the socio-political arrangements based on it, individually or collectively.

It was first and foremost Shīʿites who indulged in this vision of utopia, but it appealed to Sufis and philosophers too, insofar as one could distinguish between them: by the end of our period, most philosophers were either Sufis or Shīʿites, or both. To Rāfiḍī Shīʿites, things had gone badly wrong as soon as the Prophet died and the only rightly guided caliph was ʿAlī, who had ruled in Kufa, not in Arabia. This drastically reduced the scope of Arabism. It did not eliminate it, nor did it rule out primitivism. Both affected the Shīʿites too (if for no other reason, then because they were so prone to sunnification), but neither is a prominent feature of Shīʿite tradition. Where ʿUmar champions the simple ways of patriarchal Arabia, ʿAlī by contrast stands for a universalist vision in which there are no Arabs any more, only Muslims for whom learning and piety take priority over wealth, noble birth, and Arab ethnicity alike.[29] And where the Sunnis typically hankered for puritan solidarity, the Shīʿites tended to crave individual spirituality over and above, or even instead of, communal perfection. For the socio-political world was irredeemably corrupt, and would remain so until the Mahdi came. If one could not reform the world of organized religion and external conformity, one could try to put an end to it; and if that was not possible either, all that was left was cultivation of that inner spark of the divine which every Gnostic, whether Shīʿite or Sufi, knew him or herself

28. Ibn Ḥawqal, *Ṣūrat al-arḍ*, 210.

29. Cf. Marlow, *Hierarchy*, 14f., 28ff. But for a passage in which he too objects to Persian luxury, see Morony, *Iraq*, 262 (against silk).

to carry, so as to retrieve the heavenly home of origin, in this life or the next, individually or as member of a spiritual brotherhood.

Antinomianism could be said to be the Muslim counterpart to Western anarchism. Both are convictions to the effect that humans can live without authority, that they once did so (in Paradise or in some golden age), and that they will again, when they have perfected their nature (in this world or the next). Both typically see the individual as shackled and wish to liberate him/her. But anarchists are out to remove the law of the state, whereas antinomians wish to eliminate the law on which a religious community is based. The myth of a golden age of freedom and innocence, which was to play a key role in the development of European anarchism, appears as a charter of religious antinomianism already in Eusebius of Caesarea (d. 340), who from a medieval Muslim perspective sounds like an outright Ismaili. According to him, the Hebrews originally lived in accordance with nature (*kata physin*), exhibiting a form of piety that was free and devoid of constraint (*eleutheron kai aneimenon*), for they had reasoned their way to true monotheism at a time when all other peoples were lost in error, and for this reason they had no need of laws (which were only for the sick, as every philosopher knew). They were corrupted in Egypt, however, so Moses now gave them a law formulated as a constitution (*politeia*) suited to their gross habits, but he formulated some of it in allegorical form: it was not the naked truth, but symbols and shadows that he told them to observe. This was how things stayed until the advent of Jesus, who made the law unnecessary again.[30]

The Christians having abrogated Mosaic law, their antinomianism could only be directed against moral precepts thereafter. In that form it played a role of some importance in the later middle ages, sometimes in combination with anarchism.[31] But it was anarchism (usually including communism) that went on to acquire major political significance in the Christian West. In the Islamic world, by contrast, it was antinomianism that commanded people's attention. Anarchism is represented only by the Najdiyya, al-Aṣamm, and other Muʿtazilites, and their views on the state were not animated by a desire to remove shackles, whether political or religious: they did not see the state as an intrinsically repressive institution. By contrast, antinomianism was represented by a large number of Gnostics, Shīʿite or Sufi, philosphically inclined or otherwise, and all did wish to remove shackles, but only of the religious kind: all asserted that religious law was dispensable for salvation, not that one could live without law or government in the here and now. They did not usually spell

30. Eusebius, *Praep. Evang.*, book vii, esp. ch. 3; ch. 6, 3–4; ch. 8, 37–40.
31. Cf. the classic account by Cohn, *Pursuit of the Millennium*, esp. chs 8–13.

out the implications of their views for the socio-political order at all. Most of them clearly held that one should leave the world as it is, by withdrawing from it, transcending it, or just playing along with it under the guise of *taqiyya*. They were not usually political activists, let alone anarchists. Their utopia was spiritual.

The Qarāmiṭa

Just occasionally, however, the antinomian vision was socio-political too, most obviously in the case of the early Ismailis. Their Mahdi was expected to abrogate the law, and we are left in no doubt that he would abrogate the established order along with it. What sort of socio-political organization, if any, did they think there would be after his arrival? We do not know. They probably did not know themselves. Like twentieth-century Marxists, they envisaged the revolution as so sharp a turn for the better that the nature of life thereafter could barely even be glimpsed.

As devotees of Adam's Paradise, they implicitly cast themselves as anarchists (and indeed communists), but this was hardly their intention. Their vision of the antinomian future seems to have functioned first and foremost as a solvent, in the sense that it de-legitimated existing institutions without amounting to a model of what was to follow. According to Sunni sources, the first missionary to Iraq promised his followers that they would be kings, not that government would wither away (let alone that everything would be held in common): "I was ordered to cure this village, to enrich its inhabitants, and to deliver them and empower them over the kingdoms of this world, replacing the people now in charge," he is reported as saying to Ḥamdān Qarmaṭ. The banners of the Baḥrayn Ismailis carried the inscription, "We desire to show favour unto those who were deemed weak on earth and to make them imams and the heirs" (Q. 28:5).[32] Apparently, people were promised that the existing political roles would be reversed, not that they would be eliminated. All social and political arrangements would indeed be abolished, but the reversion to a state of chaos would be followed by the birth of a new order in which the Ismailis would rule. Beyond that it seems unlikely that anyone knew what to expect.

The Mahdi did change the world for some of them. In the 290s/910s the Ismaili peasants of the Kufan countryside were ordered to surrender increasingly large proportions of their wealth to their local missionaries, and eventually to hand over their moveable property altogether, on the grounds that this

32. Ibn al-Dawādārī, *Kanz*, vi, 45 (from Akhū Muḥsin); Ibn al-Jawzī, *Muntaẓam*, vi, 215f.; Thābit b. Sinān, *Akhbār*, 53. The verse had previously been used by the Hāshimite revolutionaries (*AA*, 285), and Muḥammad al-Nafs al-Zakiyya (Tab., iii, 209).

constituted the true harmony (*ulfa*) mentioned in the Qur'ān. (No reference was made to the absence of private property from Adam's Paradise.) Having pooled their resources, the villagers abandoned their fields and moved to an abode of emigration (*dār al-hijra*), where they took to a new life as warriors on behalf of the Mahdi and maintained themselves, one assumes, on the basis of the communal chest established by the missionaries, plus booty. This, then, was how the weak on earth were favoured in the new dispensation. In 317/930 the Ismailis of Baḥrayn sacked Mecca, massacred pilgrims, and removed the black stone as a sign that Islam as we know it was coming to an end, and in 319/931 the Mahdi manifested his presence in Baḥrayn in the form of a young Persian captive. He initiated the abolition of the law by issuing strange and, by normal Muslim standards, repulsive rules, but it ended badly: having turned against the pillars of the local community, he was soon killed himself. A second attempt seems to have been made at some point, however, for a strikingly new socio-political order was in existence some hundred years later. Muslim ritual and dietary law had vanished, there were no mosques, except for visitors, and social relations were egalitarian. In socio-economic terms, the polity was a welfare state. Politically, it exhibited the novel feature that several members of the same family ruled together as a council. The army was furnished by the Ismailis themselves and everybody participated in annual campaigns against non-Ismaili Muslims, contributing to a sense of participatory politics. How far Adam's Paradise had been invoked as a model in all this we do not know, but it is in any case hard to believe that it could have worked on a larger scale, in a more complex society and metropolitan environment. It came to an end in the 460s/1070s.[33]

The Fatimids did not engage in any socio-political experiments of any kind. They simply postponed the end of the world, as has been seen. This was also what the early Christians had done, but unlike the Christians, the Fatimids kept the law. Their Nizārī offshoot did abolish the law at Alamūt in 559/1164, but there was no real animus against it any more, and they returned to it in, or soon after, 607/1210.[34] Once again it was made clear that even as an Ismaili, one had to live in this imperfect world of externality. One might as well be a Sunni in that case, or alternatively, one could withdraw into one's inner self to cultivate the higher truth behind a mask of *taqiyya*. The antinomian utopia turned purely spiritual again.

33. On all this, see above, 201f.; Halm, *Reich*, 52ff., 57f., 225–36/Empire, 48ff., 54, 250–64 (his understanding of the events in Iraq differs from mine); Nāṣir-i Khusraw above, 276, note 95; de Goeje, 'Fin de l'empire'.

34. Cf. above, 211.

The Brethren of Purity

Among those who took to cultivation of the inner self were the tenth-century Brethren of Purity, who offered a new version of Ismaili antinomianism in their epistles. They told their readers that one day, when they had been perfected by philosophy and shed their bodies, they would live together and worship God without any need for external compulsion at all, driven by inner impulses alone, as angels. There had been no law in our original home, the *madīna fāḍila* from which we have fallen, nor would there be in the perfected state.[35] True religiosity was devoid of books, mosques, alms, *ʿulamāʾ* and all the paraphernalia of organized religion, as they have the animals say in the fable in which the animals take the humans to court. But what about the here and now? The answer was that as long as they had bodies, humans had to accept their enslavement to the law, just as animals had to accept their enslavement to humans, since it was from the union of body and soul that evil inclinations stemmed. It was by obeying humans that animals could hope to be reborn as humans, and it was by obeying God that humans could hope to acquire immortality as disembodied souls. The law was one of five oppressive forces which dominated human existence and could not be escaped. At least, it could not be escaped in the present era. The Brethren hint at a great collective transformation in the future, but it does not seem to have been messianic hopes that sustained them. They also hint that select individuals could achieve the perfection that would render the law redundant already in this life, and this comes across as what they really hoped for. Their liberation from the law would be spiritual: they would behave as if they were sources rather than subjects of the law by living as they saw fit; each one would be king in the sense of acknowledging nobody as morally superior. There was no vision of an organized society managing without rulers here, let alone an incitement to revolt.[36]

The Brethren of Purity probably typify the most common form of educated antinomianism, whether Ismaili, philosophical or Sufi: the aim was to reach an individual state of perfection in which one could ignore the law, usually in the sense of abandoning ritual worship and certain features of dietary law (such as the prohibition of wine), occasionally ignoring sexual restrictions as well. Externally, the perfected person might go on observing the law, so as not to get into trouble with his family, his neighbours, or the authorities, but privately he would live as he pleased.[37] What mattered was in any case the inner sense of

35. For their *madīna fāḍila*, see *RIS*, iv, 38.3, 171.-7.

36. Cf. below, 355f.; *RIS*, iii, 307f.

37. Cf. Ghazālī, *Munqidh*, 48 = 78f.

freedom. But whatever the variations, the freedom was envisaged as individual, not as a grand collective transformation.

The freethinkers

Abū ʿĪsā al-Warrāq, Ibn al-Rāwandī, Abū Bakr al-Rāzī, and others who denied the existence of prophethood exemplify another form of antinomianism, though the term is not normally used in connection with them: unlike the Ghulāt, the Ismailis, most philosophers, and the Sufis, they denied the very status of the law as revealed, not just its necessity for salvation. They could have condemned it as a positive obstacle to salvation, especially with reference to the bloodshed that it legalized, and perhaps some did. On the whole, though, the impression they convey is that they deemed it to be neither an obstacle nor an avenue to salvation, but simply a set of human conventions without any bearing on salvation at all (or so at least al-Rāzī). Their own relationship with the divine was spiritual, internal, and wholly private, devoid of any entanglements with social and political organization, which they saw as purely man-made institutions. But they did not usually have anything against these institutions, and most of them moved freely in polite society behind a mask of *taqiyya*. Like other antinomians, they were apolitical.[38]

Niẓāmī's communities

The degree to which antinomianism remained separate from utopian visions of political freedom is neatly illustrated by Niẓāmī's Alexander epos. Towards the end of his life, according to Niẓāmī, Alexander the Great came across a devout community of mountaineers who were Muslims without prophets; through divine inspiration (*ilhām*) and analogy (*qiyās*) with their own circumstances they had come to believe in God.[39] Here then we have a people illustrating al-Rāzī's contention that humans had a divinely implanted instinct (*ilhām*) which enabled them to reach the truth by rational enquiry when they set their minds to it.[40] Like another literary figure, Ibn Ṭufayl's Ḥayy b.Yaqẓān, they had come to know God and devised ways of worshipping Him entirely by their own intellectual efforts. They also resemble Ḥayy b.Yaqẓān in that they immediately recognized the truth of revealed religion when it was explained to them, here by Alexander, whom they recognized as a prophet. Al-Rāzī had rejected

38. Cf. above, ch. 14, 172f.; Stroumsa, *Freethinkers*.

39. *Iqbālnāme*, 224.4 = 538 (drawn to my attention by Mohsen Ashtiany); cf. Bürgel, 'Krieg und Frieden im Alexanderepos Nizamis', 102.

40. Cf. above, 172.

prophethood in the name of reason, but Niẓāmī's point is rather that reason makes all of us potential prophets, if not all equally great: Alexander knew more than the people he encountered; Muḥammad knew more than Alexander. But Niẓāmī's people have a stronger affinity with al-Rāzī than with Ḥayy b.Yaqẓān to the extent that they do not seem to have found rationalist religion to be incompatible with social life. Ḥayy withdrew to the unhinhabited island on which he had grown up after discovering that life in a community based on revelation ruled out open cultivation of philosophy, but Niẓāmī's mountaineers form a community. The reader now waits with bated breath for an account of their social and political institutions. But we are not given any.

Shortly after his encounter with these people, Alexander comes to a city where the inhabitants had no locks on their doors, no walls around their gardens, no shepherds to guard their flocks, and no police, for there was no crime among them, and no human blood was ever shed. "We consider each other members of a single family," they explained. Nobody coveted wealth, people were satisfied with necessities, property was distributed equally, and everybody would help a friend in need.[41] What Niẓāmī is describing here is a utopia rooted in pre-Islamic Iran: pacifist, egalitarian, marked by even distribution of material goods, unaffected by the Lie, this was the community that a third-century Zoroastrian heresiarch had devised, that Mazdak (d. before 540) had tried to bring about, and which lived on thereafter among the Khurramīs of medieval Iran.[42] Unlike Mazdak's vision, Niẓāmī's is only quasi-communist, but in return it is anarchist, which Mazdak's was not. A Western reader reacts by wanting to merge the two stories: the people who knew the truth without prophets ought to be the people who lived in quasi-communist equality without authority precisely because they were innocent of the prophetic law on which conventional society rested. But this was not how Niẓāmī saw it. He does not identify the religion of the quasi-Khurramī city at all. Antinomianism belonged to a different cultural strand from Khurramism, and insofar as one can tell they never met, in literature or elsewhere.

The fundamental models

Basically, there are only two ways of relating a universal truth to a particular socio-political order. We may call them the Judaic and the Buddhist. The Judaic model merges the highest truth with the social and political arrangements of its adherents by recourse to the idea of divine choice. There is only

41. *Iqbālnāme*, 224 = 538.
42. Ibid., 227ff. = 540ff. Cf. below, 346ff.; Crone, 'Zoroastrian Communism'.

one God, who is true for all human beings, but who has chosen one particular people as His special treasure and who has thus sanctified their ethnicity, polity, and law, which form part of the religion and have to be adopted (in a very etiolated form these days) by all converts to the God in question. This is the model one encounters in the first century of Islam. It uses a universal truth to sanctify the particular, and it does so by means of a revealed law: this is the institution that ties people to a specific place of worship, specific ways of doing things, a specific type of leadership, and a specific people and prophet. By contrast, the Buddhist model separates the truth from the social and political arrangements of its adherents by replacing God with an impersonal concept. There is only one cosmic law, which is true for all human beings, and it operates indifferently with respect to the various groups into which mankind is divided. To profit from this law one has to sever one's ties with this world, including one's ethnic group, polity, and law, to work on one's inner self to achieve enlightenment. The universal is here used to desacralize the particular. This is the model one encounters in Gnostic *ghuluww*.

Most religions have taken a stand in between the two extremes, with a certain flexibility in both directions. This is true of Islam as well, both in its Shīʿite and its Sunni versions. Both are products of the Judaic rather than the Buddhist model in that they operate with a unique God who legislates about this world and the next alike, and both were in principle blueprints for a polity, Sunnism much more so than Shīʿism. There was also some veneration of the Arabs as a chosen people in both, though again much more so in Sunnism than in Shīʿism. From there onwards, however, they diverge, Sunnism continuing on the line of the Judaic model and Shīʿism moving towards that of Buddhism. One sees the contrast on the tribal margins: where Sunnism produced Almohads and Wahhābism, Shīʿism produced Druzes and Ahl-i haqq. But one also sees it in the cities, especially in Iran.

Thanks to its Zoroastrian and Gnostic heritage on the one hand and various features of early Islamic history on the other (notably the fact that Iran was not arabized), the tension between law and spirituality was stronger among Iranians than elsewhere. It was evident long before Iran became a Shīʿite country, in men such as al-Warrāq, Ibn al-Rāwandī, Īrānshahrī, al-Sarakhsī, Abū Bakr al-Rāzī, al-Fārābī, Ibn Sīnā, the many Iranians among Ismaili thinkers,[43] Suhrawardī *maqtūl*, and the many Iranian Sufis whose individualist spirituality was perceived as a threat to the established order.[44] It also showed in the antinomian, or indeed anti-social, movements of wandering ascetics founded

43. Abū Ḥātim al-Rāzī, al-Nasafī, Abū Yaʿqūb al-Sijistānī, Abū 'l-Haytham al-Jurjānī, al-Kirmānī, al-Muʾayyad al-Shīrāzī, Nāsir-i Khusraw, and Naṣīr al-Dīn Ṭūsī.

44. Al-Ḥallāj, Abū Saʿīd al-Khayr, ʿAyn al-Quḍāh al-Hamadhānī.

by Iranians at the very end of our period.[45] But the sixteenth-century imposition of Shīʿism as the official religion of Iran did nothing to reduce the tension, which now produced the Nuqṭavīs, the Bābīs and, via them, the Bahāʾīs. The Bahāʾīs did what the Ismailis had shied away from doing outside Baḥrayn: they universalized and spiritualized Islam by abrogating the law, severing all connections between the faith and socio-political organization. They thereby constituted themselves as members of a new religion, precisely as the Christians had done when they abrogated Jewish law, and as in effect the Ismailis of Baḥrayn had done as well. It is hard to imagine anything like this coming out of Sunnism. Certainly, nothing did in the case of Aḥmadism, the parallel in Sunni India to the Shīʿite Bābīs from whom the Bahāʾīs sprang. Since then the pendulum in Iran has sprung in the opposite direction, towards collectivist legalism, but it is hard to believe that we have reached the end of the story. At all events, the tension was both taut and creative in medieval times. It gave Iranian Islam, and above all Iranian Sufism, a multi-dimensionality all of its own.

45. Karamustafa, *God's Unruly Friends*, esp. 3 (for the Iranian origin of the two main founders), 91 (the characterization as 'anarchist individualism'), 99 (the Iranian and other non-Arab appeal).

CHAPTER

20

THE SOCIAL ORDER

To the Arab conquerors, people were first and foremost members of descent groups such as tribes and nations rather than of social strata or classes. The key distinction was between Arabs and the rest, that is, the *ʿajam* or barbarians (especially Iranians). Arabs were free, autonomous tribesmen chosen by God to be the carriers of His last revelation and rulers of the world. Everyone else was misguided and (already or soon to be) defeated. There was no room in this simple view of things for non-Arab Muslims, yet converts soon appeared in significant numbers, introducing new ways and ideas which the Arabs not unnaturally felt to be wrong. "This community will take to innovation when three things come together: perfect prosperity, the attainment of adulthood by the children of captives, and both Arabs and non-Arabs reciting the Qurʾān," ʿUthmān is said to have predicted.[1] The children of captives (*abnāʾ al-sabāyā*) whose dire influence is here being deplored were the offspring of Arabs by non-Arab concubines, a by-product of Arab domination; the non-Arabs reciting the Qurʾān were mostly slaves and freedmen, also a product of Arab might, and both undermined the very order on which Arab power rested. Could *mawālī* (clients), as non-Arab Muslims were known, hold positions of authority over Arab Muslims? Most Arabs were outraged by the idea. Did they have the same chances of salvation as the people who had brought them the truth? The scholars affirmed it, but there was a strong sense that non-Arabs, like women in a male job market, had to be particularly good in order to succeed, and stories

1. Tab., i, 2803f. For other traditions blaming the children of converts, see Sayf, *Ridda*, 18, no. 21; Abū Zurʿa, no. 1339.

depicting non-Arab converts as better Muslims than their Arab counterparts abound.

By early ʿAbbāsid times, non-Arab Muslims were in a position sufficiently strong to generate the Shuʿūbī controversy over the relative status of Arabs and non-Arabs in Islam.[2] The Shuʿūbīs were those who felt the Arab orientation of Islam to be dated. Just as today modernity is fast becoming a global culture which merely happens to be of Western origin, so Islam was fast becoming a universalist religion which merely happened to have its roots in Arabia, or at least this was how the Shuʿūbīs saw it. They fully accepted that the truth had originally come in Arab packaging, but they held this to be a historical fact of no religious consequence. True universalism was not compatible with ethnic favouritism; the Arabs were a people like any other, and Islam was a religion that you could combine with any ethnicity and culture. The Shuʿūbīs were however up against the fact that God's own word was in Arabic, that His house was in Arabia, that His deputy was an Arab, and that many held love of the Arabs to be part of the faith.[3] There was massive resistance to the Shuʿūbīs, who were generally denounced as impious, especially by *jamāʿī* Muslims, though by origin the latter were mostly non-Arabs themselves. Both Khārijism and Shīʿism had a Shuʿūbī streak to them, the former in its claim that the caliph did not have to be an Arab (let alone a Qurashī), the latter in its insistence that the caliph had to descend from a lineage so sacred that other people's ancestry ceased to matter. "*ʿArabiyya* is not the father or progenitor of anyone, just a language," as the Shīʿites said, meaning that classical Arabic had nothing to do with ethnicity, but was simply the medium in which the high culture was expressed (like Latin in the medieval West or international English today).[4] But the controversy was never really settled. It died down to flare up again from time to time, most recently in the twentieth century, when the arguments in favour of the special status of the Arabs were recycled in support of Arab nationalism while its opponents were branded as 'Shuʿūbīs'.[5]

2. The best account is still Goldziher, *MS*, i, chs 3–5.

3. For a convenient collection of Ḥadīth to this effect, see Zayn al-Dīn al-ʿIrāqī, *al-Qurab fī maḥabbat al-ʿarab*. One is surprised by the claim in Richard, *Shīʿite Islam*, 1, that Islam is no more Arab than Christianity is Jewish.

4. Kulīnī, *Kāfī*, viii, 246, no. 342; Nuʿmān, *Daʿāʾim*, ii, no. 729 (father or mother).

5. For a nice example of the former, see al-Bazzāz (prime minister of Iraq 1965–8) in Donohue and Esposito, *Islam in Transition*, 86; for the latter, see *EI*², s.v. 'Shuʿūbiyya'.

From egalitarianism to hierarchy

Among themselves, the Arab conquerors prided themselves on their egalitarian ways. Arab tribes had no closed aristocracies or castes, only fluid hierarchies which were often challenged and contested. The present was inegalitarian, but it was always open to reshuffling, much as in modern America, which also manages to combine an egalitarian outlook with a deeply inegalitarian reality by keeping the hierarchy open.[6] The monotheist tradition reinforced the egalitarian ideal. As the fourth-century Lactantius had deemed the pagan Greeks and Romans incapable of justice because of their social differentiation ("for when all are not equal, there is no equity"),[7] so the Muslims now deemed the pre-Islamic Persians to have lived in oppressive inequality. Islam had come to move people "from the service of servants (i.e. other humans) to the service of God", as the Persians were told in one of the many accounts set on the eve of the battle at Qādisiyya in which the simple ways of the Arabs are lovingly contrasted with the decadent opulence of the Persian nobles. "People are sons of Adam and Eve, brothers born of the same father and mother," an Arab explained. Another Arab boasted that "we Arabs are equal. We do not enslave one another, except in the case of somebody at war with another"; when he condemned the fact that some Persians were lords (*arbāb*) over others, the lowly people reacted with applause, whereupon the nobles realized that their subjects (*ʿabīdunā*) had heard things they would never forget.[8] All this, of course, is to tell us that the Arab conquest of Iran was a good thing: just as the British brought proper government to the Indians, so the Arabs brought social equality to the Persians.

Social egalitarianism is still among those gifts brought by the Arabs to Iran in the tenth-century philosopher al-ʿĀmirī, himself an Iranian. Like so many others, he tells us that the Persian kings forbade their subjects to progress from one rank to another; they oppressed them and reduced them to chattels; and at the same time, he says, the Zoroastrian priests kept divine wisdom (i.e. philosophy) to themselves lest their subjects use it to scrutinize the absurd claims of Zoroastrianism. But Islam did away with all that. "All men are of Adam, and Adam is of dust," the Persians were told; this removed the barrier to social mobility, and divine wisdom now became freely available.[9] Social equality is

6. Cf. Lindholm above, 44, note 41.

7. *Divine Institutes*, v, 14, in Garnsey, *Ideas of Slavery*, 79.

8. Tab., i, 2268, 2274f.

9. ʿĀmirī, *Iʿlām*, 160, 174–6; cf. Marlow, *Hierarchy*, 88ff. Compare Tab. i, 2269, where the Persian general says that "since Ardashīr came to power the Persians have not allowed anyone from among the lowly people to leave their occupations".

also among the gifts brought by the Arabs in many modern accounts of the Arab conquest of Iran.[10]

In short, just as the Muslims saw themselves as replacing non-Arab *mulk* with *imāma*, so they prided themselves on putting an end to social hierarchies by bringing a new egalitarianism. But unlike the imamate, egalitarianism did not make it as an article of faith. Sectarian divisions are not associated with different concepts of the social order, and whereas the transformation of the imamate was tenaciously resisted, there are no complaints about the loss of egalitarianism, except insofar as it could be subsumed under the reappearance of *mulk*. Perhaps it was too tied up with ethnic issues to be seen as a development in its own right. Even after the ʿAbbāsid revolution, when everybody agreed that ethnic chauvinism was wrong, questions concerning the social order continued to be overshadowed by, or posed in terms of the relative status of Arabs and non-Arabs. It was only in the tenth-century that people began to describe their society in terms of *ṭabaqāt*, social strata, without reference to ethnic divisions.

By then, Muslim society was thoroughly elitist in organization and outlook alike. There still was not much in the way of closed social groups such as aristocrats or serfs. It is true that the members of the Prophet's family (initially both ʿAlids and ʿAbbāsids, but in the long run just the ʿAlids) had come to form a nobility monitored, in the major cities, by a 'marshal of the nobles' (*naqīb al-ashrāf*), who kept records of their births and deaths, weeded out intruders, watched over their behaviour, including their marriages, and helped them pursue financial claims. It is also true that there were caste-like formations, or indeed real castes, in marginal areas such as South Arabia and India (best known from modern anthropological studies).[11] Here the descendants of the Prophet sometimes came to form the top caste, as what one might call Muslim brahmans. But there were no castes in the Muslim heartlands, nor did the *ashrāf* here constitute an aristocracy in the European sense of a group with a hereditary right to land and a role in government. For all its prominence in pre-Islamic Iran, an aristocracy in that sense did not emerge in the Islamic world at all, thanks to the tendency for military power to be assigned to men of servile or tribal origin. Its absence gave the higher bourgeoisie, in the loose sense of wealthy, educated townsmen, an unusual cultural prominence.

In the absence or dearth of closed groups, medieval Muslims usually operated with a broad division of society into an elite (*al-khāṣṣa*) and common people (*al-ʿāmma*), or with a number of social strata or occupational groups,

10. E.g. Bausani, *The Persians*, 73.
11. Cf. *EI*[2], s.vv. 'nakīb al-ashrāf', 'sharīf'.

ranging from three to seven, identified according to the author's tastes: all were simply analytical devices, not estates or other groups endowed with corporate identity.[12] But whereas Arabian tribesmen had carried the entire culture they shared in their heads whatever their socio-economic status, the elite and the common people were now divided in both socio-economic and cultural terms, the former being schooled in the cosmopolitan high culture of which classical Arabic was the vehicle, whereas the latter were uneducated members of the many parochial cultures underneath; and the entire inegalitarian edifice tended to reproduce itself from one generation to the next, with little social mobility. Elevated descent was highly regarded, and new men were taunted with their uncouth origins. Inherited wealth was the best.[13]

Even so, one has to grant al-ʿĀmirī that Muslim society comes across as more egalitarian than that of Sāsānid Iran, for social mobility did exist, and all believers were still equal in the eyes of God – or almost so: the Shīʿites could not help singling out the Prophet's kinsmen for special favours, and Sunni scholars could not help doing the same for themselves. God might forgive a scholar's sins because of his knowledge, as even al-Ghazālī said;[14] or He would forgive seventy of their sins, but not one of those of the ignorant, as a twelfth-century scholar put it.[15] Such exceptions notwithstanding, the general sense of equidistance from God remained. Al-Bīrūnī, who recognized the similarity between the Iranian hierarchy and the Indian caste system, held the greatest barrier between Indians and Islam to be the Muslim insistence that people are equal except in terms of piety.[16]

In praise of hierarchy

By the tenth century, social stratification was generally held to be a good thing, not least by Ismailis and other thinkers influenced by philosophy. Hierarchy pervaded the universe from the cosmos at large to the human body and should therefore be exemplified at the level of human society as well, they said. Without subordination of the inferior to the superior, there would be no order. According to the Ismailis, minerals were subordinated to plants, and plants were subordinated to animals, which were subordinated to humans, and within the human species, ordinary humans were subordinated to prophets. In fact, all humans were born with different abilities: even twins reared on the

12. For details, see Marlow, *Hierarchy*, 38, 55ff., 123ff.
13. Cf. Ibn Sīnā, *SI*, *x*,10, 449 = 105.
14. Ghazālī, *Munqidh*, 55 = 91.
15. Meisami, *Sea*, 121.
16. Marlow, 'Muslim Views of the Indian Caste System', 15.

same food and taught by the same teacher would prove to have different gifts, they said. Hence there had to be subordination, which was the principle whereby things were maintained.[17] The hierarchy that the Ismailis had in mind was based on religious knowledge, not on wealth or military power. To Aristotelians, the hierarchy was based on virtue (cultivated by the study of philosophy). What both were discussing, in other words, was a chain of spiritual leadership, a ladder of salvation, which ought to be reflected in the distribution of wealth and power, but which was more important than the distribution of worldly goods. It was moral and religious leadership rather than wealth and coercive power that tended to preoccupy other people too, notably the Sufis.

That leadership based on spiritual or moral excellence ranked more highly than the mere possession of wealth or power was generally agreed (at the level of theory). But should moral excellence be rewarded with high social and political status? Ought the moral, social, and political hierarchies to coincide? Most people thought so; indeed, most people automatically assumed that by and large they actually did: then as now, they tended to equate the great with the good. It was because the great were morally superior that one had to treat nobles with love, common people with a mixture of carrot and stick, and the lowly with fear-inducing measures;[18] one should apply the *ḥudūd* according to people's rank *and* their deserts, as Ṭāhir told his son.[19] To be lowly was to be vile. Even if one held kings and their henchmen in moral contempt, it came naturally to revere high-ranking jurists and judges, whose social status could be presumed to rest on moral deserts. Only by conscious adoption of an alternative set of ideas could one declare the socio-political hierarchy not to reflect any kind of moral merit at all.

Ismailis, philosophers, and Sufis all made this declaration: all denied that the normal world of oppressive kings and Pharisaic jurists rewarded true merit and knowledge. According to the Ismailis and the philosophers, this was deplorable: the distribution of worldly wealth and influence *ought* to rest on mastery of the truth and righteousness (as they understood them). The Ismailis succeeded in bringing this about in places, too, for it was the missionaries who took the social, political, and religious leadership of Ismaili communities. The philosophers would have liked to take a similar role in Muslim society, but they had to make do with statements of principle. The philosopher king and prophet should assign people to the positions for which they were suited, they said. According to al-Fārābī, there were five basic groups in the ideal city,

17. Abū Ḥātim al-Rāzī, *Aʿlām*, 6ff.; Abū Yaʿqūb al-Sijistānī, *Ithbāt*, 16, 24ff.; *RIS*, i, 321ff.; iv, 121; Abū 'l-Fawāris, *Imāma*, 92r.ff.; cf. Pines, 'Shīʿite Terms and Conceptions', 181ff.

18. Above, 157, note 49.

19. Tab., iii, 1050.

namely the three he found in Plato's *Republic* (philosophers, soldiers, and producers of wealth such as peasants, pastoralists, and traders) plus two that he added himself (bearers of revealed religion, meaning religious scholars and theologians, and professionals such as doctors and astrologers).[20] Ibn Sīnā only has the three basic groups of Plato's *Republic*: rulers, guardians (*ḥafaẓa*), and people working with their hands, whom he calls craftsmen (*al-ṣunnāʿ*) in apparent oblivion of peasants and pastoralists, possibly because he thinks of his polity as a city in the literal sense.[21] According to both, all professional groups and sub-groups ought to be ranked on the basis of merit under leaders of their own in order to cooperate like the limbs of the human body and to be rewarded, in this world and the next, by the sort of felicity, if any, that went with their rank.[22] Everybody ought to work for the common good, as all philosophers agreed; idlers ought to be banished, and those who could not work due to physical disability ought to be maintained by the state.[23] Presumably, then, everybody would be well provided for. But this is not stated. Socio-economic organization did not interest the philosophers much.[24] In any case, the entire edifice was theoretical.

Sufism

Unlike the Ismailis and the philosophers, the Sufis fully accepted that the moral and the socio-political hierarchies were separate, and always would be. They had no wish to bring them together; on the contrary, it was precisely by spurning the things of this world that one set out on the Sufi path. Nothing delighted them more than showing up the vast gap between the worldly establishment and the bearers of genuine truth and morality. "This very hour I have learned true Islam from an old woman, and true chivalry from a water carrier," as Dhū 'l-Nūn exclaimed at the court of the ultimate guardian of the Islamic establishment, the caliph, to whose presence he has been summoned on a charge of heresy. "I learnt sincere belief from a barber," as Junayd declared.[25] As the Cynics of the ancient world had shocked their contemporaries by their

20. Fārābī, *Fuṣūl*, §53/57.

21. Ibid., §53/57; Ibn Sīnā, *SI*, *x*, 447 = 104; cf. also Marlow, *Hierarchy*, 52f

22. Ibn Sīnā, above, note 21; id., *Rīṭūrīqā*, 40f.; Fārābī, *SM*, 81 = 37f. and *MF*, 15.4.

23. Plato in Fārābī, *Talkhīṣ*, 39f.; Fārābī, *Fuṣūl*, 62/66; Ibn Sīnā, above, note 21; cf. also Marlow, *Hierarchy*, 58ff.

24. Such interest as they display in it mostly arises from their desire "to demonstrate a consistent and rational pattern by which the whole universe is governed", as Marlow remarks (*Hierarchy*, 51).

25. Arberry, *Muslim Saints and Mystics*, 91, 207.

outrageous behaviour and paradoxical statements calculated to bring out the moral irrelevance of conventional institutions, so the Sufis now delighted in violating the strict conventions of their own highly rule-bound world by looking disgusting, speaking strangely, and behaving like madmen. Like the drop-outs of the 1960s, they were dirty, long-haired, dressed in tatters, and often of no fixed address. "O God, how dirty are your friends – not a single one of them is clean," as the maid of a Baghdadi Sufi is said to have sighed.[26] Real Sufis were as kings in rags.[27] They would dismiss wealth, homes, fine clothes (or clothes altogether), good food (or food altogether, insofar as compatible with life) as irrelevancies or positive obstacles to friendship with God, and write off gender, social status, and even slavery, as distinctions of no consequence on the grounds that "freedom is freedom of the heart, nothing else";[28] they would often belittle the value of book learning too on the grounds that knowledge of God was to be found inside oneself: ink pots should be broken and books torn up, one should be a Sufi rather than a Kūfī (i.e. Ḥanafī jurist).[29] All Sufis were strangers to the normal world.

As ascetics who sought to withdraw from this world, the Sufis raised the question how far the spiritual needs of individuals could be pursued at the expense of social obligations. To renounce this world is to shed obligations to family, children, friends, students, and ultimately society at large; it is what is popularly known today as dropping out. Was it right to disappear from this world, permanently or temporarily, or did social obligations always have priority over individual desires? Where was God to be found, deep inside oneself or on the contrary in public life? Widely divergent answers were given to these questions. At one extreme, the individual soul was potentially God and the cultivation of inner life took priority over everything in this world. At the other extreme, the cultivation of inner life was reduced to mild asceticism and humility coupled with dedication to the maintenance of moral standards, by commanding right and prohibiting wrong.

It goes without saying that no society can survive on the view that individual need overrides that of the collectivity. Like the Ismailis and the philosophers, the Sufis had to swear obedience to the law, or in other words to accept the organized religion on which the social and political order rested. But again like the Ismailis and the philosophers, they often combined acceptance of the law as a socio-political necessity with belief in individual exemption from it, seeing themselves as a spiritual elite who had progressed beyond the stage

26. Schimmel, *Mystical Dimensions*, 37 (in slightly heavier language).
27. Arberry, *Doctrine of the Ṣūfis*, 2.
28. Thus Shiblī (d. 334/945) in Sulamī, *Ṭabaqāt*, 347.
29. Schimmel, *Mystical Dimensions*, 17f.

where sin could touch them. Sufi extremists went in for all the transvaluation that their Gnostic forebears had engaged in, including dismissal of the law as so many shackles tying them to the social conventions of the society into which they happened to have been born. Such antinomianism was dangerous: it encouraged criminal behaviour and gave Sufism a bad name. Al-Qushayrī (d. 465/1072) wrote a widely read manual of Sufism repeatedly stressing the need for observance of the law; al-Ghazālī also wrote a treatise against *ibāḥa*, as antinomianism was called; and many other Sufis were to distance themselves from antinomian attitudes thereafter. One could cultivate one's inner spirit *provided* that one was a good citizen; the external forms of worship had to be the starting point for higher exploration.

But even if this was accepted, the question how far one could go was far from solved. Was it commendable to violate social conventions of all kinds? Was it healthy to spend so much time in preoccupation with one's inner self? What was wrong with conformity and common sense? If one did seek to transcend this world, did one still have to marry, indeed could one do so? Was it right to seek isolation (*ʿuzla*) from normal society to live as a hermit? If yes, did such avoidance rank higher on the moral scale than assisting a large number of people, for example an entire polity? Such questions were debated from the ninth century onwards, and with particular intensity in the eleventh.[30]

To a greater or lesser degree, all Sufis stepped out of their social roles for a realm of freedom, permanently, temporarily or just momentarily, to escape from the endless demands of family and friends and the rigid rules of social etiquette, seeking to find a deeper meaning to life. Originally, they did not form a hierarchy themselves. But all places of escape fill up as news of their attractions spread, and all develop organization in the process. By the end of our period the Sufis were no longer back-packing tourists in an untouched and exotic world. The great Sufi orders were under formation and there were now Sufi hierarchies in this world reflecting the angelic hierarchies of the next. The leaders of such hierarchies, though wealthy and influential, still did not have actual political or military power, but that too was to come, especially in tribal areas, if only after our period.

Justifying socio-political inequality

Ladders of salvation apart, how was one to make sense of social inequality as it existed in the real world? "If God is wealthy, generous and magnanimous,

30. Cf. Dankoff's introduction to the *Kutadgu Bilig*, in which it is a burning issue (Yūsuf, *Wisdom*, 23ff.).

why has He favoured some of His created beings with wealth and made others poor?"[31] Granted that this was how He behaved, He could hardly expect everyone to worship Him. "Prayer is not for the poor but for the rich and powerful," as a tenth-century poet said, "Why should I pray? Where is my power, my house, my mounts, my harness, my jewelry, my girdles, my moon-faced slaves, my pretty charming slave girls?"[32] The poor were for ever envious of the rich, Ibn al-Dāya and Mubashshir b. Fātik agreed. Indeed, there was constant "war between the poor and the rich, the weak and the strong", according to Ibn al-Dāya's testaments.[33] "The masses loathe the government (*al-sulṭān*) as schoolboys loathe their teacher," al-Kindī said, casting the conflict as political rather than socio-economic, which was more common.[34] Unlike tyranny, social inequality did not generate a major debate, but from the tenth century onwards, one does find a standard argument in its justification.

Humans needed to cooperate in order to survive. This theme, which forms the standard prelude to demonstration of the necessity of the government, also serves to explain why we need to be different in order to form a whole. We must be different because we have needs so diverse that they can only be fulfilled by division of labour. Everyone has to make somebody else subservient (*sakhkhara*) to himself, as al-Jāḥiẓ had put it,[35] alluding to the Qur'ānic verse 43:32: "We have divided between them their livelihood in the present life and raised some of them above others in rank so that some of them may take others in servitude (*li-yattakhidha baʿḍuhum baʿḍan sukhriyyan*)." God had made people different in terms of appearance, character and livelihood so that they would serve one another, as al-Ṭabarī said in explanation of the same verse.[36] By cooperating as specialists in diverse things, all humans could be servants and served alike: everyone, however lowly, benefitted from other people's labour in some respects, the philosopher al-Rāzī said.[37] People were born with different abilities and aspirations that caused them to choose different occupations, and this was proof of monotheism, for if every man wanted to be a builder or tailor or scholar, the world would not survive, the Imami exegete al-Qummī explained, also with reference to Q. 43:32.[38] God made everyone subservient

31. Rāghib, *Dharīʿa*, 378.

32. Muḥammad b. Aḥmad al-Ifrīqī in Thaʿālibī, *Yatīma*, iv, 146, and elsewhere; tr. in Mez, *Renaissance*, 343f.

33. Ibn al-Dāya, ʿUhūd, 16; Marlow, *Hierarchy*, 63.

34. Cited by Ibn Wahb, *Burhān*, 423.

35. Jāḥiẓ, *Ḥayawān*, i, 42ff.

36. Ṭabarī's *Tafsīr*, xiii, 67 (where the early exegetes take the verse as a reference to slavery and service in the literal sense); similarly Fakhr al-Dīn al-Rāzī, *Tafsīr*, xxvii, 209f.

37. Rāzī, *Ṭibb al-rūḥānī*, 106 = 89 (ch. 17).

38. Qummī, *Tafsīr*, ii, 257.

(*sakhkhara*) to a particular craft by giving people different natures, so that everyone liked his own occupation, as was true even of weavers and cuppers (whose work was regarded as demeaning); if God had not done this, we all *would* have chosen the same occupation, al-Rāghib al-Iṣfahānī said.[39] Al-Bīrūnī agreed (adding an explanation of why things had prices). The Indian caste system struck him as an example of the ranking and servitude mentioned in the Qur'ān.[40]

So far, the argument only shows that we must have occupational specialization, not that there must be differentiation of wealth, prestige and privilege as well (though the Qur'ānic verse takes this for granted). If the many needs we have are equally important, why should those who fulfil them be so differently rewarded? Indeed, why should some people be positively despised for engaging in occupations indispensable for our comfort? This last question was not considered at all.[41] As to why the rewards had to be different, the answer was that without poverty or the fear of it, people would not endure hard work or undertake tasks such as weaving, cupping, dyeing, and sweeping: thus al-Rāghib al-Iṣfahānī, taking it for granted that such work was despised and forgetting his earlier argument that people chose these occupations because God has made their natures suitable for them.[42] If God gave everyone what he wanted, everyone would belong to the highest rank and nobody would need other people any more, so they would stop cooperating: thus the Shīʿite secretary Ibn Wahb, illustrating the infinite exchangeability of cause and effect in teleological arguments designed to vindicate the world as it is (we must cooperate in order to fulfil our different needs; we must have different needs in order to cooperate).[43] If all were equal, nobody would be in a position to help anyone else, al-Māwardī agreed. To him, too, cooperation was a value in its own right, not simply a way of making up for the deficiencies of human nature: God made humans weak and needy precisely because He wished them to assist one another and anything that made them do so, including poverty and wealth, existed by divine favour.[44] "If all be wealthy, they will not serve one another, as equally they will not if all be poor," Naṣīr al-Dīn Ṭūsī observed.[45] Poverty was

39. *Dharīʿa*, 375; similarly Naṣīr al-dīn Ṭūsī, *Ethics*, 190; cf. Marlow, *Hierarchy*, 148ff., citing Rāghib's *Tafṣīl al-nash'atayn* as well, and Ghazālī at 152f.

40. Bīrūnī, *Jawāhir*, 6f. = 6; id., *Hind*, 271.11 = ii, 137 (tr. wholly misunderstood).

41. Noted by Marlow, *Hierarchy*, 155.

42. Rāghib, *Dharīʿa*, 377; Marlow, *Hierarchy*, 153.

43. *Burhān*, 271f.

44. Māwardī, *Adab al-dunyā*, 144, 147 and *Tashīl al-naẓar*, 97; both cited in Marlow, *Hierarchy*, 146.

45. Naṣīr al-dīn Ṭūsī, *Ethics*, 190; cf. Marlow, *Hierarchy*, 153.

required not only to make the poor keep working for the rich but also to keep them in their place, as Niẓām al-Mulk had the Zoroastrian priests argue against the communist Mazdak: "if a man is poor he is out of necessity compelled to enter the service and hire of a rich man; thus high and low rank are manifested; when all property is shared, differences of rank will disappear from the world. The meanest wretch will be equal to the king."[46] The long and the short of it was that "if all men were equal, they would perish", as the Prophet and the philosophers were believed to have said.[47]

To a modern reader, all these arguments come across as self-serving, circular, and incoherent. But the incoherence, at least, disappears the moment one considers the kind of society they were meant to justify. In the medieval Muslim world, as in most medieval societies, people tended to be either wealthy *or* productive. There was not much in the way of a middle class distinguished by both work and a comfortable life. "If all be wealthy" translated as "if all settled down for a life of leisure based on other people's labour", which was obviously impossible. The only occupations that people would stay in when they were rich, according to al-Rāghib al-Iṣfahānī, were kingship (presumably meaning political and military leadership of all kinds), trade and secretarial work; all other occupations required poverty for their performance.[48] There is some truth to al-Rāghib's argument even under modern conditions, as is clear from the need for immigrants to service the middle classes in the wealthy West; and in a society in which wealth was generally unproductive, it seemed obvious that poverty was God-given. Society would collapse without it; nobody could imagine an alternative, or at least not on the assumption of society remaining civilized. One could think away civilization and arrive at what al-Fārābī called a *madīnat al-ḍarūra*, a primitive society in which people only collaborated for the basic necessities of life. Ibn Rushd implicitly took the tribes of pre-Islamic Arabia to have formed such a society (and Ibn Khaldūn made it explicit),[49] but who would want to live like them? Desert-dwellers were not fully developed human beings.[50] Just as one could not have civilization without tyranny, so one could not have civilization without inequality. It was a fact that one simply had to accept. God had it in His power to make all men rich, Kay Kāʾūs says, but in His wisdom He decreed that some should be rich and others poor.[51] This was

46. *SN*, 266 = 203 (ch. 44.13).

47. Rāghib, *Dharīʿa*, 376 (the Prophet); Naṣīr al-dīn Ṭūsī, *Ethics*, 190 (the philosophers); cf. Marlow, *Hierarchy*, 20, 148. Cf. also Abū 'l-Fawāris, *Imāma*, 92v.

48. *Dharīʿa*, 377.

49. Pines, 'Societies Providing for the Bare Necessities of Life'.

50. Fakhr al-dīn al-Rāzī, *al-Mabāḥith al-mashriqiyya*, ii, 523.

51. *QN*, 18.

not much of an explanation, but at least it assured people that it was all to the good.

That, of course, was the ultimate monotheist argument. Whatever existed was created by God, who knew best, so everything had to be for the best simply because it existed. Or so it was commonly felt.[52] This is why arguments in justification of the world as it was tended to be circular; it is also why they tended to be persuasive. Muslim tradition says that when God created Adam, He took out the seeds of all future human beings from Adam's loins and made a covenant with them (cf. Q. 7:172). In one story, He shows the seeds to Adam, who sees that they are all different. "O Lord," Adam says, "if you were to create them after a single model, with the same size, nature, temperament, kind, life-span and fortune [*arzāq*], then they would not oppress one another, and there would be no envy, hatred or disagreement about anything among them." God responds that Adam does not know what he is talking about. "I have made some damned and others saved, some sighted and others blind, some short and others long, some beautiful and others ugly, some learned and others ignorant, some rich and others poor, some obedient and others disobedient, some healthy and some sick, some crippled and others free of disease. The healthy will look at the one diseased and praise me for what I have saved him from; the diseased will look at the healthy and pray to me, ask me to cure him, and endure my trial with fortitude, and I will put him down for a generous reward. The rich will look to the poor and praise me and thank me, while the poor will look to the rich and pray to me and ask me," and so on; and in any case, as we are reminded, God is the great king whose prerogative it is to do what He likes.[53] It is difficult to warm to this portrait of God as a praise-addicted autocrat, but formulated in more abstract terms the message is that there could be no experience of pleasure if pain did not exist, and that in any case ultimate reality is what it is whether you like it or understand it or not. There is some sugar-coating of the bitter pill in the promise of future rewards, but since God starts by announcing that He has created some humans saved and others damned for reasons of His own, this is not much of a consolation. Yet by the sheer fact of casting ultimate reality as a personal being endowed with infinite wisdom and justice the story manages to convey a sense that evil has a moral purpose; it is simply that we cannot see the purpose, we have to take it on trust.

In another tradition the poor complain to the Prophet that the rich are better off not only in this world, but also in the next, for the rich can pray, give

52. Not all theologians agreed (cf. Ormsby, *Theodicy in Islamic Thought*).

53. Kulīnī, *Kāfī*, ii, 9f; Ibn Bābawayh, *ʿIlal al-sharāʾiʿ*, 10f. (bāb 9.4). Ibn Ḥanbal, *Zuhd*, 85, has a short version to the same effect, and cf. Ormsby, *Theodicy*, 66–9. Compare the *Clementine Homilies*, no. 19, ch. 23.

alms, go on pilgrimage, manumit slaves, and so on, thus gaining merit in all kinds of ways, whereas the poor can only pray. The Prophet responds by teaching the poor something which will be better for them than "owning the whole world and spending it in God's path": after each ritual prayer they should say "glory be to God" thirty-three times and other phrases of a similar nature up to a hundred times. This ultra-democratic road to salvation was however also open to the rich, who were soon using it too. When the poor complained that the imbalance remained, the Prophet brushed them off with the observation that "That is God's generosity: He gives it to whomsoever He wills."[54] It simply so happened that some could serve God with both their persons and their property while others could not; there was no rhyme or reason to it. But again the sheer fact that it originated in a superior being that one could relate to and love, even if one could not understand it, helped to make the seeming injustice bearable.

Unlike Latin Christians, medieval Muslims were not predisposed by their myths about the origins of mankind to think of the social order as unjust. The Stoic (ultimately Cynic) notion that private property and slavery (and originally marriage too) were conventional rather than natural institutions, and had been absent back in the days when humans lived by natural law, became a commonplace in the Latin West thanks to its fusion with the story of the Fall; but as noted already, it did not pass to the Muslims, though there may be echoes of it here and there.[55] More precisely, the Muslims followed their eastern Christian forebears in being more interested in the Stoic concept of moral slavery – being at the mercy of one's own passions – than in social and political inequality.[56] Freedom was the rejection of desire: how strange that a slave would try to purchase his own freedom whereas a free man would not try to escape the slavery of desire, which would save him in this world and the next alike, as the philosopher al-ʿĀmirī quotes earlier authorities as saying.[57] It is clear that the existence of poverty and misery was a cause of much debate (though it does not seem to have affected Sunni scholars much). Insofar as it was perceived as a social rather than an ethnic issue, however, it was debated under the rubric of theodicy (justification of evil) rather than that of social

54. Dāya, *God's Bondsmen*, 401f.; cf. Q. 62:4.

55. Cf. Dawson, *Cities of the Gods*, chs 3–4; Lovejoy and Boas, *Primitivism and Related Ideas in Antiquity*, chs 4, 10, and the references given in Crone, 'Ninth-Century Muslim Anarchists', notes 17–21; above, 262f. Schneider, *Kinderverkauf*, 28ff., suggests that the maxim *al-aṣl huwa 'l-ḥurriyya* is a residue of such notions.

56. Cf. Garnsey, *Ideas of Slavery*, 105f., 131ff., 150ff. The views of the Greek (and Syriac) church fathers still await systematic research.

57. *Saʿāda*, 166f.

order. The poor and wretched were an admonition to the rich, who would increase their praise of God, they said, crediting the poor with religious virtues and assuring them that they would receive compensation in the next world. Others were not so sure: the poor and wretched would have been better off if they had never been born, they said; God did not care about them, or their misery was inflicted by evil forces, or the stars, rather than by God, or it was punishment for sins they had committed in earlier eras.[58]

Private property

Though the Stoic idea of private property and slavery as foreign to natural law remained unknown to the Muslims, they did inherit a communist tradition from both their Greek and their Iranian forebears. Plato abolished private property and marriage alike for the ruling elite in his *Republic*: the guardians, who are both men and women, share their property; their mating is collective and regulated by the state, and the same is true of the upbringing of children; the food-producers continue to have private households with their own women, children and fields. Mazdak abolished private property and marriage for everyone in sixth-century Iran, seeking to implement the vision of a third-century heresiarch: peasants and aristocrats alike were to share everything; land and women were to be distributed equally and everyone who had less than others could freely help himself to more. His ideas lived on among the Khurramīs of early Islamic Iran.[59] Between them, Plato and Mazdak might have generated a strong communist tradition in Islam, but this they did not. Mazdakism and its Khurramī bearers had a reputation so scandalous that nobody even remotely associated with them could hope for intellectual respectability. The similarity between the Platonic and the Persian ideas had been noted by the sixth-century Agathias (in a vein hostile to the Persians),[60] but no Muslim commented on it. Al-Fārābī does not mention Plato's communist proposals at all, and al-ʿĀmirī merely has Plato recommend an ascetic lifestyle for the guardians; of the collectivization of their property, women, and children he says not a word.[61] It is only when we reach Ibn Rushd on the margins of the Muslim world in twelfth-century Spain that the proposals are suddenly taken seriously, in very much the spirit in which they had originally been made: it was by their pursuit of wealth and power for their own private satis-

58. *RIS*, iii, 429ff.

59. For all this, see Dawson, *Cities of the Gods*, 87ff; Crone, 'Kavad's Heresy' and 'Zoroastrian Communism'.

60. Crone, 'Zoroastrian Communism', 452.

61. *Saʿāda*, 399ff.

faction that families caused strife and fragmentation; only by abolishing private households altogether could the city achieve its true unity of purpose.[62]

That the private household stood in the way of internal peace and unity seems to be the fundamental idea behind all communist proposals in antiquity and early Islam, including Mazdak's. When Muḥammad and his Companions moved to Yathrib, they were paired with local Yathribīs by pacts of brotherhood (*muʾākhāt*), and each pair would share everything except their wives. (One man is said to have ceded one of his wives to his 'brother' as well.)[63] The aim of that too was social unity. Apocalyptic expectations tended to bring out a desire for such sharing. "The earth is God's, people are God's servants, and God's wealth should be divided among them equally," a tradition triggered by the fourth civil war in the early ninth century has a heavenly voice proclaim.[64] Fired by expectations of the imminent coming of the Mahdi, the Ismailis of tenth-century Iraq pooled their moveable property, as noted already, much as the early Christians had pooled theirs in the expectation of the imminent return of Christ, and they explicitly declared this to be the ultimate expression of social harmony (*ulfa*).[65] But socio-economic experimentation was rare and communism even more so. Most people undoubtedly agreed with Niẓām al-Mulk that "religion exists for the protection of wealth and wives",[66] meaning that it was a major purpose of the Sharīʿa to declare both of them sacrosanct and that accordingly it was the duty of the state to protect them. One could renounce both, as Sufi ascetics did, but one could not force anyone to share them, or even share them voluntarily as far as women were concerned, though Sufis sometimes did that too to show that they were above the things of this world. The standard response to other people's poverty was to be charitable: to give freely was what all preachers enjoined. But as noted already, the old Khurramī idea of a society in which all members form a single household

62. Cf. above, 190; cf. Dawson, *Cities of the Gods*, 43.

63. *EI*², s.v. 'muʾākhāt'. The tradition deemed Muḥammad himself too elevated for pairing with an Anṣārī and made ʿAlī his brother instead.

64. Arjomand, 'Islamic Apocalypticism', 236, citing Nuʿaym b. Ḥammād, *Fitan*, 126 (S, §591).

65. Cf. above, 202, 325f.; al-Nuwayrī in Lewis, *Islam*, ii, no. 25. For the Christians, see Acts of the Apostles, 2:44f.; 5:1–10. The sources claim that the Ismailis shared their women as well, if only for a single orgiastic night, but for a variety of reasons this is unlikely to be true.

66. *SN*, 263 = 200 (ch. 44, 8). God created possessions for people in order that they use them in obedience to God, Ibn Rajab was later to note (Kister, 'Land Property and *Jihād*', 285).

reappears in Niẓāmī's description of the remote city discovered by Alexander on his return from the land of Gog and Magog.[67]

If such ideas were alien to *sharʿī* circles, there was a strong tendency instead to worry about private property not being legitimately held. The key problem here was the state, which vitiated property relations by its violations of the law. All the money it collected was tainted because of unlawful revenues, all the money it spent was thus tainted too. Some traditionists of ascetic inclinations declared it wrong not just to accept stipends from rulers, but also to handle coins struck by them, cross bridges or pray in mosques built by them, or even to work in the torch light emitted by their police at night.[68] Some declared Baghdad to be *dār al-ghaṣb*, an abode of usurpation, because its establishment had involved violation of what they took to be the fiscal status of the area, and deemed it unlawful to live in it or to make money by letting or selling property there, except under circumstances of overriding necessity (*ḍarūra*).[69] There were ascetics, Muʿtazilites among them, who held the entire abode of Islam to be an abode of unbelief (*dār al-kufr*), and all property relations to be so vitiated that it was unlawful to make one's livelihood in any way at all: one could only beg, and then only in extreme need when overriding necessity (*ḍarūra*) made it lawful to accept even contaminated money or food. Like the anarchists, they identified the state as the chief violator of the law, the core of the evil from where the corruption spread.[70] But they did not see anything immoral about property as such. Nor did they see any way of removing or reforming the state, with which they lived in sullen coexistence. They were heirs to a long tradition in the Middle East of coping with foreign rulers. Like the ultra-orthodox Jews of Jerusalem today, they preferred their own inward-turned communities to participation in the society around them even when the rulers were their own.

Women

Women's place was at home. "Their purpose is the continuation of the lineage of the race," as Niẓām al-Mulk says, his point being that the wives of kings

67. Above, 329; cf. Bürgel, 'Krieg und Frieden im Alexanderepos Nizamis', 102f. ("eine Art kommunisticher Utopie").

68. Cf. Cooperson, *Classical Arabic Biography*, 113f., 176. For more moderate views, see Ibn Baṭṭa, 67 = 128; Ghazālī, *Iḥyāʾ*, ii, 115, 125f.

69. Cooperson, *Classical Arabic Biography*, 178, citing *TB*, i, 4ff.

70. Crone, 'Ninth-Century Muslim Anarchists', 21f. Ibn Baṭṭa, 67f = 129, once more stands for moderation: buying, selling, and all trades and occupations are valid no matter what the moral status of the amir.

should be prevented from meddling in their husbands' affairs (he does not discuss women as rulers in their own right).[71] Their intelligence was generally deemed deficient, but at the same time, they were full of wiles, so one should beware of them. One should not teach them to read and write, a tradition ascribed to ʿUmar said, and numerous authors concurred.[72] For all that, highly educated women are certainly attested (and not just in the ranks of slave-girls). If one consulted them, one should act contrary to their advice, the mirror authors say, invoking a famous Prophetic statement to this effect.[73] According to Kay Kāʾūs, "it were best for a girl not to come into existence". One should not sell her, but one should get rid of her as fast as possible.[74]

The philosophers' attitude tended to be no different, despite their devotion to Plato's *Republic*. Al-ʿĀmirī deemed the subordination of women to men to be natural, like that of slaves to their masters and children to adults, and he tacitly rewrote Plato's guardians as men alone, saying nothing about their relations with women.[75] Ibn Sīnā explained why the lawgiver must prescribe that women should be veiled, secluded, dependent on their husbands for their income, forbidden to divorce them, and limited to one each, whereas men could have several wives. All this was in accordance with wisdom: "he must own her, not she him," as he put it, explaining that it is deeply shaming for a man to share his spouse with someone else.[76]

Only Ibn Rushd paid serious attention to Plato's radical suggestions, again in the very spirit in which they had first been made.[77] Since there was nothing more harmful to a city than its citizens' saying "This is mine and this is not mine", holding women, children and property in common was conducive to virtue: it would turn the city into an organic whole.[78] If the 'weddings' were not repeated, each man would be left with a particular woman and the city would turn into one consisting of private households, he pointed out in polemics against Galen,[79] seeing with great clarity that it was for the sake of

71. *SN*, ch. 42, §1.

72. ʿUmar in Ibn Qutayba, *ʿUyūn*, iv, 78.6; Jāḥiẓ *Bayān*, ii, 180.6; Maʿarrī in Nicholson, 'Meditations', nos. 326–7; *NM* (G), 163; *QN*, 125; Naṣīr al-Dīn Ṭūsī, *Ethics*, 173. Similarly the *ḥisba* manuals of al-Shayzarī (d. 589/1193), *Nihāyat al-rutba*, 104, and Ibn al-Ukhuwwa (d. 729/1329), *Maʿlim al-qurba*, 261f.

73. Cf. above, 157, note 50.

74. *QN*, 125, 127. For the sale of children, cf. Schneider, *Kinderverkauf*, 317ff. and the traditions at 376, 379, 385f, 392.

75. *Saʿāda*, 187f.

76. Ibn Sīnā, *SI*, *x*, 449ff. = 105f.

77. *Commentary*, 52–8 = 164–73/57–66.

78. Ibid., 57f. =172 /65

79. Ibid., 56f. = 170/63f.

communal unity that Plato had abolished the households, and accepting that mating had to be regulated to ensure that the guardians produced offspring of the same quality as themselves. He also accepted that women could be warriors, philosophers, and rulers, for though he granted that men and women had different natures, he agreed with Plato that the difference was one of degree rather than of kind, and he regretted that "the competence of women is unknown . . . in these cities [i.e. in al-Andalus] since they are only taken in them for procreation and hence are placed at the service of their husbands and confined to procreation, upbringing and suckling"; for "since women in these cities are not prepared with respect to any of the human virtues, they frequently resemble plants." He held their unproductive lives to be one of the causes of poverty in al-Andalus.[80] The contrast with Ibn Sīnā's blithe endorsement of conventionality could not be greater.

Among the religious scholars, al-Ṭabarī (d. 923) stands out for holding that women could receive appointment as judges.[81] The Ḥanafīs almost agreed: women could serve in all matters on which their testimony was accepted, but not in questions to do with retaliation and the penalties known as *ḥudūd*. (Broadly speaking, one could have female judges in civil, but not criminal courts.) But according to the Shāfiʿites and Mālikites, they could not serve as judges at all: if they could adjudicate in matters of property, they could also adjudicate in matters of retaliation and the *ḥudūd*, meaning that they could even be imams, al-Shāfiʿī said, and this was obviously an absurd idea.[82] Though the attitudes of thinking men were not as uniform as might be thought, the prevailing view was that women should be confined to the domestic sphere. Exclusion from public life (*al-jumʿa wa'l-jamāʿa*) was one of the numerous afflictions with which God had punished Eve for her sin, as a misogynist account of the Fall informs us.[83] Only men could move freely in the public world, let alone hold office in it.

Slaves

Unlike the Stoics, Plato had not impugned slavery, and no medieval Muslims did so either. They did hold freedom to be, so to speak, the default condition

80. Ibid., 54 = 166/59

81. Māwardī, *Aḥkām*, 107/65 = 131/72.

82. Simnānī, *Rawḍa*, i, §§10–14, with the retort that one could be qualified for the *qaḍāʾ* without thereby being eligible as imam. He does not mention Ṭabarī's view, but claims that the Khārijites would accept women as judges in everything: this is presumably just an inference from the (unreliable) report that they would accept women as imams, which he mentions in §38 (cf. above, 57, note 11).

83. Kisāʾī, *Qiṣaṣ al-anbiyāʾ*, 50.13.

of human beings (*al-aṣl huwa 'l-ḥurriyya*),[84] meaning that people should be presumed to be free unless there was evidence to the contrary. But the rule did not generate stories about the aboriginal freedom of mankind or of how slavery had first emerged. Like government, it was assumed always to have existed. The Qurʾān takes the institution for granted. There is no reason to believe that Muḥammad intended to abolish slavery,[85] and the idea that humans could remove so entrenched a feature of the human condition did not occur to later Muslims either. Slaves merely wished to escape from their own slavery when they rebelled, not to abolish it for mankind at large, just as rebellions inspired by poverty never envisaged that the condition as such could be eliminated. Servile revolts were uncommon, however, for barrack slavery was rare.[86] We do hear of slaves (*ʿabīd*) who cultivated large estates in Umayyad Arabia, but like the blacks who cultivated the oases of Arabia and the Sahara in recent times, they were probably in the nature of serfs rather than barrack slaves (i.e. they lived much like free people, but could not leave the land and were financially exploited by their owners).[87] Plantation slavery properly speaking does not seem to have existed at all, nor do we hear of slaves working in mines, or as rowers. Rather, we find them in private homes, usually urban rather than rural, in urban professions, and above all in and around the ruling elite. Most slaves were domestic servants. Some worked for their masters outside the home, as their apprentices or agents, or as independent craftsmen and traders paying regular sums to their masters, much as they had done before the rise of Islam.[88] Still others were soldiers, from common troopers to commanders, in the public army and private retinues alike. When such slaves found their conditions unbearable, they typically killed their masters and/or ran away.

Like their Christian predecessors, the jurists accepted that all believers were equal in the eyes of God: neither *status libertatis* nor ethnicity, gender or any other human distinction mattered for purposes of salvation; in moral terms, slavery was irrelevant. A Muslim slave was not just a piece of property, but also a believer endowed with ritual obligations, if not quite like those of

84. Cf. Rosenthal, *Muslim Concept of Freedom*, 32; Schneider, *Kinderverkauf*, 23ff., who sees a Stoic residue here.

85. *Pace* Khadduri, *Islamic Conception of Justice*, 234. Compare the conviction of a nineteenth-century Christian scholar that the Church opposed it (Garnsey, *Ideas of Slavery*, 7n.).

86. There is a famous example in the Zanj of lower Iraq in the seventh to ninth centuries (cf. *EI*², s.v. 'Zandj').

87. Crone, *Roman, Provincial and Islamic Law*, 129f., notes 9, 52; Lecker, 'Biographical Notes on Ibn Shihāb al-Zuhrī', 52, cf. 55.

88. Cf. Garnsey, *Ideas of Slavery*, 2f, 6.

free men.[89] The jurists stressed that slaves had to be treated well, just as they in their turn had to serve their masters faithfully, and those who converted (as most of them did) were likely to be manumitted sooner or later. Once free, a Muslim could not legally be enslaved, whether by capture in war or other means, nor could Muslims lawfully sell themselves or their children into slavery, and there was no debt bondage or contract of indenture. The law did not grant the state, or anyone else, the right to impose forced labour (*taskhīr*) either.[90] But the jurists did not go so far as to deem all Muslims to be free by definition, since this would have enabled slaves to free themselves by converting. It is only when a community is defined by features beyond individual control, such as ethnicity or citizenship, that its members can all be deemed to be free by definition, and the Muslim community was no longer of that type.

It had however started as a community of Arabs, and for Arabs slavery was indeed abolished. "It is repulsive that Arabs should own each other now that God has made things ample and conquered the non-Arabs (for us)," ʿUmar is said to have declared on his accession; he and other Muslims agreed that "nobody can own an Arab" and that captives already taken should be redeemed.[91] The history of this idea awaits a study. It is not clear whether it was known under the Umayyads, who routinely enslaved the women and children of defeated rebels (executing the men) whether they were Arabs or not, and who do not seem to have been blamed for this, only for enslaving Muslims.[92] Yet the idea came to be accepted even by the tribesmen of Arabia itself, though they had been happy enough to enslave each other, or at least each others' women, before the rise of Islam and were not normally given to obeying Islamic precepts that greatly changed their way of life. Outside Arabia, the rule was perhaps not of great importance in practice, but it is interesting as one out of many residues of the special status of the Arabs.

The Arabs apart, some tension remained between the institution of slavery and the idea that all Muslims were slaves of God. A slave-owner was somebody who turned God's property into his own, as a fourth-century Greek church father had said (in a homily against pride rather than slavery).[93] But although some slaves were Muslims, all had been reduced to servile status thanks to

89. *EI*², s.v. "ʿabd, 3'; cf. Garnsey, *Ideas of Slavery*, 31, 70.

90. Cf. Rosenthal, *Muslim Concept of Freedom*, 77ff.

91. Tab., i, 2012; Abū ʿUbayd, *Amwāl*, 197 (who thinks that Arab men were never enslaved in the Jāhiliyya either). The rule is also credited to the Prophet (Hamidullah, *Conduct of State*, §446).

92. That Arabs could not be lawfully enslaved is however known in a story about Marwān and three tribesmen who sell themselves to him in a famine (*Aghānī*, x, 73).

93. Gregory of Nyssa in Garnsey, *Ideas of Slavery*, 81, cf. 84.

unbelief, and this made the institution acceptable. Slavery could be seen to exist for the same reason as holy war, its most important source of supply, namely that some people obstinately clung to their own erroneous beliefs even when they had heard about Islam. Slavery was a punishment for the refusal to acknowledge God, as the Ḥanafī jurist al-Bazdawī said.[94] In an Imami source ʿAlī makes the ringing statement that "Adam was not born as a slave or a slave-woman; all people are free (*al-nās kulluhum aḥrār*)", but he continues that *God* has enslaved some to others and merely recommends patience.[95] This is presumably a reference to the same view. It is also an illustration of the fact that ethnic egalitarianism got in the way of social issues, for ʿAlī's concern in that statement is not so much with the rights and wrongs of slavery as with the equality of all ethnic groups, which he here endorses regardless of how they came to form part of the Muslim community.

The philosophers were inclined to justify the institution in different terms, with reference to the idea that some peoples (such as Africans and Turks, according to Ibn Sīnā) were natural slaves.[96] Known from Aristotle and Bryson's *Oikonomikos*, this idea became sufficiently widespread to enter manuals of slave purchase.[97] It would have soured race relations in Islam, had it won out, for it built the servile status of the African or Turk into their physical features, so that they could never escape it. There was indeed a tendency in that direction already. Since it was mostly via enslavement that different-looking people entered the Muslim world, ethnic and social prejudice blended: to be a black in the Middle East was to have a slave somewhere in one's ancestral line.[98] But it was only among the bedouin that servile status actually fused with ethnicity. To them, slaves (*ʿabīd*) were blacks and blacks were *ʿabīd* for ever, even when they had been freed; no Arab woman could ever marry them; freedmen formed clearly demarcated populations under Arab protection.[99] The philosophers' idea of natural slavery would have had the same effect in the settled Muslim world, but it did not become prevalent. The jurists tied slavery to faith, which was changeable, and people generally saw mastery of the high

94. Cited in Schneider, *Kinderverkauf*, 27; cf. also Jurjānī in Rosenthal, *Muslim Concept of Freedom*, 25n.

95. Kulīnī, *Kāfī*, viii, 69, no. 26.

96. Thus ʿĀmirī, *Saʿāda*, 187f., 363.5 (reflecting Aristotle, *Politics*, 1254b); Ibn Sīnā, *SI*, *x*, 453 = 108; Ibn Bājja, *Risālat al-wadāʿ*, 136 (Rosenthal, *Muslim Concept of Freedom*, 31, underestimates the diffusion of the idea, contrast 91n.) Compare also Garnsey, *Ideas of Slavery*, 170f.

97. Plessner, *Bryson*, 164ff.; Ritter, 'Handbuch des Handelswissenschaft', 14.

98. Cf. Lewis, *Race and Slavery*, ch. 4. The idea, widespread in the United States, that the link between slavery and colour made its first appearance in the Americas is mistaken.

99. Crone, *Roman, Provincial and Islamic Law*, 44, 46 and the literature cited there.

culture as a passport to respect and prestige whatever one's colour. Three generations of freedom sufficed to remove the traces of slavery according to the jurists, whose views here seem to have reflected social reality. There was much interbreeding between people of all colours, and though the number of slaves, both black and white, taken by the Muslims over the years was very high, it was only in the desert that the populations of servile origin remained discrete. There is nothing comparable to the black population of America elsewhere in the Middle East today.[100]

Animals

The most menial of all slaves were domestic animals. Like the Jews and the Christians, medieval Muslims assumed God to have granted humans dominion over animals, or more precisely over other animals, for they fully accepted that humans were animals too; but they held humans to be superior to other animals by virtue of their faculty of reason and/or their immortal souls, and this, in their view, entitled mankind to lord it over the rest of God's creation.[101]

Still, even dumb animals were sentient beings and animal suffering generated more discussion than slavery, or more precisely more than human slavery, for animals were seen as reduced to slavery too. Sympathy for animals is attested already in the pre-Islamic Near East. Leaving aside the Zoroastrian veneration of cattle and reluctance to kill them, the sectarian circles to which Mazdak belonged (the later Khurramīs) held it wrong to inflict suffering on living beings and so were vegetarian. The Manichean position was similar. Vegetarianism was also advocated by the Neoplatonist philosopher Porphyry, a Hellenized Syrian, who adduced a pupil of Aristotle on the aboriginal form of human life in his support. (Like many other lovers of animals, both Greek and Iranian, he also believed in the transmigration of souls from animals to humans.) Muslims, too, were generally sympathetic to animals. They displayed a stronger awareness of their suffering than Latin Christians, though there was a tendency for the animal sympathizers to be heretical or marginal figures.[102]

100. Lewis, *Race and Slavery*, 84 (assigning only a limited role to concubinage and intermarriage in the explanation).

101. Cf. Q. 17:70 ("We have honoured the sons of Adam . . . and favoured them over many of the others we have created"); Q. 45:13 ("And He has subjected to you [*sakhkhara lakum*] all that is in the heavens"). For the many other verses to the same effect, see Haq, 'Islam', 111.

102. Crone, 'Kavad's Heresy', 26 and notes 111–31 thereto; Porphyry, *On Abstinence* (and Fortenbaugh and Schütrumpf [eds], *Dicaearchus of Messana*, for the pupil of Aristotle); Bousquet, 'Des animaux et de leur traitement'.

Abū ʿĪsā al-Warrāq, a ninth-century Iranian Muslim heretic generally held to have been a crypto-Manichean, wrote a *Book of Laments over Animals*, probably about animal suffering. Several ninth-century Muʿtazilites held that animals would be compensated in Paradise for undeserved suffering even though they might not live for ever. The poet and freethinker Abū 'l-Al ā' al-Maʿarrī (d. 449/1058) was a vegetarian (indeed a vegan); so too was the Iranian mystic and philosopher al-Suhrawardī (d. 587/1191).[103] Another Iranian philosopher, al-Rāzī, stressed that one should not maltreat domestic animals and that the philosophers were divided over the human right to slaughter them. People did not in his view have any right to inflict pain on any sentient creature unless it deserved it, or unless the purpose was to avert from it still greater pain. As a believer in transmigration, however, he held that killing cattle could be justified on the grounds that slaughter released the animal soul for transfer to a human body, from where it could reach immortality; and like his Zoroastrian forebears, he held the killing of snakes, scorpions, hornets, and other noxious insects to be positively meritorious.[104] But the father of the Iranian mystic ʿAbdallāh al-Anṣārī, (d. 481/1089) would not even kill noxious animals: he once spared a scorpion in his shop.[105] Much of this was alien to the Sunnis, but Prophetic Ḥadīth also lays down that domestic animals should be treated well, while enjoining the believers to kill noxious animals (snakes, scorpions, and hornets among them); and Sunni jurists hold the *muḥtasib* (market inspector and censor) responsible for ensuring that animals (and slaves) were not abused.[106]

Were humans actually wrong to treat animals as they did? This question was debated by the Brethren of Purity in a riveting fable, referred to several times already, in which humans and animals go to court over the human claim that the animals "were created for us, for our sake, and are our slaves". The animals indignantly deny it, graphically describing the many terrible ways in which humans inflict suffering on them, and denying that humans have any superiority over them. That the Brethren held it wrong to maltreat animals is

103. Stroumsa, *Freethinkers*, 44; Heemskerk, *Suffering in the Muʿtazilite Theology*, 187ff.; Nicholson, 'Meditations', nos. 320f.; cf. Margoliouth, 'Abu'l-ʿAlā al-Maʿarrī's Correspondence on Vegetarianism'; Hodgson, *Venture of Islam*, ii, 236. Note also that humans originate as vegetarians in *RIS*, ii, 203 = Goodman, *Case*, 51, but it is not a central point here.

104. Rāzī, *Sīra al-falsafiyya*, 314f./104f. = 327ff./231f.

105. Laugier de Beaurecueil, *ʿAbdullāh Anṣārī*, 26f.

106. Cook, 'Dietary Law', 263n. and the references given there; Māwardī, *Aḥkām*, 429/257 = 279; Shayzarī, *Nihāyat al-rutba*, 117f. (cf. also the fourteenth-century Ibn al-Ukhuwwa, *Maʿālim al-qurba*, 77); Haq, 'Islam', 122ff.

abundantly clear, but this was not all they had to say. They accepted that superiors had a right to enslave inferiors, so the issue was whether humans were superior to other animals. The animals deny this and demolish the arguments of their human opponents with great eloquence until, shortly before the end, the humans adduce the immortality of their souls and win the case, with an unobtrusive proviso to the effect that the animals may be liberated in the next cycle.[107] The message of the fable seems to be that just as animals are subjected to humans even though they worship God directly, without prophets, books, mosques, ritual, and all the other paraphernalia of organized religion, so humans are slaves to the law even though they also have it in them to worship God without organized religion. The animals stand both for themselves and for the natural religion that humans have lost. For the moment, both they and the humans had to endure their subjection, but humans would eventually be liberated from the law, to live by natural religion again, and the animals would be liberated by becoming humans themselves: like al-Rāzī, the Brethren held that the souls of animals used by humans would pass into human beings, enabling them to achieve immortality.[108]

The end of the fable is so abrupt that the Brethren forget to admonish people to treat animals better in the present cycle, but they tell other stories in which they declare their sympathy for all living beings, saying that they do not wish to harm any of them.[109] The Persian poet Niẓāmī (d. c. 1200) also disliked the use of violence against all living beings, animals included: "Not even an ant's wing will be harmed by me . . . better that you be injured than that others be," he said. His Muḥammad was first and foremost a missionary: "That one man should accept Islam is dearer to me than the killing of a thousand unbelievers," he presents him as saying.[110] The inhabitants of his quasi-Khurramī city avoided bloodshed to the best of their ability: they did hunt animals, but only for sustenance. Wild animals were not afraid of them, he says, picking up a theme beloved of mystics.[111] Wild animals were not afraid of the Sufi Rābiʿa al-ʿAdawiyya either: she did not eat meat.[112] Nor did Majnūn, the mad lover who symbolizes human love of God, according to Niẓāmī; like Rābiʿa, he

107. *RIS*, ii, 203–377 = *Case*, 51–202 (Goodman's translation of the final paragraph omits the proviso! It is however also mentioned at the beginning of the case; cf. *RIS*, ii, 233 = *Case*, 77).

108. *RIS*, iv, 121; cf. Pines, 'Shīʿite Terms and Conceptions', 182ff. Cf. above, 209, 327.

109. Cf. below, 377.

110. Bürgel, 'Nonviolence in the Epic Poetry of Niẓāmī', 67f.

111. Niẓāmī, *Iqbālnāme*, 230 = 543.

112. Ritter, *Meer der Seele*, 328.

roamed about and "lived with the animals always at peace".[113] Persian miniatures typically depict Majnūn sitting naked in the desert with wild animals around him.

The ancient Near Eastern Gilgamesh epic tells of how Enkidu, a wild man, came to sleep with a temple prostitute sent to him by king Gilgamesh, whereupon the wild animals shied away from him: Enkidu had been initiated into human civilization; he had eaten of the tree of knowledge. Near Eastern Jews, Christians, and Muslims similarly say that the animals rebelled against Adam and Eve after the two had eaten the forbidden fruit, or that the animals ceased to speak, having previously talked in the same language as humans.[114] The unity of being had been lost. Was civilization worth it? The Sufi answer was that it was not. Kings, cities, hierarchies, books, social life, wealth, material goods, hard work, marriage, and death: as madmen they rejected it all, trying to undo the seduction of Enkidu.

113. Bürgel, 'Nonviolence in the Epric Poetry of Niẓāmī', 75, quoting his *Laylī u Majnūn*.

114. Tennant, *Fall*, 150f, 197, 193 (citing *Bereshith Rabba*, pseudepigraphica, Philo, and Josephus); Solomon of Basra, *Book of the Bee*, 24; *RIS*, ii, 230 = *Case*, 74.

CHAPTER

21

MUSLIMS AND NON-MUSLIMS

INFIDELS

Human beings were divided into Muslims and infidels (*kuffār*, sing. *kāfir*). A Muslim was someone who surrendered to God and lived as His servant (*ʿabd allāh*, pl. *ʿibād allāh*) in a society based on His law. Infidels were rebels against God whose societies could never be more than the robbers' nests with which St Augustine had compared kingdoms devoid of justice.[1] Since they did not live by God's law, nothing they did had any moral basis. Relationships established by them were not legally valid, compacts made with them did not have to be honoured, they themselves could be freely killed, "like wild animals before the arrows and spears", as a famous thirteenth-century poet put it; their property could be taken as booty, and "all their wives and children are free spoil", as the poet said, meaning that they could be taken as slaves.[2] Bereft of divine guidance, infidels were not what we would call truly human.

Some infidels came closer to true humanity than others. Unlike pagans, indiscriminately known as polytheists (*mushrikūn*) and idolaters (*ʿabadat al-awthān*), the Jews and the Christians had received revelations from God, the Pentateuch (*al-tawrāt*) in the case of the Jews, the Gospels (*al-injīl*) in that of the Christians. They were *ahl al-kitāb*, People of the Book. But they were still infidels, for they denied that Muḥammad had brought a new revelation from God, and they had perverted their scriptures and their original faith: their

1. *City of God*, IV.4.

2. Rūmī, *Mathnawī*, i, 3318f.; cited (in slightly different wording) in Bürgel, 'Nonviolence in the Epic Poetry of Niẓāmī', 64.

monotheism was no longer pure. Those of them who had not been brought under Muslim sovereignty were outlaws on a par with the pagans.

Dār al-ḥarb

Muslims lived in *dār al-islām*, the abode of Islam, or what one might more idiomatically call the Muslim world. This was the world in which Islamic law held sway and in which there were rights and duties, human warmth, peace, and brotherhood. Infidels lived in *dār al-kufr*, the abode of unbelief, also known as *dār al-ḥarb*, the abode of war, or what one might more fashionably call the realm of 'The Other'. This was the world in which there was no legal (as opposed to de facto) order, in which no Muslim could live in the early view, and with which no Muslim could transact. The relationship between them was deemed to be one of war, whether latent or actively pursued.[3]

The antithetical relationship between the two abodes could be softened by a limited grant of rights and duties to the infidels whereby they were enabled to transact with Muslims. (For a full grant they would obviously have to convert.) Thus there could be truces with infidel polities, though there was disagreement both about the circumstances in which they were permitted and about the maximum period for which they could run (from three months to ten years or more).[4] Infidel polities could also be brought into a tributary relationship with the Muslim world on a long-term basis, causing some jurists to postulate the existence of an intermediate category of *dār al-ʿahd*, the abode of treaty.[5] And individual denizens of the abode of war, known as *ḥarbī*s, could obtain safe-conducts (sing. *amān*) enabling them to venture into Muslim territory as traders, pilgrims, ambassadors, and other travellers under the technical label of *mustaʾmin*s. Those of them who were People of the Book could even live on a permanent basis in the Muslim world, for *kitābī*s were eligible for *dhimma*, legal protection to match that of the Muslims themselves even if they did not want to convert, provided that they were willing to recognize Muslim sovereignty and display their position of inferiority by paying poll-tax (*jizya*). Whether pagans were eligible for *dhimma* was more controversial, as will be seen.

Muslims could also venture into infidel territory, subject to such conditions as the infidels might impose, but could they live there on a permanent basis, assuming that the infidels would have them? First-century Muslims took it for

3. In general, see Aghnides, *Theories of Finance*, 353ff.; Khadduri, *War and Peace*.
4. Ibn Rushd, *Bidāya*, i, 543ff. (tr. in Peters, *Jihād*, 38ff.); Qaffāl, *Ḥilya*, vii, 718ff.
5. On which, see *EI*², s.v.

granted that they could not.[6] In Mecca they had lived by pagan law, much like the early Christians in the Roman empire, but when the Prophet moved to Medina to create a Muslim polity there, emigration (*hijra*) became obligatory: a believer living under infidel rule was henceforth obliged to move to a place where Muslim law was applied and holy war conducted; separation from polytheists (*firāq al-mushrikīn*) was a fundamental duty. When the Arabs converted to Islam, they duly moved to Medina and other abodes of emigration (*dār al-hijra*), that is, the garrison cities in the conquered lands. When the Khārijites of the Umayyad period deemed their fellow-Muslims to have turned infidel, they left the garrison cities for camps of their own.

But as so often, the initial simplicity was shortlived. Many Arabs, and eventually non-Arabs too, converted without moving anywhere. They, or at least the Arabs, were deemed to be 'bedouin', translatable as quasi-Muslims: since they did not participate in the congregational prayers and holy war, except on an ad hoc basis, they did not count as full members of the Muslim community. Non-Arabs who stayed in (or were sent back to) their villages in the Umayyad period did not officially count as members at all. But the *umma* could not remain in the nature of a military camp for ever. From the later Umayyad period it began to be argued that the Prophet had abolished the duty of *hijra* when he conquered Mecca. One could now be a Muslim anywhere, "even in a fox hole". By c. 800 this had been generally accepted.

The fox hole was however envisaged as located within the caliphate. Could one be a Muslim even in the abode of unbelief?[7] By c. 800 there were Muslims who lived on a largely or wholly permanent basis outside the caliphate, usually as traders. What were their chances of salvation? Answers are hard to come by. Envisaged as a move from the countryside or desert to a garrison city, the obligation of *hijra* generated massive discussion and clear answers in the two centuries. Envisaged as a move from territory ruled by infidels to the abode of Islam, it generated little debate in our period, and certainly no clarity. Even after our period the ambivalence remained.[8] Living under infidel rule was apparently a subject that the jurists preferred to avoid unless they were in a position simply to forbid it. Some jurists in al-Andalus did forbid it in response to the Christian advance: one should not enter non-Muslim territory even for trade; it was generally forbidden for Muslims to reside in non-Muslim territory, except temporarily, or, according to others, it was strictly forbidden to

6. For what follows, see Crone, 'Hiǧra'.
7. For what follows, see Abou El Fadl, 'Islamic Law and Muslim Minorities'.
8. Abou El Fadl, 148f., 182.

enter or live in the abode of war under any circumstances.[9] If the infidels conquered Muslim land, all the Muslim inhabitants had to make a *hijra* to a place under Muslim government, and to engage in holy war for the recovery of their lost land from there, according to such jurists. But *hijra* and *jihād* for the recovery of lost land, which was to figure prominently in the Muslim response to European colonialism, still played only a subsidiary role in the period covered by this book.[10]

It was probably with reference to merchant diasporas that jurists discussed the problem of living under non-Muslim rule in the east, where al-Māwardī was among the first openly to confront it in a permissive vein: it was lawful for Muslims to live in the abode of unbelief as long as they could openly practise their religion there, he said. Or more precisely, this is what he meant. What he actually said was that all lands in which Muslims could openly practise their religion formed part of the abode of Islam.[11] Since full practice of Islam included Muslim sovereignty, he could claim to be saying no more than that all lands under Muslim sovereignty formed part of the Muslim world – a safe fall-back position in case he was accused of innovating. But in practice it is clear that he is making a concession: one could be a Muslim anywhere in the world as long as there was no persecution; one did not have to live under Muslim rule if the infidels were tolerant. Conversely, some jurists required or recommended emigration (*hijra*) from lands where wrongdoing prevailed within the realm of Islam.[12] What al-Māwardī and such jurists were conceding was that socio-political and moral borders had ceased to coincide.

Things became even more complex in 1258, when the Mongols killed the last ʿAbbāsid caliph, thereby transferring the entire eastern Muslim world to infidel sovereignty. A popular tag, eventually a Prophetic saying, had it that government could endure unbelief but not injustice. As al-Māwardī said, this was merely meant to highlight the importance of justice, not to legalize infidel government, but the Mongols in Baghdad cleverly asked an assembly of scholars for a responsum (*fatwā*) on the question whether a just infidel ruler was better than an unjust Muslim. The scholars had no choice but to answer in the affirmative.[13] They clearly did not mean it. But nor did they want to declare the eastern Muslim world to be infidel territory for lack of a Muslim ruler after

9. Thus Ibn Ḥazm, Ibn ʿAbd al-Barr, the older Ibn Rushd (the grandfather of the philosopher), and Abū Bakr b. al-ʿArabī in Abou El Fadl, 'Islamic Law and Muslim Minorities', 149, 150f.; Meier, 'Umstrittende Pflicht', 69f.

10. Meier, 'Umstrittene Pflicht', 70ff.; further references in Crone, 'Hiğra', 382.

11. Abou El Fadl, 'Islamic Law and Muslim Minorities', 150.

12. Cf. above, 182, note 68.

13. Sadan, '"Community" and "Extra-Community"', 108ff.

the fashion of the first-century Khārijites. Lands that had once formed part of *dār al-islām* remained part of it for ever, the Ḥanafīs and Shāfiʿites said, at least for as long as just a single Muslim law was applied in them.[14] Moral rectitude, once established, could not be eliminated as long as it could find expression in at least partial practice of God's law. Political sovereignty was dispensable.

Within two centuries of the conquests the *ahl al-sunna wa'l-jamāʿa* had ruled that one could be a Muslim without a rightly guided imam. Now they concluded that one could be a Muslim without a Muslim ruler of any kind. They did not say it directly, or very often or clearly, nor did they confront the next question in line, whether one could be saved even without a Muslim community, as an individual living alone among infidels. Most of them implicitly put their foot down here: morality was embodied in a law, and the law presupposed communal life. But the need for communal life was sometimes questioned, too, if only in other contexts. It was after all as strangers that the true believers lived among their own co-religionists, as the Sufis said.[15] Islam did not quite reach the point of becoming wholly detachable from its original social and political setting, and thus capable of combination with any kind of social and political order. It still has not reached that point today and perhaps it never will. But it had moved much further in that direction, by 1258, than a historian of its earliest period might have thought possible.

Jihād

Whether one could live in the abode of war or not, the abode itself was illegitimate. It had no right to exist, like states denied diplomatic recognition in modern times. Though truces could temporarily suspend hostilities between it and the abode of Islam, the relationship between them could never be one of real peace. Muslims were legally obliged to wage holy war against *dār al-ḥarb* until it ceased to exist or the world came to an end, whichever would be the sooner. It was commonly held that Jesus would return at the end of times to complete the task by breaking the crosses, killing swine, destroying churches and synagogues, and converting all *ahl al-kitāb* by persuasion or the sword. Or the Mahdi would see to it that everyone on earth became either a Muslim or a tributary, this being how God would fulfil his promise to make Islam prevail over all religion.[16]

14. Abou El Fadl, 'Islamic Law and Muslim Minorities', 161f., 183.

15. E.g. Ibn Qayyim al-Jawziyya, *Madārij al-sālikīn*, iii, 194ff.

16. *EI*², s.v, 'ʿĪsā b. Maryam', col. 84r; Arjomand, 'Islamic Apocalypticism', 242; Maqdisī, *Bad'*, ii, 183.

'Holy war' is a modern term sometimes said to be a borrowing from Greek. Islamicists often voice dissatisfaction with its use as a translation of *jihād (fī sabīl allāh)*, which literally means 'striving (in the path of God)',[17] and it certainly does not have anything in common with the Greek concept.[18] It does however seem a perfectly adequate term for warfare enjoined by God, fought for His sake, and rewarded by Him. *Jihād* was not holy in the sense of ritually distinguished from profane activities. Neither the soldiers nor their weapons were consecrated,[19] no special rules of ritual purity applied to the camp, no sacrifices were offered for victory, and no mobile sanctuaries or sacred objects were brought along to indicate God's presence.[20] The holiness lay entirely in the fact that God's will was being done. Participants who fought with the wrong intentions were not engaged in *jihād* and God would not reward them.

All the classical schools of law, Sunni, Shīʿite and Khārijite, identify holy war as an obligation with reference to Q. 2:216 ("Prescribed for you is fighting [*al-qitāl*], though it be hateful to you"). Here as elsewhere, the Qurʾān refers to the activity by a derivative of the verb meaning to fight (*qātala*), not of that meaning to strive (*jāhada*). It often mentions striving in the path of God as well, in a manner suggesting that the two activities were related (esp. 9:41), but it never actually identifies the two, and it is a bit of a mystery that *jihād* came to be the technical term for holy war.[21] Altogether, the early history of the duty is in need of further research. In the Umayyad and early ʿAbbāsid periods, holy war seems to have been widely regarded as an obligation comparable to prayer, fasting, pilgrimage, and the payment of alms, that is, as a duty incumbent on every adult individual capable of fulfilling it (meaning every free able-bodied male in this particular case, though some Khārijites would include women and slaves as well).[22] All these duties were 'pillars of Islam', it was said.[23] But there

17. E.g. Noth, *Heiliger Krieg*, 22f.; Peters, *Jihad*, 3f.

18. Cf. Thucydides, *Pelep. War*, i, 112; Aristophanes, *Birds*, 556, where it is war for the control of a sanctuary (Delphi). Since these appear to be the only attestations of the term *hieros polemos* in Greek, including Byzantine, writings (Dennis, 'Defenders of the Christian People,' 33f.), one wonders if medieval Latin *bellum sacrum* is not more likely to lie behind the modern term.

19. The early Khārijites seem to have been something of an exception: they would shave their heads before going into battle (Goldziher, *MS*, i, 248ff.).

20. Contrast the participants in the 'wars of Yahweh' (von Rad, *Holy War in Ancient Israel*, 42).

21. Cf. Sachedina, 'Development of *Jihad*', 37f.

22. Cf. Makḥūl and Saʿīd b. al-Musayyab in Ibn Abū Shayba, *Muṣannaf*, v, 351f. (in later works Saʿīd b. al-Musayyab is said to have regarded holy war as a *farḍ ʿayn*, e.g. Qaffāl, *Ḥilya*, vii, 645, but it may be doubted that he knew the term); Crone and Zimmermann, *Epistle*, 180f.

23. Cf. below, note 25. *Jihād* remained a pillar of Islam without remaining an individual duty in Imami Shīʿism (Ṭūsī, *Nihāya*, 289).

were also some who denied that *jihād* was a pillar, arguing that it was not obligatory for everyone, or not obligatory at all,[24] only commendable (*ḥasan*).[25] Both sides apparently lacked the concept of a communal duty (*farḍ kifāya*) by which the disagreement was eventually resolved. In classical law the obligation does indeed fall on all Muslims, but collectively rather than individually, meaning that some can fulfil it on behalf of all.

Since the communal obligation to wage holy war was officially discharged by the ruler and his troops, civilians could in principle have left it at that, except in emergencies, when *jihād* became an individual duty again. But volunteering remained highly meritorious, and as mentioned before, civilians would often join the official campaigns as volunteers (*mutaṭawwiʿa*) or go to live on the frontier for extended periods, attaching themselves to fortified settlements known as *ribāṭ*s, in the hope of earning a place in Paradise.[26] They fought for God's community, not the ruler's, and their zeal never generated a system of military conscription. They were also a mixed blessing from the point of view of the authorities in that they were prone to disruptive behaviour, even to the point of turning against fellow-Muslims. Those who lived in the frontier areas often seemed to have more in common with their close enemies than with their distant co-religionists.[27] For all that, few activities 'in God's path' were as highly esteemed as *jihād*, which is praised in the most extravagant terms in the religious literature.

The earliest concept of holy war

In classical law *jihād* is missionary warfare.[28] It is directed against infidels, who need not be guilty of any act of hostility against Muslims (their very existence

24. Cf. ʿAbd al-Razzāq, *Muṣannaf*, v, no. 9271; Ibn Abū Shayba, *Muṣannaf*, v, 352, where ʿAṭāʾ and ʿAmr b. Dīnār profess not to know whether the duty was universal.

25. Thus Ibn ʿUmar, bracketing it with voluntary alms, in ʿAbd al-Razzāq, *Muṣannaf*, v, no. 9279 (where Islam has four pillars), and in Ibn Abū Shayba, *Muṣannaf*, v, 352 (where it has four 'props'), 353 (five pillars). Similarly ʿAbdallāh b. al-Ḥasan, the father of al-Nafs al-Zakiyya (both d. 145/762), in Ibn Rushd, *Bidāya*, i, 533 (tr. in Peters, *Jihād*, 29). Sufyān al-Thawrī also denied that holy war was a duty, except when the infidels attacked (Sarakhsī, *Siyar*, i, 187), and Ibn Shubruma is said also to have identified it as voluntary (Maḥmaṣānī, *Awzāʿī*, 352, without reference).

26. Above, 298.

27. Cf. Darling, 'Contested Territory', esp. 145ff. For Khurasani *mujāhidūn* attacking Rayy (like Christian crusaders attacking Constantinople) in 355/966, see Miskawayh, *Tajārib*, in *Eclipse*, ii, 222ff. = v, 234ff.

28. See below, 368. In connection with the Ottoman expansion it is sometimes said that *jihād* stood for defensive warfare whereas *ghazw* was irregular raiding in which infidels often

is a cause of war), and its aim is to incorporate the infidels in the abode of Islam, preferably as converts, but alternatively as *dhimmīs*, until the whole world has been subdued. Islamicists generally assume this to have been the nature of *jihād* from the start. Thus they will debate whether the Arab conquests were motivated by a universalist conception of Islam or by worldly considerations, taking it for granted that if the conquerors were not trying to bring Islam to all mankind, they cannot have been fighting for religious reasons at all.[29] The sources regularly present the Arab invaders as inviting the infidels to convert before fighting them, suggesting a universalist conception, but their testimony is not weighty since they were compiled long after the event; and whatever the Arabs may have done during the conquests, they certainly did not display much interest in converting people after they had conquered them, except in the case of fellow-Arabs. For these reasons it has been concluded that the early conquests were not *jihād* at all.[30]

But this approach rests on a misconception. Religious and political universalism are not natural partners. Universalist religions do not normally generate attempts at world conquest, as is clear from the peaceful spread of early Buddhism, early Christianity, Manichaeism, and Bahaism. Conversely, conquerors setting out to subdue the world are not normally animated by a desire to save souls: one need only think of Alexander the Great, the Romans, or the Mongols. And why should a missionary intent be the only way in which a religious motivation could display itself?[31] The opposite of universalism is not materialism but rather particularism, and holy war is well known to have been an institution of great antiquity in the Near East without having anything to do with proselytization.

Holy war in the ancient Near East was holy in the sense of its being enjoined by the gods and fought for the extension of their land (identical with that of their servants). "The god Ashur (and) the great gods who magnify my sovereignty . . . commanded me to extend the borders of their lands," the Assyrian king Tiglath-Pileser I (d. 1076 BC) announced in one of his inscriptions.[32] "At the command of my lord Ashur my hand conquered from beyond

---

participated too (cf. Darling, 'Contested Territory', 137). No source known to me espouses this view. In the period covered by this book, *ghazw* was simply the campaigning, irregular or otherwise, by which missionary *Jihād* was carried out. Whether infidels joined or not made no difference.

29. E.g. Gabrieli, *Muhammad and the Conquests of Islam*, ch. 6.

30. Thus Watt, *Political Thought*, 18. For his apologetic intent, see his 'Theory of *Jihād*', 390: showing that the conquests were not religious in nature helps to clear Islam of the charge that it is a religion of violence.

31. Cf. the sensible remarks of Bousquet, 'Observations sur la nature et les causes,' 44ff.

32. Oded, '"The Command of the God" as a Reason for Going to War', 225.

the Lower Zab River to the Upper Sea . . . I made bow to my feet thirty kings of the Nairi countries . . . I imposed on them (regular) tribute," he declared elsewhere.[33] "I was acting only upon the trust-inspiring oracles given by Ashur, the great lord, my lord . . . I swept over Hatti in its full extent, making it look like ruin-hills left by the flood," Shalmanassar III (d. 824 BC) boasted. "The terror and glamour of Ashur, my lord, overwhelmed them . . . pillars of skulls I erected in front of the town," he says in another inscription.[34] "I have given into your hand Sihon the Amorite, king of Heshbon, and his land; begin to possess it and contend with him in battle," the god of the Israelites told Moses. "We took all his cities . . . and utterly destroyed the men, the women and the little ones," Moses reports.[35] "Kamosh (god of the Moabites) spoke to me and said, Go and take (the town of) Nebo from Israel, so I went to it by night and fought it from early dawn to midday and took it and killed everybody, 7000 men, boys, women, girls and slave girls": thus a stele by a Moabite king.[36]

In all these examples the warfare is linked with a particularist concept of religion: each people has its own patron deity, a sacralized version of themselves, whose command entitles or indeed obliges them to destroy or subdue their neighbours; each deity cares only for his own people, whom he furnishes with a divine right to conquer without concern for the fate of their victims. Each ethnic group sees its deity as bigger and better than other people's gods and find proof of this in victory. Much later, when the number of true gods had been reduced to one, the feeling of the believers was that the one and only deity had chosen them above all others: victory furnished the proof yet again. In short, holy war in the Near East was divinely enjoined imperialism. So it still seems to have been in the time of the Sasanids. "The Zoroastrians say, We do not force anyone to convert to our religion, nor do we encourage anyone. It is a religion with which God has chosen us. We do not prevent anyone from adopting it, but we only fight and use the sword against the nations to make them pay tribute and render obedience."[37]

The Arab conquerors seem to have thought of holy war along the same lines. "God says, We have written in the Psalms . . . my righteous servants shall inherit the earth," the commander of the Arab troops tells his men on the eve of the decisive battle of Qādisiyya in Iraq in 637; "now this is your inheritance and what the Lord has promised you: He permitted you to take it three years ago, and you have nourished yourselves on it, eaten off it, killed its inhabitants,

33. Pritchard, *Ancient Near Eastern Texts*,^{2} 275.

34. Ibid., 277

35. Deut. 2:24, 34.

36. Weippert, '"Heiliger Krieg" in Israel und Assyrien', 484f.

37. ʿAbd al-Jabbār, *Tathbīt*, i, 185.

collected taxes from them, and taken them prisoners until today."[38] In other words, the earth which God had promised His righteous servants was, or included, the Persian empire, which the Arabs had been living off for the three years since the invasion of Iraq began, from which they had taken rich spoils, and which they were now proposing to take in its entirety. In another story, also set before the battle of Qādisiyya, a Persian general asks an Arab prisoner-of-war what the Arabs have come for. "That which God has promised us," he replies. When the general asks him what that is, he replies "Your land, your children, and your lives if you refuse to submit (to our God)."[39] Here as in the ancient Near Eastern examples, a deity has told his people to go take the land of other people, who are casually written off as booty along with their possessions, though there is one major difference: the intended victims can now abandon their own community to join that of the invaders. Some non-Arabs did convert in the course of the conquests, to be incorporated in the new community as allies of Arab tribes.[40] But with or without conversion, the conquerors' understanding of Islam was particularist: religion was being used to validate the dominion of a single people, or to expand their ranks, not to unite mankind in a single truth above ethnic and political divisions. "I want them (Quraysh) to profess a single creed by which the Arabs will accept them as their leaders (*tudīna lahum bihā*) and the non-Arabs will pay them *jizya*," as the Prophet is supposed to have said.[41] Whatever Muḥammad may have preached, *jihād* as the bulk of the Arab tribesmen understood it was Arab imperialism at God's command. Their universalism was political.

That they should have understood their religion in a particularist vein is not surprising. Arab tribesmen were notorious ethnic chauvinists. The extremes to which they could go in their sense of being the only real people on earth is well known from the behaviour of the early twentieth-century Ikhwān of Saudi Arabia, whose naturally high self-esteem was also driven into a higher gear by religion. But the Ikhwān were at least defeated when they attempted conquest outside Arabia. By contrast, the early conquerors went from one astonishing victory to another for about a hundred years, increasingly convinced that God was in league with them to the exclusion of all others. Since the league, as they saw it, was between God and Arabs, they were offended by the existence of Arab adherents of other faiths, notably Arab Christians, whom they subjected to attempts at forced conversion from time to time while

38. Tab., i, 2289. The quotation is from Q. 21:105, citing Ps. 37:29.

39. Ibid., i, 2254.

40. Cf. Crone, *Roman, Provincial and Islamic Law*, 89.

41. Ibn Ḥanbal, *Musnad*, i, 227.-2.

leaving non-Arab Christians in peace;[42] and converts of non-Arab origin had to adopt not only the Arab God, but also the political membership and (initially via an ally, thereafter via a patron) the tribal organization of the Arabs.[43] One could not gain access to their God without becoming one of them. There were also practical considerations behind these rules, but this merely goes to show that the massive success of the conquests reinforced the particularist interests of the conquerors.

Intelligible though their outlook was, however, it was certainly archaic. Holy war of the ancient Near Eastern type might still survive among the Zoroastrians, a species of pagans, but the monotheist ancestors of Islam had left it behind. It is true that when Christians fought non-Christians, they had a sense of fighting for their own religion – their own way of life, as we would say today. Heraclius gave a strong religious colouring to his campaigns against the Persians in the 620s, when the very survival of the Byzantine empire was at stake; he is even said to have told his soldiers that they would fall as martyrs assured of eternal life, much as the Qur'ān says to the believers.[44] But such ideas still fell short of the belief that God had chosen one people over others and ordered them to go conquer the earth. The Christians found the early Muslim concept of holy war deeply offensive, both in its postulate of a blatantly partial God and in its unthinking endorsement of violence, though they were familiar with the concept from the Old Testament. It was a very tribal notion. It matched the archaism of the multipurpose polity and was one of the many areas where the injection of ancient, outdated ideas by tribal conquerors into a sophisticated world was the starting point for massive rethinking and the emergence of new institutions. The classical concept of *jihād* is an example, for it is not a mere variant on the ancient Near Eastern idea, but rather a novel conception unique to Islam.

The classical concept of jihād

"We have written in the Psalms . . . my righteous servants shall inherit the earth": like the commander at Qādisiyya, al-Ṭabarī begins a discussion of *jihād* with Q. 21:105, but the spirit in which he does so is quite different, for he continues by citing 34:28, "We have not sent thee but as a bearer of glad tidings and a warner to all mankind." According to him, all *earlier* prophets had been sent to a particular segment of humanity, but Muḥammad was favoured

42. Cf. Robinson, *Empire and Elites*, 60f.

43. Cf. *EI*², s.v. 'mawlā'.

44. Howard-Johnson, 'Official History of Heraclius' Persian Campaigns', 82, 85; cf. Q. 2:154; 3:157, 169, 195; 4:74 (where the term 'martyr' is not used).

with a general message and a universal mission (*al-risāla al-ʿāmma wa'l-daʿwa al-kāffa*).[45] Holy war as he saw it was still imperialism at God's command: to him, as to all classical jurists, its purpose was to make Islam sovereign on earth. But God's command was no longer understood as addressed to an ethnic group, only to the believers whoever they might be; and it was now linked to a religious *mission civilisatrice* rather than the satisfaction of Arab chauvinism. As the British conquerors saw themselves as bringing good government to the natives and as the French saw themselves as bringing them higher civilization, so the Muslims saw themselves as bringing salvation.[46] World religion and world conquest had married up.

Islam or death?

It is thanks to the classical definition of *jihād* as missionary warfare that the Arab conquerors were once depicted in Western literature as warriors fighting with the Qurʾān in one hand and the sword in the other. The stereotype has its roots in the sources. Thus the jurist al-Ḥalīmī (d. 403/1012) describes *jihād* as calling people to Islam and backing the call with violence (*qitāl*) where necessary.[47] *Jihād* is "the forcible mission assisted by the unsheathed sword against wrongheaded people who arrogantly refuse to accept the plain truth after it has become clear", according to al-Juwaynī (d. 478/1085),[48] God sent Muḥammad "to call to belief in God's unity by the sword" (*dāʿiyan ilā tawḥīdihi bi'l-sayf*), the fourteenth-century Ibn Rajab says.[49] "If they adopt our creed, well and good. If not, we put them to the sword," as a seventeenth-century Indian hagiography puts it, popularizing the image that was to pass to the British.[50] For all that, the stereotype is misleading, not only in connection with the conquests, but also later, when *jihād* had indubitably come to be understood as a missionary enterprise.

As the jurists saw it, holy warriors called to God's unity with the sword by venturing into *dār al-ḥarb* in order to summon the infidels to Islam. The

45. Ṭabarī, *Ikhtilāf al-fuqahāʾ*, 1, discussed in Sachedina, 'Development of *Jihad*,' 38.

46. Cf. John Stuart Mill on the sacred duty of intervention in "nations which are still barbarous" where it was "likely to be for their own benefit that they should be conquered and held in subjection by foreigners" (cited in Makdisi, *Culture of Sectarianism*, 8f.). Or, as Cecil Rhodes put it, "We happen to be the best people in the world . . . and the more of the world we inhabit, the better for humanity" (quoted in Porter, *Lion's Share*, 134).

47. Cook, *Commanding Right*, 341.

48. *Ghiyāth al-umam*, §304 (*al-daʿwa al-qahriyya al-muʾayyada bi'l-sayf al-maslūl ʿalā 'l-māriqīn alladhīna abaw wa'stakbarū baʿda wuḍūḥ al-ḥaqq al-mubīn*).

49. Ibn Rajab (d. 795/1393) in Kister, 'Land Property and Jihād', 285.

50. Darling, 'Contested Territory', 147.

summons, if actually delivered, were meant to be peaceful, and if the infidels accepted them, the war was over. In practice, they did not, of course, and the summons might not even be delivered, on the grounds that the infidels had heard them before. They were in that case to be fought until they surrendered politically. The departure from the stereotype starts here, for whether the defeated infidels should be forced to convert depended on what type of infidels they were. The key point was that all infidels had to be brought under Muslim sovereignty, not that they all had to accept Islam.

People of the Book (*ahl al-kitāb*), meaning Jews and Christians, were to be distinguished from pagans, according to most jurists. Since the Jews and the Christians had received earlier revelations from God, they could be allowed to exist. They were to be offered status as protected people (*ahl al-dhimma*) in return for payment of a demeaning poll-tax (*jizya*), the jurists said, adducing the Prophet's precedent and Q. 9:29: "Fight those who do not believe in God and the last day and do not forbid what God and His messenger have forbidden and do not practise the religion of truth, from among those who have been given the book, until they pay *jizya* out of hand, in a state of humiliation."[51] The jurists must have been hard put to find an appropriate verse, for Jews and Christians are hardly people "who do not believe in God and the last days". It would in fact have been easier for them simply to lay down that all infidels without exception were to be given the choice between Islam and death, for the Qurʾān also says, "Fight them (i.e. unbelievers) until there is no *fitna*, and the religion is entirely God's" (8:39), and "Kill the polytheists wherever you find them" (9:5; Christians were often and Jews occasionally deemed to be polytheists). But the jurists did not want so draconian a rule, so they chose to overlook the problematic aspect of the first verse and to limit the application of the two uncompromising verses to pagans.[52]

On pagans they were less inclined to compromise. The Qurʾānic verses apart, a famous Ḥadīth declared Muḥammad to have been sent to fight people until they said "there is no God but God", which was compatible with the survival of Jews and (probably) Christians, but not with that of pagans.[53] The Prophet was remembered as having given them the choice between conversion and death. But it was only Arab pagans that he had eradicated: did their non-Arab peers have to be similarly treated? After some debate, the jurists decided that the Zoroastrians (*al-majūs*) of Iran were an exception, on the grounds that

51. The meaning of *jizya ʿan yad* is uncertain (cf. most recently Rubin, 'The case of "ʿan yadin"').

52. Cf. Ibn Rushd, *Bidāya*, i, 534, 546 (tr. in Peters, *Jihad*, 30, 41); Jaṣṣāṣ, *Aḥkām al-Qurʾān*, i, 548f.

53. Cf. Ibn Rushd, *Bidāya*, i, 546 (tr. in Peters, *Jihad*, 41).

they had once possessed a book (meaning a scripture in the Judeo-Christian tradition: the Avesta did not count), and/or that the Prophet had accepted *jizya* from Zoroastrians (in eastern Arabia), instructing his followers to treat them as if they were People of the Book (*sunnū bihim sunnata ahl al-kitāb*).[54] But the jurists could not agree on other pagans. Some took the Prophet's eradication of Arab idolaters to mean that all pagans had to be given the choice between Islam or death, whatever their ethnicity. This was the position of the Shāfiʿites, for example.[55] Others argued that the Arabs were a special case and that it was the Prophet's treatment of Zoroastrians which had universal significance: all non-Arab pagans should be treated as Zoroastrians. This was the position of the Mālikīs and the Ḥanafīs.[56] In deference to the Prophet's precedent most jurists accepted that Arab pagans should be given the choice between Islam and the sword, but this was a purely theoretical concession since Arab pagans did not exist any more, and there were some who brushed even that aside, arguing that all unbelievers were eligible for *dhimmī* status, full stop.[57]

Practice was a good deal simpler than theory. Outside Arabia and Berber North Africa, successful *jihād* seems never to have been followed by coercive measures against infidels refusing to convert. Male captives might be killed or enslaved, whatever their religious affiliation. (People of the Book were not protected by Islamic law until they had accepted *dhimma*.) Captives might also be given the choice between Islam and death, or they might pronounce the confession of faith of their own accord to avoid execution: the jurists ruled that their change of status was to be accepted even though they had only converted out of fear.[58] Women and children captured in the course of the campaigns were usually enslaved, again regardless of their faith. But the conquered population at large rarely seems to have been given a choice between conversion

54. Friedmann, 'Classification', 179ff.; Sālim, *Epistle*, II, §29 and the commentary thereto. Since Zoroastrians were only quasi-*kitābī*s, Muslims could not eat their meat or marry their women, as they could those of Jews and Christians.

55. Māwardī, *Aḥkām*, 248/143 = 159; Shāfiʿī, Abū Thawr, Ibn Ḥazm and others in Ibn Rushd, *Bidāya*, i, 546; tr. in Peters, *Jihad*, 40; Friedmann, 'Classification', 183.

56. Friedmann, 'Temple of Multān', 181 and 'Classification', 183, 185. It was also the position of Awzāʿī, Abū ʿUbayd and others, cf. (in addition to Friedmann), Morabia, *Ǧihâd*, 267.

57. Thus the fourteenth-century Ibn Qayyim al-Jawziyya, on the grounds that the *jizya* verse (Q. 9:29) was simply revealed too late to benefit the pagans of Arabia (Friedmann, 'Classification', 185). The view that even Arab pagans would be eligible for *dhimmī* status if they existed is also attributed to Mālik and Abū Ḥanīfa (Friedmann, 'Classification', 183, 185n.).

58. Jaṣṣāṣ, *Aḥkām*, i, 550 (*ad* 2:256), who says he does not know of any disagreement about this; cf. also Ṭabarī, *Ikhtilāf*, 162f.

and death, and it is by omitting this point that the stereotype misleads. Once the war was over, people received *dhimma* in return for the payment of *jizya* and were generally left in peace, again whether they were pagans or People of the Book. One should not think of *jihād* as something conducted along the lines of Charlemagne's forced conversion of the Saxons.

If this disposes of the stereotyped misconception, it lands us with the opposite problem of explaining how the jurists could see holy war as a missionary enterprise at all. *Jihād* was still in the nature of divinely enjoined imperialism. The fact that the troops were meant to summon the enemy to Islam was largely symbolic; the missionary phase of the warfare came to an end the moment the invitation was refused; some male captives apart, all conquered peoples were in practice allowed to retain their religion once they had been enslaved or placed under the political control of the Muslims. How then could the jurists see the enterprise as a call to Islam backed by violence? In what way did it promote the spread of the faith? The answer, of course, is that captives apart, it did so indirectly.

Holy war spread Islam first and foremost in the sense of extending its sovereignty. Muslim rulers would move in along with *qāḍī*s and scholars to build mosques, apply Islamic law, place restrictions on the building of non-Muslim houses of worship and introduce other discriminatory measures against the original inhabitants, who were reduced to tributaries in their own land. Inevitably, they sooner or later began to convert. They were not necessarily persecuted: the Muslim record of tolerance is generally good. But those who stuck to their faith were apt to feel that history was passing them by, which easily turned into a conviction that the truth must lie elsewhere. "The *dhimmī* living among the Muslims sees the beauty of the Muslim faith and is exhorted to, and often does, accept Islam," as a Ḥanafī lawyer put it: it was for this reason that conquered people could be allowed to persist in the worst of crimes, unbelief, in return for a mere monetary consideration, the poll-tax (i.e. where it might have seemed more commendable to force them to convert or to kill them).[59] Nor should the importance of captives be underestimated. Muslim warriors routinely took large numbers of them. Leaving aside those who converted to avoid execution, some were ransomed and the rest were enslaved, usually for domestic use. Dispersed in Muslim households, slaves almost always converted, encouraged or pressurized by their masters, driven by a need to bond with others, or slowly becoming accustomed to seeing things through Muslim eyes even if they tried to resist. Though neither the *dhimmī* nor the slave had been faced with a choice between Islam and death, it would be absurd

59. Sarakhsī, *Mabsūṭ*, x, 77.-5; cited in Aghnides, *Theories of Finance*, 356.

to deny that force played a major role in their conversion. Nor do medieval jurists generally attempt to deny it. They did hold that "one should not say of someone who converts after warfare that he has been converted by force (*mukrahan*), for he is not forced when he consents (in his inner self) and becomes a genuine Muslim"; there had not in fact been any coercion at all, some said, for true belief is what is goes on in the heart, not the public confession of faith. But this was to square the use of force with the Qur'ānic statement "there is no compulsion in religion" (*lā ikrāh fī 'l-dīn*) (2:256), or to spare the feelings of the convert, not to deny the role of coercion in enabling him to see the light.[60]

The moral status of coercion

Generally speaking, medieval Muslim jurists did not worry about the legitimacy of using violence as long as it was used in accordance with God's law. *Jihād* was prescribed in the Qur'ān itself, so its moral status was not open to doubt. The Qur'ān did admittedly also make the above-mentioned declaration that "there is no compulsion in religion" (2:256), and it contains a host of other statements advocating peaceful debate with religious adversaries.[61] But 2:256 was commonly held to prohibit forced conversion of *dhimmī*s, not the warfare whereby *dhimmī* status was imposed on them, and some said that both this and the other verses enjoining toleration had been abrogated when holy war was prescribed in Medina. These views must have crystallized early, for they are entrenched in the exegetical literature from the moment of its emergence in the mid-eighth century.[62]

When the jurists of the eighth and ninth centuries evinced doubts about the legitimacy of holy war, they typically did so with reference to the qualifications of the warriors. If things were in order on the Muslim side, they were satisfied that holy war was in the best interest of the victims themselves. The infidels were "dragged to Paradise in chains", as Ḥadīth so graphically puts it.[63] But if the Muslims were led by a wrongful ruler, did his iniquity invalidate the holy war fought by or under him? As has been seen, the Shī'ites thought so,

60. Jaṣṣāṣ, *Aḥkām*, i, 548; Rāzī, *Tafsīr*, vii, 16; Ṭūsī, *Tibyān*, ii, 311; Qurṭubī, *Aḥkām*, ii, 281 (all *ad* 2:256).

61. Cf. Sachedina, 'Freedom of Conscience and Religion in the Qur'an', esp. 74ff., with a modernist interpretation to activate them.

62. Cf. Muqātil, *Tafsīr*, 134f.; Ṭabarī, *Tafsīr*, iii, 13ff.; cf. also the engaging discussion in Cook, *The Koran*, 100ff.

63. Bukhārī, *Ṣaḥiḥ*, ii, 250 (*K. al-jihād*); *'Iqd*, iii, 412.16.

but the Traditionalist, eventually Sunni, answer was that it did not.[64] Were very small numbers allowed to fight, thereby courting death? An early form of this question is said to have presented itself to the 'good' Umayyad caliph ʿUmar II (717–20), who reportedly ordered the evacuation of the Muslim populations in Spain and Transoxania, the extreme western and eastern borders of the Muslim world at the time, and prohibited further warfare when they refused to leave.[65] He did not set a *sunna* thereby, however, for the jurists rarely debate the safety of settlements, only that of the participants in battle. Holy warriors had to have a reasonable chance of success, for although it was highly meritorious to fall in holy war, it was forbidden to commit suicide. Nonetheless, there were Sunni jurists who permitted people to seek martyrdom more or less at will.[66]

Above all, however, the warriors had to have the right motivation: they had to fight with the intention of serving God's cause, not for the sake of booty. This view is amply represented in the accounts of the conquests, compiled as they were with a view to legitimating the expansion (and other things). When the Arabs are asked what they have come for, they do not usually reply "your land and your children", but rather deny being moved by material considerations. In the exchanges between the Arabs and the Persians at Qādisiyya, for example, the Persians often declare themselves convinced that the Arabs have come in search of sustenance and booty, whereupon the Arabs insist that they have only come to spread Islam.[67] Sayf b. ʿUmar even goes so far as to have the Arabs offer to go home if the Persians would convert, as has been seen.[68] It is partly because the jurists see religious motives as the opposite of a desire for material enrichment that the Islamicist literature abounds in debates whether the conquerors were animated by religious feelings or rather by a desire for booty, but Western scholars are also habituated by their Christian background to thinking of religion and worldly success as mutually exclusive. Medieval Christian jurists, much like their Muslim counterparts, ruled that the participants in 'just war' were not to fight for booty, and there is something of a tradition for thinking of *jihād* as the Islamic version of just war.[69] All this is unhelpful, however. The conquerors plainly did not see a conflict between God and material rewards, but on the contrary a causal connection: the one led to

64. Cf. above, ch. 18, 297f.

65. Crone, 'Qays and the Yemen', 23.

66. Kohlberg, 'Medieval Muslim Views on Martyrdom', 29f.; for an Imami view, see above, 123, note 51; for the Assassins, see below, 390f.

67. Tab., i, 2352. The Byzantines were also convinced that they had come for booty, cf. Dennis, 'Defenders of the Christian People', 32f.

68. Cf. above, ch. 2, 31.

69. Cf. Kelsay and Turner Johnson, *Just War and Jihad*.

the other; booty was among the good things with which God rewarded His followers. And just war was quite different from *jihād* in that it did not include war for the dissemination of the faith. Like *jihād*, it could be fought for the recovery of rightful possessions, but whereas *jihād* was always directed against infidels, the medieval theory of just war was mostly meant for the regulation of conflict within the Christian world itself.[70]

The tenth- and eleventh-century qualms

The conquered peoples, above all the Christians, Manichaeans, and other Gnostics, always held the Muslim reliance on the sword to be wrong, and this did eventually affect the Muslims themselves. As early as 634 a Greek tract had declared that the so-called prophet must be an impostor because prophets do not come with armed with the sword; some sixty years later a Syriac patriarch supposedly told the caliph ʿAbd al-Malik (d. 705) that Islam was "a religion established by the sword and not a faith confirmed by miracles",[71] and the Christians continued to express themselves in this vein for ever after, both in their vernaculars and, from the ninth century onwards, in Arabic. The Muslims do not seem to have been greatly bothered by the charges as long as their empire lasted, but things looked different when it broke up. It began to do so already in the 750s; the process accelerated in the 860s, and by 950 the entire area once controlled by the Sāsānids had come to be governed by Iranians again. Islam now had to make sense as a set of beliefs independently of Arab power, and it had to do so to Muslims whose own ancestors had more often than not been Christians or adherents of other religions opposed to the idea of religious war. This was when the non-Muslim accusations regarding Islam and the sword began to hurt.

According to a story told by the Muʿtazilite al-Khayyāṭ (d. c. 913), an Indian king once asked Hārūn al-Rashīd to send people for him to debate with. "I've heard that you spread it with the sword . . .," he said. Hārūn sent a traditionist who recited the usual "I've heard from so-and-so who heard from so-and-so," which unsurprisingly failed to impress the Indians; they concluded that Islam did indeed owe its success to the sword. Then Hārūn sent a *mutakallim*, who demolished the Indians with hardhitting dialectical arguments, so the story had a happy end: Islam was true all right; it was just the traditionists who were stupid.[72] Slightly later, the philosopher al-ʿĀmirī (d. 996)

70. Cf. *Cambridge History of Later Medieval Philosophy*, 771ff. On the whole 'booty vs religion' issue, see also Crone, *Meccan Trade and the Rise of Islam*, 244f.

71. Hoyland, *Seeing Islam as Others Saw It*, 57, 203.

72. Ibn al-Murtaḍā, *Ṭabaqāt al-muʿtazila*, 55.

took issue with 'pseudo-sophisticates' (*mutaẓarrifa*), apparently in eastern Iran, who argued that "if Islam were a religion of truth, it would be a religion of mercy; and if it were a religion of mercy, the one who calls to it would not attack people with the sword, arbitrarily strip them of their property, capture their families and enslave them; rather, he would proselytize by words and guide to it by the force of his explanations."[73] In other words, true religion was spread by peaceful proselytization whereas holy war was just a cover for rapaciousness, whatever people might say about the purity of their intentions. Or again, the Ismaili Nāṣir-i Khusraw (d. c. 1075) describes how he searched for the truth among Christians, Jews, Manicheans, and Muslim sects of all kinds: "they said that the injunctions of the *sharīʿa* do not conform with reason because Islam was established by the mere force of the sword."[74]

Here as in al-ʿĀmirī, it is impossible to tell whether the charge is made by Muslims, non-Muslims or both, but there were certainly Muslims (or ex-Muslims) such as al-Rāzī who rejected all established religions, not just Islam, on the grounds that prophets were impostors who stirred up war, as has been seen.[75] The Companions only followed Muḥammad out of a desire for raids, plunder, and worldly goods, the (Qarmaṭī) Shīʿites said according to ʿAbd al-Jabbār, who rightly saw that there was a meeting of minds between non-Muslims and heretics here, and devoted much effort to refuting accusations that the Prophet and his followers had been motivated by worldly considerations.[76]

Few adopted so extreme a position, but the legitimacy of religious imperialism is questioned elsewhere too. A tenth-century Iranian regarded Ibn Karrām, the founder of a religious movement in eastern Iran, as worthier of prophethood than Muḥammad because he, Ibn Karrām, had lived ascetically and not conducted wars.[77] Several stories in the epistles of the Brethren of Purity voice disapproval of religious violence of any kind. One, also told elsewhere, contrasts the narrow-minded bigotry of a Jew (a thin disguise for a legalistic Muslim) with the universalist attitude of a Zoroastrian, a member of a despised minority who is here made to play the role of the good Samaritan by rescuing the bigoted Jew even though the latter abuses his kindness. "As for those who do not share my religion and views, I regard it as lawful to take their lives and property and unlawful to help, advise, assist them or to feel mercy or pity for them," the Jew says. The Zoroastrian by contrast wants good for all

73. ʿĀmirī, *Iʿlām*, 186.

74. Ivanow, *Nasir-i Khusraw*, 23.

75. Cf. above, 172. Stroumsa, *Freethinkers*, 96, 106. He claimed that disputes and warfare would disappear without religion (Abū Ḥātim, *Aʿlām*, 186ff.).

76. ʿAbd al-Jabbār, i, *Tathbīt*, 8ff., 35.

77. Van Ess, *TG*, iv, 91.

mankind whether they agree with him or not; "I do not wish ill for any created beings (*lā urīdu li-aḥad min al-khalq su'an*)," he says.[78] "I believe in mercy to all living beings," he adds in one version.[79] True to his principles the Jew steals the Zoroastrian's mule and travel provisions, abandoning him in the desert; and true to his, the Zoroastrian saves the Jew when he later finds him wounded on the road, the mule having thrown him off. The Brethren of Purity also tell a variant version of this story in which the dialogue is between a redeemed friend of God and someone doomed to perdition who prides himself on fighting God's enemies, meaning those who "disagree with my persuasion and creed": if he defeats them, he will call them to his own faith and consider it lawful to kill them, take their property and enslave their offspring if they refuse; if he fails to establish control of them, he will curse them, which makes him feel good. The friend of God pronounces him spiritually sick and declares that "I do not wish ill for any created beings" (*lā urīdu li-aḥad min al-khalq su'an*).[80] "There are people who profess as part of their religion that it is lawful to shed the blood of everyone opposed to their beliefs," they elsewhere note, giving 'Jews', Khārijites, and infidels in general as their examples. Others, they say, "profess mercy and compassion to all people as part of their religion, expressing regret for sinners and praying for forgiveness on their behalf, feeling sympathy for every living animal (*kulli dhī rūḥ min al-ḥayawān*), and wishing well-being for everyone. That is the doctrine of the pious, ascetic, and upright believers, and it is the doctrine of our noble brethren."[81] God's friends and righteous servants "are at peace with themselves and people are at peace, and safe, with them. They do not wish anyone ill (*lā yurīdūna li-aḥad su'an*) and do not harbour evil for any created being, friend or foe, opponent or fellow-believer."[82]

Q. 2:256 reconsidered

The tenth- and eleventh-century qualms changed the debate about the moral status of holy war. It now came to focus almost entirely on the victims rather than the warriors; and what the early Muslims had simply taken for granted – that it was right to use violence against them – now had to be argued at length.

78. *RIS*, i, 308; Tawḥīdī, *Imtāʿ*, ii, 158 (tr. in Bürgel, 'Zoroastrianism', 207f.); *Sirr al-asrār*, 140f. A genuine Zoroastrian does in fact say precisely that in a fourteenth-century work (Zartusht-i Bahrām Pazhdu, *Zarātushtnāme*, poem 24, lines 543–5).

79. *Sirr al-asrār*, 141.

80. *RIS*, iii, 312f.

81. Ibid., iv, 44.

82. Ibid., iii, 312.5, cf. 312.2 for the subject.

In this context there was renewed discussion of *lā ikrāh fī 'l-dīn*, "There is no compulsion in religion" (2:256). The view that it referred to the rights of *dhimmī*s, or that it had been abrogated, continued to be mentioned, and some left it at that.[83] But others now read the verse differently.

How could holy war be right if there was no compulsion to religion? Many responded by interpreting the verse with reference to the distinction between inner and outer man and the different levels of religion that it entailed. At one level, religion was a prescription for collective order in this world with its do's and its don'ts, its morality, its law and its war; at another level, it offered spiritual, philosophical, or esoteric truths for individuals. This conception had the merit of marrying up well with the received account of Muḥammad's career. As pure spirituality, Islam was exemplified by the period in Mecca, where Muḥammad and his followers had lived under a pagan regime. God and Caesar here had separate domains, as one would have said if there had been a Caesar in Mecca. But in Medina, Muhammad had created a new law and polity in the name of Islam so that henceforth both the inner and the outer lives of the Muslims were governed by the same set of rules. God had filled the place of the absent Caesar. What the Christians saw as two separate departments, the religious and the secular, now had to function as two levels within the same department of religion.

It followed that the Qur'ānic declaration "There is no compulsion in religion (*lā ikrāh fī 'l-dīn*)" could only be concerned with religion at the spiritual level. It was only here that there was not, or indeed could not be, any coercion. One might well wonder what had been the point of giving Arab pagans the choice between Islam and death when inner conviction (*iʿtiqād*) was beyond compulsion, the Ḥanafī jurist al-Jaṣṣāṣ (d. 370/981) said in his comments on the verse, clearly with reference to the forced converts of his own time; his answer is that they were only forced to conform externally (*innamā ukrihū ʿalā iẓhār al-islām*), but that there certainly was a point to this, for inner conviction would eventually follow: the convert and/or their children would sooner or later become sincere believers.[84] In a similar vein the Shāfiʿite scholar Abū Bakr al-Qaffāl (d. 365/976) says that forcing people to convert by threatening to kill

83. E.g. Māwardī, *Tafsīr*, i, 271f.

84. Jaṣṣāṣ, *Aḥkām*, i, 54 9 (*ad lā ikrah*); followed by Kiyā al-Ḥarrāsī, *Aḥkām*, 340f. Compare St Augustine's legitimation of Christian warfare, here with reference to the wielder of the sword rather than the victim, by a distinction between "the deed, which takes place publicly", deemed unimportant, and "the preparation of the heart, which is internal", deemed crucial (*Cambridge History of Later Medieval Philosophy*, 772).

them is excellent, for the victims will gradually get to love the true religion and so escape eternal damnation.[85]

The Brethren of Purity also took the declaration to mean that compulsion was valid at the external level, though inner conviction could not be forced. As far as socio-political order was concerned, they said, religion and political regimes were twins: this was why there were so many wars of religion.[86] What they have in mind does not seem to be *jihād*, but rather religious warfare within the Muslim world, viewed as a regrettable, but inevitable consequence of the fact that polities were based on religious law. But they fully endorse the obligation to fight for one's faith in other passages,[87] explaining that holy war is not motivated by hostility to infidels but rather by a desire to bring them to the truth, or at least subject them to *jizya* so as to ensure the safety of the Muslims – for the very existence of infidels is dangerous, and the best form of defence is attack.[88] Though normally a ruthless activity, war as conducted by the Prophet was characterized by both mercy and kindness, for he would always start by summoning the infidels to the truth or the payment of *jizya*, and he instructed his followers not to kill old people, children, women, or religious personnel.[89] There was no denying that people sometimes had to be cured against their will, they noted elsewhere, and prophets were doctors of souls.[90] All this pertained to the lower level at which people were sick, which the Brethren clearly considered themselves to have transcended.

All the interpretations of Q. 2:256 considered so far try to restrict the meaning of the verse: it had been abrogated, it only concerned *dhimmī*s, or it referred to the spiritual realm beyond the reach of legislation. But one could also use it to widen the scope of religious freedom. This had been tried already in the eighth century, when some adduced it to prove that Zoroastrians and other non-Arab pagans were eligible for *dhimmī* status even though they were

85. In Rāzī, *Tafsīr*, viii, 192 (ad 3:110). Cf. ʿĀmirī, below, 385.

86. *RIS*, ii, 368 = *Case*, 194.

87. God revealed "How is it with you that you do not fight in the way of God . . ." (Q.4:75) when the Muslims in Mecca were persecuted by the pagans and wrote to Muḥammad in Medina for help (*RIS*, iv, 23f.). The lawgiver would engage in *al-ḥarb wa'l-qitāl* against infidels (iv, 133), without it there could be no unification of people in a single doctrine (iii, 165), and *jihād* was one of the heavy, but inescapable legal duties (iii, 308.1).

88. *RIS*, iii, 162 (epistle 31), with the adage "when Rūm is not raided it will raid." Compare Shaban's view of Sulaymān as a pacifist who wanted to put an end to war by conquering the Byzantine empire (in his *Islamic History*, [i], 129), and the British view that only when there were no foreigners any more would Britain be secure (Porter, *Lion's Share*, 131).

89. *RIS*, iii, 162f.; cf. also i, 326f., on the qualifications of soldiers.

90. Ibid., iv, 15, 16.

not People of the Book.[91] Others now used it in a spirit of tolerance again, above all the Ismailis.

Thus Abū Ḥātim al-Rāzī tells us that the verse was revealed in Medina after holy war had been prescribed: first God had told Muḥammad to fight the infidels until all the religion was His, and next He had ordered Muḥammad to leave people free to pursue the inner meaning of the revelation in which salvation lay. In other words, the verse established religious freedom, not for infidels, but for Muslims: anyone who conformed externally was to be left in peace to interpret the revelation as he wished. Like al-Jaṣṣāṣ, Abū Ḥātim distinguished between external conformance, which could be imposed by force, and inner convictions, which were beyond compulsion. But unlike al-Jaṣṣāṣ, he took the inner convictions to be beyond compulsion in the sense of protected by the law: even if they were articulated, one takes it, it was forbidden to use force in order to change them.[92]

This is also how the Fatimid Ismailis understood the verse, and not only to protect their own beliefs. When a Mālikī in North Africa asked to be excused from a debate with an Ismaili which was likely to culminate in his forced conversion or death, the missionary Abū ʿAbdallāh al-Shīʿī (d. 911) told the debater to leave the Mālikī alone, citing "There is no compulsion in religion".[93] The erratic caliph al-Ḥākim (1021–36) cited the verse in the same vein, though his record of tolerance was none too good.[94] At the *ẓāhirī* level of religion people were made to obey by compulsion and deference to authority (*bi'l-jabr wa'l-taqlīd*); at the *bāṭinī* level they followed the truth voluntarily, moved by the promises and threats relating to afterlife, not by force, as the missionary al-Maybudhī (c. 980) said.[95] (The Fatimids also used the verse to forbid attempts at forced conversion of *dhimmī*s.)[96]

The Ismailis had another argument for tolerance within the Islamic world as well. Trying to explain why ʿAlī had not taken up the sword against his co-religionists when they deprived him of the caliphate, Abū 'l-Fawāris (c. 390/1000) cites "There is no compulsion in religion" and observes that *jihād* is only a duty against people who have abandoned the confession of faith and public acts of worship, that is, apostates and infidels. He explains that nothing done under duress carried any moral meaning: it merited neither reward nor punishment and therefore did not affect the victims' chances of salvation.

91. E.g. Qatāda and others in Ṭabarī, *Tafsīr*, iii, 16; Muqātil, *Tafsīr*, 135.
92. Abū Ḥātim, *Aʿlām*, 110–12.
93. Madelung and Walker, *Advent of the Fatimids*, 70 = 123.
94. Halm, 'Der Treuhändler Gottes', 37.
95. Ivanow, *Studies in Early Persian Ismailism*, 130.
96. Thus the caliph al-Ẓāhir (d. 1036) in Lewis, *Jews of Islam*, 42.

Moreover, he said, shifting his attention to the agents, the trials and tribulations of life were due to the devils who had been given a free hand with humans for a specified time: in other words, one was rewarded morally for withstanding and enduring such hardship, not by killing the people who embodied it.[97]

This argument reappears in the Sunni theologian Fakhr al-Dīn al-Rāzī (d. 606/1209) as an argument against holy war. He identifies it as Muʿtazilite, naming Abū Muslim (al-Iṣbahānī, d. c. 320/932) and the above-mentioned al-Qaffāl among its adherents. There are problems with the attribution, but we can leave them aside.[98] The argument here goes as follows. The verse "there is no compulsion in religion" means that God did not base faith on compulsion and coercion, but rather on *al-tamakkun wa'l-ikhtiyār*, enabling people to choose (here al-Rāzī seems to be citing the Muʿtazilite exegete al-Zamakhsharī).[99] By now, he continues, the proofs of monotheism have however been presented so clearly that people have no excuse for remaining infidels any more: forced conversion and compulsion are the only methods left for dealing with them. But it is not allowed to use such methods in this world, which is an abode of trial (*dār al-ibtilāʾ*), for this would nullify the meaning of trial and testing, or, as he puts it in his own reformulation, it is incompatible with moral responsibility (*taklīf*).[100]

Wherever this argument originated, it was a powerful one in that it denied that coercion carried any reward for either the agents or the victims. The infidels would not benefit, since nothing done under duress carries any moral meaning. The holy warriors would not be rewarded either, however pure their intentions, not because all opinions were equally valid, as modern pluralists would claim, but rather because erroneous views were meant as a test of Muslim fortitude and thus had to be withstood rather than removed. Learning to tolerate the intolerable formed part of one's moral education. By this

97. Abū 'l-Fawāris, *Imāma*, 98r. The difference between religious laws is also construed as a test (*imtiḥān*), and moreover one for which we should be grateful, in Abū Ḥātim al-Rāzī, *Aʿlām*, 157f.; but the reference here is to the differences between religions, not within them.

98. The two statements attributed to Qaffāl by al-Rāzī on the subject contradict each other. Qaffāl is indeed said to have been a Muʿtazilite in his youth and to have written his *Tafsīr* before he repented. But if this *tafsīr* is al-Rāzī's source of information here, where did he find the statement in favour of forced conversion mentioned above, note 85? One would have expected that, too, to come from the *Tafsīr*. Was Qaffāl muddle-headed?

99. Cf. Zamakhsharī, *Kashshāf*, i, 387 (*ad* 2:256), where the wording is almost identical and 10:99 is also invoked ("If your Lord wanted it, all those on earth would have believed together. Will you then force people to become believers?").

100. Rāzī, *Tafsīr*, vii, 15 (*idh fī 'l-qahr wa'l-ikrāh ʿalā 'l-dīn buṭlān maʿnā al-ibtilāʾ wa'l-imtiḥān*).

complicated route the verse came to be read in what a modern reader takes to be its prima facie meaning.[101]

Al-ʿĀmirī's defence of jihād

Whatever Fakhr al-Dīn al-Rāzī's motivation may have been, his view was uncommon. Most scholars held that people had to be forcibly saved, with or without invoking the two levels of religion, and most philosophers agreed. Al-Fārābī did know of people (possibly Abū Bakr al-Rāzī) who deemed it wrong for members of the same species to seek to dominate each other,[102] but in his own opinion it was legitimate to use war "to induce and force people to what is best and most fortunate for them . . . when they do not know it themselves and do not submit to those who do know".[103] The legislator must lay down that people opposing his law should be fought, Ibn Sīnā said.[104] Nations whose conduct was not good had to be coerced to adopt the virtues, as Ibn Rushd quotes Plato as saying, noting the agreement between the Sharīʿa and philosophy here (though he seems to have regarded his contemporaries' devotion to holy war as excessive).[105] But the topic did not preoccupy the philosophers much. Only one them, al-ʿĀmirī, wrote at some length in defence of holy war, and he did so as an apologete for Islam rather than a philosopher, by way of response to the arguments of the Pseudo-Sophisticates (*mutaẓarrifa*).

Al-ʿĀmirī's response makes no mention of Q. 2:256 or the two levels of religion. Rather, he starts by offering a minimalist definition of *jihād*: it is defensive and religious in a narrow sense (concerned with the defence of temples, churches, mosques, religious books, and the like in his examples). This enables him to claim that all religions have it, even the Christians "who believe that one should assist one's religion by proselytization without use of the sword", and that the Muslims differ only in being keener to fulfil the duty than others.[106]

101. The further history of the verse is worth a study. Ibn Kathīr (d. 774/1373) also starts by expounding what is in effect al-Zamakhsharī's position, listing all the classical interpretations as other people's views at the end, though he does not have Fakhr al-Dīn al-Rāzī's unusual continuation. The modernist interpretation of the verse may have longer roots than usually assumed.

102. *MF*, ch. 18, §15, presenting it as ancient view.

103. Fārābī, *Fuṣūl*, §63/§67, where unjust war (*ḥarb jawr*) is war conducted in satisfaction of the ruler's personal desires; cf. also *Taḥṣīl*, §43; Mahdi, 'Alfarabi', 173ff.; Kraemer, 'The *Jihād* of the *Falāsifa*', esp. 303, 312f., 319.

104. *SI*, *x*, 453f., cf. 444 = 108f., cf. 102.

105. Ibn Rushd, *Commentary*, 26 = 118f./11f.; Black, *Islamic Political Thought*, 124, citing his commentary on Aristotle's *Nicomachaean Ethics*, which only survives in Latin.

106. *Iʿlām*, 147ff.

But how is this to be squared with Muḥammad's warfare and the conquests, the reader wonders: is he really going to present them as defensive after the fashion of modern apologetes?[107] The answer is no. Whether because his sense of history was too strong or because his sense of logic was too weak, he falls back on the *mission civilisatrice* argument. Muḥammad fought for the welfare of mankind. Muḥammad would not of course have used the sword if people had obeyed him of their own accord, but since they so stubbornly resisted him, he had no choice.[108] It was for their own good that he fought them. He was *not* animated by a desire for power and wealth, as is clear from the fact that he spent thirteen years suffering for his convictions in Mecca.[109] But like a good manager (*sāʾis*), he had to use the sword and the whip to save people from their own mistakes, and in this he was a mercy to mankind. The Iranians should be grateful, as al-ʿĀmirī tells them in another chapter, for the conquests liberated them from the oppressive Sāsānid polity.[110] In addition to eliminating the Iranian aristocracy and allowing for social mobility, Islam enabled the Iranians to reach the spiritual perfection that Zoroastrian priests had denied them; and it also made it possible for the Iranians themselves to "go to adjacent nations to appropriate them in accordance with the rules of *jihād*, and to make their countries flourish with the booty they acquire and to move their (victim's) children to the protection of their homes, to train them in good manners, bring them up with praiseworthy characters" and eventually to manumit them and make them say for ever, "O Lord, forgive us and our brethren who preceded us in the faith and do not place any rancour in our hearts against those who believe" (Q. 59:10). In other words, the Iranians could gain religious and worldly advantages by waging holy war against their infidel neighbours themselves (in practice meaning Turks). Once converted, their captives would seek to forget the rancour they felt against their captors and come to venerate them as earlier bearers of the true faith. "These are the ways of the Persian nation in the days of this religion," as he says.[111]

Al-ʿĀmirī's argument against the Mutaẓarrifa rests on the axiom that Islam is true: this is what justifies the Prophet's use of force to impose it. Since it was precisely the truth of Islam that the Mutaẓarrifa denied with reference to the

107. E.g. Shaltūt in Peters, *Jihad*, ch. 7.

108. *Iʿlām*, 156f. ʿĀmirī's here speaks somewhat like the British anti-imperialists who felt resentment "against those uncooperative peoples whose recalcitrance had forced Britain to take them over (as it seemed) against her will" (Porter, *Lion's Share*, 50).

109. The sufferings endured by Muḥammad and the Muslims as a weak minority in Mecca are also much stressed by ʿAbd al-Jabbār, *Tathbīt*, i, 8, 16, 20.

110. Cf. above, 334.

111. *Iʿlām*, 174–7.

Prophet's use of the sword, al-ʿĀmirī's response amounts to a most unphilosophical circular argument. For all that, it is extremely interesting in two ways. First, he finds it impossible to think of infidels as autonomous human beings. Since it was self-evident to him that humans had to obey God (as conceived by the Muslims), forcing infidels to obey did not come across to him as fundamentally different from disciplining animals or children. To him, infidels are benighted natives much as they were to well-meaning Europeans of the eighteenth and nineteenth centuries, who likewise set out to save them from themselves. Earlier Muslims had more commonly thought of infidels as rebels or outlaws who had to be brought to heel. Either way, it was impossible to conceive of them as endowed with rights. All rights came from God (as conceived by the Muslims). What right could one have to hold out against the only force and power in the universe? "Come willingly or unwillingly (*ṭawʿan aw karhan*)?" as God Himself tells Heaven and Earth in the Qurʾān (41:11). Everyone in the heaven and on earth submitted to Him "willingly or unwillingly" (3:83; 13:15). "Some of us embraced Islam willingly, others as a result of coercion," Arabs told Persians at Qādisiyya, adding that all were now pleased that they had done so.[112] God had sent Muḥammad with the religion of truth "to make it prevail over the whole religion whether the infidels like or not", as the coinage of the Umayyad period proclaimed, quoting Q. 9:33; 61:9. The purpose of holy war was to bring Islam to all mankind, voluntarily or by force, as Ibn Khaldūn was to say.[113] The long and the short of it was that people had no real choice in the matter.

Secondly, al-ʿĀmirī knew that if you captured an infidel child, he would convert and come to be grateful to you for having enslaved him. Most people knew that, and this made it difficult to entertain serious doubts about the legitimacy of holy war. Ultimately, most people liked the result. If the victims of the Western colonists in modern times had been as grateful for their Westernization as were the victims of the Arabs for their islamization, Western thinkers would probably also have found it difficult to doubt the legitimacy of their own imperialist expansion. But for a variety of reasons, the Western conquerors could not in the long run persuade their victims that their *mission civilisatrice* worked to the good of everyone concerned. Being dragged halfway to industrial modernity in chains was not comparable to being dragged to Paradise. Nor, of course, did the Western imperialists concentrate on children. It was in their internal *jihād* conducted by charitable agencies and social workers against their own lower classes that they removed children from their

112. Tab., i, 2240, 2284.
113. Below, note 116.

families in order to save them, and it was here that most people liked the result (and still do).

To most scholars, the fact that Muslims were willing to risk their lives in order to drag reluctant infidels to Paradise was a source of great pride. "Who does you a greater favour than the person who kills himself so that you may live?" as they asked the Shuʿūbīs.[114] Far from trying to hide their use of force, they often stressed that *jihād* was more strongly enjoined in their own *sharīʿa* than in that of other people.[115] Actually, as Ibn Khaldūn (d. 784/1382) noted, again with pride, Islam was the *only* religion to enjoin it. He inferred that Islam was the only universalist religion. The purpose of *jihād*, he said, was to bring Islam to all mankind, voluntarily or by force: this was why Islam united religious authority and political power; other religions were not addressed to all mankind and therefore separated the two, so that the religious leaders did not have anything to do with politics or war while the political rulers only fought for non-religious reasons.[116] There can be no better illustration of the fact that the Muslims had created a new concept of holy war by fusing religious and political universalism. It must be thanks to Ibn Khaldūn that the secondary literature so regularly identifies the conquests as motivated by either a universalist understanding of Islam or non-religious ambitions.[117]

MUSLIMS AS INFIDELS

When Muslims disagreed among themselves, they often denounced each other as infidels. This act, known as *takfīr*, was a good deal more serious than it may sound to the modern reader. To declare people to be infidels was not just to insult them (though it certainly was that), but also to declare them outlaws expelled from the community of believers, so that henceforth they could be freely robbed and killed by anyone who cared to do so. Nobody necessarily did anything of the sort. The accusers were usually scholars from one group hurling charges at another, and both parties might go on living much as before, dissociating from each other and studiously avoiding interaction except, when the authorities were weak, for purposes of fighting in the streets. But where the government took (or was made to take) an interest, *takfīr* amounted to a call for execution; where the *ʿulamāʾ* controlled the mob, it amounted to a call for assassination or lynching; and where tribal groups were involved, it amounted to a call for warfare against the miscreants. The relative roles of the state and

114. *ʿIqd*, iii, 412.18. On the Shuʿūbīs, see above, ch. 20.
115. Qaffāl in Fakhr al-Dīn Rāzī, above, note 85; ʿĀmirī, *Iʿlām*, 148.
116. Ibn Khaldūn, *Muqaddima*, 255 = i, 473.
117. Cf. above, 365.

self-help in the enforcement of beliefs is difficult to assess, but kings and crowds were the two main dangers to independent thinkers. The Brethren of Purity claimed not to be afraid of either: if they were secretive, it was because they did not want to cast pearls before swine, they said.[118] Socrates, too, had been fearless in his time: one of the remarkable aspects of his lifestyle was that "he did not practise dissimulation with either the common people or those in authority".[119] When adherents of unpopular views such as *mutakallims* and philosophers had to flee from a city, it was usually because the local scholars had acted as rabble-rousers. It was the masses that al-Suhrawardī (d. 1191) saw as the main enemy of theosophers, undoubtedly correctly, though it was by a ruler that he was killed.[120]

The Khārijites

The first Muslims to engage in *takfīr* in a systematic way were the Khārijites.[121] They held themselves to be the only believers. All other alleged Muslims were infidels who could in their opinion be killed and/or enslaved, exposed to random slaughter (*istiʿrāḍ*), and robbed of their possessions, just like the infidels beyond the borders. One could not intermarry with them, inherit from them, eat their meat, pray for their salvation or otherwise treat them as co-religionists, for they were not members of the Muslim community. One could not even live alongside them in physical terms, one had to make a *hijra* to a Muslim centre of one's own if one could, as the Prophet had left pagan Mecca for Medina. Views of this kind were systematized by the Azāriqa (with whom they have come to be associated ever since) and also by the Najdiyya. Both the Azāriqa and the Najdiyya left Basra for abodes of *hijra* of their own in the second civil war, proclaiming imamates of their own in Iran and Arabia respectively, and both waged holy war against their former co-religionists until they were defeated, in 78/697f and 73/692f respectively.

The Khārijites started a protracted debate about the status of people in error: were they believers or not? To a modern reader it is an odd question (why shouldn't they be?), but to first-century Muslims belief was first and foremost a claim to membership of the saving community. The believers were those who travelled together in serried ranks, forming a single caravan, following the same imam of guidance, moving by the same routes to the same destination. All would eventually arrive at Paradise, for "God has promised the believers,

118. *RIS*, iv, 166.
119. *Sīra*, 309 = 322/227.
120. Fakhry, *Islamic Philosophy*, 304; *EI*², s.v. 'Suhrawardī' (no. 3).
121. What follows is based on Crone and Zimmermann, *Epistle*, ch. 5.

men and women, gardens underneath which rivers flow, forever therein to dwell, and goodly dwelling-places in the gardens of Eden", as the Qur'ān says (9:72). Believers were *ahl al-janna*, people destined for Paradise, and if a man was allowed to stay in the caravan, he would get to Paradise along with the rest. How then could he be said to be in error? Conversely, if he went astray, he ceased to form part of the caravan of believers. What then could he be but an infidel? The original scheme did not have any gradations. But gradations were precisely what was needed, and from the mid-Umayyad period onwards they began to be made.

All Khārijites stuck to the classification of their opponents as infidels. In their view, the believers were few, closely knit, and chosen above all others: typically they were as tolerant of sinners within their own ranks as they were intolerant of outsiders. But after the second civil war they modified the meaning of 'infidel'. The Ibāḍīs denied that erring 'people of the *qibla*' were infidels in the sense of pagans (*mushrikūn*, *ʿabadat al-awthān*), claiming that rather they were infidels in the sense of hypocrites (*munāfiqun*) or, as they added at some point, scorners of God's grace (*kuffār niʿma*). This solution, which was also adopted by the Zaydīs,[122] made a major difference, for hypocrites had rights and duties under Islamic law whereas polytheists and idolaters did not. It followed that one could live among non-Khārijite people of the *qibla*, intermarry with them, inherit from them, eat with them and so forth, as the Muslims of the Prophet's time had lived with hypocrites in Medina. One should still rebel when one could in order to establish sovereignty over them. *Jihād* against evildoers was a cardinal duty. But one could not subject them to random slaughter, nor could one enslave their women and children. One could kill their men in battle, but their property was sacrosanct and not to be taken as booty.

Other Khārijite sects arrived at the same accommodation by different means, notably a differentiation between abodes of concealment (*kitmān*) and openness (*aʿlāniyya*). The abode of concealment was the area under 'infidel' sovereignty: here one could live among the 'infidels' and treat them as Muslims for the duration. But all ties with them had to be cut the moment one made an exodus (*khurūj*) to establish a sovereign community of one's own, for in the abode of openness one treated the 'infidels' exactly as the extremists said one should. All in all, the Khārijites never abandoned the principle that the *umma* consisted of people destined for Paradise (*ahl al-janna*). They merely mitigated the legal consequences of classifying all others as *kuffār*.

122. Ibid., 201.

The Murjiʾa

The Murjiʾites, who appeared from c. 700 onwards, began by taking a new stance on the relative status of ʿUthmān and ʿAlī.[123] To ʿUthmānīs, ʿUthmān was a believer and ʿAlī an infidel; to ʿAlawīs it was the other way round, and to Khārijites both were infidels. The Murjiʾa said that they did not know.[124] That people were either believers bound for Paradise or infidels bound for hell they did not initially doubt, but since they could not tell which one of them was bound for heaven and which one for hell, they refused to throw in their lot with either of them.

By the later Umayyad period they too had come to introduce gradations. Infidels were still bound for hell, but believers were not necessarily bound for paradise, for even people in error were believers, they said: they now professed not to know whether such 'erring believers' would go to Paradise or hell. This position scandalized their contemporaries. How could there be such a thing as an erring believer (*muʾmin ḍāll*)? It sounded like a contradiction in terms. If people in error went to Paradise along with the rest, what was the point of being law-abiding? And if they went to hell, in what sense were they different from infidels? The Murjiʾite answer was that they were believers in the sense that faith had nothing to do with acts; they were not to be excommunicated merely because they failed to behave as others said they should. But this did not dispose of the outrageous fact that their solution would send sinners to heaven or believers to hell, for ever after, *khālidīna fīhā*, as the Qurʾān says.

The obvious thing to do with a sinful believer was to send him to hell for a limited period until he was ready for Paradise, but it was with sentencing policies as with everything else at first: there were no gradations. One could not punish erring believers by a short spell in a corrective institution, he went to hell for ever or not at all. The Murjiʾite response to the question where the believing sinner would go thus had to be that they did not know: God would send him to Paradise or to hell as He saw fit. There was perfect Qurʾānic authority for this: God punishes and forgives as He wishes (Q. 48:14; cf. also 5:118; 33:24). But it turned afterlife into a kind of Russian roulette: if the sinner was in luck, he would get eternal felicity; if not, he was damned for ever. Some Murjiʾites unsurprisingly responded by sending all sinful believers to Paradise, but this sounded almost antinomian.

123. Ibid., ch. 6.

124. They practised *irjāʾ*, suspension of judgement, whence their name.

Others

The other attempts to introduce gradations left the equation of believers and *ahl al-janna* intact. Faith included works: one had to live by the law to count as a member of the saving community. But how then did the sinner avoid being expelled from it? The Muʿtazilite solution was that he was neither here nor there, so to speak; the sinner (*fāsiq*) was in a position in between (*manzila bayna manzilatayn*), meaning that he was treated as a member of the community of believers in this world and sent to hell in the next.[125] The Traditionalists (*ahl al-ḥadīth*), on the other hand, said that sinners were still Muslims: there was no question of expelling them from the community. But whether a particular Muslim was also a believer they could not tell, for a believer was still a person destined for Paradise in their view. They famously professed not to know whether they themselves were believers. If one asked them, they would respond 'God willing (*in shāʾ allāh*)', which struck the Murjiʾites as absurd: did these people doubt their own faith? But the ignorance was important for purposes of social peace. Nobody knew who was saved or damned, within certain limits. There were positions (such as Qadarism) which had been branded as infidel in Prophetic Ḥadīth, and anyone who adopted them could thus be safely denounced as an infidel by the Traditionalists. But for the rest, the sheep would be sorted from the goats on the Day of Judgement. All upright Muslims, that is, believers, would go to Paradise; all sinful Muslims would go to hell. Meanwhile, all must live together. What is more, even the sinful Muslim who was sent to hell would eventually get out, for though the concept of a graded sentencing policy never seems to have caught on in medieval Islam, it came to be accepted that all Muslims would eventually be released thanks to Muḥammad's intercession. In the last resort, then, hell remained a place for infidels: believers were indeed *ahl al-janna*, sinners and all.[126]

The significance of all this lies in the fact that it marks a transition from a tribal to a complex conception of society. To tribesmen, societies were culturally uniform: all members shared the same values; each member carried one and the same culture in his head. Muslim society could not possibly go on fulfilling these requirements after the conquests; diversity was now inevitable. This was more than the Khārijites could accept. By expelling all dissenters as infidels (or in other words by opting out as the only true believers) they hoped to create a Muslim society as uniform as the tribal one from which they hailed. But mainstream Muslims came fully to accept that the *umma* had to consist of

125. Van Ess, *TG*, ii, 260ff.; *EI*², s.v. 'Muʿtazila', and the literature cited there.

126. On all this, see Crone and Zimmermann, *Epistle*, 234ff. and the literature cited there.

a wide variety of different and even antagonistic groups pursuing diverse aims and objectives under the same general Islamic umbrella. The *umma* ceased to be a caravan taking everyone by the same route to the same destination. Sinners and upright people, believers and sinful Muslims, adherents of one legal school and the other, people moving in quite different directions under intellectual imams of their own: all these and more came to form a single community eventually known as Sunni. There was of course much more to the formation of this community than the agreement to accommodate sinners, but this was the first step allowing Islam to become precisely the kind of broad umbrella that the Khārijites could not tolerate.

Takfīr

For all that, the Muslims retained their propensity for outlawing their opponents. The early Ismailis are said to have classified their opponents in the Khārijite style, as infidels whom one might eradicate by random slaughter (*istiʿrāḍ*).[127] But like the Khārijites, they toned down their claims: actually, non-Ismailis were hypocrites at worst, mere 'weaklings' (*mustaḍʿafūn*) at best;[128] their lives and property were sacrosanct, and they were to be left in peace as long as they conformed to the law.[129] The much later Ismailis of the 'new mission' (*daʿwa jadīda*), sometimes known as Assassins, were to revise this position. Although they do not seem to have practised random slaughter, they did practise assassination (a word derived from their by-name), which some early Khārijites had endorsed as well and which they brought to a fine art by training young men for suicide missions in the hope of undermining the Seljuq establishment.[130] The young men were told that by dying for the cause they purified their souls for the realms of light (Ismailis did not believe in bodily resurrection).[131] Unlike today's suicide bombers, they could only kill one person at a time, typically high-ranking officials such as Niẓām al-Mulk (their most famous victim), and they were killed by those who witnessed the event, not by their own weapons; but then as now they struck terror among their

127. Nawbakhtī, *Firaq*, 64.

128. Qāḍī Nuʿmān, 'Risāla mudhhiba', 76f., where the *ahl al-ẓāhir* are also identified as wrongdoers (*ẓālimūn*), cited in Marquet, 'Tolerance', 211 (simplified); cf. also the scheme in Malījī, *al-Majālis al-mustanṣiriyya*, 79f.

129. Muʾayyad in Muscati, *Life and Lectures*, 152.

130. Cf. Hodgson, *Assassins*, 80ff.

131. Ibid., 83; cf. Muʾayyad on the resurrection in Muscati, *Life and Lectures*, 90f., 93–5, 105, 111ff.: bodies are subject to decay; the prophets described Paradise as a place of sensual pleasure to make themselves understood by people of low intelligence.

opponents. Though suicide was unanimously forbidden, there was a long tradition of fighting to the death in battles, and of vowing to do so, and generally speaking, the dividing line between suicide and martyrdom was thin.[132]

Assassination, secret killing, random slaughter, not to mention the ritual strangling practised by some Gnostics: all these were the weapons of people who had been cornered. Most Muslims regarded them with abhorrence. But it was not just marginal people who continued to practise *takfīr*. Religious scholars did too, though they did not necessary mean that the alleged infidels were outlaws who should be killed: the import might simply be that they were bound for hell and that one should not marry their women, eat their slaughters, and so on. In that spirit some Ashʿarites branded as infidels those who deviated from Ashʿarite doctrine, or who did not understand *kalām*, while most Muʿtazilites deemed regions dominated by Sunnis to be *dār al-kufr*.[133] "The leaders of the inmates of hell have assembled around you," as a Muʿtazilite judge joked to Niẓām al-Mulk when the latter brought him together with a Ḥanbalite and an Ashʿarite, explaining that "we declare one another to be infidels".[134] But not all *takfīr* was benign. A scholar such as al-Ṭabarī (d. 923) branded anyone who declared the Qurʾān to be created as an infidel who could be lawfully killed (*kāfir ḥalāl damuh*). So did the caliph al-Qādir in his creed of 1018.[135] ʿAbd al-Qādir al-Jīlānī (d. 1166), the Ḥanbalī founder of the Sufi order known as the Qādiriyya, added that this was true even of someone who merely held his own pronunciation of the Qurʾānic text to be created: "He is an unbeliever in almighty God whom one should not mix with, eat with, intermarry with, or have as one's neighbour; rather, he should be shunned and treated with contempt; one should not pray behind him, accept his testimony, he cannot act as marriage guardian, nor should one pray over him when he dies. If one gets hold of him, he should be asked (up to) three times to repent, as one does an apostate. If he repents, then well and good. If not, he should be killed."[136]

Many regretted this eagerness to define people out of the community, and there was much discussion of the grounds on which one could do it, most

132. Cf. above, note 66.

133. Griffel, *Apostasie und Toleranz*, 310f.; Baghdādī, *Uṣūl*, 270, cf. 340f.

134. Ibn al-Jawzī, *Muntaẓam*, ix, 90 (year 478).

135. Sourdel, 'Profession de foi', 194 = 187; Griffel, *Apostasie und Toleranz*, 112.

136. In Goldziher, *Livre de Mohammed Ibn Toumert*, 57n. For the relationship between unbelief and apostasy, see Griffel, *Apostasie und Toleranz* and 'Toleration and Exclusion'.

famously by al-Ghazālī.[137] Rejection of key articles of faith was generally held to make a person an infidel, though people disagreed over precisely what they were, whereas the disagreement over legal doctrines such as that found within and between the schools was held to be acceptable, or even commendable.[138] But some held that disagreement over points of law could make a person an infidel too, and others said that neither could. That one could not denounce anyone as an infidel on matters either doctrinal or legal is said to have been the view of jurists such as Abū Ḥanīfa, Sufyān al-Thawrī, al-Shāfiʿī, and Abū Thawr.[139]

The Brethren of Purity took the simplest view of things. In their opinion it was due to mere confusion that people had taken to "declaring one another infidels and cursing one another".[140] Here is what a rightly guided person would say: "I have surrendered my beliefs to my Lord (*aslamtu li-rabbī madhabī*), my religion is the religion of Abraham, peace be upon him, and I say as he did: 'Whoso follows me belongs to me; and whoso rebels against me, surely Thou art all-forgiving, all-compassionate' (Q. 14:36). 'If Thou chastisest them, they are Thy servants; if Thou forgivest them, Thou art the all-mighty, the all-wise' (Q. 5:118)."[141]

137. Goldziher, *Livre de Mohammed Ibn Toumert*, 59; Lewis, *Political Language*, 86; Griffel, *Apostasie und Toleranz*, esp. 312ff. and 'Toleration and Exclusion', 350ff.

138. Thus, for example, Bāqillānī (Ibish, *Al-Baqillani*, 95).

139. Cf. the conspectus of Ibn Ḥazm cited in Goldziher, *Livre de Mohammed Ibn Toumert*, 60n.

140. *RIS*, iv, 61.

141. Ibid., iii, 313.

CHAPTER

22

EPILOGUE: RELIGION, GOVERNMENT, AND SOCIETY REVISITED

As we have seen, medieval Muslims generally held the best polity to be one based on religion because people had to subordinate their individual interests to those of the collectivity when they lived together and could best be made to do so in the name of higher things. The highest of all things were God and the next world. Forming a single polity thus meant submitting to God and whoever represented Him as leader of the polity in question; vice versa, submitting to God meant entering a polity in which God set the rules of human interaction, laying down how one was to behave with other people and with Him.

In other words, revealed religion was first and foremost about collective interests. "Religions are never established for private benefit or individual advantage but always aim at collective welfare," as al-ʿĀmirī noted.[1] "The meaning of religion (*dīn*) in Arabic is communal obedience to a single leader," as the Brethren of Purity observed.[2] Modern Westerners, conditioned to thinking about religion as a relationship of spiritual love between God and an individual, or as a set of convictions about the metaphysical world, usually have trouble with this view of things, and of course there was much more to religion than collective organization by the time these statements were made. But whatever else God was about, he stood for common interests, the public order, the Muslims at large. *Māl allāh*, God's money, was synonymous with *māl al-muslimīn*, the money of the Muslims, or in other words the treasury: being

1. *Iʿlām*, 105 (*al-nafʿ al-khāṣṣī, al-fāʾida al-juzʾiyya, al-maslaḥa al-kulliyya*).

2. *RIS*, iii, 486 (*inna maʿnā al-dīn fī lughat al-ʿarab huwa al-ṭāʿa min jamāʿa li-raʾīs*). The observation appears to be etymologically correct: *dāna lahu* means to surrender or be in a state of obedience to somebody (just as *aslama* means to submit).

God's, it did not belong to any human being, but rather to all of them (or rather all those who served Him); and since it belonged to all of them, it was administered by the public authority, the government. *Ḥuqūq allāh*, God's rights, are similarly obligations (such as the *ḥudūd* penalties or the canonical taxes) which are owed to God/the Muslim community, not to any one or several members of it, and which were likewise administered by the government.[3] The imam was the deputy of God and of the Muslims, and might appear now as the one, now as the other, in one and the same work.[4] "Wherever there is a general need, there the obligation is to God," as Ibn Taymiyya was to put it.[5] "All private matters belong to the human sphere, all concerns of society to the divine," as ʿAlī is reported to have said.[6] God served to remove something from the control of private individuals. In antiquity people would free their slaves by selling them to a god: as the slave of that god they would not belong to any human being. The same is true of anything owned by God in Islam. Whatever is God's has been withdrawn from the sphere of contending human beings; it is beyond individual interest, unaffected by private desire (*hawā*), neutral, unbiased, and of equal importance to all, a public good, and thus administered by public authorities, the representatives of God. In short, it was by recourse to God that one created a public sphere.

Dividing up the governmental task

It was by recourse to God that Muḥammad had created a public sphere in Medina, but as it proved, there could be leaders of many types in that sphere. Rulership could be divided up in a variety of manners, including that conventionally known as the separation of government and religion. The reader should note that this expression is open to misunderstanding. As far as medieval Islam is concerned, it stands for a change in the manner in which God's government was executed on earth, not for a process whereby government was emptied of religious significance. It means that there ceased to be a single person endowed with the fullness of God's delegated power: scholars took over the task of guiding people; the deputy of God was left with the coercive role, which eventually passed to kings. This was a separation of power and religion comparable to that which obtained in medieval Europe, in which God kept His sword in one institution and His book in another. But in both cases

3. Johansen, 'Sacred and Religious Elements in Hanafite Law', esp. 297f.

4. Simnānī, *Rawḍa*, i, §37 (*yanūbu ʿan allāh wa-rasūlihi*), §517 (*nāʾib ʿan al-muslimīn*).

5. Ibn Taymiyya, *Ḥisba*, 26 = 54 (*wa-mā iḥtāja ilayhi al-nās ḥājatan ʿāmmatan fa'l-ḥaqq fīhi li'llah*).

6. Cited in *EI*[2], s.v. 'Bahāʾīs', col. 917a.

the sword and the book alike continued to be God's. He just did not assign both to the same keeper any more. Similarly, when amirs, sultans and kings are referred to as secular rulers, it means that they were rulers of a type that could appear in any society rather than rulers of the specific type called for by the Sharīʿa: there was nothing specifically Islamic about them. It does not mean that they had no religious role to play. However external they were to Islam by origin, and sometimes outlook too, their prime role was still as protectors of a religious institution.

It should also be noted that the dividing line between the two institutions always remained fuzzy. There was no gradual establishment of a clearer demarcation between them. Al-Ghazālī's efforts in this direction notwithstanding, medieval Muslims never acquired the sense of living in two distinct organizations, devoted to different aims, governed by different norms, and headed by different people, the king and his agents in the one case, the caliph (if any) and religious scholars in the other. In other words, one cannot speak of a separation of church and state such as that which developed in Europe from the great ecclesiastical reforms of the eleventh century onwards. Still less were the two domains separated to the point where religion was privatized and the socio-political order secularized, as was to happen in Europe in modern times. In the modern West, government devotes itself largely or wholly to secular aims by general agreement, not by failure to fulfil a supposedly religious role. Secular aims are held to override those of religion when they clash. In the modern West it is secularism that articulates the common good and religion which belongs in the realm of private interests that have to be curbed for the sake of collective welfare. Islam has itself come to be seen as a form of such private interests in the context of the growth of Muslim minorities in the West. But in the Muslim world there was no such development. Here the public domain continued to be God's. He just ceased to govern it via a single institution.

The institution that really mattered to medieval Muslims was the religious one, not the state, to which books on political thought are customarily devoted. Indeed, as observed above, they often saw the state as a kind of excrescence on the society formed by religion. It was something that came into being for the execution of religious directives and which was to that extent governed by the thinking men who formulated the directives, not by the musclemen who executed them, for all that it was the musclemen who had the power to kill, fleece, and maim the believers, including the thinkers in question.[7] Religious leaders certainly had far more regular dealings with the believers, on a much more intimate basis, than the wielders of swords. Indeed, in *milla*s of

7. Above, 170, 246f.

unbelievers under Muslim protection they sometimes ruled the believers in all respects except that they had little or no coercive power.

From this it should be clear that a book on medieval Islamic political thought cannot deal with the domain pertaining to kings alone, but must rather cover the entire public order, inclusive of all those who directed or wished to direct the believers without being wielders of the sword, such as the religious scholars, Sufi thinkers, philosophers, and saints. The degree to which their thinking amounted to political thought can of course be disputed. Most modern scholars would probably say that a great deal of it was political even when it was not focused on the agency that we call the state. Certainly, were one to limit political thought in the Islamic world to thought about that agency, one would be left with little but mirrors for princes, sermons admonishing princes, and constitutional law. Much absorbingly interesting thought about power and its uses in the public domain would be left out. Considerable effort notwithstanding, the chances are that much has been inadvertently left out of this book as well, given the vastness and the diffuse nature of the subject.

The three circles

If we think of the domains of religion, state, and society as three circles, Islamic history starts with a situation of perfect identity: only one circle is visible, it encompasses all three domains, which are completely identical. Religion had spawned a society and its government. This is the situation in the Prophet's Medina. We then have six centuries of development in which the circles gradually come apart. At the end of our period, as far as government is concerned, the overlap with religion was minimal. The Sharīʿa did cover the caliphate, holy war, taxation and other aspects of public organization, but its rules on these subjects were commonly ignored, and there was in any case a good deal more than that to politics. Government now formed an almost completely detached circle of its own, devoted to the upkeep of Islam but not generated by it. But as far as society (or at least urban society) was concerned, the overlap remained almost total. Insofar as one can tell, society continued to be based largely on the Sharīʿa in respect of marriage, divorce, succession, and commercial transactions, an admixture of customary law notwithstanding; and it continued to display its loyalty in visible ritual law.[8] In short, Muslim society was now in the nature of a church: a congregation of believers protected by a state instead of forming one on its own.

8. It is not known how far this was true of village society in our period. Among the tribes of the desert, customary law continued to prevail and ritual law was often ignored.

It is not customary to speak of Muslim society in this manner, for one usually thinks of a church as a religious organization distinct from lay society. A church is after all simply an assembly: the *ekklēsia* of God as distinct from the *ekklēsia* formed by the Athenian people, for example, as Origen explained.[9] Differently put, the church is that assembly which is devoted to worship. But it was precisely as an assembly devoted to worship that Muslim society had originated, complete with its own army and government; and though it had ceased to govern itself, it had not been divided into a religious institution and a lay society. States were too superficial in nature to generate permanent communities to match them. In the terminology with which this book began, they were mere governmental agencies, and never generated countries. The populations successively ruled by the Ṭāhirids, Saffārids, Sāmānids, Ghaznavids, and Seljuqs, for example, did not see themselves as members of an enduring kingdom of eastern Iran, or of Iran as such, within which dynasties rose and fell (as did dynasties in Byzantium or medieval England, for example); rather, each dynasty represented a shortlived kingdom of its own within the Community of Believers. The populations brought together by a common ruler were not sufficiently affected by the experience to be set apart from others on a long-term basis. The *umma* did contain groups formed without recourse to religion, such as ethnic communities, tribes and clans – all based on kinship, real or imagined. But kin groups aside, practically all the organizations that medieval Muslims belonged to were simply sub-divisions of the *umma*, such as legal schools, doctrinal movements, or Sufi brotherhoods, not communities based on alternative principles. In short, Muslim society remained an assembly devoted to worship; unlike the state, it was still organized on a religious basis.

At the end of our period we thus have a situation of minimal overlap with the Sharīʿa in government and maximal overlap as far as society is concerned. The only way the circles could continue to separate was by progressive secularization of Muslim society itself, meaning increasing reliance on manmade laws for the regulation of not just political but also social affairs and a corresponding relegation of religious life to the private sphere as something optional embodied in separate institutions of its own. This is what al-Rāzī and others dimly perceived when they rejected prophets as impostors: they saw religion as private and the socio-political order as secular, not as a church under royal protection. It was also what the early Ismailis perceived when they predicted a new era in which Muḥammad's law would be abrogated and organized religion replaced by private spirituality.

Their visions were far too radical for other Muslims, of course, but for all that the circles did continue to separate. On the one hand, customary law rose

9. Cf. Origen in Barker, *Alexander to Constantine*, 440.

to increasing prominence from the thirteenth century onwards, to be formally acknowledged as a source of law (at least by the Ḥanafīs) and eventually to generate an entire civil code, the Ottoman *Mejelle* promulgated in 1877.[10] On the other hand, the growth of the Sufi orders from about the same time onwards resulted in a profusion of optional religious institutions distinct from wider society. In the 1920s the predictions of the early Ismailis were fulfilled in Turkey, when Atatürk abolished Islamic law, though it was not as the Mahdi of the Ismailis that he did so, but rather as the secularizer of an unwilling Sunni society. This somewhat ambivalent example notwithstanding, secularization is also what many Muslims would like to bring about today, not by rejection of the Prophet, and not by messianic revolution or coercion either, but rather by peaceful reform resulting in the privatization of religion. They are the adherents of *laicisation* who perceive the remaining overlap as an archaism and hold that life would be freer, easier, and more progressive if the socio-political and the religious spheres could be made to separate completely. They would prefer to remove religion from the socio-political order to optional organizations, and they have come some way. Today, the only part of the Sharīʿa completely to have escaped the ravages of modernity is ritual law; and the Sufi orders do form a kind of church, in the sense of a religious assembly separate from society at large. But for all that, many Muslims, perhaps most, resist secularization. They want to keep society at large in the nature of a religious assembly, without any, or at least without complete loss of the overlap to which they are accustomed, which is entrenched in their heritage, and canonized by centuries of use. Collective concerns still seem to them best treated as God's. Fundamentalism poses the problem in an acute form, for if the secularists want to do away with the last remains of the overlap, the fundamentalists want to restore it as much as possible. Nobody can predict what the future will bring, but it is a safe bet that the issue will remain contentious for a long time.

10. *EI*², s.v. 'ʿurf'.

CHARTS

CHART 1: THE GENEALOGY OF THE UMMA, FROM AN UMAYYAD PERSPECTIVE

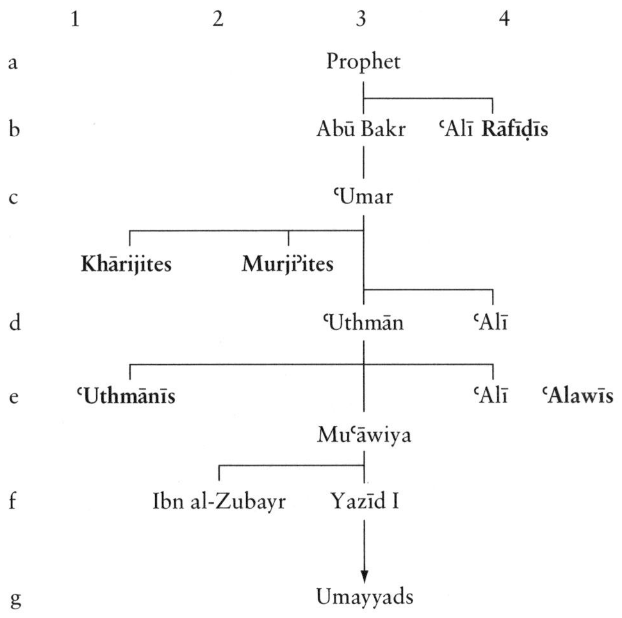

Parties are shown in bold under the last imam they share with other Muslims. Column 3 gives the succession as perceived by an ʿUthmānī of the pro-Umayyad variety: ʿUthmān is succeeded directly by Muʿāwiya, ʿAlī was just a rebel.

The ʿUthmānīs' party split when Ibn al-Zubayr refused to accept the succession of Yazīd I (line f), but no sect emerged from this schism: the adherents of the Zubayrids died out; the adherents of the Umayyads continued, but it became rare for them to be described as a religious party. The ʿUthmānī party shown is that of the Traditionalists who saw ʿUthmān as the last rightly guided caliph. ʿAlī appears three times in the chart, first as the 'caliph in exile' who was imam to the Rāfiḍīs (line b) and next as the caliph who was imam to the ʿAlawīs, some of whom rejected the caliphate of ʿUthmān (lines d) while others recognized the first part of it (line e).

All doctrinal developments above line e took place after those below it. The heresiographers, however, operate on the assumption that sects emerged at the time of the imam over whom they split off from the main body, so that their presentation often inverts the chronological sequence. (A modern sect that rejected all imams other than the Prophet himself would appear in the heresiographers as having originated at the time of the Prophet's death.)

CHART 2: THE GENEALOGY OF THE UMMA, FROM A SHĪʿITE PERSPECTIVE

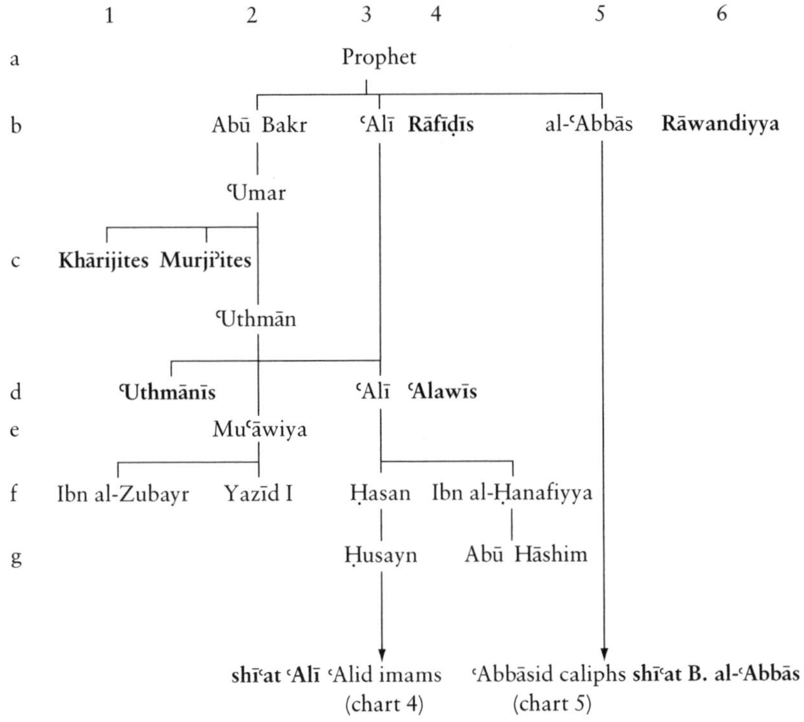

Here column 3 shows the succession as perceived by a Rāfiḍī Shīʿite: ʿAlī is the Prophet's successor, not ʿUmar's or ʿUthmān's, and remains so till his death. To more moderate Shīʿites, he only became caliph after the death of ʿUthmān, whose caliphate some rejected and others accepted, in part or in full. Most Shīʿites agreed that ʿAlī was followed by his two sons, Ḥasan and Ḥusayn, but al-Mukhtār identified ʿAlī's successor as Ibn al-Ḥanafiyya.

The ʿAbbāsids owed their rights to Abū Hāshim according to some (4, g), from al-ʿAbbās according to others (5, b), though they were eventually to accept Abū Bakr, ʿUmar, ʿUthmān, and ʿAlī as their spiritual ancestors. The Sunni four-caliphs thesis is not shown here.

CHART 3: THE GENEALOGY OF THE HĀSHIMITES (ʿABBĀSIDS AND ṬĀLIBIDS)

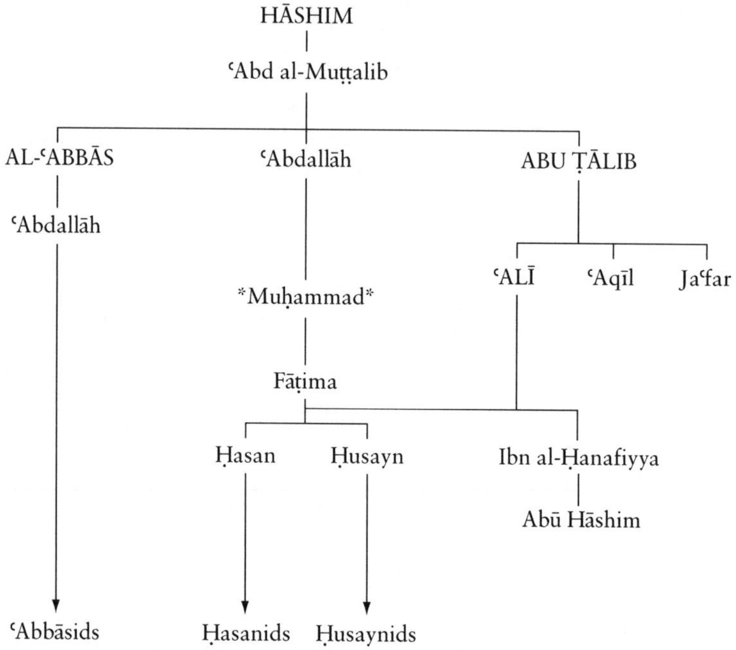

The eponymous ancestors behind the terms Hāshimites, ʿAbbāsids, Ṭālibids, and ʿAlids are written in capitals. The Prophet is asterisked.

CHART 4: THE ʿALIDS TILL 874

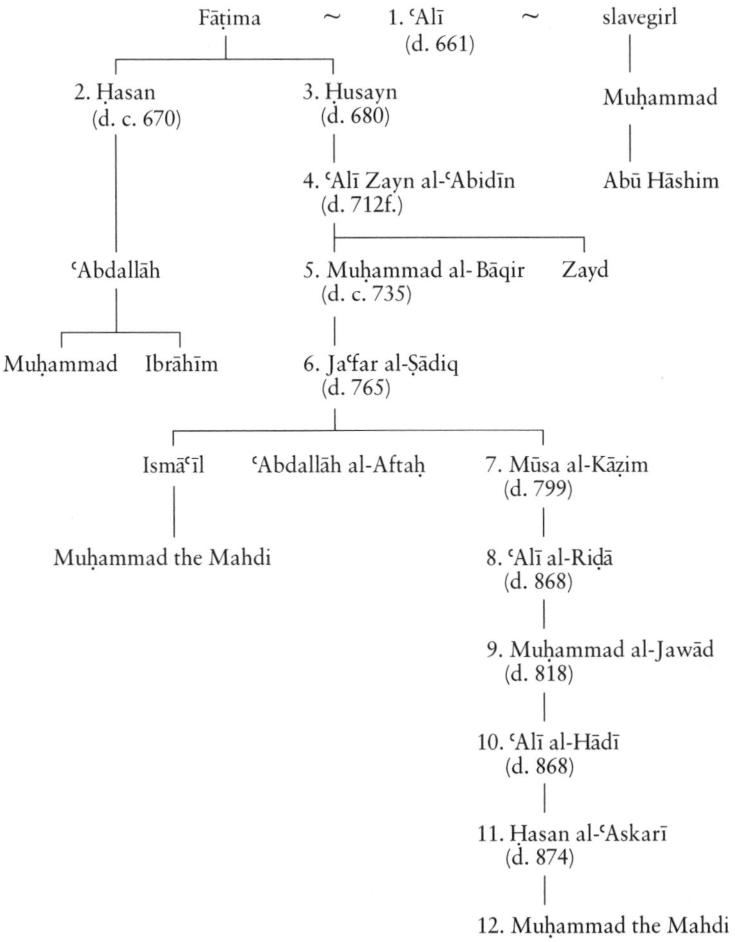

The chart only shows the main ʿAlids mentioned in this book. The twelve imams of the Imamis are numbered and shown with deathdates.

CHART 5: THE ʿABBĀSIDS TILL 861

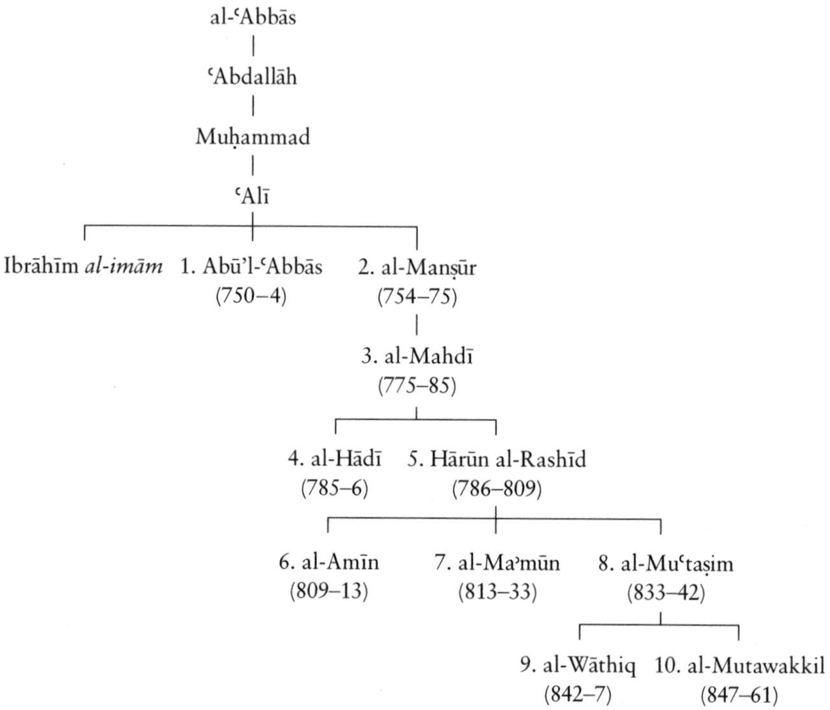

The chart is much simplified. The caliphs are numbered and shown with deathdates. For a full list of the caliphs, see chart 10.

CHART 6: THE GENEALOGY OF THE SHĪʿITE SECTS

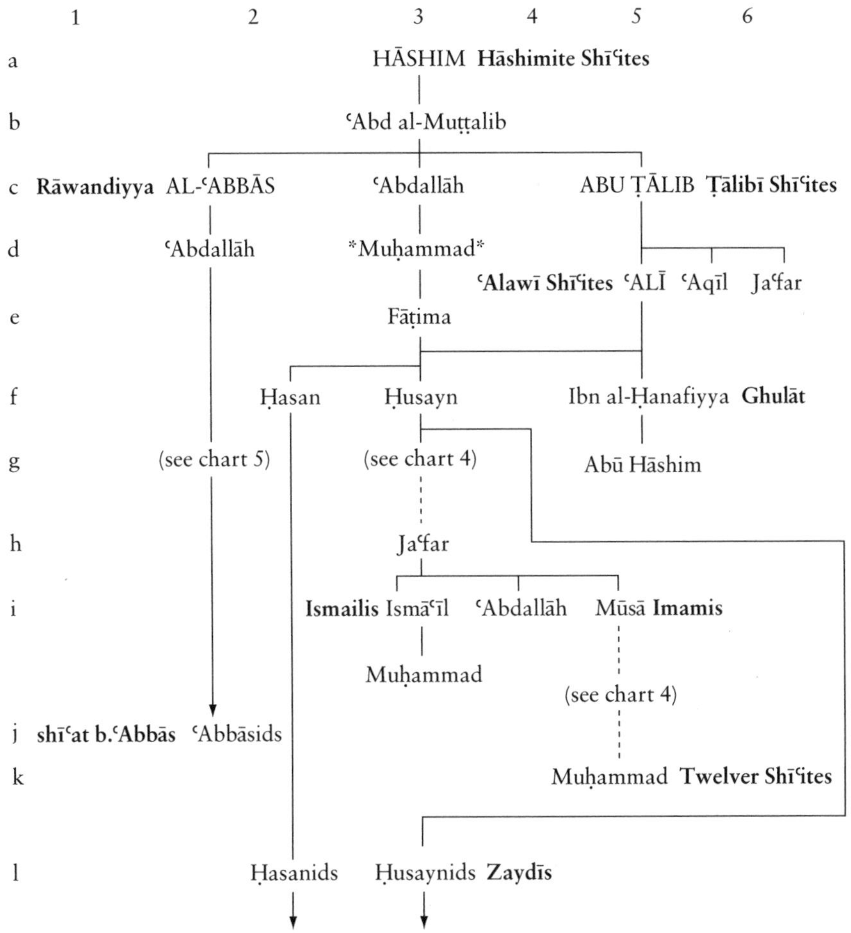

This chart shows groups formed around a real descent group rather than a line of caliphs, as in charts 1 and 2. The groups are shown in bold next to the imams in whose name they branch off from the *jamāʿa*, or from other Shīʿites. The fact that the Hāshimites were a real descent groups made Shīʿite sects much better suited to genealogical presentation than their non-Shīʿite counterparts: sects proliferate as the family tree branches out. Since real descent group are also much more ramified than a succession of caliphs, this chart is greatly simplified. In column 3 we have the direct ancestors and descendants of the Prophet. As before, eponymous ancestors are printed in capitals.

CHART 7: THE ISMAILI CYCLES

speaker prophet (*nāṭiq*)	*asās* and imams
1. Ādam	Shīth (Seth) 7 imams
2. Nūḥ	Sām (Shem) 7 imams
3. Ibrāhīm	Isḥāq or Ismāʾīl (Isaac or Ishmael) 7 imams
4. Mūsā	Hārūn (Aaron) 7 imams
5. ʿĪsā	Shamʿūn al-Ṣafā (Peter) 7 imams
6. Muḥammad	ʿAlī 7 imams: 1. Ḥasan 2. Ḥusayn 3. ʿAlī Zayn al-ʿĀbidīn 4. Muḥammad al-Bāqir 5. Jaʿfar al-Ṣādiq 6. Ismail 7. Muḥammad b. Ismāʿīl

7. Muḥammad b. Ismāʿīl returning as the Mahdi, end of history

The seven imams in the first five eras are not usually identified by name, though there is occasional reference here and there to past imams and other dignitaries. It was only the ones in the current era – the sixth – that mattered. Under the Fatimids, the cycles eventually came to be revised as follows:

1. Adam	*asās* and 7 imams
2. Noah	*asās* and 7 imams
3. Abraham	*asās* and 7 imams
4. Moses	*asās* and 7 imams
5. Jesus	*asās* and 7 imams
6. Muḥammad	*asās* and 7 heptads (i.e. 49), or an indeterminate number, of imams
7. the Mahdi	

CHART 8: THE ISMAILIS AND RELATED SECTS

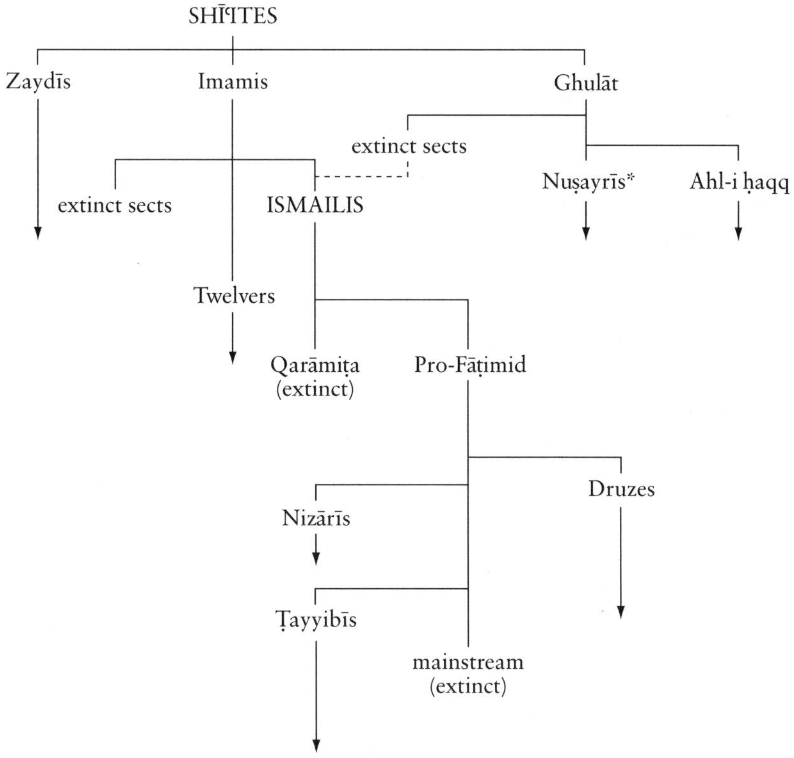

* Also known as ʿAlawīs, which is somewhat confusing to a novice in that they are very different from the ʿAlawīs of the first two centuries, and emerge much later too.

CHART 9: THE IMAMS OF THE PRO-FĀṬIMID ISMAILIS

asās (1) ʿAlī, d. 661
1 (2) al-Ḥasan, d. c. 670
2 (3) al-Ḥusayn, d. 680
3 (4) ʿAlī Zayn al-ʿĀbidīn, d. 712 or 713
4 (5) Muḥammad al-Bāqir, d. c. 735
5 (6) Jaʿfar al-Ṣādiq, d. 765
6 (7) Ismāʿīl, d. before 765
7 (1) Muḥammad b. Ismāʿīl

The *ḥujja*s in Salamiyya/imams in hiding:

1 ʿAbdallāh the elder, fl. 870s[1]
2 Aḥmad b. ʿAbdallāh,
3 Abū ʾl-Shalaghlagh, d. c. 899[2]
4 Saʿīd/ʿUbaydallāh al-Mahdī, 899–909[3]

Fāṭimid caliphs:

1 ʿUbaydallāh al-Mahdī, 909–34
2 Abū ʾl-Qāsim Muḥammad al-Qaʾīm, 934–46
3 al-Manṣūr, 946–53
4 al-Muʿizz, 953–75
5 al-ʿAzīz, 975–96
6 al-Ḥākim, 996–1021
7 al-Ẓāhir, 1021–36
8 al-Mustanṣir, 1036–94
9 al-Mustaʿlī, 1094–1101
10 al-Āmir, 1101–30
11 al-Ḥāfiẓ, 1131–49
12 al-Ẓāfir, 1149–54
13 al-Fāʾiz, 1154–60
14 al-ʿĀḍid, 1160–71

1 Known to opponents of the Ismailis as ʿAbdallāh b. Maymūn al-Qaddāḥ.

2 His real name was Abū ʿAlī Muḥammad b. Aḥmad.

3 A nephew rather than a son of his predecessor, but married to the latter's daughter. Though this was also the relationship between ʿAlī and Muḥammad, it was problematic to Saʿīd, alias ʿUbaydallāh, in his role as imam, given the requirement that imamic succession be from father to son.

The first segment gives the imams shared by the Imamis and the Ismailis. The latter sometimes number them in the same way as the Imamis, but more often they count ʿAlī separately, starting the line of imams with al-Ḥasan. There is a gap of about a century between the disappearance of Muḥammad b. Ismāʿīl and the emergence of the Ismaili sect, led by ʿAbdallāh the elder. Whether or in what sense there was an Ismaili sect before this ʿAbdallāh is uncertain. The last *ḥujja* (later imam) of the Salamiyya period was the first Fatimid caliph.

CHART 10: THE CALIPHS, 632–1258

Rāshidūn, in Medina:
Abū Bakr, 632–4
ʿUmar, 634–44
ʿUthmān, 644–56

in Kufa:
ʿAlī, 656–61

Umayyads, in Syria:
Muʿāwiya, 661–80
Yazīd I, 680–3
Marwān I, 684–5
ʿAbd al-Malik, 685–705
al-Walīd I, 705–15
Sulaymān, 715–17
ʿUmar II, 717–20
Yazīd II, 720–4
Hishām, 724–43
al-Walīd II, 743–4
Yazīd III, 744
Marwān II, 744–50

ʿAbbāsids, in Iraq:
Abū l-ʿAbbās al-Ṣaffāḥ, 750–4
al-Manṣūr, 754–75
al-Mahdī, 775–85
al-Hādī, 785–6
Hārūn al-Rashīd, 786–809
al-Amīn, 809–13
al-Maʾmūn, 813–33
al-Muʿtaṣim, 833–42
al-Wāthiq, 842–7
al-Mutawakkil, 847–61
al-Muntaṣir, 861–2
al-Mustaʿīn, 862–6
al-Muʿtazz, 866–9
al-Muhtadī, 869–70
al-Muʿtamid, 870–92
al-Muʿtaḍid, 892–902
al-Muktafī, 902–8
al-Muqtadir, 908–32
al-Qāhir, 932–4
al-Rāḍī, 934–40
al-Muttaqī, 940–4
al-Mustakfī, 944–6
al-Muṭīʿ, 946–74
al-Ṭāʾiʿ, 974–91
al-Qādir, 991–1031
al-Qāʾim, 1031–75
al-Muqtadī, 1075–94
al-Mustaẓhir, 1094–1118
al-Mustarshid, 1118–35
al-Rāshid, 1135–6
al-Muqtafī, 1136–60
al-Mustanjid, 1160–70
al-Mustaḍīʾ, 1170–80
al-Nāṣir, 1180–1225
al-Ẓāhir, 1225–6
al-Mustanṣir, 1226–42
al-Mustaʿṣim, 1242–58

CHART 11: CHRONOLOGY

c. 570	birth of Muḥammad
622	*hijra* to Medina
632	death of Muḥammad
632–4	caliphate of Abū Bakr, suppression of the *ridda*, beginning of the conquests
634–44	caliphate of ʿUmar, conquest of Syria, Egypt, Iraq, Iran
644	ʿUthmān elected caliph by *shūrā*
656	ʿUthmān killed by provincial malcontents after a siege of his house
656–61	first civil war, ʿAlī's caliphate in Kufa
661	ʿAlī murdered by a Khārijite (Ibn Muljam)
661–750	Umayyad dynasty in Syria
661–80	caliphate of Muʿāwiya, conquest of North Africa
683–92	second civil war; Ibn al-Zubayr rebels against the Umayyads in Mecca as does al-Mukhtār in Kufa, while the Azāriqa and Najdiyya Khārijites leave Basra to rebel in western Iran and Arabia respectively; but the rebels do not cooperate
692	the Umayyads reconquer Mecca from Ibn al-Zubayr, who is killed; their bombardment of the Kaʿba goes down as one of their many misdeeds
685–705	caliphate of ʿAbd al-Malik, builder of the Dome of the Rock in Jerusalem
694–714	governorship of al-Ḥajjāj in Iraq
705–15	caliphate of al-Walīd I, conquest of Transoxania, al-Andalus, and Sind
744–50	third civil war, Hāshimite revolution
750–1258	ʿAbbāsid dynasty
750–2	first Ibāḍī imamate in Oman
754–75	caliphate of al-Manṣūr, builder of Baghdad
756	al-Andalus secedes under ʿAbd al-Raḥmān I
762–3	revolt of the ʿAlids Muḥammad al-Nafs al-Zakiyya (Medina) and Ibrāhīm (Basra)
765	death of the ʿAlid scholar Jaʿfar al-Ṣādiq, sixth imam to the Imamis
767	death of Abū Ḥanīfa, foremost jurist in Kufa
778–909	Ibāḍī imamate in Tāhert (Rustumids, modern Algeria)
794–893	second Ibāḍī imamate in Oman
796	death of Mālik, foremost jurist in Medina
798	death of Abū Yūsuf, pupil of Abū Ḥanīfa
800–909	Aghlabid dynasty in Ifriqiya (modern Tunisia)
809	death of Hārūn al-Rashīd

811–13	fourth civil war pitting al-Ma'mūn against al-Amīn
817	Ma'mūn announces the succession of ʿAlī al-Riḍā
818	Ma'mūn leaves Marw for Baghdad, arriving in 819
820	death of al-Shāfiʿī
821–76	Ṭāhirid dynasty in Khurāsān and Transoxania
833	Ma'mūn institutes the inquisition (*miḥna*); he dies four months later
833–42	reign of al-Muʿtaṣim; *miḥna* of Ibn Ḥanbal, introduction of caliphal slave soldiers
842–7	reign of al-Wāthiq; *miḥna* actively maintained
847–61	reign of al-Mutawakkil, abolition of the *miḥna*
855	death of Ibn Ḥanbal, Traditionalists scholar and hero
861	assassination of al-Mutawakkil, slave soldiers take over
861–945	break up of the ʿAbbāsid caliphate
860s	rise of the Ṣaffārid dynasty in Sīstān (till 1003) and of the Ṭūlūnid dynasty in Egypt (till 905)
860	death of al-Qāsim b. Ibrāhīm, leading Zaydī scholar in Medina
869	death of al-Jāḥiẓ, Muʿtazilite littérateur
874	disappearance of the twelfth imam
897	establishment of the Zaydī imamate in Yemen (on and off till 1962)
900–1005	Sāmānid dynasty in Transoxania and Khurāsān
906–89	Ḥamdānid dynasty in Mosul
909	Fatimid conquest of North Africa
912–61	ʿAbd al-Raḥman III, founder of the Umayyad caliphate in al-Andalus
923	death of al-Ṭabarī, exegete, jurist, and chief source for the history of the Islamic world up to his own time
925	death of Abū Bakr al-Rāzī, philosopher, and physician
934	death of Abū Ḥātim al-Rāzī, Ismaili missionary
944–1004	Ḥamdānid dynasty in Aleppo
945–1055	Būyid dynasty in Iraq; other branches (with slightly different dates) in Rayy, Jibāl, Fars, and Kerman
950	death of the philosopher al-Fārābī
969	Fatimid conquest of Egypt
976–97	Sebüktegin founds the Ghaznavid dynasty
999–1030	Maḥmūd of Ghazna
1010	*Shāhnāme* of Firdawsī
1022	death of al-Mufīd, Imami scholar
1031	end of Umayyad caliphate in al-Andalus, political fragmentation
1037	death of the philosopher Ibn Sīnā

1040	Oghuz Turks led by Seljuqs defeat the Ghaznavids at Dandanqān
1048	death of the polymath al-Bīrūnī
1055	Seljuqs enter Baghdad under Ṭughril Beg
1058	death of the Sunni scholar al-Māwardī
1062	Yūsuf b. Tāshufīn, leader of the Almoravids, founds Marrakesh
1063	death of Tughril Beg, great sultan of the Seljuqs
1063–72	sultanate of Alp Arslān
1067	death of the Imami scholar al-Ṭūsī
1071	Oghuz Turks led by Alp Arslān defeat the Byzantines at Manzikert; Turks overrun Anatolia (modern Turkey)
1072–92	sultanate of Malikshāh
1085	Toledo falls to the Christians; death of the Sunni scholar al-Juwaynī
1086	Yūsuf b. Tāshufīn, Almoravid leader, begins the conquest of al-Andalus
1092	death of the vizier Niẓām al-Mulk
1095	Pope Urban preaches the first Crusade
1099	the Crusaders conquer Jerusalem
1105–18	sultanate of Muḥammad Tapar
1111	death of al-Ghazālī, foremost Sunni scholar
1118–57	sultanate of Sanjar
1127–1251	Zengid dynasty in Mosul, other branches in northern Mesopotamia; Zengids in Aleppo and Damascus, 1147–83 (conquered by the Ayyūbid Saladin)
1130	death of Ibn Tūmart, founder of the Almohad movement
1147	the Almohads evict the Almoravids, continuing till 1269 (when all of Spain apart from Granada falls to the Christians)
1150–1220	expansionist Khwārizmshāhs
1157	end of the great Seljuq sultanate; smaller branches continue
1169–1252	Ayyūbid dynasty in Egypt
1171	end of the Fatimid caliphate in Egypt
1178–1260	Ayyūbid dynasties in various Syrian cities, falling to the Mongols or Mamluks in 1260 or shortly thereafter
1187	Saladin defeats the Crusaders at Ḥattīn, retakes Jerusalem
1180–1225	the caliph al-Nāṣir
1198	death of the philosopher Ibn Rushd
1252	beginning of the Mamluk regime in Egypt
1256	the Mongols led by Hulagu capture Alamūt, putting an end to the 'New Mission'
1258	the Mongols storm Baghdad, putting an end to the caliphate
1260	the Mamluks defeat the Mongols at ʿAyn Jālūt

BIBLIOGRAPHY, ABBREVIATIONS, AND CONVENTIONS

When new editions and translations preserve the pagination of an earlier edition (usually in the margin), the references in this book are always to the original pagination. Islamicists would save themselves a great deal of trouble if they could agree always to do this, and always to preserve the original pagination (or paragraph division) when they prepare new editions and translations themselves, taking a leaf out of the book of the classicists (see below, s. v. Plato – much the same could have been said *ad* Aristotle or other Greek and Latin authors). A reference to the Leiden edition of al-Ṭabarī will take you to the passage in Ibrāhīm's edition and the English translation as well, since both preserve the pagination of the Leiden edition in the margin; by contrast, references to the pages of Ibrāhīm's edition or the English translation are dead ends. References to the pages of English translations of secondary literature are also dead ends, and it is particularly galling to have to go to the library to locate passages in the translation of a work of which one has the original on one's shelf. Where new editions or translations omit the original pagination, I sometimes give references to both. But giving multiple references to the same passage is time-consuming, I do not always do so, and I never give more than three.

When references are given in the form 4 = 20, the first figure refers to the page of the text and the second to the translation; 20.3 means page 20, line 3; and 20.-3 means page 20, line 3 up.

AA = *Akhbār al-dawla al-ʿabbāsiyya wa-fīhi akhbār al-ʿAbbās*, ed. ʿA.-ʿA. al-Dūrī and ʿA.-J. al-Muṭṭalibī, Beirut 1971.

Aalders, G. J. D., 'Nomos Empsychos', in P. Steinmetz (ed.), *Politeia und Res Publica. Beiträge . . . dem Andenken Rudolf Starks gewidmet*, Wiesbaden 1969, 315–29.

al-ʿAbbādī (d. 458/1066), *Kitāb ṭabaqāt al-fuqahāʾ aš-šāfiʿīya*, Leiden 1964.

ʿAbbās, I. (ed.), *ʿAhd Ardashīr*, Beirut 1967.

—, 'Naẓra jadīda fī baʿḍ al-kutub al-mansūba li-ibn al-Muqaffaʿ', *Majallat Majmaʿ al-Lugha al-ʿArabiyya bi-Dimashq* 52, 1977, 538–80.

ʿAbd al-Jabbār (d. 415/1025), *al-Mughnī fī abwāb al-tawḥīd wa'l-ʿadl*, vol. xx, parts 1 and 2, ed. ʿA.-Ḥ. Maḥmūd and S. Dunyā, Cairo n.d.

—, *Tathbīt dalā'il al-nubuwwa*, ed. ʿA.-K. ʿUthmān, 2 vols, Beirut 1966.

ʿAbd al-Malik b. Ḥabīb (d. 238/853), *Kitāb al-ta'rīkh*, ed. J. Aguadé, Madrid 1991.

ʿAbd al-Razzāq (d. 211/827), *al-Muṣannaf*, ed. Ḥ.-R. al-Aʿẓamī, 11 vols, Beirut 1970–2.

Abou El Fadl, Kh. M., 'Ahkam al-Bughat: Irregular Warfare and the Law of Rebellion in Islam', in J. Turner Johnson and J. Kelsay (eds), *Cross, Crescent, and Sword*, Westport, CT, 1990, ch. 7.

—, 'Islamic Law and Muslim Minorities: the Juristic Discourse on Muslim Minorities from the Second/Eighth to the Eleventh/Seventeenth Centuries', *Islamic Law and Society* 1, 1994, 141–87.

—, 'The Islamic Law of Rebellion', PhD Dissertation, 2 vols, Princeton University 1999.

Abrahamov, B., 'al-Ḳāsim ibn Ibrāhīm's Theory of the Imamate', *Arabica* 34, 1987, 80–105.

Abū 'l-Aswad al-Du'alī (d. 69/688), *Dīwān*, ed M. Ḥ. Āl Yāsīn, Beirut 1974.

Abū 'l-Faraj al-Iṣbahānī (d. 356/967), *Kitāb al-aghānī*, 24 vols, Cairo 1927–74.

—, (attrib.), *Kitāb al-ghurabā'*: see Pseudo-Iṣbahānī.

—, *Maqātil al-Ṭālibiyyīn*, ed. S. A. Ṣaqr, Cairo 1949.

Abū 'l-Fawāris Aḥmad b. Yaʿqūb (wrote c. 1000), *al-Risāla fī 'l-imāma*, ed. and tr. S. N. Makarem under the title *The Political Doctrine of the Ismāʿīlīs*, New York 1977. Cited by the folio number given in the margin of both the Arabic text and the English translation.

Abū Ḥātim al-Rāzī (d. 322/934), *Aʿlām al-nubuwwa*, ed. Ṣ. al-Ṣāwī, Tehran 1977.

Abū Hilāl al-ʿAskarī (d. 395/1005), *al-Awā'il*, ed. M. al-Miṣrī and W. Qaṣṣāb, 2 vols, Damascus 1975.

Abū Isḥāq Ibrāhīm b. Qays (d. 475/1082f.), *Mukhtaṣar al-Khiṣāl*, Oman 1984.

Abū Muṭīʿ al-Balkhī (d. 197/812f. or 199/814f.), *al-Fiqh al-absaṭ*, in M. Z. al-Kawtharī (ed.), *al-ʿĀlim wa'l-mutaʿallim*, Cairo 1368.

Abū Tammām (d. 232/846), *Hamasae Carmina*, ed. and tr. (Latin) G. G. Freytag, Bonn 1828–51. Cited as Abū Tammām, *Ḥamāsa*.

Abū Tammām (fl. fourth/tenth century) in W. Madelung and P. E. Walker, *An Ismaili Heresiography. The 'Bāb al-shayṭān' from Abū Tammām's* Kitāb al-shajara, Leiden 1998. Cited as Abū Tammām.

Abū ʿUbayd al-Qāsim b. Sallām (d. 224/828), *K. al-amwāl*, ed. M. Kh. Harrās, Cairo 1969.

Abū Yaʿlā, Ibn al-Farrā' (d. 458/1066), *al-Aḥkām al-sulṭāniyya*, ed. M. Ḥ. al-Fiqī, Cairo 1966.

—, *K. al-amr bi'l-maʿrūf wa'l-nahy ʿan al-munkar*, MS Damascus, Ẓāhiriyya, Majmūʿ no. 3779. Cf. Cook, *Commanding Right*, 129, note 116.

Abū Yaʿqūb al-Sijistānī: see al-Sijistānī.

Abū Yūsuf (d. 182/798), *Kitāb al-kharāj*, ed. I. ʿAbbās, London 1985.

Abū Zurʿa (d. 281/894), *Ta'rīkh*, ed. Sh.-A. al-Qawjānī, 2 vols, Damascus 1980.

al-*Aghānī*: see Abū 'l-Faraj al-Iṣbahānī.

Aghnides, N. P., *Mohammadan Theories of Finance*, Lahore 1961.

Akhbār majmūʿa, ed. E. Lafuente y Alcántara, Madrid 1867.

al-ʿAlawī, ʿAlī b. Muḥammad (fl. late third/ninth century), *Sīrat al-Hādī ilā 'l-Ḥaqq Yaḥyā b. al-Ḥusayn*, ed. S. al-Zakkār, Beirut 1972.

Alcinous (fl. c. 150), tr. J. Dillon, *The Handbook of Platonism*, Oxford 1993.
Amir-Moezzi, M. A., *The Divine Guide in Early Shīʿism*, Albany 1994.
al-ʿĀmirī (d. 381/992), *K. al-iʿlām bi-manāqib al-islām*, ed. A. A.-Ḥ. Ghurāb, Cairo 1967.
—, (attrib.), *al-Saʿāda wa'l-isʿād*, ed. Minovi, Tehran 1936. For the question whether Minovi was right to identify the author (given as Abū 'l-Ḥasan b. Abī Dharr) as al-ʿĀmirī, see Rowson, *Muslim Philosopher*; A. ʿA.-Ḥ. ʿAṭiyya, *al-Fikr al-siyāsī wa'l-akhlāqī ʿinda 'l-ʿĀmirī*, Cairo 1991.
Arazi, A., and ʿA. Elʿad, '"L'Epître à l'armée". Al-Maʾmūn et la seconde *Daʿwa*', part 1, *Studia Islamica* 66, 1987, 27–70.
Arberry, A., 'An Arabic Treatise on Politics', *The Islamic Quarterly* ii, 1955, 9–22.
—, (tr.), *The Doctrine of the Ṣūfīs*, Cambridge 1935.
—, (tr.), *Muslim Saints and Mystics. Episodes from the Tadhkirat al-Auliyāʾ by Farid al-Din Attar*, London 1966.
—, (tr.), *The Seven Odes*, London 1957.
Arendonk, van, C., *Les débuts de l'imamat zaidite au Yémen*, Leiden 1960. References are to the pagination of the Dutch original (Leiden 1919) given in the margin.
Aristophanes (d. 385 BC), *The Birds*, ed. and tr. J. Henderson, Cambridge, MA 2000.
Aristotle (d. 322 BC), *The Nicomachaean Ethics*, ed. and tr. H. Rackam, London and New York 1926; tr. Isḥāq b. Ḥunayn, *al-Akhlāq*, ed. ʿA.-R. Badawī, Kuwait 1979.
—, *Politics*, ed. and tr. H. Rackam, Cambridge, MA and London 1932.
—, *Rhetoric*, ed. A. Tovar, Madrid 1953; English tr. W. R. Roberts in J. Barnes (ed.), *The Complete Works of Aristotle. The Revised Oxford Translation*, 2 vols, Princeton 1984, vol. ii; Arabic tr., *Aristotle's Ars Rhetorica, the Arabic Version*, ed. M. C. Lyons, 2 vols (the second contains the glossary), Cambridge 1982.
Aristotle (attrib.), *Sirr al-asrār*: see Pseudo-Aristotle.
—, *Siyāsat al-mudun*: see Pseudo-Aristotle.
Arjomand, S. A., 'The Consolation of Theology: Absence of the Imam and Transition from Chiliasm to Law in Shiʿism', *The Journal of Religion* 76, 1996, 548–71.
—, 'Ḡayba', in *Enc. Iran.*
—, 'Imam *Absconditus* and the Beginnings of a Theology of Occultation: Imami Shiʿism circa 280–90/900 AD', *Journal of the American Oriental Society* 117, 1997, 1–12.
—, 'Islamic Apocalypticism in the Classic Period', in B. McGinn (ed.), *The Encyclopaedia of Apocalypticism*, ii, New York 1999, ch. 8.
—, 'Messianism, Millenialism and Revolution in Early Islamic History', in A. Amanat and M. Bernhardsson (eds), *Imagining the End: Visions of Apocalypse from the Ancient Middle East to Modern America*, London and New York 2002, 106–25 and 355–9.
al-Ashʿarī (d. 324/935f.), *Kitāb maqālāt al-islāmiyyīn*, ed. H. Ritter, Istanbul 1929–33.
Assmann, J., *Moses the Egyptian. The Memory of Egypt in Western Monotheism*, Cambridge, MA 1997.
ʿAthamina, Kh., 'The Tribal Kings in Pre-Islamic Arabia', *al-Qanṭara* 19, 1998, 19–37.
Augustine, Saint (d. 430), *The City of God*, tr. J. Healey, ed. R. V. G. Tasker, 2 vols, London 1945.
al-Azdī (d. 334/946), *Taʾrīkh al-Mawṣil*, ed. ʿA. Ḥabība, Cairo 1967.
al-Azmeh, A., *Muslim Kingship. Power and the Sacred in Muslim, Christian, and Pagan Polities*, London 1997.
—, 'Utopia and Islamic Political Thought', *History of Political Thought* 11, 1990, 9–19.

BA = al-Balādhurī (d. 279/892), *Ansāb al-ashrāf*, vol. ii, ed. M. B. al-Maḥmūdī, Beirut 1974; vol. iv a, ed. M. J. Kister, Jerusalem 1971; vol. v, ed. S. D. F. Goitein, Jerusalem 1936; vol. xi (*Anonyme arabische Chronik*), ed. W. Ahlwardt, Greifswald 1883. See also BF.

al-Baghdādī (d. 429/1037), *al-Farq bayna 'l-firaq*, ed. M. Badr, Cairo 1910.

—, *Uṣūl al-dīn*, Istanbul 1928.

al-Baghdādī, al-Khaṭīb (d. 463/1071): see al-Khaṭīb.

al-Balādhurī, see BA, BF.

al-Bāqillānī (d. 403/1013), *al-Tamhīd*, ed. M. M. al-Khuḍayrī and M. ʿA.-H. Abū Rīda, Cairo 1947.

Barker, E. (tr.), *From Alexander to Constantine. Passages and Documents Illustrating the History of Social and Political Ideas 336* BC – AD *337*, Oxford 1956.

—, (tr.), *Social and Political Thought in Byzantium from Justinian I to the Last Palaeologus. Passages from Byzantine Writers and Documents*, Oxford 1957.

Barthold, W., *Turkestan down to the Mongol Invasion*, 3rd edn, London 1968. First published 1900. References are to the pagination of the second Russian edition (Moscow 1963) given in the margin.

Bashear, S., 'Muslim Apocalypses and the Hour: a Case-Study in Traditional Reinterpretation', *Israel Oriental Studies* 13, 1993, 75–99.

—, 'The Title 'Fārūq' and its Association with Umar I', *Studia Islamica* 72, 1990, 47–70.

Bausani, A., *The Persians*, London 1971.

Bayhaqī (d. 470/1077), *Tārīkh*, ed. ʿA. Fayyaḍ, Mashhad 1977.

Baynes, N. H., 'Eusebius and the Christian Empire', *Annuaire de l'Institut de Philologie et d'Histoire Orientale* 2, 1933–4 (*Mélanges Bidez*), 13–18; reprinted in his *Byzantine Studies and Other Essays*, London 1955, no. 9.

al-Bazdawī (d. 493/1099), *Kashf al-asrār ʿalā uṣūl al-fiqh*, 4 vols, n.p. 1889.

Beaulieu, P.-A., 'Theodicy, Theology, Philosophy: Mesopotamia', in *Religions of the Ancient World: a Guide*, forthcoming.

Beeston, A. F. L., 'Nemara and Faw', *Bulletin of the School of Oriental and African Studies* 62, 1979, pp. 1–6.

Berman, L. V., 'Maimonides, the Disciple of Alfārābī', *Israel Oriental Studies* 4, 1974, 154–78.

Beskow, P., *Rex Gloriae. The Kingship of Christ in the Early Church*, Uppsala 1962.

BF = al-Balādhurī, *Futūḥ al-buldān*, ed. M. J. de Goeje, Leiden 1866 (repr. 1992).

Bielawski and Plezia: see Pseudo-Aristotle.

Binder, L., 'Al-Ghazālī's Theory of Islamic Government', *The Muslim World* 45, 1955, 229–41.

al-Bīrūnī (d. after 442/1050), *al-Āthār al-bāqiya ʿan al-qurūn al-khāliya*, ed. C. E. Sachau, Leipzig 1878 (repr. 1923); tr. C. E. Sachau, *The Chronology of Ancient Nations*, London 1879 (repr. 1984).

—, *Hind = K. fī taḥqīq mā li'l-Hind*, ed. E. [C.] Sachau, London 1887; tr. E. C. Sachau, *Alberuni's India*, 2 vols, London 1910.

—, *R. ifrād al-maqāl fī amr al-aẓlāl*, in his *Rasāʾil*, Hyderabad 1948, no. 2; tr. (barely intelligibly) E. S. Kennedy, *The Exhaustive Treatise on Shadows*, Aleppo 1976.

—, *K. al-jawāhir*, ed. F. Krenkow, Hyderabad 1355; tr. (introduction only) T.-D. al-Hilālī, *Die Einleitung zu al-Bīrūnī's Steinbuch*, Leipzig 1941.

al-Bisyānī, also known as al-Basyawī (fl. fourth/tenth century), *Mukhtaṣar al-Basyawī*, ed. ʿA.-Q. ʿAṭāʾ and M. ʿA. Zarqa, Oman n.d.

Black, A., *The History of Islamic Political Thought from the Prophet to the Present*, New York 2001.

Bosworth, C. E., 'An Early Arabic Mirror for Princes. Ṭāhir Dhū 'l-Yamīnain's Epistle to his Son ʿAbdallāh (206/821)', *Journal of Near Eastern Studies* 29, 1970, 25–41

—, *The Ghaznavids*, Edinburgh 1973.

—, (tr.), *The History of al-Ṭabarī*, vol. xxxii, Albany 1987.

—, 'The Imperial Policy of the Early Ghaznawids', *Islamic Studies* 1, 1962, 49–82.

—, *The New Islamic Dynasties*, New York 1996.

—, 'The Political and Dynastic History of the Iranian World (AD 1000–1217)', in *The Cambridge History of Iran*, vol. v, ed. J. A. Boyle, Cambridge 1968, 1–202.

—, *Sīstān under the Arabs*, Rome 1968.

Bourouiba, R., *Ibn Tumart*, Alger 1974.

Bousquet, G.-H., 'Des animaux et de leur traitement selon le Judaisme, le Christianisme et l'Islam', *Studia Islamica* 9, 1958, 31–48.

—, 'Observations sur la nature et les causes de la conquête arabe', *Studia Islamica* 6, 1956, 37–57.

Bowersock, G., P. Brown and O. Grabar (eds), *Late Antiquity: a Guide to the Post-Classical World*, Cambridge, MA 1999.

Brague, R., 'Note sur la traduction arabe de la *Politique*, derechef, qu'elle n'existe pas', in P. Aubenque (ed.), *Aristote politique*, Paris 1993, 423–33.

Bredow, M. von, *Der heilige Krieg (Ǧihād) aus der Sicht der målikitischen Rechtsschule*, Beirut 1994.

Brock, S. P., 'North Mesopotamia in the Late Seventh Century. Book XV of John Bar Penkāyē's Rīš Mellē', *Jerusalem Studies in Arabic and Islam* 9, 1987, 51–75.

Brockelmann, C., *Geschichte der arabischen Literatur*, 2nd edn, 2 vols, Leiden 1943–9 (references are to the original pagination); *Supplementbände*, 3 vols, Leiden 1937–42.

Bryer, D. R. W., 'The Origins of the Druze Religion', (chs 1–2), *Der Islam* 52, 1975, 47–83; ch. 3, ibid., 239–62; ch. 4, *Der Islam* 53, 1976, 5–27.

Bryson: see Plessner.

al-Bukhārī (d. 256/870), *al-Ṣaḥīḥ*, ed. L. Krehl and T. W. Juynboll, 4 vols, Leiden 1862–1908.

Bürgel, J. C., 'The Idea of Nonviolence in the Epic Poetry of Niẓāmī', *Edebiyât* 9, 1998, 61–84.

—, 'Krieg und Frieden im Alexanderepos Nizamis', in M. Bridges and J. C. Bürgel (eds), *The Problematics of Power*, Bern 1996, 91–107.

—, 'Zoroastrianism as Viewed in Medieval Islamic Sources', in J. Waardenburg (ed.), *Muslim Perceptions of Other Religions*, Oxford 1999, 202–12.

Burstein, S. M., 'The Greek Tradition from Alexander to the End of Antiquity', in C. G. Thomas (ed.), *Paths from Ancient Greece*, Leiden 1988, ch. 3.

Busse, H., *Chalif und Grosskönig. Die Buyiden im Iraq (945–1055)*, Beirut 1969.

—, 'Das Hofbudget des Chalifen al-Muʿtaḍid billāh (279/892–289/902)', *Der Islam* 43, 1967, 11–36.

—, 'The Revival of Persian Kingship under the Būyids', in D. S. Richards (ed.), *Islamic Civilisation 950–1150*, Oxford 1973, 47–69.

Butterworth, C. E. (ed.), *Philosophy, Ethics and Virtuous Rule: A Study of Averroes' Commentary on Plato's 'Republic'* (Cairo Papers in Social Science, vol. 9, monograph 1), Cairo 1986.

—, *The Political Aspects of Islamic Philosophy. Essays in Honor of Muhsin S. Mahdi*, Cambridge, MA 1992.

—, 'Die Politischen Lehren von Avicenna und Averroës', in *Pipers Handbuch der politischen Ideen*, ed. I. Fetscher and H. Münkler, vol. ii, Munich 1993, ch. 4.

Calder, N., 'Friday Prayer and the Juristic Theory of Government: Sarakhsī, Shīrāzī, Māwardī', *Bulletin of the School of Oriental and African Studies* 49, 1986, 35–47.

—, 'Judicial Authority in Imāmī Shīʿī Jurisprudence', *BRISMES Bulletin* vi, 1979, 104–8.

—, 'Legitimacy and Accommodation in Safavid Iran: the Juristic Theory of Muḥammad Bāqir al-Sabzavārī (d. 1090/1679)', *Iran* 25, 1987, 91–105.

—, 'Zakāt in Imāmī Shīʿī Jurisprudence, from the Tenth to the Sixteenth Century', *Bulletin of the School of Oriental and African Studies* 44, 1981, 468–80.

Cambridge History of Later Medieval Philosophy, from the Rediscovery of Aristotle to the Disintegration of Scholasticism, 1100–1600, ed. N. Kretzmann, A Kenny, and P. Pinborg, Cambridge 1982.

Cambridge History of Medieval Political Thought, c. 350 – c. 1450, ed. J. H. Burns, Cambridge 1988.

Canard, M., 'L'impérialisme des Fatimides et leur propagande', *Annales de l'Institut des Etudes Orientales de l'Université d'Alger* vi, 1942–7; reprinted in his *Miscellanea Orientalia*, London 1973, 156–93.

Chittick, W. C. , 'Bābā Afżal-al-dīn', in *Encyclopaedia Iranica.*

—, *The Heart of Islamic Philosophy. The Quest for Self-knowledge in the Teachings of Afḍal al-Dīn Kāshānī*, Oxford 2001.

—, (tr.), *A Shiʿite Anthology*, Albany 1981.

Chokr, M., *Zandaqa et zindīqs en Islam au second siècle de l'Hégire*, Damascus 1993.

Clement of Alexandria (d. between 211 and 216), *Stromata*, V, ed. and tr. A. le Boulluec and P. Voulet, Paris 1981.

— (attrib.), *The Clementine Homilies*, tr. in *Ante-Nicene Christian Library*, ed. A. Roberts and J. Donaldson, vol. xvii, Edinburgh 1870.

Cobb, P., *White Banners. Contention in ʿAbbasid Syria, 750–880*, Albany 2001.

Cohn, N., *The Pursuit of the Millennium*, London 1970 (first published 1957).

Conrad, L., 'Did al-Walīd I found the First Islamic Hospital?', *Aram* 6, 1994, 225–44.

Cook, D., 'Muslim Apocalyptic and *Jihād*', *Jerusalem Studies in Arabic and Islam* 20, 1996, 66–104.

Cook, M. A., *Commanding Right and Forbidding Wrong in Islamic Thought*, Cambridge 2000.

—, 'An Early Islamic Apocalyptic Chronicle', *Journal of Near Eastern Studies* 52, 1993, 25–9.

—, 'Early Islamic Dietary Law', *Jerusalem Studies in Arabic and Islam* 7, 1986, 218–77.

—, *Early Muslim Dogma, a Source-critical Study*, Cambridge 1981.

—, *Forbidding Wrong in Islam: An Introduction*, Cambridge 2003.

—, *The Koran: A Very Short Introduction*, Oxford 2000.

—, *Muhammad*, Oxford 1983.

Cooperson, M., *Classical Arabic Biography*, Cambridge 2000.

Corbin, H., *Cyclical Time and Ismaili Gnosis*, London 1983.

—, 'The Ismāʿīlī Response to the Polemic of Ghazālī', in S. H. Nasr (ed.), *Ismāʿīlī Contributions to Islamic Culture*, Tehran 1977, 69–98.
—, *Histoire de la philosophie islamique*, vol. i (no further vols published), Paris 1964.
Crone, P., 'Did al-Ghazālī Write a Mirror for Princes?', *Jerusalem Studies in Arabic and Islam* 10, 1987, 167–91.
—, '"Even an Ethiopian Slave": the Transformation of a Sunnī Tradition', *Bulletin of the School of Oriental and African Studies* 57, 1994, 59–67.
—, 'The First-Century Concept of *Hiǧra*', *Arabica* 41, 1994, 352–87.
—, 'Kavād's Heresy and Mazdak's Revolt', *Iran* 29, 1991, 21–42.
—, 'The Khārijites and the Caliphal Title', in *Studies in Islamic Middle Eastern Texts and Traditions in Memory of Norman Calder*, ed. G. R. Hawting, J. A. Mojaddedi, and A. Samely, Oxford 2000, 85–91.
—, '*Mawālī* and the Prophet's Family, an Early Shīʿite view', forthcoming in a volume ed. J. Nawas.
—, *Meccan Trade and the Rise of Islam*, Oxford and Princeton 1987.
—, 'Ninth-Century Muslim Anarchists', *Past and Present* 167, 2000, 3–28.
—, 'On the Meaning of the ʿAbbāsid Call to *al-Riḍā*,' in *The Islamic World. Essays in Honor of Bernard Lewis*, ed. C. E. Bosworth and others, Princeton 1989, 95–111.
—, *Pre-industrial Societies*, Oxford 1989.
—, 'Were the Qays and the Yemen of the Umayyad Period Political Parties?', *Der Islam* 71, 1994, 1–57.
—, *Roman, Provincial and Islamic Law*, Cambridge 1987.
—, 'Serjeant and Meccan Trade', *Arabica* 39, 1992, 216–40.
—, '*Shūrā* as an Elective Institution', *Quaderni di Studi Arabi* 19, 2001, 3–39.
—, 'The Significance of Wooden Weapons in al-Mukhtār's Revolt and the ʿAbbāsid Revolution', in *Studies in Honour of Clifford Edmund Bosworth*, vol. i, ed. I. R. Netton, Leiden 2000, 174–87.
—, *Slaves on Horses, the Evolution of the Islamic Polity*, Cambridge 1980.
—, 'A Statement by the Najdiyya Khārijites on the Dispensability of the Imamate', *Studia Islamica* 88, 1998, 55–76.
—, 'The Tribe and the State', in J. A. Hall (ed.), *States in History*, Oxford 1986, 48–77.
—, 'Tribes without Saints' (in preparation).
—, 'Zoroastrian Communism', *Comparative Studies in Society and History* 36, 1994, 447–62.
Crone, P., and M. Cook, *Hagarism. The Making of the Islamic World*, Cambridge 1977.
Crone, P., and M. Hinds, *God's Caliph. Religious Authority in the First Centuries of Islam*, Cambridge 1986.
Crone, P., and L. Treadwell, 'A New Text on Ismailism at the Sāmānid Court', in C. F. Robinson (ed.), *Texts, Documents and Artefacts. Islamic Studies in Honour of D. S. Richards*, Leiden and Boston 2003, 37–67.
Crone, P., and F. W. Zimmermann (ed., tr., comm.), *The Epistle of Sālim ibn Dhakwān*, Oxford 2001. The edition and translation are cited as Sālim, *Epistle*, the rest of the book as Crone and Zimmermann, *Epistle*.
Daftary, F., *The Ismāʿīlīs. Their History and Doctrine*, Cambridge 1990.
Dagron, G., *Empereur et prêtre. Étude sur le 'césaropapisme' byzantin*, Paris 1996.
—, 'L'empire romain d'orient au ive siècle et les traditions politiques de l'hellénisme. Le Témoignage de Thémistios', *Travaux et Mémoires* 3, 1968, 1–242.

Daiber, H., 'The Ismaili Background of Fārābī's Philosophy – Abū Ḥātim ar-Rāzī as a Forerunner of Fārābī', in U. Tworuschka (ed.), *Gottes is der Orient, Gottes is der Okzident. Festschrift für Abdoljavad Falaturi*, Cologne 1991, 143–50.

—, 'Political Philosophy', in S. H. Nasr and O. Leaman (eds), *History of Islamic Philosophy*, part II, London and New York 1996, 841–85.

—, 'The Ruler as Philosopher. A New Interpretation of al-Fārābī's View', *Mededelingen der Koninklijke Nederlandse Akademie van Wetenschappen, Afd. Letterkunde, NR* 49, Amsterdam 1986, 133–49.

Danishpazhouh, M.-T., 'An Annotated Bibliography on Government and Statecraft', in S. A. Arjomand (ed.), *Authority and Political Culture in Shīʿism*, Albany 1988, 213–39.

Dankoff, see Yūsuf Khāṣṣ.

Daou, T. Bayhom, 'The Imāmī Shīʿī Conception of the Knowledge of the Imām and the Sources of Religious Doctrine in the Formative Period: from Hishām b. al-Ḥakam (d. 179 AH) to Kulīnī (d. 329 AH)', unpublished PhD thesis, London 1996.

Darling, L. T., 'Contested Territory: Ottoman Holy War in Comparative Context', *Studia Islamica* 91, 2000, 133–63.

Davidson, H. A., *Alfarabi, Avicenna, & Averroes, on Intellect*, Oxford 1992.

Davis, D., *Epic and Sedition. The Case of Ferdowsi's Shahnameh*, Washington 1992.

Dawson, D., *Cities of the Gods. Communist Utopias in Greek Thought*, Oxford 1992.

Dāya, Najm al-Dīn Rāzī (d. 654/1256), *The Path of God's Bondsmen from Origin to Return*, tr. H. Algar, New York 1982.

Dennis, G. T., 'Defenders of the Christian People: Holy War in Byzantium', in A. E. Laiou and R. P. Mottahedeh (eds), *The Crusades from the Perspective of Byzantium and the Muslim World*, Washington 2001, 31–9.

al-Dhahabī (d. 748/1348), *Siyar aʿlām al-nubalāʾ*, ed. Sh. Arnaʾūṭ et al., 25 vols, Beirut 1981–8.

—, *Taʾrīkh al-islām wa-ṭabaqāt al-mashāhīr wa'l-aʿlām*, ed. Ḥ.-D. al-Qudsī, 6 vols, Cairo 1947–8

al-Dīnawarī (d. 282/895), *al-Akhbār al-ṭiwāl*, ed. V. Guirgass, Leiden 1888.

Dio Cocceianus Chrysostom (d. c. 120), [*Works*,] ed. and tr. J. W. Cohoon, vol. i, London and New York 1932.

Djait, H., 'Les Yamanites à Kufa au Ier siècle de l'Hégire', *Journal of the Economic and Social History of the Orient* 19, 1976, 141–81.

Donner, F. M., 'La question du messianisme dans l'Islam primitif', *Revue des Mondes Musulmans et de la Méditerranée* nos. 91–4 (= *Mahdisme et Millénarisme en Islam*, ed. M. Garcia-Arenal, Aix-en-Provence 2000), 17–27.

—, 'The Sources of Islamic Conceptions of War', in J. Kelsay and J. Turner Johnson (eds), *Just War and Jihad*, New York 1991, ch. 2.

Donohue, J. J., and J. L. Esposito, *Islam in Transition*, Oxford 1982.

Driver, G. R., and J. C. Miles (ed., tr., comm.), *The Babylonian Laws*, 2 vols, Oxford 1952.

al-Dumayjī, ʿA.-A., *al-Imāma al-ʿuẓmā ʿinda ahl al-sunna wa'l-jamāʿa*, Riyad 1987.

al-Dūrī, ʿA.-ʿA., 'al-Fikra al-mahdiyya bayna 'l-daʿwa al-ʿabbāsiyya wa'l-ʿaṣr al-ʿabbāsī 'l-awwal', in *Studia Arabica et Islamica. Festschrift for Iḥsān ʿAbbās*, ed. W. al-Qāḍī, Beirut 1981, Arabic section, 123–32.

Dvornik, F., *Early Christian and Byzantine Political Philosophy*, 2 vols, Washington 1966.

EI^1 = *Encyclopaedia of Islam*, Leiden 1913–38.

EI[2]: see *Encyclopaedia of Islam*.

Elisséeff, N., 'Un document contemporain de Nūr ad-Dīn', *Bulletin des Études Orientales* 25, 1972, 125–40.

Enc. Iran. = *Encyclopaedia Iranica*, ed. I, Yarshater, London and Boston 1982.

Encyclopaedia of Islam, 2nd edn, Leiden 1960– (abbreviated as *EI*[2]).

Endress, G., 'The Circle of al-Kindī', in G. Endress and R. Kruk (eds), *The Ancient Tradition in Christian and Islamic Hellenism*, Leiden 1997, 43–76.

—, 'The Defense of Reason: the Plea for Philosophy in the Religious Community', *Zeitschrift für Geschichte der arabisch-islamischen Wissenschaften* 6, 1990, 1–49.

Ess, J. van, *Anfänge Muslimischer Theologie*, Beirut 1977.

—, *Frühe Muʿtazilitische Häresiographie*: see Ps(eudo)-Nāshiʾ.

—, (ed.), 'Das *Kitāb al-irǧāʾ* des Ḥasan b. Muḥammad b. al-Ḥanafiyya', *Arabica* 21, 1974, 20–52.

—, *TG* = *Theologie und Gesellschaft im 2. und 3. Jahrhundert Hidschra*, Berlin and New York 1991–7.

—, *Zwischen Ḥadīt und Theologie. Studien zum Entstehen prädestinatianischer Überlieferung*, Berlin 1975.

Eusebius (d. 340), *Praeparatio Evangelica*, book vii, ed. and tr. G. Schroeder and É. des Places, *La préparation évangélique, livre VII*, Paris 1975.

Fakhry, M., *A History of Islamic Philosophy*, 2nd edn, New York 1983.

al-Fārābī (d. 339/950), *Falsafat Aflāṭūn*, ed. F. Rosenthal and R. Walzer, London 1943; tr. M. Mahdi, 'The Philosophy of Plato', in his *Alfarabi. Philosophy of Plato and Aristotle*, Glencoe 1962; rev. edn (pagination unaffected) Cornell 1969.

—, *Fuṣūl al-madanī*, ed. and tr. D. M. Dunlop, Cambridge 1961; re-edited on the basis of a new manuscript with four additional *fuṣūl* and a different paragraph numbering by F. M. Najjār, *al-Fuṣūl al-muntazaʿa*, Beirut 1971. References are given to both editions in the above order, in the form §19/21.

—, *K. al-ḥurūf*, ed. M. Mahdi, Beirut 1969.

—, *K. al-jamʿ bayna raʾyay al-ḥakīmayn Aflāṭūn wa-Arisṭūṭālis*, ed. and tr. A. N. Nadir, Beirut 1960; tr. D. Mallet, *Farabi, Deux traités philosophiques*, Damascus 1989.

—, *K. al-milla*, ed. M. Mahdi, Beirut 1968; tr. D. Mallet, *Farabi, Deux traités philosophiques*, Damascus 1989.

—, *MF* = *K. ārāʾ ahl al-madina al-fāḍila*, ed. and tr. R. Walzer, *al-Farabi on the Perfect State*, Oxford 1985. Cited by chapter and paragraph. References to Walzer, *Farabi on the Perfect State*, are to Walzer's introduction and commentary.

—, *SM* = *al-Siyāsa al-madaniyya*, ed. F. M. Najjar, Beirut 1964; partial translation (from p. 69 of Najjar's edition), based on the earlier Hyderabad edition, by F. M. Najjar in Lerner and Mahdi, *Sourcebook*, no. 2.

—, *Talkhīṣ nawāmīs Aflāṭūn*, ed. and tr. (Latin), F. Gabrieli, *Alfabius Compendium Legum Platonis*, London 1952; partial translation (to *maqāla* 3) by M. Mahdi in Lerner and Mahdi, *Sourcebook*, no. 4.

—, *Taḥṣīl al-saʿāda*, ed. J. Āl Yāsīn, Beirut 1981; tr. M. Mahdi with a different paragraph division in his *Alfarabi's Philosophy of Plato and Aristotle*, Glencoe 1962; rev. edn (pagination unaffected) Cornell 1969; partially reprinted (from §16 of Mahdi's translation, corresponding to the middle of Yāsīn's edition, §14) in Lerner and Mahdi, *Sourcebook*, no. 3. References are by paragraph, in the form §14 = §16.

al-Farazdaq (d. prob. 112/730), *Dīwān*, ed. M. I. A. al-Ṣāwī, Cairo 1936.

al-Fāsī (d. 832/1429), *Shifā' al-gharām bi-akhbār al-balad al-ḥarām*, ed. ʿU. ʿA.-S. Tadmurī, 2 vols, Beirut 1985.

Fierro, M., 'Sobre la adopción des título califal por ʿAbd al-Raḥmān III', *Estudios Árabes* 6, 1989, 33–42.

—, 'Al-Asfar Again', *Jerusalem Studies in Arabic and Islam* 22, 1998, 196–213.

—, 'The Legal Policies of the Almohad Caliphs and Ibn Rushd's *Bidāyat al-Mujtahid*,' *Journal of Islamic Studies* 10, 1999, 226–48.

—, 'Le mahdi Ibn Tûmart et al-Andalus: l'élaboration de la légitimité almohade', *Revue des Mondes Musulmans et de la Méditerranée* nos. 91–4 (= *Mahdisme et Millénarisme en Islam*, ed. M. Garcia-Arenal, Aix-en-Provence 2000), 107–24.

—, 'The *Qāḍī* as Ruler,' in *Saber Religioso y Poder Poliítico en el Islam (Actas des Simposio Internacional*, Granada 1991), Madrid 1994, 71–116.

Finer, S. E., 'Notes Towards a History of Constitutions', in V. Bogdanor (ed.), *Constitutions in Democratic Politics*, Aldershot 1988, ch. 2.

Fortenbaugh, W. W., and E. Schütrumpf (eds), *Dicaearchus of Messana. Text, Translation, and Discussion*, New Brunswick 2001.

Fouchécour, C.-H. de, *Moralia: les notions morales dans la littérature persane du 3e/9e au 7e/13e siècle*, Paris 1986.

Fradkin, H., 'The Political Thought of Ibn Ṭufayl', in C. E. Butterworth (ed.), *The Political Aspects of Islamic Philosophy. Essays in Honor of Muhsin S. Mahdi*, Cambridge, MA 1992, ch. 6.

Friedmann, Y., 'Classification of Unbelievers in Sunnī Muslim Law and Tradition', *Jerusalem Studies in Arabic and Islam* 22, 1998, 163–95.

—, *Prophecy Continuous*, Berkeley 1989.

—, 'The Temple of Multān', *Israel Oriental Studies* 2, 197, 176–82.

Gabrieli, F., *Muhammad and the Conquests of Islam*, tr. V. Luling and R. Linell, London 1968.

Galston, M., *Politics and Excellence. The Political Philosophy of Alfarabi*, Princeton 1990.

—, 'Realism and Idealism in Avicenna's Political Philosophy', *The Review of Politics* 41, 1979, 561–77.

—, 'The Theoretical and Practical Dimensions of Happiness as Portrayed in the Political Treatises of al-Fārābī', in C. E. Butterworth (ed.), *The Political Aspects of Islamic Philosophy. Essays in Honor of Muhsin S. Mahdi*, Cambridge, MA 1992, ch. 3.

Gamal, A. S., and M. Dols (eds and trs), *Medieval Islamic Medicine: Ibn Riḍwān's Treatise 'On the Prevention of Bodily Ills in Egypt'*, Berkeley 1984.

Garnsey, P., *Ideas of Slavery from Aristotle to Augustine*, Cambridge 1996.

Geddes, C. L., 'The Apostasy of ʿAlī b. al-Faḍl', *Arabian and Islamic Studies. Articles Presented to R. B. Serjeant*, London 1983, 80–5.

Gelder, G. J. van, 'Mirror for Princes or Vizor for Viziers: the Twelfth-Century Arabic Popular Encyclopaedia *Mufīd al-ʿulūm* and its Relationship with the Anonymous *Baḥr al-fawā'id*', *Bulletin of the School of Oriental and African Studies* 64, 2001, 313–38.

Gellner, E., *Conditions of Liberty. Civil Society and its Rivals*, London 1994.

George, F. W. A., 'Jean de Meung and the Myth of the Golden Age', in H. T. Barnwell, A. H. Diverres, G. F. Evans, F. W. A. George, and Vivienne Mylne (eds), *The Classical Tradition in French Literature: Essays Presented to R. C. Knight*, London 1977, 31–9.

al-Ghazālī (d. 505/1111), *Faḍāʾiḥ al-bāṭiniyya*, Amman 1993.
—, *Iḥyāʾ ʿulūm al-dīn*, Cairo 1282.
—, *al-Iqtiṣād fī 'l-iʿtiqād*, ed. A. Çubukçu and H. Atay, Ankara 1962.
—, *al-Munqidh min al-ḍalāl*, ed. and tr. (French) F. Jabre, Beirut 1959; tr. W. M. Watt, *The Faith and Practice of al-Ghazálí*, Edinburgh 1953. References are to Jabre's edition and Watt's translation.
—, (attrib.), *Naṣīḥat al-mulūk*, tr. F. R. C. Bagley, *Ghazālī's Book of Counsel for Kings*, Oxford 1964. The first half of this work is correctly ascribed, but the second half cannot be al-Ghazālī's, see Pseudo-Ghazālī.
—, *al-Qisṭās al-mustaqīm*, ed. V. Chelhot, Beirut 1959.
Gibb, H. A. R., 'Constitutional Organization', in M. Khadduri and H. J. Liebesny (eds), *Law in the Middle East*, vol. i, Washington 1955, ch. 1.
—, 'Al-Mawardī's Theory of the Caliphate', in his *Studies on the Civilization of Islam*, ed. S. J. Shaw and W. R. Polk, Princeton 1962, ch. 9 (reprinted from *Islamic Culture* 11, 1937, 291–302).
Glassen, E., *Der Mittlere Weg. Studien zur Religionspolitik und Religiosität der späteren Abbasiden-Zeit*, Wiesbaden 1981.
Goeje, M. J. de, 'La fin de l'empire des Carmathes du Bahraïn', *Journal Asiatique*, ninth series, 5, 1895, 5–30.
Goitein, S. D., *A Mediterranean Society*, vol. ii (*The Community*), Berkeley 1971.
—, 'Minority Selfrule and Government Control in Islam', *Studia Islamica* 31, 1970, 101–16.
Goldziher, I., 'Beiträge zur Literaturgeschichte der Śîʿâ und der sunnitischen Polemik', *Sitzungsberichte der Kaiserlischen Akademie der Wissenschaften zu Wien*, Phil.-Hist. Klasse 78, 1874 (facsimile reprint in his *Gesammelte Schriften*, ed. J. Desomogyi, vol. i, Hildesheim 1967), 439–524.
—, *Introduction to Islamic Theology and Law*, tr. A. and R. Hamori, Princeton 1981.
—, *Le Livre de Mohammed Ibn Toumert*, Alger 1903.
—, *MS* = *Muslim Studies*, 2 vols, London 1967–71 (references are to the pagination of the German original, 2 vols, Halle 1889–90).
—, 'Du sens propre des expressions ombre de dieu, Khalife de dieu', *Revue de l'Histoire des Religions* 35, 1987, 331–8.
Goodman, L. E. (tr.), *The Case of the Animals versus Man Before the King of the Jinn. A Tenth-Century Ecological Fable of the Pure Brethren of Basra*, Boston 1978.
—, (tr.), *Ibn Tufayl's Hayy Ibn Yaqzān*, 4th edn, Los Angeles 1994.
Griffel, F., *Apostasie und Toleranz in Islam. Die Entwickelung zu al-Ġazālī's Urteil gegen die Philosophie und die Reaktion der Philosophen*, Leiden 2000.
—, 'Toleration and Exclusion: al-Shāfiʿī and al-Ghazālī on the Treatment of Apostates', *Bulletin of the School of Oriental and African Studies* 64, 2001, 339–54.
Grignaschi, M., 'L'Origine et les métamorphoses du "Sirr al-asrâr" ', *Archives d'Histoire Doctrinale et Littéraire du Moyen Age* 51, 1976, 7–112.
—, 'Quelques spécimens de la littérature sassanide conservés dans les bibliothèques d'Istanbul', *Journal Asiatique* 254, 1966, 1–142.
—, 'Les rasāʾil Arisṭāṭālīsa ilā Iskandar de Sālim Abū 'l-ʿAlāʾ et l'activité culturelle à l'époque Omayyade', *Bulletin d'Etudes Orientales* 19, 1965–6, 7–83.
—, 'Le roman épistolaire classique conservé dans la version de Sâlim Abû 'l-ʿAlâʾ', *Le Muséon* 80, 1967, 211–64.

—, 'Un roman épistolaire gréco-arabe: la correspondence entre Aristote et Alexandre', in M. Bridges and J. Ch. Bürgel (eds), *The Problematics of Power: Eastern and Western Representations of Alexander the Great*, Bern 1996, 109–23.

Grunebaum, G. E. von, *Medieval Islam*, 2nd edn, Chicago 1961.

Guerrero, R. R., 'El compromiso político de al-Fārābī ¿Fue un filósofo šīʿī?', *Actas de las II Jornadas de Cultura Arabe e Islamica (1980)*, Madrid 1985, 463–77.

Gutas, D, *Greek Thought, Arabic Culture. The Graeco-Arabic Translation Movement in Baghdad and Early ʿAbbāsid Society*, London 1998.

—, 'Pre-Plotinian Philosophy in Arabic (Other than Platonism and Aristotelianism): a Review of the Sources', in W. Haase and H. Temporini (eds), *Aufstieg und Niedergang der römischen Welt*, part II (Principat), vol. 36.7, New York 1994, 4939–73.

al-Hādī ilā 'l-Ḥaqq (d. 298/911), *al-Aḥkām fī 'l-ḥalāl wa'l-ḥarām*, 2 vols, n.p. 1990.

Hallaq, W., 'Caliphs, Jurists and the Saljūqs in the Political Thought of Juwaynī', *The Muslim World* 74, 1984, 26–41.

Halm, H., 'The Cosmology of the pre-Fatimid Ismāʿīliyya', in F. Daftary (ed.), *Mediaeval Ismaʿili History and Thought*, Cambridge 1996, ch. 3.

—, *The Fatimids and their Traditions of Learning*, London 1997.

—, *Kosmologie und Heilslehre der frühen Ismāʿīlīya*, Wiesbaden 1978.

—, *Das Reich des Mahdi. Der Aufstieg der Fatimiden (875–973)*, Munich 1991; tr. M. Bonner, *The Empire of the Mahdi. The Rise of the Fatimids*, Leiden 1996.

—, *Shiʿa Islam: from Religion to Revolution*, Princeton 1997.

—, 'Der Treuhändler Gottes. Die Edikte des Kalifen al-Ḥākim', *Der Islam* 63, 1986, 11–72.

Hamdani, H. F., 'On the Genealogy of the Fatimid Caliphs', Publications of the American University of Cairo, School of Oriental Studies, Occasional Paper, no. 1, Cairo 1958.

al-Hamdānī (d. 521/1127), *Takmilat Taʾrīkh al-Ṭabarī*, second printing, Beirut 1961.

Hamidullah, M., *Muslim Conduct of State*, 7th edn, Lahore 1977.

—, 'Règne conjoint. La théorie et la pratique islamiques', *Rivista degli Studi Orientali* 28, 1953, 99–104.

Ḥamza al-Iṣbahānī (d. before 360/970), *Tawārīkh sinī mulūk al-arḍ wa'l-anbiyāʾ*, ed. and tr. (Latin) J. M. P. Gottwaldt, 2 vols, Leipzig 1844, 1848; ed. (with *Taʾrīkh* for *Tawārīkh* in the title) Beirut 1961. I have used the Beirut edition, but also refer to Gottwaldt's edition in parenthesis, marked G.

Haq, S. N., 'Islam', in D. Jamieson (ed.), *A Companion to Environmental Philosophy*, Oxford 2001, ch. 8.

al-Harthamī (fl. c. 820) (attrib.), *Mukhtaṣar siyāsat al-ḥurūb*, ed. ʿA.-R. ʿAwn and M. M. Ziyāda, Cairo 1964.

Hartmann, A., *An-Nāṣir li-dīn Allāh (1180–1225). Politik, Religion, Kultur in der späten Abbasidenzeit*, Berlin 1975.

Harvey, S., 'The Place of the Philosopher in the City According to Ibn Bājja', in C. E. Butterworth (ed.), *The Political Aspects of Islamic Philosophy. Essays in Honor of Muhsin S. Mahdi*, Cambridge, MA 1992, ch. 7.

Hawting, G. R., 'The Significance of the Slogan *Lā Ḥukma illā Lillāh* and the References to the *Ḥudūd* in the Traditions about the *Fitna* and the Murder of ʿUthmān', *Bulletin of the School of Oriental and African Studies* 41, 1978, 453–63.

Haykel, B. A., 'Order and Righteousness: Muḥammad ʿAlī al-Shawkānī and the Nature of the Islamic State in Yemen', unpublished D.Phil., Oxford 1997.

Heck, P., *The Construction of Knowledge in Islamic Civilization: Qudāma b. Jaʿfar and his Kitāb al-kharāj wa-ṣināʿat al-kitāba*, Leiden 2002.

Heemskerk, M. T., *Suffering in the Muʿtazilite Theology*, Leiden 2000.

Henry III, P., 'A Mirror for Justinian: The *Ekthesis* of Agapetus Diaconus', *Greek, Roman and Byzantine Studies* 8, 1967, 281–308.

Hillenbrand, C., 'Islamic Orthodoxy or Realpolitik? Al-Ghazālī's Views on Government', *Iran* 26, 1988, 81–93.

Hiyari, M., 'Qudāma b. Ǧaʿfar's Behandlung der Politik: Das Kapitel *As-siyāsa* aus seinem Vademecum für Sekretäre *Kitāb al-ḫarāǧ wa-ṣanāʿat al-kitāba*', *Der Islam* 60, 1983, 91–103.

Hobbes, T. (d. 1679), *Leviathan*, London 1994 (first published London 1651).

Hodgson, M. G. S., 'How did the Early Shīʿa become Sectarian?', *Journal of the American Oriental Society* 75, 1955, 1–13.

—, *The Order of Assassins*, the Hague 1955.

—, *The Venture of Islam*, 3 vols, Chicago 1974.

Howard-Johnson, J., 'The Official History of Heraclius' Persian Campaigns', in E. Dąbrowa (ed.), *The Roman and Byzantine Army in the East*, Krakow 1994, 57–87.

Hoyland, R. G., *Seeing Islam as Others Saw It. A Survey and Evaluation of Christian, Jewish and Zoroastrian Writings on Early Islam*, Princeton 1997.

Hunger, H., *Prooimion, Elemente der Byzantinischen Kaiseridee in den Arengen der Urkunden*, Vienna 1965.

IAH = Ibn Abī 'l-Ḥadīd (d. 655/1257), *Sharḥ nahj al-balāgha*, ed. M. A.-F. Ibrāhīm, Cairo 1965–7.

Ibish, Y., *The Political Doctrine of Al-Baqillani*, Beirut 1966.

Ibn ʿAbd al-Ḥakam (d. 257/871), *Sīrat ʿUmar b. ʿAbd al-ʿAzīz*, ed. A. ʿUbayd, 2nd printing, Damascus 1954.

Ibn ʿAbd Rabbih (d. 328/940), *al-ʿIqd al-farīd*, ed. A. A. Amīn, A. al-Zayn, and I. al-Abyārī, 7 vols, Cairo 1940–53 (cited as *ʿIqd*).

Ibn ʿAbdūn (late eleventh/early twelfth century), 'Risāla fī 'l-qaḍāʾ wa'l-ḥisba', ed. É. Lévi-Provençal in his *Trois traités hispaniques de ḥisba*, Cairo 1955; tr. É. Lévi-Provençal, *Séville musulmane au début du xiie siècle*, Paris 1947.

Ibn Abī 'l-Ḥadīd: see IAH.

Ibn Abī 'l-Rabīʿ (c. 650/1250?), *Sulūk al-mālik fī tadbīr al-mamālik*, Cairo 1329.

Ibn Abī Shayba (d. 235/849), *al-Muṣannaf*, ed. ʿA.-Kh. Khān al-Afghānī, 15 vols, Hyderabad 1386–1403.

Ibn Abī Uṣaybiʿa (d. 668/1270), *ʿUyūn al-anbāʾ fī ṭabaqāt al-aṭibbāʾ*, ed. A. Müller, 2 vols, Königsberg 1884 (repr. 1972).

Ibn ʿAsākir (d. 571/1176), *Taʾrīkh madīnat Dimashq*, vol. ix, ed. ʿA. Shīrī, Damascus n.d.

Ibn al-Athīr (d. 630/1233), *al-Kāmil fī 'l-taʾrīkh*, ed. C. J. Tornberg Leiden 1851–76, reprinted (with different pagination) Beirut, 12 vols, 1965–7. References are to the Beirut reprint unless otherwise specified.

Ibn Bābawayh (d. 381/991), *Risālat al-iʿtiqād*, Najaf 1343 = *A Shīʿite Creed*, tr. A. A. A. Fyzee, Oxford 1942.

—, *ʿIlal al-sharāʾiʿ* [Najaf 1966].

—, *ʿUyūn akhbār al-Riḍā*, ed. M. al-Ḥusaynī al-Lājawardī, 2 vols, Tehran n.d.
Ibn Bājja (d. 533/1139), *Risālat al-wadāʿ*, in M. Fakhrī (ed.), *Rasāʾil Ibn Bājja al-ilāhiyya*, Beirut 1968.
—, *Tadbīr al-mutawaḥḥid*, ed. M. A. Palacios, Madrid 1946; ed. M. Fakhrī, *Rasāʾil Ibn Bājja al-ilāhiyya*, Beirut 1968 (references are to the folio number of the unique manuscript given in both editions); partial tr. L. Berman in Lerner and Mahdi, *Sourcebook*, ch. 8.
Ibn Baṭṭa (d. 387/997), *La Profession de foi d'Ibn Baṭṭa*, ed. and tr. H. Laoust, Damascus 1958.
Ibn al-Dawādārī (d. after 736/1335), *Kanz al-durar wa-jāmiʿ al-ghurar*, vol. vi, ed. Ṣ.-D. al-Munajjid, Cairo 1961.
Ibn al-Dāya, Aḥmad b. Yūsuf (d. c. 330–40/941–51), K. *al-ʿuhūd al-yūnāniyya al-mustakhraja min rumūz kitāb al-siyāsa li-Aflaṭūn*, in ʿA.-R. Badawī (ed.), *al-Uṣūl al-yūnāniyya li'l-naẓariyyāt al-siyāsiyya fī 'l-islām*, Cairo 1954.
Ibn Ḥajar (d. 852/1449), *Rafʿ al-iṣr ʿan quḍāt al-Miṣr*, in al-Kindī, *The Governors and Judges of Egypt*, ed. R. Guest, Leiden and London 1912, 501–614.
—, *Tahdhīb al-tahdhīb*, 12 vols, Hyderabad 1325–27.
Ibn Ḥamdūn (d. 562/1167), *al-Tadhkira al-ḥamdūniyya*, ed. I. ʿAbbās and B. ʿAbbās, 10 vols, Beirut 1996
Ibn Ḥanbal, Aḥmad (d. 241/855), *al-Musnad*, 5 vols, Cairo 1895.
—, K. *al-zuhd*, ed. M. J. Sharaf, Beirut 1981.
Ibn Ḥawqal (d. after 362/973), K. *ṣūrat al-arḍ*, ed. J. H. Kramers, Leiden 1967.
Ibn Ḥazm (d. 456/1064), K. *al-faṣl fī 'l-milal wa'l-ahwāʾ wa'l-niḥal*, 5 vols in 2, Cairo 1317–21. Normally transliterated as K. *al-fiṣal*, but there does not seem to be any such word (allegedly a plural of *faṣla*), and two rhyming words was the norm in titles, not three. That K. *al-faṣl* is the correct form is persuasively argued by G. Ḥ. Āasī, 'Muslim Understanding of Other Religions: an Analytical Study of Ibn Ḥazm's *Kitāb al-faṣl fī al-Milal wa al-Ahwāʾ wa al-Nihal*', PhD Dissertation, Temple University 1986, 76ff. (drawn to by attention by Camilla Adang).
—, *Jamharat ansāb al-ʿarab*, ed. ʿA.-S. M. Hārun, Cairo 1962.
—, *al-Muḥallā*, ed. M. Shākir, 11 vols, Cairo 1928–33.
Ibn Hishām (d. 218/833 or earlier), *al-Sīra al-nabawiyya*, ed. M. al-Saqqā, I. al-Abyārī and ʿA.-Ḥ. Shalabī, 2 vols, 2nd printing, Cairo 1955.
Ibn ʿIdhārī (wrote c. 712/1312f.), K. *al-bayān al-mughrib*, ed. G. S. Colin and É. Lévi-Provençal, 2 vols, Leiden 1948–51.
Ibn Idrīs al-Ḥillī, Muḥammad (d. 598/1202), K. *al-sarāʾir*, 3 vols, Qum AH 1410.
Ibn al-Jawzī (d. 597/1200), *al-Muntaẓam*, vols v–x, Hyderabad 1357–9 (the edition used unless otherwise indicated); ed. Muḥammad and Muṣtafā al-Qādir ʿAṭā, 18 vols, Beirut 1992–3.
—, *Sīrat ʿUmar b. ʿAbd al-ʿAzīz*, ed. M.-D. al-Khaṭīb, Cairo 1331.
—, *al-Shifāʾ fī mawāʾiẓ al-mulūk wa'l-khulafāʾ*, ed. F. ʿAbd al-Munʿim Aḥmad, Alexandria 1978.
—, *Talbīs al-iblīs*, ed. M. M. al-Dimashqī [Cairo 1928]; tr. D. S. Margoliouth, [4th instalment] *Islamic Culture* 9, 1935, 87–109.
Ibn Kathīr (d. 774/1373) *al-Bidāya wa'l-nihāya,* ed. ʿA. M. Muʿawwaḍ and ʿA. A. ʿA. al-Mawjūd, vol. xiii, Beirut 1994.

—, *Tafsīr al-Qur'ān al-ʿaẓīm*, 4 vols, Cairo n.d.
Ibn Khaldūn (d. 808/1406), *al-Muqaddima*, ed. M. Quatremère, 3 vols, Paris 1858; ed. Beirut n.d.; (references are to the Beirut edition unless otherwise indicated); tr. F. Rosenthal, *The Muqaddimah*, 3 vols, 2nd edn, Princeton 1967.
Ibn al-Muqaffaʿ (d. c. 140/757), *al-Adab al-Kabīr* and *al-Risāla fī 'l-ṣaḥāba*, in *al-Majmūʿa al-kāmila li-mu'allafāt ʿAbdallāh b. al-Muqaffaʿ*, Beirut 1978 (cited by page); ed. and tr. Pellat, *Ibn al-Muqaffaʿ, 'Conseilleur' du Calife*, Paris 1976 (cited as P, by paragraph). For the fragments of his *Yatīma*, see M. Kurd ʿAlī, *Rasā'il al-bulaghā'*, Cairo 1946.
Ibn al-Murtaḍā (d. 840/1437), *Ṭabaqāt al-muʿtazila*, ed. S. Diwald-Wilzer, Beirut 1961.
Ibn al-Nadīm (d. 380/990), *Kitāb al-Fihrist*, ed. R. Tajaddud, Tehran 1971; tr. B. Dodge, *The Fihrist of Ibn al-Nadīm*, 2 vols with continuous pagination, New York 1970.
Ibn Qayyim al-Jawziyya (d. 715/1350), *Madārij al-sālikīn*, ed. M. Ḥ. al-Fiqī, 3 vols, Cairo 1955–6.
Ibn Qiba (d. before 319/931): see Modarressi.
Ibn al-Qifṭī (d. 646/1248), *Ta'rīkh al-ḥukamā'*, ed. J. Lippert, Leizig 1903.
Ibn Qutayba (d. 276/889), *K. al-ʿarab*, in Kurd ʿAlī, *Rasā'il al-bulaghā'* (q.v.).
—, (attrib.), *al-Imāma wa'l-siyāsa*: see Pseudo-Ibn Qutayba.
—, *al-Maʿārif*, ed. Th. ʿUkāsha, 2nd printing, Cairo 1969.
—, *K. al-Shiʿr wa'l-shuʿarā'*, ed. A. Shākir, 2 vols, Cairo 1966–7.
—, *Ta'wīl mukhtalif al-ḥadīth*, ed. M. Z. al-Najjār, Beirut 1966.
—, *ʿUyūn al-akhbār*, 4 vols, Cairo 1925–30.
Ibn Riḍwān (d. 453/1061): see Gamal and Dols.
Ibn Rushd (d. 595/1198), *Averroes' Commentary on Plato's 'Republic'*, ed. and tr. E. I. J. Rosenthal, Cambridge 1956; tr. R. Lerner, Ithaca and London 1974. I have used both translations, usually preferring Lerner's. References are to Rosenthal's text and translation, with no separate reference to Lerner's since it preserves the pagination of Rosenthal's text in the margin.
—, *Bidāyat al-Mujtahid*, ed. M. S. Muḥaysin and Sh. M. Ismāʿīl, 2 vols, Cairo 1970; tr. A. K. Nyazee and M. A. Rauf, 2 vols, Reading 1994–6 (not used).
—, *Compendio de Metafísica*, ed. C. Q. Rodriguez, Cordoba 1998.
—, *Talkhīṣ al-khaṭāba*, ed. M. S. Sālim, Cairo 1967; ed. and tr. M. Aouad, 3 vols, Paris 2002.
Ibn Saʿd (d. 230/845), *al-Ṭabaqāt*, ed. E. Sachau, 9 vols, Leiden 1904–40; ed. Beirut, 5 vols, 1957–60. The volumes cover the same sections in the two editions (except that some of Sachau's are divided into two parts), but the paginations differ. References are to the Sachau edition, with the different page numbers of the Beirut edition in parenthesis, marked B.
Ibn Ṣaghīr (wrote prob. c. 290/903), 'Chronique d'Ibn Ṣaghīr sur les imams rostemides de Tahert', ed. and tr. A. de C. Motylinski in *Actes du XIVe Congrès International des Orientalistes, Alger 1905*, iii, Paris 1908, 3–132.
Ibn Shahrāshūb (d. 588/1192), *Manāqib ʿAlī b. Abī Ṭālib*, ed. Y. al-Biqāʿī, 2nd printing, 5 vols, Beirut 1991.
Ibn al-Simnānī, see al-Simnānī.
Ibn Sīnā (d. 428/1037), *Rīṭūriqā = K. al-majmūʿ (aw al-ḥikma al-ʿarūḍiyya) fī maʿānī kitāb rīṭūrīqā*, ed. M. S. Sālim, Cairo n.d. (preface dated 1950).
—, *SI*, *x* = *al-Shifā'*: *al-Ilāhiyyāt*, ii (*al-maqāla al-ʿāshira*), ed. I. Madkūr, Cairo 1960; tr. M. E. Marmura, 'Healing: Metaphysics X', in R. Lerner and M. Mahdi, *Medieval Political Philosophy: a Sourcebook*, New York 1963, ch. 6.

—, *SM, viii* = *al-Shifāʾ: al-manṭiq*, viii (*al-khaṭāba*), ed. I. Madkūr, Cairo 1954.
Ibn Taghrībirdī (d. 874/1469f), *al-Nujūm al-zāhira fī mulūk Miṣr wa'l-Qāhira*, 16 vols, Cairo 1929–72.
Ibn Taymiyya (d. 728/1328), *al-Ḥisba fī 'l-islām*, Cairo 1387 = *Public Duties in Islam*, tr. M. Holland, London 1982.
—, *Minhāj al-sunna al-nabawiyya fī naqḍ kalām al-shīʿa al-qadariyya*, ed. M. R. Sālim, Cairo 1962.
—, *al-Siyāsa al-sharʿiyya*, Kuwait 1986.
Ibn al-Ṭiqṭaqā (wrote 701/1302), *al-Fakhrī*, ed. H. Derenbourg, Paris 1895 (ed. Cairo, n.d.); tr. C. E. J. Whitting, *Al Fakhri*, London 1947 (preserves Derenbourg's pagination).
Ibn Ṭufayl (d. 581/1185f), *Ḥayy b. Yaqẓān*, Beirut 1963; tr. L. E. Goodman, New York 1972.
Ibn al-Ukhuwwa (d. 729/1329), *K. maʿālim al-qurba fī aḥkām al-ḥisba*, Cairo 1976.
Ibn Wahb al-kātib (wrote c. 335/946), *Kitāb al-burhān fī wujūh al-bayān*, ed. A. Maṭlūb and Kh. al-Ḥadīthī, Baghdad 1967.
Ibn al-Wazīr (d. 840/1436), *Hidāyat al-afkār*, MS, British Library, Or. 3792.
Ibn Ẓāfir al-Azdī (d. 613/1216), *Akhbār al-duwal al-munqaṭiʿa*, ed. A. Ferré, Cairo 1972.
Idris, J. S., 'Is man the Vicegerent of God?', *Journal of Islamic Studies* 1, 1990, 99–110.
al-Ījī (d. 756/1355), *Kitāb al-mawāqif*, vol. viii, Cairo 1907.
Ikhwān al-Ṣafā: see *RIS*.
al-Imāma wa'l-siyāsa: see Pseudo-Ibn Qutayba.
Inalcik, H., 'Turkish and Iranian Political Theories and Traditions in the Kutadgu Bilig', in his *The Middle East and the Balkans under the Ottoman Empire*, Bloomington 1993
ʿIqd: see Ibn ʿAbd Rabbih.
al-ʿIrāqī: see Zayn al-Dīn.
Iṣbahānī: see Abū 'l-Faraj al-Iṣbahānī and Pseudo-Iṣbahānī.
al-Iskāfī (d. 421/1030), *Kitāb luṭf al-tadbīr*, ed. A. ʿAbd al-Bāqī, Baghdad 1964.
al-Iṣṭakhrī (wrote c. 340/951), *Masālik al-mamālik*, ed. M. J. de Goeje, Leiden 1870.
Ivanow, W., *Nasir-i Khusraw and Ismailism*, Leiden and Bombay 1948.
—, (ed.), 'K. istitār al-imām', in *Bulletin of the Faculty of Arts of the University of Egypt* 4, 1936, 93–107; tr. in W. Ivanow, *Ismaili Traditions Concerning the Rise of the Fatimids*, Oxford 1942, 157–83.
—, *Studies in Early Persian Ismailism*, Bombay 1955.
Jaʿfar b. Manṣūr al-Yaman (fourth/tenth century), *Sarāʾir wa-asrār al-nuṭaqāʾ*, ed. M. Ghālib, Beirut 1984. There is also a partial edition and translation (from al-Bāqir onwards) in W. Ivanow (ed. and tr.), *Ismaili Tradition concerning the Rise of the Fatimids*, Oxford 1942.
—, (attrib.), *Kitāb al-kashf*, ed. R. Strothmann, Islamic Research Association Series, no. 13, London 1953; ed. M. Ghālib, Beirut 1984 (cited in parenthesis as G).
—, *The Master and the Disciple*, tr. J. W. Morris, London 2001.
al-Jāḥiẓ (d. 255/869), *al-Bayān wa'l-tabyīn*, ed. ʿA.-S. M. Hārūn, 2nd printing, Cairo 1960–1.
—, *K. al-Ḥayawān*, ed. ʿA.-S. M. Hārūn, 7 vols, Cairo 1938–58.
—, 'al-Jawābāt wa-istiḥqāq al-imāma', in his *Rasāʾil*, vol. iv, 285–307.
—, 'al-Maʿāsh wa'l-maʿād', in his *Rasāʾil*, vol. i, 91–134.
—, 'Manāqib al-Turk', in his *Rasāʾil*, vol. i, 5–134.

—, 'Maqālāt al-Zaydiyya wa'l-Rāfiḍa', (also known as 'Bayān madhāhib al-shīʿa') in his *Rasāʾil*, vol. iv, 311–324.
—, 'Fī 'l-nābita', in his *Rasāʾil*, vol. ii, 7–23.
—, 'al-Nisāʾ', in his *Rasāʾil*, vol. iii, 139–59.
—, *Rasāʾil*, ed. ʿA.-S. M. Hārūn, 4 vols, Cairo 1964–79.
—, 'Risāla fī 'l-ḥakamayn', ed. C. Pellat, *al-Mashriq* 52, 1958, 417–91
—, (attrib.), *Tāj*: see Pseudo-Jāḥiẓ.
al-Jahshiyārī (d. 331/942), *Kitāb al-wuzarāʾ wa'l-kuttāb*, ed. M. al-Saqqā and others, Cairo 1938.
al-Jaṣṣāṣ (d. 370/981), *Aḥkām al-Qurʾān*, 3 vols, Beirut 1994.
Johansen, B., 'Eigentum, Familie und Obrigkeit im Hanafitischen Strafrecht', in his *Contingency in a Sacred Law*, Leiden 1999, 349–420 (reprinted with new pagination from *Die Welt des Islams* 19, 1979).
—, 'La mise en scene du vol par les jurists musulmans', in M. P. di Bella (ed.), *Vols et Sanctions en Mediterranee*, Amsterdam 1998, 41–74.
—, 'Sacred and Religious Element[s] in Hanafite Law', in E. Gellner and J.-C. Vatin (eds), *Islam et Politique au Maghreb*, Paris 1981, 281–301.
Judah Halevi (wrote 1140), *Kitāb al-radd wa'l-dalīl fī 'l-dīn al-dhalīl (al-Kitāb al-Khazarī)*, ed. D. H. Baneth and H. Ben-Shammai, Jerusalen 1977 = *Book of Kuzari*, tr. H. Hirschfeld, New York 1946.
al-Juwaynī, Abū 'l-Maʿālī (d. 478/1085), *Ghiyāth al-umam fī 'ltiyāth al-ẓulam*, ed. ʿAbd al-ʿAẓīm al-Dīb, 2nd edn, Cairo 1401/1981f. The edition by Kh. al-Manṣūr, Beirut 1997, preserves the paragraph numbering of al-Dīb's edition.
—, *K. al-Irshād ilā qawāṭiʿ al-adilla fī uṣūl al-iʿtiqād*, ed. M. Y. Mūsā and ʿA. ʿA.-M. ʿAbd al-Ḥamīd, Cairo 1950.
K. = *Kitāb*.
Karamustafa, A. T., *God's Unruly Friends. Dervish Groups in the Islamic Later Middle Period, 1200–1550*, Salt Lake City, 1994.
Kāshif, S. I. (ed.), *al-Siyar wa'l-jawābāt li-ʿulamāʾ wa-aʾimmat ʿumān*, 2 vols, Cairo 1986.
Kay Kāʾūs (wrote 475/1082), *Qābūsnāma*, tr. R. Levy, *A Mirror for Princes*, London 1951.
Kelsay, J., and J. J. Turner Johnson (eds), *Just War and Jihad. Historical and Theoretical Perspectives on War and Peace in Western and Islamic Traditions*, New York 1991.
Kennedy, E. S., 'The World Year Concept in Islamic Astrology', *Proceedings of the Tenth International Congress of the History of Science*, Paris 1964, 23–43 (reprinted in his *Studies in the Islamic Exact Sciences*, ed. D. A. King and M. H. Kennedy, Beirut 1983, 351–68). References are to the original pagination.
Khadduri, M., *The Islamic Conception of Justice*, Baltimore and London 1984.
—, *War and Peace in the Law of Islam*, Baltimore 1955.
Khalīfa b. Khayyāṭ (d. 240/854, or 230 or 240), *Taʾrīkh*, ed. S. Zakkār, Damascus 1967–8
al-Khaṭīb al-Baghdādī (d. 463/1071), *Sharaf aṣḥāb al-ḥadīth*, ed. M. S. Haṭîboğlu, Ankara 1972.
—, *Taʾrīkh Baghdād*, 14 vols, Cairo 1931 (abbreviated as *TB*).
Khomeini, *Islam and Revolution. Writings and Declarations of Imam Khomeini*, tr. H. Algar, Berkeley 1981.
al-Kirmānī, Ḥamīd al-Dīn (d. 412/1021), 'al-Risāla al-wāʿiẓa', in *Majmūʾ at rasāʾil al-Kirmānī*, ed. M. Ghālib, Beirut 1983.

al-Kisāʾī (unknown), *Qiṣaṣ al-anbiyāʾ, ed. I. Eisenberg, Leiden 1922.*
Kister, M. J., 'Land Property and *Jihād*', *Journal of the Economic and Social History of the Orient* 34, 1991, 270–311.
Kitāb al-irjāʾ, see Ess, van J.
Kitāb al-rushd, ed. M. K. Hussein in The Ismaili Society, *Collectanea*, vol. i, Leiden 1948, 185–213; tr. W. Ivanow, *Studies in Early Persian Ismailism*, 2nd edn, Bombay 1955, 29–59.
Kiyā al-Ḥarrāsī (d. 504/1110), *Aḥkām al-Qurʾān*, ed. M. M. ʿAlī and ʿI. ʿA. ʿI. ʿAṭiyya, Cairo 1974–5.
Kohlberg, E., 'Abū Turāb', *Bulletin of the School of Oriental and African Studies* 41, 1978, 347–52.
—, 'The Development of the Imāmī Shīʿī Doctrine of *Jihād*', *Zeitschrift der Deutschen Morgenländischen Gesellschaft* 126, 1976, 64–86.
—, 'Imam and Community in the Pre-Ghayba Period', in S. A. Arjomand (ed.), *Authority and Political Culture in Shiʿism*, Albany 1988, ch. 2.
—, 'From Imāmiyya to Ithnā-ʿashariyya', *Bulletin of the School of Oriental and African Studies* 39, 1976, 521–34.
—, *A Medieval Muslim Scholar at Work. Ibn Ṭāwūs and his Library*, Leiden 1992.
—, 'Medieval Muslim Views on Martyrdom', *Koninklijke Nederlandse Akademie van Wetenschappen*, NR, part 60, no. 7, 1997, 281–307.
—, 'In Praise of the Few', in *Studies in Islamic and Middle Eastern Texts and Traditions in Memory of Norman Calder*, ed. G. R. Hawting, J. A. Mojaddedi, and A. Samely, Oxford 2000, 149–62.
—, 'Some Imāmī Shīʿī Views on the *Ṣaḥāba*', *Jerusalem Studies in Arabic and Islam* 5, 1984, 143–75.
—, 'Some Zaydī Views on the Companions of the Prophet', *Bulletin of the School of Oriental and African Studies* 39, 1976, 91–8.
—, 'Taqiyya in Shīʿī Theology and Religion', in H. G. Kippenberg and G. G. Stroumsa (eds), *Secrecy and Concealment, Studies in the History of Mediterranean and Near Eastern Religions*, Leiden 1995, 345–80.
Kraemer, J., 'The *Jihād* of the *Falāsifa*', *Jerusalem Studies in Arabic and Islam* 10, 1987, 288–324.
—, *Philosophy in the Renaissance of Islam*, Leiden 1986.
Kraus, P., 'Beiträge zur islamischen Ketzergeschichte. Das *Kitāb az-Zumurrud* des Ibn ar-Rāwandī', *Rivista degli Studi Orientali* 14, 1933, 93–129, 335–79.
—, 'Zu Ibn al-Muqaffaʿ', *Rivista degli Studi Orientali* 14, 1934, 1–20.
al-Kulīnī (d. 329/941), *al-Kāfī*, ed. ʿA. A. al-Ghaffārī, 8 vols, Tehran 1381.
al-Kumayt b. Zayd (d. 126/743), *Die Hāšimijjāt des Kumait*, ed. and tr. J. Horovitz, Leiden 1904.
Kurd ʿAlī, M. (ed.), *Rasāʾil al-bulaghāʾ*, 2nd printing, Cairo 1954.
Kuthayyir ʿAzza (d. 105/723), *Dīwān*, ed. and tr. H. Pérès, 2 vols, Algiers and Paris 1928–30.
Lactantius (d. c. 320), *The Divine Institutes*, books i–vii, tr. M. F. McDonald, Washington 1964.
Lalani, A. R., *Early Shīʿī Thought. The Teachings of Imam Muḥammad al-Bāqir*, London 2000.

Lambton, A. K. S., 'The Dilemma of Government in Islamic Persia: the *Siyāsat-nāma* of Niẓām al-Mulk', *Iran* 22, 1984, 55–66.
—, 'The Internal Structure of the Saljuq Empire', in *The Cambridge History of Iran*, vol. v, ed. J. A. Boyle, Cambridge 1968, 203–82.
—, 'Islamic Mirrors for Princes', in *Atti del Convegno Internazionale sul Tema: La Persia nel Mediovo*, Rome 1971, 419–42.
—, 'Justice in the Medieval Persian Theory of Kingship', *Studia Islamica* 17, 1962, 91–119.
—, *State and Government in Medieval Islam*, Oxford 1981.
Lameer, J., *Al-Fārābī and Aristotelian Syllogistics*, Leiden 1994.
Land, J. P. N. (ed. with a Latin tr.), *Anecdota Syriaca*, vol. iv, Leiden 1875.
Landau-Tasseron, E., 'The "Cyclical Reform": a Study of the *Mujaddid* Traditions', *Studia Islamica* 70, 1989, 79–117.
Laoust, H., *La politique de Ġazālī*, Paris 1970.
Laugier de Beaurecueil, S. de, *Khwāja ʿAbdullāh Anṣārī*, Beirut 1965.
Leaman, O., 'Ibn Bājja on Society and Philosophy', *Der Islam* 57, 1980, 109–19.
Lecker, M., 'Biographical Notes on Ibn Shihāb al-Zuhrī', *Journal of Semitic Studies*, 41, 1996, 21–63.
Lecomte, G., *Ibn Qutayba. L'homme et son oeuvre, ses idées*, Damascus 1965.
Leder, S., 'Aspekte arabischer und persischer Fürstenspiegel', in *Erlesenes*, ed. W. Beltz and S. Günther (*Hallesche Beiträge zur Orientwissenschaft* 25), Halle 1998, 120–51 (also in A. de Benedictis (ed.), *Specula principum*, Frankfurt 1999).
Lerner, R., and M. Mahdi, *Medieval Political Philosophy: a Sourcebook*, Glencoe 1963.
Lev, Y., *State and Society in Fatimid Egypt*, Leiden 1991.
Lewis, B., (tr.), *Islam from the Prophet Muhammad to the Capture of Constantinople*, 2 vols, Oxford 1974.
—, *The Jews of Islam*, London 1984.
—, *The Political Language of Islam*, Chicago and London 1988.
—, *Race and Slavery in the Middle East*, Oxford 1990.
—, 'The Regnal Titles of the First Abbasid Caliphs', *Dr. Zakir Husain Presentation Volume*, New Delhi 1968, 13–22.
Lindholm, C., *The Islamic Middle East. An Historical Anthropology*, Oxford 1996.
—, 'Kinship Structure and Political Authority: the Middle East and Central Asia', *Comparative Studies in Society and History* 28, 1986, 334–55.
—, 'Quandaries of Command in Egalitarian Societies: Examples from Swat and Morocco', in J. Cole (ed.), *Comparing Muslim Societies: Knowledge and the State in a World Civilization*, Ann Arbor 1992, 63–94.
Little, D., 'A New Look at *al-Aḥkām al-Sulṭāniyya*', *The Muslim World* 64, 1974, 1–15.
Lovejoy, A. O., and G. Boas, *Primitivism and Related Ideas in Antiquity*, Baltimore and London 1935 (repr. 1997).
Luther (d. 1546), 'On Secular Authority', in H. Höpfl (tr.), *Luther and Calvin on Secular Authority*, Cambridge 1991.
al-Maʿarrī: see Nicholson.
Macdonald, D. B., *Development of Muslim Theology, Jurisprudence and Constitutional Theory*, New York 1903 (repr. Beirut 1965).
Madelung, W., 'Abū 'l-ʿAmayṭar the Sufyānī', *Jerusalem Studies in Arabic and Islam* 24, 2000, 327–42.

—, 'The Account of the Ismāʿīlīs in *Firaq al-Shīʿa*', in Stern, *Studies* (q.v.), 47–55.
—, (ed.), *Arabic Texts Concerning the History of the Zaydī Imāms*, Beirut 1987.
—, 'The Assumption of the Title Shāhānshāh by the Būyids and 'the Reign of the Daylam (*Dawlat al-Daylam*)', *Journal of Near Eastern Studies* 28, 1969, 84–108, 169–83.
—, 'Authority in Twelver Shiism in the Absence of the Imam', in G. Makdisi, D. Sourdel, and J. Sourdel-Thomine (eds), *La notion de'authorité au moyen âge*, Paris 1982, 163–73.
—, 'Fatimiden und Baḥrainqarmaṭen', *Der Islam* 34, 1959, 34–88; tr. A. Azodi, 'The Fatimids and the Qarmaṭīs of Baḥrayn', in F. Daftary (ed.), *Mediaeval Ismaʿili History and Thought*, Cambridge 1996, ch. 2 (omits the original pagination). Cited in that order, separated by a slash.
—, 'Frühe muʿtazilitische Häresiographie?': see Pseudo-Nāshiʾ.
—, 'The Hāshimiyyāt of al-Kumayt and Hāshimī Shiʿism', *Studia Islamica* 70, 1989, 5–26.
—, 'Has the *Hijra* come to an End?', *Revue des Etudies Islamiques* 54, 1986, 225–37.
—, *Der Imam al-Qāsim ibn Ibrāhīm und die Glaubenslehre der Zaiditen*, Berlin 1965.
—, 'Das Imamat in der frühen ismailitischen Lehre', *Der Islam* 37, 1961, 43–135.
—, 'Naṣīr al-Dīn Ṭūsī's Ethics between Philosophy, Shiʿism, and Sufism', in R. G. Hovannisian (ed.), *Ethics in Islam*, Malibu 1985, 85–101.
—, 'New Documents concerning al-Maʾmūn, al-Faḍl b. Sahl and ʿAlī al-Riḍā', in *Studia Arabica et Islamica. Festschrift for Iḥsān ʿAbbās*, ed. W. al-Qāḍī, Beirut 1981.
—, *Religious Trends in Early Islamic Iran*, Albany 1988, 333–46.
—, 'Shiite Discussions of the Legality of the *Kharāj*', in *Proceedings of the Ninth Congress of the Union Européenne des Arabisants et Islamisants*, ed. R. Peters, Leiden 1981, 193–202.
—, *The Succession to Muḥammad*, Cambridge 1997.
—, 'The Sufyānī between Tradition and History', *Studia Islamica* 63, 1984, 5–48.
—, 'A Treatise of the Sharīf al-Murtaḍā on the Legality of Working for the Government', *Bulletin of the School of Oriental and African Studies* 43, 1980, 18–31.
—, and P. E. Walker (eds and trs), *The Advent of the Fatimids. A Contemporary Shiʿi Witness: Ibn al-Haytham's Kitāb al-Munāẓarāt*, London 2000.
al-Maghnīsāwī (wrote 939/1532), *Sharḥ al-fiqh al-akbar*, in *al-Rasāʾil al-sabʿa fī 'l-ʿaqāʾid*, 3rd printing, Hyderabad 1980; tr. Wensinck, *Creed* (q.v.).
Mahdi, M., 'Alfarabi', in L. Strauss and J. Cropsey (eds), *History of Political Philosophy*, Chicago 1963, 160–80.
—, *Alfarabi and the Foundation of Islamic Political Philosophy*, Chicago 2001.
—, 'Al-Fārābī's Imperfect State', *Journal of the American Oriental Society* 110, 1990, 691–725.
—, 'Alfarabi', in *Encyclopaedia Iranica*.
Maḥmaṣānī, Ṣ., *al-Awzāʿī wa-taʿlīmuhu al-insāniyya wa'l-qānūniyya*, Beirut 1978.
al-Majālis al-mustanṣiriyya, see al-Malījī.
Makdisi, G., 'Autograph Diary of an Eleventh-Century Historian of Baghdād', II–III, *Bulletin of the School of Oriental and African Studies* 18, 1956, 239–60; 19, 1957, 13–48.
—, *Ibn ʿAqil et la résurgence de l'Islam traditionaliste au XIe siècle*, Damascus 1963.
—, *Ibn ʿAqil. Religion and Culture in Classical Islam*, Edinburgh 1997. Cited as *Ibn ʿAqil*.

—, 'The Marriage of Ṭughril Beg', *International Journal of Middle East Studies* 1, 1970, 259–75; facsimile reprint in his *History and Politics in Eleventh-Century Baghdad*, Aldershot 1990, no. 9.

—, 'Les rapports entre calife et sulṭân à l'époque saljûqide', *International Journal of Middle East Studies* 6, 1975, 228–36; facsimile reprint in his *History and Politics in Eleventh-Century Baghdad*, Aldershot 1990, no. 7.

Makdisi, U., *The Culture of Sectarianism*, Berkeley 2000.

al-Malījī (wrote 451/1059f), *al-Majālis al-mustanṣiriyya*, ed. M. K. Ḥusayn, [Cairo 1947]. On the author (not named in the publication), see Daftary, *Ismāʿīlīs*, 641, note 160.

Manzalaoui, M., 'The Pseudo-Aristotelian *Kitāb Sirr al-Asrār*', *Oriens* 23–4, 1974, 147–257.

al-Maqdisī, *Aḥsan al-taqāsīm*: see al-Muqaddasī.

al-Maqdisī, Muṭahhar b. Ṭāhir (wrote c. 355/966), *Kitāb al-badʾ waʾl-taʾrīkh*, ed. and tr. G. Huart, Paris 1899–1919 (reprinted without the translation, n.p., n.d.).

Margoliouth, D. S., 'Abū ʾl-ʿAlā al-Maʿarrī's Correspondence on Vegetarianism', *Journal of the Royal Asiatic Society* 1902, 289–332.

Mārī b. Sulaymān (mid-sixth/twelfth century) in *Maris Amri et Slibae De Patriarchis Nestorianorum Commentaria*, ed. and tr. (Latin) H. Gismondi, part i, Rome 1899.

Marín, M., 'Muslim Religious Practices in al-Andalus (2nd/8th–4th/10th Centuries)', in S. Kh. Jayyusi (ed.), *The Legacy of Muslim Spain*, Leiden 1994, 878–94.

—, '*Šūrā* et *ahl al-Šūrā* dans al-Andalus', *Studia Islamica* 62, 1985, 25–51.

Marín-Guzman, R., 'The Causes of the Revolt of ʿUmar ibn Ḥafṣūn in al-Andalus (880–928)', *Arabica* 42, 1995, 180–221.

Markus, R. A., *Saeculum: History and Society in the Theology of St Augustine*, Cambridge 1970.

Marlow, L., *Hierarchy and Egalitarianism in Islamic Thought*, Cambridge 1997.

—, 'Kings, Prophets and the ʿUlamāʾ in Mediaeval Islamic Advice Literature', *Studia Islamica* 81, 1995, 101–20.

—, 'Some Classical Muslim Views of the Indian Caste System', *The Muslim World* 85, 1995, 1–22.

Marmura, M. E. , 'Avicenna's Theory of Prophecy in the Light of Ashʿarite Theology', in W. S. McCullough (ed.), *The Seed of Wisdom. Essays in Honour of T. J. Meek*, Toronto 1964, 159–78.

—, 'The Islamic Philosophers' Conception of Islam', in R. G. Hovannisian and S. Vryonis (eds), *Islam's Understanding of Itself*, Malibu 1983, 87–102.

—, 'The Philosopher and Society: Some Medieval Arabic Discussions', *Arab Studies Quarterly* 1, 1979, 309–23.

Marquet, Y., 'La Tolérance dans l'Ismailisme médiéval', in U. Vermeulen and D. de Smet (eds.), *Philosophy and Arts in the Islamic World*, Leiden 1998, 209–18.

al-Masʿūdī (d. 345/956 or 346), *Murūj al-dhahab* (cited as MM) ed. C. Barbier de Meynard and A. J. B. Pavet de Courteille, Paris 1861–77 (cited by volume and page); ed. C. Pellat, Beirut 1966–79 (cited by volume and paragraph).

—, *Kitāb al-tanbīh waʾl-ishrāf*, ed. M. J. de Goeje, Leiden 1894.

al-Māturīdī (d. 333/944), *K. al-Tawḥīd*, ed. F. Kholeif, Beirut 1970.

al-Māwardī (d. 450/1058), *Adab al-dunyā waʾl-dīn*, ed. M. al-Saqqā, Cairo 1973.

—, *K. al-aḥkām al-sulṭāniyya*, ed. M. Enger, Bonn 1853; ed. Cairo, 3rd printing, 1973; French tr. E. Fagnan, *Les Status Gouvernementaux*, Alger 1915 (repr. 1984); English tr. W. H. Wahba , *The Ordinances of Government*, Reading 1996; also A. Yate, London 1996. References are to Enger's edition, the Cairo edition and Wahba's translation in that order, in the form in the form 111/67 = 74f. No separate references are necessary for Fagnan's translation, which preserves the pagination of Enger's edition.

—, *Aʿlām al-nubuwwa*, ed. M. M. al-Baghdādī, Beirut 1987.

—, *Tafsīr al-Qurʾān*, ed Kh. M. Khiḍr, 4 vols, Kuwait 1982.

—, *Tashīl al-naẓar wa-taʿjīl al-ẓafar fī akhlāq al-malik wa-siyāsat al-mulk*, ed. R. al-Sayyid, Beirut 1987.

—, (attrib.), *Naṣīḥat al-mulūk*: see Pseudo-Māwardī.

McDermott, M. J., *The Theology of al-Shaikh al-Mufīd (d. 413/1022)*, Beirut 1978.

Meier, F., 'Über die umstrittende Pflicht des Muslims, bei nichtmuslimischer Besetzung seines Lands auszuwandern', *Der Islam* 68, 1991, 65–86.

Meisami, J. S., *Persian Historiography to the end of the Twelfth Century*, Edinburgh 1999.

—, (tr.), *The Sea of Precious Virtues (Baḥr al-Favāʾid). A Medieval Islamic Mirror for Princes*, Salt Lake City 1991.

Melchert, C., 'Religious Policies of the Caliphs from al-Mutawakkil to al-Muqtadir', *Islamic Law and Society* 3, 1996, 316–42.

Mez, A., *The Renaissance of Islam*, tr. S. Kh. Bakhsh and D. S. Margoliouth, Patna 1937.

Mikhail, H., *Politics and Revelation, Mawardi and After*, Edinburgh 1995.

Milan, P. B., 'The Golden Age and the Political Theory of Jean de Meun: a Myth in the *Rose* Scholarship', *Symposium* 23, 1969, 137–49.

Milliot, L., *Introduction à l'étude du droit musulman*, Paris 1953.

Miskawayh (d. 421/1030), *Tajārib al-umam*, in H. F. Amedroz and D. S.

Margoliouth (eds and trs), *The Eclipse of the ʿAbbāsid Caliphate*, vols i–ii, iv–v, Oxford 1920–1.

MM = see al-Masʿūdī, *Murūj*.

Modarressi, H., *Crisis and Consolidation in the Formative Period of Shīʿite Islam. Abū Jaʿfar ibn Qiba al-Rāzī and His Contribution to Imamite Shīʿite Thought*, Princeton 1993. The texts and translations are cited as Ibn Qiba, 'Ghayba' and 'Naqḍ kitāb al-ishhād', the rest of the book as Modarressi, *Crisis*.

Momen, M., *An Introduction to Shīʿi Islam*, New Haven and London 1985.

Monnot, G., *Penseurs musulmans et religions iraniennes*, Paris 1974.

Morabia, A., *Le Ǧihâd dans l'Islam médiéval. Le 'combat sacré' des origines au XIIᵉ siècle*, Paris 1993.

Morony, M. G, *Iraq after the Muslim Conquest*, Princeton 1984.

Morrall, J. B., *Political Thought in Medieval Times*, London 1958.

Morris, J. W. (ed. and tr.), *The Master and the Disciple*, London 2001.

Mottahedeh, R. P., and R. al-Sayyid, 'The Idea of *Jihād* in Islam before the Crusades', in A. E. Laiou and R. P. Mottahedeh (eds), *The Crusades from the Perspective of Byzantium and the Muslim World*, Washington 2001, 23–9.

al-Mubarrad (d. 286/900), *al-Kāmil*, ed. A. M. Shākir and Z. Mubārak, 3 vols, Cairo 1936–7; ed. W. Wright, Leipzig 1864–92. References are to the Cairo edition unless otherwise noted. References to Wright are given in parentheses, using the abbreviation W.

al-Mufīd (d. 413/1022), *K. al-irshād*, tr. I. K. A. Howard, London 1981.

—, *al-Muqniʿa*, 2nd printing, Qum 1410.
al-Muqaddasī (wrote c. 375/985), *Aḥsan al-taqāsīm fī maʿrifat al-aqālīm*, ed. M. J. de Goeje, Leiden 1906; tr. B. A. Collins, Reading 1994 (not used). The correct form of the name is Maqdisī, but since there are so many authors of that name, the old habit of calling him Muqaddasī is quite useful.
Muqātil b. Sulaymān (d. 150/767), *Tafsīr*, ed. ʿA. M. Shiḥāta, vol. i, Cairo 1979.
Murad, H. Q., '*Jabr* and *Qadar* in Early Islam: a Reappraisal of their Political and Religious Implications', in W. B. Hallaq and D. P. Little (eds.), *Islamic Studies Presented to Charles J. Adams*, Leiden 1991, 117–32.
al-Murādī (d. 489/1096), Abū Bakr Muḥammad b. al-Ḥasan al-Ḥaḍramī al-Qayrawānī, *Kitāb al-ishāra ilā adab al-imāra*, ed. R. al-Sayyid, Beirut 1981.
Muscati, J., *Life and Lectures of the Grand Missionary Al-Muayyad-Fid-Din al-Shirazi*, Karachi 1950.
Muslim b. al-Ḥajjāj (d. 261/875), *al-Ṣaḥīḥ*, 8 vols, Cairo 1916.
Nadler, R., *Die Umayyadenkalifen im Spiegel ihrer zeitgenössischen Dichter*, Inaugural-Dissertation, Erlangen-Nürnberg 1990.
Nagel, T., 'Ein früher Bericht über den Aufstand von Muḥammad b. ʿAbdallāh im Jahre 145 h', *Der Islam* 46, 1970, 227–62.
—, *Die Festung des Glaubens*, Munich 1988.
—, *Rechtleitung und Kalifat*, Bonn 1975.
—, *Staat und Glaubensgemeinschaft im Islam*, 2 vols, Z(rich and Munich 1981.
—, 'Über die Ursprünge der Religionspolitik der ersten Seldschukischen Sultane', *Zeitschrift der Deutschen Morgenländischen Geselleschaft, Supplement ii (XVIII. Deutscher Orientalistentag*), Wiesbaden 1974, 241–8.
Nahj al-balāgha, compiled by al-Sharīf al-Rāḍī (d. 406/1016), with the commentary of Muḥammad ʿAbduh, Beirut 1993.
Najjar, F., 'Democracy in Islamic Political Philosophy', *Studia Islamica* 51, 1980, 107–22.
—, 'Fārābī's Political Philosophy and Shīʿism', *Studia Islamica* 14, 1961, 57–72.
Narshakhī (wrote 332/943f), *Tārīkh-i Bukhārā*, ed. C. Schefer, Paris 1982; repr. Amsterdam 1975. The section used in this book was added by a later author, probably Muḥammad b. Ẓufar (wrote 574/1178f.), cf. *EI*², s.v. 'Narshakhī'.
al-Nasafī (d. 318/930), 'Le Kitāb al-radd ʿalā l-bidaʿ d'Abū Muṭīʿ Makḥūl al-Nasafī', ed. M. Bernand, *Annales Islamologiques* 16, 1980, 39–126.
al-Nasawī (d. 647/1249f.), *Sīrat al-sulṭān Jalāl al-dīn Mankubirtī*, ed. Ḥ. A. Ḥamdī, Cairo 1953.
Nāshiʾ (attrib.), see Ps(eudo)-Nāshiʾ.
Nashwān al-Ḥimyarī (d. 573/1178), *al-Ḥūr al-ʿīn*, ed. K. Muṣṭafā, Baghdad 1948.
Naṣīr al-Dīn Ṭūsī, see Ṭūsī.
Nāṣir-i Khusraw (d. c. 470/1077), *Book of Travels (Safarnāme)*, tr. W. M. Thackston, Albany 1986.
Naṣr b. Muzāḥim (d. 212/827), *Waqʿat Ṣiffīn*, 2nd edn ed. ʿA.-S. M. Hārūn, Cairo 1962.
Nasr, S. H., 'Afdal al-Din Kashani and the Philosophical World of Khwaja Nasir al-Din Tusi', in M. E. Marmura (ed.), *Islamic Theology and Philosophy: Studies in Honor of George F. Hourani*, Albany 1984, ch. 16.
al-Nawbakhtī (d. c. 300/912), *Firaq al-shīʿa*, ed. H. Ritter, Istanbul 1931.
al-Naysābūrī (fl. late fourth/tenth century), *Ithbāt al-imāma*, ed. M. Ghālib, Beirut 1984.

Nazim, M. (ed. and tr.), 'The *Pand-Nāmah* of Subuktigīn', *Journal of the Royal Asiatic Society* 1933, 605–28.
Nemesius (d. before 400), *De Natura Hominis*, ed. M. Morani, Leipzig 1987 (cited by paragraph); tr. N. Telfer, *Cyril of Jerusalem and Nemesius of Emesa* (Library of Christian Classics, iv), London 1955 (cited by page).
Netton, I. R., *Muslim Neoplatonists. An Introduction to the Thought of the Brethren of Purity*, Edinburgh 1991.
Newman, A. J., *The Formative Period of Twelver Shīʿism. Ḥadīth as Discourse between Qum and Baghdad*, London 2000.
Nicholson, R. A. (ed. and tr.), 'The Meditations of Maʿarrí', in his *Studies in Islamic Poetry*, Cambridge 1921, 43–289.
Niẓām al-Mulk (d. 485/1092), *Siyāsatnāme* (abbreviated *SN*), ed. H. Darke, *Siyar al-mulūk*, 2nd edn, Tehran 1985; tr. H. Darke, *The Book of Government or Rules for Kings*, London 1960.
Niẓāmī (d. 599/1202), *Iqbālnāme*, ed. W. Dastgirdī, Tehran 1334; tr. J. Ch. Bürgel, *Das Alexanderbuch*, Zürich 1991.
Niẓāmī ʿArūḍī Samarqandī (d. after 547/1152), *Chahár Maqála*, tr. E. G. Browne, London 1921 (repr. from *Journal of the Royal Asiatic Society* July and October 1899).
NM (G): the *Naṣīḥat al-mulūk* attributed to al-Ghazālī, see Pseudo-Ghazālī.
NM (M): the *Naṣīḥat al-mulūk* attributed to al-Māwardī, see Pseudo-Māwardī.
Noth, A., *Heiliger Krieg und Heiliger Kampf in Islam und Christentum*, Bonn 1966.
Nuʿaym b. Ḥammād (d. 229/844), *al-Fitan*, ed. S. Zakkār, Mecca [1991] (cited by page); ed. M. al-Shūrī, Beirut 1997 (cited as S, by paragraph).
al-Nuʿmān b. Muḥammad, al-Qāḍī (d. 363/974), *Daʿāʾim al-islām*, ed. A. ʿA. A. Fayḍī, 2 vols, 3rd printing, Cairo 1969.
—, *K. al-himma fī ādāb atbāʿ al-aʾimma*, ed. M. K. Ḥusayn, Cairo n.d.
—, *R. iftitāḥ al-daʿwa*, ed. W. al-Qāḍī, Beirut 1970.
—, 'al-Risāla al-mudhhiba', in ʿA. Tāmir (ed.), *Khams rasāʾil ismāʿīliyya*, Salamiyya 1956, 27–87.
—, *Taʾwīl al-daʿāʾim*, ed. M. Ḥ. al-Aʿẓamī, 3 vols, Cairo 1969–74.
al-Nuʿmānī, Ibn Abī Zaynab (mid-fourth/tenth century), *al-Ghayba*, Beirut 1983.
Oded, B., 'The "Command of the God" as a Reason for Going to War in the Assyrian Royal Inscriptions', in M. Cogan and I. Ephʿal (eds), *Ah, Assyria . . . Studies in Assyrian History and Ancient Near Eastern Historiography Presented to Hayim Tadmor*, Jerusalem 1991, 223–30.
O'Meara, D. J., 'Aspects of Political Philosophy in Iamblichus', in H. J. Blumenthal and E. J. Clark (eds), *The Divine Iamblichus*, Bristol 1993, 65–73.
—, 'The Justinianic Dialogue "On Political Science" and its Neoplatonic Sources', in K. Ierodiakonou (ed.), *Byzantine Philosophy and its Sources*, Oxford 2002, 49–62.
—, 'Neoplatonist Conceptions of the Philosopher-King', in J. van Ophuijsen (ed.), *Plato and Platonism*, Washington D.C., 1999, no. 13.
—, 'Plato's *Republic* in the School of Iamblichus', in M. Vegetti and M. Abbate (eds), *La Repubblica di Platone nella traditione antica*, Napoli 1999, 193–205.
—, 'Religion as Abbild der Philosophie. Zum Neuplatonischen Hintergrund der Lehre al-Farabis', in T. Kobusch and M. Erder (eds), *Metaphysik und Religion. Zur Signatur des spätantiken Denkens*, Leipzig 2002, 343–53.

—, 'Vie politique et divinisation dans la philosophie néoplatonicienne', in M.-O. Goulet-Cazé and others (eds), *Chercheurs de Sagesse. Hommage à Jean Pépin*, Paris 1992, 501–10.

l'Orange, H. P., *Studies on the Icononography of Cosmic Kingship in the Ancient World*, Oslo 1953.

Origen (d. 254 or 255), *Contra Celsum*, tr. H. Chadwick, Cambridge 1953.

Ormsby, E. L., *Theodicy in Islamic Thought. The Dispute over al-Ghazālī's 'Best of all Possible Worlds'*, Princeton 1984.

Paul, J., *Herrscher, Gemeinwesen, Vermittler: Ostiran und Transoxanien in vormongolischer Zeit*, Beirut 1996.

Peters, R., *Islam and Colonialism. The Doctrine of Jihad in Modern History*, the Hague 1979.

—, (tr.), *Jihad in Classical and Modern Islam, a Reader*, Princeton 1996.

Pines, S., 'The Limitations of Human Knowledge According to al-Fārābī, Ibn Bājja, and Maimonides', in I. Twersky (ed.), *Studies in Mediaeval Jewish History and Literature*, Cambridge, MA 1979 (facsimile reprint in his *Collected Works*, vol. v, *Studies in the History of Jewish Thought*, ed. W. Z. Harvey and M. Idel, Jerusalem 1997), 82–109.

—, 'La loi naturelle et la société: la doctrine politico-théologique d'Ibn Zurʿa, philosophe chrétien de Baghdad', *Scripta Hierosolymitana* 9 (facsimile reprint in his *Collected Works*, vol. iii, *Studies in the History of Arabic Philosophy*, ed. S.Stroumsa, Jerusalem 1996), 154–90.

—, 'Shīʿite Terms and Conceptions in Judah Halevi's *Kuzari*', *Jerusalem Studies in Arabic and Islam* 2, 1980 (facsimile reprint in his *Collected Works*, vol. v, *Studies in the History of Jewish Thought*, ed. W. Z. Harvey and M. Idel), Jerusalem 1997), 165–251.

—, 'The Societies Providing for the Bare Necessities of Life according to Ibn Khaldūn and to the Philosophers', *Studia Islamica* 34, 1971 (facsimile reprint in his *Collected Works*, vol. iii, *Studies in the History of Arabic Philosophy*, ed. S. Stroumsa, Jerusalem 1996), 125–38.

Plato (d. 347 BC), *The Laws*, ed. and tr. R. G. Bury, Cambridge MA 1926. The quaint-looking references are to the pages of Stephanus' edition of 1578, subdivided into segments marked 'a' to 'e', reproduced in all scholarly editions of Plato's works, and generally used as reference points by classicists so that passages can be located regardless of what edition or translation one happens to be using.

—, *The Republic*, ed. and tr. P. Storey, Cambridge MA 1937. For the references, see the preceding item.

Plessner, M. (ed.), *Der Oikonomikos des Neupytagoreers 'Bryson' und sein Einfluss auf die islamische Wissenschaft*, Heidelberg 1928.

Plutarch, *Lives*, ed. and tr. B. Perrin, ix, Cambridge, MA and London 1950.

Porter, B., *The Lion's Share. A Short History of British Imperialism 1850–1983*, 2nd edn, London and New York 1984.

Porphyry (d. c. 305), *On Abstinence from Killing Animals*, tr. G. Clark, Ithaca 2000.

Praechter, K., 'Antikes in der Grabrede des Georgios Akropolites auf Johannes Dukas', *Byzantinische Zeitschrift* 14, 1905, pp. 479–91.

Pritchard, J. B. (ed.), *Ancient Near Eastern Texts Relating to the Old Testament*, 2nd edn, Princeton 1955.

Proclus (d. 485), *Sur le premier Alcibiade de Platon*, ed. and tr. A. Ph. Segonds, 2 vols, Paris 1985–6.

Ps. = Pseudo. Falsely attributed books continue to referred to by the names of their alleged authors, prefixed by 'Pseudo-' or qualified by 'attributed to', when the real author of the work remains uncertain or unknown.

Pseudo-Aristotle, *Fī siyāsat al-mudun*, ed. and tr. J. Bielawski with an extended commentary by M. Plezia, 'Lettre d'Aristote à Alexandre sur la politique envers les cités', *Archiwum Filologiczne* 25, 1970, 6–206 (the confusing layout notwithstanding, the text and translation are cited by section and line). On this text, see also Grignaschi, items 3–5, and Stern, *Aristotle on the World State.*

Pseudo-Aristotle, *Sirr al-asrār*, ed. ʿA.-R. Badawī, *al-Uṣūl al-yūnāniyya li'l-naẓariyyāt al-siyāsiyya fī 'l-islām*, Cairo 1954, pp. 65–171. On this work, see Grignaschi, item 1, and Manzalaoui.

Pseudo-Ghazālī (anon., before 595/1199): author of the second half of al-Ghazālī's *Naṣīḥat al-mulūk* (q.v.), i.e. the part which is a mirror, cf. Crone, 'Did al-Ghazālī write a Mirror for Princes?'.

Pseudo-Ibn Qutayba (Ibn al-Qūṭiya[?], d. 367/977): *al-Imāma wa'l-siyāsa*, Cairo 1969. For the authorship, see Lecomte, *Ibn Qutayba*, 174–6.

Pseudo-Iṣbahānī (anon., wrote c. 380/990): Abū 'l-Faraj al-Iṣbahānī (attrib.), *Kitāb al-ghurabāʾ*, ed. Ṣ.-D. al-Munajjid, Beirut 1972 = *The Book of Strangers*, tr. P. Crone and S. Moreh, Princeton 2000 (with a discussion of the authorship in ch. 4).

Pseudo-Jāḥiẓ (probably al-Taghlabī/Thaʿlabī, d. 250/864), *Kitāb al-tāj*, ed. A. Z. Pacha, Cairo 1914; tr. C. Pellat, *Le livre de la couronne*, Paris 1954. On the authorship, see Schoeler, *Kitāb al-Tāǧ*.

Pseudo-Māwardī, *Naṣḥīat al-mulūk*, ed. Kh. M. Khiḍr, Kuwait 1983. There is another edition (which I would have used had I known about it earlier) by F. ʿAbd al-Munʿim Aḥmad, Alexandria 1988, which also has a critical introduction showing that the book cannot be by al-Māwardī, since the legal positions adopted in the book are mostly Ḥanafī (whereas al-Māwardī was a Shāfiʿite jurist). Aḥmad tentatively suggests that the book is by Abū Zayd al-Balkhī (d. 322/934). This remains to be examined, but he is certainly right that the book was written in eastern Iran (cf. Khiḍr's edition, 83f., 168, 169).

Pseudo-Nāshiʾ (probably Jaʿfar b. Ḥarb, d. 236/850): in J. van Ess (ed.), *Frühe Muʿtazilitische Häresiographie*, Beirut 1971. For the authorship, see W. Madelung, 'Frühe muʿtazilitische Häresiographie: das *Kitāb al-Uṣūl* des Ǧaʿfar b. Ḥarb?', *Der Islam* 57, 1980, 220–36.

Pseudo-Thaʿālibī (anon., seventh/thirteenth century), *Tuḥfat al-wuzarāʾ*, ed. Ḥ. ʿA. al-Rāwī and I. M. al-Ṣaffār, Baghdad 1977. For the authorship, see the critical introduction by R. Heinecke to her edition, *Tuḥfat al-wuzarāʾ. Das Wesir-Spiegel eines unbekannten Kompilators aus den ersten Hälfte des 7./13. Jahurhunderts*, Beirut 1975.

Pseudo-Zayd b. ʿAlī (Abū Khālid al-Wāsiṭī?, fl. later second/eighth century), *Majmūʿ al-fiqh*, ed. E. Griffini, Milan 1919. For the authorship, see van Ess, *TG*, i, 262.

Q = Qurʾān, Egptian standard edition.

al-Qāḍī, W., 'The Development of the Term *Ghulāt* in Muslim Literature with Special Reference to the Kaysāniyya', in *Akten des VII. Kongresses für Arabistik und Islamwissenschaft*, ed. A. Dietrich, Göttingen 1976, 295–319.

—, 'An Early Fāṭimid Political Document', *Studia Islamica* 48, 1978, 71–108.

—, 'The Religious Foundations of Late Umayyad Ideology and Practice', in *Saber Religioso y Poder Político en el Islam (Actas des Simposio Internacional, Granada 1991)*, Madrid 1994, 231–73.

—, 'The Term 'Khalīfa' in Early Exegetical Literature', *Die Welt des Islams* 28, 1988, 392–411.

al-Qaffāl al-Shāshī, Abū Bakr Muḥammad b. Aḥmad (d. 507/1113), *Ḥilyat al-ʿulamāʾ fī maʿrifat madhāhib al-fuqahāʾ*, vol. vii, ed. Y. A. I. Darādkah, Amman 1985.

QN: see Kay Kāʾūs, *Qābūsnāma*.

Qudāma b. Jaʿfar (d. 337/948 or earlier), *al-Kharāj wa-ṣināʿat al-kitāba*, ed. M. Ḥ. al-Zubaydī, Baghdad 1981.

al-Qummī, Abū 'l-Ḥasan ʿAlī b. Ibrāhīm (early fourth/tenth century), *Tafsīr*, 2 vols, Beirut 1991.

al-Qummī, Saʿd b. ʿAbdallāh (d. c. 300/912), *Kitāb al-maqālāt wa'l-firaq*, ed. J. Mashkūr, Tehran 1963.

al-Qurṭubī (d. 671/1273), *al-Jāmiʿ li-aḥkām al Qurʾān*, 20 vols, Cairo 1967.

R. = *Risāla.*

Rad, G. von, *Holy War in Ancient Israel*, tr. M. J. Dawn, Grand Rapids, MI 1991 (German original 1958).

al-Rāghib al-Iṣbahānī (d. c. 400/1010), *al-Dharīʿa ilā makārim al-sharīʿa*, ed. A. Y. al-ʿAjamī, n.p. 1414.

Rahman, F., *Prophecy in Islam. Philosophy and Orthodoxy*, London 1958.

Rasāʾil Ikhwān al-Ṣafā: see *RIS*.

al-Rāzī, Abū Bakr (d. 313/925 or 323), *al-Sīra al-falsafiyya*, ed. and tr. P. Kraus, 'Raziana I: La Conduite du Philosophe', *Orientalia* 4, 1935, 300–34; reprinted with new pagination in al-Rāzī, *al-Rasāʾil al-falsafiyya*, ed. P. Kraus, Cairo 1939, 97–111; also tr. C. E. Butterworth, 'The Book of the Philosophic Life', *Interpretation* 20, 1993, 227–36. References are to both editions and both translations, the original one first, separated by a slash.

—, *al-Ṭibb al-rūḥānī*, ed. ʿA.-L. al-ʿĪd, Cairo 1978; tr. A. J. Arberry, *The Spiritual Physick of Rhazes*, London 1950.

al-Rāzī, Abū Ḥātim: see Abū Ḥātim.

al-Rāzī, Fakhr al-Dīn (d. 606/1209), *K. al-arbaʿīn fī uṣūl al-dīn*, Hyderabad 1353.

—, *K. al-mabāḥith al-mashriqiyya fī ʿilm al-ilāhiyyāt wa'l-ṭabīʿiyyāt*, 2 vols, Hyderabad 1343.

—, *K. muḥaṣṣal afkār al-mutaqaddimīn wa'l-mutaʾakhkhirīn min al-ʿulamāʾ wa'l-ḥukamāʾ wa'l-mutakallimīn*, Cairo 1323.

—, *al-Tafsīr al-kabīr*, 32 vols in 16, Tehran 1413.

Rāzī, Najm al-Dīn, see Dāya

RCEA = *Répertoire chronologique d'épigraphie arabe*, Cairo 1931–.

Rebstock, U., *Die Ibāḍiten im Maġrib (2./8.-4./10. Jh.)*, Berlin 1983.

Reinhart, A. K., *Before Revelation*, Albany 1995.

Richard, Y., *Shīʿite Islam*, Oxford 1995.

Richter, G., *Studien zur Geschichte der älteren arabischen Fürstenspiegel*, Leipzig 1932.

Ringgren, H., 'Some Religious Aspects of the Caliphate', *Studies in the History of Religions* (supplements to *Numen*), iv: *The sacral kingship, la regalità sacra*, Leiden 1959, 737–48.

RIS = *Rasāʾil Ikhwan al-Ṣafā*, Beirut 1957. Users of other editions are referred to D. R. Blumenthal, 'A Comparative Table of the Bombay, Cairo, and Beirut Editions of the *Rasāʾil Iḫwān al-Ṣafāʾ*', *Arabica* 21, 1974, 186–203.

Ritter, H., 'Ein arabisches Handbuch der Handelswissenschaft', *Der Islam* 7, 1917, 1–91.

—, *Das Meer der Seele*, Leiden 1978.

Robinson, C., *Empire and Elites after the Muslim Conquest, the Transformation of Northern Mesopotamia*, Cambridge 2000.

—, 'Prophecy and Holy Men in Early Islam', in J. Howard-Johnston and P. A. Hayward (eds), *The Cult of Saints in Late Antiquity and the Middle Ages*, Oxford 1999, 241–62.

Rosenthal, E. I. J., 'The Place of Politics in the Philosophy of al-Farabi', *Islamic Culture* 29, 1955, 157–78 (facsimile reprint in his *Studia Semitica*, vol. ii, Cambridge 1971, no. 5).

Rosenthal, F., 'Abū Zayd al-Balkhī on Politics', in C. E. Bosworth and others (eds), *The Islamic World from Classical to Modern Times. Essays in Honor of Bernard Lewis*, Princeton 1989, 287–301.

—, *Aḥmad b. aṭ-Ṭayyib al-Saraḫsî*, New Haven 1943.

—, 'Arabic Books and Manuscripts': see al-Thaʿālibī.

—, *The Classical Heritage in Islam*, London and New York 1975.

—, 'On the Knowledge of Plato's Philosophy in the Islamic World', *Islamic Culture* 14, 1940, 387–422; facsimile reprint in his *Greek Philosophy in the Arab World*, Aldershot 1990, no. 2.

—, *The Muslim Concept of Freedom*, Leiden 1960.

Rotter, G., *Die Umayyaden und der zweite Bürgerkrieg (680–92)*, Wiesbaden 1982.

Rowson, E. K. (ed. and tr.), *A Muslim Philosopher on the Soul and its Fate: al-ʿĀmirī's Kitāb al-Amad ʿalā 'l-abad*, New Haven 1988.

Rubin, U., 'Quran and *Tafsīr*. The case of "*ʿan yadin*", *Der Islam* 70, 1993, 133–44.

Rūmī (d. 672/1273), *Mathnawī*, ed. R. A. Nicholson, 8 vols, London 1925–40.

Runia, D. T., 'God and Man in Philo of Alexandria', *Journal of Theological Studies* 39, 1988, 48–75; facsimile reprint in his *Exegesis and Philosophy. Studies on Philo of Alexandria*, Aldershot 1990, no. 12.

Ryan, W. F., and C. B. Schmitt (eds), *Pseudo-Aristotle, the Secret of Secrets: Sources and Influences*, London 1982.

Sachedina, A. A., 'The Development of *Jihad* in Islamic Revelation and History', in J. Turner Johnson and J. Kelsay (eds), *Cross, Crescent and Sword*, Westport, CT, 1990, ch. 2.

—, 'Freedom of Conscience and Religion in the Qur'an', in D. Little, J. Kelsay, and A. A. Sachedina, *Human Rights and the Conflict of Cultures: Western and Islamic Perspectives on Religious Liberty*, Columbia, SC, 1988.

—, *Islamic Messianism. The Idea of the Mahdī in Twelver Shīʿism*, Albany 1981.

—, *The Just Ruler in Shīʿite Islam. The Comprehensive Authority of the Jurist in Imamite Jurisprudence*, Oxford 1988.

—, 'A Treatise on the Occultation of the Twelfth Imāmite Imam', *Studia Islamica* 48, 1978, 109–24.

Sadan, J., 'A "Closed-Circuit" Saying on Practical Justice', *Jerusalem Studies in Arabic and Islam* 10, 1987, 325–41.

—, 'Community' and 'Extra-Community', *Israel Oriental Studies* 10, 1980, 102–15.

al-Sadūsī, Muʾarrij b. ʿAmr (d. 195/810, or 174, or 200), *K. Ḥadhf min nasab Quraysh*, ed. Ṣ.-D. al-Munajjid, Cairo 1960.

Sālim (probably later second/eighth century, but incorporating an earlier account of Murji'ism), see Crone and Zimmermann.
al-Sālimī, ʿA. (d. 1332/1914), *Tuḥfat al-aʿyān bi-sīrat ahl ʿUmān*, 2 vols in one, Cairo 1961.
Salinger, G., 'A Muslim Mirror for Princes', *The Muslim World* 46, 1956, 24–39.
Sanders, P., *Ritual, Politics, and the City in Fatimid Cairo*, Albany 1994.
Sanhoury, A., *Le Califat*, Paris 1926.
al-Sarakhsī (d. 483/1090), *K. al-mabsūṭ*, 30 vols in 15, Cairo 1324.
—, *Sharḥ K. al-siyar al-kabīr li-Muḥammad b. al-Ḥasan al-Shaybānī*, ed. Ṣ.-D. al-Munajjid, 5 vols, Cairo 1971–2.
Sartori, G., 'Constitutionalism: a Preliminary Discussion', *American Political Science Review* 56, 1962, 853–64.
Sayf b. ʿUmar (d. before 193/809), *Kitāb al-ridda wa'l-futūḥ wa-kitāb al-jamal wa maṣīr ʿA'isha wa-ʿAlī*, ed. Q. al-Samarrai, Leiden 1995.
Schacht, J., *An Introduction to Islamic Law*, Oxford 1964.
Schimmel, A., *Mystical Dimensions of Islam*, Chapel Hill 1975.
Schneider, I., *Kinderverkauf und Schuldknechtschaft*, Stuttgart 1999.
Schoeler, G., 'Verfasser und titel des dem Ğāḥiẓ zugeschriebenen sog. *Kitāb al-Tāğ*', *Zeitschrift der Deutschen Morgenl(ndischen Gesellschaft* 130, 1980, 217–25.
Sea of Precious Virtue: see Meisami.
Seneca, *Letters*, in R. Campbell (tr.), *Letters from a Stoic*, London 1969.
Serjeant, R. B., 'A Zaidī Manual of Ḥisbah of the 3rd Century (H)', *Rivista degli Studi Orientali*, xxviii, 1953, 1–34.
Shaban, M. A., *Islamic History [i], AD 600–750*, Cambridge 1971.
—, *Islamic History, ii, AD 750–1055*, Cambridge 1976.
al-Shāfiʿī (d. 204/820), *al-Risāla*, ed. A. M. Shākir, Cairo 1940; tr. M. Khaddurī, 2nd edn, Cambridge 1987.
al-Shahrastānī (d. 548/1153), *K. al-milal wa'l-niḥal*, ed. W. Cureton, 2 vols, London 1842–46; tr. D. Gimaret and G. Monnot, *Livres des religions et des sectes*, 2 vols, UNESCO 1986 (which preserves the paginations of both Badrān's and Cureton's pagination).
—, *K. nihāyat al-aqdām fī ʿilm al-kalām*, ed. with a summary tr. A. Guillaume, London 1934.
Sharon, M., *Black Banners from the East. The Establishment of the ʿAbbāsid State – Incubation of a Revolt*, Jerusalem and Leiden 1983.
Shayzarī, ʿAbd al-Raḥmān b. Naṣr (d. 589/1193), *al-Nahj al-maslūk fī siyāsat al-mulūk*, ed. M. A. Damaj, Beirut 1994.
—, *Nihāyat al-rutba fī ṭalab al-ḥisba*, ed. al-Sayyid al-Baz al-ʿArīnī, Beirut 1969.
al-Sijistānī, Abū Yaʿqūb (d. after 361/971), *Kitāb al-iftikhār*, ed. M. Ghālib, [Beirut] 1980.
—, *Kitāb ithbāt al-nubū'āt*, ed. ʿA. Tāmir, Beirut 1966.
—, 'Tuḥfat al-mustajībīn', in ʿA. Tāmir (ed.), *Khams rasā'il ismāʿīliyya*, Salamiyya 1956, 146–55.
—, *The Wellsprings of Wisdom*, tr. P. E. Walker, Salt Lake City 1994.
Simidchieva, M., '*Siyāsat-nāme* Revisited: the Question of Authenticity', in *Proceedings of the Second European Conference of Iranian Studies*, ed. B. G. Fragner and others, Rome 1995, 657–74.

Simnānī, Ibn al- (493/1100), *Rawḍat al-quḍāh wa-ṭarīq al-najah*, ed. Ṣ-D. al-Nāhī, 4 vols, Baghdad 1970–74. Cited by volume and pararaph, except towards the end of the book, where the paragraph division disappears. The Ḥanafī biographical dictionaries give the author's name as ʿAlī b. Muḥammad al-Raḥbī, adding that he was known as Ibn al-Simnānī because he claimed to be the son of the Ḥanafī jurist al-Simnānī (on whom, see *EI*², s.v.). This is correctly reported in the editorial introduction along with the deathdate given here. The editor nonetheless gives the author's name as al-Simnānī and his deathdate as 499 on the title page, and both have now passed into the library catalogues.

Sirr al-asrār: see Pseudo-Aristotle.

SN: see Niẓām al-Mulk, *Siyāsatnāma*.

Solomon of Basra (fl. c. 1222), *The Book of the Bee*, ed. and tr. E. A. W. Budge, Oxford 1886.

Sorabji, R., (ed.), *Aristotle Transformed. The Ancient Commentators and their Influence*, London 1990.

Sourdel, D., 'Une profession de foi de l'historien al-Ṭabarī', *Revue des Etudes Islamiques* 36, 1968, 177–99.

Sperl, S., 'Islamic Kingship and Arabic Panegyric Poetry in the Early Ninth Century', *Journal of Arabic Literature* 8, 1977, 20–35.

Stern, S. M., *Aristotle on the World State*, Oxford 1968.

—, 'Cairo as the Centre of the Ismāʿīlī Movement', in his *Studies* [q.v.], 234–56 (reprinted with new pagination from *Colloque international sur l'histoire du Caire*, Cairo 1972, 437–50).

—, 'A Collection of Treatises by ʿAbd al-Laṭīf al-Baghdādī', *Islamic Studies* 1, 1962, 53–70.

—, 'The Constitution of the Islamic City' in , in D. S. Richards (ed.), *Islamic Civilisation 950–1150*, Oxford 1973, 25–50.

—, 'Heterodox Ismāʿīlism at the time of al-Muʿizz', in his *Studies* [q.v.], 257–288 (reprinted with new pagination from *Bulletin of the School of Oriental and African Studies* 17, 1955, 10–33).

—, 'Al-Masʿūdī and the Philosopher al-Fārābī', in his *Medieval Arabic and Hebrew Thought*, London 1983, no. XV (facsimile reprint from *Al-Masʿūdī Millenary Commemoration Volume*, Aligarh 1960, 28–41).

—, 'New Information about the Authors of the "Epistles of the Sincere Brethren", in his *Studies* [q.v.], 155–76 (reprinted with new pagination from *Islamic Studies* 4, 1964, 405–28).

—, *Studies in Early Ismāʿīlism*, Jerusalem and Leiden 1983.

Strothmann, R., *Das Staatsrecht der Zaiditen*, Strassburg 1912.

Stroumsa, S., *Freethinkers of Medieval Islam. Ibn al-Rāwandī, Abū Bakr al-Rāzī and Their Impact on Islamic Thought*, Leiden 1999.

al-Sulamī (d. 412/1021), *Ṭabaqāt al-ṣūfiyya*, ed. J. Pedersen, Leiden 1960.

Sulaym = *Kitāb Sulaym b. Qays al-Hilālī*, ed. M. Bāqir Anṣārī, 3 vols (the third contains the edition), Qum 1955.

Tab., see al-Ṭabarī, *Taʾrīkh*.

al-Ṭabarī (d. 310/923), *Jāmiʿ al-bayān ʿan tafsīr al-qurʾān*, 15 vols, Beirut 1988.

—, *Das Konstantinopler Fragment des Kitāb ikhtilāf al-fuqahāʾ*, ed. J. Schacht, Leiden 1933.

—, *Taʾrīkh al-rusul wa'l-mulūk*, ed. M. J. de Goeje and others, Leiden 1879–1901; ed. M. A.-F. Ibrāhīm, 10 vols, Cairo 1960–9; tr. various, *The History of al-Ṭabarī*, ed. E. Yarshater, 39 vols, Albany 1989–98 (cited as Tab.). References are to the Leiden edition, which works for all three.

Talbi, M., *L'Émirat aghlabide*, Paris 1966.

Talmon-Heller, D., 'Religion in the Public Sphere: Rulers, Scholars and Commoners In Syria under Zangid and Ayyubid Rule', in *The Public Sphere in Muslim Societies*, ed. M. Hoexter, Sh. N. Eistenstadt, and N. Levtzion, Albany 2002, 49–64.

al-Tanūkhī, *Nishwār al-muḥāḍara*, ed. ʿA. Shāljī, 8 vols, Beirut 1971–2; partial translation by D. S. Margoliouth, *The Table-talk of a Mesopotamian Judge*, parts ii and vii (repr. from *Islamic Culture* 3–6, 1929–32), Hyderabad n.d.

Tārīkh-i Sīstān, ed. M.-Sh. Bahār, Tehran 1314; tr. M. Gold, Rome 1976.

al-Tawḥīdī (d. 414/1023), *Kitāb al-imtāʿ wa'l-muʿānasa*, ed. A. Amīn and A. al-Zayn, 3 vols, Cairo 1939–44.

TB, see al-Khaṭīb al-Baghdādī.

Tennant, F. R., *The Sources of the Doctrines of the Fall and Original Sin*, Cambridge 1903.

al-Thaʿālibī (d. 429/1038), *Ādāb al-mulūk*, ed. J. al-ʿAtiyya, Beirut 1990.

—, *Ghurar akhbār mulūk al-furs wa-siyarihim*, ed. and tr. H. Zotenberg, Paris 1900 (repr. Tehran 1963). It is not certain that this work is by the same Thaʿālibī, but as things stand, it seems to be, cf. F. Rosenthal, 'From Arabic Books and Manuscripts III: the Author of the Ġurar as-Siyar', *Journal of the American Oriental Society* 58, 3, 1950, 181–2.

—, (attrib.), *Tuḥfat al-wuzarāʾ*, see Pseudo-Thaʿālibī.

—, *Yatīmat al-dahr*, 4 vols, Cairo 1934,

Thābit b. Sinān (d. 363/974), *Taʾrīkh akhbār al-qarāmiṭa*, ed. S. Zakkār, Beirut 1971.

Themistius (d. 388), *Risālat Thāmistiyūs ilā Yūliyān al-malik fī 'l-siyāsa wa-tadbīr al-mulk* ed. M. S. Sālim, Cairo 1970; re-edited with a Latin translation by I. Shahid, *Epistula de re publica gerenda*, Cambridge, MA 1974. Cited in the above order, by pages, separated by a slash.

Theophanes: *The Chronicle of Theophanes Confessor*, tr. C. Mango and R. Scott, Oxford 1997. References are to the year since the creation, *anno mundi* (AM).

Thucydides (d. c. 400 BC), *History of the Peleponnesian War*, ed. and tr. C. Foster Smith, 4 vols, Cambridge, MA and London 1919–21.

al-Tījānī (d. after 711/1311), *Riḥla*, ed. Ḥ. Ḥ. ʿAbd al-Wahhāb, Tunis 1958.

al-Ṭurṭūshī (d. 520/1126), *Sirāj al-mulūk*, Cairo 1935.

al-Ṭūsī, Abū Jaʿfar (d. 460/1067), *K. al-khilāf*, 6 vols, Qum 1407–14.

—, *al-Mabsūṭ fī fiqh al-imāmiyya*, ed. M. T. al-Kashfī, 8 vols, Qum 1351–87.

—, *al-Nihāya*, Beirut 1970.

—, *al-Tibyān fī tafsīr al-qurʾān*, 10 vols, Najaf 1957–63.

Ṭūsī, Naṣīr al-Dīn (d. 672/1274), *The Nasirean Ethics*, tr. G. M. Wickens, London 1964.

Tyan, E., *Le Califat (Institutions du droit public musulman)*, i, Paris 1954.

—, *Histoire de l'Organisation judiciaire en pays d'Islam*, 2 vols, Paris 1938–43.

ʿUyūn wa'l-ḥadāʾiq fī akhbār al-ḥaqāʾiq, Kitāb al-, part iii, ed. M. J. de Goeje, Leiden 1871; part iv, 1 and 2, ed. ʿU. al-Saʿīdī, Damascus 1972–3.

Vatikiotis, P. J., *The Fatimid Theory of State*, Lahore 1957.

Wakīʿ (d. c. 306/918), *Akhbār al-quḍāh*, ed. ʿA.-ʿA. M. al-Marāghī, 3 vols, Cairo 1947–50.
Walker, P. E., *Ḥamīd al-Dīn al-Kirmānī. Ismaili Thought in the Age of al-Ḥakīm*, London 1999.
Wallis, R. T., *Neoplatonism*, 2nd edn by L. P. Gerson, London and Indianapolis 1995.
Walzer, M., *Regicide and Revolution*, London 1974.
—, *The Revolution of the Saints: a Study in the Origins of Radical Politics*, New York 1971 (first published 1965).
Walzer, R., see al-Fārābī, *FM*.
al-Wansharīsī (d. 914/1508), *al-Miʿyār al-muʿrib*, 13 vols, Rabat 1981.
Wasserstein, D., *The Rise and Fall of the Party-Kings. Politics and Society in Islamic Spain, 1002–1086*, Princeton 1985.
Watt, W. M., *The Formative Period of Islamic Thought*, Edinburgh 1973.
—, 'God's Caliph. Qurʾānic Interpretations and Umayyad Claims', in C. E. Bosworth (ed.), *Iran and Islam, in Memory of Vladimir Minorsky*, Edinburgh 1971, 565–74.
—, *Islamic Philosophy and Theology*, Edinburgh 1962.
—, *Islamic Political Thought*, Edinburgh 1968.
—, 'The Significance of the Theory of *Jihād*', in *Akten ses VII. Kongresses für Arabistik und Islamwissenschaft, Göttingen 1974*, ed. A. Dietrich, Göttingen 1976, 390–4.
al-Wazīr al-Maghribī (d. 418/1027), *Kitāb al-siyāsa*, ed. S. al-Dahhān, Damascus 1948.
Weippert, M., '"Heiliger Krieg" in Israel und Assyrien', *Zeitschrift für die alttestamentliche Wissenschaft* 84, 1972, 460–93.
Wensinck, A. J., *Muhammad and the Jews of Medina*, tr. W. Behn, Freiburg im Breisgau 1975.
—, 'Muhammad und die Propheten', *Acta Orientalia* 2, 1924, 168–98.
—, *The Muslim Creed*, Cambridge 1932.
Wensinck et al., *Concordances et indices de la tradition musulmane*, Leiden 1936–69.
Westerink, L. G., 'The Alexandrian Commentators and the Introductions to their Commentaries', in R. Sorabji (ed.), *Aristotle Transformed. The Ancient Commentators and their Influence*, Ithaca 1990, 325–48.
Wilkinson, J. C., *The Imamate Tradition of Oman*, Cambridge 1987.
Wörterbuch der klassischen arabischen Sprache, ed. M. Ullmann and others, 2 vols to date (covering *kāf* and *lām*), Wiesbaden 1970–
al-Yaʿqūbī: see YB and YT.
YB = al-Yaʿqūbī (d. after 292/905), *K. al-Buldān*, ed. M. J. de Goeje, Leiden 1892.
YT = al-Yaʿqūbī, *Taʾrīkh*, ed. M. Th. Houtsma, 2 vols, Leiden 1883.
Yūsuf Khāṣṣ Ḥājib (wrote 462/1069f), *Wisdom of Royal Glory (Kutadgu Bilig), a Turko-Islamic Mirror for Princes*, tr. R. Dankoff, Chicago and London 1983.
al-Zamakhsharī (d. 538/1144), *al-Kashshāf*, 2 vols, Cairo 1966.
Zaman, Muhammad Qasim, *Religion and Politics under the Early ʿAbbāsids. The Emergence of the Proto-Sunnī Elite*, Leiden 1997.
Zartusht-i Bahrām Pazhdu (eighth/fourteenth century), *Zarātushtnāme*, ed. F. Rosenberg, rev. M. Dabir-Siyāqī, Tehran 1959.
Zayd b. ʿAlī (d. 122/740) (attrib.), *Majmūʿ al-fiqh*: see Pseudo-Zayd.
Zayn al-dīn al-ʿIrāqī (d. 806/1403), *al-Qurab fī maḥabbat al-ʿarab*, ed. I. Ḥilmī al-Qādirī, Alexandria 1961.

Ziai, H., 'The Source and Nature of Authority: a Study of al-Suhrawardī's Illuminationist Political Doctrine', in C. E. Butterworth (ed.), *The Political Aspects of Islamic Philosophy. Essays in Honor of Muhsin S. Mahdi*, Cambridge, MA 1992, ch. 8.

—, 'al-Suhrawardī, Shihāb al-Dīn Yaḥyā', in *EI*².

Zimmermann, F. W., *Al-Farabi's Commentary and Short Treatise on Aristotle's De Interpretatione*, Oxford 1981.

—, 'Review of J. van Ess, *Anfänge muslimischer Theologie*', in *International Journal of Middle East Studies* 16, 1984, 437–41.

al-Zubayr b. Bakkār (d. 256/870), *al-Akhbār al-Muwaffaqiyyāt*, ed. S. M. al-ʿĀnī, Baghdad 1972.

INDEX AND GLOSSARY

Main entries are in bold. Square brackets around figures indicate that the subject is being discussed without use of the entry word or, where applicable, that provided in the parenthetical gloss. Figures over 398 are introduced by an asterisk, indicating that they refer to the charts. As is customary, the definite article 'al-' is ignored for purposes of alphabetization.

Glosses are only provided when the requisite information is not given on first occurence of the word, when the word is mentioned several times without the information being repeated, or when the word is ambivalent in some way. No doubt the reader will find inconsistencies: I hope I have erred on the side or repetition rather than omission. Dates are not usually given, as the reader can find them in the charts, chronology or bibliography. The index does not cover the last two items.